1-708-857-40

$\mathcal{E}$conomics by Design:

Principles and Issues

Robert A. Collinge
Ronald M. Ayers

The University of Texas at San Antonio

Prentice Hall,   Upper Saddle River, NJ 07458

Executive Editor:	Leah Jewell
Editorial Assistant:	Kristin Kaiser
Editor-in-Chief:	James Boyd
Marketing Manager:	Sandra Steiner
Production Editor:	Louise Rothman
Production Coordinator:	Renee Pelletier
Managing Editor:	Carol Burgett
Manufacturing Supervisor:	Arnold Vila
Manufacturing Manager:	Vincent Scelta
Senior Designer:	Ann France
Design Director:	Patricia Wosczyk
Interior Design:	Chris Wolf
Cover Design:	Maureen Eide
Illustrator (Interior):	University Graphics, Inc.
Composition:	University Graphics, Inc.
Cover Art/Photo:	Daryl Stevens Illustration

© 1997 by Prentice-Hall, Inc.
A Simon & Schuster Company
Upper Saddle River, New Jersey 07458

Collinge, Robert A.
　　Economics by design: Principles and Issues / by Robert A. Collinge and Ronald M.
　　Ayers.
　　　　　p.　cm.
　　Includes bibliographical reference and index.
　　ISBN 0-13-373788-8
　　1. Economics.　I. Ayers, Ronald M.　II. Title.
HB171.5.C845　1996
330—dc20　　　　　　　　　　　　　　　　　　　　　　96-32847
　　　　　　　　　　　　　　　　　　　　　　　　　　　　　CIP

Prentice-Hall International (UK) Limited, London
Prentice-Hall of Australia Pty. Limited, Sydney
Prentice-Hall Canada, Inc., Toronto
Prentice-Hall Hispanoamericana, S.A., Mexico
Prentice-Hall of India Private Limited, New Delhi
Prentice-Hall of Japan, Inc., Tokyo
Simon & Schuster Asia Pte. Ltd., Singapore
Editora Prentice-Hall do Brasil, Ltda., Rio de Janeiro

Printed in the United States of America

10　9　8　7　6　5　4　3　2　1

*T*o Mary, Mom, Dad, and my students, for their insights and encouragement.

RAC

*T*o my mother and father, my former professors at the University of New Orleans and Tulane University, and the ever-patient Coco.

RMA

Contents in Brief

*N*avigator's Guide

A Quick Reference to the Modular Layout of *Economics by Design*

- Easy-to-use modular chapter layout providing an abundance of material for maximum flexibility in picking and choosing topics and level of coverage.

- Fifteen chapters, each containing three learning modules.

- Lively yet concise presentation of basic economic principles in TRAVELING THE ECONOMICS EXPRESSWAY modules—includes numerous brief applications and examples to engage student interest.

- Wide-ranging, in-depth discussion of economic issues in EXPLORING ISSUES modules—choose from two Explorations per chapter to apply chapter principles.

- Selected principles extended and developed in MASTERING ROADSIDE CHALLENGES modules—choose from two Challenges per chapter to further the formation of economic proficiencies.

Contents

PART TWO
The Power of Prices

PART THREE

The Energy of the Marketplace

PART FIVE
Aggregates for the Big Picture

Preface

Substance, Access, Interest—

These are the goals of *Economics by Design: Principles and Issues.* The text is appropriate for an issues-oriented course that teaches essential economic principles in either one or two terms. *Economics by Design* strives for a clear, crisp, and accurate presentation of the central components of mainstream economic theory, along with issues prominent in today's world.

The text is designed in a unique modular format that allows a choice of principles and issues to cover. The fifteen chapters, each with three learning modules, offer a plentiful array of material to allow instructors who teach the one-term course to customize their courses—emphasizing essentials or issues, as desired. Using *Economics by Design* as the primary text in a two-term micro-macro sequence allows the instructor to comfortably intersperse theory and application in a manner that traditional nonmodular principles texts do not allow.

Economics by Design motivates learning and promotes retention by systematically combining up-to-date theory and application. The material meets high standards of conceptual rigor, but is easy to grasp because of the intuitive, application-oriented manner in which it is presented. At all times, *Economics by Design* strives to keep the presentation accessible and interesting.

Economics by Design *Is Flexible and User-Friendly*

With a conversational style attractive to today's diverse student body, *Economics by Design* motivates readers to learn what they *need* to know and uncover what they might *want* to know. This approach is founded in the age of interactive information—it places the user at the controls.

The user can select the material to be covered, along with its sequence and degree of depth. *Economics by Design* offers the casual reader an opportunity to get up to speed quickly in the topic areas he or she chooses. While appropriate for a terminal survey/

issues course in economics, this approach also allows the flexibility needed for a one-term principles course. *Economics by Design* can thus prepare students for additional courses at advanced levels, up to and including the pre-MBA level.

Get behind the Wheel, . . .

Economics by Design is an information highway, beckoning the reader into a journey of economic discovery. This is an open road with multiple access ramps, broad vistas, rest stops, and challenges along the way. The reader has the option to speed from start to finish or to explore particular interests more thoroughly. The flexibility of this framework allows the reader or instructor the option to navigate a personally chosen course.

Each chapter in *Economics by Design* is composed of three learning modules: Traveling the Economics Expressway, Exploring Issues, and Mastering Roadside Challenges. The first two modules cover essential principles and issues, respectively. The third module is typically more advanced and assumes familiarity with the material covered in the Expressway module.

. . . Turn the Key, and Go!

The first module, Traveling the Economics Expressway, commences with the symbolic icon of car keys. The goal in this module is to provide novices with "key" concepts in a concise and engaging manner that allows them to get up to speed quickly in their study of economics. The user will become familiar with straightforward graphical analysis. However, complex graphs and equations that would slow the reader's progress are avoided.

Readers who wish to cover the basics quickly might stop when their journey on the Expressway is over. If limited time is a problem, instructors might wish to assign only this module in particular chapters. The result will be an ability to analyze and understand the subject when it is encountered in person, on the news, or in other courses.

Explore Issues

The second module in each chapter consists of two Explorations, denoted by the icon of a road that beckons the explorer forward. Explorations offer an opportunity to examine various dimensions of economic issues, including the ethical dimensions currently emphasized by accrediting bodies. These investigations provide a refreshing change of pace, giving readers the option to venture off the main road and explore the economic landscape. Sometimes the second Exploration is an educational short story. Because educational fiction is an effective pedagogical technique that promotes interest and retention, seven of the thirty Explorations take this form.

Explorations invite the reader to ponder the application of economic analysis to issues of the day. The reader will find that economics is no irrelevant tome of theory, but rather is active and ongoing. The presence of Explorations integrated into their appropriate chapters eliminates the need to assign a separate readings book or to place articles on reserve. Explorations enhance students' abilities to retain and apply the theoretical material in the chapter.

*P*repare to Be Challenged!

The final module in each chapter is entitled Mastering Roadside Challenges. Challenges, identified by an icon showing a rock climber working his or her way up a difficult cliff, allow students to hone analytical or other skills that relate to the subject of the chapter. The Challenges draw students into the practice of economics and would be especially appropriate in the one- or two-term principles class or an honors survey class. As with the Explorations, instructors can assign or omit Challenges as they wish. Students who work through the Challenges will possess a solid foundation for intermediate-level study in economics.

Economics by Design *offers a Superior Organization*

Economics by Design surpasses other texts by simultaneously emphasizing quality in content, writing, and pedagogy. Some one-term texts wander from issue to issue with little apparent organization, offering no more than a scattershot of principles along the way. While courses using such texts may seem compelling at the time, students leave without a systematic grounding in economic fundamentals. Without a solid foundation in essential economic principles, students do not learn to "think economics" and thus find it difficult to apply economic concepts in the future.

Other one-term texts go to the opposite extreme, with so much emphasis on the dry development of theory that their fragmentary sprinklings of applications do little to captivate student interests. The instructor who seeks to provide this learning stimulus with outside readings is burdened with the task of identifying appropriate readings, tracking them down in the library, complying with copyright laws, and then integrating them with the principles.

In contrast to one-term texts, two-term principles texts tend to be weighted down with excess detail that is irrelevant for most students. Through concise writing and the elimination of peripheral topics, *Economics by Design* avoids this problem. This text offers ample material for a two-term sequence that covers economic principles in greater depth than the one-term course while also stressing the relevance of economics to issues of the day.

Table P-1 identifies possible course designs for five alternative courses. The table refers to the three modules: **A.** Economics Expressway; **B.** Exploring Issues (two Explorations per chapter); **C.** Roadside Challenges (two per chapter).

Chapters	Survey/Issues	Principles	Pre-MBA Principles	Micro Principles	Macro Principles
1 Roadmap for Economics	A,B	A,C	A,B,C	A,B,C	A,B,C
2 Production, Growth, and Trade	A,B	A,C	A,B,C	A,B,C	A,B,C
3 Market Prices: Supply and Demand	A,B	A,C	A,B,C	A,B,C	A,B,C
4 Efficiency and Political Prices	A,B	A,C	A,B,C	A,B,C	
5 Into the International Marketplace	A,B	A,C	A,B,C	A,B,C	A,B,C
6 The Firm	A,B	A,C	A,B,C	A,B,C	
7 Market Models	A,B	A,C	A,B,C	A,B,C	
8 Income from Labor and Human Capital	A,B	A,C	A,B,C	A,B,C	
9 Government's Role in Production	A,B	A,C	A,B,C	A,B,C	
10 Taxation and Public Choice	A,B	A,C	A,B,C	A,B,C	A,B,C
11 Measuring the Macroeconomy	A,B	A,C	A,B,C		A,B,C
12 Employment, Output, and Fiscal Policy	A,B	A,C	A,B,C		A,B,C
13 Money, Banking, and Monetary Policy	A,B	A,C	A,B,C		A,B,C
14 Policy for the Long Run	A,B	A,C	A,B,C		A,B,C
15 Global Economic Themes	A,B			A,B,C	A,B,C
Discretionary Additions	Elements of C	Elements of B			
Discretionary Deletions	Elements of B	Elements of C	Elements of B	Elements of A, B, C	Elements of A, B, C

TABLE P-1 *Possible Course Designs for Single-Term Courses*

Note: Some instructors teaching the one-term principles or survey/issues course may wish to delete certain chapters entirely, especially if they desire a deeper coverage of the topics in the remaining chapters. To emphasize issues, instructors have the option of eliminating various Expressways while still covering the Explorations that follow. This approach would typically require the instructor to provide a limited amount of background material.

With Integrated Coverage of International Topics, . . .

Internationally oriented material is woven throughout *Economics by Design*. In recognition that markets are global in scope, a full chapter on the international economy is introduced in the first third of the book. This chapter is written so that it can be covered at any point later in the course, if desired. In addition, internationally oriented issues and principles are brought up in context wherever appropriate. The result is that coverage of issues and principles relating to international trade and finance recurs throughout the book.

*E*conomics by Design Is Complete and Self-Contained—

Economics by Design offers consistent pedagogical aids to speed the learning process. For example, graphs are captioned with concise, self-contained explanations to reduce back-and-forth page flipping. In addition, terminology has always been a **barrier to entry** into the field of economics. In order to surmount this barrier, each significant new term is in color (witness the preceding sentence), as are significant other terms that have been mentioned peripherally in earlier chapters. Where possible, the meaning of terms is made clear in context, so that the pace of conceptual learning is not obstructed. A list of selected terms—those colored in the text—is included at the end of each chapter. Definitions of all selected terms are then compiled in a glossary at the end of the book. If a term is of secondary importance, it is italized and not designated as a selected term.

Each chapter of *Economics by Design* concludes with Study by Design, a concise workbook that provides two ways to study. The first is grounded in the recognition that today's students are busy. Some studying must be done at odd moments, such as on the bus or over a quick cup of coffee between classes. To facilitate this process, Study by Design commences with a section called *SpeedStudy*, a speedy review and self-test that students consistently report to be a very useful learning aid. This self-test encourages students to begin the process of evaluating their level of understanding and helps them to quickly bring to light any weaknesses in their learning.

SpeedStudy is followed by The MasterMind, which is intended for longer study sessions in which the student's goal is to master the material in the chapter. Included in this section are thought questions, problems, and a multiple-choice self-test. Study by Design concludes with detailed suggestions for possible term papers. These suggestions encourage students to investigate economic issues on their own or at the discretion of the instructor.

Economics by Design offers a full complement of ancillary materials, including a study guide, printed test bank, computerized test bank, instructor's manual with lecture notes, transparencies, and the ABC News/Prentice Hall Video Library. In contrast to other texts, the authors of *Economics by Design* have personally composed the study guide, test bank of over 3,500 questions, and instructor's manual, which provides consistency in writing style and coverage between the text and the questions, notes, and other materials in these ancillaries.

*C*onventional and Innovative at the Same Time

Economics by Design offers enhanced adoptability, to make the tasks involved in class preparation and teaching as easy as possible for instructors. Preparing a course outline with a text that presents a radically different arrangement of topics would take up too much of a busy instructor's valuable time. To promote the efficient use of preparation time, topics are both familiar and up-to-date. The material is also arranged in the conventional micro-first fashion. Teachers who adopt *Economics by Design* will find that, with minimal rearranging and rewriting of their notes, they can teach in the manner they find comfortable. Flexibility, modern content, currency of the issues, and an engaging style are the advantages built into *Economics by Design*.

A World of Thanks!

Our debts are many. To start, we would like to thank the economics profession, past and present, for putting together the rich body of economic theory from which we draw. In a text of this sort, the vast majority of the individuals responsible for developing these economic ideas must inevitably go uncited. Still, without their anonymous contributions, this text could not have been written.

More personally, our thanks go to the many professional colleagues and students who have shared their thoughts along the way. We have adopted many suggestions at the behest of our students. Their input has been extensive because, in whole or in part, *Economics by Design* has been class-tested at our university for over two years. Class-testing occurred in multiple sections of each of three different courses: the one-term survey/issues course, the two-term principles course, and the one-term micro-macro principles course for entering MBA students without prior exposure to economics.

We would also like to thank the hard-working people at Prentice Hall for bringing a complete product to market. Special thanks go to Leah Jewell, who gave us room to run with creative ideas on presenting economic fundamentals and issues. The involvement of Leah, Louise Rothman and Carol Burgett at every step of the way has always been constructive. We also thank Kristin Kaiser, editorial assistant, and Sandra Gormley of University Graphics.

We are grateful for the detailed, thought-provoking comments and suggestions of this text's many reviewers. Their input has been incorporated throughout to improve the quality of *Economics by Design*. Any deficiencies that remain are, of course, the responsibility of the other author . . . whichever one of us that may be! The following reviewers have assisted us: George Beardsley, *California Polytechnic State University;* John Conant, *Indiana State University;* Mousumi Duttaray, *Indiana University;* Dan Fuller, *Weber State University;* Anthony Greco, *University of Southwestern Louisiana;* Jan Hansen, *University of Wisconsin;* Matthew Hyle, *Winona State University;* Rose Kilburn, *Modesto Junior College;* Steven Lile, *Western Kentucky University;* Jose Mendez, *Arizona State University;* Wayne Plumly, *Valdosta State University;* David Sollars, *Auburn University at Montgomery;* Darlene Voeltz, *Rochester Community College;* Richard Welch, *University of Texas—San Antonio;* Jim Wheeler, *Vance Granville Community College;* and Larry Wilson, *Sandhills Community College.*

R.A.C.
R.M.A.

*R*oadmap for Economics

A Look Ahead

Economics provides a key to understanding numerous aspects of the world around us. Some are trumpeted in newspaper headlines about the big public policy issues of the day. Others affect us quite personally. For example, economics can explain why the price of textbooks is greater than the price of novels; why some people earn more than others; why some business firms advertise, while others do not; and how countries can all gain through international trade.

This chapter sweeps across the economic landscape. Scarce resources and unlimited wants force us to make economic choices. We will see that these choices can involve the big macroeconomic issues or the more detailed microeconomic issues. The importance of the price system is revealed, and some basic economic questions are examined. The chapter continues by discussing methods of economic analysis. It is seen that economists employ models, which highlight important aspects of the world around us, to explain how the world works. Popular perception to the contrary, the best models are often the simplest—like a roadmap!

DESTINATIONS

*M*odule A

As you zip along the Economics Expressway you will arrive at an ability to

- describe how scarce resources and unlimited wants lead to the study of economics;
- identify three basic questions that all economies must answer;
- recognize the strengths of the marketplace and motivations for government involvement;
- understand what a model is and why models are best kept simple;
- distinguish techniques used in economic research.

*M*odule B

Upon leaving the Expressway to explore issues you will be able to

- explain how the lack of economic incentives in communism led to its downfall;
- describe the opportunities for students and professionals in the realm of economics.

*M*odule C

Mastering Roadside Challenges will allow you to hone analytical skills by

- graphing direct and inverse relationships;
- identifying seven basic sources of economic data.

Scarce Resources, Unlimited Wants

Economics studies the allocation of scarce resources in response to unlimited wants.

Economics is about choice. Both individually and as a society, we seek to choose wisely. We are forced to choose because resources are scarce, and it takes resources to produce the goods and services we want.

Securing the most value from resources is the objective of economic choice. At a personal level, we each have our own economy. We have limited income to spend on the many things we want. For example, we might forgo the new Jaguar we've long dreamed of in order to pay tuition at Highbrow College. Usually, however, resource **scarcity** does not force us into all-or-nothing decisions. We might be able to purchase a used Dodge Neon and still afford tuition at Home State University.

Every time something is scarce we must make a choice. We commonly make choices at **the margin**, meaning incrementally. Decision making at the margin is about the choice of a little more of this and a little less of that. It's about weighing and balancing benefits and costs. Should I eat the last slice of pizza? What is the best use of the next hour of my time? What should I do with the last dollar in my pocket? If we are wise in the use of our money and our time, we get more for them.

Businesses also face alternatives and make decisions at the margin. Should another worker be hired, or should scarce funds instead be used to upgrade the office computer system? Should one more item be added to the restaurant's menu? Should one be deleted? Should the restaurant stay open later, or close earlier? Should it increase overtime, or cut it back? In sum, business decisions are often made one increment at a time.

Economics looks more broadly at the interactions of households, businesses, and government within the framework of national and international economies. Indeed, most people think of a nation's economy when they think of economics, which brings up some different issues than occur at the personal and business levels. For example, individuals and businesses often focus on spending money wisely. More generally, though, money is just one part of the economic puzzle. From the point of view of a nation's economy, money is little more than grease for the wheels of commerce—a convenience that helps us reach our economic ends. Scarce resources lead to scarce goods, whether or not money is involved.

For example, if everything were declared to be "free," supermarkets, department stores, discount stores, and other retailers would quickly be picked bare. People would complain that they did not take home everything they wanted or that they arrived too late to obtain anything at all. This is often what happens during humanitarian relief efforts, in which food and other aid is distributed from the back of a truck. The result seen in Somalia and other recipient countries is that the fastest and strongest, rather than the neediest, get the goods. Free distribution is not an economical way to allocate scarce resources and the goods and services they produce.

Resource allocation refers to the manner in which resources are used. When society makes choices about what will be consumed, and thus about what to give up, it is making decisions about the allocation of resources. Consider the choices facing the U.S. in 1957. The Soviet Union had placed the first satellite, *Sputnik*, into orbit around the earth. America panicked—its citizens demanded that the U.S. catch up. As a consequence, the nation engaged in a deliberate reallocation of educational resources toward mathematics and science. The space race was on, and by 1969 human footprints marked the surface of the moon.

Most decisions about the allocation of resources are less dramatic than the decisions leading to the space race. For example, labor resources are allocated according to changes in consumer spending. The change in consumer preferences during the 1990s in favor of cotton instead of synthetic fibers in clothing resulted in more jobs than otherwise in cotton farming and processing. Similarly, the housing boom of the mid-1990s created greater demand for skilled construction workers. Workers who assembled appliances and those who manufactured brick, insulation, and the thousands of other inputs going into new homes also benefited.

QuickCheck

Would $2 million dollars satisfy all of your wants?

Answer: It would be quite difficult to discover someone with $2 million dollars who would decline to accept a third million. Even billionaires would accept another billion, if only to better endow their trust funds. Unless you would actually decline to accept that third million, then $2 million dollars does not satisfy all of your wants. Essentially, your wants are unlimited.

OBSERVATION POINT: Scavenging, Tinkering, and the Home Workshop—Changing Visions of the American Dream

At the end of World War II, a generation of soldiers returned to civilian life. This same generation had grown up in the deprivation of the Great Depression. Adversity breeds resourcefulness. Blemished apples and soft bananas from someone's trash, a piece of tin found in a dump, and a few lengths of lumber that have fallen from a passing truck—each can serve a purpose when you're needy. Later, on foreign fields of battle, the skills developed by scavenging goods and tinkering with balky equipment were highly prized.

Scavenging and tinkering were a way of life, and ways of life influence choices. When the GIs came home to start careers and families, they set their sights on their dream homes, complete with workshops. Builders responded by setting aside a small area in the garage of most new houses built during the postwar construction boom. A man now had a place for his tools, his scrap lumber, his nuts and bolts found in the streets. He had a place to build that bookcase instead of wasting money by buying it at the furniture store. With a spot to work on things that broke down, it was the American dream.

Today? Modern microprocessors can confound the most resolute tinkerers. Even broken toasters are thrown out rather than repaired, because most people are too busy with their jobs to spend their time tinkering. Builders' selling efforts these days focus on high ceilings, fireplaces, and luxury baths, not workshops. The American dream? Each new generation defines it in its own way.

Surveying the Economic Landscape

Microeconomic Issues

Microeconomics is about the individual components of the economy and includes individuals acting as consumers or as workers. It also includes **firms**, businesses that produce goods or services. The industries in which firms operate are also included in the realm of microeconomics; an **industry** is composed of firms producing similar outputs.

Microeconomics revolves around the interaction of consumers and producers in markets. **Markets** can take physical, electronic, or other forms. The common characteristic of all markets is that they facilitate the voluntary exchange of resources, goods, and services. Market prices serve as the signals that guide the allocation of resources. Indeed, another name for microeconomics is *price theory*, since participants in the economy make choices based upon *incentives* (motivations) provided by prices.

Microeconomic questions often affect our lives each day. Suppose you decide to go on vacation. What will be your destination? Will you use the services of a travel agent? At which hotel will you stay? If you decide to fly, which airline will you choose? Is the fare lower if you purchase tickets in advance? Why do many airlines reduce the fare if you stay over a Saturday night? How are ticket prices related to government regulation of the airlines? Should government regulate airplane noise? If so, how? As you can see, the list of microeconomic questions is long.

Macroeconomic Issues

Macroeconomics looks at the big picture. It concentrates on analysis of economic *aggregates*, total values for the economy as a whole. The most important aggregate is *gross domestic product (GDP)*, which measures the value of the total output produced by the economy. GDP is obtained by adding up the values of all goods and services produced.

Macroeconomic issues are often raised in the news. Employment, economic growth, interest rates, money, inflation, and the federal budget deficit are examples of macroeconomic issues that will be addressed in this book.

Macroeconomics was first considered a separate field of study following the work of John Maynard Keynes in the 1930s. Keynes suggested macro answers to the problems of the Great Depression, answers that seemed lacking in the microeconomic mainstream of economic thought. The field of macroeconomics became quite popular in the 1950s and 1960s, which led to economics students being served up economic principles in nearly equal doses of micro and macro. However, in recent years, macroeconomics has focused on establishing a solid microeconomic foundation. Thus, the distinction between microeconomics and macroeconomics has been blurring, with more and more micro analysis being applied to macro issues.

✓ QUICKCHECK

The debate over the desirability of free trade among nations has been much in the news. Can you identify both macroeconomic and microeconomic aspects of this issue?

Answer: The ability of free trade to spur the growth of the economy is a macro issue. A micro issue involves which workers would gain and which would lose jobs. While issues are often pigeonholed as macro or micro, many issues have aspects of both.

A

*W*hat, How, and for Whom?

Every economy must answer three basic economic questions:

1. **What?** What goods and services will be produced and offered for sale and in what quantities? Clothing, compact discs, medical services, fast food, and many other items are offered for sale. What is the reason that these things are readily available for purchase, but other items, such as 78 RPM records, are not?
2. **How?** How will goods and services be produced? There are numerous production techniques available to produce most things. Some methods of production are hundreds of years old, utilizing simple hand tools and much labor. Alternative production methods employ computers, robots, and other high-technology inputs in combination with less labor. How are these decisions made, and why are new production techniques constantly being developed?
3. **For whom?** Who will consume the goods and services that are produced? People who live on Poverty Row consume less than those who live on Park Avenue, so income and wealth matter. What determines the income and wealth of an individual or family? If a family's income is not large enough to allow family members to consume the necessities of life, should income be redistributed from others who are wealthier?

When it comes to deciding what, how, and for whom, government might make the decisions by decree. If so, the economy is termed **command and control**. Alternatively, government might stay out of the picture and allow economic choices to be made entirely in the marketplace. In that case, the economy is characterized by laissez-faire free markets, also termed laissez-faire capitalism. Laissez faire means "let it be." Freedom of choice in both production and consumption is a defining characteristic of **free markets**. Free markets are often called capitalistic, where the term *capitalism* emphasizes the private ownership of resources. Private property is also an essential ingredient in a free-market economy.

In practice, countries always have **mixed economies**, meaning that countries choose a combination of markets and command and control. Figure 1A-1 illustrates this spectrum of choice. Different countries choose different combinations, perhaps influenced by custom, tradition, religion, and other factors.

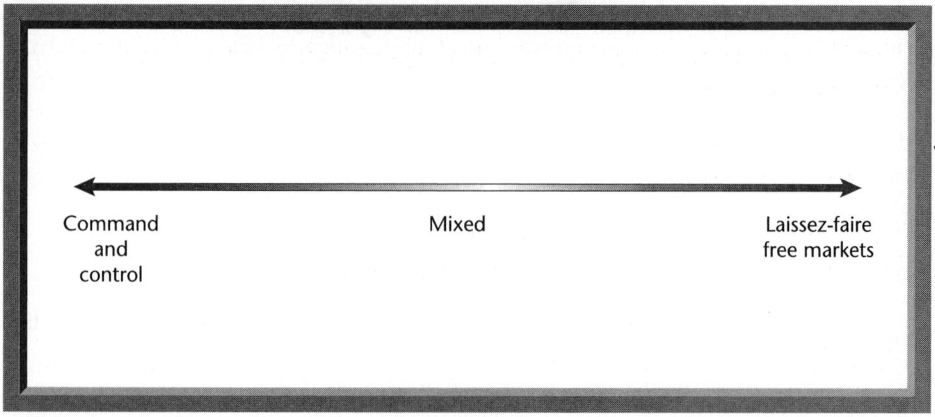

Figure 1A-1   The Spectrum of economic systems. Command and control involves government allocation of resources. Laissez faire is characterized by private resource allocation. In reality, all countries have mixed economies, with the mix varying from country to country.

In the United States, for example, federal, state, and local governments are directly responsible for almost one-fifth of aggregate output and employment. Even when government is not directly involved, it often influences the private marketplace through regulation, taxation, and other means. For example, federal, state, and local government revenue in the U.S. totals about one-third of the value of U.S. output, with about half of that revenue going to finance *transfer payments* that transfer income from some citizens to others. For example, Social Security recipients and holders of government debt both receive transfer payments.

Two primary economic objectives can guide countries in choosing how much government to mix with free markets. The first objective is equity, which refers to fairness. While we often intuitively sense what is fair, the concept of equity is difficult to pin down. While there are commonly accepted principles of equity that apply in certain circumstances, such as to taxation (discussed in chapter 10), equity is ultimately a matter of personal opinion. Well-meaning people can reasonably disagree about what is equitable, and their views cannot be proved or disproved.

The second economic objective is efficiency, which means that resources are used in ways that provide the most value, that maximize the size of the economic pie. Economic efficiency means that no one can be made better off without someone else becoming worse off. Economic efficiency has two components:

- **Technological efficiency**, which implies getting the greatest quantity of output for the resources that are being used. For any given output, then, a least-cost production technique must be chosen.
- **Allocative efficiency**, which involves choosing the most valuable mix of outputs to produce. For example, the economy might be able to produce the greatest possible amount of toothpicks from the resources at its disposal. That choice would be technologically efficient. However, if the economy produces nothing but toothpicks, consumers would not be getting the greatest value from the economy's resources. The economy would be allocatively inefficient, because the wrong mix of goods would have been chosen.

There is frequently a tradeoff between efficiency and equity. More equity may result in less efficiency, and vice versa. For example, many people believe that, for the sake of equity, tax systems should be something like Robin Hood—taxes should take from the rich and give to the poor. However, as tax rates rise, incentives to work and invest fall. Thus the more redistributional is the tax system, the less productive the economy is likely to be. The economic pie may be divided more equitably, but its size would be diminished. The result is inefficiency.

Command and Control—Who Needs Markets?

The marketplace seems cluttered with choices. Aren't all these choices wasteful? Wouldn't it be better to do away with seemingly unnecessary variety, skip all the advertising, and just have government run the economy for the good of us all?

Throughout history, many countries have turned to economic dictators who promised to eliminate the perceived disorder of the marketplace. Unfortunately, even the most well-meaning *central planners* who make decisions in a command-and-control economy cannot know our desires as well as we can know them ourselves. Moreover, nothing ensures that only the most well-meaning central planners will rise to the top. The result is often *inefficiency*, in which resources are squandered on the production of the wrong goods and services or wasted through use of the wrong production techniques.

Governments subscribing to command-and-control methods of resource allocation also must apportion the incomes of workers, thereby determining the distribution of goods and services. If government miscalculates, as in Communist Cuba, it may well be forced to implement *rationing* of goods, which permits consumers to buy only limited amounts of essential goods that are in short supply. Rationing by government is inefficient because it wastes resources. While government may attempt to ration equitably, its prospects for success are dubious.

The Invisible Hand and the Price System— Who Needs Government?

Is it not mysterious that goods and services are regularly offered for sale in quantities that satisfy the wants of consumers? After all, there is no commander-in-chief ordering an army of workers to bring those goods to market. In his seminal work *The Wealth of Nations* (1776), Adam Smith explained this mystery. Smith described how the **invisible hand** of the marketplace leads the economy to produce an efficient variety of goods and services, with efficient production methods as well. Guided by this invisible hand, producers acting in their own self-interests provide consumers with greater value than even the most well-intentioned of governments.

The reason for the invisible hand is straightforward. To prosper in the competitive marketplace, producers must provide customers with things that they value. Those producers who are best at doing so thrive. Those who pick the wrong goods and services to produce, or produce them in an inferior manner, lose out.

All participants in a market economy, including consumers, businesses, and investors, make choices on the basis of information conveyed by market prices. The collection of prices in all markets is termed the *price system*. **Prices provide information about scarcity.** For example, you could probably not afford to hire your friend's favorite rock star to perform at her birthday party. The scarce talents of superstars generally command a price that only a larger audience can pay.

More specifically, prices of all goods and services reflect the value of the scarce resources used in their production. For example, suppose the market price of a color television is $150, while a CD player costs $100. That price differential tells us that the resources incorporated in the television are 50 percent more valuable than the resources embodied in the CD player. If the resources used in making televisions are actually 80 percent more valuable, producers would shift resources over time away from the production of televisions and into the production of CD players. They would stop when the price differential also reached 80 percent.

Price changes lead to changes in both consumer and firm behavior. When gasoline prices increased in the 1970s, consumers responded by increasing their purchases of smaller automobiles. The allocation of resources was adjusted as a consequence. To increase gas mileage, auto makers reduced vehicle weights by replacing heavy steel with aluminum, plastics, and other lightweight materials.

In sum, in a free-market economy, consumer spending determines what will be produced. In response to market prices, as though guided by an invisible hand, free-market choices ordinarily bring about allocative efficiency in answering the "what" question. Firms seeking to "make money" choose least-cost production techniques, thus accomplishing technological efficiency in answering the "how" question. The "for whom" question is answered by the market-determined incomes of workers and others who provide economic resources.

The Mix in the Middle

Since government often fails the test of efficiency, why not get rid of government altogether? Let markets reign supreme! While it may sometimes sound tempting, getting rid of all government would be neither possible nor efficient. For one thing, any country that abolished its government would soon find itself ruled by gangs, clans, or even the government of another country. Moreover, there are many goods and services that markets fail to provide efficiently. **Market failures occur when markets fail to achieve efficiency.** Market failures include the following:

- **Public goods**—goods that are jointly consumed and nonexcludable, such as national defense and highways. While people value these goods, they usually are unwilling to pay for them unless government forces them to do so. The reason is that anyone can consume a public good, whether or not that person has helped pay for it.
- **Externalities**—side effects of production or consumption that affect third parties who have no say in the matter. For example, smoking a cigar in a crowded room creates an externality to others in the room who must breathe the smoke. Yet, without government action, neither the buyer nor seller of the cigar has any need to consider these external effects on others. Other types of pollution, such as motor vehicle exhaust or industrial pollution of air and water, can create more severe externalities.
- **Market power**—the ability to affect market prices, caused by a lack of competition. Market power can result in higher prices and less output, as is often true of an unregulated *monopoly*, a market with only one seller. Significant market power can nullify the invisible hand of the marketplace, which relies on competition to achieve efficiency.

Sometimes market failures are minor, such as the externality experienced by the rest of the class when a student distracts the instructor by showing up late. When market failures are more significant, government action may be needed. However, not all government policies are equally efficient. Many of the most efficient public policies do not abandon markets. Rather, markets can often be steered back on course with public policies that are minimally disruptive to the workings of the invisible hand.

Government is also concerned with equity. The distribution of income in the free marketplace rewards those who provide the most value to others. To some extent this arrangement seems fair. To some extent, it does not. For example, through no fault of their own, some people are incapable of providing much of value in the marketplace. This situation could be due to physical impairment or the lack of opportunity to acquire knowledge and skills. Government may attempt to promote equity by redistributing income, by providing social services, and by other means.

Firms and workers pursue their own self-interests in a mixed economy, but within limits placed upon them by government. If consumers demand a particular good or service, the market is free to meet that demand subject to regulations on production techniques, worker pay, product safety, and so forth. Some products are even banned. The sale of heroin is outlawed, the sale of antibiotics controlled by prescription, and the use of tobacco discouraged by mandatory warning labels. **The major command-and-control techniques used by government in a mixed economy are the following:**

- **Government production,** such as national defense, highways, public education, postal services, and parks. Government produces about 19 percent of U.S. national output.
- **Income redistribution,** such as housing subsidies, food stamps, Medicaid, and other services for the poor. Income redistribution accounts for about 15 percent of U.S. national income.
- **Taxation,** which takes about one-third of U.S. income. Major taxes include sales taxes, property taxes, income taxes, Social Security taxes, and other taxes assessed by the various levels of government.
- **Regulations,** such as minimum wage laws, price controls, or any of the various controls over how products are to be produced and what products can be offered for sale. For example, government regulates both workplace and product safety.
- **Mandates,** which are directives for citizens, firms, or lower levels of government to perform specified actions. Examples include requirements that firms provide access to the handicapped and health care and other benefits to their employees.

There is ongoing debate in most countries over how much government is the right amount. For example, even if market failures are identified, will government action be an improvement? If so, which policy alternatives are most promising? Does government go too far in trying to correct inequities, or not far enough? Finding the proper mix of government and markets is an unending source of political contention.

The Mix in the United States and around the World

Figure 1A-2 shows the fraction of total economic activity directly accounted for by government in selected countries, including the United States. These data show that some nations more closely approximate pure capitalism than do others. These data also understate the significance of government because of the indirect effects of government regulations upon costs in the private sector of the economy.

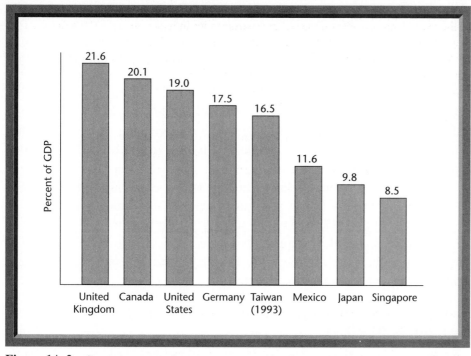

Figure 1A-2 Government purchases as a percentage of gross domestic product (GDP), Selected Countries, 1994.

Source: Economic Report of the President, 1996, Table B-1, *International Financial Statistics*, March 1996, and *Europa World Yearbook*, 1995.

Unlike in the nineteenth and early twentieth century, the U.S. can no longer lay claim to a relatively laissez-faire free-market economy. The transition to an activist government has occurred in response to a perception that government action provides the only available outlet for correcting inequities and failures in the marketplace. At the other extreme, few governments still promote central planning of their economies, because widespread use of command and control failed to achieve higher living standards for their citizens.

For example, Vietnam and China, although self-identified as communist countries, have adjusted their centrally planned economies toward greater reliance upon free markets. By 1996 only Cuba and North Korea still adhered to the command-and-control model that characterized the old Soviet Union. However, throughout the world, governments do plan in key economic sectors and still use command-and-control techniques as one of their policy tools.

Governments often own critical firms and resources. For example, while many U.S. citizens think of Europe as capitalist, some European governments own large industrial companies that are of significant importance to their economies. Until 1994, for example, the large French automaker known as Renault was owned by the government of France. Since then, the French government has sold much of Renault to private investors. This is an example of the worldwide trend toward privatization. *Privatization* occurs when government sells off publicly owned businesses to private investors or contracts with private industry to provide goods or services that had previously been produced by government. Countries turn to privatization to achieve greater efficiency.

OBSERVATION POINT: Intertwining Economic and Political Philosophies

Economics is concerned with obtaining the most value from society's scarce resources. What is value? Who is to judge? In a democracy, it seems natural that citizens should judge value for themselves. Is this approach best? The philosophical and political issues run deep.

During the eighteenth and nineteenth centuries, economics was called political economy. Prior to that, it was usually referred to as moral philosophy, to emphasize the philosophical nature of seeking human betterment. The term *political economy* makes clear that politics and economics intertwine. Although the name has been shortened to *economics*, the link between economics, politics, and philosophy remains as important as ever.

*E*conomic Analysis

The practice of economics often calls for analysis of complex issues. Sometimes these issues involve value judgements; sometimes they are factual. In either case, economic analysis is improved by following some basic methodologies.

Positive and Normative Economics

Economic pronouncements are in abundant supply from an array of sources. Media commentators, politicians, ordinary citizens, and even economists are often remarkably eager to share their purported insights. How can we make sense of this mishmash of opinions? Is it truly nothing but opinion?

With some sorting, unsupported opinions can be separated from thoughtful analysis. A good start distinguishes between normative and positive economic statements. **Normative statements** have to do with behavioral norms, which are judgments as to what is good or bad. Examples of normative statements often include "ought" or "should" in them. They imply that something deserves to happen, such as: "The federal government ought to balance its budget."

Positive statements have to do with fact. They may involve current, historical, or even future fact. Positive statements concern what is, was, or will be. The accuracy of positive statements can be checked against facts, although verifying predictions about the future will have to wait until that future arrives. Sometimes it is also hard to judge the accuracy of a statement, although in principle it could be done. For example, "A balanced federal budget will lead to lower interest rates" is a positive statement that would be difficult to verify.

Positive economic statements are not necessarily true. However, factual evidence may be introduced to support or refute any positive economic statement. Professional economists generally deal in positive economics, although they might assume some ba-

	Macroeconomics	Microeconomics
TABLE 1A-1 *Categorizing Economic Statements*		
Positive	The unemployment rate is rising.	So many people have switched to eating chicken, I think I'll lose my job at the beef-packing plant.
Normative	The unemployment rate is too high.	People should eat more fish!

sic normative goals, such as goals of efficiency and equity. Table 1A-1 provides examples of positive and normative statements, categorized by whether the subject matter is microeconomics or macroeconomics.

Finding Fallacies

It is easy to fall into error when reasoning about economic problems. Fallacious reasoning leads to false conclusions. One example is the *fallacy of composition*. This error in thinking occurs when it is assumed that what is true at the micro level must also be true at the macro level. In other words, the fallacy of composition involves the observation of a truth about some individual component of the economy accompanied by the assumption that this truth will also apply to the economy at large. For example, "Engine Charlie" Wilson, head of General Motors in the 1950s, was widely ridiculed in the press for allegedly saying, "What's good for General Motors is good for the country."

Another fallacy in reasoning occurs when we observe an association between two events and then mistakenly assert that one of the events caused the other. This *fallacy of causation* is an easy mistake to make and can lead to unwarranted conclusions. For example, the manager of a firm may interpret increased sales as a visible sign of brilliant management, when in fact sales took off because of blunders at competing companies or because of an expanding economy.

✔ QUICKCHECK

Is there a fallacy in each of the following statements? If not, is the statement normative or positive?

a. The federal government collects more tax revenue than any state government.
b. Because the catering service that I own is profitable, the catering industry must be profitable.
c. After the tornado hit Central City, Uncle Sam moved too slowly in providing aid.

Answers:

a. Positive. The statement can be checked for its factual accuracy.
b. The fallacy of composition.
c. Normative. The statement implies that the government should have moved more quickly, without telling us what is meant by *too slowly*. A positive version of the statement might read as follows: "After the tornado hit Central City, it took two weeks for aid to reach the stricken population. Officials predict a quicker response to future disasters."

*E*conomic Modeling: The Route to Higher-Level Understanding

Economics makes extensive use of **models**. A model is a simplified version of reality that emphasizes features central to answering the questions we ask of it. Different models answer different questions. For example, a roadmap is a model. The wide red lines that designate interstate highways let us know of major high-speed routes. The circles and yellow splotches show us the locations of towns and larger cities. If our goal is high-speed driving, we want the map kept simple, since we seek to read it quickly.

Economists are often criticized for using models that omit features of the real world. This criticism is unmerited, unless the omitted features are essential in answering the questions asked. Similarly, a roadmap eliminates many features of the terrain, such as trees, houses, and hills. That lack would be inappropriate if the map is for surveying or hiking. For driving, though, including those details would reduce the map's usefulness. Note also that a good model need not be totally realistic, even in the features it does include. After all, from a helicopter we would not actually find huge red lines connecting black circles and yellow splotches. The roadmap is merely representative, as a good model should be.

An example of a model is shown in Figure 1A-3, which uses the notion of a roadmap to represent the layout of chapters in this book. *Economics by Design* involves Expressway Driving in which many features on the economic landscape are surveyed. There is

Figure 1A-3   Chapter roadmap.

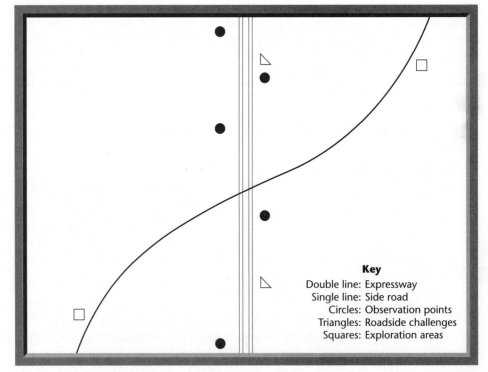

Key
Double line: Expressway
Single line: Side road
Circles: Observation points
Triangles: Roadside challenges
Squares: Exploration areas

also the option to go on Explorations to further examine the surrounding countryside. Alongside the road there are Challenges, which allow learners to develop their analytical skills by examining the economic terrain up close. Note that, while this model illustrates the chapter layout, the actual book looks nothing like the model. Yet, nevertheless, the model conveys the concept, which is its purpose.

There is an important principle to keep in mind when building a model, whether it applies to economics or otherwise. This is the principle of **Occam's razor**, formulated by the English philosopher William of Occam (1300–1349, approximately). Occam argued that reasoning is improved by focusing one's thinking on the most essential elements of an issue. He suggested using a figurative razor to cut away the unnecessary elements from analysis. Occam's razor is a vivid and simple concept. Its use increases the likelihood that modeling will lead to correct conclusions.

Economic models seek to explain the choices people make and the consequences of those choices. Examples of such models explain prices, unemployment, economic growth, and more. Economic models may involve graphs, numbers, or mathematics. Some economic models are quite simple yet amazingly powerful, as we shall see in the following chapters. Other economic models are exceedingly complex, involving advanced mathematics and statistics. Some models consist of hundreds or even thousands of equations stored in computer memory. Even large, complex models are simplified versions of reality.

A

Experimental Economics

Since the mid-1970s economists have discovered something that psychologists have known for a long time—that experiments with laboratory animals can provide insights into human behavior. One experiment confirmed that rats, like humans, will consume less of a good when the price of the good is increased and more when price is decreased. Price was how many times the rat had to push a lever to obtain food or drink.

Economists also experiment on human subjects. These experiments often place paid college student volunteers in an environment that simulates some aspect of economic reality and forces them to make economic decisions. Good decisions result in higher pay for the volunteers. Of course, economic experimentation can go only so far. We would not want to see economists given the power to throw half the population of the country out of work just to see what the effect would be on consumer spending!

Theories and Tests

The preponderance of economic research involves the development and testing of theories about human behavior. *Theories* represent thoughts that are organized toward answering selected questions. **A theory is a statement about how the world works.** Tests of theories are of two types. Theories are first tested for their internal logic. Does a theory make sense? Sometimes the testing stops there. On other occasions, theories are tested by collecting data, which is evaluated to see whether the facts, as revealed by the data, are consistent with the theory. Testing of theories allows us to judge their value.

Support for a theory may be obtained through evidence developed by *econometrics*, the blend of theory, mathematics, and statistics that is a cornerstone of much applied economic research. In simple form, econometrics is used to look for indicators that two or more things are related to each other in a certain way. For example, econometrics might be used to estimate the effect that rising incomes have on people's decisions to buy pickup trucks.

OBSERVATION POINT: Crafting the Tools—The Nobel Laureates

The annual Nobel Memorial Prize in Economic Science, established in 1968, is the most coveted honor that can be bestowed upon a living economist. In addition to the honor and the acclaim, the Prize pays about $1 million to the winner or winners. The 1994 and 1995 winners were honored for their work in developing *game theory* and *rational expectations*, respectively. These topics are addressed in chapters 7 and 14. Many other Nobel-honored tools of analysis have also made their way into the mainstream of economics and thus into this book.

Nobel winners have also been recognized for work in macroeconomics, monetary economics, the economics of information, and the "Austrian school" of economics, a body of thought that favors a laissez-faire approach to markets. Recent winners have broadened the scope of economics to include analysis of government choice, discrimination, crime, families, and the interplay between law and economics. Other Nobels have been awarded for work on the role of railroads in the development of the U.S. and on the economics of slavery.

Research and Practical Application

Economists respond to happenings in the world around them. Whether their writings are scholarly or popular, economists' research interests often involve questions that have practical application, even when their research papers would not appear practical to the lay reader.

Numerous journals publish economic research. The most prestigious journal is *The American Economic Review.* Lengthier research is put forward in the form of scholarly books. Many scholarly writings involve complex arguments and specialized research techniques and are understandable only to economists with graduate degrees. Before scholarly research is published, it is put through a review process in which other economists judge the merits of the research. The review process, although imperfect, seeks to ensure that errors are eliminated from research before it is published. From the beginning of an idea to final publication can take years.

A prerequisite to much of this research is extensive training in the fields of mathematics and statistics. This approach has become a source of controversy among economists. Many economists view mathematics and statistics as the only way to lift economics from the realm of art to the heights of true science. Mathematical models test whether economic theories are right or wrong. Generally, the most prestigious economic research is highly mathematical in nature.

Other economists believe that the economics profession has become unjustifiably "clubby," with mathematical prowess often used as a self-serving barrier to entry to protect the status of the mathematical elite. These dissenting economists point out that mathematical models in economics often violate the principle of Occam's razor and provide limited insight into actual economies. These economists would not eliminate mathematics. Rather, they emphasize that insight and practical application of economic ideas are equally significant and rarely require years of specialized study in higher math as a prerequisite.

Economists frequently offer their perspectives to the general public. For example, Nobel laureate Milton Friedman topped the best-seller list with *Free to Choose*, a book advocating limited government and reliance upon markets. The general public has also embraced the works of Professor John Kenneth Galbraith of Harvard University. In contrast to Friedman's writings, Galbraith's books and magazine articles promote expanding the economic role of government. Authorship of nontechnical books, textbooks, magazine and newspaper articles, and media interviews and appearances are outlets that allow economists to communicate with the general public.

EXPRESS STUDY TRUE OR FALSE

1. Goods and services are the same as ~~resources~~. *outputs*
2. Industry studies are an example of ~~macro~~economic analysis. *micro*
3. Taxation is a command-and-control method employed in mixed economies.
4. Markets fail to achieve an efficient allocation of resources when there are public goods or externalities.
5. The fallacy of composition is an error in reasoning that involves attributing causality to an event. *Causation*
6. Econometrics is concerned with ~~making economics understandable to the general public~~. *statistical methods of analyzing economic data*

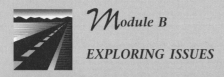

EXPLORATION 1
"From each according to . . . , To each according to . . . "?

Choosing the right mix of government and free enterprise involves questions of economics, philosophy, and politics. Economic incentives can lead to the success or downfall of political systems.

The *Communist Manifesto* was written by Karl Marx and Friedrich Engels in 1847 as a proclamation for the League of the Just, a secret international organization aimed at overcoming the exploitation of labor. The *Communist Manifesto* was a short book—little more than a pamphlet by today's standards. However, its influence in the field of political economy for a time rivaled Adam Smith's very lengthy *The Wealth of Nations*, first published in 1776. *Political economy* was the term used in the eighteenth and nineteenth centuries to describe the study of what we now call economics. Even today, some use the term to accentuate the close ties between economic analysis and public policy. Nowhere are these ties more apparent than in the two books just mentioned.

On the one hand, *The Wealth of Nations* provided the intellectual basis for the system of free markets found in the U.S. Constitution. James Madison, Thomas Jefferson, and the other founding fathers were well acquainted with Adam Smith's analysis of the virtues of competitive markets. On the other hand, the *Communist Manifesto* served as the intellectual basis for a very different kind of government, one founded on the notion of class warfare between owners of capital and labor resources. This idea was used to justify a strong central government that would allocate resources equitably. Equity was taken to mean, as Karl Marx stated in 1875, "from each according to his abilities, to each according to his needs."

*T*he Communist Philosophy . . .

> *All I ask is a tall ship and a star to steer her by.*
> — *John Masefield, 1878–1967, poet*

What does a person need? A chicken in every pot? Will rice and beans do? A glass of wine and a loaf of bread? Love? Peace and quiet? We each have different ideas when it comes to fulfilling our personal needs. People want more, and yet make do with less. How is a government to know about diverse needs?

Partly because needs are so hard to pin down, the task of following Marx's philosophy has proved difficult in practice. The result is that Marxist governments have tended to expound a philosophy of **egalitarianism**, in which everyone is supposed to get the same access to everything from soap to medical care. If people can make do with what they get, they must be getting what they need, right?

. . . ignores Personal Incentives . . .

The problem with using egalitarianism as the rule to allocate a country's output is that egalitarianism provides no incentive for people to be productive. If a country distributes the same amounts to all, its people are not motivated to do their best. Since the Communist credo requires that each person produce according to that person's abilities, the lack of incentives to do so became a serious problem.

In a communist economy, smart people act stupid. The reason is simple. The smarter you act, the more will be expected of you. To live well, you are well advised to keep your head down and act as if you're no better than anyone else. It used to be said in the former Soviet Union that those whose heads stuck above the crowd got them chopped off!

. . . and Led to Its Own Collapse.

With a central authority attempting to direct the what, how, and for whom of production, bad choices were made and resources were squandered. Everyone had a job, but productivity and purchasing power lagged badly. As put by disgruntled workers in Eastern Europe and the Soviet Union, "We pretend to work, and they pretend to pay us."

Actually, the USSR was quite effective at spurring economic growth when the problem was lack of physical capital, such as tractors. Indeed, the Soviet Union became known for its tractor factories. But a modern economy requires education, training, and the freedom and incentive to express creativity. On this score, communism failed badly.

It was small wonder that, over time, the comparatively free markets of the West led to a dramatically better standard of living than was available in the communist economies of the East. Exposed to this better way of life through the global reach of the media, residents of Eastern Europe and the Soviet Union became disillusioned with communism. Cynicism reigned. When the Communist apparatus was in jeopardy and it seemed safe to do so, there was a groundswell of support for its demise. Communism was not a philosophy worth fighting for, and so it collapsed with only a whimper.

Still, there is nostalgia for the relative order and security that was provided by the Communist State. While living standards were low, life was not crassly commercial. The stress of getting ahead in the job market or business world was absent, since opportunities were confined to the Communist party. Moreover, the advent of comparatively free markets has been rough, with many people finding their paltry living standards declining still further. Then, too, there is the matter of pride. With insufficient conviction to rally to the philosophy of communism, many former Communists have instead turned to the rallying cry of nationalism, risking its attendant danger of war. This risk was fulfilled in the conflict between the Serbs, Croats, and Bosnians in the former communist country of Yugoslavia.

B

*T*he Marketplace Is Better at "from Each" . . .

Nationalism does not by itself answer the economic questions of resource allocation. Whatever their governmental leanings, nations can choose their own economic system. They are usually well served to allow relatively free markets, if their goal is to get the most value for their citizens from the resources they possess. Even China recognized this fact, leaving behind Mao Tse Tung's castigation of "Capitalist Roaders" in favor of moving in the direction of free markets.

Free markets offer people opportunity—the opportunity to get ahead or to fall behind. The market rewards people who use their abilities to satisfy their fellow citizens, so long as that satisfaction is embodied in a good or service that can be sold in the marketplace. "Build a better mousetrap, and the world will beat a path to your door."

The free market does not work through altruism. Rather, as Adam Smith put it, it is as though producers are guided by an invisible hand. The invisible hand of the marketplace means that people acting in their own self-interests will more effectively serve the public interest than could even the most well-meaning of governments or altruistic of philanthropists. In the marketplace, the myriad of decisions by individual customers determines what is and is not valuable enough to produce. The marketplace rewards those best able to offer goods and services of value to others. The better a person is at providing value to others, the more will be that person's income. In this way, each person has an incentive to develop his or her productive potential.

. . . but Lacks Compassion.

Firms in the private marketplace offer products that people are willing to pay for or they go out of business. The money to pay for successful products comes from incomes or inheritances that depend upon people's abilities. The marketplace rewards ability with more income. That seems fair, to some extent.

The problem arises that, through no fault of their own, people do not all have the same potential. Furthermore, people may develop their potentials in ways that seem productive at the time, but turn out not to be. For example, elevator operators found their skills obsolete when the ingenuity of manufacturers created automatic elevators. That example reflects the changing opportunities in society, but hardly seems fair to many of the people whose livelihoods are involved.

In other cases people find themselves with disabilities that prevent them from reaching their full potential to provide for others. This situation does not mean that they are worth any less as humans, although the free market tends to pay them less. Again, that does not seem fair. Likewise, situations can arise in most people's lives that prevent them from following their desired paths. The free market appears not to care.

While not immoral, the market is amoral—it seems to turn a blind eye to questions of equity. Sometimes the market seems fair, such as by rewarding those who follow through on ideas that are of benefit to others. However, the free market is fair only by coincidence. Many issues of equity must be addressed through other means.

*A*ttempts by Government to Correct Inequities . . .

Private charities are an attempt to correct inequities. Still, many people think that fairness requires help from all who have the ability. Enter government, with its ability to tax. Specifically, government imposes taxes that take from those who can afford to give and that give to those in need.

There's that word, again—need! What is a need? To the extent that government seeks to take from each in accordance with ability and give to each according to need, it finds itself back in the communist dilemma. Government becomes the arbiter of what people need. Government also becomes a drag on productivity, which leads modern economies to search for the mix in the middle. On the one hand, pure communism shrinks the economic pie badly. On the other hand, laissez-faire capitalism bakes a big pie, but may slice it very unequally.

. . . bring Tough Choices.

How does a government decide where to draw the line on taxes and redistributional spending? In the political process, it may look to voters. Some voters will always want more redistribution; others will desire less. In many cases, the amount of redistribution depends upon the taxes that the individual voters expect to face. Low-income voters tend to want more and high-income voters less. It is the voters in the middle who usually decide elections. Where that middle lies will be affected by the extent to which those voters are paying burdensome taxes. It also depends on perceptions among those voters about whether high taxes along with generous spending make staying in poverty too easy and escaping it too difficult.

*R*awls' Philosophy of the Original Position Can Illuminate . . .

Does political economy offer any help in making these choices? Perhaps economic philosophy can once more shed some light. In particular, imagine that we place ourselves in the original position. As described by twentieth-century political philosopher John Rawls, the **original position** occurs prior to when we have assumed identities as separate people. We do not know who we will become nor how much of those qualities that help us become wealthy we would have. From that position, we must contemplate the risk of becoming an individual the free market leaves behind. Of course, we could also be someone able to thrive in the marketplace.

. . . the Nature of the Trade-offs We Face . . .

The original position gives us a unique perspective. We might be at either the receiving or giving end of the tax system. What kinds of government policies would we support?

We would not want to be left out in the cold. For this reason, Rawls suggests that

B

we choose a *maxi-min* philosophy, in which government attempts to maximize the well-being of the least well-off person in the economy, the person on the bottom rung of the economic ladder. The focus would be on improving the lot of those who are worst off, whoever they may be.

Alternatively, since the size of the economic pie is generally larger when government keeps taxes low, we might choose to take our chances. After all, while the risk is higher, so is the expected standard of living. We also might doubt government's ability to identify the needy. We might even mistrust government's will to fairly implement a policy to reward the neediest, even if identifying them were possible.

Most likely, we would choose a *safety net* to protect us from some but not all risks. This approach is the basis for such government programs as unemployment insurance and Social Security. We also figure that individuals are better positioned to know their own needs than government could ever be. Thus we want freedom and opportunity to go along with security.

. . . but We Will Still Argue.

Exactly how much freedom and opportunity should we mix with exactly how much insurance against life's pitfalls? Debate will continue on and on and on. The issues are important to our lives, and we will have different perspectives. On that we can agree.

PROSPECTING FOR NEW INSIGHTS

1. JESSE: The values in this country have eroded. Drugs, promiscuous sex, obscenities—you name it, people just do whatever they want. I like the idea of a strong central government that maintains the American way of life. We need freedom and opportunity within limits, where government keeps us from going too far.

   PAUL: I hear you, but you've missed the point. The point of the American way is to be answerable to yourself. Yes, when people harm others or take their property, government needs to intervene. Otherwise, it's just one group imposing its version of morality on everybody else.

   This exchange illustrates that the mix in the middle involves much more than just how high taxes are and how much social insurance there is. What are some of the other points of contention in how "free" free markets should be?

2. Many people think that, the more democratic is a country, the greater reliance it will place upon free markets. Do you think this is true? Explain.

The work lives of two fictional professors of economics reveal insights into both the practice of economics and opportunities for students studying the subject.

Real World Problems—The Role of Economics

Professor Caleb Skinner hurried across the campus of Pinnacle State University, his heels drumming a staccato beat against the brick walkway. As was too often the case, he was nearly late for class again. Another phone call from a staffer at the House Committee on Economic Growth assured his waiting students of a few minutes to socialize, study, or just sleep. At least his appearance before the Committee was over. Testifying before Congress was a rush, but it was also stressful.

"Cal!" Without turning, Cal recognized the voice of a colleague, friend, and business partner. Barely slowing down, he swiveled, swept his hand through the air in a waving motion, and returned the greeting, "Jeff, what's up?"

The two professors marched together in lockstep. "I just called Deborah Martinez in Seattle. She wants us to fly up next week, meet the marketing people, and get to work on the project." Cal recognized the name Deborah Martinez, although he had never spoken to her.

"So the President of the Fish Council of America herself has invited us to a command performance. Well, OK. Let's get together this afternoon and see what we might be able to do for them. If anyone can figure out why consumers are eating less fish and what can be done about it, we can."

Cal's mind quickly ran over the successes enjoyed by Econ-O-Calc, the consulting firm he and Professor Thomas Jefferson Johnson had started five years ago. They had taken on dozens of jobs for firms, trade associations, and attorneys. Like most colleges, the large state university employing Skinner and Johnson encouraged faculty members to consult in their spare time, in the belief that such work can help faculty keep their skills up-to-date. The handsome sum of additional income the partners earned by consulting was nice too.

The Economics Profession

Cal Skinner and Jeff Johnson exemplify academic economists. Economics professors teach their classes, participate in university and community affairs, conduct research, and possibly do consulting work. A Ph.D. (Doctor of Philosophy) degree, which typically takes at least four years of intense study beyond a Bachelors, is required to become a full-time faculty member at most schools.

Economists are also employed in industry and government. In industry the duties of economists are varied. Some forecast the future of the economy, focusing on interest rates, inflation, wages, and other macroeconomic variables, and then analyze the implications of their forecasts for their employers. Others engage in work related to marketing or maintaining good company relations with investors. Many find work with consulting firms that specialize in supplying economic expertise to companies on a job-by-job basis. Some economists are entrepreneurs who publish newsletters dealing with trends and forecasts. Increasingly, with the globalization of the economy, an international perspective is required of business economists. Salaries in industry tend to be higher than those in academia.

Government economists tend to spend their time doing policy-oriented research. New legislation and regulations have economic impacts, which economists attempt to estimate. Virtually all government branches and agencies employ economists, with nearly 40 percent of all economists working for government. Median salaries in government are similar to those in academia.

"Gong, gong, gong, . . ." Cal was startled by the repetition of the deep, resonant tones coming from the grandfather clock in the entry hallway. Midnight, and he was still working. Nothing new about that. His wife and two children had gone to bed several hours earlier, but he had been at the desk in the study since dinner, rewriting a "revise and resubmit" for *The Worldwide Journal of Economics*.

His research paper, "A Paradigm for Stabilizing Economic Growth: Theory and Empirical Evidence," would be published soon. First, though, he had to abide by the editor's request that he make the changes suggested by three anonymous reviewers, all experts in the topic Cal had written about, who had volunteered their time to critique research papers submitted to the journal. For his part, Cal also volunteered to review the submissions of other authors.

Cal was at an impasse in his revision of the paper. "Perhaps it's just fatigue," he thought. He considered calling Jeff, to pick Jeff's brain for his expertise on dynamic optimization, a mathematical technique Cal utilized for the first time when writing this paper. It had taken every moment of his spare time in the past six months to learn the technique. Even so, he was still a bit shaky in applying it. It was Jeff who first pointed out to him that the method would be perfect for this paper. Jeff would still be awake and working too. Cal thought a moment longer and finally decided to creep to bed. He would see Jeff tomorrow morning between classes.

*E*conomics in the Political Arena

Cal's thoughts drifted toward a stimulating class discussion that occurred earlier in the day. The questions raised in class had reaffirmed Cal's belief that ECO 101 students are fully able to grasp sophisticated economic concepts.

"Professor Skinner, why do we keep throwing money at problems?" Leslie's question seemed more a comment than a real question. She continued, "Everybody knows that most government programs have failed. Crime and pollution are everywhere . . ."

"Wait a minute," Lester interrupted, "that's not right. Lots of government programs have made a difference. FHA-insured mortgages have taken people from slums and turned them into homeowners. Civil rights legislation has eliminated racial segregation and most overt discrimination. Even this university, one of the finest in the country, is proof that public education can be just as good as that provided by the elite private universities."

Cal mediated the difference of opinion by asking a question. "Class, who can help us explain the contradiction inherent in the apparent success of some government programs and apparent failure of others?" He had not finished asking the question before Melinda's hand shot up. Cal nodded in her direction to indicate permission to speak.

"It seems to me that market-based government programs perform well, while those relying on bureaucratic command and control are beset by red tape, inefficiency, and high costs. Lots of government programs involve broad legislation, with bureaucrats entrusted with filling in the details and administering the programs. Implementing government programs this way just asks for problems."

As Cal put away his papers for the night, he made a mental note to prepare a class assignment that would reflect the debate. His teaching philosophy favored getting students out of the classroom once a semester. Perhaps the class could survey the residents of a public housing project, and use the results in a report on housing the poor.

Pursuing the Study of Economics: Insights and Opportunities

Like Cal Skinner, Jeff Johnson enjoyed a feeling of accomplishment from public service. He served as vice-president of a professional organization, the Continental Economics Association. He helped plan the association's annual meetings, which brought together economists from the U.S., Canada, and Mexico to present and discuss their research. Occasionally, he was interviewed by the media. He also gave speeches on economic matters before civic groups. But his first love was the periodic visits to high schools, where he promoted economics as a major for better students. "No doubt about it," he always said at the conclusion of his presentations, "economics is not the easiest subject, but a bright student who is willing to work should be able to succeed."

Each presentation began with a brief overview of how economics is used. Johnson caught the attention of his audience by noting that a major in economics can pay well. For example, mid-career men with undergraduate economics degrees were reported to have earned a median salary of $49,377 in 1993, which was within $4,000 of engineering, the top-paying major for this group. Mid-career women with economics degrees received a median salary of $49,170 in 1993, an amount that exceeded the earnings of women with any other undergraduate major.* Table 1B2-1 shows an exhibit Johnson displayed to students that summarizes the clients and employers served by economists.

During each presentation, Johnson also described the duties of economists in academia, industry, and government. He pointed out that many economics majors find employment as management trainees in banking, retailing, and marketing. Others become sales trainees, research assistants, or administrative assistants. Many have gone on to take top positions in industry and government. Employers seek economics majors for their analytical abilities and their general grasp of the way the world works. Also, Johnson related that, in his experience, law schools preferred economics majors. Table 1B2-2 shows

B

*Source: Daniel E. Hecker, Earnings of College Graduates, 1993, *Monthly Labor Review*, December 1995, Table 3, page 6.

TABLE 1B2-1 *Who Needs Economic Analysis?*

Lawyers	Accountants
Engineers	Health services administrators
Government	Education administrators
Unions	Environmental scientists
Trade associations	Urban and regional planners
Nonprofit organizations	

Source: Occupational Outlook Handbook, 1994–1995.

another of Johnson's exhibits. The table lists related occupations in which economics training is especially useful.

He emphasized that graduate training was required to advance within the economics profession. A major asset possessed by job seekers is experience in conducting research, developing surveys, and analyzing data. A facility with mathematics and statistics is useful for analyzing business trends, forecasting sales, and planning purchasing and production. Strong computer skills are also valuable. Johnson pointed out that calculus and statistics courses are necessary, and depending on which specialty in economics a student might pursue, finance and accounting could be helpful. Among the economics courses, Johnson noted that the basic theory courses are required and that mathematical economics and econometrics courses should also be taken.

As he entered the departmental mail room, Jeff Johnson's thoughts were far from the public service requirements of his job. "Where is that check from the Fish Council?" he mused. The work he and Skinner had performed for the Fish Council had identified the problem and offered solutions. Johnson was ready to be paid. But the absence of a check was quickly forgotten as he opened an envelope postmarked Mexico City. He began to read the following letter from Guillermo Esquivel, the resident of the Mexican capital who had received his master's degree from the department last year:

> *Dear Professor Johnson,*
> *I thought you might be interested in knowing that I am applying everything I have learned about economics. My job allows me to help my country, as when my research helped convince my fellow citizens of the wisdom of free trade. Your letter of recommendation helped me to get this job, and for that I shall always be grateful.*
> *Guillermo*

Johnson turned to leave the departmental mail room and walk the twenty paces to his office. It was time to prepare for class. As he placed Guillermo's letter in the file

TABLE 1B2-2 *Related Occupations*

Financial analysts	Financial managers
Underwriters	Accountants and auditors
Actuaries	Securities and financial services salespeople
Credit analysts	Loan officers and budget officers

Source: Occupational Outlook Handbook, 1994–1995.

folder in his left hand, he briefly reflected on the satisfaction his job brought him. "This economics is much more than a job to me," he thought. "I don't get rich, but I don't worry. Oh yes, no doubt the Fish Council will get around to sending that check some day."

PROSPECTING FOR NEW INSIGHTS

1. Describe elements of this story that involve positive economics. Describe other elements that involve normative economics.
2. Professors at many universities perform their jobs subject to the principle of publish or perish. This means that professors must meet a quota for an amount of creative, published research that is established by university administrators. Those professors who fail to met the quota are subject to penalties and sometimes even lose their jobs.
   a. Does the publish or perish policy change a professor's incentives to allocate more time to research and less to teaching?
   b. What are the advantages and disadvantages of publish or perish from a student's point of view?
   c. How does the policy relate to scarcity?

B

Module C

MASTERING ROADSIDE CHALLENGES

CHALLENGE 1
Working with Graphs

Economists draw graphs in order to clarify thoughts and show relationships. Each of the two axes of a graph is labeled with the name of a variable of interest to the economist, where a variable can represent anything that can change. For example, the selling price of a good is a variable because it can take one of a variety of values. So is the quantity sold of a good.

Within the axes, a relationship between two variables is shown by a line known as a curve. Curves that slope upward to the right show a **direct relationship**, also termed a **positive relationship**, between the variables. Curves that slope downward to the right show an **inverse relationship**, also termed a **negative relationship**.

An example will help. Suppose we are interested in the relationship between the average yearly sales of umbrellas and the average yearly quantity of rainfall, measured in inches. Hypothetical data for five communities are given in Table 1C1-1.

The relationship between rainfall and umbrellas sales is clearly positive, because increases in rainfall are associated with a greater number of umbrellas sold. In Figure 1C1-1, the data are plotted with rainfall measured on the horizontal axis and umbrella sales on the vertical axis. A curve is drawn through the plot of points. The curve slopes upward to the right, again confirming the direct relationship between two variables.

In contrast, Figure 1C1-2 shows a curve that slopes downward to the right, indicating an inverse relationship between variables. The axes are labeled to show the relationship between the sales of woolen coats and the average January temperature in five cities.

✔ QUICKCHECK

Use the data in Figure 1C1-2 to create a table similar to Table 1C1-1. Verify that the numbers in the table show an inverse relationship.

The slope of a line is the change in the variable measured on the vertical axis divided by the change in the variable measured on the horizontal axis. This value is sometimes referred to as the rise over the run. In Figure 1C1-1, the slope of the curve equals 100 divided by 10, which equals 10. The slope of the curve in Figure 1C1-2 equals minus 10. When one variable depends on another, the first variable is termed a *dependent variable*, and the second is termed an *independent variable*. Since variations in rainfall cause differences in umbrella sales, rainfall is the independent variable and umbrella sales the dependent variable.

Graphs can also be used to show a change in the relationship between the variables.

TABLE 1C1-1	*Hypothetical Data on Rainfall and Umbrella Sales*		
Data Point	Community	Yearly Rainfall	Umbrella Sales
A	Center City	30 inches	100 units
B	Moose Haven	40 inches	200 units
C	Blountville	50 inches	300 units
D	Houckton	60 inches	400 units
E	Echo Ridge	70 inches	500 units

A change in the relationship between two variables is indicated by a shift in a curve. For example, suppose umbrellas become a fashion accessory, carried even when it is not raining. The curve in Figure 1C1-1 would shift up, as shown in Figure 1C1-3. In this example, the sales of umbrellas increase by 100 units in each community.

Not all curves are linear, meaning straight lines. Some curves are curved. However, in this book many relationships will be portrayed graphically as linear. This approach simplifies the analysis, in keeping with the principle of Occam's razor, and allows us to focus our attention on the analysis rather than the shape of the curve. When curves are drawn as nonlinear, the nonlinearity will typically be important to the analysis. For example, in the next chapter the curve called the production possibility frontier is shown as nonlinear because the nonlinearity has significant implications.

Figure 1C1-1 **A positive relationship** between two variables is represented by a curve that slopes upward to the right.

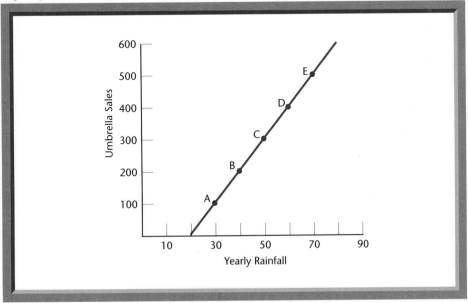

C

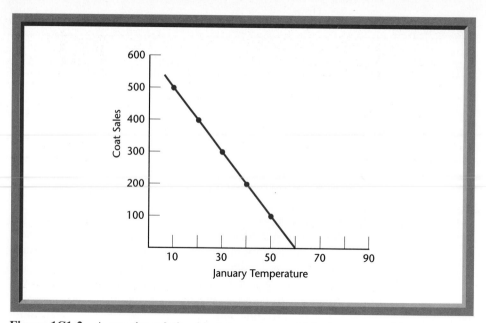

Figure 1C1-2 A negative relationship between two variables is represented by a curve that slopes downward.

Figure 1C1-3 A shift in a curve occurs when the curve changes position. A shift represents a new relationship between the variables.

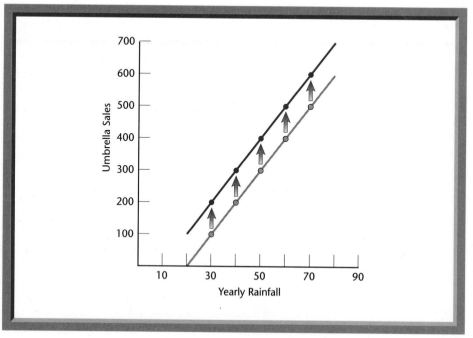

Data provide the raw material of empirical economic research. Economists utilize data to support their hypotheses. Much of these data are collected by various levels of government. Important nongovernmental sources of data include industry trade associations, the United Nations, the Organization for Economic Cooperation and Development (OECD), the International Monetary Fund (IMF), Standard and Poor's, Moody's, and Robert Morris Associates.

A short list of useful sources of data follows. If you are interested in finding data on a specific subject, the *American Statistics Index* (ASI), which is found in many university libraries, is especially useful. It indexes data available in U.S. government publications, by subject.

1. *Economic Report of the President*. Annual. Roughly one half of the book is a compilation of numerous data tables from among those issued by government agencies. The text is written by the President's Council of Economic Advisers and provides a professional assessment of the performance of the economy. Written to be understood by the general public, the *Economic Report* is probably the best place for both novices and experts to start a general search for data about the U.S. economy.
2. *International Financial Statistics*. Monthly. Published by the International Monetary Fund in English and other languages, the book presents several hundred large pages of finely printed economic data on the world at large and on specific countries throughout the world. The focus is on the financial side of economic activity, such as inflation, interest rates, government budgets, and exchange rates. There are also data on a variety of nonfinancial features of world economies, such as the composition of exports and imports. To promote easy access, the IMF also provides a CD-ROM version.
3. *Federal Reserve Bulletin*. Monthly. The user will find extensive data on money, banking, interest rates, and finance, along with news relating to the financial environment. Also featured are articles that analyze economic developments. Articles are written to be accessible to the general reader.
4. *Survey of Current Business.* Quarterly. This publication of the U.S. Department of Commerce is a rich source of data on business conditions.
5. *City and County Data Book*. Annual. What is the population of your hometown? What is the average age of its residents? Average income? This data source provides information about the economies of U.S. cities and counties.
6. *Statistical Abstract of the U.S.* Annual. This source contains hundreds of data tables, packed full of facts about the U.S.
7. **The Internet.** There are numerous sites relating to economics and economic data, many of which are offered by the federal government and by universities. For example, using Netscape or another web browser, a search for "economic," "data," and "government" will offer links to many of these sites.

Before you initiate a data search, there are a few things you should know. Data may be time-series or cross-sectional. **Time-series data** show the values of a variable as time passes. The unemployment rate for the U.S. for each of the last twenty years is an example of time-series data. **Cross-sectional data** are fixed at a moment in time, but vary in some other way. The 1996 unemployment rates for each of the fifty states are an example of cross-sectional data.

Some warnings regarding the use of data are in order. The first caveat is to read the footnotes, which are often present in data tables. Footnotes provide information about how data are defined. Some data will be *seasonally adjusted*. This means that the data have been adjusted from the actual numbers to remove the effect of predictable seasonal changes. For example, department store sales are highest in December because of the importance of Christmas. The seasonal adjustment of these data would adjust for the increase in sales, thus allowing the underlying trend to reveal itself.

Other data are preliminary, meaning that the data may not have been completely tabulated at the time of publication. Preliminary data will be revised later and then published in corrected form. The process of revising data can sometimes go on for years. Competent researchers are careful in drawing conclusions based upon preliminary data.

The definition or method of collecting data sometimes changes over time. Drawing valid statistical conclusions becomes difficult or impossible, because newer data is incompatible with older data. Changes in data definitions or methods of collection are almost always noted, usually in a footnote.

C

Study by Design

SpeedStudy

SpeedReview

Economics is the study of how to allocate scarce resources to satisfy unlimited wants. Scarcity forces us to make choices, both individually and collectively. Three questions that every economy must answer are what, how, and for whom. These questions may be answered by government command and control or by laissez-faire free markets. In practice, countries choose a mix of both.

Economic issues are categorized into macroeconomics and microeconomics. Within these fields, analysis can be either positive or normative. Economic reasoning can be impaired by various common fallacies. Economics uses models, simplified versions of reality that shed light on economic relationships. Some models are highly mathematical.

SpeedStudy True or False Self-Test

A1. The essence of scarcity is a lack of money.

A2. Wants are limited.

A3. Without scarcity, there would be no need for economics.

A4. Consumer decisions about what to buy will affect the allocation of resources.

A5. Microeconomics is about the big public policy issues.

A6. An industry is a group of firms producing a similar output.

A7. Allocative efficiency requires the use of a least-cost production technique.

A8. If there is market failure, there is inefficiency.

A9. The following is a normative statement: "Movies today are too violent."

A10. Economic models built on the principle of Occam's razor will include as many details of the real world as possible.

B11. In the last three centuries, there has been little relationship between political and economic ideas.

B12. Lack of incentives for efficiency was a root cause of communism's failure.

B13. Economists are employed in industry, government, and academia.

B14. Unlike the hard sciences, economics does not require much proficiency in mathematics and statistics.

C15. A curve with a negative slope shows a direct relationship between variables.

C16. If there is a change in the relationship between variables, we can illustrate the change by a shift in a curve.

C17. An example of cross-sectional data is the current inflation rate in the countries of Europe.

C18. A good source of data on money and banking is the *Federal Reserve Bulletin*.

The MasterMind

Selected Terms Along the Way

MasterMind Multiple Choice Self-Test

A1. Decision making at the margin is about
   a. all-or-nothing choices.
   b. choices involving money.
   c. incremental choices.
   d. normative economics.

A2. The "what" question is about
   a. the choice of production methods.
   b. the distribution of income.
   c. mixed economies.
   d. the choice of goods and services.

A3. Which of the following is *not* an advantage of market allocation of resources over central government allocation of resources?
   a. Markets distribute income in the most equitable manner possible.
   b. Market prices allocate resources to their highest valued uses.
   c. People out for their own self-interest in the marketplace have more incentive to provide products of value to others than would government bureaucrats.
   d. Competition among firms causes products to be produced in the most technologically efficient manner.

A4. Which of the following is the best example of a positive economic statement?
   a. New York should repeal its income tax.
   b. An increase in the minimum wage is likely to increase unemployment.
   c. It is unfair to subsidize farmers.
   d. The price of gasoline is just fine!

A5. "The proud dog ran to the fence to bark furiously at the letter carrier, who soon moved on to neighboring homes. Satisfied that her barking had driven the intruder away, the dog returned to her nap." This scenario illustrates
   a. Occam's razor.
   b. a normative statement.
   c. the fallacy of composition.
   d. the fallacy of causation.

B6. Which is *not* consistent with a maxi-min philosophy?
   a. Helping the least well-off.
   b. A safety net of social programs.
   c. Lower taxes.
   d. Redistributing income from the rich.

B7. Economists in government spend the majority of their time
   a. teaching.
   b. doing policy-oriented research.
   c. consulting.
   d. making forecasts.

C8. Direct relationships between variables are illustrated graphically by
   a. curves that slope upward to the right.
   b. curves that slope downward to the right.
   c. curves that are horizontal.
   d. curves that are vertical.

C9. Preliminary data
   a. are the best type of data to use.
   b. will be revised later.
   c. are not available in the United States.
   d. are always seasonally adjusted.

MasterMind Questions and Problems

A1. Describe how scarcity affects the following decision makers:
   a. the President of the United States.
   b. a business executive.
   c. a city manager.

A2. Are people a resource? Does it matter whether a person is employed or unemployed? Explain.

A3. During World War II, sugar, gasoline, meat, and other goods were rationed by the U.S. government. Families were issued ration cards that allowed them to buy a government-determined quantity of rationed goods. Why would the government bypass the price system in time of war? Is government rationing, rather than rationing by price, a good idea? How does government rationing affect the allocation of resources?

A4. If farmers stopped farming or transportation workers quit shipping the food that farmers grow, we might wake up one morning to discover our cupboards bare. Why don't we lose sleep over that possibility? What causes the food and other goods to appear in stores?

A5. Explain how choices made between government spending taxpayer money, or taxpayers spending that money themselves, affect the allocation of society's resources.

B6. At this point in your life, are you personally in what Rawls termed the original position? To what extent does the idea of original position shed light on the conventional wisdom, which says that radical youth become conservative in middle age?

B7. Plot an imaginary calendar for an economics professor's day, including each major activity described in Exploration 2.

C8. Do you think that a college student's grade in a course and the amount of time spent studying the subject are positively or negatively related? Draw a graph, label the axes, and show the relationship between grades and study time. Do you think the relationship is necessarily linear? What factors other than study time affect grades? How do they affect the position of the curve you have drawn?

C9. Each day the *Wall Street Journal* publishes stories that focus on the latest economic statistics. Why do business decision makers find this information worthwhile? Could lack of data lead to more wrong decisions?

Future Explorations: Mapping out Term Papers

1. Adam Smith and the Invisible Hand
This paper will require you to study Adam Smith's *The Wealth of Nations* and secondary sources that refer to the invisible hand of the marketplace. Your goal is to explain in your own words the meaning and significance of Smith's ideas about competition and the invisible hand.

2. **The Nobel Prize in Economics: The Winners and Their Contributions to Knowledge**

   This paper starts with a brief autobiographical sketch of several people who have won the Nobel Prize in economics. Describe the specialty field that each is known for. Sketch their ideas. Do the Nobel Prize winners describe the practical application of their ideas? (Hint: The better-known winners such as Milton Friedman and Paul Samuelson will be easier.)

3. **The Economics Journals: The Current Issues**

   Locate several recent copies of the *American Economic Review* or the *Journal of Political Economy* and report on the contents by annotating several articles from each copy. Select articles that relate to practical application or current issues. Be sure to comment on each author's use of graphs and mathematics.

Answer Key

ExpressStudy True or False	SpeedStudy True or False Self-Test		MasterMind Multiple Choice Self-Test
1. F	1. F	10. F	1. c
2. F	2. F	11. F	2. d
3. T	3. T	12. T	3. a
4. T	4. T	13. T	4. b
5. F	5. F	14. F	5. d
6. F	6. T	15. F	6. c
	7. F	16. T	7. b
	8. T	17. T	8. a
	9. T	18. T	9. b

CHAPTER

Two

Production, Growth, and Trade

A Look Ahead

What does the word *model* call to mind? A swimsuit model? A model citizen? A model airplane? In this chapter, we will model the essence of economics—scarcity and choice. While designed for different purposes, this economic model shares a common trait with these other models—yes, even the swimsuit model. That trait is simplicity, to highlight the features that are significant.

Economics is about common sense. By organizing this common sense systematically, we can shed light on a diverse array of questions that concern our personal lives and the choices our country makes. For example, the same model that tells us what career opportunities appear most promising can also be used to explain why countries are not well served to protect either their high-paying or low-paying industries. We will also find out why economics pervades life on earth and even makes its way aboard the starship *Enterprise*.

The basic model of economics developed in this chapter explains the mundane, such as which products a country chooses to produce and how producers respond to prices. It also reveals the sublime, such as the rise and fall of nations and governments. Future chapters investigate the details behind the broad scope of economics that we glimpse here.

DESTINATIONS

*M*odule A

As you zip along the Expressway you will arrive at an ability to

- analyze trade-offs facing both individuals and countries;
- depict what it means for marginal opportunity costs to increase;
- model a country's production possibilities, and how these possibilities respond to technological development;
- describe how economies can grow faster if they are willing to cut back on current consumption;
- explain why people and countries gain from trade, even if they do not have an absolute advantage in anything.

*M*odule B

Upon leaving the Expressway to explore issues you will be able to

- identify how the information highway represents capital that solves some but not all information problems in the economy;
- point out how the incentives for population growth are likely to be inefficient.

*M*odule C

Mastering Roadside Challenges will allow you to hone analytical skills by

- computing comparative advantage as a basis for mutually beneficial trade;
- illustrating why countries are well served to separate their choices of what to produce from their choices of what to consume.

Scarcity and Choice

There is no such thing as a free lunch.

Economics exists because resources are scarce relative to our wants. Scarcity means we have to make choices. Take lunch for example. Suppose your school cafeteria holds a Student Appreciation Day and offers a free sandwich buffet between noon and 1:00 next Thursday. Would you go? Your decision depends upon opportunity costs.

Opportunity Costs

Opportunity costs represent the value of foregone alternatives. Perhaps you contemplate how good the cafeteria's sandwiches are, relative to other things you could eat. You might also consider how pleasant the surroundings are, relative to other lunch spots. You would also want to check your calendar—your time may be needed for something of higher priority, such as studying for an exam. If you choose to eat the cafeteria's sandwiches, you must give up the value of alternative ways to spend that time. While no money is taken, the lunch is in reality far from free.

The money you pay for an item could have alternatively been spent on something else. The value of the best alternative use of that money is an opportunity cost, but not usually the only opportunity cost. The value of foregone alternative uses of time or other nonmonetary resources must also be included. To compute your own opportunity cost of going to college, for example, you must compute what you would be doing if you were not in school. Would you be working? Then the cost of a semester is tuition plus the foregone earnings from the job you would have had. Maybe you would have been spending all of your time at the beach. That, too, has an opportunity cost. Only you can know how high it is, because only you can know what value you receive from lying in the sun and listening to the surf.

OBSERVATION POINT: "The Grass is Always Greener . . .

. . . on the other side of the fence," the saying goes. Take marriage, for example. How many married men and women do not catch themselves envying the freedom of their single friends—freedom to meet new people and do what they want, when they want to do it? How many of those single friends do not look back with envy of their own, seeing the warmth and security of sharing one's life with someone special? Oh, those opportunity costs! We cannot have it all!

A

Resources

Resources are usually divided into the categories of land, labor, capital, and entrepreneurship. **Land** refers to all natural resources in their natural states. These gifts of nature include such things as minerals, water, soil, and location. For example, neither motor oil nor gasoline would be considered as land. Rather, both are products that make use of land as an input. The crude oil from which the motor oil and gasoline were derived is land.

Labor refers to people's capacity to work. It ignores the increased productivity from acquired skills and abilities, which constitute **human capital**. Human capital is a special case of an economy's third resource, capital. **Capital** is anything that is produced in order to increase productivity in the future. Along with human capital, there is also *physical capital*, which includes buildings, machinery, and other equipment. For example, a college education adds to human capital, and the classroom in which that education was obtained is physical capital. The classroom aids in the production of an education, and the education aids in productivity at the workplace.

> CAUTION: The definition of *capital* used in economics differs from that used in finance. *Financial capital* refers to financial instruments, such as stocks, bonds, and money.

Entrepreneurship is taking personal initiative to combine resources in productive ways. Rather than accepting jobs where orders are handed down from above, entrepreneurs blaze new trails in the world of commerce. If you start your own business, you are an entrepreneur. Entrepreneurs take risks, but have the potential to become the economy's movers and shakers. Countries tap the creative potential of entrepreneurship in order to improve the value they get from other resources. In the process, the entrepreneurs themselves are sometimes handsomely rewarded.

The possibilities for combining an economy's resources depends upon technology. **Technology** refers to possible techniques of production. As technologies change, the relative values of various resources also change. For example, natural harbors declined in significance due to the technology of air transportation. While the value of land around harbors diminished, air travel increased the importance of other resources, such as the human capital needed to pilot the planes.

✓ QUICKCHECK

What economic benefits would enrolling in college offer the prospective student?

Answer: A college education provides students with both capital and goods for current consumption. The capital is human capital, meaning the skills and abilities college imparts, which increase productivity in the workplace. The consumption goods include such things as gaining perspective on life, learning interesting things, meeting interesting people, and having a good time. Such consumption goods have different values to different students, which is one good reason why some people major in ecology, some in education, and others in economics, even when aptitude tests might recommend different choices.

A

OBSERVATION POINT: The Entrepreneurial Road to Riches—Sam Walton, Bill Gates, . . . and You?

One in two hundred, they say—the odds of striking it rich as an entrepreneur may not be great, but the potential payoff does motivate people to try. How can a person win at the entrepreneurial gamble?

The answer is to offer a product that fills an unmet niche in the mass market. Former economics major Sam Walton used the concept of one-stop shopping at everyday low prices in cities and towns across America. The success of Wal-Mart catapulted the Walton family to first place among America's wealthy. Bill Gates amassed his fortune by positioning Microsoft to provide the industry-standard interface for the personal computer. The more user-friendly, the more money rolls in.

The common theme to the success stories of America's modern entrepreneurs is insight into what the public likes to do and how they could do it better or more conveniently. Talk on the phone? Craig McCaw said "take it with you," and took home $11.5 billion dollars from his sale of McCaw Cellular Communications Corporation. Chat over coffee? Howard Shultze earned his fortune by opening Starbucks Coffee Company as a place to hang out over a steaming brew. FedEx your important papers? That was Fred Smith's idea. Linda Wascher saw The Limited catapult its parent company, Warneco, onto the Fortune 100 list of America's largest companies. It was Domino's that delivered for Tom Monaghan, and Motown that recorded Berry Gordy's profit.

Do you have the next good idea, just waiting to take the world by storm? Are you willing to take the risk to find out? If so, you are ready to join the ranks of the entrepreneurs.

Production Possibilities

Modeling Scarcity and Choice

Recall that a model is a simplified version of reality. Following the principles of Occam's razor discussed in chapter 1, a good model emphasizes only those features pertinent to solving the problem at hand. This section will model the essence of economics—scarcity and choice. An economy's scarce resources limit its options. The economy thus must make choices about what to produce. We can model these options, and the choices among them, with a **production possibility frontier.**

The production possibility frontier illustrates scarcity and choice by assuming that only two goods can be produced. This simplification is appropriate, because understanding choice between any two goods allows the understanding of choice between each good and any other. It is termed a frontier because it represents the limits of output possibilities, given current resources and technology. Frontiers of knowledge and capability are made to be expanded, and the production possibility frontier is no exception. Over time, as resources are accumulated and new techniques learned, the production possibility frontier will expand outward.

Consider the fictional economy of Hermit Island, inhabited exclusively by Herschel the Hermit. Herschel has the island to himself, and it provides for all his material needs. Still, he must spend time to feed himself. His options are to catch fish or harvest coconuts. He values both of these foods in his diet and can spend up to eight hours a day to obtain them. Table 2A-1 and Figure 2A-1 illustrate a production possibility frontier for Herschel's economy.

The graph reveals the same information as the table, but does so in a manner that, with practice, can be interpreted at a glance. For example, the combination of three fish and sixteen coconuts can be read from the third line of the table or seen as point C on the graph. Point D on the graph shows the combination of two fish and nineteen coconuts.

Relationships among data are more readily apparent in the graph than in the table. For example, a basic message of the production possibility frontier is that, as more fish are caught, fewer coconuts are collected. A glance at the graph reveals this relationship. The inverse relationship between fish and coconuts illustrates the opportunity cost of Herschel using his limited resource, time.

As Herschel increases his catch from zero fish to a maximum of five fish, we see

TABLE 2A-1	*Production Possibility Frontier*	
Data Point	Fish Caught per Day	Coconuts Collected per Day
A	5	0
B	4	10
C	3	16
D	2	19
E	1	21
F	0	22

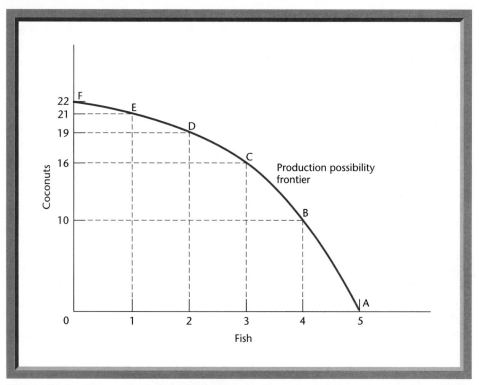

Figure 2A-1 **The production possibility frontier** illustrates an economy's options from which to choose.

the number of coconuts he collects drop at a nonlinear rate. In other words, the opportunity cost of the first fish is only one coconut. The opportunity cost of two fish is giving up three coconuts. The opportunity cost of five fish is twenty-two coconuts. Table 2A-2 illustrates this opportunity cost, where the *marginal opportunity cost* refers to the additional opportunity cost from catching one more fish. **Marginal** is a word that pops up frequently in economics. It always means incremental, pertaining to one additional unit of something.

TABLE 2A-2 *Opportunity Costs*

Data Point	Fish Caught per Day	Opportunity Cost (number of coconuts forgone)	Marginal Opportunity Cost (change in number of coconuts foregone)
F	0	0	undefined
E	1	1	1
D	2	3	2
C	3	6	3
B	4	12	6
A	5	22	10

These numbers illustrate a principle known as **the law of increasing cost, which says that as an economy adds to its production of any one good, the marginal opportunity cost of that good will rise.** This principle explains why the production possibility frontier appears bowed outward. To understand this law, let us examine further the economy of Hermit Island.

Each working hour of the day, Herschel has to choose between fishing and gathering coconuts. The most productive fishing occurs at certain hours of the day when the fish are biting. While all hours are equally well suited to gathering coconuts, Herschel knows that the number of coconuts gathered per hour declines as he spends more hours per day gathering, because he gathers the most accessible coconuts first. Knocking a few hours off of coconut gathering to fish during feeding time allows him to catch some fish at a cost of relatively few coconuts. Adding more hours to his fishing time leads to less and less incremental productivity in fishing and takes away increasingly more productive hours in gathering. The result is the law of increasing cost.

Stated more broadly, in producing any good X, an economy first uses resources that are best suited to producing X. If the economy keeps adding to the production of good X, it uses resources that are increasingly less well suited to X, but increasingly better suited to other goods (Y). The result is that Y production drops at an increasingly rapid rate as X production increases. The root cause of the law of increasing marginal opportunity costs is thus that resources are not equally well suited to the production of different goods.

For instance, classrooms are well suited to producing human capital, but not well

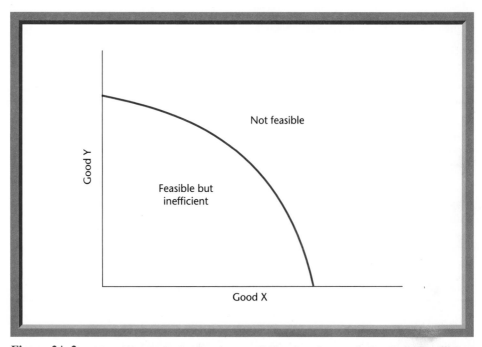

Figure 2A-2   All points on the production possibility frontier are technologically efficient and feasible. Points within the production possibility frontier are also feasible, but are not technologically efficient. Points outside the frontier cannot be reached with current resources and technology.

suited to producing automobiles. Resources are often specialized to perform limited tasks: fish hooks are great for fishing, cooktops for cooking, coal mines for mining coal, etc. They can sometimes be used for other purposes, but will not be as productive in these uses. For example, coal mines are fine places to grow mushrooms and have led to commercial production under such brand names as Moonlight Mushrooms. However, until the coal seams play out, the coal output is likely to be of higher value.

Figure 2A-2 shows the general notion of the production possibility frontier. This idea can be conveyed on a graph without numbers, since the idea transcends any particular numbers. (If you have trouble with a graph without numbers, however, just add some illustrative numbers.) All points within or along the frontier are feasible combinations of goods X and Y. For the economy to be at a point on the production possibility frontier, it must use all of its resources and use them efficiently. If the economy acquires more resources, its entire production possibility frontier shifts outward, such as shown in Figure 2A-3. **Whenever the production possibility frontier shifts outward, the economy is said to have experienced** economic growth, which allows it to produce more output. In sum,

- Every point along the production possibility frontier is technologically efficient.
- Points inside the frontier imply some unemployed or misallocated resources and are thus inefficient.
- Points outside the frontier are unattainable with current resources and technology.

✓ **QUICKCHECK**

Are all points along a production possibility frontier equally efficient? Is an economy indifferent among them?

Answer: All points on the production possibility frontier are technologically efficient, meaning that it is impossible to produce more of one good without giving up some of the other. However, while technological efficiency is necessary for overall economic efficiency, it is also necessary to choose the point that is allocatively efficient. People may be quite willing to give up one good for more of another. Thus, not all points on the production possibility frontier are allocatively efficient, and an economy is not indifferent among those points. In response to consumer demand, however, competitive markets will ordinarily choose points that are allocatively efficient.

Technological Change—The General and the Specific

Technological change can increase productivity generally, as has been the case with better information flows made possible by modern computers and telecommunications. Oftentimes, however, technological change is specific to an industry. For example, a biotechnological advance might improve cucumber yields but have no effect on the steel industry.

Figure 2A-4 illustrates the difference between general growth and specialized growth, where the economy starts from the original production possibility frontier. In the case of general growth, productivity in both the pretzel and pumpkin industries increases. In the case of specialized growth, productivity increases in only one industry.

The production possibility frontiers labeled Specialized Growth in Figure 2A-4 indicate technological improvement in only the pretzel industry. To see why growth occurred in the pretzel industry but not the pumpkin industry, consider the output of each

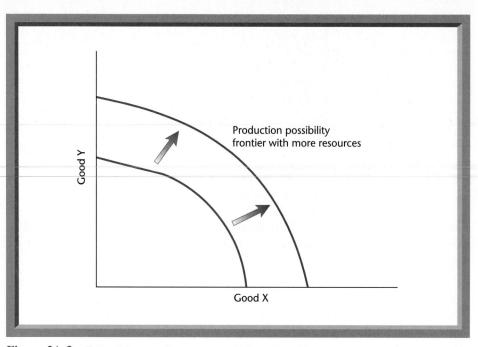

Figure 2A-3 Economic growth can be caused by an increase in resources.

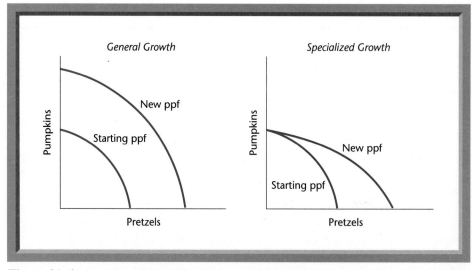

Figure 2A-4 Broad-reaching technological change brings general growth, which shifts the entire production possibility frontier (ppf) outward. **Specialized technological change brings specialized growth,** which causes the production possibility frontier to rotate in the direction of the industry to which the new technology applies.

good separately when none of the other is produced. When no pretzels are produced, the technological change has not affected the production possibility for pumpkins, because the point on the vertical axis is the same as before. However, when no pumpkins are produced, the technological change has allowed an increase in the possible output of pretzels. We know this because the intercept on the horizontal axis is to the right of where it was before. Whatever that maximum quantity of pretzels had been, it is now higher. Hence the technological change applied only to the pretzel industry. **Specialized growth thus pivots the production possibility frontier in the direction of more output in the industry affected by the technological change.**

Modeling Growth—Impoverished Countries Face a Difficult Trade-off

Land, labor, capital, and entrepreneurship—these are the resources the economy has to work with. Production possibilities will depend upon how much of each resource the economy has and upon the technology that is available to make use of those resources. As resources increase or technology improves, production possibilities grow. In the event of natural disasters, the exhaustion of natural resources, or anything else that causes an economy's resource base to shrink, the country's production possibilities will also shrink. This effect would be just opposite to that depicted in Figure 2A-3.

For example, suppose we return to the economy of Hermit Island. Herschel might construct some netting to use in catching fish and some additional netting to collect the coconuts as they fall to the ground. The nets are capital goods that allow him to catch more fish and collect more coconuts per hour. This shifts Herschel's production possibility frontier outward. Alternatively, were Herschel to overfish, and a coconut blight to strike, too, fewer fish and coconuts would be available. His production possibility frontier would shift inward.

In more complex economies, economic growth does not necessarily mean that standards of living improve in the country. That depends in part on whether the economy measures the right things when it tabulates growth. It also depends upon population. After all, if an economy grows by adding the resource of labor, that also involves more mouths to feed. Thus, economic growth is often measured on a **per capita** basis, meaning output per person.

Economies have relatively little control over how much land and labor they have. They have more influence over capital and entrepreneurship. How much entrepreneurship a country possesses will depend upon such things as culture and whether entrepreneurs are well rewarded for their risk-taking. To amass more capital, an economy must also provide incentives for capital creation. Since capital represents output that is produced now for the purpose of increasing productivity later, the creation of capital comes at the expense of current consumption. Figure 2A-5 illustrates this choice.

For example, at point A the economy is devoting nearly all of its resources to consumption goods. The result is that its stock of capital decreases over time, because of equipment wearing out, buildings falling into disrepair, and other forms of **depreciation** As its stock of capital falls, its production possibility frontier shifts inward. Point B, in contrast, trades off some current consumption for a significant amount of *capital formation*, meaning that it adds to its stock of capital. The result is that its production possibility frontier shifts out over time.

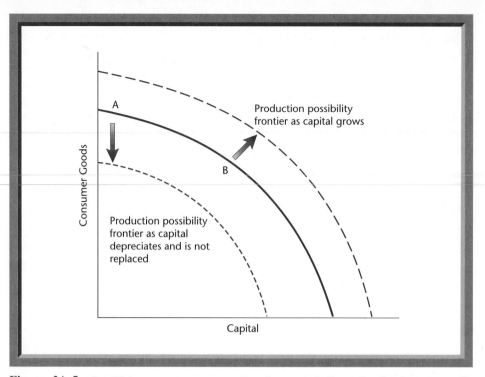

Figure 2A-5 **Sacrificing current consumption for capital formation hastens economic growth,** but may be painful in the present. For example, choosing point **B** provides the capital needed to expand production possibilities over time. In contrast, choosing point **A** allows for more current consumption, but shrinks the production possibility frontier over time. This is because not enough new capital is produced to offset the depreciation of existing capital.

When an economy is characterized by widespread poverty, the route to economic growth involves particularly tough trade-offs. In Herschel's case, he was forced to subsist on fewer fish and coconuts while he spent time weaving the nets. More generally, the only way to ameliorate poverty is to channel resources into amassing capital. Those resources are taken away from the production of goods that meet current needs, such as food and housing.

OBSERVATION POINT: From the Shah to the Ayatollah—A Slippery Path to Growth

Imagine holding the reins as your country emerges from its long slumber to stand tall and fearless in the new day ahead. Such was the dream of the Shah of Iran, absolute ruler of a country with a fabulous wealth of oil reserves.

With OPEC having dramatically increased the price of oil in the 1970s, Shah Mohammad Reza Pahlavi embarked on a rapid modernization of his country. His goal was for Iran to catch up with the West in prestige, living standards, and culture. Resources were channeled to highways, oil refineries, schools, dams, and other capital infrastructure. Seemingly overnight, Iran's economy was to be transformed from agricultural to industrial.

With all this change going on, lifestyles were disrupted and animosity seethed among Iran's traditionally oriented Islamic population. Improving living standards remained but a distant promise as change in the here and now was imposed from above. The more discontent simmered, the more its expression was harshly suppressed by SAVAK, the Shah's fearsome secret police.

A bump in the road? A rough spot to traverse before the journey's glorious end? That may have been the idea. The reality was a revolution in 1979, which overthrew the Shah in favor of Islamic fundamentalist Ayatollah Ruholla Khomeini. Rather than join the West, Iran attempted to cut itself off from Western culture. Instead of developing capital infrastructure, Iran poured its resources into more than a decade's worth of warfare with its neighbor, Iraq. As for the Shah's vision, it remained but a shimmering mirage in the Iranian desert.

A

*C*ircular Flow and the Role of Money

Production possibility frontiers are about possibilities. What a market economy will actually choose to produce is decided through the interaction of consumers and businesses. In effect, consumers vote with their money for the assortment of goods and services that is offered. **Money** is a medium of exchange. As such, money is used to make purchases. Money also serves other purposes. For example, money can measure the value of things, even if they are not actually bought and sold—"That view is worth a million dollars!" Likewise, money can store value for future spending.

Without money, people would be forced to exchange goods directly, a situation known as **barter**. Barter is unworkable in a complicated economy. For example, to buy this textbook, you would be forced to provide something the bookstore would want in return. What do you have? Would you offer a chicken? What if the bookstore will only accept Buffalo wings? Yes, the possibilities become convoluted quickly. Money comes to the rescue—it greases the wheels of commerce.

Many things have served as money through the years. In prisoner-of-war camps in World War II, cigarettes served as money. Traditionally, gold, silver, and other scarce metals have served as money. Such monies are termed *commodity monies*. Unfortunately, the use of commodity money leads to worries over *debasement*, in which people combine less valuable metals with the gold or silver or merely chip or shave off pieces.

Since gold and silver are subject to debasement and are also hard to transport, they were often replaced by paper. The paper money could be nothing more than warehouse receipts for precious metals held in storage. Still, this practice led to a worry about counterfeit receipts and also about the integrity of the warehouse. Paper money was more readily accepted if issued by government. These days, however, government prints up paper currency without even pretending to back it with gold or silver. Such money is called *fiat money*. People accept this as money, in part because government accepts it as payment.

A critical condition for gold, currency, or any other item to be accepted as money is that the quantity of the item must be restricted. Whereas additional gold may be mined, only the mythical King Midas could manufacture gold from other sources. Despite many years of trying, the alchemists in the middle ages never succeeded in turning lead into gold. Likewise, individuals must not be able to print government currencies, or those currencies would lose their value as money. That is why counterfeiting is illegal. Government must also be careful about printing too much currency if it wishes its currency to retain value as money.

Figure 2A-6 illustrates the **circular flow** model of economic activity, which depicts how markets use the medium of money to determine what goods and services are produced and who gets to buy them. The top part of the diagram illustrates the *output market* in which producers sell goods and services to consumers. The actual assortment of goods and services is determined by how much households are willing to pay relative to business firms' production costs.

The bottom part of the diagram shows the *input market*, which illustrates that households supply the resources of land, labor, capital, and entrepreneurship. All of these resources are ultimately owned by people, who make up households. The sale of resources to business provides the income that households use to buy products. Indeed, since it is people who own businesses, business profits also belong to households. Hence, the circular flow of inputs and outputs is maintained by a counterflow of dollars.

The circular flow model can be expanded in many respects. For example, it could be expanded to show that government influences the mix of goods that are produced and the manner in which resources are used. Likewise, it can be expanded to include foreign commerce. However, the circular flow model is something like a pictograph on the walls of a prehistoric cave. It is a good picture for conveying the basic essence of economic activity, just as a pictograph can convey the notion of a successful hunt for winter game. More de-

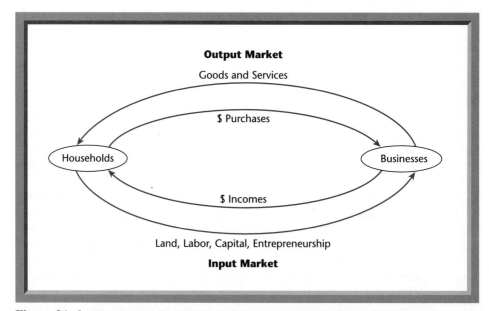

Figure 2A-6   The circular flow diagram shows that household income depends on the sale of resources and that household spending determines outputs and the value of those resources.

tailed stories are probably better told with more abstract languages. Analytical graphs, of which the production possibility frontier is an example, represent one such language.

Expanding Consumption Possibilities through Trade

Economies are fortunate to have other economies to trade with. This is true for national economies, regional economies, local economies, and even personal economies. For example, we each have our own production possibilities. Yet, if we tried to rely only upon these production possibilities, we would be hard-pressed to live as well as Herschel the Hermit. Thus, we trade. We trade our labor services for income, to allow us to purchase what we want. We trade so that we can consume more quantity and variety than we could produce on our own. Cities, states, and countries trade among themselves for the same reasons individuals trade with one another.

Specialization according to Comparative Advantage—The Basis for Trade

In order to gain from trade, an economy must specialize according to its **comparative advantage**. **An economy has a comparative advantage in producing a good if it can produce that good at a lower opportunity cost than could other economies.** This means the economy chooses to produce those things it does well relative to other things it could be doing. Contrary to popular belief, trade is not based on **absolute advantage**, which refers to the ability to produce something with fewer resources than others could.

For example, Mr. Spock of "Star Trek" is known for his logical mind. He is able to learn new scientific knowledge with little effort. He is a master at chess. Indeed, it is likely that he could clean the passageways of the starship *Enterprise* more effectively than any other crew member. After all, his logical mind would lead him to choose the most effective way to get the job done. Yet, Mr. Spock does not mop the floors and scrub the walls. That would be illogical.

Spock's scarce time could be put to better use than cleaning the starship's passageways, since the opportunity cost of his doing so would be high. Even though Spock has an absolute advantage in almost everything he would choose to undertake, he has a comparative advantage only in things he does relatively well. Spock is many times more efficient than others at scientific research, which is why he holds the post of science officer. He is only slightly more efficient at mopping the floors, which is why he does not hold the post of janitor. Spock does not have a comparative advantage at being a janitor.

In order to gain from trade, it is not necessary to have an absolute advantage at anything. Even if a person cannot do anything well, he or she can still do some things relatively better than other things. For example, it might take Charlie Brown longer to mow yards than it would take other people. Yet, if that is what Charlie were to do best, he would mow yards. Other people would be delighted to hire him because he would charge less than their own time is worth. It is unimportant that it takes him longer.

Thus, both well-endowed and poorly endowed people gain from trade. Likewise, well-endowed and poorly endowed regions and countries also gain from trade. The resulting *consumption possibilities* will be greater for the well-endowed than for the poorly endowed. Still, through trade, both types of economies can consume more than they could produce on their own.

In other words, while a country is constrained to produce along or inside its production possibility frontier, it can exchange some of its own output for the output of other countries. Goods and services a country sells to other countries are termed **exports**. Exports are in effect traded for **imports**, which are goods and services a country buys from other countries. Through this trade, a country can consume a combination of goods and services that lies outside its production possibility frontier. (Challenge 2 in this chapter graphs the possibilities for an economy to consume beyond its production possibility frontier.)

Small countries gain proportionally more from international trade than do large countries. This is because, the larger is the country, the more opportunities there are to specialize internally. For example, the U.S. produces potatoes in Maine and Idaho for sale throughout the other states. Likewise, Michigan specializes in automobile production, Texas in oil and gas production, and so forth. If the U.S. were broken into fifty different countries, this trade among states would all be international. As it is, the tremendous diversity of resources found within the United States leads it to have one of the smallest proportions of international trade relative to its output of any country in the world.

Figure 2A-7 shows the proportion of various countries' exports relative to their outputs. The smaller the country, typically, the higher that ratio is, and the more it gains from trade.

Economists do not spend a great deal of time attempting to compute the goods in which countries have their comparative advantages. The reason is that markets do that quite effectively on their own. If a country has a comparative advantage in a good, it can produce that good cheaply relative to other goods it could produce. These will be the goods it can offer at the best prices in the international marketplace. Thus, without any economic research, economies engaging in international trade naturally tend to export those goods for which they have a comparative advantage and import the rest.

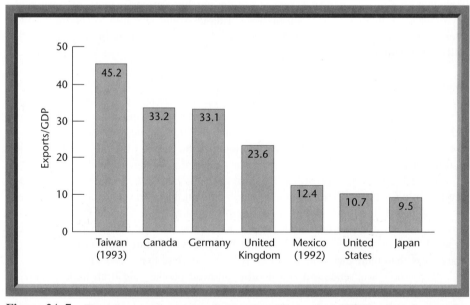

Figure 2A-7   Exports as a percentage of gross domestic product (GDP), selected countries, 1994.

Source: Calculated from country tables, *Internatonal Financial Statistics.* December 1995; and *Europa World Yearbook*, 1995.

Effects of International Trade on Earnings Opportunities in the U.S.

Although international trade increases the aggregate value of a country's consumption possibilities, that does not mean that all residents share in those gains. The primary purpose of international trade, like the purpose of market trade within countries, is to promote efficiency. Sometimes the efficiency gains seem unfair, especially to workers who find their jobs and lives disrupted. This is because, while aggregate job totals may not be much affected by foreign commerce, opportunities in specific industries and types of occupations can change markedly. When industries are hit particularly hard by imports, U.S. law allows for various types of *trade adjustment assistance*, designed to ease the transition from industries on the decline to ones with more promise.

Changes in job opportunities caused by trade often seem unfair to workers whose jobs are lost. However, the problem is mainly a function of markets themselves rather than of whether markets are international. Markets typically promote efficiency, not necessarily equity. With or without foreign trade, jobs and lives are disrupted when products decline in popularity, when technological change affects the manner in which products are produced, and when the fortunes of individual companies rise or fall. These changes are brought about by competition in response to consumer demand. While sometimes disruptive to individual lives, the evolving nature of the U.S. market economy has been essential to maintaining America's high standard of living.

The U.S. has an abundance of both physical and human capital relative to most, but not all, other countries. This means that the U.S. is likely to have a comparative advantage in goods that are *capital intensive*. In other words, for the U.S. to gain from international trade, it specializes in exporting goods that use a high proportion of capital in their production. Thus, the U.S. is known for its exports of airplanes, financial services, and movies. In turn, it imports goods that use a high proportion of labor and land, such as textiles and crude oil.

There are exceptions. For example, Japan is in some respects more capital intensive than the U.S., which explains why Japan exports so many electronic goods to this country. Over all, though, international trade causes the U.S. to specialize somewhat in capital-intensive goods. Exports thus increase the demand for capital in the U.S. and increase the prices paid for capital. The prices paid for capital represent income to owners of capital, including human capital.

By increasing the return to human capital in the U.S., international trade opens up attractive employment opportunities for those who have acquired skills and abilities. For example, the return to a college education is higher than it would be without international trade. Conversely, job opportunities for unskilled labor are harmed by international trade, as imports of labor-intensive goods lead to lower wages and fewer job openings. The result? Competition among workers to obtain burger-flipping jobs is likely to become increasingly intense. In contrast, it is competition among employers to hire the well-educated and skilled workers that promises to intensify as time goes by.

OBSERVATION POINT: Protecting Jobs ... at a Price

"Don't export our good jobs!" "Don't trade with low-wage countries—they'll take our jobs!" We hear the first argument made about U.S. trade with Japan. The second argument comes from opponents of trade with Mexico, China, and other developing countries. Together, the message is simple—don't trade!

While the message may be simple, it is also unsound. For example, should a country prohibit its industries from buying foreign steel? If it does, it is devoting resources to a high-cost industry in which it does not have a comparative advantage. For the sake of transferring a relatively few workers into high-paying jobs, the country would be shrinking the overall value that it gets from its resources. Steel workers are better off, but the country suffers.

The same holds true for protecting low-wage jobs, such as in the textile industry. While it may be a tool for income redistribution, that redistribution is actually a form of make-work project. Better value for the money could be obtained by importing textiles from other countries. For government to change the mix of goods to favor either high-wage or low-wage industries can only reduce possibilities for consumption. The result is a smaller economic pie that is sliced to favor the protected industry.

The U.S. does protect certain jobs, through restricting imports of textiles, steel, and various other products. For example, protection of the U.S. steel industry in the 1980s was associated with a 20 to 40 percent increase in steel prices from 1984 to 1990. These higher prices decreased the international competitiveness of U.S. steel-using industries. The higher costs from protectionist programs are also felt directly by consumers. For example, protectionist policies in place between 1980 and 1984 were estimated to have added $620 to the price of automobiles sold in the U.S. Such cost increases translated into an estimated $160,000 cost of each autoworker's job that was saved.

EXPRESS STUDY TRUE OR FALSE

1. Human capital is created when a person acquires knowledge and skills that can increase his or her earnings.
2. If you decide to buy a Butterfinger candy bar instead of an equally priced Almond Joy, the opportunity cost of your purchase is the value you would have received from that Almond Joy.
3. In the circular flow model of economic activity, resources are assumed to be owned by businesses.
4. There is only one point on the production possibility frontier that is technologically efficient.
5. A country that trades with other countries can consume outside its production possibility frontier.
6. Relative to most countries, the U.S. has a comparative advantage in goods that are produced with a high proportion of capital, including human capital.

An information superhighway involves investing in capital and technology, which expands future production and consumption possibilities. While an information superhighway cannot solve all information problems, its presence does suggest a different mix of outputs and of government regulations.

$\mathcal{V}$isions of Information Superhighways

Railroads, highways, maps—there is something compelling about these things. They are each capital that offers personal freedom and power. They take us where we want to go, even if only in our minds. Is it any wonder, then, that we use the terminology of highways to talk about the new vistas being opened by technology? It is like the development of the U.S. highway and interstate highway systems that opened up America for all to explore.

For physical highways, construction has slowed. For communication highways, construction has accelerated. Both of these highway systems represent a capital investment that facilitates economic growth. There is an important difference, however, in terms of the engine for that growth. With roadways, it has been largely government that has amassed the capital. Building the interstate highways has been a *public works project*—one directed by government. Government has also been instrumental in creating the Internet, the information highway of the 90s. However, other elements of the information highway have been built primarily with private money. This manner of construction harks back to the railroads of the nineteenth century.

Railroads had a challenge to overcome, which markets helped answer. At first, there was little standardization. This quickly led to problems, however, as equipment designed for one gauge of track could not pass onto other rail lines of different gauges. To keep costs down, locomotive and boxcar manufacturers also did not wish to be manufacturing equipment of different gauge, height, and weight, depending upon the construction of the buyers' railroads. Railroads adopted common standards of design; competition would not allow them to do otherwise. Still, for many farmers and manufacturers dependent upon the railroads for access to markets, competition often seemed lacking. Government intervened with regulations to protect these users' interests. Government also used land grants to subsidize new construction. Government is likely to intervene along the information highway, too.

State governments took the lead in constructing highways in the U.S. States had strong interests in highways that brought in business from elsewhere. They had little interest, however, in highways that allowed travelers to pass through quickly on their journeys between other states. For example, why should Pennsylvania spend money to build and maintain its portion of the interstate highway linking Buffalo, New York, and Cleveland, Ohio? Thus, the federal government intervened to set guidelines and provide incentives, as it may do again in the construction and operation of privately owned information highways.

*I*nnovation and Capital Formation

The development of information highways expands a country's production possibilities for nearly all types of services and goods, including both new capital and consumer goods. The effect on production possibilities for goods and services is illustrated in Figure 2B1-1. How much those possibilities are expanded, however, will depend on specific goods and services and on the type of highway that is constructed. What type is best? Government planners cannot know, in part because the production possibilities are in a constant state of flux in response to technological change. For example, should the information highway be constructed of fiber optic lines? What of cellular or other wireless technologies? The possibilities keep evolving. To know which is best requires an assessment of costs and benefits of alternatives.

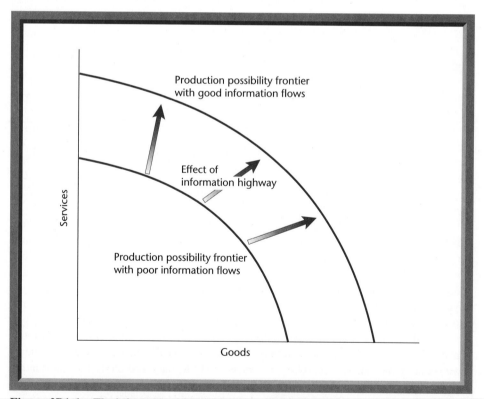

Figure 2B1-1   The information highway improves information flows, which has the effect of shifting the production possibility frontier outward for nearly all types of goods and services.

Economic efficiency requires the economy to maximize benefits relative to costs. The marketplace does this through a plethora of decisions made by businesses and consumers. For example, companies will not string billions of dollars worth of fiber-optic cables unless they are convinced that other technologies will not soon make those cables obsolete. Even if the cost of creating capital is known, its value depends upon technological development.

The value of capital depends also upon other capital. For example, the set of encyclopedias on your shelf is a form of capital, waiting to increase your productivity in future years. However, if an information highway allows you on-line access to a continuously updated encyclopedia, that physical set may become just more clutter that gets in the way of productivity.

Capital formation and technological change go hand in hand. New *hardware* systems, such as personal computers interconnected by a web of fiber-optic cables, in turn bring forth new *software* that provides the brainpower to make use of the hardware's potential. While both hardware and software are capital, how much potential can be extracted from the hardware depends upon the creativity of software designers. Together, both allow greater access to information, which in turn increases productivity throughout the economy.

For example, research in virtually all fields is more easily done with fingertip access to the libraries of the world. Likewise, instantaneous access to medical records promotes productivity in health care. Shopping from home can save time and gasoline and even reduce pollution. This is the information economy in action.

While the physical capital of hardware and software are necessary, human capital also plays a critical role. For example, advertisements frequently tout the whiz-bang things that computers can do. Yet, when people go to the expense of actually buying the advertised hardware and software, the purchases often merely take up space—they require an investment in human capital to extract their whiz-bang capabilities. For this reason, people may quite rationally decide to use seemingly obsolete hardware and software. By the same token, if accessing information flows requires too much human capital, the information highway will not be user-friendly, and the information economy will be dominated by a technical elite.

How much effort is put into user-friendliness and other aspects of information systems depends upon consumer willingness to pay. "Build a better mousetrap, and the world will beat a path to your door." How much the world is willing to pay for that better mousetrap determines how much effort will be put into mousetrap innovation. The same holds true for innovation in the hardware and software capital that underlie the information economy.

*R*egulation—*Along the Way and Down the Road*

Is there a role for government in the information economy? We have seen government design and help finance the Internet. Yet, many people worry about misuse of government power on these information routes. We do not want Big Brother eavesdropping on our private conversations. Likewise, we fear for the privacy of our personal financial and medical records.

Government does choose to regulate the information highway for various reasons. For example, a locality's telephone lines are typically owned by a single company, as is its ca-

B

ble television network. Since competition in the marketplace is what keeps prices in line with costs, and since such competition appears to be missing, government may choose to regulate the prices charged by these companies. This may in turn become regulation of prices charged along the information highway if local telephone or cable lines serve as access points.

Such regulation brings objections. One objection is that, even though only one firm may be providing a particular product, there are many similar products that serve as effective competition. In the case of local telephone service, for example, various forms of wireless competition exist. Even cable television companies sometimes offer telephone service. The danger is that, by regulating one service, innovation and potential competition are kept at bay. In contrast, if a local telephone service were to charge excessively high prices, would not competitors offering the same or similar services enter the market and provide competition?

Government also uses its regulatory powers to promote equity. Here too there is controversy, since not everyone has the same opinions about what constitutes equity. For example, should all U.S. citizens be entitled to the same access to the information highway? Proponents of equal access argue that the economy will become separated into information haves and have-nots if information service providers are allowed to serve only profitable markets.

For everyone to have equal access to information would involve a massive amount of investment that private companies would not undertake on their own. Such investment would be needed to provide services to out-of-the-way places, and even to small- and medium-sized cities. This investment has opportunity costs and would surely slow development of the highway itself. Opponents of equal access point out that large cities are served by an extensive system of expressways, whereas small towns are connected by narrower roads. Should a system of information highways be any different?

What of the information itself? Should government regulate its content? Should there be complete freedom of speech and expression, even if children might be in the audience? In areas of pornography and criminal activity, we might want government to provide some guidelines for information that is accessible to all. If government monitors content, however, where does it stop? Would it censor everything that government officials think would be unsuitable for the most impressionable children? Would it censor anything that does not pass a test of political correctness?

There is even the question of which government would do the regulating, since information flows are increasingly global. In December 1995, for example, the online service CompuServe sparked a global outcry when it temporarily blocked access for all of its subscribers to 200 newsgroups on the Internet. At the behest of a Bavarian prosecutor, Munich police had suggested that CompuServe "scrutinize" these newsgroups for violation of German law. The list of newsgroups included chat groups about AIDS and other topics of interest to homosexuals. Other governments might have found those topics acceptable, but added different sites to the list.

While there are tough philosophical questions about information content, we should not discount the power of the marketplace to solve many of them. For example, protecting children at home from pornography is far from impossible. In response to market demand, creative software writers have developed programs to block access to a wide array of materials available. One company, Surfwatchers Software, Inc., advertises the ability to block over one thousand Internet sites containing sexually explicit text and pictures. Parents can remain in charge, but must pay the market price.

Informational Asymmetries in an Information Economy

Informational asymmetries occur when one person has access to more information than another on a subject of mutual interest. For example, the seller of a used car usually knows more about its condition than the buyer can know, even if the buyer has the car tested. Likewise, the buyer of health insurance knows more about his or her own likelihood of sickness and injury than the insurance company can know. Even easy access to information along the information highway will not resolve such asymmetries.

Informational asymmetries are responsible for several puzzling facets of modern life. For example, the value of an automobile drops by a couple of thousand dollars as soon as it is first sold. The reason is that buyers of used cars are aware of informational asymmetries. They know what they don't know! Thus, used car buyers figure that there is probably a reason the car is being sold so quickly. The buyer infers that it is likely to have problems, even if the car is actually okay.

In the case of health insurance, the buyer of an individual policy winds up paying a much higher premium than if the same person bought the same policy as a member of an employer group plan. The reason is that the insurance company figures that workers are hired for reasons unrelated to their need for insurance. In contrast, an individual who goes to the trouble of lining up a personal health insurance policy is **signaling**—sending a message to—the insurance company that he or she is more likely to need that coverage. Since insurance claims cost money, the insurance company charges more for the policy, even if the signal is incorrect.

There are still other ways that informational asymmetries will continue to affect our lives. Are you studying at one of the top ten universities in the country? If you are, you will find that your degree will be worth a great deal more in the job market than degrees held by people who have acquired an equal amount of knowledge at lesser-known schools. This is the problem of *credentialism*. Employers use credentials as a way to ensure that their employees are intelligent and well trained. Since grading standards vary from school to school, and since the job interview process cannot hope to uncover all of an applicant's skills and abilities, employers pay more for degrees from schools they have heard of and trust. It often seems inequitable, but it can be efficient.

Informational asymmetries provide at least part of the explanation for another phenomenon observed in the labor market—cronyism. *Cronyism* occurs when employers hire friends, relatives, fellow church members, and so forth. That may be a profitable business practice if these employees are more reliable than strangers. While it seems unfair to applicants outside the group of cronies, cronyism probably does serve to reduce job turnover and minimize false credentials. In short, at a cost of equity, cronyism offers a way to circumvent asymmetric information.

Implications of an Information Economy

In November 1994 an obscure mathematician in Virginia humbled the mighty Intel Corporation by reporting that Intel's Pentium computer chip could not be relied upon to do complex mathematical calculations. The mathematician noted this failing in an Internet forum, which spread the news rapidly through the country. Intel at first made light of the problem. However, in response to an uproar among users, Intel was eventually forced to offer free replacements for the defective chips. Could such a thing have happened a decade ago? Would anyone have listened?

The rapid dissemination of information has changed how the world operates. It offers the potential for much more radical change in the future. For example, the 1930s saw the implementation of banking regulation to protect unwitting investors from losing their money in unsafe banks. With information at everyone's fingertips, however, investors can merely call upon databanks provided by government or private ratings companies to determine the bank's reliability. Perhaps banking insurance is becoming unnecessary.

Banking is but one example. With ever more information at our fingertips, we can expect to see more and more changes in the possibilities for both private-sector production and government regulation. Clever entrepreneurs try to predict such changes and profit from them. Their profit is ours, too, if they help us better cope with the expanding information economy.

PROSPECTING FOR NEW INSIGHTS

1. In the spirit of the concluding section, identify some possible future production possibilities that can be brought about by an information superhighway. How might readily available information change the role for government in areas other than banking?

2. Suppose it requires at least one thousand dollars to buy the equipment necessary to connect into the information highway and additional money to access much of the information, games, movies, etc., that are available there. Should government subsidize this access by legislating reduced rates for the poor? Explain, making reference to the benefits and to the problems that would arise.

EXPLORATION 2
Population Growth on a Finite Planet—Must the Outlook be Dismal?

Economics has been seen as a dismal attempt to temporarily improve living standards, with the inevitable result that population growth will drive them down again. So far, improvements in resources and technology have more than compensated for growing numbers of mouths to feed. Some economic incentives are for lower birthrates. Other incentives push birthrates higher.

Labor is a resource that can increase output—the size of the economic pie. However, increased labor is ordinarily associated with increased population—the number of people sharing that pie. This brings economic problems.

The effects of population growth intrude into our lives. For example, we can relive our nation's history by visiting Civil War battlefields in Northern Virginia . . . if we can make our way through Washington's urban sprawl that has engulfed them. "Grow, grow, grow!" the business and political cheerleaders chant. But do we really want to be surrounded by ever more neighbors? Some people view such questions as beyond the purview of academic disciplines. They might be surprised to learn how central the issue of population growth has been in the history of economics.

*T*he Dismal Science

Most students think they know why economics is called **the dismal science**. They envision struggling through an entire term of tough material and tough grading—a dismal prospect!

In truth, the term has very different origins, dating back to the early nineteenth century. At that time, Thomas Robert Malthus popularized the notion that economics could only hope to delay the day of reckoning, in which the world's population finds itself at the brink of starvation. According to this *Malthusian* view, starvation is the only force that can keep population in check. While economics can temporarily improve the world, the inevitability of population growth and the limits of the earth's capacity to produce must inevitably reduce us all to no more than a subsistence existence. A dismal thought indeed!

Yet, the world has come a long way since the early 1800s, and both population and living standards have increased dramatically. For the most part, people of the world are much farther removed from starvation now than then. Since the earth has not expanded, something else must have happened. That something is technology. Technological change has enabled the world to get much more output for its resources than ever imagined by Malthus.

There is still room for concern. If the world continues to experience the same population growth rate that it has over the course of the twentieth century, it must ultimately fill every nook and cranny with people. There would be no room to produce the food to feed them. Since population grows geometrically, it doubles according to the **rule of seventy-two,** which states that doubling time equals seventy-two divided by the rate of growth. At a modest growth rate of 3 percent, then, the world's population would double every twenty-four years. As population keeps doubling, where are those people to go?

Fortunately, there are economic incentives that put a brake on excessive population growth. Specifically, as countries become wealthier, the opportunity cost of people's time rises. Because children take time, people choose to have fewer of them. This is especially true in countries that provide reliable retirement benefits for the elderly. Otherwise, the cost of raising children is offset by the expectation that those children will provide for their parents' retirement.

*T*he Price of Parenting: The Signals Are Distorted

The world has seen its population grow rapidly, from 2.9 billion in 1960 to an estimated 5.73 billion in 1995. A longer perspective, as seen in Figure 2B2-1, shows that population has exploded over the last three and a half centuries. Part of the reason for this growth is that advances in medicine and hygiene have lowered death rates, thereby increasing longevity. Birthrates have also been high, however, especially among the segments of the population least able to afford raising children.

To get a handle on why some segments of the population have higher birthrates than others, consider the costs and benefits of having and raising a family. Some of these costs are **private costs**, meaning that the parents pay. Such costs include the time and income the parents must forego to raise their children, as well as the explicit expenses they incur.

Other costs are **external costs**, meaning that they are borne by others. While some external costs arise from such things as overcrowding, the largest component of external costs involves expenses to other taxpayers, such as to finance the schools that the children attend or to finance the help that government provides to the parents.

To the extent that the costs of rearing children are external, parents face a price of children that does not reflect the full cost of those children to society. *Ceteris paribus* (other things being equal), we can expect the quantity of children demanded to rise because of this inefficiently low price. While few people would choose to have children for the explicit reason of receiving extra welfare benefits, the variety of taxpayer subsidies aimed at rearing children reduces the cost of those children dramatically, especially for people with lower incomes.

B

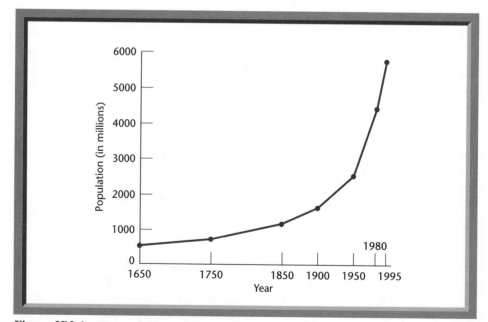

Figure 2B2-1   The exploding world population.

Source: 1996 World Almanac and Book of Facts, p. 838.

The lower cost of children promotes population growth in two ways. First, it affects parents' benefit-cost calculations by increasing the proportion of benefits to costs. Parents will rationally choose larger family sizes than they otherwise would have. Second, it increases the number of unplanned pregnancies. Because the cost of "mistakes" is lower, fewer precautions are taken and more unintended pregnancies occur. For both reasons, the existence of external costs results in a more rapidly growing population.

The children themselves can add both positive and negative externalities, depending on their future contributions in life. Unfortunately, the welfare check to single mothers provides incentives that discourage a cohesive family unit and may thus reduce the quality of child rearing. Specifically, for the mother to receive welfare benefits, it is often necessary for the father to drop out of sight. Sometimes this is done explicitly—the father departs and is not seen again. Other times, it is done fraudulently—the father is still in the family, but keeps out of the sight of the welfare caseworkers. Either way, child rearing is disrupted.

When making the decision as to whether to have children, parents will also consider the benefits. Benefits are received by the parents and the rest of society. Once the children are created, the benefits also go to the children themselves. Benefits to the parents are *private benefits*, because the parents make the choice. Benefits to the children and to the rest of society are mostly external, although the parents may be concerned with some of these benefits, especially those going to their own children. An example of an *external benefit* is that the world is well served by the contributions of many individuals, both famous and obscure. An external cost is that the world is not well served by ever-increasing demands on its scarce natural resources resulting from additional people on the planet.

While taxpayers shoulder many of the costs of additional children, those children do grow up to be taxpayers in their own rights. The children would, on balance, provide an external benefit in terms of taxation if they wind up paying more in taxes than they add in costs. For instance, our current problems with financing Social Security stem in large part from a decline in the birthrate following the post-World War II baby boom. While extra babies in the 1960s would have reduced the stresses on Social Security during their working years now, however, it would also add more recipients later. Thus, the logic of promoting population growth in order to provide external benefits from more taxpayers is rather shaky.

*P*romoting the Well-Being of Children

When a country seeks to obtain an efficient population growth rate, it faces a fundamental problem. Efficiency calls for parents to face the full costs and benefits of having children. Otherwise, the parents' benefit-cost calculations would not coincide with those of society at large. However, the decision about whether to have children is only one aspect to the issue of population growth. The other is the well-being of the children themselves. The goal of providing the incentive for parents to choose their family size efficiently often conflicts with the goal of equity to children once they are created.

For example, efficiency would suggest that parents should pay all costs of rearing children, including costs of food, shelter, and education. However, equity suggests that children should have comparable opportunities. A child born into poverty does not choose to be there, any more than a child born in more comfortable circumstances. Thus, from the point of view of equal opportunity in things that matter, it makes sense for taxpayers to subsidize the infant formula, schooling, school lunches, and other elements necessary to bring up the less fortunate child. The trade-off is that those subsidies increase the number of children born into poverty.

This is a dilemma. We wish children to be raised well. A good upbringing does not mean that the children have no hurdles to overcome, but does mean that the hurdles should not be too high. Yet, in well-intentioned efforts to make life easier for existing children, we find ourselves encouraging births into households with the least opportunities in preference to births into more financially secure households. There is no obvious, widely acceptable solution to this dilemma.

Replacing the Resources That Limit Growth

While prices are distorted when it comes to the incentives to have children, prices do come to our rescue in other ways. It has often seemed impossible that the earth could support many more people. However, the world's population keeps growing, and the world keeps supporting that growth. In large part, the saving grace has been technological advancement, spurred on by prices that signal when resources are getting scarce.

Periodically, resources appear to be running out. Well before any resource actually does run out, the perception that it might drives the price higher. For example, when oil supplies dwindled in the 1970s and concerns arose about the world using up this nonrenewable resource, prices surged higher. After all, if you have oil in the ground, and if you think the world's oil is running out, wouldn't you want to forego pumping now so that you could sell your oil at a lucrative price in the future when the world runs out? Since the same incentives face all owners of a nonrenewable resource, the result is that prices rise in the present because resources are hoarded for the future.

When the price of a nonrenewable resource rises, the market is motivated to do two things. First, it explores for more. In the 1970s, the high price of oil resulted in major new finds in Mexico, Alaska, the North Sea, and elsewhere. The market also develops substitutes. In the case of oil, such substitutes include technology to give motor vehicles more miles per gallon and insulation to reduce the energy costs of homes. Alternative energy sources were also developed, but did not take hold because the search for new supplies was so successful that oil prices dropped back down.

Other examples abound. At one time, copper seemed to provide a limit to growth, since the world's copper supplies seemed to be running out and since copper was needed for electricity and telephone connections. We know what happened. The rising price of copper spurred new technologies, such as fiber optics, that greatly reduced the world's need for copper. In the realm of food, too, technology has so far been very successful at increasing yields per acre more rapidly than necessary to meet the needs of a growing population. As price has risen, technology has responded.

The Options Before Us

We know the world cannot sustain an ever-increasing population. Even if we could feed everyone, we might wish to avoid the other stresses of a crowded planet. Unfortunately, prices do not provide the signals necessary for an efficient population growth rate. Moreover, making price signals efficient would not be equitable.

When prices are not used to allocate resources, government turns to command-and-control alternatives. For example, China prohibits a family from having more than one child. The penalty for violating this law can be forced sterilization. Some people have suggested similar options for the U.S., although usually only as a condition of receiving extra welfare benefits. Along the same lines, others suggest the less draconian, but still risky, measure of birth control implants. Still, U.S. citizens value their personal freedoms and are uncomfortable with allowing government to be too intimately involved with personal choices. Lacking a consensus for action, we do nothing and watch our population grow.

Despite an inefficiently high growth rate, the price system has spurred technological change that has more than kept pace with population growth. After looking for two centuries, people have yet to meet insurmountable limits to growth. Will they ever come? Do we need to take action at all? If so, what should that action be? Population growth is a sensitive issue because it involves people's lives and personal choices. Addressing this issue remains a challenge for our future.

PROSPECTING FOR NEW INSIGHTS

1. Ecosystems have carrying capacities for the species within them. Do you think there is a comparable carrying capacity for humans within the world's ecosystem? If so, how far do you think we are from that capacity, and what would be the consequences of overshooting it?
2. What roles do religious beliefs play in either promoting or hindering a solution to the world's population problems? Explain.

B

$\mathcal{M}$odule C

MASTERING ROADSIDE CHALLENGES

CHALLENGE 1
Specialization According to Comparative Advantage—Computation and Market Revelation

Economists are not usually called upon to identify the goods for which individuals and countries have comparative advantages. Rather, the marketplace reveals this information automatically. To see why, we can compute comparative advantage in a simple example and then interpret market prices to see why individuals or businesses will choose to produce accordingly, even when they have not done the computation.

Suppose there are two countries: Eastland and Westland. Both countries produce only corn and baseballs. For simplicity, we will assume that all corn is identical and that the baseballs are also interchangeable. The productivity of workers is shown in Table 2C1-1. Note that Eastland's workers are more productive at both manufacturing baseballs and harvesting corn. Eastland has an absolute advantage in both corn and baseballs. However, because a worker cannot do two things at one time, countries must allocate each worker to producing either one good or the other. To maximize its gains from trade, each country chooses according to its comparative advantage.

The key to computing comparative advantage is to measure opportunity cost. In this case, the choices are simple. To produce corn, a country must allocate labor away from baseballs and thus forego baseballs. Likewise, to produce baseballs, a country must forego corn. Thus, the opportunity cost of corn is in terms of baseballs foregone, and the opportunity cost of baseballs is in terms of corn foregone. Next is some simple algebra to compute the opportunity cost of a single baseball or unit of corn, so as to allow comparison of opportunity costs between countries. Applying this math to Table 2C1-1 yields the results shown in Table 2C1-2. By specializing according to this comparative advantage, countries will gain the most from trade.

In the real world, in which products are produced with various types of capital and other resources, computing comparative advantage in this way would be difficult. Fortunately, the market automatically generates specialization according to comparative advantage. This is because the market prices of resources reflect the value of those resources in alternative uses, that is, their opportunity costs. Competition ensures that the prices of

TABLE 2C1-1	*Productivity per Worker in Eastland and Westland*	
Country	**Corn**	**Baseballs**
Eastland	10 units per day	4 per day
Westland	5 units per day	3 per day

TABLE 2C1-2 *Computing Opportunity Cost and Comparative Advantage*

Product Location	Opportunity Cost (C is corn and B is baseballs)	Opportunity Cost per Unit
Corn in Eastland	10C = 4B	2/5 baseball (.4B)*
Corn in Westland	5C = 3B	3/5 baseball (.6B)
Baseballs in Eastland	4B = 10C	5/2 corn (2.5C)
Baseballs in Westland	3B = 5C	5/3 corn (1.67C)**

*Lower opportunity cost per unit of corn implies comparative advantage in Eastland.

**Lower opportunity cost per unit of baseballs implies comparative advantage in Westland.

goods within a country equal the sum of the opportunity costs of the resources used in their production.

For example, consider Table 2C1-3, showing the pretrade prices of corn and baseballs in Eastland and Westland. Prices in Eastland are given in yen (¥) and prices in Westland in pounds (£). The information in that table would lead to the same opportunity costs and comparative advantage figures listed in Table 2C1-2, without any computation of labor productivity. The relative prices of corn and baseballs in Eastland imply that a baseball costs the equivalent of 2.5 units of corn. In Westland, a baseball effectively costs 1.67 units of corn. Likewise, corn costs 2/5 of a baseball in Eastland and 3/5 of a baseball in Westland, just as in Table 2C1-2.

Were the two countries to trade, the price of a baseball would settle somewhere between these figures, such as at two units of corn per baseball. At such a price, each country would export the good for which it has a comparative advantage and import the other good. Both countries would then see their consumption possibilities expand beyond their production possibilities. Applying this result to the real world, we find countries exporting goods they have comparative advantages in and importing goods for which they do not.

Exceptions can occur when government intervenes, such as by subsidizing selected exports. There are also many goods that are not directly traded. For example, Big Mac hamburgers are always produced locally at McDonald's' restaurants around the world. For goods that are not traded, the reason usually is that transportation, storage, and other costs associated with the trade itself outweigh the gains of comparative advantage.

TABLE 2C1-3 *Relative Prices within Countries in the Absence of Trade*

Country	Corn	Baseballs
Eastland	¥200	¥500
Westland	£30	£50

C

People specialize in production according to their interests and income opportunities. They then use the income they earn to buy the things they want. Note that this is a two-part decision. First they decide what to produce; then they decide what to consume. The economies of countries engaged in international trade operate the same way.

Figure 2C2-1 shows how international trade allows a country to consume outside its production possibility frontier. For example, a country might be able to exchange one unit of good Y for two units of good X, where X and Y can be any two goods, such as food and clothing. The country can trade with other countries at this relative price. The result is a **consumption possibility frontier** with a slope of −1Y/2X, which is seen in Figure 2C2-1 as a line tangent to the production possibility frontier.

A country could produce at any point on its production possibility frontier and still trade. However, it must produce at the production point shown in Figure 2C2-1 in order to reach the consumption possibility frontier, which maximizes its consumption opportunities. At that production point only, the production possibility frontier has a slope that is identical to the slope of the consumption possibility frontier. The consumption possibility frontier includes that production point, but otherwise lies outside the production pos-

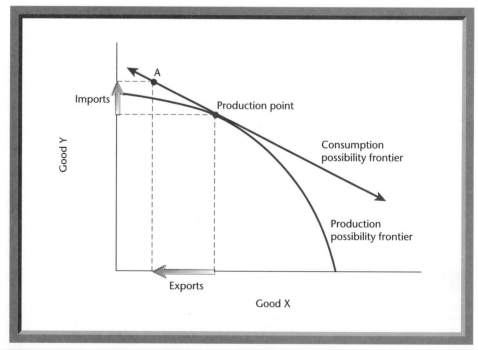

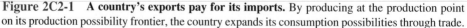

Figure 2C2-1 A country's exports pay for its imports. By producing at the production point on its production possibility frontier, the country expands its consumption possibilities through trade.

C

sibility frontier. The country can consume at any point along or within this consumption possibility frontier. The consumption possibility frontier must be tangent to the production point shown in the figure, otherwise part of the consumption possibility frontier would lie within the production possibility frontier, which would not maximize consumption.

Suppose the country consumes at point A. In this case it is consuming more of good Y than it is producing, meaning that it imports good Y. To obtain this extra Y, it is forced to consume less of good X than it produces, meaning that it exports good X. Thus the exports of good X allow the country to buy the imports of good Y. These quantities are shown in Figure 2C2-1.

Without trade, the country was forced to consume along or within its production possibility frontier. Trade has thus expanded its consumption possibilities. The country can consume more of both goods than it could before. Since economies exist in order to achieve the most consumption, not just to produce for its own sake, countries that specialize according to comparative advantage gain from international trade. The invisible hand of free-market prices signals them to do so.

C

Study by Design

SpeedStudy

SpeedReview

Whatever choices people make, there are always opportunity costs. These opportunity costs are illustrated by the production possibility frontier. The production possibility frontier represents various combinations of two goods that would be technologically efficient. Economic growth expands the frontier. Such growth can occur if a country adds more capital or other resources. Trade according to comparative advantage allows individuals, regions, or countries to consume beyond their production possibility frontiers. Within a country, this trade involves a circular flow of money to exchange inputs for outputs.

SpeedStudy True or False Self-Test

A1. Other things being equal, if a country produces more capital goods, its production possibility frontier will shift outward over time.

A2. If you start your own business, you are an entrepreneur.

A3. The axes of the production possibility frontier are labeled price and quantity. *one good or service for another*

A4. The circular flow model of economic activity shows how the value of goods must equal the value of services. *resource input*

A5. When we make economic decisions, our goal is always to maximize the opportunity cost of our actions. *minimize*

A6. Technological change in the widget industry will pivot the production possibility frontier in the direction of more widgets.

A7. Economic growth is represented on a production possibility frontier as a shift outward of that frontier.

A8. To gain from trade, a country must be able to do something better or with fewer resources than the other country. *doesn't have to*

A9. The countries of Superior and Wannabee produce nothing but fish and movies. The residents of Superior are far better suited to both activities than are the residents of Wannabee. This means that Superior has a comparative advantage in both goods. *absolute*

A10. With international trade, a country is able to produce outside its production possibility frontier. *consume*

B11. The value of one type of capital depends in part on the amount of other capital.

B12. Asymmetric information explains why it does not matter in the job market where college degrees are from.

B13. The quantity demanded of children is greater when the price of having children is lowered by government subsidies.

B14. The Exploration on population growth suggests that the world is running out of resources and that markets are incapable of dealing with the problem.

C15. If workers in Country A can produce 10 widgets or 10 gizmos per day, while workers in Country B can produce 5 widgets or 1 gizmo per day, the two countries can both gain from trade if Country B specializes in the production of widgets.

C16. Suppose there are only two countries, Goodfonutn and Superior, both of which produce only bats and balls. Assume that workers in Goodfonutn could produce 1 bat or 1 ball per day. Assume that workers in Superior could produce 3 bats or 5 balls per day. True or false: Under these assumptions, workers in Goodfonutn would specialize in producing bats and would export some of these bats in exchange for imports of balls.

C17. The consumption possibility frontier touches the production possibility frontier at one point only.

C18. A country that engages in international trade cannot know which goods to produce until it determines which goods it wants to consume.

The MasterMind

Selected Terms Along the Way

opportunity costs, 39
land, 40
labor, 40
human capital, 40
capital, 40
entrepreneurship, 40
technology, 40
production possibility frontier, 42
marginal, 43
law of increasing cost, 44

economic growth, 45
per capita, 47
depreciation, 47
money, 49
barter, 49
circular flow, 50
comparative advantage, 51
absolute advantage, 51
exports, 52

imports, 53

informational asymmetries, 59
signaling, 59
the dismal science, 61
rule of seventy-two, 61
private costs, 62
external costs, 62

consumption possibility frontier, 68

MasterMind Multiple Choice Self-Test

A1. The opportunity cost of a new city police contract is

   a. the amount of money it takes in order to provide the city with the most highly qualified personnel.

   b. the value of the other goods and services that the city and taxpayers will be forced to give up in order to pay for the contract.

   c. the cost to victims of crimes that the new contract would prevent.

   d. the value of the opportunities that city policemen acquire by accepting it.

A2. A production possibility curve depicts the trade-off between

   a. demand and supply.

   b. price and quantity.

   c. one output and another output.

   d. equity and efficiency.

A3. Which of the following is most likely to cause the production possibility curve to shift outward?

   a. A decrease in the unemployment rate.

   b. Increasing the production of capital goods.

   c. An increase in the unemployment rate.

   d. A decrease in population.

A4. As a general economic rule, economic well-being in a country is _____ by allowing imports, and _____ by allowing exports.

   a. increased; increased

   b. decreased; increased

   c. increased; decreased

   d. decreased; decreased

A5. A country has a comparative advantage in the production of a good if it can produce that good _____ than can other countries.

   a. with fewer raw materials

   b. at a lower opportunity cost

   c. at a higher quality

   d. with fewer labor hours

B6. In Exploration I, the information highway is primarily viewed as

   a. land.

   b. labor.

   c. capital.

   d. a consumption good.

B7. The Malthusian view of population is that

   a. people will voluntarily limit the size of their families.

   b. starvation is the solution to overpopulation problems.

   c. forced sterilization of the population must be implemented.

d. overpopulation is not a problem because resources keep growing and technology keeps
improving.

C8. Suppose one acre of land is able to produce
5,000 bushels of rice or 6,000 bushels of wheat
in Louisiana. In Arkansas, one acre of land can
produce 3,000 bushels of rice or 4,000 bushels
of wheat. Arkansas has a comparative advantage over Louisiana in

a. only wheat.

b. only rice.

c. both wheat and rice.

d. neither wheat nor rice.

C9. Suppose dirt and fish are the only two goods in
the world. If the country of Waterland imports
fish, it is likely to also

a. import dirt.

b. export fish.

c. export dirt.

d. export both fish and dirt.

MasterMind Questions and Problems

A1. Do management skills differ from entrepreneurial skills? Explain.

A2. What would a straight-line production possibility frontier between coconuts and fish on Hermit Island say about opportunity costs? Does
the law of increasing marginal opportunity cost
still apply in this case?

A3. Draw the original production possibility frontier
in Figure 2A-4. How does the frontier change
when technological change affects only the
pumpkin industry?

A4. California and France both produce wine.

a. Without international trade U.S. consumers
would be unable to consume French wines,
but they would still be able to consume California wines. Would this arrangement be better for the United States as a whole? For any
particular groups within the U.S.?

b. Do you think France imports U.S. wines?
Explain.

A5. Succinctly evaluate the validity of the following:

a. "The U.S. is losing its competitive edge to
other countries with more diligent and skilled
workers. The problem is that we are becoming increasingly incapable of producing anything that other countries would want to buy.
We are fast on our way to becoming a nation
of burger flippers."

b. "The U.S. standard of living has been the
envy of the world. Unfortunately, because
we have allowed imports from countries
where working conditions are dismal and labor is cheap, our own standard of living is
rapidly being pulled down to match the competition."

B6. Would you expect credentialism to grow more
important, less important, or stay at its current
level of importance as the information superhighway develops over time?

B7. Explain how problems of overpopulation can
create tensions between countries that might
lead to war.

C8. Suppose there are only two countries, A and B.
Country A is endowed with abundant resources
of all types and a highly intelligent and motivated labor force. Country B has few natural resources, and its workers cannot seem to do anything well. Both countries are self-sufficient,
each subsisting upon goods X and Y. The price
of both X and Y in country A is $1. In country
B, the price of X is £1 and the price of Y is £2.
Neither country trades with the other, but both
are meeting now to consider removing trade
barriers so that trade could occur.

a. If trade were to occur, what would be its pattern, that is, which country would specialize
in which product(s)? Why?

b. As trade minister for country A, would you
recommend free trade? Why or why not?
What if you were minister for country B?

C9. a. Draw an outwardly bowed production possibility frontier between sneakers and stereos, labeling the horizontal axis as sneakers. Suppose it takes two sneakers to buy one stereo. Draw carefully a consumption possibility frontier that is consistent with this ratio. Label the slope and the production point. Label a consumption point that would be consistent with a free-market choice to export sneakers.

Label the amount of sneakers exported and the amount of stereos imported.

b. Without labels, repeat the graph above. Suppose the price of stereos rises to three sneakers each. Draw and label another consumption possibility frontier, production point, and consumption point. Indicate the new amount of sneaker exports.

Future Explorations: Mapping out Term Papers

1. The Effect of War on Production Possibilities
When a country goes to war, it is forced to allocate resources away from producing both consumption goods and capital goods. By itself, the reduction in the production of capital goods would cause a country's production possibility frontier to shift inward over time. Yet, after World War II, the economies of Germany, Japan, and the U.S. boomed. This paper explains why. The paper also looks at other countries that saw their economies set back by war and discusses why those economies did not perform as well.

2. Fit to Print?—The Economics of Growth and Trade
Politicians and newspaper columnists often take positions about economic matters. This paper gathers some statements about international trade that have been reported in newspapers or magazines. Each statement is then analyzed to see if it is consistent with the principles of comparative advantage and gains from trade. In addition, some statements about economic growth may also be gathered. These statements are analyzed for an understanding of the trade-off between equity and incentives for capital formation.

3. Overcoming Scarcity: A Report on Technological Change
Technological change can help the economy to obtain more output with fewer resources. This paper highlights a few modern technological changes, such as the personal computer, the robot on the assembly line, and the personal fax machine. The paper then discusses each in terms of its ability to make us more productive.

Answer Key

ExpressStudy
True or False

1. T
2. T
3. F
4. F
5. T
6. T

SpeedStudy True
or False Self-Test

1. T	10. F
2. T	11. T
3. F	12. F
4. F	13. T
5. F	14. F
6. T	15. T
7. T	16. T
8. F	17. T
9. F	18. F

MasterMind Multiple
Choice Self-Test

1. b
2. c
3. b
4. a
5. b
6. c
7. b
8. a
9. c

*M*arket Prices: Supply and Demand

A Look Ahead

"Teach a parrot to say 'supply and demand,' and you have an economist!" That tongue-in-cheek quip has been handed down for decades in introductory economics courses. While not literally true (we hope), it does point out how central the concepts of supply and demand are to economic analysis. Supply and demand analysis cuts to the heart of most economic questions. We can use it to interpret the varied markets within our economy and the interaction of our markets with those of other countries. Supply and demand analysis also lets us explore the effects of public policies and other aspects of human behavior.

Why do college professors get paid more than drugstore clerks? Why does Shaquille O'Neal get paid more than a college professor (or just about anyone else)? Polly the parrot knows the answer: "Squawk, supply and demand!" Why do textbooks cost more than romance novels? Why do movies contain sex and violence? Why is the air polluted? Why do diamonds cost more than water? The answers? You guessed it . . . "Squawk!"

Of course, you would not be well advised to answer all economic questions with "supply and demand" and leave it at that. Rather, the study of supply and demand analysis must be done with care and precision if it is to reveal reliable answers to the economic questions we ask of it. This chapter examines the characteristics of demand and supply, and looks at the how demand and supply interact in the marketplace to determine the prices we pay. Later chapters make use of this material to answer the previous questions and many more.

DESTINATIONS

*M*odule A

As you zip along the Expressway you will arrive at an ability to

- distinguish between the general notions of supply and demand used in ordinary conversation and the precise notions employed in the study of economics;
- explain what it means to shift demand and supply, and why shifts might occur;
- describe how the marketplace settles upon the equilibrium price and quantity;
- measure the responsiveness of one variable to another;
- identify how a price change can increase, decrease, or not change a firm's revenues, depending upon the elasticity of demand facing that firm.

*M*odule B

Upon leaving the Expressway to explore issues you will be able to

- interpret why the war on drugs increases crime associated with drug use;
- discuss how vouchers use competition to improve the quality of schooling.

*M*odule C

Mastering Roadside Challenges will allow you to hone analytical skills by

- mastering the eight possible shifts of supply and demand;
- computing the elasticity of demand and its effects on consumer spending.

*T*he Answer to Economic Questions—
Supply and Demand

Supply and demand analysis plays such a central role in answering economic questions that it should come as no surprise that the economics profession attaches very specific definitions to these concepts. The economic definitions of supply and demand are much more precise than the fuzzy notion that demand is something a person wants or needs and supply is what is offered. Rather, supply and demand are both defined as relationships between price and quantity. Supply relates the quantity offered for sale to each of various possible prices. Demand does the same, except now the relationship is between the various possible prices and the associated quantities that would actually be purchased. We start by looking at demand.

*D*emand

> **Demand** *relates the quantity of a good that consumers will purchase at each of various possible prices, over some period of time, ceteris paribus.*

Demand is a relationship, not a single quantity. For a given price, demand will tell us a specific quantity that consumers will purchase. This quantity is termed the **quantity demanded**. In other words, demand relates quantity demanded to price over the range of possible prices. To emphasize that demand is a relationship and not just a single point, demand is also sometimes called a *demand schedule* or, more generally, a *demand curve*.

   Demand must be defined for a set period of time. For example, demand for milk will be quite different if the period in question is one day, one week, or one year. Moreover, anything else that might influence the quantity demanded must be held constant. This is termed the *ceteris paribus* condition. It means that we only look at one relationship at a time, where *ceteris paribus* is the Latin for holding all else equal. (It is always either italicized or underlined.)

   Suppose we want to know how an increase in water rates will affect the amount of water used to sprinkle lawns. We know that the quantity of water demanded will depend on various things besides the price. To avoid mixing up the effects of price and rainfall, for example, we might estimate one demand curve for times of normal rainfall and another for times of drought. This approach allows us to focus exclusively on the relationship between price and quantity demanded.

By Word, by Table, by Graph

There are various ways to express relationships. One is to provide a table of data. Another is to show that data with a graph. For example, the data in Table 3A-1 make up a demand schedule. The data from Table 3A-1 can be plotted on a graph to form a demand curve, shown in Figure 3A-1, where the horizontal axis is labeled Quantity to denote the quantity demanded at each possible price. Since price is measured in dollars, the dollar sign provides the label for the vertical axis.

Note how the graph pictures an inverse relationship between price and quantity demanded. As price rises, quantity falls. As price falls, quantity rises. This relationship is termed the *law of demand*. It is an empirical law, meaning that no one enforces it, but buyers almost always adhere to it.

You've heard the saying "a picture is worth a thousand words." That saying usually applies to supply and demand analysis. While a table of data can be useful for applications calling for numerical calculations, a graph is ordinarily better suited for broader messages, such as the inverse relationship between price and quantity demanded. When the specific data are less important than the general nature of the relationship, it is common to draw a graph without attaching any specific numbers to that graph, as is done in many of the graphs in this chapter and the rest of this book.

If you are uncomfortable with a graph without numbers, recall the simple solution mentioned in chapter 2: Add some numbers. Even though the numbers would be artificial, the graphical relationship may then become easier to comprehend. For example, we could have labeled Figure 3A-1 with different numbers or with no numbers at all. The graph would still impart the notion that price and quantity vary inversely.

Focusing Thoughts *with* Ceteris Paribus

Price is not the only factor that influences how much people buy. Quantities purchased are also dictated by income, tastes, the prices of other goods, and various other factors. By holding all but price constant, the *ceteris paribus* assumption lets us focus on one thing at a time. This approach provides order to what otherwise might seem like a jumble of simultaneous changes.

What happens to demand when other things change? Changes in other aspects of the world have the potential to *shift* the entire demand curve, leading to a new relationship between price and quantity. Things that shift demand are termed demand's **shift factors**. An *increase in demand* occurs when demand shifts to the right. A *decrease in demand* occurs when demand shifts to the left. Figure 3A-2 summarizes these shifts. Note

TABLE 3A-1	*Demand*	
Data Point	**Price ($)**	**Quantity Demanded**
A	5	0
B	4	1
C	3	2
E	2	3
F	1	4
G	0	5

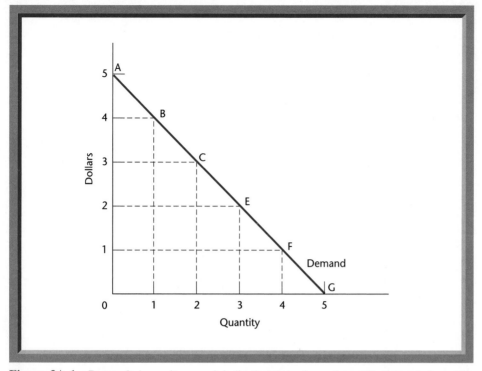

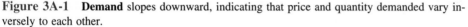

Figure 3A-1 Demand slopes downward, indicating that price and quantity demanded vary inversely to each other.

that a change in the price of the good neither increases nor decreases demand—demand does not shift. Rather, a price change would change the quantity demanded, which involves moving along the same demand curve.

Consider an example of demand shifting. For instance, a boom in new home construction is generally associated with higher home prices. This association does not mean that consumers buy more homes because the price of homes has risen. Rather, something else has changed. Perhaps a surging economy is responsible for higher consumer income and thus greater home purchases despite higher home prices. In this case, price and quantity rise together, because some other factor is at work—a change in consumer income. To the extent that higher income causes consumers to buy more of a good at any given price, the higher income has increased demand, such as depicted by the rightward pointing arrow in Figure 3A-2.

✔ QUICKCHECK

Would an increase in price decrease demand?

Answer: No, a change in the price of a good represents a movement along demand. In contrast, to decrease demand would entail shifting the entire demand curve to the left. Since price is not a shift factor, that shift does not occur.

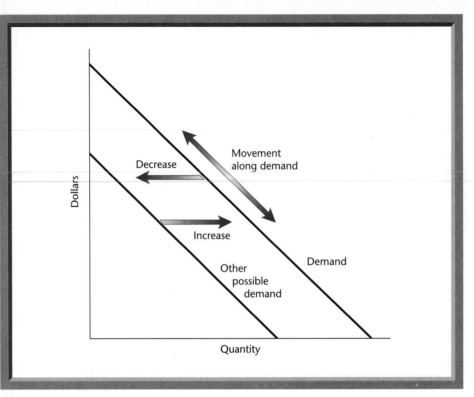

Figure 3A-2 **Demand shifts** when there is a change in a shift factor. A change in price does not shift demand. Rather, a price change causes a movement along the demand curve to a new quantity demanded.

Things That Shift Demand

Some things are more likely to shift demand than are other things. As mentioned, consumer income is a likely shift factor. For **normal goods,** an increase in income shifts demand to the right. However, there are many goods that people buy less of as their incomes rise. These are termed **inferior goods.** An increase in income shifts the demand for inferior goods to the left. Is there anything you would buy less of as your income increases? Perhaps you would eat fewer hot dogs and cans of tuna, and more steak and fresh fish. If so, for you, hot dogs and tuna would be inferior goods, and steak and fresh fish would be normal goods.

Changes in the prices of substitutes and complements also shift demand. A **substitute** is something that takes the place of something else. Different brands of coffee are substitutes. So are coffee and tea. A **complement** is a good that goes with another good, such as ketchup on hot dogs or cream in coffee. The degree to which one good complements or substitutes for another will vary according to each person's tastes and preferences. For example, many coffee drinkers prefer to take their coffee black. For them coffee and cream are not complements. Likewise, to the extent a consumer is loyal to a particular brand of a product, other brands might not be viewed as acceptable substitutes unless the price difference is dramatic.

What would happen to demand for a good if the price of a substitute changes? To answer questions like this one, it often helps to be specific. For example, consider how much Sparkle Beach laundry detergent shoppers purchase at various possible prices. Those quantities would go up or down depending upon the prices of Tide, Surf, All, and other possible substitutes. If the price of the substitutes rises, *ceteris paribus*, shoppers buy more Sparkle Beach. Their demand for Sparkle Beach shifts out. Likewise, should the substitutes be reduced in price, *ceteris paribus*, shoppers would buy less Sparkle Beach— demand shifts in. Thus, demand shifts directly with a change in the price of a substitute.

Conversely, demand shifts inversely to a change in the price of a complement. Since complements are the opposite of substitutes, a change in the price of a complement shifts demand in the opposite direction from what would occur if there were a change in the price of a substitute. For example, cheese slices are complementary to sandwich meats. An increase in the price of sandwich meats would decrease consumption of those meats and anything that goes with them. Demand for cheese slices would shift to the left. Likewise, a decrease in the price of sandwich meats would shift demand for cheese slices to the right.

Changes in *tastes and preferences* will also shift demand. Over time, as some items become more popular, their demand curves shift out. Other items see their popularity fade and their demand curves shift in. Producers often use advertising in an attempt to influence tastes and preferences toward their particular brand of product.

OBSERVATION POINT: New Coke? Or Old Coke in a New Bottle?

Remember New Coke? In 1985 the Coca-Cola Company stopped making their traditional Coca-Cola. They instead introduced a reformulated New Coke to better compete with Pepsi. It seems that taste tests favored Pepsi over traditional Coke, but favored New Coke over Pepsi. Market research notwithstanding, however, New Coke was a flop.

"Bring back 'the real thing'!" cried Coke customers, and back it came under the name Coca-Cola Classic. Curiously, even though the formula is the same as that of traditional Coke, Coke Classic has proven more popular. Was it the publicity? The near loss of something millions of Coke drinkers took for granted? Was it nostalgia? In any case, the demand for Coke shifted to the right, and that was just fine with the corporate officers in Atlanta.

What worked once could work again. No, the Coca-Cola Company is not out to deprive us of that which we cherish. Rather, it is the floppy plastic Coke bottle that is in danger of oblivion. With advances in plastic making, the Coca-Cola Company now offers plastic bottles in the same general shape as its traditional glass bottle. Will these freshly minted versions of the old Coke bottle permanently replace the shapeless plastic bottles that dominated the 1970s and 1980s? If the shapely bottles significantly increase demand for Coke, you can bet they'll stay!

TABLE 3A-2 *Changes in Demand*

Demand Shifts to the LEFT When	Demand Shifts to the RIGHT When
The prices of substitutes decrease.	The prices of substitutes increase.
The prices of complements increase.	The prices of complements decrease.
The good is normal and income decreases.	The good is normal and income increases.
The good is inferior and income increases.	The good is inferior and income decreases.
Population decreases.	Population increases.
Consumers expect prices to decrease in the future.	Consumers expect prices to increase in the future.

A

Changes in population, in expectations about future prices and incomes, or in many other factors can cause demand to shift. Population is a shift factor that applies to market demand. Demand will increase or decrease to the extent that population increases or decreases. Interestingly, a change in consumer *expectations* about future prices or income will itself shift demand in the present. For example, if you expect prices to fall in the future, you might put off your purchases now, in effect shifting your current demand curve to the left. You would be treating future purchases as a substitute for current purchases. For some products, other factors could be significant, such as a bout of frigid weather that shifts the demand for mittens to the right.

Summing up, when consumers buy less of a good at each price, demand shifts to the left. When consumers buy more of a good at each price, demand shifts to the right. Table 3A-2 summarizes these shifts. Changing tastes and preferences could shift demand in either direction. **A change in the price of the good causes a change in the quantity demanded, but does not shift demand.** Rather, a change in price causes a movement along the demand curve.

✓ **QuickCheck**

After reaching a low of about 6.75% in October of 1993, interest rates on 30-year home mortgages rose to nearly 8% by the spring of 1994. In response to this upturn in mortgage interest rates, lenders saw a record number of consumers seek to finance or refinance mortgages in early 1994. In short, the interest rate is the price of a home mortgage, and consumers bought more mortgages when the price started rising. Does this behavior violate the law of demand?

Answer: No, the law of demand is not violated. Rather, there was a change in expectations, which resulted in demand shifting outward. Specifically, consumers observed that rates, which had been falling until October 1993, were starting to rise. Customers began expecting prices to rise rather than fall in the future. With customers anxious to buy sooner rather than later, the entire demand curve for mortgages shifted to the right. As it turned out, consumer expectations were quite correct, as mortgage rates continued to rise throughout that year.

Supply

> **Supply** *relates the quantity of a good that will be offered for sale at each of various possible prices, over some period of time, ceteris paribus.*

The first thing to note about supply is its symmetry with demand. Supply tells us the quantity that will be offered for sale at various prices. This quantity is termed the **quantity supplied**. Note that supply and quantity supplied are not synonyms. Supply refers to the entire schedule that relates price and quantity and is thus also called a *supply schedule* or *supply curve*. Quantity supplied is the quantity associated with a single point on that schedule. As price changes, quantity supplied changes, but supply does not.

Supply is often referred to as the supply schedule or supply curve in order to emphasize that it is not any single quantity. Like demand, supply must be specified for a set period of time, such as a day, month, or year. The *ceteris paribus* clause makes sure that other things are held constant, so that we can focus clearly on the relationship between price and quantity supplied.

By Word, by Table, by Graph

Just as with demand, supply can be presented as a table or as a graph. An example of supply is listed in Table 3A-3 and graphed in Figure 3A-3. In contrast to the downward-sloping demand curve, supply nearly always slopes upward to the right. This direct relationship between price and quantity supplied is known as the *law of supply*. As price rises, the quantity offered for sale increases, because the higher revenue per unit sold means that some additional units now become profitable to produce and sell.

Ceteris Paribus—*Same Meaning, Different Shift Factors*

Changes in *ceteris paribus* conditions would shift supply. While changes in *ceteris paribus* conditions also shift demand, the most important shift factors are likely to differ. Remember that for demand, the most important shift factors are income, prices of substitutes and complements, tastes and preferences, and expectations of future prices and incomes. For supply, changes in expectations as to future prices are still important. However, the other important shift factors are different. In addition to expectations as to future prices, supply's important shift factors include (1) prices of inputs, (2) technological change, and (3) government or union restrictions on the manner in which production occurs.

TABLE 3A-3 *Supply*

Data Point	Price ($)	Quantity Supplied
H	5	4
I	4	3
J	3	2
K	2	1
L	1	0
M	0	0

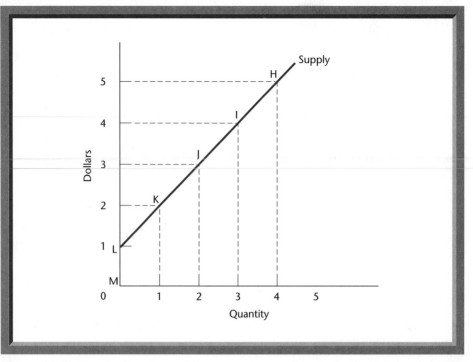

Figure 3A-3 **Supply** slopes upward because an increase in price leads to a greater quantity supplied.

Why would expectations of future prices be important to a seller? To answer that question, suppose you own an oil field and that it costs you $1 per barrel to pump your crude oil from the ground. How much oil would you offer for sale if the price were $15? $20? Why wouldn't you pump your oil field dry if the selling price were $1.50?

For each possible current price, you would ask yourself how likely it would be for the price to go higher in the future. If you think prices are on their way up, you would put off your pumping until later. If you expect prices to remain flat or to drop in the future, you would pump more now. If your expectations change, your entire supply schedule for pumping oil in the present would shift. For example, if you become convinced that the world is about to run out of oil, your supply curve in the present would shift far to the left, so that you would retain plenty of oil to sell at high prices in the future.

If wages or other input prices fall, firms see their expenses drop and are willing to produce more at any given price. Hence a decline in input prices *increases* supply, meaning that supply shifts to the right. Were input prices to increase, supply would *decrease*, meaning that it would shift to the left. In that case, fewer units are offered for sale at any given price. In general, supply will vary inversely with changes in input prices.

Firms adopt technological change in order to produce more output per unit of input, which has the same effect as a decrease in input prices. Technological change in the production of any good shifts its supply to the right.

When government or labor unions restrict the way that firms do business, the effect is an increase in per unit production cost. For example, the Environmental Protection Agency requires automobiles to meet exhaust-gas emission standards, such as with catalytic converters. To cover the cost of the catalytic converters, the auto makers require a higher price for the autos they sell. For any given price, then, the producers offer fewer units for sale. Thus, the supply curve shifts to the left.

Likewise, if unions succeed in obtaining costly benefits or in restricting the amount of work firms can expect from any given worker, the result will be a similar increase in expenses per unit of output. This result is why government or union restrictions on the manner in which production occurs have the effect of decreasing supply—supply shifts to the left.

Other shift factors could also be important in some applications. For example, some products are produced jointly, such as beef and leather. An increase in the popularity and price of beef would lead to a movement up the supply curve for beef. The greater quantity supplied of beef means that more cattle are raised for slaughter, which has the effect of shifting the supply of leather to the right. In brief, more leather would be offered for sale at each price of leather, in response to people consuming more steak and hamburger.

Summing up, when producers offer to sell less of a good at each price, supply decreases. When producers offer to sell more of a good at each price, supply increases. Table 3A-4 summarizes these shifts. **Note that a change in the price of the good causes a change in the quantity supplied, but does not shift supply.** Rather, a change in price causes a movement along the supply curve.

OBSERVATION POINT: The Livestock Gourmet on a Hot Summer Day

While humans huddle by their air conditioners to escape the sweltering summer sun, life is good for some Iowa pigs and cattle—they enjoy a gourmet feast of tasty wet corn feed. On particularly hot days farmers in the vicinity of the Cargill corn processing plant in Eddyville, Iowa, can buy this high-quality feed for a very low price. It's not that Cargill pities overheated animals. Rather, it is the availability of electricity that shifts out Cargill's supply of wet feed.

The many air conditioners that run on exceptionally hot days stresses the ability of the local electric company to provide power. The ensuing power shortage leads to electricity cutbacks for industry, including Cargill. Cargill is left with huge piles of perishable wet feed, because there isn't enough electricity to dry and store it. The result is that, although power curtailment is not one of the more common things that shift supply, it's one that leaves some cows very contented.

TABLE 3A-4	*Changes in Supply*
Supply Shifts to the LEFT When	**Supply Shifts to the RIGHT When**
Sellers expect price to rise in the future.	Sellers expect price to decline in the future.
The price of labor or any other input rises.	The price of labor or any other input falls.
The price of a product produced jointly falls.	The price of a product produced jointly rises.
Government or union restrictions on production practices increase cost.	Technological change lowers cost.

*E*quilibrium—*Demand Meets Supply and the Market Clears*

Demand can be one individual's or the market's as a whole. Likewise, supply can be from one firm or all firms in the market. The market is the bringing together of buyers and sellers. While most people think of a market as a physical location, markets usually extend well beyond any single place. Markets can be local, regional, national, or multinational in scale. For example, gold, crude oil, and many other commodities are sold in global markets, with only minor variations in price throughout the world.

Market demand is the summation of all the individuals' demands in that market. Summing individuals' demands is straightforward if you remember to add quantities, not prices. For each price, the quantity demanded in the marketplace is the sum of the quantities demanded by all consumers. An example will demonstrate this process.

For our example, we will consider a market with two consumers, Jack and Jill. Jack and Jill are both interested in purchasing—what else?—pails of water. Jack is a laid-back sort of fellow who has no interest in climbing the hill to get water for himself. He is quite willing to pay for at least some of the water he uses. Jill, in contrast, sees climbing the hill as good aerobic exercise, but is worried about tumbling down. The different demands of Jack and Jill can be combined into a market demand, as shown in Table 3A-5 and Figure 3A-4. In each case, it is quantities that are added, not prices.

Market supply is the schedule depicting the total quantity offered for sale in the market at each price. To obtain market supply, merely add the quantities offered for sale by all sellers at each price. Graphically, market supply is the horizontal summation of each seller's supply curve. Continuing with the example, Table 3A-6 and Figure 3A-5 show the supplies of two sellers of pails of water—Wally and Wanda—and how their supplies sum to market supply.

When supply and demand meet in the marketplace, a market price is created. While individual sellers are free to price their products however they wish, there will be only one price that *clears the market*, such that the quantity supplied equals the quantity demanded. **The market-clearing price and the resulting quantity traded comprise what is known as the market equilibrium, meaning that there is no tendency for either price or quantity to change,** *ceteris paribus.*

Market equilibrium is determined by the intersection of supply and demand, as

TABLE 3A-5 *Market Demand Sums the Quantities Demanded by Each Buyer*

Price ($)	Jack's Quantity Demanded	Jill's Quantity Demanded	Market Quantity Demanded
5	1	0	1
4	2	1	3
3	3	2	5
2	4	3	7
1	5	4	9
0	6	5	11

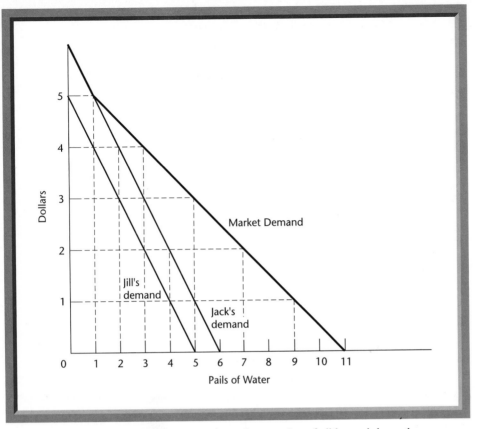

Figure 3A-4 **Market demand** is the horizontal summation of all buyers' demands.

TABLE 3A-6 *Market Supply Sums the Quantities Supplied by Each Seller*

Price ($)	Wally's Quantity Supplied	Wanda's Quantity Supplied	Market Quantity Supplied
5	4	5	9
4	3	4	7
3	2	3	5
2	1	2	3
1	0	1	1
0	0	0	0

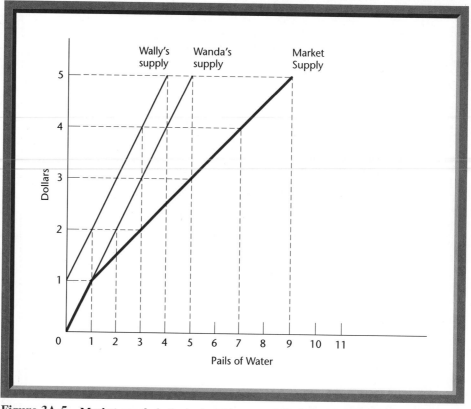

Figure 3A-5 **Market supply** is the horizontal summation of all sellers' supplies.

shown in Table 3A-7 and Figure 3A-6. This price and quantity combination is labeled P*
and Q*, respectively, at a price of $3 and a quantity of five pails.

At any price above P*, there would be a **surplus**, representing the excess of quantity supplied over quantity demanded. For example, a price of $4 would be too high and result in a surplus of four pails. In that case, Wally and Wanda would compete with each other for sales by lowering price. More generally, in any market in which a surplus oc-

TABLE 3A-7 *Market Equilibrium at a Price of $3*

Price ($)	Quantity Demanded	Quantity Supplied	Surplus (or Shortage)
5	1	9	8
4	3	7	4
3	5	5	0
2	7	3	(4)
1	9	1	(8)
0	11	0	(11)

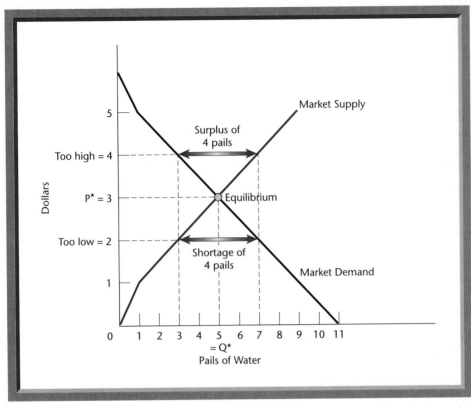

Figure 3A-6   Market equilibrium occurs at a price of $3 and a quantity of 5 pails. Any price above $3 would lead to a surplus. Any price below $3 would cause a shortage. Neither surpluses nor shortages will persist in a free market.

curs, some sellers would cut their prices slightly so as to be the ones that make the sales. Other suppliers would then be without customers, and would consequently lower their own prices enough to capture customers from their competitors. This leapfrogging process would continue until the quantity demanded and supplied are equal, which occurs at the equilibrium price of P*.

A price that is too low results in a **shortage**, equal to the amount by which quantity demanded exceeds quantity supplied. For example, a price of $2 would result in a shortage of four pails. Because there is not enough water to meet demand at that price, Jack and Jill would scramble to be first to buy. More generally, whenever there is a shortage in any market, buyers compete against each other for the limited quantities of the goods that are offered for sale at that price. For sellers shortages provide an opportunity both to raise prices and to increase sales, a doubly appealing prospect. Price would thus rise to P*, the point at which the shortage disappears. Thus, without any guidance, the invisible hand of the free market eliminates either surpluses or shortages, and leads to the equilibrium at which the market clears.

Suppose one of the shift factors for either supply or demand were to change. For example, suppose an increase in consumer income or decrease in the price of a complement shifts demand to the right. One of the most common mistakes students make is to think this shift in demand would also shift supply. It would not, because demand is not a shift factor for supply. Rather, the rightward shift in demand leads to a movement up the supply curve and results in a new, higher, equilibrium price and quantity.

For practice, you might draw the basic supply and demand diagram, and then sketch a few shifts in either demand or supply. Note the effect on the equilibrium price and quantity. Note also that shifting demand does not cause a shift in supply or vice versa.

✓ **QUICKCHECK**

In the example represented by Figure 3A-6, how much would be sold if the price is $4? If the price is $2?

_____

Answer: Remember that each sale requires both a buyer and a seller. Thus, if the price is $4, three pails of water would be sold. If the price is $2, again three pails of water would be sold.

Elasticity—Measuring Responsiveness

The concept of **elasticity** measures the responsiveness of one thing to another. Elasticity is defined with respect to any two variables. Although the names of the variables may change, the formula remains the same, as follows:

$$\frac{\text{Percentage change in one variable (Y)}}{\text{Percentage change in other variable (X)}}$$

For example, if Y changes by 20% in response to a 10% change in X, the elasticity equals 2, obtained by dividing 20% by 10%.

Elasticity has a broad range of application. Farmers might be interested in the elasticity of plant growth with respect to fertilizer application. Perhaps you would be interested in the elasticity of your class grade with respect to study time. If that elasticity is high, a small percentage increase in your study time would lead to a large percentage increase in your grade. You would be well rewarded to study more. In contrast, if the elasticity is low, the two variables are not much related. Sleep late!

The Elasticity of Demand and Its Effects on Consumer Spending

In economics, some elasticities are more significant than others. The most significant is the price elasticity of demand, which is often abbreviated as simply elasticity of demand. The **elasticity of demand** measures the responsiveness of quantity demanded to price. Its formula is given by the percentage change in quantity demanded, divided by the percentage change in price. Since price and quantity demanded are inversely related, the computation of the elasticity of demand will always be negative. For convenience, economists often refer to the elasticity of demand by its absolute value, meaning that the negative sign is dropped.

In absolute value, the elasticity of demand can fall within three ranges. These ranges, summarized in Figure 3A-7, are as follows:

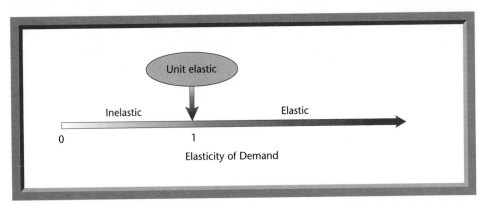

Figure 3A-7 **Price elasticity of demand** can range from zero to infinity (in absolute value).

1. **Inelastic demand:** Elasticity of demand lies between 0 and 1; in this range, the quantity demanded is relatively unresponsive to price.
2. **Unit elastic demand:** Elasticity of demand = 1; in this range, the quantity demanded changes proportionally to changes in price.
3. **Elastic demand:** Elasticity of demand is greater than 1; in this range, the quantity demanded is relatively responsive to changes in price.

In general, the more substitutes there are for a product, or the greater the fraction of a person's budget it takes to buy the product, the greater will be its elasticity of demand. Thus, demand for Domino's Pizza is quite elastic, because there are many close substitutes, including other brands of pizza and other types of fast food. Demand for drinking water is quite inelastic, because it takes a tiny fraction of the budget and there are no close substitutes.

Demand for college textbooks is inelastic, meaning that even significant increases in the price of a textbook will not deter students from buying copies. The reason is that textbooks are tied to courses. Once students register for the courses, there are no longer any close substitute for the courses' texts. Moreover, since a bad text can conflict with good teaching, instructors who assign texts give first priority to their contents rather than to their prices.

Consumer spending translates into revenue for sellers. That revenue equals the quantity sold multiplied by the price received. In other words

$$\text{Total revenue} = \text{price} \times \text{quantity}$$

Most people assume that when price increases, sellers earn more revenue. However, this assumption is often not true, because quantity demanded falls any time price rises. An increase in price will bring in more revenue only if demand is inelastic, meaning that the fall in quantity demanded is less significant than the rise in price. In contrast, were demand to be elastic, the quantity demanded would be quite responsive to price. Any increase in price would cause a proportionally greater fall in the quantity sold and thus would lower total revenue. Table 3A-8 summarizes the effects on total revenue of a price change.

For example, if demand is elastic, the quantity demanded is very responsive to price changes. The effect of lower prices is to increase purchases so much that revenues actually rise. This result has occurred in many industries, ranging from air travel to comput-

TABLE 3A-8	*The Effect of a Change in Price Upon Revenues*
Change in Price	**Effect upon Sales Revenues**
Higher Price	If demand is inelastic, revenue rises.
	If demand is unit elastic, revenue remains constant.
	If demand is elastic, revenue falls.
Lower Price	If demand is inelastic, revenue falls.
	If demand is unit elastic, revenue remains constant.
	If demand is elastic, revenue rises.

ing. When computing power was very expensive twenty years ago, the revenues of the computer industry were a mere fraction of current revenues, now that computing power is cheap. This illustrates another point as follows: **The longer the time period involved, the greater will be the elasticity of demand.** Time lets people adjust, to substitute toward goods that become relatively less expensive and away from those that become relatively more expensive.

The elasticity of demand will vary along most demand curves. Along a downward-sloping straight-line demand curve, the rule is that demand is unit elastic at the midpoint, elastic above the midpoint, and inelastic below the midpoint. Remember, the lower is the point on a straight-line demand curve, the lower will be its elasticity. The reason is that, when we move down the demand curve, any **percentage** change in price becomes larger relative to the corresponding **percentage** change in quantity. This relationship is shown in Figure 3A-8.

✓ **QUICKCHECK**

Suppose Wally's Water Works enters a new market. Wally initially sets the price of water at $5 per pail, but wonders if he should charge less. If Wally faces an elasticity of demand equal to 1/3, why would he regret lowering his price? What if the elasticity is 3?

Answer: An elasticity of demand equal to 1/3 means that demand is inelastic. If Wally lowers his price, his increase in sales will not be enough to make up for the loss of revenue per unit. In other words, keeping the price at $5 per pail means that he sells fewer pails but makes more total revenue than if the price is lower. In contrast, an elasticity of demand equal to 3 would mean that Wally faces an elastic demand for his water. In that case, a price reduction would lead to such a large percentage increase in sales that Wally's revenues would rise.

OBSERVATION POINT: **Sin Taxes—Is It Morality We're After?**

Cigarettes and alcohol are taxed at much higher rates than virtually any other good. The reason is partly because these "goods" are seen as bad. Just as important, it is because the elasticity of demand is low relative to that of other goods.

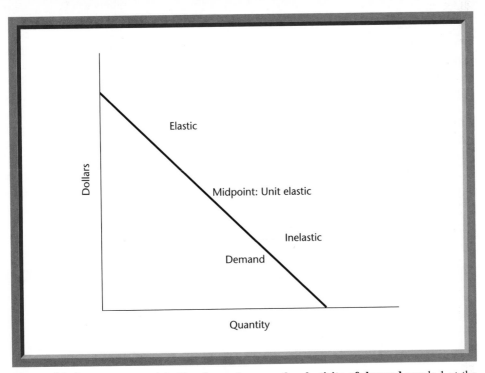

Figure 3A-8 **Along a straight-line demand curve, the elasticity of demand** equals 1 at the midpoint, is higher above that point and lower below it.

If the elasticity were high, people could more easily switch to other goods with lower tax rates. That would cut into tax revenues, which is exactly what happened after Congress passed five luxury taxes in 1990. Higher tax rates on yachts and other luxuries actually brought in less revenue, because so many people refused to buy these items at the higher prices the tax implied. Four of the five luxury taxes were repealed for this reason—demand was too elastic. Because elasticity is higher at higher prices, the amount of extra revenue government could collect by raising alcohol and tobacco taxes is also limited. Proposals to finance health care through taxes on alcohol and tobacco overlook this fact of economic life.

Cigarettes and alcoholic beverages are not the only goods with low elasticities of demand. Milk has a low elasticity of demand, and yet milk is not taxed at all in most places. It seems that the so-called sin aspect of smoking and drinking means that the public, even smokers and drinkers, are less willing to fight higher taxes on those items. Moreover, smoking and drinking can have some harmful effects on others, whereas what could be more wholesome than milk?

A caution is in order about taxing sin. If goods are singled out for high taxes because they are bad, it is important to figure out just how bad. Let the punishment fit the crime.

The Extremes of Demand Elasticity

There are three extreme cases in which elasticity is constant throughout the demand curve. These are shown as cases 1 through 3 in Figure 3A-9. Case 1 depicts a demand that is *perfectly inelastic*, meaning that the quantity demanded will not depend upon price. While demand for some goods is highly inelastic, there aren't any goods that do not show as least some responsiveness to price. For example, demand for insulin or certain pharmaceutical drugs is highly inelastic. However, to the extent that patients must actually pay more when price increases for these necessities, they will skimp on their dosages and thus buy less.

Case 2 depicts a demand that is unit elastic throughout. This shape is referred to as a rectangular hyperbola, because any rectangle drawn under that demand curve will have the same area. Because demand relates price and quantity, when price is multiplied by

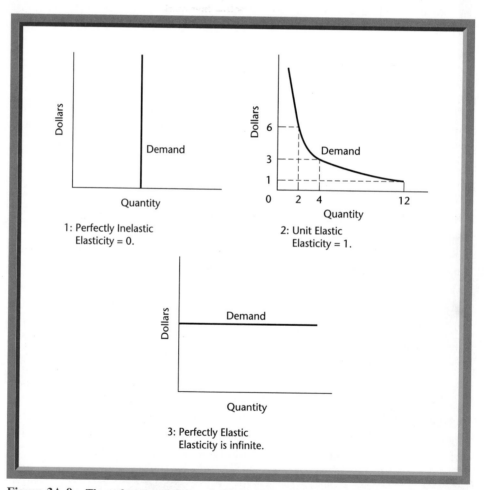

Figure 3A-9   These three special cases hold elasticity constant at each point along demand.

quantity, the result is a rectangle. The area of the rectangle equals total revenue. Thus total revenue does not change in response to changes in price, as is necessary for demand to be unit elastic. In this example, whether the price is $1, $3, or $6, the total revenue is $12, which is the area of either the 1×12, 3×4, or 6×2 rectangle.

For demand to be unit elastic throughout, the same amount will be spent, no matter the price. This scenario occurs only if the buyers have a preset budget that must be fully spent. For example, Congress authorizes a certain amount of money to be spent filling the strategic petroleum reserve each year. The total amount authorized is always spent, without regard to the price of oil.

Case 3 depicts a demand that is *perfectly elastic* throughout. In other words, the slightest increase in price over some threshold leads to a complete loss of sales. At any price at or below this threshold, unlimited quantities could be sold. This demand is a close approximation to demand facing the firm in the competitive marketplace. For example, if you are a Nebraska wheat farmer, you would sell none of your grain if you price it at even one penny more than the market price set by the interaction of buyers and sellers in the commodity exchanges of Chicago. At or below that market price, however, you could sell all you could produce, no matter how large your farm.

Three Other Elasticities

Three additional elasticities are also referred to frequently. First is the **elasticity of supply**, which measures the responsiveness of quantity supplied to price. Its formula is given by the percentage change in quantity supplied divided by the percentage change in price. Since price and quantity supplied are directly related to each other, the elasticity of supply will always be positive. The elasticity of supply can fall within the following three ranges:

1. **Inelastic supply:** Elasticity of supply lies between 0 and 1; in this range, the quantity supplied is relatively unresponsive to price.
2. **Unit elastic supply:** Elasticity of supply = 1; in this range, the quantity supplied changes proportionally to changes in price.
3. **Elastic supply:** Elasticity of supply is greater than 1; in this range, the quantity supplied is relatively responsive to changes in price.

Contrast the description of elasticity of supply and that of elasticity of demand. Note that, with the exception of substituting supply for demand, the definitions are identical.

Another elasticity, the **income elasticity of demand**, measures how the quantity demanded responds to income. It is computed by dividing the percentage change in quantity demanded by the percentage change in income. If the income elasticity of demand is positive, an increase in income increases the quantity demanded. **A positive income elasticity of demand indicates the good is normal.** Conversely, **a negative income elasticity of demand indicates the good is inferior**, because consumption falls when income rises. Thus, we would expect the income elasticity of demand to be positive for cellular phones and negative for canned luncheon meat.

Finally, the **cross elasticity of demand** measures how the quantity demanded of one good responds to changes in the price of another good. Its formula is given by the percentage change in the quantity demanded of one good divided by the percentage change in the price of the other. If this value is positive, the quantity demanded of the first good changes in the same direction as the price of the other good. **A positive cross elasticity of demand indicates the goods are substitutes,** such as Coke for Pepsi. Thus, if the price of Pepsi increases, so does demand for Coke.

If the cross elasticity of demand is negative, the quantity demanded of the good falls as the price of the other good rises, and vice versa. Thus **a negative cross elasticity of demand indicates that the goods are complements,** such as popcorn and movies. If movie tickets become more expensive, fewer people go to the movie theater and less popcorn is sold.

EXPRESS STUDY TRUE OR FALSE

1. A decrease in income decreases demand for a normal good.
2. A decrease in price shifts demand to the right.
3. An increase in supply increases demand.
4. If the market clears, there is neither a surplus nor a shortage.
5. If demand is elastic, an increase in price will decrease revenues.
6. The cross elasticity of demand between peanut butter and jelly is positive.

EXPLORATION 1
Crime and the Market for Drugs

The war on drugs causes expenditures on drugs to increase. Increased spending on drugs increases the crime and violence that the war on drugs is intended to fight.

The United States has the highest proportion of its citizens behind bars of any "first-world" country. Sixty percent of those prisoners are convicted on drug-related charges. It sometimes appears that recreational drugs are ripping apart our social fabric. Yet, the more we fight the problem, the worse it seems. How can this be?

Many images come to mind when the word *drugs* is mentioned. There are the wonder drugs that have helped the sick. There is the contrasting image of eggs in the frying pan—"your brain on drugs." The violence of the drug cartels involved in the production and sale of cocaine and the pathos of the cocaine babies born to addicted mothers both come to mind. There are the AIDS patients who have shared dirty needles and the thieves stealing to support their habits. Also woven in are the counterculture of the 1960s and the creativity of such classic writers and poets as Edgar Allen Poe and Samuel Coleridge.

We need to do some sorting. Suppose we put aside questions of whether drug use is moral and of where to draw the line on drug laws. Instead, let's employ economic analysis to solve the dilemma of why toughening up our enforcement of drug laws seems to make drug-related problems worse. Then we will examine the implications of changing the direction of public policy away from the so-called drug war.

The Market for Drugs . . .

Illegal drugs are sold in markets, in many ways much like the markets for other goods. One difference is that information is not readily available about sources of supply, since this information could be used by law enforcement agencies. Nor is product quality ensured by government regulation or legal recourse. In the drug market, it is truly **caveat emptor**—let the buyer beware!

One consequence is that drug users tend to connect with only one or two dealers, who then have an interest in maintaining quality standards to ensure the customer comes back. In turn, most dealers are connected to only one or two wholesalers. Since competition keeps prices down, this reduction of competition causes higher prices.

... Sees Violent Crime on the Supply Side ...

On the supply side of the marketplace, government enforcement of drug laws pushes prices up even more dramatically by increasing the risk associated with dealing drugs. This will drive out the most *risk averse* suppliers and add a **risk premium** to prices. Who will remain? Some remaining suppliers will be those who shrug off the risk, perhaps because they enjoy it or have become accustomed to the lifestyle. For the most part, however, competition will select those suppliers who are best at circumventing the law. Usually that involves the insurance of hooking up with a powerful criminal organization.

From street gangs on up to the reputed drug Mafia, organized crime flourishes under tough drug law enforcement. These organizations offer both connections and firepower to the dealers. In addition, because the drug dealer cannot turn to the police for protection, that dealer becomes easy prey for organized criminals. Here is one source of crime associated with drugs—turf battles in which criminal organizations seek to dominate the sales of drugs in an area.

While having criminals killing criminals could be the subject of an intriguing debate, there are also unintended third parties who get caught in the crossfire. Furthermore, the survivors are those criminals who are best at violence. We see this in the violence of the drug trade along the U.S. border with Mexico and within Colombia, the major source of cocaine.

—*W*itness Colombia—

In Colombia, the dominance of the Medellin drug cartel came to an end with the gunning down of Pablo Escobar, the drug king. Although the dominance of the Medellin cartel merely gave way to dominance by the rival Cali cartel, most people breathed a sigh of relief. After all, the Cali cartel was known to be less violent.

Quickly after the Cali cartel came to prominence, the bosses of that cartel sought government clemency. After all, life had become dangerous for them, and they were already rich. Was this the end of drug violence in Colombia?

Unfortunately, a new generation of brutal gun-toting drug lords has replaced the old guard of the Cali cartel. The harsh law enforcement had driven out all but the most violence-prone from the top ranks of the leading cartel. Thus, while the new drug lords have learned to avoid directing the wrath of the world at any one of them personally, the overall climate of violence in Colombia's drug-producing areas continues unabated.

... Crime for Cash to Buy Drugs, ...

Why is there drug-related crime by drug users? Perhaps a small fraction has to do with the drugs impairing the user's judgment. Far and away the primary cause, however, is money. Tough enforcement of the drug laws makes it much more expensive to support a drug habit.

Drug users are often addicted to the drugs they use and would go to great lengths to avoid doing without. In other words, the demand for drugs is inelastic because the quantity purchased does not drop proportionally to increases in price. This means that, the tougher we enforce our drug laws, the more money drug users need. Moreover, the tougher we punish a convicted drug offender for the drug use itself, the less the user cares about adding other crimes to the list. Thus, while many addicts can support their habits with legally earned income, others think little of resorting to robberies, burglaries, and other crimes.

. . . and More Addictive Drugs.

Tough enforcement of our drug laws has also had the perverse effect of increasing the popularity of the most highly addictive drugs. This effect occurs as users substitute more addictive drugs for less addictive ones. Why would users want to do this?

The answer has to do with bulk. The bulkier the drug, the more likely it is to be intercepted. This is why marijuana grown in the U.S. today is likely to be much more potent than that grown in the 1960s. More potent drugs cut down on bulk. Unfortunately, the least bulky drugs also tend to be the most addictive. For instance, "cracking" cocaine to form crack requires only a small amount of cocaine, a drug with very little bulk. The relatively lower cost and highly addictive nature of crack has led it to pervade the cities of our country.

Tough enforcement of drug laws causes more violence on the supply side, more money-related crime by addicts, and substitution of more addictive drugs. What about the alternative route of backing off on law enforcement efforts, or even of legalizing some or all drugs altogether?

There are Alternatives to the Current War on Drugs . . .

There are numerous possible drug control policies between the current war on drugs and a *laissez faire* hands off strategy. At the extreme, if all drugs were legalized, that would seem to suggest including prescription pharmaceuticals. Should drugstores allow the customer to point and buy "three of those green ones, one of those big red capsules, and twelve of the yellow ones with dots?" In this portion of the Exploration, we look at the implications of moving away from the current war on drugs without specifying the details of how far that movement goes.

Figure 3B1-1 depicts the market for drugs, where the model is deliberately nonspecific as to exactly what sort of drugs these are. The addictive nature of drugs leads to an inelastic demand curve. The market price and quantity of drugs in the free market, denoted P_{fm} and Q_{fm}, is determined by the intersection of free market supply and demand. The drug war, denoted by subscript dw, causes the price to be higher and the quantity to be lower, *ceteris paribus*.

. . . that Might or Might Not Increase Usage.

Relative to the outcome under the drug war, the free market would appear to offer both good news and bad news. The good news is that the quantity of spending, given by P multiplied by Q, would be lower without the drug war. This means less crime to raise

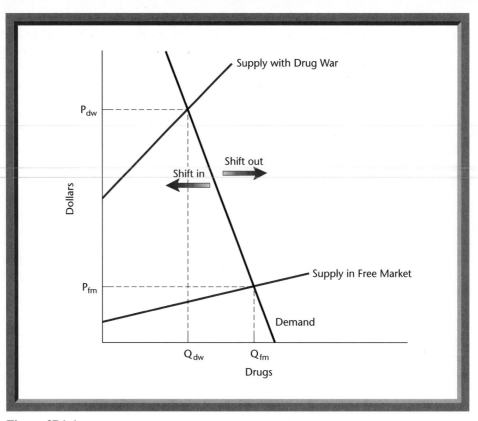

Figure 3B1-1   Law enforcement affects the market for drugs. fm = Free market; dw = drug war.

money to buy drugs. Since drugs would be sold by legitimate businesses in the free market, the violent territorial crime of the drug rings would also largely disappear. The bad news is that drug use would rise, *ceteris paribus*, because demand always shows an inverse relationship between price and quantity.

Keep in mind that the demand curve keeps constant everything but price. But moving away from the drug war entails more than just a drop in price. For example, the entire demand curve would shift outward to the extent that users no longer fear being arrested, which would lead to greater usage. Alternatively, the demand curve might shift inward to the extent that drug usage constitutes less of an antiauthority rebellion and is seen more as a matter of responsible personal behavior.

*D*rug Pushers Would Lose Their Jobs at School . . .

There is another factor that would shift demand inward, one that obliterates one of the most disreputable groups in our society. Specifically, without the risk premium on prices to pay for their fancy cars and lavish lifestyles, drug pushers would be out of business.

There would be no incentive to lure schoolchildren to drug use, because there would be no money in it. Without their wads of cash and the power it buys, pushers would lose their ill-bought status as role models for many of our children. Free from the pressure of pushers, and without drugs exemplifying rebellion against authority, fewer kids would turn to drugs. How far this change would shift the demand curve in, though, is anybody's guess.

Some people suggest legalization of many drugs, but only if we impose high sales taxes to discourage purchases and pay for drug-related problems. This policy would be akin to taxing cigarettes in proportion to their **external costs**—those not captured in the marketplace. While taxes can be reasonable, a prohibitively high tax would reopen the doors to criminal pushers and modern-day bootleggers.

Interestingly, some of the biggest unseen proponents of tough drug laws are the drug pushers and their suppliers. Do you know why? Without tough drug laws, these dealers would be out of business. Of course proponents include others with much purer intentions. As the saying goes, "Politics makes strange bedfellows."

. . . and Free Markets Would Keep Usage Down in the Workplace . . .

Moving away from the drug war toward legalization does raise many questions. Some people are concerned about whether quality would diminish in the workplace, especially when that quality involves personal safety. For example, with drug use legal, what would prevent aircraft maintenance and flight crews from being so "stoned" that it would be unsafe to fly in their planes?

The answer is that, without government prohibitions, the free market would provide its own incentives for a clear-headed workforce. The incredibly high cost of a plane crash in terms of replacing the equipment and settling lawsuits would give airlines strong incentives to screen their personnel for drugs, alcohol, or other judgment-impairing problems. In general, companies that employ workers with impaired judgment would lose out in the competitive marketplace to those firms that are more effective at screening out problem workers.

B

. . . but Problems of Addiction Will Persist.

Legal or illegal, drugs do cause problems for both users and innocent victims. For example, driving-under-the-influence laws have reduced but not eliminated problems of drunk driving. Would a similar approach provide pedestrians and other drivers adequate protection from drivers hallucinating under the influence of LSD?

Questions of law aside, recreational drugs are the source of serious problems. For example, everyone's heart goes out to babies born addicted to cocaine. Viewing addicted babies and other heart-wrenching consequences of addiction can evoke a rage in which drug abuse becomes something to be wiped out at all costs. Should we act on that rage and escalate the current war on drugs? Alternatively, would backing off on the drug war lead to less addiction and more voluntary treatment? You be the judge.

1. TERRI: Drug users are wasting away their lives and not being productive members of society.

PAUL: That's their choice. People should be free to do as they please.

What do you think? Should a person have the right to be unproductive? Who will determine which lifestyles are unproductive?

2. PAUL: Government should not be trying to make personal decisions for us. It would make good economic sense to decriminalize recreational drugs and treat them like alcohol and tobacco. But no one can talk about that, you know.

TERRI: Recreational drugs need to stay illegal, because they're bad for the both users and society. Government shouldn't condone the use of harmful substances. What's more, drug laws give people the incentive to avoid doing wrong.

Find elements in both Paul's and Terri's arguments that make good economic sense. Why would Paul suggest that people are afraid to talk about decriminalizing drugs? Explain why debate on drug-related issues is often heated, and why well-meaning people disagree.

EXPLORATION 2
Empowering the Consumer—Vouchers for Education

B

The market for primary and secondary education is both similar to, and different from, other markets. A school voucher plan can promote competition and choice at the levels of primary and secondary education.

For most goods and services, consumers know what they buy. With education, in contrast, the idea is to learn. Consumers cannot know exactly what that learning will be. If they did, they would not need to learn it.

To the extent possible, consumers do pick and choose when it comes to education. While most apparent at the college level, consumers also try to be selective at the elementary and high school levels. For example, consumers seek to live in public school districts with the best reputations, which drives up property values in those districts. Public schools also face competition from private schools. Private schools are frequently perceived as a **superior good**. Superior goods are normal goods that people buy more than in proportion to increases in their incomes. This explains why private schools are able to charge high tuitions and still attract students from the free public schools.

Efficiency in the marketplace comes about through competition. Competition would be more intense if private and public schools each had equal access to tax dollars. Should public policy promote competition in this way and let parents and students pick the winners?

The Demand Side and the Public Interest

Demand for education depends upon income and wealth. Thus, whatever the price of educational quality, the quantities chosen will be less in poor neighborhoods than in rich ones. Likewise, residents of poorer neighborhoods choose to buy lower quality cuts of meat and models of automobiles than do their counterparts in wealthier neighborhoods. This is the marketplace in action.

While most of us want others to have opportunities for adequate incomes, we do not usually focus our concerns on the types of vehicles they drive or on whether they choose hamburger or steak. In contrast, we do worry about variations in the quality of education between rich and poor districts. The reason is that, unlike most other goods that parents buy, education is likely to have a long-lasting impact on the prosperity of their children. Indeed, kids that are forced to make do with low-quality food and second-hand autos may be motivated to strive harder to succeed in life. In contrast, with defective educational tools and without being stimulated to learn more on their own, children with inferior educations possess less opportunity for future success.

Public schools are usually financed through local property taxes, which are at the discretion of local voters. Because demand for education is lower in poor districts, voters choose smaller budgets per pupils in those districts. In order to increase demand, poor school districts' resources are sometimes augmented with wealth transfers from elsewhere. These transfers can take many forms, such as grants from higher levels of government to low-income school districts, or even inclusion of some of the richer districts' property on the tax rolls of poorer districts.

Robin Hood plans that take from purportedly rich school districts and give to poor ones have some obvious appeal. Especially to those on the receiving end of the transfers, the plans seem fair. However, three cautions are in order. First, to the extent government transfers incomes from the haves to the have-nots, it is also taking away incentives to work hard and get ahead. If these policies are carried to the extreme of complete egalitarianism, in which everyone is guaranteed as much wealth as everyone else, there would be no incentive to work. National output would drop to nearly nothing, and we would all be equally impoverished.

A second caution has to do with the nature of collective choice. If most voters think that the level of spending they choose will be paid in part with money from elsewhere, they will choose to spend more because the price to them is lower. People are not as careful with other people's money as with their own.

The third caution concerns choice of family size. Again, the issue is one of price. To the extent that government helps pay for education, it is paying part of the cost of raising children. Parents then have less incentive to limit the size of their families. This is the law of demand in action. As the price of having children drops, the quantity chosen increases.

B

The Supply Side—Choice at a Price

Like all markets, the market for education is composed of a demand side and a supply side. As we have seen, the demand side is much like that of other markets, except that government has more interest in the amount people choose to purchase. On the supply side, however, the market for primary and secondary education in the United States differs dramatically from other markets. The reasons revolve around government.

The invisible hand of the free market achieves efficiency by allowing profit-seeking firms to compete for the affections of the consumer. Successful firms provide products that are the most valuable to consumers. Unfortunately, there is very little competition in the markets for primary and secondary education in the U.S.

While consumers are free to shop around for schools, the price is high. For instance, to switch from one "free" public school to another, parent-consumers must pull up their stakes and relocate. The monetary and nonmonetary costs of that action could be daunting. Alternatively, the parents could send their children to one of a handful of accessible private schools. Here too, considering tuition and transportation expenditures, the cost of choice is still quite high.

The result is that, rather than effective competition in the marketplace, primary and secondary education is provided largely through the "command and control" mechanism of government. This does not mean that those in education are not motivated to do right by the children in their classes. Still, because different people have different perspectives on educational quality, it is likely that the characteristics of education in America today would change if more competition were allowed.

Many educators point to the expertise of educational professionals as reason enough for them to call the shots. Other educators are more supportive, seeing competition as providing the checks and balances that keep expenses down and quality up. For evidence they point to statistics showing that public schools spend much more per pupil than do private schools, despite the private schools having a better reputation for quality. They say that parents should be allowed to shop for the best value in schools. Would parents shop well, or would the experts pick better?

School Vouchers Let the Parents Decide

To bring about more competition, government could issue vouchers for education—educational vouchers or school vouchers for short. **Vouchers** specify an amount that the holder can spend, but restrict that spending to a certain category of goods. For example, food stamps are vouchers that low-income recipients are allowed to use toward food purchases. School vouchers would be issued free of charge to parents on the basis of the grade levels of their children and would be spendable only on education for those children.

The amount of educational vouchers could vary, but might best be set equal to the estimated cost of providing a basic level of education for the appropriate grade level. Some parents, such as those of physically challenged children, would receive larger vouchers to compensate for their children's special needs. Vouchers could then be spent for education at the specified grade level in any accredited school. Parents would be free to supplement vouchers with extra money of their own. In this way, schools would compete to receive parents' vouchers. Schools could no longer count on politically defined school districts to provide them with a captive group of customers.

With a voucher plan in place, there would no longer be a necessity for the government to own any public schools. Not only would the operation of the schools be driven by market demand, but so too would their locations and designs. Despite its advantages, however, such a radical change from the status quo might prove difficult to get through the political process. Most actual legislative proposals for school vouchers retain support for publicly owned schools.

What of religion? Would allowing parents to spend their vouchers on church-run schools violate the separation of church and state that Americans hold dear? To answer this question, consider where the voucher money comes from. Under the present system, taxpayers pay for the public schools and get their money back only if they send their children there. In other words, the government takes taxpayers' money and offers to return it only if they keep their children out of religious or other private schools. That policy can be viewed as actively discouraging religion.

The basic notion of vouchers is much more evenhanded. With a pure voucher system, taxpayers are offered the opportunity to get their tax money back if they send children to any school, public or private. It would no longer be relevant whether the school is religious or sectarian. Curiously, most existing and proposed voucher plans would explicitly restrict spending to government-owned public schools.

*T*he Spectrum of Control

Some people worry that vouchers would lead to segregated, unequal schools. These critics imagine a collection of elitist schools filled with the most gifted. Alongside would be other schools for the "leftovers," those whose parents don't care, those with learning disabilities, immigrants with language difficulties, etc. Must vouchers lead to such a grim outcome?

The answer is that vouchers are very flexible and can be designed to meet a wide variety of objectives. For example, vouchers could be specified to apply only to schools meeting certain educational standards. Those standards need not be restricted to academic coverage, but could also include admission policies and actions to promote diversity. Indeed, anything required of our current system of public and private schools can be incorporated into vouchers, too.

While it is necessary to tie vouchers to some legitimate criteria of what schooling should consist of, there is a danger in going too far toward command and control. If we rigidly specify exactly what a school must do to qualify for voucher expenditures, then we lose the invisible hand of the marketplace that provides products consumers want. Choice has value to consumers. That value will be lost if the educational products must by law be identical.

As an example, consider mainstreaming, a philosophy that is currently popular among educators. Mainstreaming consists of placing physically challenged students in the same classes as everyone else, rather than isolating them in separate classes. Interpreters or other aides provide special assistance as necessary. The idea is to promote tolerance and prevent stigmatization. Opponents claim that the challenged are often better able to advance if grouped according to their special needs. Those holding this view would ar-

B

gue that the hard-of-hearing, for instance, perform better and feel better about themselves in classes designed exclusively for them.

Should we all debate this issue and then mandate one philosophy over another? The alternative is to let the marketplace make the decision. Some schools would offer one approach; others would offer the other. Parents, gauging their own children's experiences, would over time move their children to the schools offering what they perceive as the better way. This is what the marketplace does well, if allowed the opportunity.

Would a school voucher plan wreak havoc on school busing? After all, it would hardly make sense to have multiple bus systems crisscrossing one another so as to pick up scattered clusters of kids. That would mean more gas, wasted time, and a wastefully large number of buses. Someone would have to pay for that busing.

Again, the marketplace has the answer. Schools that locate near one another at relatively central locations could share the same bus routes. Third-party operators of school buses would contract their services to more than one school. Schools that save time and money in this manner would find themselves with a competitive advantage over those that do not. In short, rather than being wasteful, the marketplace is likely to offer an improvement over politically located schools. The invisible hand of the marketplace would position schools in areas that provide the most net value to their customers.

*W*ho Should Do the Choosing?

The marketplace promotes diversity. When it comes to purely personal goods, such as what shows to watch and what to eat for dinner, diversity obviously promotes our well-being. However, education is not purely personal. To the extent that parents choose for their children, it is the children that bear most of the consequences of that choice. Allowing not-yet-educated children to choose on their own does not seem to offer much of an alternative. Yet, leaving school choice to the collective public sector raises the specter of unresponsive bureaucracies that trap the poor but not the rich. How much weight should be assigned to each concern is a matter of hot debate.

PROSPECTING FOR NEW INSIGHTS

1. MIA: Choice is okay for some things, but not for education. We should all learn the same things so we can get started on an equal footing. Anyway, parents often either don't know or don't care about what gets taught at school!

    PAUL: That puts too much power in the hands of the educational elite, telling us what and how to learn. Anyway, "different strokes for different folks." Kids have different needs and aspirations, and nobody is in a better position to judge that than the parents and kids themselves.

    Should educational opportunities be different? If so, how different? Is it better to leave choice to parents and children, or to the experts? Is there a happy medium?

2. CLEO: I think voucher amounts should vary with household income. The more income, the less help—it's only fair. Still, most people should pay something

out of their own pockets to educate the kids they chose to have. Keeps our taxes down!

Mo: Free education for only the needy gives everybody an incentive to hold down family size except the poor. I think education should be free for everyone. Your income shouldn't have anything to do with how much voucher power you have.

Evaluate Cleo's and Mo's ideas. If a voucher plan is to be used, should the voucher amount depend upon a person's income?

B

MASTERING ROADSIDE CHALLENGES

CHALLENGE 1
How Market Equilibrium is Affected by Shifts in Supply and Demand

There are only eight possible ways in which supply and demand can shift. Table 3C1-1 lists all eight and labels them as cases 1 through 8. The two columns on the right side of Table 3C1-1 list the effects of the shifts on the market equilibrium price and quantity, labeled P* and Q* respectively. These are filled in for only the first four cases. Figure 3C1-1 shows these cases graphically.

The final four cases are nothing more than combinations of the first four. Once you have mastered cases 1 through 4, you might try your hand at filling in the blank spaces associated with cases 5 through 8. Some of the blank spaces must be filled in with Unknown to indicate that the direction in which the equilibrium price or quantity will move cannot be known without further information. You should avoid looking at the remainder of this section until you have filled in the blanks in Table 3C1-1.

Cases 5 through 8 are combinations of the first four and are best analyzed in that manner, as presented in Table 3C1-2. For instance, consider case 5. When demand shifts to the right, *ceteris paribus*, P* and Q* both increase. When supply shifts to the right, *ceteris paribus*, Q* increases but P* decreases. By themselves, both shifts pull quantity higher. However, the shifts in demand and supply pull price in opposite directions. We cannot know which will be the stronger pull without additional information.

Figure 3C1-2 illustrates this effect by showing three alternative shifts in demand. D1 represents a shift in demand that is weaker than the shift in supply. The result is a lower equilibrium price. In contrast, were D2 to be the shift in demand, the downward and upward pulls on price would just balance and price would not change. D3 represents a shift in demand that dominates the shift in supply and drives price higher.

TABLE 3C1-1 *The Eight Cases of Shifting Demand and Supply*

Case	Demand	Supply	P*	Q*
1	No change	Right	Fall	Rise
2	No change	Left	Rise	Fall
3	Right	No change	Rise	Rise
4	Left	No change	Fall	Fall
5	Right	Right	—	—
6	Left	Left	—	—
7	Right	Left	—	—
8	Left	Right	—	—

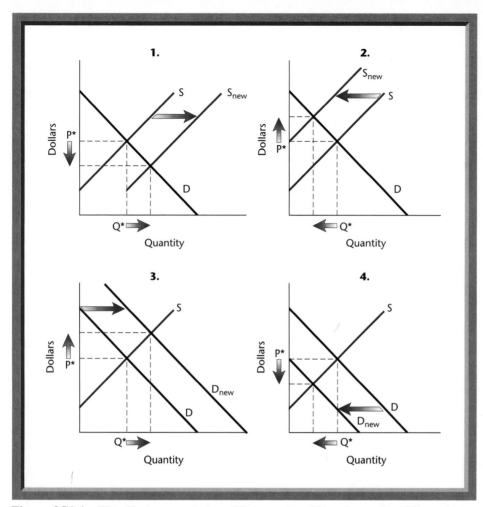

Figure 3C1-1 **The effects on market equilibrium price (P*) and quantity (Q*) can be ex-**plained by a shift in either demand (D) or supply (S), as shown in these four cases. When demand and supply shift simultaneously, the result can be analyzed by combining the pertinent two of the four cases shown.

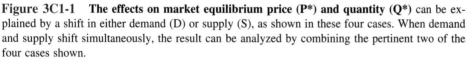

TABLE 3C1-2	*Cases 5 through 8 Combine Cases 1 through 4*			
Case	**Demand**	**Supply**	**P***	**Q***
5: 1 and 3	Right	Right	Unknown	Rise
6: 2 and 4	Left	Left	Unknown	Fall
7: 2 and 3	Right	Left	Rise	Unknown
8: 1 and 4	Left	Right	Fall	Unknown

C

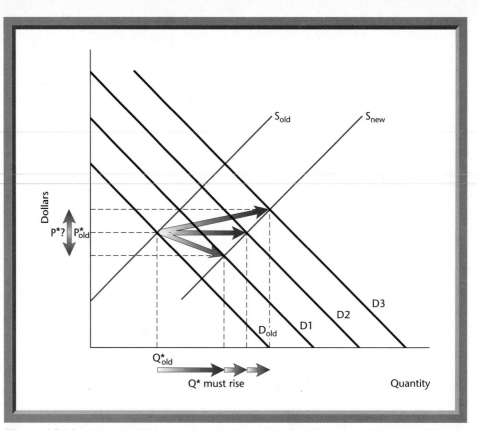

Figure 3C1-2   Case 5—When supply and demand both shift to the right, the equilibrium quantity increases. If demand (D1) shifts less than proportionally to the change in supply, price falls. If demand (D2) shifts proportionally, price remains constant. If Demand (D3) shifts more than proportionally, price rises. Thus, **without knowing the magnitude of the shift, the effect on price cannot be determined.** This example represents a combination of cases 1 and 3 from Table 3C1-1.

To truly master all the possible shifts in demand and supply, try working backwards. For example, suppose price rises and quantity falls. What could have caused this situation? One possibility is that supply shifts to the left, *ceteris paribus*, as listed in case 2. But that is not the only possibility. For instance, case 6 could have occurred if both demand and supply shifted to the left, but the supply shift was the more dominant of the two. Likewise for case 7.

Can you apply this analysis? For example, how would you interpret the observation that the price of video camcorders has fallen in the last ten years, and people are now buying more? Analytically, it could be case 1, in which demand stays constant while supply shifts right. More likely, however, case 5 applies, in which both demand and supply shift to the right. Demand shifted as camcorders became an increasingly popular addition to the gadgets of modern life. However, the increase in supply has been even more pronounced, which explains why prices have fallen.

C

All elasticities have the same basic formula, that being the percentage change in one variable divided by the percentage change in another as follows: $\%\Delta Y / \%\Delta X$. Different elasticities merely name the variables differently. Therefore, if you know how to compute one elasticity, you can merely substitute variables to compute any other elasticity. Hence the challenge of computing an elasticity is in being able to compute a percentage change.

In common usage, a percentage change is defined as the change in something divided by what it started out as. For example, if a person's weight rises from 100 pounds to 150 pounds, we say that their weight has risen by 50 percent, that is, by 50/100. Curiously, if the person's weight were to drop to 100 pounds after being at 150 pounds, the percentage change would be -33%, that is, $-50/150 = -1/3$. In other words, weight rose by half but fell by one third.

This type of measure will not do for the computation of elasticities. Rather, a measure is needed that is independent of the direction in which the variables are changing. That measure of percentage change is provided by the **midpoint formula**, which computes percentage change as the change in the variable divided by an amount halfway between the starting and ending amount. Consider the variable Y, which changes from an initial value of Y_0 to a value of Y_1. Symbolically, the midpoint formula to compute the percentage change in Y is as follows:

$$\%\Delta Y = \frac{\Delta Y}{\text{base}}$$

where ΔY equals $Y_1 - Y_0$, and the base equals $(Y_0 + Y_1)/2$. Likewise, the percentage change in variable X would be computed as follows:

$$\%\Delta X = \frac{\Delta X}{\text{base}}$$

where ΔX equals $X_1 - X_0$, and the base equals $(X_0 + X_1)/2$. To compute the elasticity of Y with respect to X, simply divide $\%\Delta Y$ by the $\%\Delta X$ as follows:

$$\frac{\Delta Y}{(Y_0 + Y_1)/2} \div \frac{\Delta X}{(X_0 + X_1)/2}$$

This is equivalent to the following shortcut formula, which gives the same result:

$$\frac{\Delta Y}{Y_0 + Y_1} \div \frac{\Delta X}{X_0 + X_1}$$

This Challenge focuses on the elasticity of demand. Recall that the elasticity of demand is defined as the percentage change in quantity demanded divided by the percentage change in price. Data from Table 3A-1 in the Expressway module are repeated in the first three columns of Table 3C2-1. The final two columns of this table contain the rev-

C

TABLE 3C2-1 *Demand and Revenue*

Data Point	Price ($)	Quantity Demanded	Total Revenue ($) = P × Q	Marginal Revenue ($) = Δ(P × Q)/ΔQ
A	5	0	0	Undefined
B	4	1	4	4
C	3	2	6	2
E	2	3	6	0
F	1	4	4	−2
G	0	5	0	−4

enue implications of demand. **Total revenue** equals price multiplied by quantity: P × Q. **Marginal revenue** is defined as the change in total revenue associated with one additional unit of output, as follows:

Marginal revenue = Δtotal revenue/Δquantity of output

Table 3C2-2 uses the shortcut formula described above to compute elasticity between each pair of data points in Table 3C2-1. Because the application is to the price elasticity of demand, variable Y is quantity and X is price:

$$\frac{\Delta Q}{Q_0 + Q_1} \div \frac{\Delta P}{(P_0 + P_1)}.$$

Equivalently, the price elasticity of demand can be computed as

$$\frac{P_0 + P_1}{Q_0 + Q_1} \times \frac{\Delta Q}{\Delta P}$$

because dividing one fraction by a second is the same as multiplying the first fraction by the reciprocal of the second.[1] For example, in computing the elasticity between points B and C, (1/3)/(1/7) = 1/3 × 7/1 = 7/3. For convenience, the elasticity of demand is expressed in terms of its absolute value, meaning that negative signs are dropped. Otherwise the elasticity of demand would always be negative, because price and quantity demanded always move opposite to each other.

Figure 3C2-1 plots the relationships between demand, marginal revenue, and elasticity we derived earlier. Figure 3C2-2 shows the more general relationships between these variables. Note the following:

- Marginal revenue is positive and total revenue is rising when demand is elastic.
- Marginal revenue is zero and total revenue is at a maximum when demand is unit elastic.
- Marginal revenue is negative and total revenue is declining when demand is inelastic.

C

---

[1]Calculus can be used to compute elasticity at a single point on a demand curve with a known functional form. The formula is P/Q × dQ/dP.

Computing the Elasticity of Demand, Shortcut Method

(a) Between Points	(b) $\dfrac{\Delta P}{P_0 + P_1}$	(c) $\dfrac{\Delta Q}{Q_0 + Q_1}$	(d) Elasticity of Demand = (c)/(b)
A and B	1/9	1/1 = 1	9
B and C	1/7	1/3	7/3
C and E	1/5	1/5	1
E and F	1/3	1/7	3/7
F and G	1/1 = 1	1/9	1/9

Figure 3C2-1 **The data from Table 3C2-1** show the typical relationship between demand (D), elasticity, total revenue, and marginal revenue.

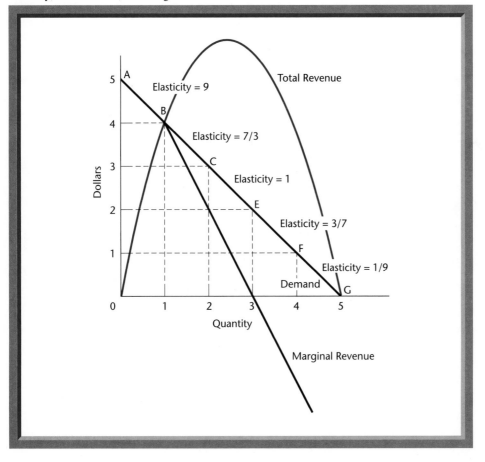

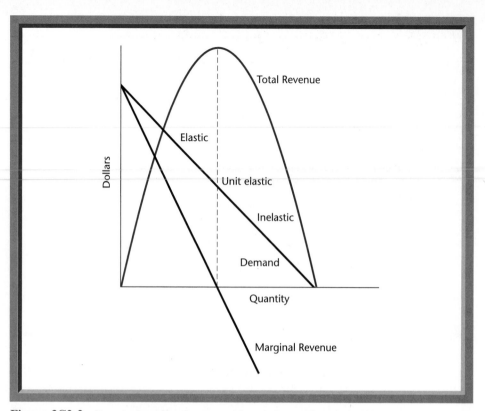

Figure 3C2-2 **In actual application,** quantities are large. The relationships between demand, revenue, and elasticity will appear as shown. Note that marginal revenue starts where the demand curve intersects the vertical axis, slopes down twice as fast as demand, and thus intersects the horizontal axis below the midpoint of demand, where elasticity equals 1.

✓ QUICKCHECK

Elasticities and the relationship between demand and revenue usually strike students as difficult until they have engaged in hands-on computation. Work through Tables 3C2-1 and 3C2-2 to verify that all the information is correct.

C

Study by Design

SpeedStudy

SpeedReview

Supply and demand analysis captures the essential role of competition in the free marketplace Economists assign very specific meanings to the concepts of supply and demand, which characterize market allocation of resources. The interaction of supply and demand leads to a market equilibrium price and quantity, from which there is no tendency to change. Various factors can shift supply and demand curves. When this happens, price and quantity adjust to a new market equilibrium. Being able to read these adjustments can make for successful business opportunities and effective public policy. The technical concept of elasticity allows for detailed study of responsiveness, such as of quantity supplied or demanded to price. The elasticity of demand is particularly important for its insight into revenue effects of price changes.

SpeedStudy True or False Self-Test

A1. If price rises, demand falls. *the quantity demanded* *falls*

A2. *Ceteris paribus*, if the price of Coca-Cola rises, the quantity sold of Pepsi will fall. *rise*

A3. If something happens that leads producers to expect price to rise in the future, supply will initially shift to the left.

A4. Technological change has the effect of shifting supply to the left. *right*

A5. Market demand is the horizontal summation of all buyers' demands.

A6. If the market clears, there is likely to be a shortage. *it is at equilibrium* *neither surplus or* *shortage*

A7. In general, elasticity measures the responsiveness of one variable to a change in another variable.

A8. If demand is elastic and price rises, total spending by consumers also rises. *falls*

A9. If demand is completely elastic throughout, it will be a horizontal line.

A10. The cross elasticity of demand will be positive for a normal good. *income*

B11. If demand for illegal drugs is inelastic, a crackdown by authorities is likely to increase spending on those drugs.

B12. Drug pushers would probably lose their businesses if drugs were to be legalized.

B13. Educational vouchers would allow parents to shop for schools.

B14. Government spends about the same amount of your tax money on your children whether or not you send them to a religious school. *more* *if*

C15. If demand shifts to the right and supply shifts to the left, we know that price will rise.

C16. If demand shifts to the right and supply shifts to the left, we know that quantity will not change.

C17. If, to sell the eighth unit of output, price must be lowered from $9 to $8, then the marginal revenue from that eighth unit is $1.

C18. If you can sell seven units of output for $9 each, and eight units for $8 each, the price elasticity of demand is 1. *17/15 or 1.13*

The MasterMind

Selected Terms Along the Way

demand, 77
quantity demanded, 77
ceteris paribus, 77
shift factors, 78
normal goods, 80
inferior goods, 80
substitutes, 80
complements, 80
supply, 83
quantity supplied, 83

market equilibrium, 86
surplus, 88
shortage, 89
elasticity, 90
elasticity of demand, 90
inelastic, 91
unit elastic, 91
elastic, 91
elasticity of supply, 95
income elasticity of demand, 95

cross elasticity of demand, 95

caveat emptor, 97
risk premium, 98
external costs, 101
superior goods, 102
vouchers, 104

midpoint formula, 111
total revenue, 112
marginal revenue, 112

MasterMind Multiple Choice Self-Test

A1. Which of the following would shift the demand for butter to the right?

   a. An increase in the price of margarine.
   b. A decrease in the price of margarine.
   c. Cheaper milking machines.
   d. An increase in the supply of butter.

A2. To arrive at market supply, individual producers' supply curves are

   a. added horizontally.
   b. added vertically.
   c. first added vertically, then divided horizontally.
   d. averaged.

A3. Suppose it is found that eating toast makes a person smarter. The effect this finding will have in the market for jelly will be to shift

   a. both demand and supply for jelly to the right.
   b. both demand and supply for jelly to the left.
   c. neither demand nor supply for jelly, but increase price.
   d. demand for jelly to the right, but not change supply of jelly.

A4. If the elasticity of demand equals 17, an increase in price would cause total revenues to

   a. increase.
   b. decrease.
   c. remain the same.

   d. increase sharply at first, but then decrease over time until, after seventeen months, revenues return to what they had initially been.

A5. Along a downward-sloping straight-line demand curve, the elasticity of demand

   a. is constant at all points, and has a value greater than 1.
   b. is constant at all points, and has the value of 1.
   c. is constant at all points, and has a value less than 1.
   d. has a value of 1 at the midpoint, a value greater than 1 above the midpoint, and a value less than 1 below the midpoint.

B6. If the government were to legalize the use and sale of addictive recreational drugs, it is most likely that there would be

   a. an increase in the number of commercial airline crashes, as pilots and air traffic controllers come to work "strung out" on drugs.
   b. a sharp decline in the income of drug pushers.
   c. an increase in the amount of money people spend on drugs.
   d. an increase in violence among suppliers.

B7. School voucher plans would do all of the following *except*

   a. increase the amount of control that parents have over schools.

b. threaten contracts negotiated by teachers' unions with the public schools.

c. violate the separation between church and state.

d. increase the amount of choices available.

C8. Suppose that new 3-D seismographic techniques allow oil producers to identify new oil fields more easily. Suppose also that high costs of vacations abroad cause an upsurge in the number of people vacationing by automobile. Supply and demand analysis reveals that

a. the price and quantity sold of gasoline will both rise.

b. the quantity sold of gasoline will rise, al-

though the direction of price movement cannot be known without more information.

c. the price of gasoline will fall, although we cannot know what will happen to quantity without more information.

d. the price of gasoline will fall and the quantity sold will rise.

C9. If consumers buy nine gizmos at a price of $9 and ten gizmos at a price of $8, then marginal revenue for the tenth gizmo is

a. $9.

b. $8.

c. $1.

d. −$1.

MasterMind Questions and Problems

A1. Draw a single graph indicating some person's demand curve for hot dogs (D). Be sure to label the axes of your graph. On this graph, indicate what market demand would be if there were only two people willing to buy hot dogs, and if each had a demand curve identical to the one you just drew. Label this curve Mkt D.

A2. Let Jack and Jill be the only two consumers in the market for pails of water. Their demand schedules are as follows:

Price	Jack's Quantity	Jill's Quantity
$1	10	15
$2	5	10
$3	0	5
$4	0	0

a. Compute market demand.

b. Compute the quantities purchased in total and by Jack and Jill individually if the price per unit is $2.

c. Graph Jack's demand and Jill's demand on separate graphs. Note that, if you connect the data points you are given, you are actually inferring additional data. For example, connecting the data points on Jack's demand implies that Jack would be willing to purchase 2.5 pails of water at a price of $2.50 per pail.

A3. Fill in the surplus or shortage in the table be-

low. In each case identify whether the number is a surplus, shortage, or neither. Identify the equilibrium price, and explain why a price above equilibrium would not last.

Price	Quantity Demanded	Quantity Supplied	Surplus or Shortage
$7	12	30	_____
$6	15	25	_____
$5	19	19	_____
$4	23	10	_____

A4. Durango Bob, owner of Durango Danceland, must decide if he should offer a Saturday night happy hour and drink specials. He knows that, even without special promotions, Saturday night is his busiest night. Being reluctant to experiment with promotions on such a successful night, he decided to experiment on Wednesday nights, when business is slower. After counting up his receipts for a few weeks with Wednesday promotions in place, he concludes that revenues rise when his prices fall.

a. Is demand at Durango Danceland elastic on Wednesday nights?

b. To determine whether it is profitable to permanently lower prices on Wednesday nights, it is not enough to know that revenues rise. What else must be considered?

A5. In the question above, Durango Bob did not consider the role of substitutes.

   a. The elasticity of demand at Durango Danceland will depend upon the cross elasticity of demand between Durango Danceland and other dance halls. Thus Durango Bob must keep an eye on the actions of his competitors. Explain.

   b. Even if it is sensible to have promotions on Wednesday nights, the same might not apply to Saturday nights. Explain, using the concept of cross elasticity of demand between Wednesday and Saturday nights at Durango Danceland.

B6. List four factors that might shift demand for recreational drugs. Also list four factors that might shift supply. For each, note the direction that demand or supply would shift.

B7. Describe the essential characteristics of a school voucher plan. What is its objective? Without examining the details, explain in general how this objective is achieved.

C8. Using a graph of supply and demand, demonstrate how a leftward shift in demand, accompanied by a rightward shift in supply, can result in the equilibrium quantity rising. On a separate graph, demonstrate how the equilibrium could alternatively have fallen.

C9. Suppose consumers buy twenty-five units at a price of $20, or twenty-six units at a price of $19.

   a. Compute the elasticity of demand between these points. Is demand elastic?

   b. Compute the marginal revenue from selling the twenty-sixth unit.

Future Explorations: Mapping out Term Papers

1. Plug that Gusher—We'll Get Rich Later!

This paper examines how expectations of future prices influence producers' decisions on how much to supply. Using oil as an example, the paper lists some alternative visions of the future, and interprets how these visions could affect supply today. For example, the paper explains why an expected decrease in the price of wind power or solar power would increase the supply of oil, even before those alternative energy sources are actually cost-effective.

2. If the Customers Don't Come, Raise Prices!

This paper applies the idea of price elasticity of demand to explain how, when businesses are doing poorly, they sometimes lower prices and other times raise them in order to bring in more revenue. For example, some struggling airlines and computer companies have been known to eliminate "sales" in order to return to profitability. In other cases, companies discount their prices to drum up business. The paper will give examples of circumstances under which each makes sense.

3. Prohibition: Fighting Supply and Demand

This paper studies the changes in the market for alcohol during and after prohibition. The focus is upon price, spending, and quality of the product, along with unwanted side effects. These side effects included increased violence and alcoholism. The paper also explores the options that faced legitimate producers of alcohol prior to prohibition. Upon enactment of prohibition, some producers went out of business, some went underground, and some turned to other products. Dire predictions of increased crime and alcoholism after the repeal of prohibition proved unfounded.

Answer Key

**ExpressStudy
True or False**

1. T
2. F
3. F
4. T
5. T
6. F

**SpeedStudy True
or False Self-Test**

1. F   10. F
2. F   11. T
3. T   12. T
4. F   13. T
5. T   14. F
6. F   15. T
7. T   16. F
8. F   17. T
9. T   18. F

**MasterMind Multiple
Choice Self-Test**

1. a
2. a
3. d
4. b
5. d
6. b
7. c
8. b
9. d

$\mathcal{E}$ fficiency and Political Prices

A Look Ahead

In newspaper stories and the public mind, equity appears to be of much greater concern than efficiency. That is partly because, although people are often confused about what makes an economy tick, everyone has a sense of what is fair and unfair. Indeed, the concept of a fair price has held a prominent place in economic thought from the days of the medieval religious philosophers and before. In contrast, the understanding of economic efficiency has been a much more recent development . . . within the last two or three centuries!

We will see how, in the absence of market failures, a competitive market equilibrium efficiently maximizes the value an economy obtains from the use of its resources. We then examine what happens when government seeks to impose a purportedly fair price in order to promote equity. Policies to promote equity come at different prices in terms of efficiency. If we choose to go this route, we need to shop among policy alternatives. The policy of substituting political prices for market prices usually turns out to be a high-cost choice. By forcing price away from the market equilibrium, many advantages of market allocation are defeated. Sometimes the effect is to harm the very people the policies intend to help.

DESTINATIONS

Module A

As you zip along the Expressway you will arrive at an ability to

- describe how a market equilibrium can maximize social surplus;
- relate the central role of price in allocating resources efficiently;
- interpret why rent controls are easy to enact, but hard to remove;
- explain how minimum wage laws do not fulfill the intentions of their supporters;
- decipher why well-meaning attempts to improve upon market prices often result in unintended and unfortunate consequences.

Module B

When you leave the Expressway to explore issues you will discover

- why people both desire and fear government involvement in health insurance;
- the consequences of federal policies that reduce the price of risk.

Module C

Mastering Roadside Challenges will allow you to hone analytical skills by

- explaining how utility-maximizing behavior lies behind consumer demand;
- describing how graphical analysis can show some but not all of the inefficiencies of politically set prices.

Efficiency in the Marketplace—Maximizing Surplus Value

For a market economy to be efficient implies that it produces the most value from the resources at its disposal. How can that value be measured? In practical terms, the value of a good to a consumer is how much money the person would be willing to pay for it. For example, if you think gizmos are worth more than gadgets, you are willing to pay more for gizmos than for gadgets. Note that what you are willing to pay is usually not what you in fact do pay.

Figure 4A-1 illustrates the value of buying and selling to the buyers and sellers. The demand and supply curves in Figure 4A-1 are shown unit-by-unit, like stair steps. This

Figure 4A-1 **Consumer surplus and producer surplus** are created for each unit of output, up to the last unit sold.

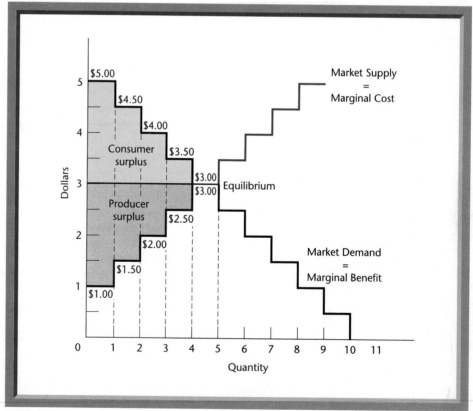

depiction allows the surplus value from each incremental unit to be represented by the height of a rectangle.

Consider first the supply curve, which tells how much will be offered for sale at each price. Because it takes a price of at least $1 to elicit the first unit of output, that first unit of output must have a **marginal cost** of $1. In other words, the resources used to produce that good are worth $1. Likewise, the second unit of output would not be offered for sale at less than $1.50, meaning that its marginal cost is $1.50. More generally, the supply curve represents marginal cost.

The demand curve represents the schedule of **marginal benefit** to consumers. In other words, someone values that first unit of output at $5. We know this, because someone would purchase that unit at a market price of $5, but not higher. Likewise, the market price would have to drop to $4.50 for the second unit to be sold to someone, indicating that $4.50 is its value. By the same token, the third unit is valued at $4, the fourth at $3.50 and so on.

Markets are efficient to the extent that they maximize *surplus value*, which is the difference between how much a good is worth and how much it costs to produce. For consumers, surplus value is the difference between the most they would have been willing to pay for the items they purchase and the price they actually pay. This difference between maximum willingness-to-pay and price is termed **consumer surplus**. More succinctly, **consumer surplus equals demand minus the market price.** In Figure 4A-1, because the market price is $3, consumer surplus equals $2 for the first unit, $1.50 for the second, $1 for the third, $0.50 for the fourth, and nothing for the fifth unit purchased. Adding these together, total consumer surplus is seen to equal $5.

Correspondingly, sellers receive **producer surplus**, given by the difference between the prices they receive and the minimum they would have been willing to sell their goods for. In brief, **producer surplus equals the market price minus supply.** The market price of $3 in Figure 4A-1 leaves the producer of the first unit a producer surplus of $3 − $1 = $2. The next four units sold generate $1.50, $1, $0.50, and $0 in producer surplus, respectively, leading to a total of $5 in producer surplus.

Social surplus is the sum of producer and consumer surplus, which equals $10 in the example above. Social surplus is the total value the economy gains by having this good produced and consumed. Without externalities or other market failures, the intersection of demand and supply leads to a quantity that maximizes social surplus, the goal of economic efficiency. Efficiency is achieved because demand and supply represent **marginal social benefit** and **marginal social cost**, respectively, where the term *social* reflects that both consumers and producers are part of society.

Any time marginal social benefit exceeds marginal social cost, an economy generates value by producing more of the good. If marginal social cost exceeds marginal social benefit, the economy would generate more value with less output. In summary, the *rule of efficiency* states that **the efficient output occurs when marginal social benefit equals marginal social cost.**

Figure 4A-2 illustrates how the market price elicits the quantity that maximizes social surplus. Any higher price would cause consumers to buy less. Any lower price would cause producers to offer less for sale. Thus, any price other than the market equilibrium price would reduce the quantity actually sold in the marketplace, which in turn would reduce social surplus. For example, at the quantity $Q_{too\ little}$ in Figure 4A-2, social surplus is reduced by the triangular area **A** relative to what it would be with a free market price.

Some people question whether money is an appropriate measuring rod for social ben-

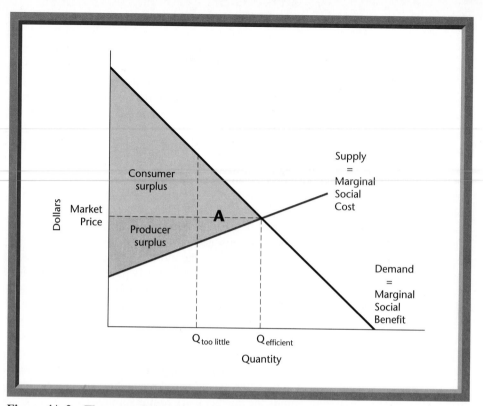

Figure 4A-2 The competitive market price maximizes social surplus, because that price elicits a quantity for which marginal benefit (demand) equals marginal cost (supply). Any other price
would cause a smaller quantity and less social surplus. For example, $Q_{too\ little}$ would reduce social
surplus by the triangular area **A.**

efits. For example, among other things, a consumer's demand for a good depends upon the
utility—satisfaction—the person receives from the good. Demand also depends upon the
person's financial status. The more money people have, the more they are able to pay,
which brings up questions of equity in the distribution of income. However, the best distribution of income is a separate issue from efficiency in the spending of that income. While
both efficiency and equity are valid economic goals, they are best analyzed separately.

✓ **QUICKCHECK**

Suppose coffee costs $1 per cup at Handy Stop Shop and $1.05 per cup at Gas'n N
Goin' next door. If you buy coffee at Handy Stop Shop, does this mean your consumer surplus from coffee is only five cents?

Answer: No, consumer surplus does not depend upon alternative prices for the same product. Rather, it
asks you what is the most you would be willing to pay to avoid doing without the product altogether and
then subtracts the price you actually pay. Thus, whatever your consumer surplus from a cup of coffee
may be, it is five cents more if you buy your coffee at Handy Stop Shop than at Gas'n N Goin'.

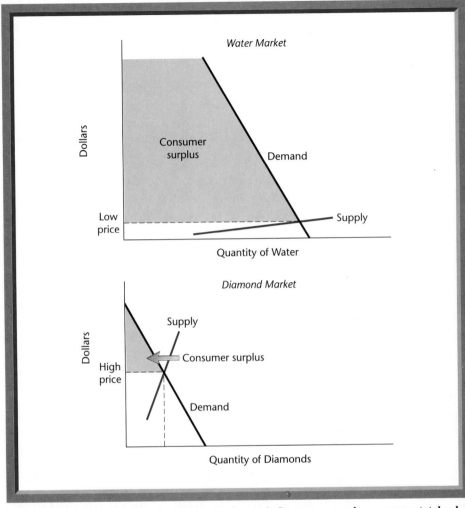

Price measures the value of a marginal unit of a good. Consumer surplus measures total value from all units of that good. Although the price of water is lower than the price of diamonds, water's total value is higher.

OBSERVATION POINT: The Paradox of Diamonds and Water

Some necessities that have a great deal of intrinsic worth are priced lower than luxuries we could easily do without. For example, people pay much more for a diamond than for a glass of water, which seems paradoxical.

The paradox disappears when we realize that a price tells the value of a good *at the margin*. Sure, the last bit of water is not worth much when water is plentiful. But the prospect of losing access to water altogether reveals just how valuable water can be. Witness the costly network of dams and aqueducts serving the burgeoning metropolises of Southern California. Witness also the billions of dollars spent on desalinization plants in the deserts of Saudi Arabia. At a personal level, imagine yourself stranded without water in Death Valley. Which would seem the better bargain—a diamond for a nickel or a glass of water for a one hundred dollar bill?

In short, as seen in the accompanying figure on the previous page, the consumer surplus from water purchases is vastly greater than the consumer surplus from diamond purchases. It is consumer surplus that truly measures the total value consumers receive from the things they buy.

*H*olding Prices Down

In 1973, the Organization of Petroleum Exporting Countries (OPEC) succeeded in restricting oil supplies to Western countries. Because demand for oil is quite inelastic, the OPEC action caused a dramatic spike upward in energy prices. In response, Congress enacted temporary gasoline price controls, which capped price increases and cut into social surplus. This action caused fuel shortages, with drivers losing much time and patience in long lines at the gas pumps. While sometimes ignored in the political process, economic analysis can be used to forestall such problems.

The problem of gasoline shortages and wasteful gas lines has little to do with gasoline and much to do with the economics of holding prices below the market equilibrium. A law that restricts price from rising above a certain level is called a **price ceiling**. Price ceilings cause numerous problems, which are magnified when ceilings are imposed broadly under **price freezes**, where price freezes prohibit a wide array of prices from rising. The transition back to market prices is often quite difficult. For example, consider a policy that continues in effect today in many cities. That is the policy of **rent controls**, which limit rent increases to below what the market would bear.

Promoting Affordable Housing—Are Rent Controls the Answer?

With rising populations in competition for scarce land, major cities sometimes choose rent controls as a way to insulate tenants from higher housing costs. Rent controls hold the monthly price of occupying apartments and rental houses to below its equilibrium level. Price tries to rise, but bumps up against the rent control ceiling. As we will see, the long-term consequences often differ from what proponents have in mind.

Figure 4A-3 illustrates a housing market with rent controls in place. For these rent controls to be meaningful, the ceiling price must be set below the market equilibrium price, P^*. The result is a housing shortage, as labeled, in which less housing is offered, Q_S, but more housing is demanded, Q_D, than would have been the case at the market equilibrium quantity of Q^*. The amount of housing actually leased will be the lesser of the two, Q_S, with the difference between that amount and the quantity demanded equaling the shortage.

Note that demand for rental housing is inelastic, meaning that the quantity demanded is not very responsive to changes in price. Still, renters are unwilling to rent as many apartments when prices are high as when they are low. For example, what would be your own reaction and that of your friends if rents were to rise substantially?

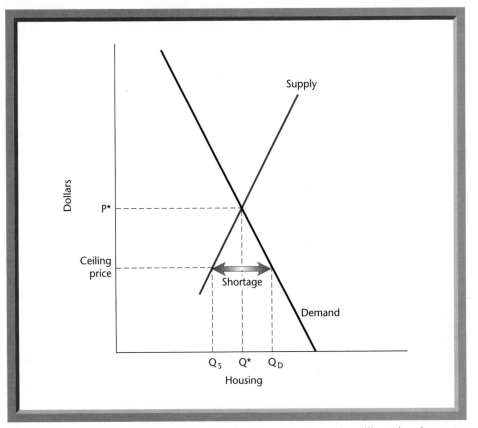

Figure 4A-3 **Rent controls create housing shortages.** The lower the ceiling price, the greater the shortage.

As rents rise, young adults become more hesitant about leaving home to set out on their own. Other people choose to share rental homes and apartments with roommates. How many roommates they choose depends on how high rents go. Still others live on their own, but rent smaller and less desirable quarters than they would have preferred. For all these reasons, demand for rental housing slopes down.

The supply of rental housing slopes upward, even in the short run before new construction has a chance to occur. Do you believe this? If your town has a special event that attracts an unusually large number of tourists, look around to see what happens. Perhaps the special event is when the leaves change color in the fall. Perhaps it is winter ski season. In New Orleans, the special event is Mardi Gras. In Louisville, it is Derby Week. During these events, some permanent residents move out and lease their homes to out-of-town visitors. Others partition off their homes or rent out extra rooms. In Atlanta, for example, some homeowners picked up an extra $500 per day per bedroom during the 1996 Olympics. In these ways, even without new construction, the quantity of rental housing supplied rises in response to higher prices.

If increases in market rents are expected to last, builders seeking profit will construct new housing units. The result is a rightward shift in supply and a downward movement in price as time passes. This is what happened after the San Francisco earthquake and fire of 1906. Initially rents jumped in response to the suddenly diminished supply of housing. However, this jump in rents prompted builders from all over to converge on San Francisco in order to participate in the construction boom. High rents did not last, because profit-driven builders quickly replaced the burnt homes. Within a year, the classified ads of the local papers offered a wide assortment of apartments for rent at rates comparable to those before the fire.

EFFECTS ON REAL ESTATE DEVELOPMENT   What would have happened in San Francisco had rent controls been in place? There would have been no influx of builders, because there would have been no surge in prices and thus no extra profit to attract them. The burned-out housing would not have been replaced. If you do not agree, consider the experience of Washington, DC, a city with rent controls firmly entrenched.

Washington suffered through violent disturbances in the 1960s in response to the assassination of Martin Luther King. Whole city blocks were pockmarked with burned-out homes and businesses. Yet times have changed. The population of the Washington metropolitan area has more than quadrupled since the 1960s, and land in the downtown business district commands enormous prices. Even so, just on the edge of the business district lies an area known as the frontier zone. Here can still be found burned-out hulks of buildings from over three decades ago. Why haven't these buildings been cleared to make way for new, close-in housing for Washington's many commuters? The answer can be found in rent controls.

Under rent controls, it is not possible to evict tenants in order to renovate and upgrade properties. There would be no point in undertaking the renovations and upgrades if rents cannot rise. Because there are many rent-controlled properties throughout the frontier zone and the rest of the city, developers know that they cannot turn these city blocks into high-quality living environments. After all, living among the often low-income tenants in the hodgepodge of rent-controlled apartments is unlikely to appeal to the higher-income tenants developers want. In the Northeast and Southeast quadrants of Washington, the result has been little development and a wide array of crumbling rent-controlled housing.

Other cities have similar stories to tell. New York has seen rent-controlled housing crumble for decades. Taking first prize, though, is Paris, France. Paris has had some rent controls in place for over two hundred years. The rent-controlled apartment houses in Paris have seen little modernization in that time, with few apartment units containing their own plumbing facilities. In the rent-controlled period between 1914 and 1948, almost no new rental housing was constructed in all of France.

OBSERVATION POINT: Trump Tower—Shelter for the Homeless?

From the lavish heights of Trump Tower, pedestrians strolling through Central Park and midtown Manhattan seem little more than tiny specks. It would be easy to forget that these are human beings with dreams and problems of their own—some even without homes. Donald Trump did not forget.

To build Trump Tower, the preexisting rent-controlled apartment building on the site had to be demolished. It would violate the law to simply evict the tenants in order to make way for higher-priced housing. Instead, tenants were presented with generous buyout offers which most, but not all, accepted. This left a building that was partially occupied and thus could not be torn down.

What was "The Donald" to do? Rather than let the precious apartment space go to waste while so many New Yorkers roamed the streets, Donald Trump generously planned to open the building's doors to the homeless. No charge! Perhaps not surprisingly, the remaining paying tenants were not well disposed toward their prospective neighbors. Negotiations progressed quickly. The renters agreed to Donald's buyout offers, and the building was demolished. Trump Tower was born.

ONE TENANT, ONE VOTE, BUT NO APARTMENT?   Rent controls sound good to tenants. They are at first, but not for all and not for long. At first, tenants see no noticeable change except lower rents. Later they see deterioration in the quality of their apartments. After all, with below-market prices and an increasing housing shortage, landlords have every incentive to skimp on maintenance.

Tenants often have few alternatives. When a significant portion of a city's residential land is taken up with rent-controlled housing, that makes other land more scarce and able to command higher rents. This effect shows up in a dramatic difference between controlled and uncontrolled rents. Tenants are stuck—they can't afford to move.

Without rent controls, it is commonplace for tenants to move from apartment to apartment as their lifestyles change. Flexibility is usually why they are renters in the first place. Rent controls make that difficult. Whether currently a renter or not, finding the next apartment may seem like an impossible challenge. Even if a renter can find a new home, the renter is likely to have incurred significant **search costs**, these being the value of the time and resources spent on looking. For instance, New Yorkers are rumored to read the obituaries to find the address of the next vacant apartment. Some New Yorkers jump even more quickly. With the right connections, they can monitor hospital and nursing home admissions to have an edge in the competition for the upcoming apartments.

Rent controls promote discrimination. Landlords can pick and choose among a great many applicants and need not rent to the first person in line. The law allows landlords to discriminate on the basis of such factors as reliability, responsibility, and references. They are legally entitled to reject poor credit risks, as many students are perceived to be. Who can prove differently if landlords also discriminate on the illegal basis of race, creed, gender, or handicap?

With all the problems of rent controls, why are they enacted in the first place? The answer is both political and social. There are many more tenants than landlords. Many of those tenants are ignorant of the long-term consequences of rent control. Others plan on buying houses or moving out of town before the consequences of rent controls get serious. In the meantime, tenants gain lower rents. In addition, rent controls serve to perpetuate the existing socioeconomic characteristics of a community.

Although rent controls do great damage over time, they are always hard to remove, and for good reason. The longer rent controls are in place, the more the housing supply shrinks, as lack of maintenance leads some apartments to deteriorate beyond repair. This is reflected by a leftward shift in supply. Likewise, demand shifts to the right as populations increase over time. The result is an increasing shortage of rent-controlled housing, as shown in Figure 4A-4.

Unfortunately, were rent controls to be removed, rents would initially skyrocket to far above where they would have been had rent controls never been imposed. Such an equilibrium is labeled P** in Figure 4A-4. Builders must be convinced that rent controls are a thing of the past before they will invest in much new construction. New construction would cause supply to shift to the right and rents to fall. In the interim, however, sensible tenants would not vote for immediate draconian rent increases. Hopes that rents will drop and housing quality improve somewhere down the line hardly seem persuasive to someone struggling to meet next month's rent.

A

Figure 4A-4 **Rent controls increase housing shortages over time** because of the combination of the increase in demand and the decrease in supply.

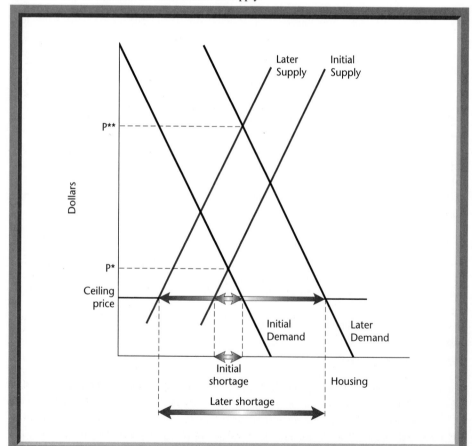

HOUSING VOUCHERS FOR THE POOR—AN ALTERNATIVE TO RENT CONTROLS   Government need not resort to rent controls in order to ensure affordable housing. One alternative is to identify the needy and assign them housing vouchers. **Housing vouchers** are government grants that the recipient can spend only on housing. Thus, even though the price of rental housing may be high, housing vouchers can bring it within reach of impoverished tenants.

In contrast to rent controls, housing vouchers cost the government money. Rent controls also cost money, but the cost is borne by landlords, and is also seen in the extra search costs incurred by renters. The budgetary cost of housing vouchers has kept them from being more widely adopted, even though they have been advocated by various public figures, such as Jack Kemp when he was Secretary of Housing and Urban Development in the administration of President Bush.

Antigouging Laws

Price gouging—the practice of hiking up prices to exploit temporary surges in demand—may be what the crew of the starship *Enterprise* could expect of the greedy Ferengi traders. Here in the United States, however, many municipalities have enacted antigouging laws, designed to hold prices down in the event of disasters. This practice can cause problems.

High prices prevent shortages and allocate sought-after goods to those who value them the most. Profitably high prices also motivate rapid restocking, which means that prices do not stay high for long. For example, when hurricanes move toward the coast, oceanfront homeowners seek out plywood to board up their windows. If stores can raise prices, they have an incentive to send out extra trucks for new supplies. Otherwise, homeowners must scramble to snatch up supplies before the shelves go bare. If homeowners are lucky, stores might use the occasion to generate good will and restock promptly despite the extra costs.

OBSERVATION POINT: Scalping the Stones

Laws vary over *ticket scalping*—the practice of buying tickets at the price set by concert promoters and then reselling at whatever the market will bear. Scalping is a form of **arbitrage**, which means buying low and selling high. This directs goods to their highest-valued uses, thus efficiently allocating seats at concerts, ball games, and other events.

As for equity, however, try asking fans of the Rolling Stones or other groups with sold-out performances. Good seats are snared quickly by scalpers, many of whom hire numerous stand-ins to buy up blocks of tickets. For example, one ticket reseller paid over $20 per person to hire nearly 150 people, including brothers of a college fraternity. All the job required was to stand in line to buy tickets. Who could blame Stones' fans for crying that they "can't get no satisfaction"?

Some fans—those willing to spend extra money to avoid the time in line—were glad for the choice and convenience offered by the scalpers. Those fans would find it inequitable to be denied that choice. Other fans saw things differently.

Promoters offer equal access to below-market ticket prices in order to stir interest in the event. Most fans view this equal access as equitable and democratic. Everyone, rich or poor, has the same opportunity, even if that means standing in line and maybe losing out. This notion of equity leaves no room for scalping.

Views will differ over what is equitable and over how to balance efficiency and equity when the two conflict. Yes, in the words of Mick Jagger, "You can't always get what you want!"

Price Freezes—The Price of What?

Price freezes that prohibit increases in most prices are sometimes imposed as a seemingly obvious way to control inflation. However, to the extent price freezes prevent prices from rising, they result in shortages and misallocations. The problems with price freezes are merely a wider manifestation of the problems of price ceilings, such as rent controls. Unfortunately, because the coverage of a price freeze is broader, the problems are greater.

Price freezes are difficult to enforce and not widely used. For example, suppose we freeze the price of candy bars. If candy bar manufacturers desire to raise prices without breaking the law, all they need to do is come out with a variation on the products that are controlled. For example, they might keep price constant, but lower the number of ounces. Alternatively, they might introduce similar products and cut down on their production of the controlled product.

Such strategies are widely adopted whenever price controls take hold. To outlaw those practices would not only freeze prices, but also freeze the mix of products available to the consumer. It would be a bureaucratic nightmare for government to try to distinguish new products that are worth producing from those that merely serve to defeat the price freeze.

OBSERVATION POINT: A Squeeze on Charmin

In 1971, in an attempt to combat inflation, President Nixon signed a price freeze into law. Shortly afterward, Canadian paper companies increased the price of wood fiber, which eroded the profits of tissue manufacturers. Johnny Carson, true to his form as host of the "Tonight Show," could not pass up this touchy subject.

In his opening monologue, Johnny joked about toilet paper shortages in New Jersey. Guess what? Even though it had not really been very difficult to find toilet paper in New Jersey, a shortage quickly developed. People rushed to the stores to snatch up all brands of tissue. Manufacturers had no special incentive to restock, so the shelves stayed bare. Thus was the start of the Great Toilet Paper Squeeze of 1971!

Black Markets as a Safety Valve

Any time government tries to hold prices below market equilibrium, it provides profit opportunities to those willing to take advantage of them. **Black market** activity is said to occur when goods are bought and sold illegally. Under rent controls, for example, it is not uncommon to hear of prospective tenants bribing landlords for an apartment. Sometimes this black market may seem somewhat gray, as when the bribes are merely offers of gifts, or agreements to "fix up the place."

The black market is nothing more than the free market trying to assert itself when government has attempted to influence that market through taxes or regulation. Regulation could take the form of price controls or the outright ban of market activities. In either case, it is hard to keep willing buyers and sellers from negotiating mutually beneficial deals.

Governments often owe a debt of gratitude to black markets that temper destructive policies. For example, Cubans rely heavily on the black market in their country. If they had to depend upon government rations, they could not obtain enough food to survive. Similarly, the shelves were often bare in the formerly communist countries of Asia and Eastern Europe. These countries relied in large measure on the industriousness of black marketers to keep their economies going. For example, the government of the Soviet Union legalized private for-profit agricultural production on approximately three percent of its arable land. Despite its relatively small acreage, this market-driven component of agriculture produced almost one third as much output as did the entire socialized sector with its abundance of land.

*P*ropping Prices Up

Although consumers are better off when prices are low, producers prefer them high. Both groups often turn to government for help. If politics dictates propping up prices, government can establish a **price floor**, also termed a **price support**, which sets a minimum price that producers are guaranteed to receive. One way to implement a price floor is for government to agree to buy at that floor price. This approach can cause surpluses to pile up at taxpayer expense, as in the case of agricultural price supports. Note that the term *surplus* in this context refers to a quantity of output, specifically the excess of what is produced over what is consumed. This concept differs from social surplus, which refers to a dollar value of gains to consumers and producers.

Government can support prices without buying up any surplus quantity. Rather, it can simply forbid buyers from paying less than some price minimum. Minimum wage laws exemplify this approach. Both methods are discussed in the sections that follow.

Agricultural Price Supports—Economics and Politics in Conflict

Only two percent of the United States labor force currently derives a living from agriculture. It is therefore surprising that agricultural price supports have been in place in the U.S. from the Great Depression through most of the 1990s. With passage of the *Freedom to Farm Act* in the spring of 1996, the stage was set for the possible permanent elimination of U.S. agricultural price supports. The Freedom to Farm Act phases out agricultural price supports over time, with the timetable varying from one agricultural commodity to another. Instead, farmers are to receive subsidies based on their needs, rather than on crop prices. The Freedom to Farm Act is an experiment that is scheduled to expire by 2003, when agricultural price supports will be re-established unless additional legislation is passed. There is good reason for this experiment, as this section reveals.

Agricultural price supports have often been justified on two counts. One is that they sustain the lifestyle of the family farm, an American tradition. However, family farming continued to decline, and a disproportionate amount of price support payments went to large farms and agribusiness. The second justification was that they ensured a plentiful supply of food for American consumers. This line of reasoning does not withstand the logic of economic analysis.

Figure 4A-5 shows the effects of an agricultural price support, such as for milk, corn, or wheat. By holding price above the equilibrium, there will be more farmers, and there will be more agricultural production. In other words, the quantity supplied, Q_S, is higher than the market equilibrium quantity of Q^*. However, the quantity demanded, Q_D, is lower, leading to a surplus as shown in Figure 4A-5. Thus, while more is produced, less is purchased. This behavior has led to agricultural surpluses averaging several billion dollars' worth of foodstuffs annually in the U.S. Eliminating agricultural price supports can be expected to cause American consumers to pay less and buy more.

The primary effect of agricultural price supports is to transfer money from con-

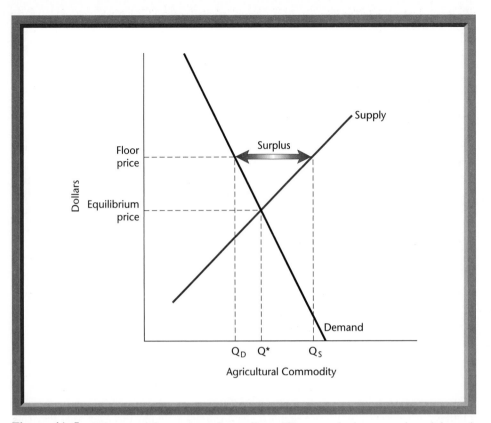

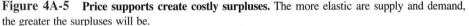

Figure 4A-5 Price supports create costly surpluses. The more elastic are supply and demand, the greater the surpluses will be.

sumers and taxpayers to farmers. This transfer occurs in two ways. First, for each unit of price-supported food that consumers buy, they pay more than they otherwise would have. Figure 4A-6 shows this extra amount as the gray shaded rectangle in the upper left. The area of this rectangle equals the quantity consumers purchase multiplied by the price difference. This amount is nothing but a transfer of income from consumers to producers—there is no net cost to the economy.

Second, because the price is maintained above the market equilibrium, a surplus results, which government agrees to buy. The amount government pays is shown as the blue shaded rectangle on the right in Figure 4A-6. The area of that rectangle equals the quantity of surplus that is generated multiplied by the price per unit of that surplus. Government attempts to avoid passing this surplus along to anyone who would otherwise be a purchaser in the marketplace. To do so would merely mean more of a surplus that government would be forced to buy, because those who received from government would buy less from farmers.

One option is to give the surplus quantity away in a relatively unpalatable form, such as by turning excess milk into powdered milk. Another option is to export the surplus in a manner that does not compete with other agricultural exports. For example, for-

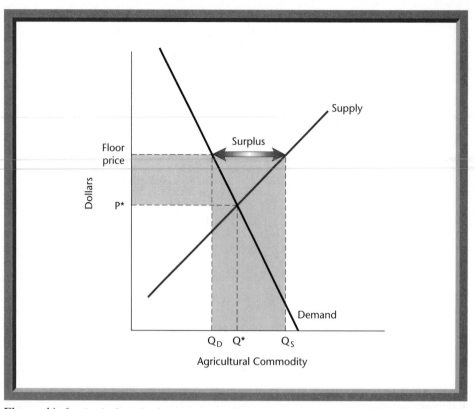

Figure 4A-6 Agricultural price supports cause consumers to pay more for what they continue to buy (*gray shaded area*), and taxpayers to pay for the surplus (*blue shaded area*).

eign aid to impoverished countries might work, to the extent that the aid does not supplant other food imports from the donor country. However, recipient countries often fear becoming too dependent upon food aid based on unpredictable agricultural surpluses. The dependency arises when farmers in those countries are driven out of business by the low food prices that years of plentiful food aid brings.

There are other options. To rid itself of surplus butter, for example, Denmark offers it for a reduced price if the buyer agrees to export that butter by baking it into Danish butter cookies. Still another common practice is to store surplus commodities until they are no longer edible and then discard them. It's like the fate of leftover food in a refrigerator!

However government disposes of agricultural surpluses, it has paid much more for these goods than they are worth in the uses to which they are put. In 1993, for example, the federal government spent $20.5 billion on agriculture, most of which went toward price support programs. It would be significantly cheaper merely to identify needy farmers and write them checks, as pointed out by backers of the Freedom to Farm Act. To some extent, government had indeed written checks to needy farmers. Government actually paid some farmers not to produce—to put aside some acreage for awhile in order to eliminate the need for government to buy the output. In response, until government officials caught on, clever farmers employed such strategies as reducing acreage by planting every other row. The extra sunlight led to extra crop yield, which partially defeated the purpose of leaving aside acreage.

It makes more economic sense to pay farmers not to produce than to squander resources on production that will be wasted. Still, such direct payments may seem too *transparent*, meaning that it becomes obvious to voters what is going on. Agricultural lobbyists would prefer that voters not focus on this aspect of the program and thus do not advocate the mere writing of checks to farmers. The 1996 Freedom to Farm Act took a middle approach by allowing payments to needy farmers, but without restricting acreage. Whether U.S. agricultural price supports will be reestablished in the future remains an open question.

The Minimum Wage

The minimum wage has become a cherished American tradition since its enactment in the 1930s. We all remember that first job. We remember how hard we worked to find it, and how we deserved no less than that minimum wage for the work we did. For many, the job served as a springboard toward great success in life. Backing for the minimum wage also arises out of American compassion for the downtrodden. Americans cherish the notion that no one should be exploited. On the face of it, the minimum wage seems like a good protection against such exploitation. On closer examination, however, it is not.

People support the minimum wage because it increases the price of relatively unskilled labor. That is also its problem. The higher wage means that more people are willing to work. These extra workers include many college and college-bound students already on the road to success. However, the higher wage also means that fewer jobs are offered. Fast food restaurants, car washes, and other businesses "make do" with fewer people, but train and work them harder. They also may replace some labor with capital, such as automated dishwashers and car-washing equipment.

The result is a surplus of labor, or shortage of jobs, depending upon how you look at it. The least employable—those with poor language, computational, or social skills—are out of luck. They cannot get that first job they need to start climbing the ladder of success. They cannot join the "jobs club"—it has become too exclusive.

Figure 4A-7 shows how minimum wage laws increase the number of people seeking low-skill work while decreasing the number of jobs available. For example, Tony would not have worked for the equilibrium wage. With a minimum wage, however, Tony might wind up taking Dave's job, even though Dave would have been willing to work for less. Because higher wages are offset by fewer jobs, there is no guarantee that minimum wage laws actually increase the total amount firms spend to employ low-skill workers. Firms will spend more only if their demand for low-skill labor is inelastic.

Interestingly, as was the case with rent controls, minimum wage requirements promote discrimination. With numerous applicants for each job opening, employers can pick and choose as they wish. It would be quite difficult to prove if they choose to discriminate on an illegal basis. While the pay is higher, the jobs and extra pay go to those applicants who need help the least. Is it a coincidence that unemployment rates are so high among black teenagers in America's inner cities? In 1994, this unemployment rate averaged over 35 percent, more than five times the rate for the population at large.

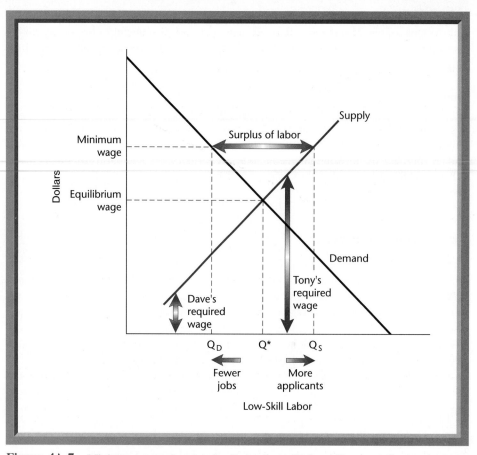

Figure 4A-7   Minimum wage laws make it tough to find a job, especially for the least-experienced and least-skilled job seekers. The higher wage causes fewer jobs and more applicants. Some of the new applicants (such as Tony) take jobs from others who need the jobs more desperately (such as Dave).

There are alternatives to the minimum wage that target the problem of low wages without controlling price. One alternative is to subsidize the earnings of low-income workers. Indeed, such a subsidy is already embedded in the U.S. personal income tax—the earned income tax credit. The drawback is that earnings subsidies come at a high budgetary cost, because they reduce government tax collections. Minimum wage laws also have high costs, but these costs are borne by businesses, consumers, and those unable to find a job. However, the costs of minimum wage laws do not show up on the government budget.

OBSERVATION POINT: Snatching Hope from the Homeless

The homeless often carry a disturbing sign—"Will Work for Food." Can't homeless people find jobs and money for homes? Advocates for the homeless are quick to point out that many of the homeless are eager to find steady work. More often than not, however, there are no steady jobs offered to them.

Lack of a home is itself an impediment to finding a job. For example, employers may worry about the employee's personal health and hygiene, and about whether or not the employee is a drifter. For these reasons, potential employers are usually unwilling to pay the minimum wage to the homeless. There are too many other applicants with fewer problems. While employers would be willing to offer jobs at lower wages, that would be illegal.

The homeless are thus caught in the grips of a political vise. Minimum wages are one side of this vise. On the other side, many of the "flophouses" that offered cheap nightly lodging have closed down. The residents could not afford rent increases that would be needed to pay the expense of renovation. The law demands such renovation to provide accessibility for the physically challenged. It also requires security from hazards such as fires, lead in pipes and paint, and asbestos. Such government policies are intended to add fairness to what is sold in the marketplace. Together with minimum wages, however, those policies block access to those markets for the very people who need it most, the homeless.

A

EXPRESS STUDY TRUE OR FALSE

1. In the absence of market failures, a market equilibrium price is efficient.
2. When a surge in demand causes the price of a good to rise dramatically, economists say that a ~~shortage exists.~~ the higher price clears the market, *s*
3. Rent controls make discrimination less costly and harder to prove.
4. Under a housing voucher plan, it makes ~~good sense~~ to read the obituaries in order to identify which apartments are likely to come up for rent. there would be no apt. shortage
5. Agricultural price supports ~~make~~ food cheaper to buy. raise prices and decrease qua – consumed
6. Minimum wage laws are likely to prevent those with the poorest work skills from finding a job.

Module B

EXPLORING ISSUES

EXPLORATION 1
Health Care—Issues of Insurance and Its Coverage

Inefficient pricing incentives under health insurance can distort the choices of both patients and providers. Government efforts to widen health care coverage while reining in costs solve some problems but make others worse.

Twiddle your thumbs? Read a book? What do you do while you wait for hours in the doctor's office before being seen for five minutes? While this may be an exaggeration, in all too many cases it is not. Why doesn't the competitive market take your time and preferences into account? Don't markets respond to what consumers demand? The answers can be found in large part by examining the intertwining roles of insurance and government.

Because health problems can be complicated, the health care marketplace is characterized by an extraordinary degree of reliance on the expertise and judgment of professionals. Some of the calls are tough. For instance, how much should we spend to prolong the life of a terminally ill patient or exceptionally premature baby? Do we allow the use of marijuana or heroin for the terminally ill? What of assisted suicide? The kinds of economic and ethical choices needed to make those judgments put health care in a league apart from other goods.

Quality Gives Way to Quantity ...

For both physicians and patients, health insurance alters incentives. This is true of traditional plans in which the patient pays a copayment of a percentage of costs over some deductible amount. For example, the patient might pay 20 percent of yearly health care expenses over a $300 deductible. Incentives are also altered by *health maintenance organizations (HMOs)*, a recently popular form of health insurance. In an HMO plan, patients are assigned a primary care physician, who refers them to specialists as needed. The patient pays a flat fee of $10 or so per visit.

Under either plan, the cost of care is subsidized by the insurance company in exchange for annual insurance premiums. Because the per unit price of health care is reduced, patients seek more of it. This is the problem of **moral hazard**, which is illustrated in Figure 4B1-1. Moral hazard leads patients to consume too much medical care.

The problem of moral hazard also faces health care professionals, to the extent that insurance changes their incentives to treat patients. Under the traditional copayment/deductible plan, for example, the incentive is to overtreat patients, because insurance will

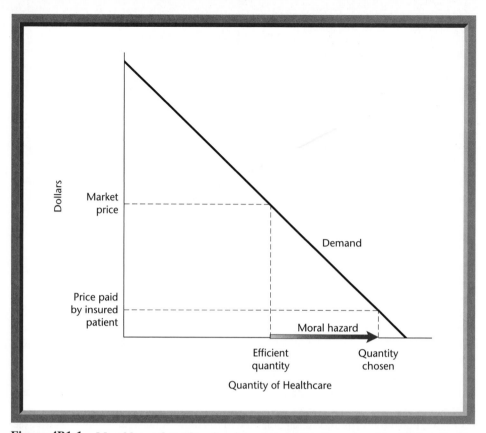

Figure 4B1-1 **Moral hazard results when insurance lowers the price of health care for the recipient, thus causing an increase in the quantity of services demanded.** This figure illustrates moral hazard facing a patient who must pay only 20 percent of actual costs. The result is an increase in consumption of healthcare services relative to what would occur if the patient faced an efficient market price.

reimburse for the time and other expenses involved in that treatment. However, an HMO plan primarily rewards its primary care physicians according to how many patients have selected them. The physician has an incentive to sign up as many patients as possible, but treat each one as little as possible. In this case, moral hazard can lead physicians to skimp on the amount of service they provide. For example, a full waiting room minimizes unplanned downtime from canceled appointments and unexpectedly quick visits, and is thus increasingly common in the offices of primary care physicians. It saves the physician money, but at the expense of patients' time.

. . . as Individuals Worry About Access to Health Care.

The list of insurance-related issues in health care goes on. Consider the nurse or parcel delivery woman with chronic back pain who cannot switch jobs without losing her employer-provided insurance coverage of her ailment. Her problem? Preexisting condition.

In 1996, Congress debated legislation to prohibit insurers from considering preexisting conditions. The final outcome of these deliberations remains to be seen, with thorny issues to be resolved. For example, if insurers were forced to ignore all preexisting conditions, people wouldn't buy insurance until they need medical care. This behavior would lead to dramatic increases in insurance premiums, and a much lower percentage of the public insured.

In a country with **universal coverage**, in which everyone has equal access to the health care bureaucracy, the problem of ensuring preexisting conditions does not arise. However, patients would sometimes choose to pay for treatment out of their own pockets. This choice could be motivated by the bureaucracy classifying irritating medical conditions as noncritical, and thus subjecting those patients to a prolonged wait until the long queue of higher-priority patients clears. What kind of treatment do patients receive? How much treatment? For how long? On whose authority? The answers depend on individuals, government, and insurance.

*I*ndividuals Must Belong to Groups . . .

Individuals have few options when it comes to choosing the type of health insurance plan that best suits their needs. The reason rests upon the nature of insurance itself. The nurse with the back pain would be delighted to find an insurer willing to pay for all treatments that might be helpful. Unfortunately, private insurance companies are the same as all other companies in the competitive marketplace. They are in business to provide a positive return to their investors, not to give away services that cost more than the value of the premiums they receive.

Consequently, insurance companies try to distinguish between ex ante (before the fact) and ex post (after the fact) conditions. The laws of probability allow insurers to cover conditions ex ante. Suppose you have the same chance as everybody else of coming down with some medical condition. By covering many people, most of whom will have no cause to file claims, the insurer can profitably offer you coverage at a fraction of treatment costs.

Ex post is another story altogether. If you already have a condition, the insurance company could make money only if they charged you at least the full cost of treatment. That would be no insurance at all! In other words, once you come down with a condition, you lose your option of initiating insurance coverage.

. . . to Obtain Coverage at Affordable Rates.

If you do not have any particular medical problems, you still cannot get an individual policy at a price approaching that of a group insurance plan. Even if you attempt to purchase insurance with coverage identical to that offered by employers, you would be charged a great deal more.

The competitive marketplace would not allow companies to offer individuals the same low insurance premiums as large employers. The reason revolves around information. Even if you do not have any particular condition yet, you probably know much better than the insurance company which conditions you would be most susceptible to. This is the problem of **adverse selection**—those who seek out insurance coverage are the most likely to need it.

Because of adverse selection, the expected cost to the insurance company of writing an individual policy is much higher than the expected cost per person under a group policy. Insurance companies that survive in the marketplace must know this, and thus charge individuals a higher price to reflect the higher costs. The lowest rates go to groups that are likely to be healthier than average, such as pools of employees at large businesses.

*U*niversal *Coverage Has Allure . . .*

Health care expenses can vary dramatically and unpredictably from person to person. This uncertainty motivates us to want insurance. We want others to be covered, too, including the sick and injured who cannot help themselves. This is a motivation for universal coverage, which requires government action to achieve.

Universal coverage would overcome the problem of adverse selection—we would all be in the same group. By forcing everyone to participate, universal coverage would also avoid the free-rider problem. This problem occurs if people figure that some safety net level of coverage will be available to them whether they contribute insurance premiums or not.

. . . but Leaves Problems.

Universal coverage raises a new set of issues. For example, if everyone is to be covered, what should that coverage consist of? Should we eliminate all choice? Who should pay? What about malpractice?

Universal coverage does not solve problems of moral hazard, and adds new problems of its own. For example, the problem of moral hazard on the part of the physician occurs if government employs physicians directly. To see the moral hazard, put yourself in the position of a physician motivated by nothing but self-interest. Your salary is determined exclusively by your rank and the number of hours you agree to work. How much of your time and the government's money would you spend per patient?

Your answer is probably "it depends." If your supervisors do not reward you for productivity, you might spend all of your time on a handful of patients and get to know those patients well. However, this lavish treatment would come at the expense of seeing fewer other patients and would result in a high cost per patient. Conversely, if your path to advancing in rank is to process the greatest number of patients at the lowest cost per patient, you would have the incentive toward superficial exploration and treatment.

*H*ealth *Care Costs Keep Rising, . . .*

Our spending on health care goes up each year, even after adjusting for inflation. For instance, health care expenditures account for roughly 14 percent of U.S. spending, compared to about 10 percent of spending in Canada and 7 percent of spending in Japan, as shown in Figure 4B1-2. What accounts for these discrepancies?

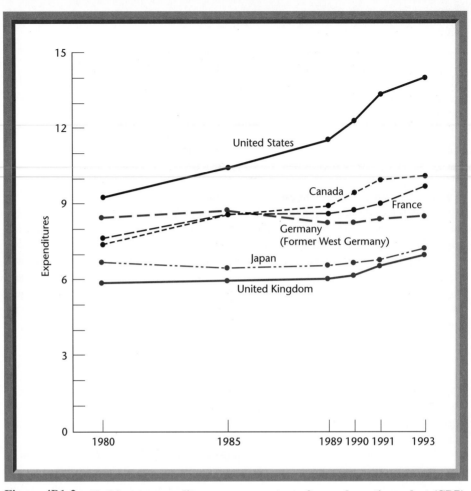

Figure 4B1-2   Health care expenditures as a percentage of gross domestic product (GDP), selected countries, 1980–1993.

Source: 1995 Statistical Abstract of the U.S., Table No. 1369.

We often hear complaints that high malpractice insurance awards increase the cost of health insurance. A survey by Lewin-VH1, Inc., suggests that doctors and hospitals paid over $11 billion in malpractice insurance premiums in 1991. They practiced an additional $20 billion worth of *defensive medicine*, extra treatment motivated by a desire to avoid lawsuits. What would be the remedies against malpractice under universal coverage? Could consumers sue the government? Could consumers shop around?

Another part of health care's rising cost lies in what we buy. Over time, health care has come to include increasingly elaborate techniques, some of which other countries view as unnecessary luxuries or frivolities. In addition, however, it often seems that drugs, doctors, tests, and everything else associated with health care simply cost too much. What happens if we control these prices?

... and Price Controls Hold Little Allure.

Consider price controls on physician services, implemented by a flat fee per service, for each category of service performed. This approach is often denoted as a single fee per *diagnostic-related group*. The problem becomes one of physician incentives. Would physicians thoroughly explore tough cases when they get the same amount of pay on the easy ones?

In 1993 President Clinton proposed that Americans be provided with national health insurance that offers each citizen complete freedom to chose their own doctors. However, doctors would be forced to charge the same "community standard" price. The effects of such a policy might surprise its backers. Doctors with the best reputations would be flooded with potential patients. The competitive response would have these superior doctors turn many patients away and keep others waiting. There would be long waits prior to scheduled appointments, and then long waits in the office before patients would be seen. The patients wind up paying extra, but the payments are in time, not money.

Likewise, doctors with good reputations cannot be expected to spend time on tricky cases when they could process the easy ones much faster for more money. The result is inefficiency. The best doctors would take the easy cases, leaving the tough ones for the less highly skilled.

Whoever pays, . . .

Health care ranks with food, shelter, and clothing as one of life's most important and expensive consumption goods. For health care to be provided to us all, it must be financed through a hefty tax, even if the tax is hidden.

For example, the Clinton administration strongly advocated universal health coverage that would be financed in large part by the hidden tax of unfunded **employer mandates**, which are benefits that government requires businesses to offer. In that case, the employer would shoulder the burden directly, but respond with such actions as paying lower wages and scaling back plans for hiring and business expansion. Explicit tax dollars would supplement those mandates in order to cover the unemployed.

B

... universal Coverage Conflicts with Productivity . . .

Both universal health insurance and the taxes needed to finance it have the effect of reducing incentives for productivity. As work effort slackens and investment slows, the size of the economic pies shrinks. Unfortunately, there is no obvious way to escape such consequences—it is in the nature of what happens when government offers life's necessities for free.

Perhaps health care policy should follow the lead of some other public assistance programs, where most people go to great lengths to avoid being a recipient. For example, public housing available to the poor is often so undesirable that none but the truly desperate would live there. What do you think—should we offer universal second-rate medical coverage? What would be covered? Would it provide enough incentive for most of us to find our own first-rate coverage? Would it be unjust to the truly needy? What other alternative would be better?

. . . and Other Countries Face the Same Tough Choices.

Perhaps the experience of other countries can help us to answer these numerous questions. For example, England offers universal health insurance coverage. Most residents who can afford it supplement that coverage with private insurance, because the waiting times and quality of care are widely deemed inferior to that offered by private insurers. Similarly, the U.S. has for many years served as a safety valve for Canada's publicly run insurance system. It is commonplace for Canadian citizens seeking to avoid interminably long waits or seeking top-notch care to cross the border and frequent U.S. doctors.

Choice offers a safety valve that we might wish to retain. Expanding coverage and holding down costs are also worthy goals. How do we proceed? Should government do more? Or less?

PROSPECTING FOR NEW INSIGHTS

1. JUAN: Government's got it backwards. We need less health insurance, not more. We already waste too much time and money on that bureaucratic mess. People should learn to accept a little risk in their lives. Government could do some real good by outlawing insurance coverage of health expenses below $2,500 per year per person. Anybody who can't scrounge that up would qualify for welfare, anyway. Result? No more health insurance fiasco.

   PAUL: Let's not forget to abolish the Food and Drug Administration, while we're at it. If it weren't for their multiyear "worthless until proven otherwise" testing processes, we could actually afford medications. Then, if we could abolish prescriptions, we wouldn't need to pay all those doctors.

   Have Juan and Paul simply gone off the deep end, or is there some economic basis for their proposals? Is it economic to prohibit consumption of insurance for people's own good? If government were to enact universal coverage with $2,500 deductibles, do you think the program would get more generous over time? Why?

2. a. Should government pursue the goal of universal health insurance coverage?

   b. During the debate over health care reform, strong opposition arose to having employer mandates to fund health insurance. What drawbacks would arise from using this funding method?

   c. If mandates are not to be used, what alternative would you find preferable?

Government-provided insurance lowers the price of risk for consumers to below the free-market price. People thus take riskier actions at taxpayer expense, such as building in flood plains or depositing their money in risky banks. In this story, as in real life, government resorts to policies that restrict free choice in order to reduce insurance expenditures.

Rising Waters

"Rona! Get the baby! River's rising fast!"

With groggy eyes, Rona glanced at the clock. Nearly 3 A.M., it read. She looked toward Sally Ann. How could that baby still be asleep, with the wind howling so, and the thunder, lightning, and all that rain? Just my luck, Rona thought. If it was quiet outside, it would be Sally Ann doing the howling at this hour.

"Rona!" Jake implored, "we've gotta leave here. Now! You take the pickup—I'll grab the Harley!"

It took only a few minutes to gather up some things. Still, the way the water was running over the driveway, it was beginning to seem like a few minutes too long. Thank goodness we don't all live in the bottomlands, thought Rona. With the rain and darkness, I can barely even see to keep this truck on the road.

Rona tried to distract herself. "Funny thing, Sally Ann. Without thinking, I've got my seat belt on and you strapped in your child seat. Bet Jake's got on his helmet, too! Don't want to be a burden on the public, you know, like we would be if we all get in a wreck and can't support ourselves any more. Anyway, it's the law. Think that's why they made those laws?" Sally Ann wasn't listening. "Hush now. I know it's scary, but we'll be safe at Aunt Donie's house real soon. Shhh." Rona wasn't sure if she was talking more to Sally Ann or to herself.

The Aftermath

"Federal Disaster Area Declared along Whippoorwill Creek," trumpeted the Byerly County Weekly Gazette. Having already heard the news through word of mouth, Jake and Rona found themselves standing in line at a temporary office of FOME, the Federal Office to Manage Emergencies.[1]

---

[1]FOME is our fictional alternative to FEMA, the Federal Emergency Management Administration. The policies discussed below are similar to some currently under consideration, but not implemented as of this writing. Current policy is that, when a home is destroyed, Federal flood assistance is provided only if the rebuilding occurs away from the flood plain. Assistance is reduced if the homeowner is covered by private insurance.

B

"Yes Ma'am, I understand you work out of your home. Still, there's nothing we can do about your computer and files. We can help you rebuild your house, though, as soon as we get our new rules from Washington. Should be through any day now. One thing—you might not be getting as much help as your neighbors, because you bought private flood insurance to cover some of your losses. We know you need help, but the ones without any insurance need it more."

"So what was the point in our spending money on private insurance? Everybody in the valley knew that flooding was a danger." Rona wondered why she asked the question, since she didn't want to hear the answer.

"You said your private insurance won't compensate you nearly enough to offset all the losses. Still, it will help, and will probably cover you better than we would. We have to take this into account. In dispersing federal funds, you understand, we must seek out the neediest recipients."

*B*andits *of the Beltway*

All the floods, earthquakes, hurricanes, and other natural disasters striking the U.S. in recent years were busting the budget of FOME. FOME wanted to consider alternatives to keep down costs. This is where the consulting firm of GZQ, Inc., comes in.

Beltway bandits, they are called, those seemingly faceless masses of consultants scattered within striking distance of I-495, the interstate highway encircling Washington, DC. Bureaucrats and bandits, all raiding the public trough, some would say. That's not the way Ralph Flores and Joe Peterson of GZQ see it. They see themselves as part of a patriotic army, the huge number of Americans needed to design and administer all the federal programs that make the country great. It's better for federal agencies to get contract advice from GZQ and other consultants than to maintain the staff to do it all in-house. The more diversity of opinion, the better.

"Okay, Joe, we know that by subsidizing housing reconstruction after flood disasters, we take away some of the incentive for people to avoid building in a flood plain. If the public is going to build, the U.S. government is going to feel obligated to help them again and again, whenever flooding occurs. You propose a solution. If I understand you correctly, you envision that flood plains be reserved for farming and public access. We are to condemn all residential structures currently standing, paying fair market value. Then we prohibit new construction. Did I get that right?" Brenda Phillips, contract officer for FOME, seemed receptive.

"Yes, you did, Ms. Phillips. The undertaking would be expensive, but would prevent many future expenses. In addition, it would open up a variety of recreational opportunities, such as hiking, fishing, and even viewing. See, I have brought a model showing homes sprinkled on picturesque hillsides, each with a scenic view of the green riverway below. The residents would be better off than they were before."

"Let me add to that," interposed Ralph. "What we propose is essentially the same as is currently done in the case of reservoirs. The land is condemned and bought up. New construction is prohibited. The only difference is that we don't propose to build an expensive reservoir and artificially flood the land. This plan blends the people with the naturescape."

"Gonna let old Mother Nature flood the land for you," Brenda laughed. "Maybe I should say 'old Parent Nature.' Thank you, gentlemen. You can expect to hear back from me soon. I will probably ask that you make a formal presentation to our committee. We need to move quickly, though, so be ready!"

Back by the Whippoorwill

The rules were in. Government would cover a fraction of the cost of rebuilding. There was a catch, though. No reconstruction could take place within the flood plain, not even without government money. "Maybe somebody else would have bought your house by the time the next flood comes," the woman at the agency told Rona. "We don't want you or anyone else to be in a position where you will need our help. You'll have to rebuild elsewhere."

"Nothing against you personally, Ma'am," the agency woman went on. "You see, any time there's insurance, that cuts the price of risk. Same's true when folks get government assistance to cope with accidents or disasters. When the price goes down, people take more risks. In insurance lingo, that's known as the problem of *moral hazard*. Private insurance can't do much to stop it. We in government can, by making rules and regulations that force people to behave safely. Not only is that good for people, but it saves a lot of tax dollars, too."

Rona was caught off guard. She had deep roots in this valley, and wanted to rebuild right where she'd been, even if that meant forgoing government aid. It wasn't that she'd never left home before. It was only a couple years ago that she moved back from a three-year sojourn in Charlottestown. She had enjoyed her position as a loan officer at the First State Bank of Charlottestown and was looking forward to advancing to a Vice Presidency. Then came the news. The Resolution Trust Company ordered First State Bank closed because of insufficient assets. Rona figured she'd had enough of the city anyway, and was glad to return to Whippoorwill Creek.

Rona was pretty proud of herself, actually. While she wasn't earning half as much as a Vice Presidency of a bank would have paid, her current job as a syndicated financial columnist let Rona stay at home with Sally Ann. Lately she was even bringing in more money than Jake. She could move, but she did not want to.

"Jake, I'm tired of government insurance pushing us around, and there being absolutely nothing we can do about it. If it weren't for government insuring bank deposits, I'd be VP now and we'd be living in Charlottestown with all of our things."

"What do you mean?"

"If it wasn't for Federal Deposit Insurance, our bank customers would have shopped for banks that invested wisely, even if they didn't pay as much interest as some of the others. They would have paid attention to safety ratings in *Consumer Banking Digest*, or some such. First State Bank would still be in business. As it was, all the customers cared about was how high the interest rates were on their deposits. The only way we could pay rates as high as the other banks was to take on a lot of high-risk investments.

"All the banks were forced to play that game," Rona continued, "or else lose out in competition for deposits. Fail sooner or fail later was the choice we faced. Of course, First State picked later. When the economy finally did go sour, then ka-boom!" Rona flung her hands high. "Not many of the little banks survived the fallout.

"You know, Jake, I don't understand this business of government insurance. They say that it's there to help us. But it costs so much, we're hit with all kinds of rules and regulations to keep us from needing that help. Like that government woman said, insurance cuts the price of taking risks. Then, when people try to take more risks, government tries to stop them. Why not just leave the price of risk alone, and let that price deter most people from taking risks? People willing to pay the price can then take all the risks they want to. I mean, I love our land, and I want to stay on it even if that means risking another flood. This flood stole things that meant a lot to me. Now government wants to steal our land, too. It's too much."

"It sure does seem like government wants to keep us out of trouble," Jake agreed. "It's not just us, of course. Remember Jim Dyer, and how he planned to build a vacation cabin on Assateague Beach until Maryland condemned his land? I guess they thought it was too risky for people like Jim to be building near the Atlantic shoreline. They didn't want to be rescuing him and rebuilding his house. They didn't know Jim!"

"That's my point! Government doesn't want to pay for the risks we take, so they don't let us take them. Why don't they let us do as we please, and just not bail us out if we get into trouble?"

"Don't get mad, but think about the other side of the coin. A lot of people are real gullible. If a bank opened up next door, and the building was impressive and the bank officers acted important, they wouldn't think twice about depositing their life savings there. They would just assume that government wouldn't let the bank open its doors unless it was safe. They need banking insurance to keep them from stumbling into risks they never dreamed existed. It wouldn't be right for them to lose their life's savings, and it wouldn't be right for government not to help them out if they did. Don't get me wrong, I'm not saying I like government regulation. I'm just saying I see how it's justified."

"I'm talked out," Rona sighed. "I need space to sort things out."

*W*atching the River Flow

Rona wandered down to her favorite spot, a rocky outcropping under a massive old black walnut tree. Here she could listen to the murmur of the water as it meandered lazily by on its long journey to the sea. She looked at the tree, still standing after the ravages of the flood. "You're a survivor, you are. A little the worse for wear, but you'll make it. How many more floods are you destined to endure? Do you wish you could run for the high ground?" she wondered.

From a distance, as if in answer to her unspoken questions, came a haunting call. "Whip-o-whil, whip-o-whil, whip-o-whil!" The whippoorwill was a bird she never saw, but often heard in the stillness of the evening. She fell silent to listen. "Yes, friend Whippoorwill," she breathed quietly. "Come what may, this is my home."

PROSPECTING FOR NEW INSIGHTS

1. Joe, of the consulting firm, GZQ, presented a picturesque model of a so-called naturescape with homes scattered upon hillsides overlooking a verdant valley. He contrasted this land use plan with the scattering of homes in the valley that existed prior to the flood. He then suggested that the residents would be better off under the plan

than under the patchwork result of the free market, in which many residents chose to live in the valley.

a. Would you prefer to live in the planned naturescape, or in an unplanned community? Bear in mind that the free market allows you to choose a home that is constructed on a hillside, although such homes cost more to build and command higher prices than ones built on flat land.

b. Do you think the existence of federal flood insurance has any influence on the free-market pattern of land use?

2. Rona drew a parallel between bank insurance and flood insurance. Suppose the federal government were to cut back on these types of insurance.

a. Since individuals do not like risk, explain how private insurance coverage could substitute for federal insurance in these areas.

b. What would the government do about those people who elected not to make use of this private insurance and then suffered catastrophic financial losses in the event of a flood or bank failure?

B

Module C

MASTERING ROADSIDE CHALLENGES

CHALLENGE 1
Utility Theory—A Guide to Consumer Choice

Consumer demand holds a special place in economic analysis. It is the driving force behind production. It is also used to measure consumer surplus, the value to consumers of that production. This Challenge looks behind the demand curve to find out what motivates consumer choice.

The law of demand states that consumers buy more of an item when its price falls, implying that demand slopes downward. One reason is that consumers usually derive more enjoyment from the first unit of a good than from the second, more from the second than from the third, and so forth. For example, you might be "dying to see a movie," but probably not if you just saw one yesterday.

In the language of economics, consumer preferences usually abide by the **law of diminishing marginal utility**. **Marginal utility** refers to the satisfaction that a consumer receives from an incremental increase in consumption. Marginal utility is the change in *total utility* associated with increased consumption of a good.

$$\text{Marginal utility} = \frac{\Delta\text{total utility}}{\Delta\text{quantity consumed}}$$

The law of diminishing marginal utility decrees that the first unit of a good is the most satisfying, after which additional units provide progressively less and less additional utility. There is even a **satiation point**, beyond which additional consumption actually reduces total utility. While we are all free to behave foolishly, we usually regret consuming past our satiation points. Figure 4C1-1 illustrates total utility and marginal utility. Note that marginal utility is zero when total utility is at a maximum, which occurs at the satiation point.

There are exceptions to the law of diminishing marginal utility, such as goods a person would rather do without altogether than try to consume in small amounts. For some addictive goods, such as cigarettes, consumers often prefer to either consume large quantities or quit "cold turkey." One cigarette per day just will not do!

One can imagine utility coming in units—"utils." However, there is no way to measure utility accurately or to compare utility convincingly across different consumers. For example, who can really say whether their satisfaction is more than, less than, or identical to the satisfaction of someone else? Although none of us can measure utility, we all judge it when we decide how to spend our budgets. Whether we prefer to emphasize Saturday night hot spots, mountain-biking trips, or social causes, we each allocate our budgets in the ways that maximize our perceptions of our own utility.

To do that, we attempt to divide our spending so that the last dollar spent on each good provides the same marginal utility, whatever the good may be. The marginal utility of a dollar we spend on a good equals the marginal utility of the good itself (MU-

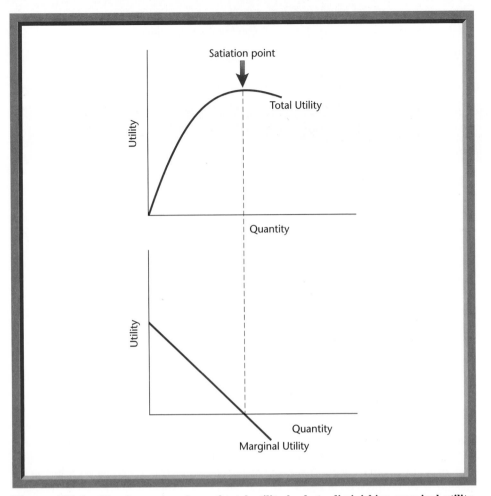

Figure 4C1-1   The decreasing slope of total utility leads to diminishing marginal utility, which lies behind the downward slope of the demand curve. Marginal utility is zero at the satiation point.

$_{good}$) divided by the price we pay for it (P_{good}). For this to be equal for all goods means that

$$\frac{MU_X}{P_X} = \frac{MU_Y}{P_Y} \text{ for all goods X and Y}$$

To understand why this equality characterizes consumer choice, consider what would happen if a consumer receives greater marginal utility from dollars spent on X than on Y. If X and Y are cars and computers, respectively, the consumer could cut down on purchases of computing power, peripheral equipment, and software. Instead, the extra money could be used to maintain or upgrade that special automobile. Even though the budget would be the same, total utility would be greater.

We would each be quick to seize such opportunities. By doing so, however, we reallocate our spending until the opportunities are no longer there. This means that the marginal utility per dollar we spend on each good will be the same.

CHALLENGE 2
Identifying the Inefficiencies of Nonmarket Prices

Both price supports and price ceilings involve transfer payments and real opportunity costs within the economy. A **transfer payment** is merely the redistribution of income from one group to another. Transfer payments often provide the political motivation for enacting the nonmarket prices. Transfer payments may be intended to promote equity. Although transfer payments themselves are not inefficient, the process of achieving them often is inefficient.

The *real opportunity cost* of production represents the value of output forgone by devoting resources to produce the good in question. Real opportunity costs are not themselves inefficient. However, they lead to inefficiencies if the output that is produced is not allocated to consumers who value it more than the costs of production.

Consider the case of a price support, as shown in Figure 4C2-1. Figure 4C2-1 can be viewed as an elaboration upon the agricultural price support analysis of Figure 4A-6. Consumers are forced to pay higher prices and respond by consuming less. The higher prices transfer surplus value from consumers to producers, as shown. There is also a loss in social surplus, given by the triangle labeled accordingly.

Taxpayers must pay for surplus production. Note that surplus production represents a quantity that is overproduced and is not the same as social surplus, which represents a value from consumption. Some of the tax payment covers the social surplus loss. However, most of the tax payment covers the real opportunity cost of production, with the remaining amount representing a pure transfer from taxpayers to producers. The inefficiency equals the social surplus loss plus the opportunity cost of the excess production, minus the value to which that excess production is put. This value is likely to be quite low, since the highest valued uses have already been met by consumers buying the product in the marketplace.

Now consider the case of a price ceiling. Here, too, there are transfers and real costs. Figure 4C2-2 reproduces Figure 4A-3's sketch of the market for rental housing. Because the ceiling price is below the market equilibrium price, P^*, the quantity of housing supplied, Q_S, drops below the equilibrium quantity, Q^*. One effect is to lower rental payments by tenants. For those units of housing that continue to be sold, total rental payments fall by an amount equal to the shaded rectangle in Figure 4C2-2. This amount equals the price difference multiplied by the number of units of housing sold. That rectangular amount is purely a transfer from landlords to tenants.

Suppose that, to achieve the decrease in housing, we somehow manage to deny housing only to those for whom housing is least valuable. This means the quantity of housing supplied is somehow allotted to those who are willing to pay the most for it. In this case, the housing that is no longer provided, $Q^* - Q_S$, would have had a value equal to the area under the demand curve between those quantities. However, landlords would

C

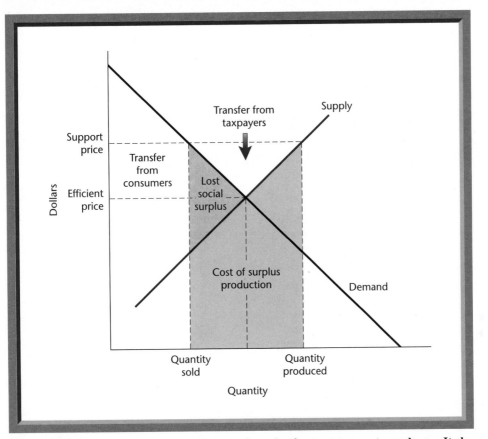

Figure 4C2-1 A price support transfers surplus value from consumers to producers. It also has real opportunity costs. Taxpayers pay the multipart rectangle on the right, which has three components: (1) a transfer from taxpayers to producers, (2) the opportunity cost of the extra production, (3) the loss in surplus value from the reduction in the quantity sold in the marketplace. The latter two costs are real. The inefficiency of the surplus equals the difference between these real costs and the value to which the surplus is ultimately put.

have required at least as much payment as given by the area under the supply curve between Q^* and Q_S. The difference, shown as the shaded triangle, represents a loss of social surplus caused by rent controls. While there is no money changing hands, this triangle represents a real cost to the economy.

The loss of social surplus is actually likely to be much greater than shown, as apartments are not necessarily assigned to those who value them most. For example, Monica may value an apartment highly, but be unable to find one. Figure 4C2-2 illustrates this value to Monica with a double-headed arrow. The valuable rent-controlled apartments may be occupied by other renters, such as Karen, who value those apartments only slightly above their rent-controlled prices. Figure 4C2-2 shows a possible value of apartment living to Karen. A free market would have Monica outbid Karen for an apartment. Rent control laws, however, do not allow this market competition and thus do not assign the apartments to maximize their value in use.

There are still more costs, which do not appear in Figure 4C2-2. For example, de-

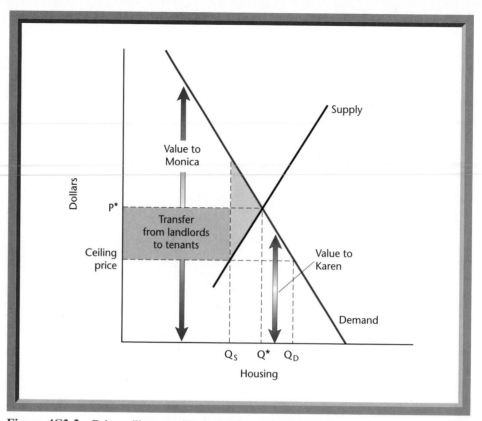

Figure 4C2-2 Price ceilings are illustrated by rent controls. Rent controls transfer social surplus from landlords to tenants. They also cause inefficiency, equal to the area of the shaded triangle if apartments are allocated efficiently. Normally, apartments will be allocated inefficiently, and costs will be higher.

terioration in the quality of housing would lower demand and thus shrink consumer surplus. In addition, discrimination in housing can lead not only to misallocation of apartments, but also to costly social tension. As discussed in the Expressway, costs are likely to worsen over time.

C

Study by Design

SpeedStudy

SpeedReview

Markets have proven to be an efficient way to maximize surplus value, and thus provide for a vibrant economy. For the sake of equity, government often seeks to change free-market prices. Unfortunately, because price signals are basic to how markets operate, changing these signals sacrifices market efficiency. When prices are kept higher than the market equilibrium price, production rises and consumption falls, leading to a surplus. When prices are held below the market equilibrium, a shortage is the result. Surpluses and shortages are not the only inefficiencies. Without market equilibrium prices, there is no assurance that those goods that are produced will go to their most valuable uses. Likewise, minimum wage laws make illegal discrimination easier and entering the workforce harder.

SpeedStudy True or False Self-Test

A1. For an economy to be efficient, it must eliminate producer surplus.

A2. Consumer surplus is greater for diamonds than for water.

A3. For a price ceiling to be effective, it must be above the market equilibrium price.

A4. Rent controls provide a good way to fight discrimination in housing.

A5. Rent controls are usually in the short-term interest of renters.

A6. Price gouging in response to natural disasters can be an efficient way to allocate scarce goods.

A7. Price freezes are likely to result in many "new" products, which are really only minor variations on other products.

A8. Despite being difficult to sell politically, economic analysis suggests that agricultural price supports are an efficient way to provide an income to farmers.

A9. The best way to get rid of surpluses that are accumulated under price support programs is for government to auction off those surpluses in the free market.

A10. Minimum wage laws make it easy for employers to discriminate.

B11. The problem of moral hazard forces individuals to join groups in order to obtain insurance coverage.

B12. If all physicians are forced to charge the same schedule of fees, health care costs would decline without any loss of competition or efficiency.

B13. In the absence of land-use restrictions, the provision of flood insurance by government can lead to overbuilding on flood plains.

B14. According to the analysis presented in Exploration II, the bank failures of the late 1980s and early 1990s were primarily the result of fraudulent activities by bankers.

C15. The law of diminishing marginal utility states that total utility falls as consumers purchase more of a good.

C16. Consumers attempt to allocate their budgets so that the marginal utility of the last dollar they spend on any one good is the same as for any other good.

C17. The presence of a price ceiling means that some consumers who value a good quite highly may be unable to buy it.

C18. A price support increases the market equilibrium quantity.

The MasterMind

Selected Terms Along the Way

MasterMind Multiple Choice Self-Test

A1. If Yvette would be willing to pay up to $10 for one gizmo, up to $8 for a second, and up to $6 for a third, and the price of gizmos is $6 apiece, then Yvette's consumer surplus totals
   a. $24.
   b. $18.
   c. $6.
   d. $4.

A2. Housing vouchers offer an alternative to rent controls by
   a. ensuring that landlords keep their words to keep rents low.
   b. giving prospective tenants the ability to pay higher rents.
   c. setting up detailed standards to which landlords must adhere in order to qualify for permits to offer rental units.
   d. constructing new, low-rent public housing on government-owned land.

A3. Ticket scalping is most likely to be
   a. neither efficient nor equitable.
   b. equitable, but not efficient.
   c. efficient, but of questionable equity.
   d. both efficient and equitable, but very unfair.

A4. Abolishing agricultural price supports leads to
   a. farmers growing more food.
   b. farmers growing the same amount of food.
   c. consumers buying more food.
   d. more consumers going hungry.

A5. Minimum wage laws would be most likely to *decrease*
   a. the number of homeless people without jobs.
   b. opportunities for the least employable to gain job experience.
   c. discrimination in the job market.
   d. wages paid for unskilled labor.

B6. Which of the following best illustrates the problem of adverse selection?
   a. Doctor Jones keep patients waiting for long periods in waiting areas.
   b. After Connie became pregnant, she sought to buy insurance coverage for herself and her baby.
   c. Patients have the incentive to overuse medical services.
   d. Medical quality is down while quantity is up.

B7. Government insurance, whether it be flood insurance or bank insurance, is likely to cause people to behave in a manner that involves more
   a. money.
   b. private insurance.
   c. discrimination.
   d. risk.

C8. If the price of A rises and the price of B falls, and given that a consumer responds by buying less A and more B, then the
   a. marginal utility of A rises and the marginal utility of B falls.
   b. marginal utility of A falls and the marginal utility of B rises.
   c. marginal utility of A and B remain equal.
   d. change in the marginal utility of A and B cannot be predicted.

C9. The benefits of price ceilings are received by
   a. consumers able to buy the product.
   b. producers able to sell the product.
   c. all consumers.
   d. all producers.

MasterMind Questions and Problems

A1. Compute consumer and producer surplus in the market for pails of water, described in chapter 3, Figure 3A-6.

A2. Rent controls lower rents for those lucky enough to have apartments. However, there are several problems.
   a. List five problems with rent controls, and briefly note why each occurs.
   b. Given all the problems with rent controls, why are they ever enacted in a democratic society?

A3. Goals of efficiency and equity are often in conflict. Using the issue of price gouging as an illustration, explain why it is so difficult to agree on what is equitable.

A4. Draw a graph representing the market for unskilled labor. Label the axes of this graph. Suppose that there is a minimum wage in this market that prevents price from reaching equilibrium. Depict the following:
   a. supply;
   b. demand;
   c. price (wage) in the presence of the minimum wage law;
   d. amount of any surplus or shortage (indicate which);
   e. quantity of labor actually employed.

A5. Minimum wage laws are a widely cherished American tradition. Although the laws seem caring and do raise wages for minimum wage labor, there are many problems. List five problems caused by minimum wage laws and

briefly indicate why each occurs. Why are minimum wage laws so popular?

B6. Describe the incentive effects on the provider and recipient of each of the following:
   a. health maintenance organizations, in which primary care physicians are rewarded mainly according to the number of patients they see;
   b. payment according to diagnostic-related groups;
   c. free choice of physicians and unlimited insurance coverage, combined with a 20 percent payment of all costs by the patient.

B7. Any kind of insurance lowers the price of taking risks. This leads to the problem of moral hazard, which government can counter by making laws that deter risky activities. Explain how mandatory seat belt laws and mandatory motorcycle helmet laws can be viewed as remedying moral hazard, given that accident victims often impose medical costs that are subsidized by government. Are there drawbacks to this approach? Explain.

C8. Suppose the marginal utility per dollar that Angela spends on each product is 20. Angela buys seven bags of pasta at $2 apiece. What is the marginal utility of Angela's seventh bag of pasta? Explain.

C9. Explain why graphical analysis cannot depict all the inefficiencies of price ceilings and price supports.

Future Explorations: Mapping out Term Papers

1. **Who are the Homeless?**

   This paper reports the findings of journalists and others as to why people are homeless. It is found that some people are homeless by necessity, such as through poverty or mental illness. Some are even homeless by choice. This paper describes various public policies that are designed to ensure safe housing, but can also drive up housing prices and, therefore, homelessness. The paper concludes with a discussion of the pros and cons of alternatives to those policies.

2. **Should Price Gouging Be Illegal?**

   This paper reports on instances of price gouging following natural disasters. Examples of offensive price gouging are given, such as reports of people selling chlorinated water from their swimming pool to Los Angeles residents who were left without water after the 1993 earthquake. The paper examines whether equity and efficiency conflict, since allowing prices to rise sharply does correct the problem of shortages and thus would appear efficient.

3. **Piecework: Issues and Policies**

   Piecework occurs when people work at home and sell their output by the piece. The most common piecework involves the manufacture of women's garments. However, this sort of piecework is outlawed by the Fair Labor Standards Act. This paper explains why enforcement of minimum wage laws and child labor laws might make it sensible to outlaw piecework. The paper also looks at the alternative view that piecework allows people to avoid commuting and daycare expenses. The paper uses economic analysis to show how allowing piecework would increase supply and thus lower prices to consumers.

Answer Key

ExpressStudy True or False	SpeedStudy True or False Self-Test		MasterMind Multiple Choice Self-Test
1. T	1. F	10. T	1. c
2. F	2. F	11. F	2. b
3. T	3. F	12. F	3. c
4. F	4. F	13. T	4. c
5. F	5. T	14. F	5. b
6. T	6. T	15. F	6. b
	7. T	16. T	7. d
	8. F	17. T	8. a
	9. F	18. F	9. a

*I*nto the International Marketplace

A Look Ahead

Countries rely upon each other more than ever before in history. Yet, no field of economics is more controversial and less understood by the public than international trade. This fact comes as no surprise, since international trade involves all of the elements associated with the economy within a country's borders—its *domestic* economy. In addition, international trade must also take into account foreign currencies and conflicting interests among countries. Nevertheless, a little systematic analysis based on the principles of supply and demand sheds a huge amount of light on this area that at first seems so murky.

This chapter first examines current trade statistics for the United States, as measured by its balance of payments accounts. Supply and demand analysis is then used to interpret exchange rates, the prices of each country's currency in terms of other currencies. The chapter proceeds to examine some common instruments of trade policy and why they are used. To some extent, countries of the world have recognized the folly of "beggar-thy-neighbor" restrictions on trade. This perspective has led to regional trading blocs, a major multination trade accord termed the GATT, and the establishment of the World Trade Organization to enforce the GATT.

DESTINATIONS

*M*odule A

As you zip along the Expressway you will arrive at an ability to

- explain why a trade deficit does not imply a balance of payments deficit;
- interpret exchange rates and explain how forces of supply and demand determine their values;
- describe why an appreciating dollar helps U.S. consumers, but hurts U.S. producers;
- analyze how trade costs jobs in some industries, but not in the aggregate;
- predict the effects of tariffs, quotas, and other nontariff barriers to trade.

*M*odule B

When you leave the Expressway to explore issues you will be able to

- discuss how the many arguments against free trade apply selectively, if at all;
- use game theory to explain how trade strategy blends economics and politics.

*M*odule C

Mastering Roadside Challenges will allow you to hone analytical skills by

- explaining why a weaker dollar increases the trade deficit in the short run, but not the long run;
- identifying the magnitude and distribution of gains and losses from a tariff.

The advertisers of Madison Avenue tell us to be patriotic and "Buy American!" But what is American and what is foreign? What is a Mercury Tracer that is sold in the U.S., but assembled in Mexico with parts from around the world? What is a Toyota Camry built in Kentucky with some components from Japan? How about a Nissan Altima that is manufactured in Tennessee? The challenge of distinguishing U.S. from foreign products does not stop with the auto industry. From McDonald's hamburgers sold in Moscow to the Japanese purchase and later sale of Radio City Music Hall in Manhattan, the United States is increasingly "going global." To see how global, we need only check the balance of payments accounts.

Going Global—Balance of Payments Accounting

As discussed in chapter 2, countries trade with one another in order to increase their standards of living. Each country records the details of trade in its **balance of payments accounts**. For example, the balance of payments accounts of the United States measure the various types of economic interactions the U.S. has with other countries. Knowing the gist of balance of payments accounting aids greatly in understanding issues of international commerce.

The balance of payments accounts contain subaccounts that categorize the major types of international economic interactions. The two primary subaccounts are the current account and the capital account, discussed in the sections that follow.

The Current Account

The **current account** measures the value of exports and imports and certain other international transactions. Exports are U.S. goods and services sold to foreigners, and imports are foreign goods and services brought into the U.S. Figures 5A-1 and 5A-2 show the major imports and exports of the United States.

Note that the U.S. imports the same categories of goods that it exports. One reason is that the specific goods within these categories can differ significantly. For example, the imported Mercedes is quite different from the exported Jeep Cherokee, even though they are both automotive. Another reason is that many subcategories of goods are included in the broad categories shown. For example, within the category of capital goods, the U.S. exports about $22 billion more in aircraft and related equipment than it imports. However, also within the category of capital goods, the U.S. exports about $13 billion dollars less in computers and related equipment than it imports.

The balance on the current account is the dollar value of exports minus the dollar value of imports, adjusted for certain other international transactions. Since exports and

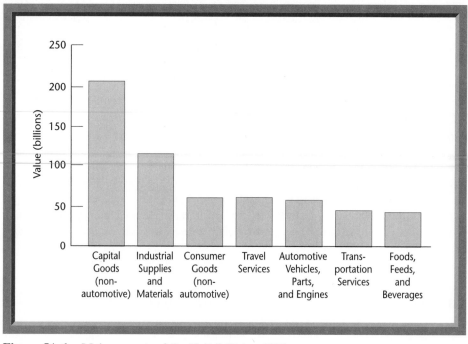

Figure 5A-1   Major exports of the United States, 1994.

Source: U.S. Department of Commerce, *Survey of Current Business*, August 1995, p. 18, Table 4.3 and p. 34, Table 3.

imports can consist of either goods or services, the current account includes the **merchandise trade account** to record trade in goods, and the **services account** to record trade in services.

The balance on the merchandise trade account is termed the **balance of trade**. The balance of trade is currently in deficit, meaning that the dollar value of imported goods exceeds the dollar value of exported goods. In 1994, the deficit stood at $151 billion, which represents 2.2 percent of the $6.9 trillion U.S. gross domestic product. Figure 5A-3 (on page 166) illustrates the values of the U.S. current account since 1979.

Figure 5A-4 (on page 167) shows a time series of current account values as a percentage of total U.S. output. Although the figures for the United States show a significant degree of foreign involvement, the figures for other countries show much more. The reason is straightforward. The larger and more diverse is a country, the more possibilities there are to specialize and trade within that country's borders. For example, the U.S. engages in a large amount of trade across state borders. Were the states of the U.S. to become fifty separate countries, the selling of Idaho potatoes in Utah would show up in the merchandise trade account. Likewise, the Harvard education of the Idaho potato farmer would become an entry into the services account. Thus, as a percentage of their outputs, smaller countries engage in much more international trade than do large countries.

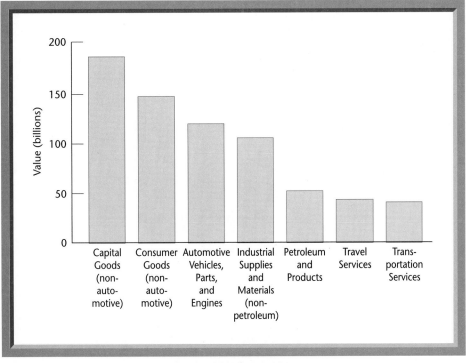

Figure 5A-2   Major imports of the United States, 1994.

Source: U.S. Department of Commerce, *Survey of Current Business*, August 1995, p. 18, Table 4.3 and p. 34, Table 3.

The Capital Account

The **capital account** looks at flows of investment into and out of the United States. Investments can be *direct investments* or *financial investments*.[1] Direct investments imply foreign control, such as Japanese ownership of U.S. golf courses and manufacturing plants. Financial investments include foreign purchases of stocks and bonds, such as Japanese purchases of U.S. government Treasury bonds. The country with the most foreign investment in the United States in 1994 was Japan, followed by the United Kingdom and the Netherlands.

The balance on the capital account is the dollar value of capital inflows minus the dollar value of capital outflows. *Capital inflows* represent dollars foreigners spend on investments in the U.S. *Capital outflows* represent dollars U.S. residents spend on investments abroad. Thus, when looking at the direction of dollar movements, capital inflows are similar to exports, and capital outflows are similar to imports. In recent years, capital inflows have exceeded outflows, meaning that the capital account has been in surplus. The surplus equaled $165.5 billion in 1994.

---

[1]Interest, dividends, profits, or other returns on investment are included in the current account.

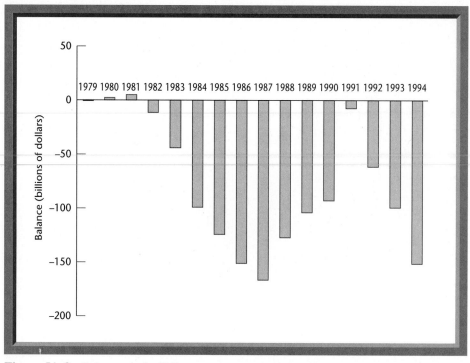

Figure 5A-3   Balance on the U.S. current account, 1979–1994.

Source: *1996 Economic Report of the President*, Table B-99.

Balancing Payments

The balance of payments accounts taken as a whole must have a balance that equals zero. The reason is that, when goods and investments are exchanged among willing buyers and sellers, each buyer and seller must always receive something of equal market value in exchange. For example, consider an export. The recorded worth of both the product sold and dollars received is exactly the same. However, under principles of double-entry bookkeeping, these entries go into different accounts. The result is that, while individual subaccounts can have surpluses and deficits, the overall market value of what is lost and what is gained must be in balance.

Even though the market value of what enters and leaves the country is said to be equal when transactions are voluntary, countries still gain from trade. How can this be? The answer lies in the nature of any kind of trade. Sellers value the goods or investments they sell at less than market value, or they would not care to sell them. Likewise, buyers value the goods and investments they buy at more than market value, or they would not care to buy them. Thus, whenever international transactions occur, both parties gain. These gains are not measured in the balance of payments accounts, because they would be impossible for government statisticians to know.

There are other items in the balance of payments accounts, such as changes in foreign currency holdings and in foreign aid. Although the balance of payments must by definition balance when all such accounts are included, the statistical data are imprecise. To

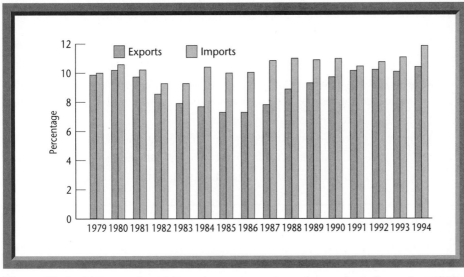

Figure 5A-4 **U.S. exports and imports as a percentage of gross domestic product (GDP), 1979–1994.**

Source: Calculated from data in the *1996 Economic Report of the President*, Table B-1.

force the accounts into balance, it is necessary to include an entry termed *statistical discrepancy*. The statistical discrepancy is quite large, because data collection is subject to large errors. For example, the statistical discrepancy in 1994 equaled −$14.3 billion. Table 5A-1 summarizes the most important components of the balance of payments accounts.

OBSERVATION POINT: It Must Be UFOs!

When all countries' trade deficits and surpluses are added together, the world as a whole has a very substantial trade deficit. That can mean only one thing—the world engages in secret trade with other planets. What's more, the world imports more than it exports! Are alien beings using the difference to buy up planet earth?

TABLE 5A-1	1994 Balance of Payments: Selected Accounts for the United States (all entries in billions of U.S. dollars)		
Balance of Payments Accounts	Exports, Capital Inflows, and Other (+) Entries	Imports, Capital Outflows, and Other (−) Entries	Balance: + = Surplus − = Deficit
Current Account	$838.82	$990.07	−$151.25
(1) Merchandise Trade	$502.49	$668.58	−$166.1
(2) Services	$198.72	$138.83	+$59.89
Capital Account	$291.37	$125.85	+$165.52

Source: International Economic Trends, Annual Edition 1995, (Federal Reserve Bank of Saint Louis), pp. 20, 21.
Note: Totals do not add up exactly, due to omitted accounts and rounding.

Do they arrive in their unidentified flying objects to scout good investment opportunities?

Perhaps you are a skeptic and seek another answer. Yes, it could be the statisticians who are pulling the hoax this time. You see, much trade goes unrecorded. For that which is recorded, costs may be inappropriately overstated and revenues understated for tax purposes. Since imports involve costs and exports revenues, statistics are biased toward exaggerating trade deficits.

You have a choice. You can accept the authority of the balance of payments accounts and reconcile yourself to the presence of alien traders—statistical proof of life on other planets. Otherwise, you should take both with a big grain of salt.

A

> ✓ **QUICKCHECK**
>
> Many people worry about a balance of payments deficit. Are such worries justified?
>
> ---
>
> *Answer:* No, the balance of payments accounts cannot run a deficit, although individual subaccounts can and do. When people worry about a balance of payments deficit they probably have in mind the merchandise trade account deficit or the current account deficit. Usually such worries revolve around the value of lost jobs. As will be discussed shortly, such worries have little economic basis.

*F*oreign *Exchange*

The U.S. balance of payments accounts use dollars as the unit of measure. However, each country has its own currency. How is it that the dollars spent on imports and investments abroad turn into the currencies of the other countries involved? How do other countries' currencies turn into dollars? The answer lies in the *foreign exchange market*, in which currencies are bought and sold for one another.

Market Equilibrium Exchange Rates—How Many Yen Can a Dollar Buy?

Figure 5A-5 illustrates a market for Japanese yen in exchange for U.S. dollars. The horseshoe-shaped arrow indicates that, with minor exceptions, dollars coming from the United States never physically make it to Japan. Likewise, yen from Japan never make it to the United States. Rather, currencies are exchanged for one another, with most exchanges processed electronically through major financial centers, such as New York, Tokyo, and London. Although global in nature, the basic operation of this market is easily understood using supply and demand analysis, as depicted in the center of Figure 5A-5.

As usual with supply and demand analysis, the horizontal axis represents quantity, and the vertical axis represents price. Quantity is the total amount of one currency, and price is its value per unit in terms of the other. That price is termed an **exchange rate**. In our example, we look at the quantity of yen and see its price in terms of dollars per yen. The market equilibrium exchange rate is labeled XR* in Figure 5A-5. In early 1996, that exchange rate was roughly $.01/yen.

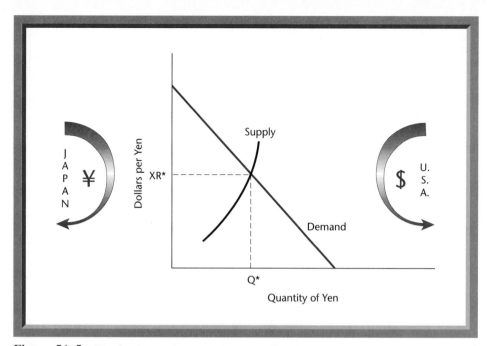

Figure 5A-5 **The foreign exchange market—buying yen with dollars.** All dollars spent on yen are bought by others spending yen for dollars. In essence, the dollars bounce back to be spent in the U.S., and the yen bounce back to be spent in Japan.

At the market equilibrium exchange rate, the total quantity of yen offered for sale, Q*, is just equal to the total quantity of yen purchased. Moreover, the total number of dollars being spent for yen is just equal to the total number of dollars being received by those selling yen. In other words, all dollars that U.S. residents spend on Japanese imports are received by sellers of yen. Those sellers would not agree to the sale unless they had something to spend those dollars on.

Those on the demand side for yen include U.S. buyers of imported goods and services from Japan. They also include U.S. investors interested in such things as Japanese property, stocks, and bonds. Those supplying yen have the same sort of interests, except now the roles are reversed. They may be wanting U.S. goods or services, or U.S. investments. The exchange of currencies thus represents the exchange of goods, services, and investments—both buyers and sellers have a use for each other's currencies.

Return flows of dollars may be indirect. For example, a U.S. importer of Japanese fax machines would enter the foreign exchange market to buy yen with dollars. The sellers of the yen may need dollars in order to pay for oil from Iran, because Iran prices its oil in dollars. Iranian oil sellers have no use for dollars in their own country, but might deposit them in a dollar-denominated account in a European or other foreign bank. Such deposits are termed *Eurodollars*, even if the bank is not in Europe. The bank, in turn, may spend these dollars to buy U.S. investments. Finally, the dollars have returned to the U.S. Although it sounds like a long process, all these transactions are likely to occur in such rapid-fire progression that the dollars may be considered to travel directly from the importer back to the U.S. economy.

Exchange rates can greatly affect the prices we see at our local stores. For example, imported products will seem cheaper if the dollar is strong. A *strong dollar* buys relatively more of other currencies than a *weak dollar*. U.S. consumers and U.S. tourists abroad both like a strong dollar. For example, suppose a ceramic vase costs 30 pesos in Mexico. If the exchange rate is three pesos per dollar, the vase costs the U.S. tourist $10. On the other hand, if the exchange rate is six pesos per dollar the vase costs only $5. Moreover, not only does a stronger dollar mean that the price of imports is lower to U.S. citizens, it also means that U.S. firms must keep their own prices lower to the extent that their products and the products of other countries are substitutes.

On the other hand, U.S. producers and foreign tourists in the U.S. prefer a weak dollar. A weak dollar means that U.S. goods and services seem cheap to foreigners, and foreign goods and services seem expensive to U.S. citizens. For example, while the exchange rate in 1995 was a little less than one hundred yen per dollar (a penny per yen), it was well over 200 yen per dollar ten years earlier. Relative to then, the Japanese tourist has over double the spending power in the U.S., and the U.S. tourist has a little less than half the spending power in Japan.

Currency Appreciation and Depreciation

Currency appreciation occurs when a currency gets stronger; currency depreciation when it gets weaker. In the previous paragraph, the yen appreciated against the dollar, and the dollar depreciated against the yen. The depreciation of the dollar against the yen since the early 1980s can be traced to an increase in U.S. demand for yen, which drives the dollar price of those yen higher. Much of this increase in demand is the result of the appetite of American consumers for Japanese electronics and automobiles.

Figure 5A-6 illustrates this currency appreciation and depreciation. In order to illustrate the basic concepts of appreciation and depreciation, the figure is kept simple. In practice, because of the many influences on currency supply and demand, both shift frequently, which means that market exchange rates rarely stay the same for long.

Governments often intervene in the foreign exchange markets in an attempt to maintain exchange rates within *target zones*. In terms of supply and demand analysis, this means that governments seek to support the price of a currency to keep it from depreciating too much, or place a ceiling on the price of a currency to keep it from appreciating too much. Since governments have no ability to enforce price ceilings and supports in international currency markets, they must resort to buying up weak currencies and selling strong currencies. In effect, they simply enter into the marketplace on either the demand or supply side, depending upon which direction they seek to push price. However, because of the huge volume of currencies being exchanged, government intervention has limited practical effect. For example, **the value of currencies exchanged worldwide in a single week exceeds the value of an entire year's worth of U.S. output.**

This was not always the case. In the period after World War II, governments from around the world adhered to the *Bretton Woods agreement*. The Bretton Woods agreement was a treaty signed in 1944 at Bretton Woods, New Hampshire, by most of the world's major trading countries. This agreement *pegged* the dollar to gold ($35/ounce) and all other currencies to the dollar, thereby implying *fixed exchange rates*. Governments agreed to take whatever actions would be necessary to maintain these rates.

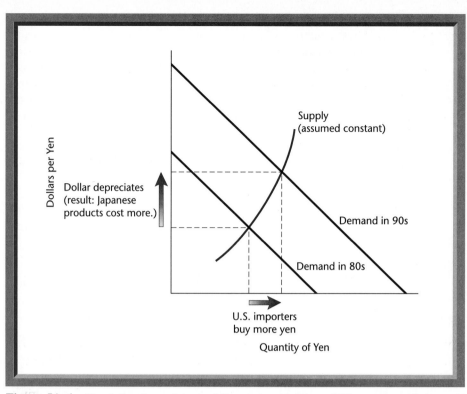

Figure 5A-6   The dollar depreciates and the yen appreciates as U.S. consumers desire more Japanese products.

As world commerce grew over the next thirty years, however, the size of currency transactions overwhelmed the ability of governments to follow through on that agreement. The system of fixed exchange rates was modified in stages and ultimately abandoned as unworkable during a run on the dollar in 1972. This run consisted of dollar selling that overwhelmed governments' abilities to maintain the agreement, thereby precipitating a financial crisis. American tourists abroad felt this crisis personally, as many tourists were stranded, unable to find anyone willing to risk accepting their rapidly depreciating currency. Since then, exchange rates have been allowed to **float** to whatever level the market dictates. However, **because governments still take actions intended to affect market exchange rates, the system is sometimes referred to as a *dirty float* or *managed float.***

Some governments try harder than others to manage their exchange rates. For example, the Mexican government supported the peso at a rate of roughly 3.5 pesos per dollar throughout most of 1994. In late December of that year, however, Mexico was forced to let its currency float freely until the rate adjusted to market equilibrium. The Mexican government did not own enough dollars to keep buying pesos, which would have been required to keep the value of the peso up.

In November and December, 1994, the exchange rate surged to about six pesos per dollar, nearly double its previous value. This abrupt depreciation of the peso dramatically increased the purchasing power of dollars in Mexico and decreased the purchasing power of pesos in the U.S. Mexico was forced to abandon its policy of supporting the peso because it had nearly exhausted its holdings of foreign currencies, termed *foreign reserves*. The Mexican government had spent nearly ten billion dollars worth of these foreign reserves to buy back its own pesos.

When the peso fell, U.S. investors saw the value of their investments in Mexico drop by billions of dollars. Likewise, U.S. merchants along the border saw dramatic drops in their pre-Christmas sales to Mexican nationals. It was small consolation that the peso's depreciation made Mexican vacations cost less for U.S. tourists or that Mexicans with investments in the U.S. reaped windfall gains.

OBSERVATION POINT: A Little Change in Exchange Rates, a Big Change in Wealth

In 1993 George Soros earned notoriety and about a billion dollars at the expense of the British government. Mr. Soros' secret? Bet on the ultimate triumph of free-market prices. Specifically, he speculated against the British pound and other European currencies that governments were most aggressive in supporting.

Speculators in international currencies stand to win or lose enormous sums of money each time exchange rates change. These speculators love to see governments try to maintain fixed exchange rates. They make the bet that governments cannot succeed in keeping exchange rates far from the free-market equilibrium. If governments attempt to keep the price of a particular currency down, speculators contract to buy that currency. If it stays cheap, the speculators can probably sell the currency for what they paid. On the other hand, if governments cannot maintain the targeted exchange rate, the speculators profit handsomely.

It is not only speculators that seem to get rich or poor quickly because of the currency markets. Curiously, the wealth of entire countries appears to rise and fall dramatically, merely because exchange rates fluctuate. The reason is that to measure the wealth of one country in terms of another, the common measuring rod is the currency of one of the countries. Did Japan's wealth really increase nearly threefold since the early 1980s relative to the wealth of the United States, merely because the yen appreciated threefold against the dollar? Of course not! If all Japanese tried to convert their assets into U.S. dollars, the increase in the supply of yen would cause the yen to depreciate precipitously. Still, we measure with the tools we have.

✔ QuickCheck

Does the U.S. trade deficit with Japan mean that the Japanese are accumulating many U.S. dollars that they will spend later? Explain.

Answer: If the question concerns actual U.S. currency, the answer is no, since the foreign exchange markets mean that almost all dollars bounce back to the U.S. before they ever reach Japan. For example, while running a trade deficit with Japan, the U.S. concurrently runs a capital account surplus, implying that the Japanese are accumulating investments in the U.S., such as stocks, bonds, factories, and real estate. These investments could be converted into dollars down the road and allow the Japanese indeed to spend more dollars later.

*T*he Fallacy of Lost Jobs

The effects of trade on jobs and income opportunities is perhaps the most controversial aspect of international trade. We are frequently assaulted with claims that it is somehow unpatriotic to buy imports. The reasoning is that every dollar spent on an imported product provides jobs abroad to make that product. Those are jobs that would have gone to American workers if only the buyer had chosen to spend his or her money on a product that is American made. This line of reasoning is misleading. While true up to a point, it misses the return flow of dollars into other jobs.

Imports cost jobs in specific industries—those that produce products in competition with the imports. However, **buying imported goods and services does not imply any reduction in aggregate employment.** The reason is that dollars that are spent on products abroad bump up against the currency market and are immediately bounced right back into the U.S. economy. To buy foreign products, we must directly or indirectly buy foreign currencies. Sellers of those currencies are buyers of dollars. They would not buy the dollars unless they intend to spend or invest them.

Some dollars do circulate abroad as the currency of choice in countries whose citizens place more faith in the purchasing power of the U.S. currency than they do in their own country's currency. The U.S. benefits when dollars stay abroad, since this allows government to create and spend extra money without raising taxes and without causing inflation. The result is akin to gifts of goods and services from other countries in exchange for pieces of paper.

Unfortunately, relatively few dollars actually leave the country for long. Rather, the vast bulk of dollars spent on imports is respent by foreigners in the U.S. on other things. These other things could be U.S. goods, services, or investments. To see how much of each, we need only refer back to the balance of payments accounts.

One way in which dollars return home is for foreigners to buy our goods and services. Without the dollars we send abroad to pay for imports, foreigners would not have the money to buy our exports. Still, as we have seen, there is a deficit in the current account. Since that deficit represents the dollar value by which our imports exceed our exports, and has recently totaled between 1 and 2 percent of our national output, could the U.S. shave one or two percentage points off its unemployment rate by eliminating both imports and exports?

The answer is clearly no. Indeed, the U.S. tried something like this in 1930, when it passed the *Smoot-Hawley Act* that raised import **tariffs**—taxes on imports—to an average rate of 52 percent on over 20,000 products, a level that was so prohibitively high that imports nearly ceased. Not surprisingly, so did exports. What did surprise a lot of people was that the action was followed by even higher unemployment rates. More recently, the 1980s and early 1990s saw significant declines in U.S. unemployment, even as the U.S. trade deficit was at all-time record high levels. This evidence supports the conclusion that there is no systematic relationship between trade deficits and unemployment rates.

Dollars that do not return to buy U.S. exports return in other ways or are replaced. For example, there is currently about $250 billion in U.S. cash circulating outside the U.S. Unless those dollars return to command U.S. goods and services, they no longer have any bearing on the U.S. economy. This has allowed the federal government to replace them

A

by printing and spending an extra $250 billion dollars, without the need to worry about causing inflation.

Foreign purchases of U.S. investments bring dollars back into the U.S. economy just as surely as do foreign purchases of U.S. exports. Dollars spent on golf courses, factories, stocks, and bonds provide jobs indirectly. For example, sales of U.S. Treasury bonds to foreigners take dollars that might have alternatively been spent on U.S. exports. However, that spending power is not lost. It is merely transferred to the U.S. government. Thus, whether the return flow is direct or indirect, it still finances jobs.

This return flow of dollars often escapes the public consciousness. One reason is that it is much easier to focus television cameras on unemployed individuals than on logical analysis. People whose jobs have been lost to imports are easy to find. Job opportunities gained in the growing export industries make for less poignant newsreel footage. Even more difficult is to track down specific jobs attributable to foreign purchases of government bonds, stocks, and real estate, because this money is circulated throughout the U.S. economy as it is spent by the sellers of these investments.

Protecting American jobs is but one line of reasoning in support of trade restrictions. Although the list of possible rationales for restricting trade is long, the applicability of the arguments is limited and often open to question. (See Exploration 1 in this chapter for a discussion of several such arguments.)

*T*rade Policy Options

Despite free trade offering countries economic advantages, all major countries have some restrictions on trade. For better or worse, countries often seek to protect individual industries or sectors of their economies from foreign competition. Policies that accomplish this goal are termed *protectionist*. American humorist Mark Twain recognized the allure of protectionism when he wrote that free traders win all the arguments, but protectionists win all the votes. However, today, recognizing the dangers of trade wars, most of the major trading countries of the world have signed the **General Agreement on Tariffs and Trade (GATT)**, which limits the use of protectionist policies.

Protectionist policies come in two basic forms: tariffs and nontariff barriers. **Nontariff barriers (NTBs)** can be either **quotas**,—quantity restrictions on imports—or any of a variety of other actions that make importing more difficult. Consider the tariff.

Import Tariffs

Demand for an imported product tells the quantities of the product consumers would purchase from foreign sources at each possible price. This demand is sometimes called *residual demand*, since it represents demand that is left over after consumers have bought from domestic suppliers. Because buyers have the ability to substitute domestically made products for foreign-made products, the demand for imports is typically more elastic than market demand as a whole. Likewise, because suppliers have many countries to sell in, import supply to any one country is also relatively elastic.

Tariffs increase the cost of selling imported products. This increase in turn increases the prices of those products in the domestic market and, by the law of demand discussed in chapter 3, reduces the quantity that will be sold. That is how a tariff restricts imports. Figure 5A-7 illustrates how a tariff raises the price and decreases the quantity of

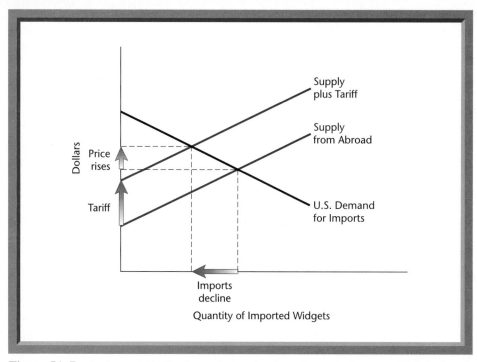

Figure 5A-7 An import tariff raises prices and reduces imports. Import tariffs help American producers at the expense of consumers.

imports, relative to what would have occurred in the free market. Note that the increase in price is less than the amount of the tariff, indicating that importers are often not able merely to pass along the entire tariff to consumers.

By raising barriers to the entry of foreign products, **tariffs can be viewed as a form of price support for domestic producers.** The higher price of imports causes the demand curve to shift to the right for domestic products that are close substitutes. For example, an import tariff on Toshiba laptop computers increases demand for Dell, Compaq, and IBM laptop computers, which in turn causes a new, higher, equilibrium price and quantity for those products. The higher price and quantity sold by domestic producers are why an import tariff is said to protect those producers from foreign competition.

Tariffs are said to be **transparent**, meaning that their effects upon prices are clear for all to see. The U.S. has an extensive array of tariffs, most of which are currently below 6 percent and falling. Most other major trading countries also have similar tariffs. With some exceptions, tariff rates are kept low by the GATT.

Quotas and Other Nontariff Barriers to Trade

Import quotas are an alternative to import tariffs and can accomplish the same goals. Unlike an import tariff, an import quota restricts the quantity of imports directly. GATT limits the extent to which countries can impose import quotas, but does allow quotas for agricultural products and to avoid disruption to countries' domestic economies. While not as widespread as tariffs, most countries have some import quotas.

For example, the U.S. restricts the import of sugar through a set of country-by-country quotas. These sugar import quotas increase the cost of sugar in the U.S. to about double what it is in the rest of the world. Consumers feel the effects when they buy sugar and sweetened products. Indeed, a primary reason for the use of corn sweetener in U.S. soft drinks is the high price of sugar in the U.S. Even so, because U.S. sugar prices are increased indirectly through quotas, rather than directly through a corresponding tariff that would exceed 100 percent, U.S. consumers tend to be unaware of how much extra the quota forces them to pay for sugar. In other words, quotas are not as transparent as tariffs.

In an attempt to increase transparency, sugar import quotas are scheduled to be replaced by tariffs by the year 2004. Agricultural interests oppose converting sugar import quotas to tariffs. They worry that consumers will object to protecting U.S. sugar interests if the effect of the protectionist policy upon the price of sugar becomes too obvious.

As an alternative to import quotas, the U.S. and some other countries have chosen to negotiate **voluntary export restraints (VERs)**, in which individual exporting countries agree to limit the quantities they export. For example, the *multifiber agreement*, currently also scheduled for elimination by 2004, sets country-by-country quotas on clothing exports to the United States and some other countries. The alternative would be for the U.S. or other importing countries to impose import quotas.

The U.S. offers to forgo quotas in favor of VERs in order to maintain good relations with the governments of the other countries involved. Exporting countries know that, if they do not agree to the VERs, they may face either quotas or some other retaliatory action. Exporting countries can also charge higher prices per unit under a VER than they could if they face import quotas. Exporting countries charge more because they are not competing against each other—they each have their preassigned VERs and are not allowed to fill those of other exporting countries.

Quotas and VERs are examples of nontariff barriers to trade (NTBs), which include all ways that countries inhibit imports without resorting to tariffs. Most NTBs do not restrict imports explicitly; their effects are even less transparent than quotas. For example, paperwork and red tape delays can inhibit trade. Under the administration of President Salinas, for example, Mexico established a clever system to fight some of its hidden NTBs. The policy was that any application for importing a product into Mexico would be automatically approved, if not acted upon within ninety days. Prior to that time, in the absence of illegal bribery, applications were often delayed so long that the market opportunity to sell the product had long since vanished.

Sometimes, NTBs are incidental to accomplishing other objectives. For example, the U.S. inspects the manufacturing processes of some products made domestically. It cannot do that for most imports, and so resorts to sampling. For this reason, entire lots of such things as canned foods from China have been discarded because sampling revealed some to be contaminated, labeled improperly, or otherwise not up to U.S. standards. While sampling does increase the cost of importing and is thus an NTB, its primary purpose is to protect public safety.

At other times, the effects on trade are intentional, but hard to prove. For example, Japan made it difficult to sell Louisville Slugger baseball bats in its country for many years, because the bats did not meet Japan's guidelines for use in baseball games. Since the Louisville Slugger was the best-selling bat in the world market, U.S. trade negotiators asserted that the Japanese regulators set their standards for bats with an eye toward restricting competition from U.S. imports.

Still other times, motives conflict. In the early 1990s, Europe would not allow the import or sale of beef from cattle fed the bovine growth hormone. While illegal in Europe, use of bovine growth hormone was allowed in the U.S. Since the U.S. government would not certify its beef exports as hormone-free, the U.S. was barred from exporting beef to Europe. That ban was lifted after the U.S. restricted imports of some minor European products and threatened to go much further if the Europeans did not back down. Since buyers in either the U.S. or Europe could always contract with cattle ranchers for whatever sort of animals they desire, U.S. negotiators argued that no government certification would be necessary.

OBSERVATION POINT: Made in Mexico, Brick by Brick

Americans have no legal right to know which state is responsible for producing the goods they buy. By law, however, they do have a right to know the country of origin for imports. This information must be labeled on each imported item.

A

The law applies to all products, including bricks from Mexico. No big deal, perhaps, except when you realize that brick kilns in Mexico are rarely high-tech. The cost of imprinting *Mexico* into each brick bound for El Norté is a significant fraction of the entire cost of producing that brick. If that NTB cuts down on Mexican brick exports, U.S. brick makers don't complain!

Trade Strategy

Countries design their trade policies with a strategy in mind. Strategies usually contain a mix of political and economic objectives. These strategies run the gamut from broadly ranging trade agreements through regional trading blocs to the selection of specific firms and industries to protect and promote.

Trading Blocs, the GATT, and the World Trade Organization

The broadest trade strategy is embodied in the multilateral General Agreement on Tariffs and Trade. This agreement is termed *multilateral* because multiple nations have joined in. Specifically, the GATT was initially signed in 1947 by the major trading countries of the world at that time. Over the intervening years, the agreement has been updated and new countries have been added. Since 1995, the GATT has been administered by the **World Trade Organization (WTO)**, an organization similar to the United Nations, but with a focus on matters of international commerce.

The initial impetus for the GATT agreement was the prohibitively high tariffs imposed by the U.S. and some other countries during the Great Depression of the 1930s. The GATT required significant tariff reductions. The high tariffs were deemed to have harmed the world economically. Furthermore, the high tariffs promoted political animosity and isolationism among countries and led to economic tensions that contributed to World War II.

The GATT agreement has been strengthened through rounds of trade negotiations that have achieved further reductions in tariffs, and also restrictions upon quotas and other

NTBs. For example, the *Uruguay round* of negotiations took eight years of often contentious bargaining before being ratified by the United States and other countries in late 1994.

The Uruguay round established the World Trade Organization to enforce the GATT. Prior to the WTO, the GATT had been administered through a bureaucracy headquartered in Geneva. This bureaucracy had limited enforcement power, however, since individual member countries could veto many of its actions. The WTO, also based in Geneva, has greater enforcement authority and cannot have its actions vetoed by any single country. This point was contentious in the Uruguay round, since the U.S. and other countries worried about losing national sovereignty.

The Uruguay round addressed a number of other thorny issues. These issues include the following:

- Tariffs: Tariffs have been cut by an average of about 40 percent worldwide on thousands of products and eliminated altogether on others, such as beer, toys, and paper. After a phase-in period, the percentage of products that can be imported *duty-free* into industrialized countries will more than double to 44% of all imported goods.
- Agricultural subsidies: *Subsidies* represent financial assistance to domestic producers. This assistance can lead to inefficient patterns of trade. After particularly heated debate, countries agreed to reduce trade-distorting subsidies to agriculture. Agricultural subsidies have been estimated to cost consumers $160 billion per year.
- Services: For the first time, global trade rules will be interpreted to cover services. To reach agreement, many of the details were left vague, especially in regard to banking and other financial services.
- *Intellectual property rights:* New rules were enacted to better protect patents and copyrights, including rights to copy computer software.

In addition to joining the GATT, most countries have also gone the route of forming regional **trading blocs**. For example, the European Community is considered a trading bloc, because it has lower trade barriers among its member countries than to the rest of the world. The United States, by signing the **North American Free Trade Agreement (NAFTA)** with Canada and Mexico, joined into a North American trading bloc. This bloc is envisioned to expand southward to include Chile and some other countries of Central and South America. As of this writing, the proposed *Americas Free Trade Accord (AFTA)* has not yet been formed.

To the extent that regional trading blocs reduce tariffs and other trade restrictions, the trading blocs promote trade among their members. This trade can come from two sources. First is **trade creation**, which involves an increase in world trade. The trade creation effect is efficient, since it allows countries to specialize according to comparative advantage.

The second effect is **trade diversion**, which represents trade that would have occurred with countries outside the trading bloc, but that is diverted to countries within a trading bloc in response to lower tariff rates. An example of trade diversion would be if the NAFTA induced IBM to assemble its laptop computers in Mexico instead of Malaysia. Trade diversion is inefficient, since it causes trade to respond to price signals from government—relative tariff rates—rather than to comparative advantage.

Economists generally support regional trading blocs as a step toward free trade. However, even supporters of regional agreements have reservations about trade-diversion effects. There are also concerns that regional trading blocs may turn inward and erect higher barriers to the rest of the world. Not only would contentious trading blocs jeopardize gains from trade, they could also be a threat to world peace.

Strategic Trade Initiatives

Government planners might seek to attract, protect, and develop industries that can dominate their markets worldwide. That is a lesson many Americans have taken from Japanese successes in the automobile and electronics industries, industries that were protected and promoted by the Japanese government. Europe has also taken the track of creating its own industrial dynamo, by subsidizing and offering guaranteed markets for European Airbus airplanes. **Strategic trade initiatives** are the plans to accomplish this goal. Strategic trade initiatives hold the potential to better a country's position in the world. However, other countries consider that to be unfair.

A

Strategic trade initiatives also have huge risks. Sometimes, as in the case of Airbus, the cost of government subsidies is enormous. Moreover, success is not assured. For example, along with autos, the Japanese shipbuilding industry was also promoted by Japanese industrial policy. That industry is today characterized by massive surplus capacity, with entire shipyards lying idle. Despite government support, the Japanese shipbuilding industry has been unable to compete with the shipbuilding industries of Korea and other countries. These countries have currencies that are weaker than the yen, and so can sell their ships at lower prices in the world market.

The possibilities for success in strategic trade initiatives are limited. Success requires that government identify an industry where a few firms can dominate the world market or where there are such synergies among firms that a few core firms can serve as a magnet for a large portion of their worldwide industry. This task is not easy for anyone. Moreover, government strategists in search of visionary economic analysis can also be swayed by the more immediate pressures of politics. Will the targeted industries be true world leaders? The danger is that targeted industries will merely be those with the greatest political clout.

EXPRESS STUDY TRUE OR FALSE

1. The United States has a balance of ~~payments~~ *trade* deficit.
2. The United States ~~has~~ a balance of payments ~~surplus~~. *out always balance althou*
3. An appreciation in the dollar means that consumers pay less for imports.
4. Elimination of the U.S. balance of trade deficit would ~~cause the U.S. unemployment~~ *have no longer term effect on the aggregate* rate to drop.
5. When other countries voluntarily limit their exports to the U.S., the U.S. pays ~~less~~ *more* per unit for those exports.
6. The United States belongs to a regional trading bloc.

EXPLORATION 1
Point/Counterpoint—So Many Reasons Not to Trade!

There are many possible exceptions to the rule that free trade is desirable because it increases a country's consumption possibilities. However, objections to free trade frequently have limited applicability or are based on shaky assumptions.

Individuals, regions, and countries can specialize according to their respective comparative advantages and gain from trading with each other. We each do that—no one in modern society is self-sufficient. When we earn incomes that allow us to buy the things we want, we are specializing and gaining from trade. Regions specialize and trade with other regions within a country. Countries do the same with other countries. A country that specializes and trades with other countries will be able to consume more than it could produce on its own. As a general rule, then, restricting trade to protect either high-wage jobs or low-wage jobs is inefficient—it cuts down on the size of the economic pie.

Since the purpose of economic activity is to consume, not to produce for the sake of keeping busy, why restrict imports? Yet countries do impose restrictions on trade, especially on imports. Sometimes the reasons make economic sense. More often, the reasons have much more to do with politics than with sound economics. This Exploration examines some of the special circumstances under which trade restrictions have been justified. In each case, caution is in order.

Infant Industries—Where Are Investors?

Developing countries often try to nurture new industries they hope will one day become a source of export earnings. These **infant industries**, are thought to need protection in the rough world marketplace. The infant industry argument claims that government must first identify promising industries and then erect import barriers to protect them. When the infants grow strong enough to fend for themselves, government should remove the barriers.

The infant industry argument is unconvincing if markets function efficiently. In the free marketplace, **venture capitalists** and other private investors will often support firms through many years of losses. They will do so if they expect that the firms will eventually become profitable and reward their patience. If private investors do not foresee profits down the road, they will withhold their funds, and the businesses will fail.

Unfortunately, there is much less assurance that government will pick industries that are likely to survive on their own. Governments often use political considerations to select "infant" industries. Even if governments do attempt careful economic analysis, such analyses are unlikely to match those of investors with their own money at risk. The result is that governments around the world have protected industries that never grew strong enough to withstand foreign competition. By requiring government subsidies to stay afloat, and by charging prices above prices in the rest of the world, such industries have proven to be expensive for governments and consumers alike.

*N*ational Defense—*Valid but Overused*

If imports or exports seriously threaten national defense, it makes sense to restrict them. No one denies this fact. However, translating national defense interests into policy is often not easy. When is the threat serious? For example, the U.S. Department of Defense has advocated restrictions on the export of computers and technology. However, if the U.S. is an unreliable supplier to other countries, will new technologies evolve elsewhere in places where the government allows producers to reap the profits from exports? Also, what weight should be put on civilian uses for products that could also be used in war? The judgments are often difficult.

On occasion, the judgments are easy. For example, is it necessary to protect the jobs of uniform makers and shoe makers in order to preserve the national security of the United States? If you work in or earn investment income from those industries, self-interest might prompt you to argue "yes!" That argument was indeed made to the U.S. International Trade Commission in the mid-1980s.

U.S. leather footwear manufacturing was in trouble, due to inexpensive imports from Brazil and Italy. It looked as if the leather footwear industry might follow the same route as the athletic shoe industry. With few exceptions, the athletic shoe industry had already abandoned the U.S. in favor of manufacturing facilities in the Far East. The argument to protect remaining U.S. shoemakers went along the following lines:

> *Without any shoe industry within its borders, what would the U.S. do in*
> *wartime if it were to run short of combat boots? Look what happened to the*
> *armies of Napoleon in Russia and to the Confederate armies in the U.S.*
> *Civil War. The soldiers of these armies marched so much that they wore*
> *out their boots. Unable to provide replacements, France and the*
> *Confederacy went down in defeat.*

Yes, this argument is far-fetched. Few people envision that a modern war would pit the U.S. against Brazil, Italy, and countries of the Far East in years of ground warfare. Even if that were likely, a simple solution would be to stockpile extra boots. Nevertheless, when the security of an industry's profits and its workers' livelihoods are at stake, the more ammunition the better!

*E*nergy Security—Drain America First?

While foreign armies are unlikely to threaten U.S. security, the U.S. might be susceptible to the threat of economic blackmail. Because the U.S. imports over half of the oil it uses, this seems to be its most vulnerable point. Despite having an abundance of coal and natural gas, the U.S. relies upon oil to provide most of its fuel and electricity. Oil is a critical energy source for transportation, heating, and production. Without energy, U.S. industry would grind to a halt.

The OPEC oil embargo of 1973 was an example of economic blackmail in action. The aim of the embargo was to punish the U.S. for its support of Israeli policy. While the embargo did not appear to affect U.S. policy, the U.S. paid the price of long gasoline lines and high energy prices. To prevent such blackmail in the future, some people argue in favor of an oil import tariff that would raise the price of imported oil and wean the U.S. from its dependency on that oil.

If the U.S. raises the price of imported oil, U.S. producers will substitute domestic oil, which increases the price of domestic oil. The higher price would prompt increased production from existing oil fields and increased drilling for new supplies. Since oil is a nonrenewable resource, opponents of oil import restrictions argue that they would "drain America first." This means that, as U.S. wells are pumped dry more quickly, the U.S. would be forced to rely even more heavily on foreign supplies in the future.

Higher oil prices in the U.S. from import restrictions would cause additional undesirable effects. For example, while oil import restrictions would reduce the immediate risk of economic blackmail, it would shrink the economic pie over time. The economy can grow faster and stronger with cheaper energy and thus be better positioned to weather energy disruptions if they ever do materialize. In addition, higher oil prices would prompt the substitution of coal and nuclear power, both of which can harm the environment. For coal, the side effects are particulates, which lead to sooty air and acid rain. For nuclear power, the side effect is the risk of a catastrophic accident. These effects add up to a high price for a doubtful energy security.

B

*E*nvironmental, Health and Safety Standards—A Level Playing Field without a Game

Some U.S. industries cannot produce products as cheaply as products from abroad, because companies abroad do not have to pay for protecting the environment or the health and safety of their workers. Should the U.S. attempt to estimate the extra costs of producing in the U.S., and then add that cost to imports by imposing an appropriate set of tariffs? Some critics of current trade policy suggest that this approach is the only way to achieve a *level playing field*.

There is merit to this argument, insofar as the environmental or other damages reach U.S. territory or otherwise affect U.S. citizens. For example, the effect of chlorofluorocarbons—chemicals named by scientists as the culprit in creating a hole in the world's ozone layer—does not depend upon which country is the source of chlorofluorocarbon emissions. Likewise, the U.S. may have an interest in ensuring that the tuna it imports has been caught in a dolphin-friendly manner.

If carried to an extreme, leveling the playing field would remove the very basis for trade itself, comparative advantage. After all, if all firms have identical costs, there is much less reason to trade. For the U.S. to impose its own environmental standards upon other countries, when environmental effects are localized, would benefit neither the U.S. nor those countries. Such action could easily be interpreted by those countries' citizens as an act of U.S. arrogance or imperialism.

For example, environmental costs of production in poor countries are often less than in the U.S. because of weaker laws or law enforcement. Higher levels of pollution are likely to be efficient for these countries, because environmental quality is a normal good—as incomes rise, people demand more. Poor countries value extra income to spend on food, shelter, and other goods more highly than extra environmental quality. Thus, poor countries have a higher opportunity cost of environmental quality and might efficiently specialize in industries with a higher pollution content. In contrast, by valuing environmental quality highly, U.S. citizens are better off when those industries go elsewhere.

External Benefits—How Much and What Policy?

Sometimes the actions of an industry provide *external benefits*, meaning benefits that go to other individuals or industries. This concept has motivated many regions and countries to compete for high-tech industries in the hopes that there will be spinoff benefits. For example, entrepreneurs and innovators often have their start in high-tech firms. Promoting entrepreneurship and innovation has value to a country and can justify favorable treatment of such industries. By restricting imports of high-tech or other selected products, trade barriers may allow the domestic industries that produce similar products to flourish.

At least three cautions are in order, however. First, trade restrictions are likely to be inferior to other policies designed to target external benefits more directly. For example, if a firm creates external benefits that can be measured, those benefits would be promoted more effectively through direct payment for those effects in proportion to their value. In short, government could use a direct subsidy to pay for external benefits. Trade restrictions involve an implicit, indirect subsidy, with undesirable side effects upon consumers.

The second caution is closely related. Sometimes the amount of external benefits is highly questionable and easily manipulated in the political process. For example, high defense budgets were justified for many years on the basis of spillover benefits to the civilian economy. This policy was followed despite considerable evidence that external benefits per dollar of defense spending were likely to be much lower than external benefits from most other types of spending.

Third, benefits that appear to be external often are not. For example, if people think they can acquire valuable human capital by working at the XYZ company, then the XYZ company can attract those workers for less pay. The lower wages make competing with imports easier. No policy action is needed, to the extent that external benefits are captured in wages. Thus, while external benefits can justify restricting trade, the justification is often unconvincing.

Dumping—Rarely Strategic

Dumping is defined as the selling of a good for less than its cost of production. A company may engage in dumping for various reasons. One common reason is that the company overestimates demand and produces too much. It then seeks to salvage what revenues it can from its bloated inventories.

A second common reason is that a company may be selling output at a price that covers wages, materials, and other operating expenses of production, but does not cover the cost of its capital and other *fixed costs* that it must pay whether it produces or not. Even though the company loses money, it would lose more by not selling.

A third reason, related to the second, revolves around different elasticities of demand in different markets. A company may dump a product in a country where its elasticity of demand is high, perhaps caused by intense competition from other companies in its industry. The company covers its capital costs by charging a higher price in markets where it faces less competition. Lower prices where competition is heavy are familiar occurrences within a country, as well as internationally. This is one reason why the same brand of gasoline sold along an interstate highway at the edge of a city is often priced much higher than when sold in the city itself.

Dumping for each of the above reasons occurs within a country, as well as in international trade. However, it is only in international trade that dumping is illegal, according to the GATT. If a company is charging a lower price in a foreign market than it does at home, and if that lower price does not cover its fixed costs, the company is guilty of dumping. Indeed, since a foreign company's capital costs are often hard to measure, the U.S. presumes dumping whenever a foreign company charges less in the U.S. than it does at home, irrespective of its costs. U.S. law allows for the imposition of antidumping tariffs, such as those imposed in the early 1990s on Japanese computer chips.

Why worry about dumping? After all, aren't U.S. consumers being offered a bargain? In most cases, the U.S. would be better off to accept the low prices and spend the savings on other products. The only time to worry is when there is **strategic dumping**—dumping that is intended to drive the competition out of business, so that the firms doing the dumping can monopolize output and drive prices up in the future. However, in most industries, the prospects for successful strategic dumping are highly questionable. After all, in a world marketplace, there are many potential competitors lurking in the wings. Even companies that have been driven out of a particular line of business can often reenter it in the future, should an increase in price make it profitable to do so.

Why All the Argument?

Sometimes objections to free trade are well-intentioned, and occasionally these objections are valid. However, mixed in with valid arguments to restrict trade are many arguments that can best be described as self-serving. It is in the interests of U.S. producers to restrict trade, if the goods and services they offer are in competition with imports. After all, this competition keeps prices and profits lower than they would otherwise be. Competition forces businesses to find ways to economize and become more efficient. They do not like this competitive pressure.

Of course, many U.S. companies have no interest in restricting imports, especially companies that use imported components or produce products for the export market. U.S. consumers are also poorly served by import restrictions, since these restrictions drive up consumer prices and thus reduce purchasing power. Curiously, consumers often seem unaware of their own interests. They may believe that importing products is somehow unpatriotic, since they perceive that importing products is equivalent to exporting jobs. Actually, this view fails to take into account the return flow of dollars—dollars return to the U.S. to buy exports and investments, thus creating other jobs.

If the arguments for and against free trade were to be counted, free trade would come up very short. However, the number of objections is not important. It is the validity of those objections that matters. In that respect, with minor exception, free trade offers the best chance of maintaining and improving the standard of living the world now enjoys.

PROSPECTING FOR NEW INSIGHTS

1. a. One way that the dollars spent by U.S. citizens on imports return to this country is through investment. Is foreign investment in the U.S. good for the country?

   b. Some people claim that allowing the Japanese to own U.S. assets is comparable to a U.S. surrender to Japan in World War II. Others contend that foreign ownership of U.S. assets, subject to U.S. law, is very different from a foreign power conquering the U.S. and establishing its own laws. What do you think? Explain.

2. What would be the effect on trade and U.S. output if the U.S. required all other countries to meet U.S. labor and environmental standards pertaining to production bound for the U.S.? Would this approach be good for the U.S.? Explain.

B

EXPLORATION 2
EDUCATIONAL SHORT STORY
The Trade Game

The interaction between politics and economics in the formation of trade policy serves as the backdrop for this story. The modern economic notion of game theory is seen to shed light on trade policy strategy. Although the people and plot are fictional, the government agencies, policies, and issues are real.

Seth Blakestrom surveyed the maps and charts that surrounded him as he sat ramrod straight at his giant oak desk. There were the military maps, to remind him of his days in the armed forces. Then there were charts of football strategies to remind him of when he coached Langley Junior High. Most prominent of all, though, were the political maps.

With their bright shadings of blue and red, these political maps brought Seth memories of battles gone by and battles to come. Seth thought of his long journey behind the political scenes. First he'd been a campaign advisor. That led to a position as Congressional staffer, and then to an appointment as a Commissioner at the International Trade Commission (ITC), the Congressional agency responsible for dealing with trade-related disputes. As Commissioner, Seth came to appreciate the sentiments of U.S. industries hit by competition from imports. While the political dimensions of these concerns were never far from mind, the ITC's staff made sure that Seth did acquire some appreciation of the economic issues involved.

It was only natural that the newly elected President should select Seth to be his personal "Aide for Trade." Seth prided himself on being a savvy operator who could get things done. With his background in politics, his involvement in making strategic decisions, the experience of coaching a winning team, and a taste of economic analysis, Seth thought he had the perfect background for the job.

Sweet Deals—Bad Economics, but Good Politics

With a slight tap, the door swung open. "Mr. President!" Seth exclaimed as he jumped to his feet. President Clifford Todd casually acknowledged the greeting as he ambled into the room. He gestured for Seth to be seated.

"Seth, you've been here only three months, and this clutter is already threatening to engulf the room," the President chuckled, "but that isn't what I came to discuss. Last month, you called my attention to an Internet newsgroup on sugar import restrictions. Well, the media's gotten wind of that newsgroup and is tapping it for ammunition to blast the sugar quotas. The farm lobby's upset. For example, maybe you saw the political cartoon about the Haitians wielding sugar cane over the heads of U.S. farmers, the one with farmers whimpering for help and cowering behind Uncle Sam. Farm-state representatives don't like that kind of thing."

"Between thee and me, Mr. President, it has always seemed remarkable to me how resilient the sugar quotas are. After all, by setting country-by-country import quotas for such countries as the Philippines, Grenada, and Haiti, we deny these countries export earnings. Then we spend money in an attempt to keep them stable and democratic. Who benefits? It's the . . ."

"Seth, you know who benefits," President Todd interrupted. "Our constituents in agriculture benefit. The sugar cane growers in Hawaii, Louisiana, and Texas benefit. The sugar beet growers in Minnesota and North Dakota benefit. Corn growers and manufacturers of corn sweeteners benefit, and you know how many states grow corn. By sticking together as a cohesive lobby, all of agriculture benefits, and agriculture is important in a great many states. No matter their populations, each of those states has two Senators. We've got to listen."

"Mr. President, it's your call. With Internet forums and other forms of town meeting discussions, though, I suggest we not discount public awareness. In the past, the only people who would pay attention to import tariffs and quotas were those whose jobs were directly at stake. I think the public is better educated than they used to be, though, and they'll hold it against us and our party if we appear to kowtow to special interests. People don't like paying twice as much for sugar as they would if the quotas were scrapped. They also resent that soft drinks have so much corn sweetener because sugar is so expensive. It really might be better if we deflect the issue rather than meet it head on."

"What do you mean?"

"Well, Mr. President, I learned something during my stint as an ITC Commissioner. We viewed ourselves as lightning rods there. Members of Congress often knew it was not in the interests of America to protect various industries. But, if an industry in the district of one of these members sought protection, the Congressional Representative would not want to say no. Quite the opposite, actually. Each member wanted to be able to champion the cause of his or her constituent industry. Members never want to seem ineffective, either, when it comes to a vote. The solution is to set up the objective ITC to evaluate each case on its merits. Members of Congress can then rant and rave if they want to and hope the ITC drags its feet or ignores them. It's great to have somebody else to blame!"

"Your point?"

"We can do the same thing. You see, we can assure our agricultural constituents that we are doing all we can to keep tariff barriers high. Unfortunately, our hands are tied. In order to open up foreign markets to U.S. exports, we have had to sign this multilateral GATT accord. Alas, we must be bound by the same rules, and thus are bound to lower some of our import barriers. This way, we ease off on sugar quotas and are forced to replace them with tariffs by 2004. Then maybe we can gradually phase those out, too. The word here is *gradual*. We must look like we're on the right road. So what if we drive at five miles per hour?"

"Well, Seth, you might be right. Farmers won't like the road, but at least non–sugar farmers will probably accept traveling it at slow speed. After all, we export a lot more farm commodities than we import. I believe that Senators will recognize the strategy and will approve."

*W*ill Bluffing Win the Game of Global Trade?

"Seth, there is another matter that I have come here to discuss. Ever since Cindy Choi took over the job of U.S. Trade Representative (USTR), she has come under criticism for being too soft on our trading partners. Personally, I think its that last name of hers. Just because her husband was born in Korea, people wonder if she really has America's best interests at heart. I thought the country was beyond that; I thought having a mix of nationalities would be good for the job. Be that as it may, be advised that Cindy isn't getting any meaningful concessions out of her Japanese counterpart, Tomiko Yu. I'm afraid we're going to be criticized for being too soft on the Japanese. As far as Cindy goes, I bet there'll be plenty of 'I told you so's.' "

"Now wait a minute, Seth. Before you say anything, let me also inform you that your memo on the game theory approach to trade has attracted a lot of discussion among my inner circle. **Game theory** has really been in the news, ever since those three economists won the 1994 Nobel Prize for that notion of playing economic games with the same sorts of strategies as might be found in poker, chess, and the like. It raises intriguing possibilities, and I want your opinion. Do you think it's time to do some bluffing?"

"Mr. President, you may have noted that I laid out some strategies in my memo, but did not make a recommendation. The reason is that I am not in a position to judge the policy responses of the Japanese. Let me briefly review these for you." Seth swept aside some of the papers piled on his desk. Underneath a glass top lay photos of a little boy and girl.

"Nice family, Seth."

B

"Thank you, Mr. President. Brian and Sally are in high school now. I've had some trouble meshing my visitation rights and the demands of this job. I'm not complaining, though. The kids and I have a great time when we do get together." Seth covered the pictures with a sheet of paper containing a box diagram that read "Payoff Matrix."

Payoff Matrix

	Trade War by U.S.	Free Trade by U.S.
Trade War by Japan	Japan = $2 billion U.S. = $2 billion	Japan = $70 billion U.S. = $25 billion
Free Trade by Japan	Japan = $25 billion U.S. = $70 billion	Japan = $60 billion U.S. = $60 billion

"I have sketched out the basic strategy questions. The numbers are meant to illustrate the gains from trade. The gains from trade will be quite different from the dollar value of the trade itself, since that value basically measures cost, not benefit. Gains from trade measures the net addition to a country's consumer and producer surplus. Should I explain what is meant by surplus value?"

"No, I first learned that concept when I studied supply and demand in a required course at my alma mater, Pinnacle State U. Glad they made me learn that, because it's a good frame of reference. Some of those basic concepts—like supply and demand, *ceteris paribus*, surplus value, and elasticity—I use a lot."

"Moving right along, then, the numbers are just gross approximations. A lot depends upon the details of *trade war* and *free trade*. As you can see, Mr. President, both countries lose badly if we engage in a major trade war. Between the two of us, both countries gain the most if both remove trade barriers and practice free trade. Trouble is, when just one country practices free trade, the other country can often gain by manipulating the **terms of trade**, which is the price of a country's exports relative to the price of its imports."

"Can you give me an example, Seth?"

"Sure. Any time a country has market power, it can influence the price it pays or receives for its products. Suppose the U.S. has market power in the oil market. If that is the case, we could restrict oil imports and drive down prices, *ceteris paribus*. Of course, that might motivate the oil exporters to reinvigorate OPEC. If so, the strategy backfires."

"What about Japan, specifically?"

"Same holds for U.S. trade with Japan. Let's say we slap tariffs on all sorts of imports from Japan. That reduces U.S. spending on Japanese products, which dries up the supply of dollars in exchange for yen. The result is that it costs more yen to buy a dollar. This means two things. First, it means our exports go down. U.S. producers wouldn't like that. Second, because the dollar becomes stronger, it means that each dollar we spend buys more yen. Importing Japanese goods would be cheaper, just like oil in the other example. While our consumers would pay a little bit more because of the tariff, most of that revenue would be offset by price cuts made by Japanese exporters. It's as though we can raise U.S. government revenue by taxing the Japanese."

"Seth, I think that's what they're doing to us. They're making it hard for U.S. companies to sell in Japan, which means that the yen is stronger than it otherwise would be. If we take action to make their sales more difficult in the U.S., then maybe we can use that as a meaningful bargaining chip to get barriers lowered in both countries."

"Mr. President, there are dangers. The Japanese public and most government officials do not believe that Japanese trade barriers are any harsher than those in the U.S. They claim that most barriers to U.S. sales in Japan are merely cultural. They believe that U.S. companies who do their cultural homework can and do succeed in Japan. If we go raising trade barriers, the perception over there will be that we are behaving aggressively. They are not going to react positively if they think we are trying to bludgeon them into submitting to unreasonable requests. After all, we would not take kindly to another country trying to twist our arms, either."

"So you think the strategy could backfire?"

"I think that's very possible. Rather than moving toward free trade, we'd risk heading into an outright trade war in which neither country gains. We could generate bad blood between us that could cause a long-term feud or worse. We came very close to that in June of 1995, when President Clinton committed the U.S. to imposing 100 percent retaliatory tariffs on Japanese luxury cars, unless Japan gave U.S. automakers greater access to Japanese auto markets. The Japanese offered some last-minute concessions that averted a full-blown trade war. Trouble is, they almost called our bluff. They truly believed that U.S. automakers were not trying very hard to sell in Japan. U.S. cars even came with steering wheels on the wrong side for Japanese highways, although this practice is starting to change."

"You speak of risks and dangers. Has there ever been any long-term fallout?"

"Good question, Mr. President. Some people say that trade wars contributed to World War II. On a more mundane scale, we do have evidence that policies enacted in strategic trade games are hard to remove once the games are over. For example, the U.S. currently imposes a 25 percent duty on pickup trucks imported from Europe. Of course, we don't see pickups from Europe, and never did. The policy was enacted decades ago as a signal that we really would pass punitive trade policies if the Europeans did not back off on some objectionable policies of their own. The Europeans backed off, but the tariff remains. There is no constituency to remove it: American consumers haven't ever considered buying a European pickup, and so don't care; American producers don't want to see the birth of competition from European imports."

B

"Maybe so, Seth, but public perception here at home is important. Public sentiment calls for getting tough with other countries that have trade policies not to our liking. Why, some politicians are even threatening to build a third political party on a platform opposing free trade. I've got the reputation of Cindy Choi and this administration to think of, so I'm inclined to risk a hard line. Enough for now, though. I'm being signalled to appear at a photo op session with the winner of the Global Village Award."

PROSPECTING FOR NEW INSIGHTS

1. Explain why restrictions on sugar imports into the United States make little economic sense. Why do they survive the political process?

2. a. Do you think other countries are playing economic games with the U.S.? If so, what are the objectives? What strategies are used to achieve these objectives?

   b. Do you think that people in most countries believe that their countries are victimized by the other countries of the world? Explain whether such beliefs are justified and, if not, why the perception would exist.

CHALLENGE 1
The J-Curve—Taming Trade Deficits Takes Time

The U.S. trade deficit is due in part to government borrowing and other factors that attract foreign investment. These investment demands in turn increase demand for the U.S. currency, thus increasing its price. The resulting stronger dollar makes U.S. exports more expensive and imports cheaper.

The U.S. trade deficit would diminish if the dollar were to weaken. However, before that occurs, a weaker dollar would initially make the trade deficit larger. This phenomenon is known as the **J-curve**, because the time path of the balance of trade in response to a currency depreciation resembles the letter *J*, as shown in Figure 5C1-1. The J-curve also applies to the balance on the current account, which includes services as well as goods. The reason for this J-curve has to do with elasticities, specifically the elasticity of U.S. demand for imports, and of foreign demand for U.S. exports.

Figure 5C1-1 The J-Curve in response to a depreciating dollar shows that the trade deficit first rises due to more dollars being spent on higher-priced imports. Smaller import volumes and larger export volumes as time passes cause the deficit to decline later.

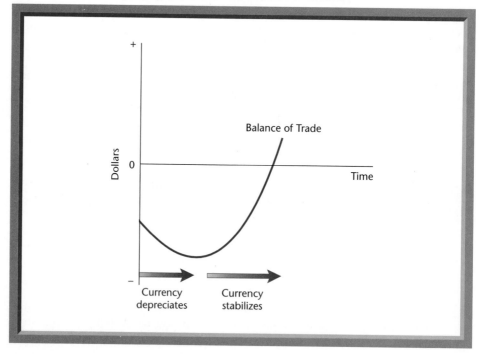

When the dollar depreciates, other countries will find U.S. goods and services cheaper. As they buy more, the U.S. receives more dollars for its exports. This effect improves the balance of trade. However, this improvement is gradual, since purchasing decisions are often made months or years in advance.

In the meantime, U.S. importers are forced to pay more dollars per unit for items that they import. This causes them to make plans to reduce the quantity that they import. Here, too, plans must often be made in advance. At first, U.S. importers will cut back a little. As time goes by, importers will be better able to line up alternative sources of their products or find U.S. products that substitute. U.S. producers will expand their operations in order to provide those substitutes, but this process takes time. Thus, quantities imported will drop slightly at first and more precipitously later. However, *spending* on imports will initially rise, as the increase in the price of imports more than offsets the decreased quantity. In other words, the demand for imports is initially inelastic.

The longer is the period of time involved, the more elastic is demand for imports. As the volume of imports shrinks over time, the number of dollars spent on imports also shrinks. Thus, as time passes, not only does the U.S. sell increasingly larger amounts of exports, but it also reduces its spending on imports as well. Over time, then, the balance of trade improves. It could even become positive, as is shown in Figure 5C1-1.

✓ QUICKCHECK

What would the J-curve look like in response to an appreciating currency?

Answer: The J-curve would appear upside down.

CHALLENGE 2
Identifying the Distributional Implications of Tariffs and Quotas

The government treasury gains revenues when a tariff is imposed on imports. Domestic producers also gain from an import tariff, since the tariff reduces competition from imports and thus allows for higher prices in the home market. By this same token, though, domestic consumers are worse off. Two gainers and one loser, it seems. Does this mean that an import tariff increases a country's well-being?

To answer that question, it is necessary to measure the value of the gains and losses. This measurement need not involve complex data collection. Rather, logic and a simple model are all that is needed. This model assumes that the U.S. is a **price taker** in the world market for some homogeneous good, such as peanuts. Being a price taker in this context means that changing the quantity of U.S. imports will not affect the world price of this product. The assumption of price taking implies that the U.S. faces a horizontal supply curve from the rest of the world, as shown in Figure 5C2-1. Note that the supply price from the rest of the world must be below the equilibrium price in the absence of

C

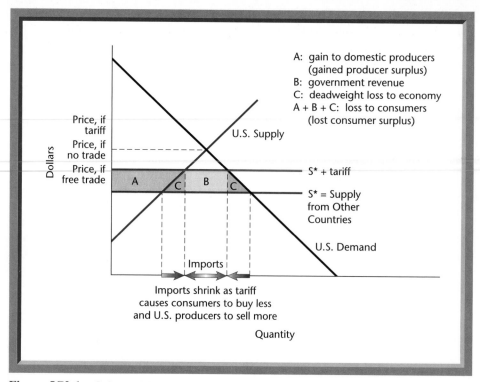

Figure 5C2-1   Gains and losses from a tariff on imports.

trade, given by the intersection of U.S. supply and demand. Unless the world price is lower, the U.S. would not import.

At the world price, U.S. producers will produce the quantity on the U.S. supply curve corresponding to that price, and U.S. consumers would buy the quantity demanded given by the demand curve. The difference is the amount that is imported. Consumers would not be willing to pay U.S. producers any more than the price they pay for imports, since the product is homogeneous and available from foreign producers at that price. When a tariff is imposed, the effective price of imports becomes the world price plus the tariff. This higher price causes U.S. consumers to cut back consumption and U.S. producers to increase production in response to that higher price. The difference comes out of imports, as shown by the arrows in Figure 5C2-1.

The higher price in the U.S. market causes U.S. producers to gain producer surplus equal to the shaded area *A*. Government receives tariff revenues corresponding to the quantity imported multiplied by the tariff rate. This amount equals the shaded area *B*. However, these two gains are more than offset by the loss of consumer surplus, equal to areas *A* + *B* + *C*. Area *C* comes in two parts, one corresponding to goods that are replaced by higher-cost domestic production, and the other to goods that are no longer purchased at all. Area *C* is referred to as **deadweight loss**, since it represents a loss of efficiency to the economy as a whole, rather than merely a transfer of benefits from one component of society to another.

C

The analysis in Figure 5C2-1 applies directly to a tariff. It also applies to import quotas that allow the same amount of imports as would have occurred with the tariff. With import quotas, however, government collects no tariff revenues. Instead, holders of import permits capture the difference between the world price and the higher domestic price. If government sells the permits to the highest bidders, it can collect this amount as public revenues. In this way, the effects of the tariff and quota can become equivalent.

C

Study by Design

SpeedStudy

SpeedReview

The balance of payments accounts measure a country's interaction with the rest of the world. Many people worry that a deficit in the merchandise trade sub-account means that jobs are lost to other countries. In fact, jobs are lost in specific industries, but not in the aggregate. The dollars the U.S. spends on imports, for example, never make it to other countries. Rather, they run into the foreign exchange market and bounce back into the U.S. as spending on U.S. exports or on investment in the U.S. The foreign exchange market balances currency flows through its market-equilibrium price, termed the exchange rate.

Often with little basis in economics, countries do choose to restrict trade with tariff and nontariff barriers. By signing the latest GATT revisions, countries agree to limit their protectionist policies and allow the World Trade Organization to enforce that they do. Countries are increasingly joining regional trading blocs that reduce trade barriers still further within those blocs.

SpeedStudy True or False Self-Test

A1. When Japanese investors buy U.S. golf courses, their purchases show up in the capital account of the U.S. balance of payments accounts.

A2. The statistical discrepancy is of small magnitude and little significance in the U.S. balance of payments accounts.

A3. The balance on the U.S. current account equals the dollar value of exported goods and services minus the dollar value of imported goods and services.

A4. The persistent U.S. trade deficit in recent years means that the number of U.S. dollars that have left the country and have not returned has risen dramatically.

A5. If foreign investors increase their investments in the U.S., the dollar is likely to appreciate.

A6. Tariffs bring in government revenues, but have no effect on the quantity of goods traded.

A7. Other countries would prefer that the U.S. negotiate import quotas rather than voluntary export restraints.

A8. Both VERs and import quotas drive up prices to U.S. consumers.

A9. A sugar import quota benefits producers of corn-based sweeteners.

A10. Economists usually call for greater restrictions on imports than politicians will agree to.

B11. In the absence of government protection, private investors are likely to support infant industries that promise to mature into profitable companies in the future.

B12. It is often difficult to determine in practice the extent to which imports or exports truly threaten national defense.

B13. U.S. sugar import quotas benefit U.S. consumers of sugar by lowering the price of sugar in the U.S.

B14. In international trade, game theory involves assessing the uncertain outcomes of alternative trade strategies.

C15. If a country's currency appreciates, the balance on its trade account will at first rise, and then fall.

C16. An appreciating dollar would cause the U.S. trade deficit to become larger initially, but shrink over time.

C17. When a price-taking country imposes an import tariff or other trade restriction, the gains to the country's producers will exceed the loss to the country's consumers.

C18. When a tariff is imposed on imports of gizmos by a price-taking country, both the country's gizmo producers and government treasury will benefit.

The MasterMind

Selected Terms along the Way

balance of payments
accounts, 163
current account, 163
merchandise trade
account, 163
services account, 164
balance of trade, 164
capital account, 165
exchange rate, 168
appreciation, 170
depreciation, 170
float, 171
tariff, 173

General Agreement on Tariffs
and Trade (GATT), 174
nontariff barriers (NTBs), 174
quota, 174
transparent, 175
voluntary export restraints
(VERs), 176
World Trade Organization
(WTO), 177
trading blocs, 178
North American Free Trade
Agreement (NAFTA), 178
trade creation, 178

trade diversion, 178
strategic trade initiatives, 179

infant industries, 180
venture capitalists, 180
dumping, 184
strategic dumping, 184
game theory, 187
terms of trade, 188

J-curve, 190
price taker, 191
deadweight loss, 192

MasterMind Multiple Choice Self-Test

A1. When an American firm invests overseas, this
action is

   a. a capital outflow.

   b. a capital inflow.

   c. not included in the balance of payments
   accounts.

   d. a merchandise export.

A2. International exchange rates

   a. are pegged.

   b. are freely floating.

   c. float, but the float is dirty.

   d. floated for awhile, but than sank.

A3. Currently, currency exchange rates are determined primarily

   a. in the marketplace.

   b. by the International Monetary Fund.

   c. by international gold flows.

   d. in accordance with the Bretton Woods
   agreement.

A4. Depreciation in a country's currency will
cause

   a. the country's exports to drop.

   b. an increase in the number of tourists visiting
   that country.

   c. windfall gains to speculators holding large
   quantities of that country's currency.

   d. widespread fear of contracting the disease,
   and hence a reluctance to accept payment in
   that currency.

A5. A voluntary export restraint (VER) can have the
same effects as an import quota, except that, unlike the import quota, the VER is likely to

   a. raise prices to domestic consumers.

   b. lower prices to domestic consumers.

   c. raise prices paid by importers.

   d. lower prices paid by importers.

B6. The Europeans have been accused of dumping
steel on the U.S. market. If true,

   a. U.S. producers of steel lose more than U.S.
   consumers of steel gain while the dumping
   occurs.

   b. the Europeans are pricing their steel sold in
   the U.S. below the price for which it is sold
   in Europe and possibly below cost.

   c. the U.S. need for steelmaking capacity during wartime clearly requires that retaliatory
   action be taken until this dumping is stopped.

   d. the quality of products made with dumped
   European steel is unreliable.

B7. Economists emphasize that the world gains the most when all countries

    a. allow free trade.

    b. prohibit all foreign trade.

    c. restrict imports but not exports.

    d. restrict exports but not imports.

C8. At first, if the dollar depreciates against the Japanese yen, U.S. consumers will import _____ Japanese goods, and pay _____ dollars for those imports.

    a. more; fewer

    b. fewer; more

    c. more; more

    d. fewer; fewer

C9. If the U.S. imposes a tariff on the import of tin, which of the following groups will lose?

    a. U.S. tin producers.

    b. The U.S. Treasury.

    c. U.S. producers of substitutes for tin.

    d. The U.S. economy as a whole.

MasterMind Questions and Problems

A1. a. The U.S. runs a trade deficit. Specifically, what does this mean? Briefly distinguish the trade deficit from the current account deficit.

    b. Suppose the U.S. decides to eliminate the current account deficit by prohibiting all imports and exports. Would this approach reduce unemployment in the U.S.? Explain.

A2. Suppose Japanese investors decide to cash in their U.S. investments. What would be the effect upon the exchange rate between the dollar and yen? Why would Japanese investors be unlikely to follow this course of action?

A3. The Arts & Entertainment Cable Network has advertised its monthly magazine at a price of $18 U.S., or $23 Canadian. Which is stronger, the U.S. dollar or the Canadian dollar? Why?

A4. Suppose the Federal government adopts the policy of "What's good for General Motors is good for the country." To this end, the government decides to prohibit the import of all motor vehicles from other counties. Assuming other countries do not change their own trade policies, what would be the impact on the value of the dollar relative to other currencies? What would be the effect on the quantity of other items imported?

A5. What purposes would be served by converting quotas or other NTBs into tariffs?

B6. a. Describe and evaluate the validity of the infant industry argument for protecting vulnerable domestic industry from foreign competition.

    b. Define dumping and evaluate the desirability of imposing antidumping tariffs when it is found to occur.

B7. Suppose you have been appointed trade advisor to the U.S. President. You are asked to brief the President on possible U.S. trade policy toward Japan, laying out the two best options available and the pros and cons of each. The President, being an intelligent person, can be expected to follow your reasoning and select his or her own course of action.

    a. Present your briefing on the first option.

    b. Present your briefing on the second option.

    c. In the course of your briefing, the President asks for your professional assessment of whether free trade is all to the good. What do you say?

C8. Graph and explain the J-curve. Be sure to label the axes of your graph.

C9. Suppose that, once sugar import quotas expire, the United States imposes a significant import duty on imported sugar. Using a graph of import demand and supply, explain the impact of this tariff. Who gains? Who loses? What is the net effect? Show any deadweight loss. What economic arguments could be used to justify this tariff? What arguments could be used to oppose it?

Future Explorations: Mapping out Term Papers

1. **The Evolution of Exchange Rates**
   In the past, countries have attempted to control the price of their currencies in terms of gold and other currencies. For example, the Bretton Woods agreement following World War II established a set of exchange rates, in which currencies were pegged to the dollar, and the dollar was pegged to gold. This paper describes that system and the forces that led to its collapse. The paper goes on to survey some arguments as to whether such a system can and should return to replace the current managed float.

2. **Free Trade in the Americas**
   This paper examines the evolution of hemispheric trade agreements, from the Free Trade Agreement between the U.S. and Canada, through the 1994 NAFTA, to the current status of trade in the Americas. The paper examines issues that were raised in debates over these agreements and attempts to assess whether these concerns were justified.

3. **International Economic Cooperation: Policies toward Atmospheric Ozone Depletion**
   Numerous industrialized countries are responsible for manufacturing products that lead to depletion of the world's ozone layer. This paper examines how countries have attempted to cooperate to resolve this problem, such as through the 1987 Montreal Protocol to phase out production of chlorofluorocarbons that form the ozone-attacking fluoride gas. The paper also looks at points of contention among countries. For example, nonindustrial countries argue that the industrialized countries should be spending much more to remedy the problem. In response, industrialized countries argue that the products are consumed in all countries, and thus the burden of change should be spread around.

Answer Key

ExpressStudy True or False	SpeedStudy True or False Self-Test		MasterMind Multiple Choice Self-Test
1. F	1. T	10. F	1. a
2. F	2. F	11. T	2. c
3. T	3. T	12. T	3. a
4. F	4. F	13. F	4. b
5. F	5. T	14. T	5. c
6. T	6. F	15. T	6. b
	7. F	16. F	7. a
	8. T	17. F	8. b
	9. T	18. T	9. d

$\mathcal{M}$*odule A*

$\mathcal{M}$*odule B*

$\mathcal{M}$*odule C*

A Look Ahead

Rockefeller, Iaccoca, Walton, Perot, Sony, Trump: the names are familiar. We read about them in the history books and in newspapers. They were, or are, just a few of the best known of the world's business leaders. Our familiarity with them illustrates the central role of business in the economy and in our lives.

Business firms can be small, large, or somewhere in between. They range from the neighborhood newspaper carrier to billion-dollar multinational corporations. As diverse as firms are, they share a common goal: profit. Profit allows a firm to survive. The survival instinct forces owners and managers to master various conceptual notions relating to revenue and cost. Business leaders who think in these terms are better able to succeed in their quest for profit. With this in mind, the firm must choose its structure and output, as we will examine in this chapter.

DESTINATIONS

*M*odule A

As you zip along the Expressway you will arrive at an ability to

- identify the legal forms and methods of financing a business;
- relate the significance of the law of diminishing returns;
- explain the rule of profit maximization;
- distinguish between economies and diseconomies of scale;
- analyze the effects of technological change and innovation.

*M*odule B

Upon leaving the Expressway to explore issues you will be able to

- recount some of the many hurdles new businesses must overcome;
- describe the lessons government can learn from its experience with farm policy.

*M*odule C

Mastering Roadside Challenges will allow you to hone analytical skills by

- deriving the relationship between a firm's input and output decisions;
- demonstrating the effects of price on a firm's profit and supply.

Firms take *inputs* of resources and produce *outputs* of goods and services to be sold in the marketplace. The desire for profit motivates firms to produce. This profit objective guides the legal, financial, and economic decisions firms must make.

Students can be viewed as producers, too. As a student you are not producing output for sale, so you can't be called a firm. But you do take resources and employ them in the production of an output. You purchase inputs of textbooks, paper, pencils, pens, and computer disks. You then combine them with the input of your time to produce outputs of new skills and knowledge.

Legal Form: Proprietorship, Partnership, and Corporation

A firm can choose to operate in one of the following three legal forms: sole proprietorship, partnership, or corporation. Which should it be?

Consider the personal implications if you open a business. If you commence in a less than formal fashion, you'll become a *sole proprietorship*—a business with a single owner. You may want to visit City Hall and file a dba (doing business as), which lets the public know that you are the operator of a business recognizable by the name you select for your firm. Or you might just print business cards and go. You can hire employees if you wish, but remember that you'll be legally liable for injuries caused to or by the employees acting in the course of their duties. You'll also be personally liable for all debts and taxes of the business. If your firm doesn't earn enough income from sales, you will have to raid your personal resources to pay off your creditors and the tax collector. You'll report the business' profits, if there are any, on your personal tax return.

If you can find one or more people with whom to start your business, you can form a partnership. *Partnerships* are similar to proprietorships. Each partner can hire employees. Each partner is also liable for business debts that the business is unable to pay. What if you don't wish to be responsible for the debts of your partner? Are you sure your partner is honest and trustworthy? If not, then form a *limited partnership*. Limited partners are liable only for the amount of their investment in the firm. If the firm earns profits, they are reported on each partner's personal tax return, along with a tax filing that provides information on the partnership.

To avoid the disadvantages of proprietorships and partnerships, many firms are formed as corporations. A **corporation** is a legal entity separate from the people who own, manage, and otherwise direct its affairs. Ownership and ultimate control are in the hands of stockholders, although working control is in the hands of a board of directors. Some of the members of the board of directors may also be stockholders. Corporations tend to be big business. While they account for only about 10 percent of businesses in the U.S., they earn over 80 percent of the revenues.

The major advantages to the corporate form of existence are *limited liability* and *perpetual existence*. Limited liability means that the owners are not personally liable for the debts of the business. In practical terms, if you choose to incorporate and the business fails, creditors cannot lay claim to your personal assets, such as your house or car. Perpetual existence means the corporation can outlive its owners, providing that it avoids dissolution through bankruptcy.

Corporations offer the most flexibility in raising funds because of the possibility of public offerings of shares of stock. When corporations distribute monies earned to their shareholders, these sums are called *dividends*. For a small business, filing fees, taxes, and other expenses that are required of new corporations could offset the advantages of incorporating.

OBSERVATION POINT: Taking Stock of Stocks

"Hey stockbroker, it's a hot tip! Buy me 100 shares of Intel Corporation at market. Do it now, before the price goes up!" Who is this eager investor buying from? It's not from Intel—it sells stock only occasionally, in large public offerings. No, the shares come from a stockholder who told another broker, "Get me out of Intel while the gettin's good!" Although portfolio adjustments may also be motivated by cash needs, risk adjustment, and other factors, buyers usually expect the price to rise, while sellers expect it to fall.

This is not your typical market transaction, in which both the buyer and seller gain. Rather, it is a gamble, the results of which will be apparent over time. The way to win at this gamble is for the investor to apply knowledge of the firm and its markets in a better way than other players in the stock market.

Want a little inside information to help you out? Here's a tip. They say that markets rise when excess cash is being poured into stock and fall when investors raise cash by selling stock. Don't you believe them! When buyers trade cash for stock, there must be sellers trading stock for cash. This is true each day, for each transaction, no matter what direction the market takes.

*A*lternative Methods of Finance

Firms have three basic sources of *financial capital*, the money needed to start or grow a business. Firms can

- **Use retained earnings**—funds the firm has saved;
- **Borrow**—by taking out bank loans or issuing **bonds**, promises to repay borrowed funds with interest at a specified future date;
- **Issue shares of stock**—but only if the firm is a corporation.

For small firms, which may have recently started up, access to the stock market is probably not an option. It is difficult for them to raise financial capital through the issuance of stock, because the costs of going public are high and most investors would find the stock too risky. Startup firms with the prospect of large profits in the future may turn to *venture capitalists*, persons or firms that specialize in providing money and advice to promising undercapitalized companies. However, most small firms must initially rely on the personal savings of their owners and their owners' friends and relatives. Larger firms have the option of attracting investors by going public with an initial public offering (IPO) of new shares of stock.

There are also differences in the availability of borrowed funds between large and small firms. Small firms have little hope of raising money by issuing bonds because investors would fear *default*, a situation in which a firm is unable to repay its debts. Large firms have easier access to the bond market at lower interest rates. The interest rate that a particular bond must offer to attract buyers depends in large part upon its rating by Moody's, Standard and Poor's, and other independent ratings services.

Businesses also seek loans from *financial intermediaries*, including banks, pension funds, insurance companies, credit unions, mutual funds, and finance companies. Many firms find bank credit to be essential, but sometimes hard to come by. For the most part, bank loans to businesses are short term. As such their primary function is to provide operating funds rather than investment dollars. Banks are sometimes willing to help finance small firms, especially when the firms can offer collateral for their loans. *Collateral* is something of value, such as real estate or equipment, which a firm pledges to turn over to the bank in the event of default.

When firms look to sources outside themselves for financing, they are said to be seeking *external funds*. Stocks, bonds, and loans provide external funds. Loans provide over 60 percent of external funds for U.S. business, with bonds providing about 30 percent and stocks about 2 percent. (Other sources of external funds provide the remainder.) External funds are not, however, the primary source of funds for firms. All the external sources of funds—including stocks, bonds, and loans—provide only about 25 percent of the funds that firms use.

Internal funds, also called *retained earnings*, are the monies that a firm earns and has left after paying all expenses, including taxes and dividends. Retained earnings make up the bulk of funds that finance U.S. firms, because retained earnings avoid the *transaction costs* associated with other methods. Thus, retained earnings are typically the cheapest way to finance operations.

While most firms use a combination of retained earnings and external funds to finance growth, there are exceptions. For example, White Castle Hamburgers started in the 1930s as a single store in Columbus, Ohio. True to its depression-era upbringing, it financed its growth into a multistate chain of frugal eating without using a penny of debt or other external funds.

*P*roduction and the Law of Diminishing Returns

The relationship between the amounts of inputs and the quantities of output a firm produces is called its **production function**. Firms employ numerous inputs. However, economists usually model the firm as if it employs only two inputs: labor and capital. Labor is mental and physical effort. Capital is in the physical sense, including buildings, tools, equipment, and machines. Economists often refer to the quantities of labor, capital, and output as unspecified units. It may be helpful to think of a unit of labor as an hour of work and a unit of capital as an hour's use of machinery.

Production and employment decisions are made by firms in either a long-run or a short-run context. In the **long run**, all inputs are *variable*, meaning that their quantities can be changed. In the **short run**, at least one input is fixed. The quantity of a *fixed* input cannot be adjusted. Capital is assumed to be fixed in the short run, while labor is assumed to be variable. Labor is variable because an increase or decrease in the number of hours of labor employed can typically be accomplished relatively quickly. Capital is fixed since it is difficult to vary many types of capital quickly.

Modeling production with only two inputs highlights the distinction between variable and fixed inputs. The implications pertaining to labor apply in the real world to any variable input, including variable capital inputs such as pencils and light bulbs. Likewise, the connotations for capital apply to any fixed input, including long-term employment contracts.

Short-run decision making by the firm focuses only upon the variable input. For instance, in your favorite supermarket, another cashier can quickly be put to work when long lines build up, assuming an idle cash register is available. The number of cashiers to put on duty is an example of a short-run decision about a variable input.

While the number of cash registers is fixed in the short run, the long run offers enough time to make adjustments. With a sufficiently long period of time available, a supermarket is able to add checkout lanes or even build a larger store. Hence, in the long run, both labor and capital are variable for a supermarket, factory, or any other firm.

When labor is combined with a fixed amount of capital, the additional output from additional units of labor is termed the *marginal product of labor*, or **marginal product** for short.

$$\text{Marginal product} = \frac{\Delta \text{output}}{\Delta \text{labor}}$$

where the triangle (Greek delta) represents difference. Distinguish this value from **average product**, which is the average quantity of output produced per worker, as follows:

$$\text{Average product} = \frac{\text{total output}}{\text{total labor}}$$

For example, consider a firm that increases its employment of labor from 100 workers to 101 workers and experiences an increase in total output from 50,000 units to 51,000 units. The marginal product is 1,000 units for the 101st worker. Average product for 100 workers is 50,000/100, which equals 500 units, and for 101 workers is 51,000/101, which equals approximately 505 units.

Notice that average product increased in the preceding example. Any average, including average product, changes in a predictable direction, depending upon the corresponding marginal value. Average product will increase when marginal product is greater than the initial average product, decrease when marginal product is less than average product, and remain constant when marginal product is equal to average product.

The relationship between averages and marginals is more general than just the relationship between average and marginal product. For instance, consider Joyce, who has an average grade of 82 in her economics course after having taken the first two tests. When she takes the next text, which is the marginal test, her average grade will increase if her grade is greater than 82 or decrease if it is less than 82. Her average remains the same if she gets exactly 82 on that third test.

Marginal product is subject to the **law of diminishing returns**, which states

> When additional units of labor or any other variable input are added in the short run, the marginal product of the variable input must eventually decrease.

The law of diminishing returns applies in the short run, implying that capital is fixed. Once a firm reaches the point of diminishing returns, each successive unit of labor will add less and less to total production. The law assumes that all labor is of equal quality, which signifies that diminishing returns occur for reasons other than those relating to labor quality. For example, when the 101st worker in the previous example has a marginal product equal to 1000 units of output, the law suggests that a 102d worker, who is just as intelligent, skilled, and energetic as the 101st, will nonetheless exhibit a marginal product of less than 1,000 units.

The explanation for the law of diminishing returns is found in the common-sense proposition that adding more and more labor to a fixed amount of capital reduces the amount of capital each unit of labor has to work with. Eventually, the effect of less capital per worker reveals itself in the form of diminishing returns.

For example, consider the Chance Clothing Company, a small clothing factory with only ten sewing machines. If the Chance family employs ten workers, each worker has one machine to operate. But if the number of workers is increased to twenty, the number of machines per worker is only one-half. The additional workers would have no capital of their own to work with and would probably be employed to unroll fabric and assist in other ways to help the machine operators work faster. Thus, while the total daily output of the factory would increase, the marginal products of the helpers would be less than that of the operators.

The principle of diminishing marginal returns applies to all types of businesses. Table 6A-1 and the corresponding Figure 6A-1 illustrate marginal and average product for Ali's King-of-Ribs Restaurant. Ali has a relatively small building. At first, marginal product rises because his employees can specialize. In Ali's case, the major specializations are the tasks of taking orders, cooking, and cleaning up.

After the third worker, there are fewer possibilities for specialization. Ali's restaurant has reached the point of diminishing returns. For example, the next three workers might "float," relieving the cashier of tending the drive-through window, helping with cleanup, or doing whatever other tasks seem most important at the time.

There is a danger from hiring too many employees. "Too many cooks spoil the ribs,"

TABLE 6A-1 *Marginal and Average Product*

Labor	Output (Q of meals/hour)	Marginal Product ($\Delta Q/\Delta L$)	Average Product (Q/L)
0	0	Undefined	Undefined
1	3	3	3
2	10	7	5
3	20	10	6.7
4	27	7	6.75
5	31	4	6.2
6	32	1	5.3
7	30	−2	4.3

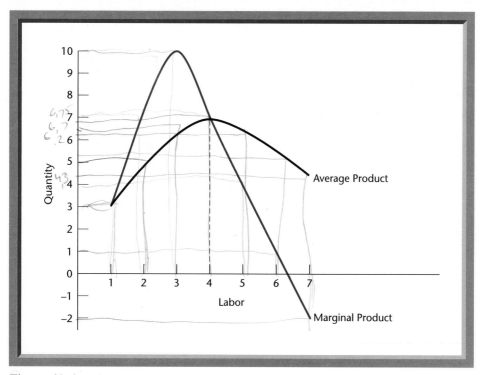

Figure 6A-1 **The marginal and average products of labor** are shown in their typical shapes.

Ali always says, as he imagines excess employees with little to do, chatting and getting in each other's way instead of attending to customers. Suppose Ali mistakenly continues to increase employment to seven workers while keeping his capital constant. In that event, he will reach *negative returns*, in which marginal product is negative. Because output is higher with fewer employees, firms seek to avoid negative returns.

Table 6A-1 and Figure 6A-1 summarize Ali's short-run production opportunities. Observe that marginal product intersects average product at the maximum point on average product but in the declining portion of marginal product. The reason is that average product is pulled up when marginal product lies above it and pulled down when marginal product lies below it.

✓ QUICKCHECK

Explain how a student faces the law of diminishing returns.

Answer: A student combines ability—an input that is fixed in the short-run—with the variable input of time. The output is knowledge as measured by an examination grade. When studying, a point is reached at which each succeeding minute of study time adds less and less to the student's knowledge. Sometimes students press their studying beyond diminishing returns and into negative returns, which start when an additional minute of continuous studying begins to result in mental confusion. Economics professors hear that excuse all the time: "I studied too much for the exam." If returns drop that far, get some rest to refresh your abilities, and try again later.

*T*he Goal: Profit Maximization

What do firms hope to achieve? The answer, "Make money!" is too vague. Certainly revenue, the income from sales, is necessary for the continued existence of a firm. But revenue is only part of the equation. Costs, the expenses a firm incurs, are equally important. **Profit** is the difference between *total revenue* and *total cost*, as follows:

Profit = total revenue − total cost

Economists usually assume that firms seek to maximize profit. Profits are an important source of funds for modernization and expansion that can keep a firm competitive. While a firm's managers might have motivations other than profit, firms that do not maximize profit are likely to be deserted by investors and find themselves in financial trouble. Managers that fail to maximize profit must also fear losing their jobs to shareholder revolts or takeovers.

The profit figures stated in corporate annual reports and in the news media are collected by accountants. Firms sometimes pull out of a particular business or operation even when it is profitable according to accounting data. When a copper mining company shut down its profitable mines in Bisbee, Arizona, in the 1970s, for example, its workers were outraged. Critics of the company bemoaned the heartless corporation that would dare throw so many people out of work, even when the mine was profitable. Clearly, the concept of accounting profit was not adequate to explain the company's decision. To explain this and other facets of business behavior, economists need a different method to measure profit than that used by accountants.

*E*conomic Profit and Opportunity Cost

The key to understanding why reportedly profitable firms sometimes go out of business is to recognize the distinction between accounting profit and economic profit. All costs measured by accountants are termed *explicit costs*. However, there are other costs, which accountants do not measure. Specifically, there are **implicit opportunity costs** associated with the value that the capital investments and entrepreneur's time would have in their best alternative uses.

Successful companies are well aware of their implicit costs. To judge whether it is allocating its investments wisely, for example, the General Electric Company requires each of its divisions to compute imputed interest on the factories, machines, and other capital that they possess. *Imputed interest* is an implicit cost because it measures the return the investment would have had elsewhere. When capital is found to have imputed interest that exceeds the value of its productivity, then economic profit would be higher if the capital is reassigned to another task. Imputed interest and other implicit costs are added to explicit costs to obtain total economic costs.

Consider an implicit cost at Alonzo's Big Time Chocolate Factory. Alonzo finished paying off the factory's mortgage on its building years ago. Although there is no monthly mortgage or other explicit cost associated with Alonzo's use of the building, implicit opportunity costs could be substantial. Suppose Alonzo receives an offer from another firm, Kandyland Kids, to rent the building for $1,000 per month. By turning down this sum of money and using the factory for his own operations, Alonzo incurs an implicit cost of $1,000 per month. If this offer is the best alternative use of the factory, its opportunity cost is $1,000. In practice, measuring implicit cost is difficult because alternatives are not always known with certainty.

Economic cost also includes economic *depreciation* over time, which is the loss of market value of capital caused by wear and tear, obsolescence, or other events. For example, if Alonzo originally paid $100,000 for his factory, but it could be sold today for only $70,000, then it has depreciated by $30,000. Accounting measures of depreciation are formulas meant to approximate economic depreciation. Approximations are needed because separately estimating the economic depreciation of a firm's every asset would be an extraordinarily expensive task.

The difference between total revenue and total economic cost is *economic profit*, or just *profit* throughout this book. When revenue exactly equals the sum of all costs, including implicit opportunity costs, the firm is said to be earning a **normal profit**. From an economic perspective, **normal profit is a cost.** A firm that earns normal profit will report a positive accounting profit, even though its economic profit is zero. The normal profit provides just enough revenue to compensate the firm's owners for the time, money, and other resources they have invested in the firm, as measured by the implicit cost of those owner-supplied inputs.

Accounting profit in excess of normal profit is called *excess profit*. **Economic profits are excess profits.** Alternatively, when revenue falls short of covering all economic costs, a firm incurs an *economic loss*, or just *loss* from here on.

✓ **QUICKCHECK**

Can you explain why the owners of the copper mine decided to close it?

Answer: Although the firm earned an accounting profit, it incurred economic losses. The firm's opportunity cost of keeping its capital tied up in the copper mine was the return that it could earn by selling those assets and investing the proceeds elsewhere. After closing the U.S. mine, the company invested in an overseas mine that offered higher expected profit.

OBSERVATION POINT: Michael Douglas and the Price of a Can of Coke

In the movie *Falling Down* it is clear that the main character, played by Michael Douglas, is having a "bad hair day." In one memorable scene, he walks into a seedy neighborhood grocery to place a call. When the store clerk abruptly refuses to provide change without a purchase, Douglas' character selects a can of Coke. "Eighty-five cents," barks the clerk. Douglas angrily responds that fifteen cents in change is not enough for a phone call. Tempers flare, and Douglas trashes the store, while furiously insisting that Cokes are worth only fifty cents.

Was the Coke worth eighty-five cents? No one forces customers to buy. If the store is making excessive profits, other "greedy" entrepreneurs would move into the neighborhood to get a share of those profits. Prices would fall. However, losses from shoplifting, vandalism, and robbery mean that the cost of doing business in high-crime areas can be substantial. Without the prospect of economic profit, new competitors stay away.

It appears that the customer is not always right. In this case he forgot the implicit cost of risk, which the price must cover. On a better day, perhaps he will remember his economics . . . and his telephone calling card.

Profit Maximization in the Short Run

What do Alonzo's Big Time Chocolate Factory, the Chance Clothing Company, and Ali's King-of-Ribs Restaurant have in common? If these businesses are to be profitable, their owners must pay attention to both revenue and cost.

A firm receives revenue by selling its output of goods or services. Total revenue is calculated by multiplying the quantity sold by the unit price. For example, when the Chance Clothing Company sells 5,000 T-shirts for $5 each, it earns $25,000 of total revenue. Costs arise when Chance acquires inputs, such as the services of labor, sewing machines, and fabric.

A Closer Look at Costs

In the short run, firms have both fixed and variable costs. A firm's **fixed cost** is associated with its fixed inputs. Total fixed cost remains constant regardless of the amount of production. For example, a firm will pay the same amount of property taxes, property insurance, rent, and executive salaries whether the firm produces its maximum output, produces nothing, or produces somewhere in between.

Variable cost increases as output rises and declines as output falls, because a firm's use of variable inputs varies directly with production. Raw materials costs, the wages of hourly labor, and shipping expenses are examples of variable costs. *Total cost* includes *total fixed cost* and *total variable cost*.

$$\text{Total cost} = \text{total fixed cost} + \text{total variable cost}$$

Observe some cost calculations performed by Wendy Webster, owner of WW Wholesale Flour. Wendy has calculated her total fixed cost to equal $200. If she produces six tons of flour, she will incur an additional $460 of total variable cost. Her total cost of producing six tons of flour would thus equal $660. By dividing total expenses by total output, Wendy calculates the per unit cost of a ton of flour to be $110. Per unit cost is called **average cost**, which equals total cost divided by the quantity of output.

$$\text{Average cost} = \frac{\text{total cost}}{\text{quantity}}$$

It may be that Wendy will produce and sell additional flour sometime soon. In that case she ought to be thinking about the amount by which total expenses will grow when she increases her output. In the short run, the amount of capital—the amount of floor space and the number of machines—is fixed. When Wendy spends more on labor and raw materials in order to increase output, the total variable cost of production will increase. **Marginal cost** is the additional cost of an additional unit of output.

$$\text{Marginal cost} = \frac{\Delta\text{total cost}}{\Delta\text{quantity}} = \frac{\Delta\text{total variable cost}}{\Delta\text{quantity}}$$

Note that the change in the total cost as quantity increases must exactly equal the change in the total variable cost. The reason is that total fixed costs do not change.

At some point Wendy will encounter rising marginal costs, because the smaller the marginal product of an additional worker, the greater the marginal cost of additional output. Thus the law of diminishing marginal product leads to rising marginal costs.

At WW Wholesale Flour, the additional cost of increasing production from six tons to seven tons will be greater than encountered when output was expanded from five tons to six tons. Table 6A-2 shows the effects on cost of marginal changes in output around six tons. While production increases by a constant one ton per row, total cost increases by a greater increment as output increases, thereby implying a rising marginal cost.

A

✔ **QUICKCHECK**

Explain why marginal cost must eventually rise.

_____

Answer: The law of diminishing returns means that a firm has to add a greater amount of variable input to expand production by one more unit, which means that input requirements rise for marginal units of output. Because inputs are costly, the marginal cost of output rises.

Decision Making at the Margin

WW Wholesale Flour is a type of firm called a **price taker**, which means that the firm has no choice but to sell its output for the going market price. Every additional ton of flour Wendy sells adds an amount of revenue equal to the market price of a ton of flour. This additional income is termed **marginal revenue**.

$$\text{Marginal revenue} = \frac{\Delta\text{total revenue}}{\Delta\text{quantity}}$$

Any time another ton is sold that has a marginal revenue greater than marginal cost, Wendy's profit will rise. Because Wendy has seen that marginal cost rises as output ex-

---

TABLE 6A-2 *Selected Costs for WW Wholesale Flour*

Output (Q per day)	Total Cost (TC)	Marginal Cost (ΔTC/ΔQ)	Average Cost (TC/Q)
4	$400	?	$100
5	$500	$100	$100
6	$660	$160	$110
7	$910	$250	$130

pands, she knows that a point will be reached at which the marginal cost of the next ton of flour will exceed its marginal revenue. When the marginal cost is greater than the marginal revenue, profit will fall. For example, if the market price is $160 per ton, ton five increases profit by $60 because the additional revenue equals the price of $160, while the offsetting additional cost is the marginal cost of $100. By a similar calculation, ton seven subtracts $90 from profit. Wendy can do no better than to produce six tons, exactly. This reasoning allows Wendy to identify the profit-maximizing quantity of flour to produce.

Rule of profit maximization:

Produce to the point where marginal revenue = marginal cost.

Some ideas deserve more emphasis than others. This is one. We've even taught it to Polly the parrot. Ask her how many crackers the cracker company will sell. **"Squawk! Marginal revenue equals marginal cost!"** Polly may not know much economics, but she knows the essential rule firms must follow to maximize profits. Whether they are price takers or not, firms will adjust output in accordance with her sage advice.

✔ **QUICKCHECK**

Why would a price taker expand production if the last unit it produced could be sold at a price that exceeded marginal cost?

_____

Answer: Every additional unit of production would add more to revenue than to cost (marginal revenue greater than marginal cost). The firm should keep producing until the equality stated in the rule of profit maximization is reached. These additional units would increase profit.

Marginal cost varies inversely with the marginal product of labor. The smaller the marginal product of an additional worker, the greater the marginal cost of additional output. By the same token, the lower is the average product of employees, the greater will be the average cost of the output that is produced. Thus, as can be seen in Figure 6A-2, the general appearance of the marginal and average cost curves is opposite to the corresponding marginal and average product curves shown in Figure 6A-1. The result is that marginal cost is shaped like the letter *J*, while average cost is shaped more like the letter *U*. Average cost is at a minimum where marginal cost intersects it.

Marginal revenue to a price-taking firm equals the going market price and is illustrated in Figure 6A-2 by a horizontal line. Equating marginal revenue to marginal cost leads to a profit-maximizing quantity of Q*. If average cost at this quantity is less than average revenue, given by the market price, the firm will earn a profit. If average cost at Q* exceeds price, the firm will incur a loss. Because Figure 6A-2 shows that price exceeds average cost at Q*, this firm is earning a profit.

Table 6A-3 summarizes the maximization of profit at WW Wholesale Flour, using the cost data in Table 6A-2. The final row in Table 6A-3 shows Wendy's *profit per unit*, which is defined as the difference between price and average cost. Average cost was calculated earlier as $110. By subtracting $110 from the price of $160, profit per unit is seen to be $50.

If changes in demand and supply cause the price to increase, WW's output could

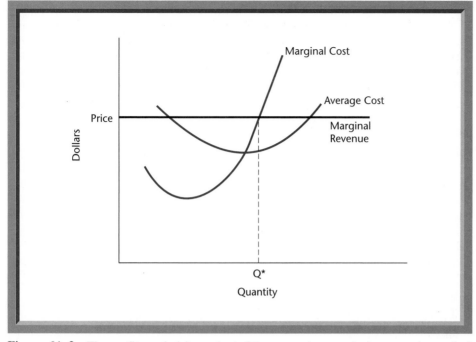

Figure 6A-2   The profit-maximizing output, Q*, occurs when marginal cost equals marginal revenue. For a price-taking firm, marginal revenue is identical to the market price. This firm is profitable, because price exceeds average cost at Q*.

change. By referring back to the data in Table 6A-2, it should be clear that an increase in market price to $250 or more would cause WW to expand production to seven tons. Wendy's total profit would then rise to $840.

Sometimes the maximum attainable total economic profit is equal to zero, a situation called break even. *Break even* occurs when the quantity that equates marginal revenue and marginal cost is also the quantity that causes total revenue to equal total cost. When a price-taking firm breaks even, price equals the minimum value of average cost. Graphically, break even would be shown by a price line tangent to the minimum point of

TABLE 6A-3	*Current Economic Data for WW Wholesale Flour, a Price Taker*
(1) Price per ton (market price)	$160
(2) Quantity (per day)	6 tons
(3) Total revenue	$960
(4) Total variable cost	$460
(5) Total fixed cost	$200
(6) Total cost	$660
(7) Total economic profit	$300
(8) Profit per unit	$50

the average cost curve. The quantity produced at break even would be the quantity associated with that minimum point on the average cost curve.

In general, the firm equates marginal revenue to marginal cost to determine its quantity. However, when price is so low that revenues are insufficient to pay variable costs, the firm can avoid paying those costs by cutting production to zero units. This process is called **shutdown**. To shut down means to cease production temporarily, leaving the firm with no output and no revenue. Since fixed costs must be paid even if the firm produces nothing, shutting down results in a loss that is equal to the firm's fixed cost. The *shutdown rule* is as follows:

Shut down when total revenue is less than total variable cost.

The shutdown rule identifies the *only* exception to the rule of equating marginal cost to marginal revenue. **Shutdown occurs in the short run.** If a firm incurs continuing losses, it will **exit** the industry, meaning that it will go out of business. This action is the opposite to the *entry* of new firms, which would occur if the industry appears profitable. **Entry and exit occur in the long run.**

✓ **QUICKCHECK**

What is WW's profit if price equals $100? What if price falls to $70? What if the price continues to fall?

Answer: If the price is $100, total revenue and total cost both equal $500. Profit would be zero, causing WW to break even. If price fell to $70, the profit-maximizing quantity would fall to four tons. This quantity would minimize the loss, which would equal $120. If price continued to fall, WW would lose more money, but not over $200, which is the point at which it would shut down.

OBSERVATION POINT: "Gifted Psychics" and Other Denizens of Late-Night Cable

What do Kenny Kingston, Ron Popeil, Anthony Robbins, and Cher have in common? Answer: They have all been stars of cable TV infomercials, those half-hour commercials disguised as talk shows and typically shown in the wee hours of the morning. Kingston claims to be "the official psychic to the Royal Family;" Popeil demonstrates the virtues of his Ronco food dehydrator; Robbins is a success guru; and Cher has pitched health and beauty products.

Is there magic at night that brings out this different side of television life? Actually, broadcasters have fixed costs that must be met whether they are on or off the air. Some stations do sign off. Others choose to compete for the small nighttime market. How do they profit when they cannot charge advertisers enough to cover the costs of producing a show? Let the advertisers turn their ads into their own shows, infomercials. Although the revenues are low, they are enough to cover broadcasters' variable costs, with a little left over to go toward fixed costs. So stay awake, night owls, to witness profit maximization in action.

The Long Run

The long run is the period of time it takes for all inputs to become variable. Since no production can occur without at least some fixed inputs, such as equipment and a place to use it in, the long run is also termed the *planning horizon*. The firm will choose among different technologies, requiring different proportions of various sorts of capital and labor.

Economies of Scale

When technology and cost conditions favor an increase in the scale of production, we say that the firm experiences **economies of scale**. *Scale* means the size of operations. Firms that produce on a large scale have a high volume of production. When the *cost per unit* drops as the firm proportionally expands its use of all its inputs, then economies of scale are present. For example, doubling the size of a firm might allow it to more than double the amount of output. That benefit would occur if the greater scale allowed more efficient use of inputs. The result would be a lower per unit cost—*long-run average cost*.

Diseconomies of scale result in increasing per unit cost of output as firm size increases. This condition may occur if the organization grows beyond a size that can easily be managed.

When all economies of scale have been achieved and diseconomies averted, the firm is said to experience **constant returns to scale**. There is usually a range of possible firm sizes that exhibit constant returns to scale. Within this range, a proportional change in all inputs leads to the same proportional change in output. For example, if this region of constant returns to scale is sufficiently large, doubling the amount of inputs will double the amount of output.

Price takers seek to reach constant returns to scale, because such firms have the lowest possible per unit costs, giving them a competitive advantage over other firms that have not achieved constant returns to scale. The relationship between the scale of production and possible economies, diseconomies, or constant returns to scale is illustrated in Figure 6A-3.

Suppose that Alonzo's Big Time Chocolate Factory faces fierce competition from other chocolate candy makers. As Alonzo's strategic planner, you are asked to recommend the most profitable course of action. Being an excellent businessperson, you begin thinking about adjusting the size of Alonzo's operations, including the size of the plant, the number of people employed, and the amounts of cocoa, sugar, and other raw materials Alonzo orders. As you contemplate expanding the scale of operations, you wonder

- Would a larger plant allow a more productive layout of machines?
- Can larger machines be found that produce chocolate more cheaply than current machines?
- Can jobs be broken down into a narrower range of tasks so that specialization of labor can be achieved?
- Will suppliers give discounts for the larger orders you will be placing in the future?

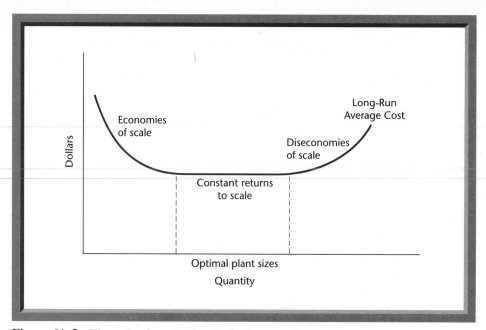

Figure 6A-3 **The scale of production.** In the long run, firms seek to minimize average costs.

Affirmative answers to any of these questions suggest that there are still economies of scale to be achieved; you have not yet reached constant returns to scale. A larger operation would lower your per unit costs. If the answers are negative, the factory should not expand. Indeed, if Alonzo's is in the range of diseconomies of scale, it should reduce its per unit costs by downsizing.

Innovation and Technological Change

Long-run average cost can shift down over time in response to innovation and technological change. Technological change—an advance in knowledge—often leads firms to adopt *innovations*, creative techniques that often embody advances in knowledge. Innovations change the way firms do business. Sometimes an innovation is implemented only by the firm that develops it; at other times innovation is diffused throughout the marketplace. The spread of technological change across firms takes time, because some firms will remain unaware of innovations or have doubts about their applicability.

Beginning in the late 1970s, for example, the technological change embodied in the new personal computers (PCs) presented firms with fresh choices. Imagine yourself managing an office at that time. The question foremost on your mind might have been, should we replace our typewriters with PCs? Electric typewriters were relatively cheap and easy to use. The new PCs offered enhanced productivity of typists, but were expensive and required extensive training to use. Would PCs be cost-effective? You would have to decide. Such decisions involve risk because uncertainty is a fact of life in business.

Innovation may focus on the production process or on the product. Some innovation, like computerizing an office, affects the production function by increasing the quantity of output or reducing the amount of inputs employed. Other innovation creates new products and markets. For instance, the invention of silicon chips made personal computers feasible, thus creating by 1995 the single most important product in home electronics.

In choosing whether to adopt new technologies, the same principle applies as in any business decision. The goal is to maximize profit. If a firm expects the marginal revenue from an action to exceed its marginal cost, the rule says, "Do it!" If not, don't.

OBSERVATION POINT: An American in Tokyo

Next to the Emperor, U.S. citizen W. Edwards Deming was quite possibly the most honored person in post-World War II Japan. That's because he taught that nation's industrialists the value of statistical quality control. As a consequence of his vision, the label "Made in Japan," which had previously identified shoddy goods, came to be associated with world-class quality.

Ironically, for years Deming's principles were ignored in the U.S. His focus on quality rather than quantity and on the long run rather than the short run was at odds with the teaching of more popular management gurus in the U.S. However, by the time of his death at the age of 93, Deming had lived to see his philosophies permeate the executive suites of U.S. business. That's an innovation for which all consumers can be thankful. Today, in his honor, the U.S. Commerce Department bestows the prestigious Deming Award upon firms that exemplify Deming's commitment to quality.

A

EXPRESS STUDY TRUE OR FALSE

1. Partnerships obtain financing by issuing shares of stock. *[handwritten: ONLY CORP.]*
2. The value that a firm's capital would have in alternative uses is called an ~~explicit~~ cost. *[handwritten: IMPLICIT]*
3. Marginal cost measures the increase in costs that results from an increase in output.
4. To maximize profits in the short run, a firm must always minimize average costs.
5. If total revenue is below total variable cost, a firm loses the least money if it shuts down.
6. Diseconomies of scale result in higher per unit costs.

[handwritten margin notes: PRODUCE TO THE POINT AT WHICH MC. COSTS = MR, WHETHER OR NOT THIS OUTPUT MIN. AVG. COSTS]

Module B
EXPLORING ISSUES

EXPLORATION 1
Mind Your Own Business—Start Up a Firm in the Land of Opportunity

---

Starting a business requires courage. It also requires the making of many choices and the surmounting of many problems. For example, as businesses grow, they confront the problem of incentives within the organization that may conflict with the firm's goals of maximum profit.

Acting as an Entrepreneur?

Act 1: Scene 1

Graduation Day! Your emotions are running high. You've wished for this day for four long years. As you climb on stage to receive your diploma, the cheers of family and friends ring loudly through the auditorium. Sheepskin in hand, the world a dizzy blur, you grin broadly as you retake your seat surrounded by fellow college graduates. However, a nagging thought flashes quickly across your mind as you subconsciously note the seemingly endless number of black-robed, freshly-minted alumni. You wonder how many of them already have jobs. How many college graduates did the placement office say were turned out every year? Oh yes, 1.1 million in the spring graduation of 1993 alone.

Act 1: Scene 2

Party time! Only days ago you were just a college student struggling with final exams. Now you're the centerpiece of your own graduation party. You should be having fun, but you're not. Previously unknown fears are creeping into your very soul. Fears of the consequences of unemployment. You don't have a job. Not that you haven't tried. What were you told at the placement office? Something about a slow economy; too many graduates. Oh well. There's time to think of such things later. Your friends and family are urging you to open your presents. Forcing a smile, you turn toward the pile of brightly wrapped gifts. Oh no! Why did the DJ hired for the party have to play the old 50s song "Get a Job" at this exact moment?

Act 2: Scene 1

One full month has passed since graduation. No job yet. What to do? The seed of an idea has been sprouting in your fertile mind. It's too daring a concept to speak out loud. Surely people will laugh. Become an entrepreneur? Start your own business? No, the idea is simply too wild.

*I*t's Time to Decide

No more play-acting—you take the plunge! Unemployment is not for you. You will create your own job by starting your own business. You write great computer software, are a fabulous cook, and your college years have trained you for a career in business. Economists would say that you've built a healthy stock of *human capital*, the skills and training embedded within you. Of course, while the U.S. is the land of opportunity, those opportunity costs could be significant. But for you, the opportunity cost of entrepreneurship is giving up the daytime soaps on TV that you've become unwittingly hooked on during your spell of unemployment. Giving up the soaps is a cost you're willing to pay.

While you possess human capital, your financial capital is limited. Before you write your business plan, a document you will use to convince others that your ideas for your business are sound, you must ponder the question of how to raise funds. The amount of start-up capital you require will, of course, depend upon the type of business you wish to operate. So the first consideration for you involves questions relating to entry. You will think twice about industries with significant *barriers to entry*. These are things that reduce the survival rate of new firms and make it extra difficult to start a new business.

For you, deciding what to do is easy. Your cooking, computer, and business skills have convinced you that developing and marketing computer software designed to teach people how to cook will lead you into the entrepreneur's hall of fame. You plan to call your firm Cooking with Computers. Congratulations! According to the Entrepreneurial Research Consortium, you'll be joining the seven million people (4 percent of U.S. adults) who try to start a business at any point in time. Because many who try do not succeed, only 706,537 new businesses actually started in the U.S. in 1993. You refuse to think about the hall of shame, though. A total of 86,133 businesses failed that year.

*S*ocial Responsibilities: What Are They?

Your first thoughts as an entrepreneur concern your social responsibilities. Some firms donate money or employee time to nonprofit organizations whose interests may focus on the environment or the homeless, for example. You remember a question raised in your college economics class: "Would you approve of this practice if you were a shareholder in such a firm?" This is a normative question.

Normative economics is addressed to what ought to be, and people's opinions in such matters can differ. Therefore, it should not be surprising that economists fall into two camps on the social responsibility of business. The majority view is that the greatest responsibility of business is to maximize the amount of profit the firm earns while letting the shareholders make individual decisions about how much they wish to contribute to their favorite causes. A second opinion is that businesses are in a leadership position and are able to be better informed about social problems than are individuals. This approach empowers business with the responsibility to promote the social good.

A person's views on this issue depend upon more than simply how much the person cares about a particular set of social problems. Many people who wish to see business act in accordance with profit maximization might care very deeply about social issues. Nonetheless, they may oppose the notion of business involvement in social issues on the grounds that businesses are not any better equipped than individuals to make these decisions. On the other hand, should not business lead by example? You decide to save that thought, and direct your attention to earning the profit that would make such questions relevant.

The Principal-Agent Problem

You aim to get big. You will have many employees and managers to guide them. Unfortunately, you will be forced to cope with the **principal-agent problem**. This problem exists because of the difficulties of making managers, who are called agents, act in perfect accord with the will of principals, the shareholders. While the old homily, "If you want something done right, do it yourself," may be useful to those who have the time and the skills necessary to apply it, there are situations when everyone lacks either the skills or the time to get something done. In a business setting, agency costs can reduce profits. The owners may not be aware that profits are not as large as they should be and that agency costs are the cause.

How do hired managers impose agency costs on a firm? There are several potential sources. When the owners *delegate* a job, meaning that someone is assigned the responsibility of performing a task with some goal in mind, communication between the parties may fail. The owners may know exactly what they want done, but communicating that knowledge to someone else may prove difficult. The problem could be at either end. The owners may not express themselves well. The agent to whom the job is being delegated may not be a good listener. Whatever the shortcomings of the two parties, its essence is the failure to communicate.

A second problem facing the owners is selecting someone who has the abilities to perform the job. *Imperfect information* about the abilities and skills of agents means that an agent may be selected who is incapable of performing all of the required tasks.

Another source of agency costs arises from differences in the interests of agents and principals. It is not hard to see how profit, the major interest of the principal, might conflict with a multitude of agent's interests. For example, managers may spend the firm's money in ways that contribute little to the revenue of the business. Company-paid country club memberships, first-class travel arrangements, a company jet, a limousine and chauffeur, and expensive office furnishings that add nothing to profit will be purchased if the agent can convince the principal that such spending is productive. What labor economists call *shirking*, but most everyone else refers to as goofing off or laziness, is also likely to become part of the agent's regular behavior.

As important as the principal-agent problem is, it is no surprise that solutions, however imperfect, have been devised to minimize its consequences. One avenue open to the owners is to keep a close eye on the agent's activities. But time spent on monitoring has an opportunity cost. There will be less time to spend on other activities of importance to the principal.

The principal might decide to share ownership of the company with the agent. It is not uncommon for executives to receive part of their compensation in the form of stock in the enterprise. The theory behind this strategy is that the harder and more effectively agents work, the more their stock will be worth. This makes their interests and the interests of principals coincide more closely. But will their interests match completely? It is doubtful because so much of the success of a business is outside the control of any one agent. So shirking is not likely to be eliminated altogether.

Most compensation plans that award stock do so in relationship to the firm's performance. But all such **incentive pay** is not in this form. Cash bonuses are another possibility. Whatever the nature of the scheme, its purpose is to bring everyone's interests into closer alignment.

If your business faced the task of devising a scheme of incentive pay as a reward for exemplary performance, how would you measure such performance? If sales doubled in the previous year, would managers deserve bonuses? Not if your competitors' sales tripled! If your company's stock doubled in price, but the overall stock market had tripled, would a well-designed plan of compensation award bonuses to your managers? The point is that markets are often competitive. Only with carefully selected benchmarks is it possible to interpret performance.

*T*he Businessperson as Hollywood Villain

You are ready to take the plunge, but find yourself curiously reluctant to admit it to your family. After deep soul searching, you fathom why. It's the media! It occurs to you that the bad guys in movies and TV shows are often written into scripts as evil, corrupt, greedy businesspeople. You think of J. R. Ewing, the conniving oilman on the long-running "Dallas" series. The implications of such stereotypes disturb you.

You refuse to be swayed by unreasonable prejudices. You know that a society that disdains businesspeople as too selfish risks killing the goose that lays the golden eggs. You've seen that living standards rise where the spirit of business enterprise is strong. Successes in Taiwan, Singapore, and the other emerging tigers of Asia spring to your mind.

Seeking profit in business is not a **zero-sum game**. In zero-sum games, the winner wins only what the loser loses. In contrast, business is a *positive-sum game*, offering the reward of profit to firms that are best at responding to consumer wishes. Positive-sum games offer everyone the chance at benefits, although not necessarily equally. Why does society put black hats on the heads of businesspeople? Is it envy? Then again, some of the biggest paychecks in the world go to Hollywood entertainers who scorn the success of others in business.

*T*o Action!

There is so much to understand; there are so many problems to anticipate, so many decisions to make . . . and you haven't even opened for business yet! You have yet to acquaint yourself with the details of labor law, health and safety regulation, affirmative action, fixed and variable costs. . . . The task is daunting, but wait! You remember your hero, Indiana Jones, and how he survived the life-threatening challenges in *The Temple of Doom*. "If Indiana can prevail," you say to yourself, "I can, too. Onward, the perils of business await!"

B

1. How would you go about deciding what kind of business to start? Where would your start-up financial capital come from?
2. What is your attitude toward the social responsibility of business? For example, should businesses contribute to charity, or is that a personal decision?

EXPLORATION 2
Adjusting to Technological Change—Lessons from the Family Farm

Despite costly subsidies paid to farmers, family farming has continued its steady decline. Rather than teach farmers how to survive, government might learn from farmers about how to cope with its own problems.

The country, indeed much of the world, is fed by crops grown on American farms. You might think that farmers would be handsomely rewarded for keeping the rest of us from starvation. Some farmers are wealthy. They are the survivors of an exodus from farming that has seen the farm population dwindle from 30 percent of the U.S. population in 1920 to less than 2 percent today. Even so, we have seen various events organized to raise money to ease the financial pain felt by the many smaller farmers who must struggle to stay afloat.

Competitive pressures in the marketplace have brought about this disturbing state of affairs. Have government policies helped or merely compounded the problems? There are lessons to be learned down on the farm, lessons that concern the adjustments of markets to technological change. Change is necessary, but disruptive. The sturdy farmer has faced it directly. Government, too, has learned from those experiences.

*F*arm Aid—Willie Nelson and Company Didn't Get There First

In recent years, singer Willie Nelson assembled the major stars of country music to perform concerts under the Farm Aid banner. The purpose of these shows was to raise money to promote family farming. It would seem that everyone admires such activities. Only the heartless could ignore the sight of farmers and their families packing up their belongings and moving from foreclosed farms. It's more than a job that is lost; it's a way of life, one that lots of city folks admire.

There is a puzzle, though. Aid for American farmers has been around for many decades. Franklin Delano Roosevelt's New Deal of the 1930s aimed to solve some of the same problems that continue to plague the farm sector today. Other farm programs even predate the New Deal era. Despite government farm aid, though, problems continue to plague the family farmer.

*F*ewer Farm Families, More Food

Sometimes markets work so well that old problems are replaced by new ones that are just as troublesome as the old. In farming the problem is too much good land. It is easy, but not quite correct, to think of land as a fixed resource. After all, there are only so many acres of land. Unless the U.S. follows the example of the Netherlands and reclaims land from the sea, there is no possibility of increased supplies of land. Although it might seem as if the supply curve of land should be drawn as a vertical line, this reasoning ignores improvements to the quality of the land, its ability to produce crops. Achieving this improvement is what agricultural research, much of it sponsored by the federal government, is often about.

Such government-sponsored research has proven quite successful at raising crop yields. The supply of high-quality farmland can also be increased through the scientific application of modern fertilizers and through crop rotation practices. But technological change on the farm embodies much more.

Industry has also provided for the farmer. A generation or two ago it was the faithful mule that supplied the power to prepare soil for planting. Today, mules have largely been replaced by tractors. Other kinds of more specialized mechanical planting and harvesting equipment have also been introduced over the long run. The effect has been to increase the productivity of the farmer. The same number of hours spent farming result in more farm output as productivity rises.

Technological change has also included the development of new crop varieties. Better seeds mean more food even if nothing else changes on the farm. Every technological improvement shifts the supply curve of food to the right, *ceteris paribus*.

Many kinds of farming approximate **purely competitive** markets, in which all firms must sell at the same market price, despite some of them having cost advantages over others. The result of pure competition is that technological change affects farmers in varying ways. Some farmers will find it easy to adopt new techniques: others will not be able to do so without difficulty. The first group will profit, even as the second group suffers. Those farmers who are unable to sell their crops at the market price without suffering economic losses will, in the long run, be forced to leave their farms.

For example, farmers in the choppy hills of Tennessee are at a disadvantage to their counterparts in the Kansas plains when it comes to employing the modern technology of huge combines and other types of farm equipment. Yet, if they produce the same product, they must sell it for the same price. As technological change takes hold, that price drops. Farmers must adopt the changes or exit the industry.

*C*orporate Farming—Can Government Fight Economies of Scale?

Tragedy for one family can be opportunity for another. When one family stops farming or moves off the farm, an opportunity is created for another to expand its operations by buying or leasing the land. As evidence, the average number of acres per farm has been increasing steadily during the twentieth century, rising from 146 acres in 1900 to 461 acres in 1990. Other aspects of the farm problem can be understood by referring to data on farm income, population, and productivity, as shown in Table 6B2-1. Note the ups and downs in farm income. These fluctuations make it difficult for small farms to keep going. Also note the uptrend in productivity, reflecting technological improvements.

Even though farms disappear, farmland is usually not abandoned. Rather, it becomes part of someone else's farm. When one farmer loses money working a particular piece of acreage, why should another farmer be able to take it over and earn a profit?

An important reason is economies of scale in farming, such as those associated with the use of large-scale equipment, which causes the average cost of farm output to decrease as farms grow larger. For example, farmers waste less time maneuvering their combines when their fields are large. This means that a bushel of corn, wheat, or other commodity can be produced at a lower per unit cost on large farms. Economies of scale are identified with the downward sloping part of the U-shaped long-run average cost curve. Economies of scale do have limits, though. Since bringing in the crop and equipment uses time and fuel, fields that extend too far can lead to diseconomies of scale, in which average costs rise.

Then there is government aid to consider. Government programs to help farmers have had a triple focus. To put more income into the hands of farmers, government has (1) restricted the supply of farm output to drive up crop prices; (2) increased demand by seeking out new markets for agricultural commodities, especially overseas markets, to increase prices of those goods; and (3) set prices of farm outputs above market equilibriums through agricultural price supports, which are maintained through *deficiency payments* that compensate farmers for the difference between the support price and any lower market price.

TABLE 6B2-1 *Farm Income, Population, and Productivity, 1979–94*

Year	Net Farm Income (billions of dollars)	Farm Population (millions of persons)	Productivity Index—Farm Output per Unit of Farm Labor
1979	$27.4	6.2	89
1980	16.1	6.1	89
1981	26.9	5.9	98
1982	23.8	5.6	100
1983	14.2	5.8	92
1984	26.1	5.7	104
1985	28.8	5.4	114
1986	31.1	5.2	117
1987	38.0	5.0	121
1988	37.5	5.0	111
1989	45.0	4.8	121
1990	44.8	4.6	126
1991	38.4	4.6	125
1992	47.9	NA	141
1993	42.1	NA	133
1994	46.7	NA	NA

Source: 1996 Economic Report of the President, Tables B-93, B-95, and B-96, NA = not available.

To use agricultural price supports to keep every farmer in business would require a price of output that would provide even the highest cost producer with at least a normal profit. Consider the three graphs in Figure 6B2-1. Farmer A is the low-cost producer, farmer B the medium-cost producer, and farmer C the high-cost producer. Don't forget that each cost curve includes an allowance for the farmer's implicit opportunity cost.

Farmer C may be the high-cost producer because he or she has higher explicit costs arising from poorer quality of land or poor management skills. Farmer C might also have excellent opportunities for earning income off the farm. In that case, farmer C's higher costs result from higher implicit opportunity costs. To keep farmer C farming, the government would have to manipulate prices so that all of farmer C's costs are covered by price. In the process, farmers A and B would grow wealthy on excess profits.

There are several objections to crop prices that keep all farmers farming. For one thing, consumers have to pay the higher prices. Since food is a necessity, high food prices hit the poor the hardest. For example, according to an analysis by Public Voice for Food and Health Policy, agricultural price supports added 33 cents to the price of a jar of peanut butter and 18 cents to the price of a gallon of milk in 1995. In total, price supports are estimated to have cost consumers an extra $4.5 billion dollars per year, most of which went to large operations rather than to small family farms.

Another problem concerns where to draw the line at government efforts to help people whose incomes are not enough to keep them in their present line of work. For example, many college professors find it difficult to support a family on their earnings. Should the government institute policies to increase college tuitions so that professors can be paid more? College students would be well aware of the costs. In general, the incomes of any category of producers cannot be raised without costs to others in society.

Since agricultural price supports are so expensive, why doesn't the government simply eliminate price supports, and replace them with subsidies to needy farmers? Actually, the Freedom to Farm Act of 1996 does just that. After 63 years, government has chosen to abandon most efforts to support prices and restrict supply. Farmers can grow what is most profitable and plant as much acreage as they wish, unlike under the system of price

B

Figure 6B2-1   Low-cost, medium-cost, and high-cost farmers.

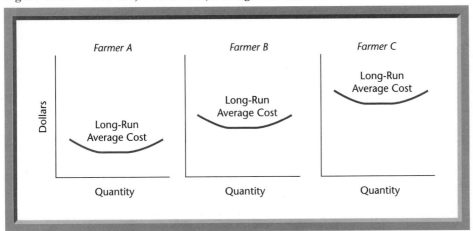

supports. However, supports for peanuts, sugar, and dairy products were left in place by the act. Furthermore, when the act expires in 2002, price supports are scheduled to be reimplemented, unless additional action is taken in the interim.

*W*hat Washington Has Learned from the Heartland

Over six decades of price supports failed to stop the exodus from the farm. For this, we should be grateful. If 30 percent of Americans were still to live on farms, as was true in 1920, many goods and services that we enjoy consuming would simply not be available. People would be growing food instead of, for example, assembling cars, building houses, and making movies. Besides, people frequently prefer to live in cities, suburbs, and small towns rather than on farms. We can take comfort that many of those who left farming did so because of attractive job opportunities elsewhere.

The history of government farm policy has been to fight the market, which has been telling us there are too many farmers. Until 1996, government chose to ignore the market's message. If government truly had wished to keep farmers on the farm, it would have been better served to outlaw all technological change in farming. If farmers were forced to stick with the farming techniques of a century ago, the country would need many more farmers today. That policy alternative is, of course, ridiculous. Still, government policies have prolonged the pain of market adjustment, and in the process forced us all to pay more for breakfast, lunch, and dinner.

In farm policy, as in the case of many other government policies, Washington has a choice to make. It can fight the market or work with it. Fighting the market means trying to stop or slow down the changes that occur as markets evolve. Working with the market means accepting change, but trying to ease the pain experienced by those who are adversely affected by that change. When to back off is a lesson learned the hard way by many onetime farmers. The recent changes in farm policy suggest that government lent an ear.

B

PROSPECTING FOR NEW INSIGHTS

1. Identify some technological advances that have changed the face of farming. Were these good for farmers? Why did they adopt them? Explain.
2. Do you view government's long-term efforts to help farmers as more a failure or more a success? What policies toward farming would be best? Should these policies be applied to other occupations also? Explain.

CHALLENGE 1
Relating Production to Cost

A firm uses a combination of resource inputs to produce an output. Specifically, output is a function of the quantities of capital and labor employed. This production function will vary among firms, depending upon the types of outputs they produce.

In the short run, the firm can vary only its labor input. This special case of the production function is known as the firm's *product curve*, because it can be shown easily by a two-dimensional curve that relates total labor input to the quantity of output produced. The Expressway section introduced the marginal and average product curves. These curves imply a **total product** curve similar to that shown in Figure 6C1-1. The slope of the total product curve equals marginal product. For example, the ranges of increasing, decreasing, and negative marginal product are each noted in this figure.

Figure 6C1-2 reverses the axes of Figure 6C1-1 to show the labor requirements for

Figure 6C1-1 **The total product of labor** shows output as a function of labor inputs, holding capital fixed.

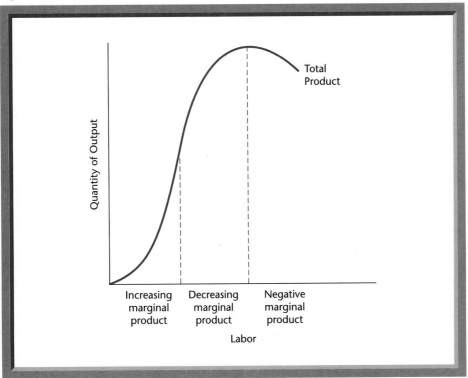

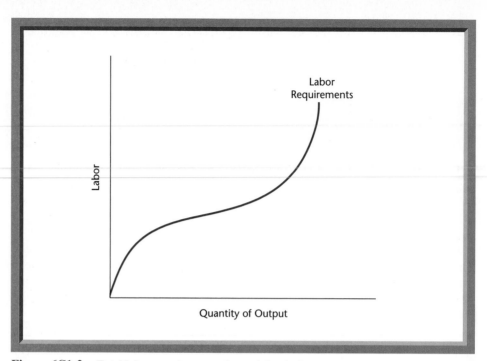

Figure 6C1-2 **Total labor requirements** for each level of output are revealed by looking at the total product curve from a different perspective.

any given level of output. The relationship between labor and output in these two figures is identical. The labor required to produce any particular amount of output, when multiplied by the cost per unit of that labor, reveals total variable cost. When the price per unit of labor is the wage rate, then total variable cost is the wage rate multiplied by the quantity of labor. As seen in Figure 6C1-3, the shape of total variable cost is identical to that of the labor requirements curve in the prior figure. The only difference is that the vertical axis is now denominated in dollars rather than units of labor.

Figure 6C1-3 also shows total cost and total fixed cost. Total fixed cost is constant at all outputs. Thus, when total fixed and variable costs are added, the total cost curve appears as nothing more than a vertical displacement of total variable cost. This means that **the slopes of both total cost and total variable cost are identical. These slopes equal marginal cost.** Marginal cost first falls and then rises, as shown in Figure 6C1-3.

Figure 6C1-4 shows typical marginal cost, average cost, and average variable cost curves, where *average variable cost* equals total variable cost divided by output. Marginal cost intersects both average cost and average variable cost at their respective minimum points. The reason these minimums do not occur at the same outputs is that *average fixed cost*, equal to total fixed cost divided by output, declines as output increases.

Average cost = average fixed cost + average variable cost

$$\frac{TC}{Q} = \frac{TFC}{Q} + \frac{TVC}{Q}$$

C

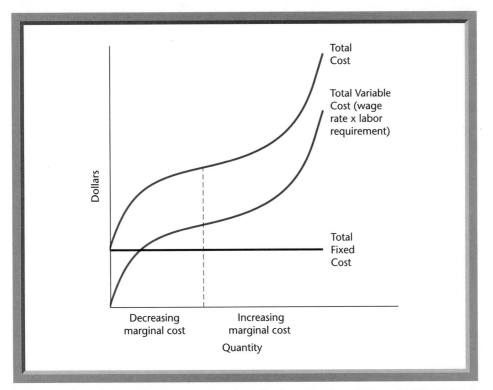

Figure 6C1-3   The total cost curve adds total fixed and total variable costs. Marginal cost is the slope of either total cost or total variable cost.

Figure 6C1-4   Typical shapes of marginal cost, average cost, and average variable cost will be as shown. Average fixed cost is the difference between average cost and average variable cost.

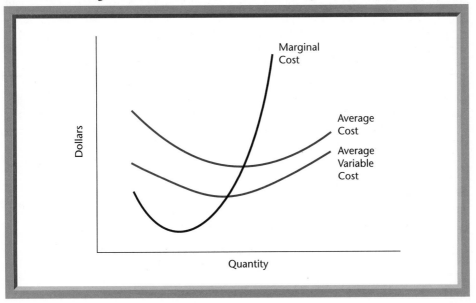

Table 6C1-1 expands Table 6A-2 in the Expressway to illustrate how to compute the various cost measures. Notice that average variable cost starts to rise before average cost, because average fixed cost is constantly declining as output increases.

A little more algebra reveals the inverse relationship between marginal cost and marginal product and between average variable cost and average product. Whatever wage is being paid for the marginal unit of labor, when divided by the output of that labor, reveals the marginal cost per unit of output. Thus the lower is marginal productivity, the higher is marginal cost.

For example, if a firm pays $10 for an extra hour of work and the worker produces five widgets in that hour, the marginal cost per widget is $2. If marginal product falls to four widgets per hour, marginal cost rises to $2.50.

$$\text{Marginal cost} = \frac{\text{wage rate}}{\text{marginal product}}$$

Dividing the wage rate by average product reveals the average variable cost of output. If the wage rate is $10 and the average product is six widgets, for example, the average variable cost of producing a widget would be $1.67. Average variable cost varies inversely with average product.

$$\text{Average variable cost} = \frac{\text{wage rate}}{\text{average product}}$$

TABLE 6C1-1	WW's Costs in Detail (all costs stated in dollars)						
Output (Q)	Total Cost (TC)	Total Fixed Cost (TFC)	Total Variable Cost (TVC)	Marginal Cost (ΔTVC/ ΔQ)	Average Cost (TC/Q)	Average Variable Cost (TVC/Q)	Average Fixed Cost (TFC/Q)
4	400	200	200	?	100	50	50
5	500	200	300	100	100	60	40
6	660	200	460	160	110	76.67	33.33
7	910	200	710	250	130	101.43	28.57

C

A firm seeks to maximize profit, where profit equals total revenue minus total cost. Profit is driven by costs and by price. It is useful to express profit in terms of price, since price is the most widely reported feature of the marketplace. *Ceteris paribus*, profits and prices move in the same direction.

If a firm sells all of its output at a single price, that price is the firm's *revenue per unit* of that output, otherwise known as **average revenue**.

$$\text{Average revenue} = \frac{\text{total revenue}}{\text{quantity}} = \text{price}$$

Multiplying average revenue by quantity thus equals total revenue. By the same token, multiplying average cost by quantity would yield total cost. Thus, a firm's profits can be expressed as

$$\text{Profit} = \text{quantity} \times (\text{average revenue} - \text{average cost})$$

Figure 6C2-1   A profitable firm. The profits shown are maximized, because the firm produces to the point where marginal cost equals marginal revenue.

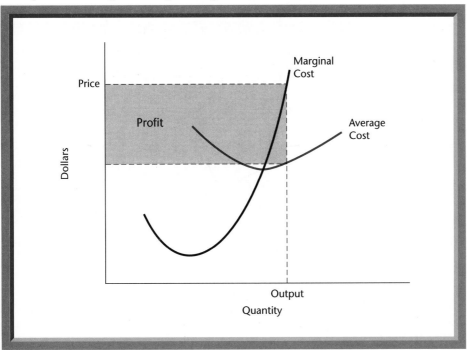

or equivalently,

$$\text{Profit} = \text{quantity} \times (\text{price} - \text{average cost}).$$

Figure 6C2-1 illustrates a profitable firm producing the profit-maximizing output given by the intersection of marginal cost and marginal revenue. The vertical difference between price and average cost at the quantity of output the firm produces is the average profit per unit of output. When this average profit is multiplied by the quantity produced, the result equals total profit, as shown by the shaded box.

Figure 6C2-2 depicts the same firm as in Figure 6C2-1. The only difference is that the firm is now facing a loss due to a drop in the market price. While the firm still produces the quantity for which marginal cost equals marginal revenue, that quantity is now lower. The firm has minimized its loss, the shaded rectangle.

If the price drops below average variable cost, the firm should immediately shut down, which corresponds to the shutdown rule stated in the Expressway. That rule is that the firm should shut down if its total revenue does not cover total variable cost. By dividing both total revenue and total variable cost by the quantity of output, the shutdown rule can equivalently be stated as follows in terms of average revenue (price) and per unit costs: **Shut down if price is less than average variable cost.** When price falls that low, shutting down minimizes the loss, which is limited to fixed costs. Table 6C2-1 summarizes the profit-maximizing decisions of the firm.

Figure 6C2-2   A firm with a loss. This firm minimizes its loss by producing to where marginal cost equals marginal revenue. If price dropped below the minimum point on average variable cost, the firm would cease production and lose its total fixed cost.

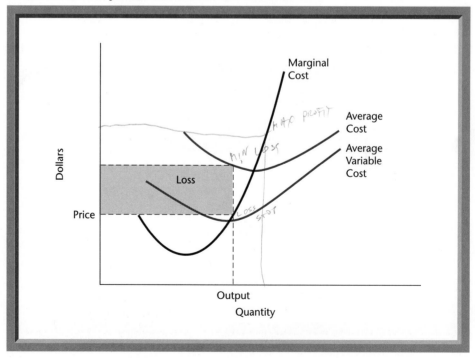

Comparison of Revenues and Costs	Set MR = MC and Produce?	Outcome
Price > average cost or Total revenue > total cost	Yes	Economic profit
Price < average cost and Price > average variable cost or Total revenue < total cost and Total revenue > total variable cost	Yes	Loss
Price = average cost or Total revenue = total cost	Yes	Break even (normal profit)
Price < average variable cost or Total revenue < total variable cost	No	Shutdown (loss equal to total fixed cost)

A price-taking firm is at the mercy of the marketplace, because market supply and demand determine the selling price of its goods. The firm contributes to market supply, since market supply is the sum of the quantities offered for sale by all firms in the industry at each possible price.

At any price above the shutdown price, the firm equates marginal revenue and marginal cost. Because the price-taking firm's marginal revenue equals the market price, the firm produces the quantity associated with its marginal cost curve at that price. Hence,

Figure 6C2-3   The firm's supply is part of the market supply. The firm's supply is that portion of its marginal cost curve that exceeds average variable cost. In the market shown, there are one thousand identical firms.

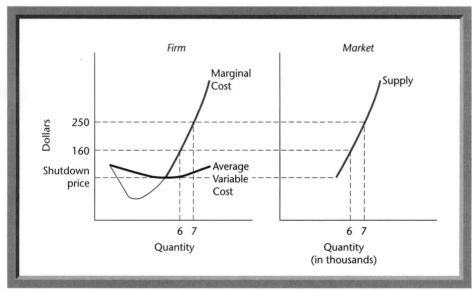

the firm's supply curve is that part of its marginal cost curve that lies above average variable cost. This supply curve shows the quantity that the firm will offer for sale at each of various possible prices.

The supply curve for WW Wholesale Flour is seen in Figure 6C2-3 in the graph on the left. At a market price of $160, the marginal revenue curve intersects the firm's supply curve at six units of output. If market price rises, WW sells more. In the graph, a price of $250 intersects the supply curve at seven units of output. That quantity makes marginal revenue equal to marginal cost. Also shown in the graph is a typical average variable cost curve. If the market price falls below the minimum point of the average variable cost curve, Wendy will shut down WW Wholesale Flour and offer no flour for sale. This circumstance is illustrated in Figure 6C2-3 as the shutdown price.

What of market supply? Sum the quantities indicated by each firm's supply curve at any price. For example, if there were 999 price takers in addition to WW, each producing six tons of flour, the total quantity supplied to the market would equal 6,000 tons (six tons multiplied by 1,000 firms). Similarly, at a price of $250, the quantity supplied to the market would equal 7,000 tons. The market supply curve is shown on the right in Figure 6C2-3.

C

Study By Design

SpeedStudy

SpeedReview

Business firms supply consumers with goods and services. Sole proprietorships, partnerships, and corporations are the legal forms that firms may take. Production creates various kinds of costs for the firm. In the short run there are both fixed and variable costs. To maximize profit, the firm produces where marginal revenue equals marginal cost, with one exception. If the firm loses so much money that it cannot cover all variable costs, it minimizes its loss by shutting down. In the long run all inputs are variable, meaning that firms can enter or exit the industry and that all costs are variable. Economies and diseconomies of scale are responsible for decreases and increases in average costs when all inputs are changed proportionally.

SpeedStudy True or False Self-Test

A1. Economists usually assume the goal of a firm is to maximize profits.

A2. Accountants calculate profit as the difference between explicit cost and implicit cost.

A3. Sole proprietorships offer their owners limited liability.

A4. U.S. firms find external funds are more important than internal funds.

A5. Total fixed cost equals zero when output equals zero.

A6. The rule of profit maximization is to produce until marginal revenue equals marginal cost.

A7. Marginal revenue equals price for a price taker.

A8. Average cost is calculated by dividing the change in total cost by the change in output.

A9. In the long run there are no fixed costs.

A10. The planning horizon is somewhere between the short run and long run.

B11. It is easy to avoid agency costs.

B12. The principal-agent problem implies that profits may not be maximized.

B13. Farming is an example of a purely competitive industry.

B14. The government imposes price ceilings on farm goods to help farmers.

C15. The slope of total cost equals average cost.

C16. Marginal cost equals the wage rate divided by marginal product.

C17. A graphical representation of loss would be a rectangle with a vertical height equal to the difference between price and average variable cost.

C18. A firm should shut down in the short run if price is less than average variable cost.

The MasterMind

Selected Terms along the Way

corporation, 200
bond, 201
production function, 202
long run, 203
short run, 203
marginal product, 203
average product, 203
law of diminishing returns, 204
profit, 206
implicit opportunity costs, 206

normal profit, 207
fixed cost, 208
variable cost, 208
average cost, 208
marginal cost, 209
price taker, 209
marginal revenue, 209
shutdown, 212
exit, 212
economies of scale, 213

diseconomies of scale, 213
constant returns to scale, 213

principal-agent problem, 218
incentive pay, 219
zero-sum game, 219
purely competitive, 221

total product, 225
average revenue, 229
firm's supply curve, 232

MasterMind Multiple Choice Self-Test

A1. The term that best describes a business you start by yourself is

   a. sole proprietorship.

   b. partnership.

   c. sinking ship.

   d. corporation.

A2. The law of diminishing returns states that

   a. when all inputs change at the same time, marginal product declines.

   b. when a variable input changes, marginal product will eventually decline.

   c. marginal cost declines.

   d. in the long run, total production will decline when all inputs are increased at the same time.

A3. Given the following cost data for RM Motors, a manufacturer of light utility vehicles, what is the marginal cost of a fourth vehicle?

Q	Total cost
0	$100
1	150
2	175
3	205
4	245
5	290

   a. $100

   b. $245

   c. $40

   d. $45

A4. A price-taking firm is currently producing 1,000 units of output. The market price of the output equals $5 per unit. Its total fixed costs equal $200, while its total variable costs are currently $150. Which statement is correct?

   a. This firm is minimizing its loss.

   b. This firm is maximizing profit.

   c. This firm is earning a profit, but it is impossible to say from the information given whether the firm is maximizing profit.

   d. This firm is at break even, but it could earn a profit if it increased its selling price.

A5. Economies of scale occur in the _____. If economies of scale are present, cost _____ with increases in output.

   a. long run; falls

   b. long run; increases

   c. short run; falls

   d. short run; increases

B6. Which best describes the principal-agent problem?

   a. Don't put all your eggs in one basket.

   b. Put all your eggs in one basket and watch that basket.

c. If you want something done right, do it yourself.

d. The attorney who represents himself has a fool for a client.

B7. Farming approximates which market structure?

a. Perfectly competitive.

b. Purely competitive.

c. Monopolistically competitive.

d. Oligopolistic.

C8. Calculate the average variable cost of four units of output from the following information.

Output	Total Cost
0	$100
1	150
2	190
3	250
4	350
5	500

a. $100

b. $350

c. $250

d. $62.50

C9. A price-taking firm's short-run supply curve is

a. its total revenue curve.

b. its average cost curve.

c. its marginal revenue curve.

d. its marginal cost curve.

MasterMind Questions and Problems

A1. In light of the advantages that corporations possess, why do you think the proprietorship and partnership forms still exist? In your answer, consider the costs and benefits of each form, including the means of financing.

A2. Provide examples of plausible opportunity costs in each of the following instances:

a. $10,000 cash invested in a firm by its owner.

b. an extra 15 hours of work per week performed for no monetary payment by a business owner.

c. a business owner's personal automobile used for business purposes.

A3. Categorize each of the following expenses incurred by Alonzo's Big Time Chocolate Factory as either fixed or variable:

a. the monthly payment Alonzo makes to the local telephone company;

b. payments to his insurance company for automobile insurance on the company car;

c. payments to the local utility for electricity to operate the candy-mixing machines;

d. Alonzo's salary as chief executive officer of the company;

e. payroll expenses.

A4. Explain why it would make no sense for a price taker to set a selling price that differs from the market price.

A5. Price scanning by bar code is common in supermarkets today. Not too many years ago, however, the price of every item purchased was entered by hand. Explain in practical terms how scanners lower costs. Must every supermarket install scanners in order to compete? Why or why not?

B6. Could there be a principal-agent problem in the management of nonprofit organizations such as schools, hospitals, and charities? Do you see any evidence for the existence of this problem on your campus? Do you think that looking at your school's budget would be informative?

B7. Why have farmers been singled out for favorable treatment by government rather than other groups, such as teachers? What would likely happen to the number of farmers if they lost their privileged status?

C8. Using the data below, compute total cost, average fixed cost, average variable cost, average cost, and marginal cost for each output. Total fixed cost is $100.

Output	Total Variable Cost
0	$0
1	50
2	90
3	140
4	200
5	300
6	500

C9. Using the data from the problem above, calculate profit at each level of output when the output can be sold for $75 per unit. Which output maximizes profit? How much is the profit?

Future Explorations: Mapping out Term Papers

1. Profits and the U.S. Firm
The purpose of this paper is to examine the profitability of American businesses in the last twenty years. How large are these profits in relation to sales? In relation to investment in capital? What has been the trend in profitability? Do American business firms make outrageous profits? In researching this topic, the goal is to put profits in perspective.

2. Is the Profit-Maximization Hypothesis a Good One?
Alternatives to profit maximization will be examined. Of special interest is the theory of "satisficing" as developed by Nobel-winner Herbert Simon. The paper discusses why profit maximization is assumed by economists and what difference it would make to economic analysis if alternative objectives are recognized.

3. American Firms Overseas: Impacts at Home and Abroad
When U.S. firms produce in foreign countries, are they welcomed or resented by the local population? Do they hurt or help economic development? Does the U.S. federal government impede or aid firms that wish to relocate overseas? The goals of this paper are to research the issues associated with U.S. business in foreign lands. The effects of this business on the U.S. economy are considered.

Answer Key

**ExpressStudy
True or False**

1. F
2. F
3. T
4. F
5. T
6. T

**SpeedStudy True
or False Self-Test**

1. T
2. F
3. F
4. F
5. F
6. T
7. T
8. F
9. T
10. F
11. F
12. T
13. T
14. F
15. F
16. T
17. F
18. T

**MasterMind Multiple
Choice Self-Test**

1. a
2. b
3. c
4. c
5. a
6. c
7. b
8. d
9. d

*M*arket Models

A LOOK AHEAD

North, south, east, west—every scout learns to navigate by the four points of the compass. In economics, too, there are four directions to take in the study of market models: perfect competition, monopoly, monopolistic competition, and oligopoly. Just as the North Star provided a shining reference for ancient travelers, the model of perfect competition offers a benchmark of economic efficiency against which real world markets can be measured.

An examination of the four market models permits greater understanding of various business behaviors and strategies and the manner in which prices are established. This chapter investigates pricing, output, profit, product differentiation, and other forms of business conduct.

DESTINATIONS

*M*odule A

As you zip along the Expressway you will arrive at an ability to

- characterize the range of market types;
- explain why the model of perfect competition is somewhat unrealistic, but still quite useful;
- state the meaning and significance of mutual interdependence;
- describe product differentiation and its implications;
- relate how and why firms charge some consumers more than others for the same products.

*M*odule B

Upon leaving the Expressway to explore issues you will be able to

- assess the merits of protecting the U.S. Postal Service from competition;
- interpret how perfect competition precludes discrimination on the basis of anything but productivity.

*M*odule C

Mastering Roadside Challenges will allow you to hone analytical skills by

- distinguishing among increasing-cost, decreasing-cost, and constant-cost industries;
- deriving output, price, and profit for a price-making firm.

The interaction of supply and demand in the marketplace creates a single market price. The simplest model of this interaction is called **perfect competition**, which assumes the existence of many identical firms selling at the market price. However, perfect competition is only one type of *market structure*, the way a market operates.

Individual sellers often have at least a bit of control over the prices of their outputs. When this occurs, firms are said to possess **market power**. Market power arises from barriers to entry. **Barriers to entry** exist when investors or entrepreneurs find obstacles to joining a profitable industry. Barriers to entry include anything that makes producing and selling output more difficult for a new firm than for an existing firm.

Market power can lead to **monopoly**, which is a market with only one seller of a good without close substitutes. Alternatively, if market power is weaker, the market structure will be *imperfect competition*, which takes one of two forms:

- **Oligopoly**—a market with more than one seller, where at least one of those sellers can significantly influence price; usually characterized by a few significant sellers;
- **Monopolistic competition**—a market with numerous firms, each of which has only a slight ability to control price.

Market power is greatest for monopoly firms, less for oligopoly firms, and slight for firms in monopolistic competition. Figure 7A-1 arranges the market models from left to right according to increasing market power.

Figure 7A-1 **Market models** can be arranged according to the amounts of market power that firms possess.

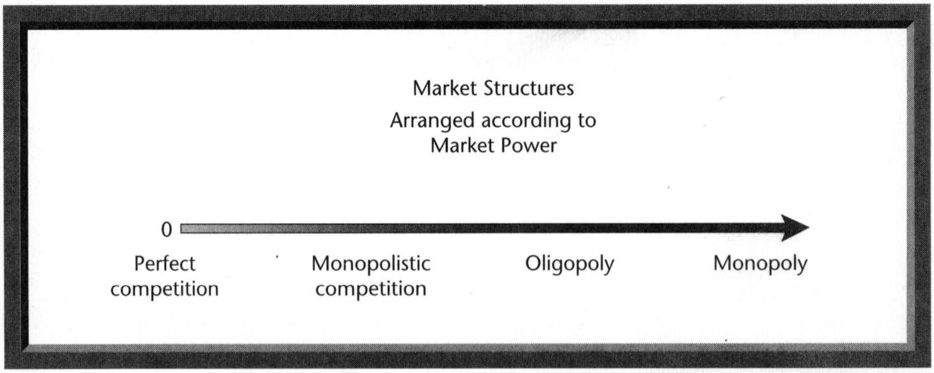

Market Structures
Arranged according to
Market Power

0

| Perfect competition | Monopolistic competition | Oligopoly | Monopoly |

*P*erfect Competition

Perfect competition is characterized by the following:

- **Numerous buyers and sellers,** implying that each firm is a price taker.
- **A homogeneous product. Homogeneous products** are identical across all firms in an industry; the output of any single firm is identical to that of any other. For example, the #2 grade yellow corn produced by Farmer Brown, Farmer Jones, and other farmers is homogeneous because there are no differences between their crops. Because products are identical, individual firms reap no benefits from advertising. Thus individual firms do no advertising in perfect competition.
- **No barriers to the entry and exit of firms.** It is easy for firms to start up or leave the industry.
- **Fully informed buyers and sellers.** Both buyers and sellers know the market price and any other pertinent information.
- **Identical firms,** All firms have access to the same production technologies and face the same prices for inputs. This assumption makes modeling easier.[1]

The focus of perfect competition is on price taking. Supply and demand establish a single market price, which becomes the selling price for individual firms. This means that, whatever the elasticity of market demand, **the demand curve facing a single firm is perfectly elastic (horizontal) at the market price.** The firm is able to sell as much as it wishes at that price, but cannot sell anything if it charges more. This concept is shown in Figure 7A-2. In contrast, *price making* is found in the three other forms of market structure.

The firm's demand will shift up or down as market price rises or falls, caused by shifts in market demand or supply. In the short run, the market price could be sufficiently high that the firm earns economic profits, or it could be so low that the firm loses money. However, **the long-run equilibrium market price results in zero economic profits for perfectly competitive firms.**

Profits are zero in the long run because positive profits would attract new entrants that shift the market supply to the right. Entry would continue to occur until profits fall to zero. Likewise, losses would prompt exit that shifts the market supply curve to the left. That would continue until price rises to the zero-profit level. In addition, firms are forced to achieve all possible economies of scale, since to do otherwise would leave them with higher costs than their competitors. The result is that all firms choose to produce in the range of constant returns to scale.

Examples of businesses that can be understood with the perfectly competitive model include farms, ranches, dealers in gold and silver bullion, copper mines, steel producers, aluminum refiners, and lumber producers. Outputs are roughly homogeneous within each of these markets. Within a particular grade, all corn is alike, beef is beef, aluminum ingots vary negligibly from one refinery to another, and so forth. Information about the market prices of these items is widely available in media reports on *commodities*, a term used to describe homogeneous goods.

---

[1]When differences among firms are important, such as in analyzing pollution by firms in different natural environments, it would be appropriate to use the model of *pure competition*. Pure competition is merely perfect competition without the assumption of identical firms. In general usage, *competition* and *competitive* refer to either pure or perfectly competitive markets.

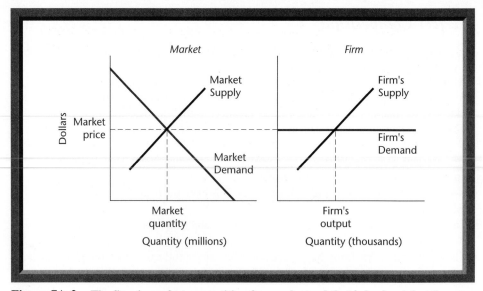

Figure 7A-2   The firm in perfect competition faces a demand that is horizontal at the market price, because each firm is a price taker. The intersection of market demand and market supply sets market price.

Perfect competition illuminates how markets allocate resources efficiently. Perfectly competitive firms produce output up to the point where price equals marginal cost. At that point, every unit produced is valued by consumers as greater than or equal to marginal cost. The next unit of output would increase cost more than the value placed upon it by consumers. It should not and will not be produced if the market is competitive. Since competition also forces firms to keep costs to a minimum, perfect competition is both allocatively and technologically efficient.

✓ **QUICKCHECK**

If you owned a gold coin of known weight and purity, but without collector value, how would you learn what price to ask if you were selling it?

Answer: You would be a price taker who would sell at the going market price for gold. This price changes often as supply and demand shift. The price at any given moment can be found on commodity exchanges, such as the Chicago Mercantile Exchange, also known as the Comex.

OBSERVATION POINT: Old McDonald Farms Again!

Old McDonald had a farm. Like so many others in the competitive agricultural industry, lack of profit drove him out of business. Exit was painful and distressing. Still, it was also easy, given the well-developed markets for land and used farm equipment. Now he wants back in, eager to sell chickens to health-conscious consumers. Entry is easy, too, although it may take time and effort. The necessary skills can be acquired in an agricultural program at college or, as in the case of old McDonald, by experience.

Entry also takes land, equipment, and other inputs, depending on the type of farming involved. For Old McDonald to raise more chickens, he will need a coop. Although land and chicken coops are expensive, this is not much of a barrier to entry in today's world. The reason is that farmers have access to borrowed funds through the banking system. They are also able to lease land and equipment. So, keep your ears open for an "ee-yi-ee-yi-oh" hollered in gratitude for the easy exit and entry in his competitive industry. It lets Old McDonald farm again.

*B*arriers to Entry

When there are barriers to entry, the "come on in" signal sent by economic profit cannot be acted upon. By impeding the invisible hand, barriers to entry call into question the efficiency of resource allocation in the free market.

Barriers take a multitude of forms when created by government. For example, tariffs and import quotas limit the ability of foreign competitors to challenge domestic firms. Government licensing of occupations and businesses is a form of barrier. In some cities, a single taxicab company is granted an *exclusive franchise*, a type of government-licensed monopoly that allows no one else to legally provide taxi service. Another government barrier is patent protection. The patent laws stop unauthorized parties from using an invention or process that has patent protection.

Firms may attempt to erect barriers in order to protect themselves from new competitors. Research and development, conducted in search of patentable outputs, is one avenue toward market power. Advertising expenditures provide another. If advertising creates customer loyalty for existing firms, new entry is made more difficult. Still another barrier occurs when a firm gains control of an essential input. Lack of that essential input deprives other firms of the opportunity to produce the output. The Aluminum Company of America (ALCOA) pursued this strategy during the early decades of the twentieth century.

OBSERVATION POINT: Is the American Medical Association Hazardous to Your Health?

The American Medical Association (AMA) is not a government agency. Nevertheless, this professional association has much to say about the availability of health care. Not only does it have power over the standards for licensing physicians, but it also has considerable input into setting standards for medical schools. Some critics of the current U.S. health care system accuse the AMA of setting unnecessarily high standards, which serve as barriers to entry into the medical profession. The purpose? Critics contend that the motivation is more income for physicians. The AMA responds that medicine is a life or death proposition, and that only the best physicians should be allowed to serve the public.

Assessing Market Power

Market power can be measured by the *four-firm concentration ratio*, which is the fraction of total sales in an industry accounted for by the four largest firms. Larger concentration ratios show that the four largest firms sell a larger fraction of total industry sales. In a pure monopoly market, the monopolist accounts for 100 percent of sales. Therefore, the four-firm concentration ratio equals 100. The ratio for oligopolies with only two, three, or four firms will also always equal 100, standing for 100 percent.

Table 7A-1 shows four-firm concentration ratios for a selection of industries. The interpretation of each concentration ratio is straightforward. The larger the number, the greater the market power, and the less is competition. The smaller the number, the less the market power, and the greater is competition.

The ability of a firm to set the selling price of its output depends upon its demand curve. Price takers have horizontal demand curves. They have no choice but to sell at the market price. Firms that possess market power have downward-sloping demand curves. The steeper the demand curve, the more market power the firm has, and the greater its ability to raise price.

Figure 7A-3 shows three firms with varying degrees of market power. The first firm is a price taker in a competitive market and thus has no market power. The second firm's demand curve barely deviates from the horizontal. Therefore, its market power is negligible. It can raise its selling price only slightly, because there are many close substitutes for its product. The third firm has more market power, because it faces little or no competition. Its demand curve is rather steep, and its ability to set price is substantial.

No firm's market power is absolute, because no firm can raise prices without reducing the quantity that consumers will buy. Observe the third firm in Figure 7A-3. If it raises price enough, it will reach the point where the demand curve intersects the price axis. At that point the quantity demanded equals zero. The firm would never want to raise price that high.

TABLE 7A-1 *Four-Firm Concentration Ratios for Selected U.S. Manufacturing Industries, 1992*

Industry	Concentration Ratio (Percent)
Meat packing plants	50
Cigarettes	93
Knit outerwear mills	46
Wood household furniture	20
Paper mills	29
Book publishing	23
Petroleum refining	30
Luggage	43
Electronic computers	45
Aircraft	79

Source: 1992 Census of Manufactures report MC92-5-2.

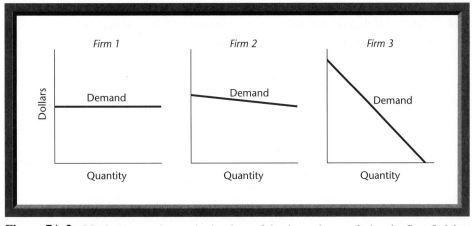

Figure 7A-3 **Market power** is seen in the slope of the demand curve facing the firm. Judging from the steep slope of its demand, firm 3 has the most market power. Firm 1 is a price taker and has no market power.

✔ **QuickCheck**

State the four-firm concentration ratio in each of the following scenarios: (a) Five firms of equal size make up the industry, (b) 100 firms of equal size make up the industry. In which scenario is there more competition?

Answer: (a) 80. Each firm will have a 20 percent market share. Therefore, four of the five firms will sell 80 percent of industry output. (b) 4. Any one firm will have a 1 percent market share; four firms will have a 4 percent share. In scenario (b) there is more competition.

Antitrust Issues and Interpretations

The first U.S. antitrust law was the *Sherman Antitrust Act* of 1890. This act is the foundation of antitrust policy and is enforced by the Justice Department. The focus of the act is on conduct, although specific illegal actions are not spelled out. In general, it prohibits contracts, combinations, and conspiracies in restraint of trade. It also forbids attempts to monopolize markets, but does not make monopoly itself illegal.

In 1914 the *Clayton Act* was passed. It supplements the Sherman Act by listing specific illegal actions, such as acquiring stock in a competing firm when that action would lessen competition. In the same year, the *Federal Trade Commission (FTC)* was created to oversee markets. Additional antitrust legislation includes the *Robinson-Patman Act* of 1936 and the *Celler-Kefauver Antimerger Act* of 1950. The purpose of these laws is to prevent firms from taking anticompetitive actions that would give them excessive market power.

A firm cannot be sure whether or not it is violating the antitrust laws, because enforcement has varied from one presidential administration to the next. It is difficult to know in advance how the FTC and the Justice Department will react to particular conduct. Under President Reagan, for example, prior strict interpretations of antitrust law were set aside in favor of less government involvement in the marketplace. Even though the meticulousness of enforcement of the antitrust laws seesaws back and forth with changes in presidential administrations, firms have the incentive to steer clear of even the suspicion of guilt. That incentive is the treble damages clause of the Sherman Act. Violators of the law can be forced to pay up to three times the amount of damages they inflict on other firms.

*M*onopoly—*Are There No Good Substitutes?*

A monopoly is characterized by a single firm selling an output for which there are no close substitutes. Goods substitute for one another when they fill the same need. For example, if there is only one seller of a good, is the seller a monopolist? Not if another good serves the same purpose. In that case, consumers who are dissatisfied with the price or quality of one good can stop buying it and obtain equivalent satisfaction by purchasing the other.

Whether there are close substitutes for a good or service is often not obvious. Consider your local electric company. It is not feasible for most people to install windmills or solar panels in their backyards to generate their own power. The electric cable that serves you is owned by a single firm, a local monopoly. What about cable television? Usually only one cable company provides service in an area. However, if satellite dishes, network television, theaters, and other recreation are good substitutes, then local cable companies are not truly monopolists.

Monopolies occur for two reasons. One involves government—government-issued patents, copyrights, and other restrictions can prevent the entry of new businesses. Such restrictions may have the economic justification of promoting research and development.

Monopoly can also arise naturally in the marketplace. **Natural monopoly** occurs when one firm can supply the entire market at a lower per unit cost than could two or more separate firms. This situation can happen if there are substantial economies of scale. A potential entrant will think twice about challenging a natural monopolist. To realize economies of scale, the entrant would need to start large, so large that the entrant and the established firm could not both survive. Few investors would be willing to finance such a challenge.

For example, imagine three or four water suppliers each burying water mains along a street, with each seller competing for the business of the nearby residents. A single firm could eliminate this wasteful duplication of effort and in the process lower the average costs of providing service. Water companies and local gas and electric companies are examples of *public utilities*, which are usually natural monopolies.

OBSERVATION POINT: Finding Monopoly—The Case of Cellophane

The existence of substitutes was the central issue in one famous court case involving the alleged monopoly held by DuPont, the producer of cellophane. While monopoly itself is not illegal, anticompetitive behavior to create one can be. The court considered evidence regarding the numerous substitutes for cellophane, a clear packaging material. These substitutes included wax paper and aluminum foil. The final decision reasoned that cellophane was one of many packaging materials produced by a number of firms. The availability of substitutes and the relatively low market share for cellophane relative to the market for packaging materials were facts that influenced the court to exonerate DuPont. The court reasoned that DuPont did not have a monopoly, because the market was for packaging materials, not just cellophane.

Selecting the Monopoly Quantity and Price

Let's follow the steps that a hypothetical monopoly firm will take in maximizing profit. Suppose that eccentric inventor Archibald Swift, after years of research and development, has finally perfected a device that will allow anyone to learn any subject simply by attaching a headband before going to bed. The device fills the user's mind with knowledge while he or she sleeps. Archibald has formed a corporation, BrainPrinting, Inc., to produce and market the patented product. BrainPrinting is an unregulated monopoly firm. There are no close substitutes for its product, and government regulators do not control its price or output.

At what price should BrainPrinters be offered for sale? Archibald will attempt to select the price that maximizes profit. He feels that maximum profit is his just reward for years of work on this breakthrough invention. He also reasons that his firm holds 100 percent of the demand for this device, since there is no similar product able to compete with it. That means that his firm is facing the market demand curve for while-you-sleep learning machines.

Archibald knows that market demand curves are downward sloping. As a monopolist, if he wants another sale, he will have to offer potential buyers a lower price. The lower price would then apply to every unit of output that he offers for sale. This means that the marginal revenue from an extra BrainPrinter would equal the price of that BrainPrinter minus the price reduction on every other brain printer he sells. Thus, **for a firm with a downward-sloping demand curve, marginal revenue is less than price.**

To ascertain demand, Archibald test-markets BrainPrinters to a sample of college students. In the test, the demand schedule for BrainPrinters shows that a price of $12 leads to zero sales, $11 to one sale, $10 to two sales, $9 to three sales, $8 to four sales, and so forth. Multiplying each price by the corresponding quantity, the total revenue figures are $0, $11, $20, $27, $32, et cetera. Since marginal revenue is the change in total revenue resulting from an additional sale, the respective marginal revenue figures are $11, $9, $7, and $5, and so forth. This confirms that, as quantity increases for a price maker, marginal revenue drops faster than price.

For example, the price reduction from $10 to $9 allows the firm to sell three units, but also causes the revenue from the sale of the first two units, which would be $20 at the $10 price, to drop to $18. This drop of $2 means that total revenue will not rise by the full amount of the $9 price. Total revenue rises by only $7, which equals the price of $9 minus the decrease of $2 on the first two units.

To find the profit-maximizing price and quantity, Archibald will calculate the marginal revenue at various quantities. He will then compare marginal revenue to marginal cost at each quantity. At some point the two must be equal, because marginal revenue declines as more output is produced and sold, while marginal cost rises because of the law of diminishing returns.

Archibald has ascertained that the marginal revenue and marginal cost of Brain-Printers are equal at a quantity of four units. Four units command a price of $8.00. Multiplying price by quantity results in $32.00 of total revenue. Archibald has also ascertained that total costs equal $15.00 at a quantity of four units. The firm's total profit is hence $17.00, the difference between total revenue and total cost. Table 7A-2 presents the cost, revenue, and profit data for BrainPrinting, Inc.'s profit-maximizing output.

✓ **QUICKCHECK**

What is the value of marginal revenue at four units of output? Is marginal cost equal to that value?

Answer: Marginal revenue equals $5. Since four units is the profit-maximizing output, marginal cost must also equal $5.

To summarize, monopolies boost their profit by decreasing output and raising price above what would prevail in a perfectly competitive market. Output is selected first, according to the marginal revenue equals marginal cost rule. Then price is set as high as the market will bear, as indicated by demand. This two-step process is illustrated in Figure 7A-4. (A complete numerical example is worked out in Challenge 2.)

Addressing the Inefficiencies of Monopoly

A profit-maximizing monopolist sets price higher than marginal cost. Thus the marginal cost of additional output is less than its marginal benefit to consumers, as measured by the demand curve. The monopolist thus produces an output that is inefficiently small, because its price is inefficiently high. Figure 7A-4 notes the efficient quantity, which occurs where marginal cost intersects the demand curve. At that quantity, the marginal value of the last unit equals its marginal cost.

TABLE 7A-2 Maximum Profit in BrainPrinting, Inc., a Monopoly

BrainPrinting, Inc.	Data
Price	$8.00
Quantity	4 units
Total revenue	$32.00
Explicit costs	$6.00
Implicit costs	$9.00
Total costs	$15.00
Total profit	$17.00
Profit per unit	$4.25

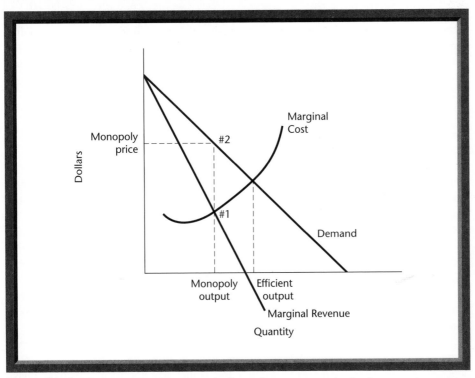

Figure 7A-4 **The unregulated monopoly firm** selects output and price in a two-step manner: #1 The firm produces until marginal cost equals marginal revenue; #2 The firm charges the highest price that will sell that output.

The invisible hand of the competitive marketplace means that deviations from efficient resource allocation are self-correcting. **In monopoly, inefficiencies can persist indefinitely.** However, although an unregulated monopoly will not produce an efficient quantity at each point in time, it does generate profits that allow it the wherewithal to invest in research and development to enhance its monopoly status. Competitive firms have neither the incentive nor financial ability to pursue this course. Thus, while producing too little and charging too much in the short run, a monopoly that earns excess profits might offer the consumer improved products in the long run.

While the monopolist does not face competition directly, it does face the threat of *potential competition* from new producers or new products. If a monopolist prices its product too high, new substitutes may be developed that draw away the monopolist's customers. Alternatively, a new firm may take the risk of challenging the monopolist's turf. To avoid these possibilities, the monopolist might practice **limit pricing**, which is charging the highest price customers will pay, subject to the limit that the price not be so high that it attracts potential competitors.

Alternatively, government may hold down the price a monopolist can charge. Most commonly, government employs *rate-of-return regulation*, which prevents the monopolist from charging a price that would generate excess profit. At the lower price that results under regulation, more output is sold, and the monopolist comes closer to the allocatively efficient ideal noted in Figure 7A-4.

A problem with rate-of-return regulation is that the regulated monopolist has little incentive to control costs or to provide innovative services. Thus, over time, regulation can impede change in production techniques and in the development of new products. The concern that regulation causes inefficiencies over time has led to the **deregulation** of some monopolies and oligopolies. Nonetheless, at least some regulation at both the state and federal level remains the norm for local public utilities.

Oligopoly—An Array of Models

Numerous markets are characterized by oligopoly, in which there are a few significant firms. In oligopoly, each significant firm's actions affect the other firms in the industry. Oligopoly firms are **mutually interdependent**, with the actions taken by one firm inducing other firms to take counteractions. Thus strategy and counterstrategy is the norm in oligopolistic markets. Mutual interdependence frequently revolves around the pricing decisions of oligopoly firms. The example afforded by the cut in the price of Marlboro cigarettes in 1995 is instructive. The price of Marlboros was lowered in response to the growing market share of generic brands. Rival cigarette manufacturers were then also forced to lower the prices of their leading brands in order to avoid losing sales to Marlboro.

Mutual interdependence can also involve product design. For instance, when Chrysler added a driver's-side sliding door option on its minivans in 1995, mutual interdependence forced Ford and GM to do the same. If they had not, their sales would have suffered.

The cigarette and automobile industries are examples of oligopolies that produce differentiated products. Each brand of cigarette offers smokers unique flavor, packaging, and other features. Each vehicle differs from competing models. Styling, color, horsepower, and interior design are just a few of the ways that cars are differentiated. Output of oligopolies is not always differentiated, however. Steel, aluminum, and copper are homogeneous commodities produced by oligopolistic firms.

Cartels

If firms would stop competing with each other, they could raise prices and earn greater joint profits. Oligopoly firms that agree to stop competing are said to form a **cartel**, a form of oligopoly characterized by collusion. The objective of a cartel is to increase price to the profit-maximizing monopoly price. The higher price implies a smaller output, which must then be allocated among the members of the cartel.

Cartels are likely to exist only in oligopoly industries, because large numbers of firms would be unlikely to agree on a selling price. However, cartels are difficult to keep together for several reasons:

- They are **illegal** in the U.S. according to the antitrust statutes. Cartels in the U.S. operate in secrecy.
- Any member firm has an incentive to **cheat,** by undercutting the monopoly price established by the cartel. By secretly selling at a lower price than other cartel members, a member could increase its sales and hence profits at the expense of its partners.
- A cartel member can **drop out** if it becomes unhappy with any aspect of the cartel

agreement. Cartel prices are sustained by limits on production for each member. Production quotas also limit the profits of each member.

- If barriers to entry are not absolute, high cartel profits could induce **competition** from new entrants or existing firms who are not members of the cartel.
- Over time, higher prices can lead to the development of **substitutes** for the cartel's product.

In the case of the Organization of Petroleum Exporting Countries (OPEC), the best known cartel, high oil prices spurred exploration, which in turn led to major oil finds in Alaska, Mexico, and the North Sea. Because OPEC did not control these new oil fields, the added oil supplies negatively affected OPEC's ability to set price. Likewise, the higher prices prompted the development of energy-efficient homes and automobiles that reduced demand for OPEC oil.

Game Theory

The mathematics of **game theory** can be employed to deepen the understanding of oligopoly markets. The method analyzes the behavior of parties whose interests conflict. The tool of analysis is the *payoff matrix*, showing the gains or losses from making a decision when mutual interdependence is present.

In game theory, as in life, the outcome of one player's decision will also depend on a decision made by another. For example, a firm cannot reason out the effect of a price cut on its profits unless it considers what competitors will do. If competitors leave their price untouched, the effects on the price-cutting firm will be very different than if competitors cut their price to match or outdo the price cut of the first price cutter.

An example of a game is illustrated by the *prisoner's dilemma*. Two persons, A and B, who are suspected by police of being partners in the commission of a crime, are arrested. Interrogation takes place in separate rooms, where each prisoner is told the following:

> *If your partner confesses, while you keep your mouth shut, we'll throw the book at you. Your partner will get off with one year in jail, but you'll do twenty years of hard time. On the other hand, if you confess while your partner keeps quiet, you will get one year of jail time, while your partner gets twenty. If you both confess, you'll both get five years in the slammer. If you both clam up, we've still got the evidence to send you away for three years in the pokey.*

Table 7A-3 summarizes the situation. Studying the payoff matrix reveals that whatever A does, B is better off confessing. Whatever B does, A is better off confessing. Guilt or innocence makes no difference. Collusion between A and B, in the form an oath by both to keep quiet, offers a lighter sentence than the five years they both receive by confessing. However, the police have separated them for the very purpose of preventing collusion. The police have in effect stacked the deck, preventing the pursuit by A and B of their joint interests.

The predicament faced in the game applies to the members of a cartel. By cooperating among themselves and raising price while cutting quantity, the member firms making up the cartel can achieve the greatest profit. But reasoned self-interest says that it pays

TABLE 7A-3	*Payoff Matrix—Prisoner's Dilemma*	
	A confesses	**A keeps quiet**
B confesses	A gets 5 years B gets 5 years	A gets 20 years B gets 1 year
B keeps quiet	A gets 1 year B gets 20 years	A gets 3 years B gets 3 years

to cheat on the arrangement by increasing sales through secret price cuts. If a member cheats while other members do not, the cheater is better off. If a member does not cheat while other members do, the honest member suffers. No matter what the other members do, a particular member of the cartel is better off by cheating. Cheating is a major reason that OPEC's power has dwindled over time.

As in poker, chess, and other games, many additional strategies also provide insights into oligopoly behavior. Some strategies are quite complex and involve the use of advanced mathematics. The use of game theory to study oligopoly behavior formed the basis for the 1994 Nobel Prize in economics.

Other Models

Oligopoly is the only market structure in which there are many separate models. The reason is that different oligopoly industries behave differently. The models of contestable markets, price leadership, and the dominant firm with a competitive fringe give a flavor of these other models.

Contestable markets occur when new rivals can enter or exit the market quickly and cheaply. Contestability can characterize either oligopoly or monopoly. The "quick in and quick out" characteristic of contestable markets limits the ability of the firm or firms already in the market to raise prices. If prices become too high in a contestable market, entry of new firms will occur since entry is easy. Congressional deregulation of the airline industry in the late 1970s has brought contestable markets to life in the airports of our major cities. In contrast, the automobile industry is costly and difficult to enter and thus does not meet the criteria of a contestable market.

The **price leadership** model observes that in some oligopolistic industries, when one firm changes its selling price, the remaining firms in the industry copy that change. The firm initiating the price change is called the price leader; the copycats are termed followers. At one time or another the cigarette, automobile, and steel industries have exhibited the pattern of price leadership. In effect, the followers in a price-leadership oligopoly have voluntarily placed themselves in the role of price takers. They count on their leader to set a good price without resorting to illegal collusion.

The *dominant firm with a competitive fringe* is a combination of the competitive and monopoly models. The dominant firm, typically the largest in the industry, has a cost advantage over many smaller fringe firms. The dominant firm has no control over other producers, and thus allows them to produce as much as they want at the market price. However, the production decisions of the dominant firm force that price to below what it would be if the competitive fringe firms were the only suppliers. This lower price allows the dominant firm a significant share of the market.

The dominant-firm-with-a-competitive-fringe model describes the worldwide crude oil market, in which the OPEC cartel takes the role of the dominant firm and the many smaller non-OPEC producers are the competitive fringe. OPEC has no choice but to allow non-OPEC oil producers to sell as much as they want at the world price of oil. However, OPEC has no problem selling its own oil because it sets the world oil price at a level that ensures that quantity demanded far exceeds the quantity supplied by the competitive fringe. OPEC production makes up the difference. Of course, if OPEC were to withhold its oil from the market, the market-clearing price of oil would be dramatically higher.

Mergers, Leveraged Buyouts, and Corporate Raiders

Mergers have the potential to reduce competition in an industry. This is why the Justice Department's merger guidelines describe the kinds of mergers that are likely to be challenged. To meet with government approval, a merger must not significantly reduce competition. Mergers between firms operating across the country are evaluated on the basis of their effect on competition in the nationwide market. Mergers between firms that operate locally are checked for their impact on local competition.

Horizontal integration occurs when a firm merges with another in the same line of business. The acquisition of Gulf Oil by Chevron in the 1980s is an example. Economies of scale can arise from horizontal mergers. To achieve economies, Chevron converted Gulf's chain of gas stations to the Chevron brand. Thus the historic orange disc that stood in front of Gulf stations for generations came down, to be replaced by the Chevron logo. More recent examples of horizontal integration are also to be found. The numerous bank mergers of the 1990s are thought to have been motivated primarily in hopes of attaining economies of scale.

A firm might acquire another firm that supplies it with an input, or it might acquire another firm that retails its output to consumers. Either case is termed **vertical integration**. The objective in the first instance is to secure reliable delivery of the input. In the second, it is to ensure a ready market for the firm's output. An example of vertical integration occurred in 1995 when the Walt Disney Company and the ABC television network joined forces to become a powerful producer and distributor of television programming.

A third type of merger is termed **conglomerate merger**. This variety of merger brings together firms whose lines of business have no obvious relationship to each other. The acquisition of Columbia Pictures by Coca-Cola in 1981 fell into this category.

In the 1990s the trend has been away from the conglomerate merger, with many former conglomerates splitting into separate firms. For example, Coca-Cola ultimately came to recognize that a soft-drink maker has no special expertise in filmmaking and sold its Columbia Pictures unit to Sony. In 1995 AT&T proceeded to split itself into three separate firms. Even the ITT Corporation, which once epitomized conglomerates, has now divided itself into separate companies. Under one corporate aegis, ITT's holdings had ranged from the New York Knicks basketball team, to Hartford Insurance, to the manufacture of high-tech military equipment. These firms were worth more to investors as separate companies than as parts of conglomerates.

In the 1980s leveraged buyouts (LBOs) became popular as a means of transferring ownership of firms. Unlike mergers, LBOs transfer ownership to the managers of a firm. Wait a minute, you say. How could the managers of a firm raise millions or even billions of dollars to buy the firm they manage? The answer is to borrow. Bank loans can finance the purchase. Once a buyout is complete, the managers can repay the banks with money raised when the firm issues bonds for that purpose.

These bonds are often called *junk bonds*. That less-than-flattering moniker refers to the high yield (interest rate) they carry because of their high risk of default. Investors in junk bonds take the risk that they will not be repaid. Highly leveraged firms, those with much debt, could sink under the weight of that debt. Junk bonds are gambles that sometimes fail. Other times, as in the leveraged buyout of RJR Nabisco, junk bonds pay off handsomely for investors, firms, and consumers alike.

Other high-profile activities in the 1980s involved *corporate raiders*. These dashing titans of high finance sometimes still seek out targets for hostile takeovers. Gaining control of a corporation usually means offering stockholders a price for their stock that is higher than the current market price. Two or more raiders sometimes try to take over the same firm. Battles for takeover rights can create expectations that the next offer to buy stock will go even higher than the last offer. That expectation can lead to a great deal of buying and selling of the target firm's stock as speculators seek profits.

Why do corporate raiders try to take over firms that do not want to be taken over? After the takeover, raiders may plan to sell assets to other companies able to use them more efficiently or to install new management capable of bringing the firm to a higher level of profitability. Either would be good for the economy. However, increasing the efficiency of a firm often means massive layoffs of workers. Critics of corporate raiders focus on this aspect of mergers and have proposed laws that would make takeovers more difficult.

Another criticism of raiders is that they artificially drive up the price of a stock in order to sell their shares at an unfair profit. Alternatively, the motive may be *greenmail*. Managers who suspect that they will lose their jobs in the event of a successful takeover will be motivated to stop that takeover. Greenmail uses corporate funds to purchase stock owned by the raider, thus providing the raider with a profit. Critics of greenmail charge that such profit is unearned, undeserved, and should be outlawed. There are also various colorfully named strategies to deter would-be raiders and, not coincidentally, lessen the pain of unemployment for managers who lose their jobs. For example, *golden parachutes*, built into some corporate executives' employment contracts, richly reward these executives in the event of a hostile takeover.

✔ QUICKCHECK

Would a hostile takeover increase or decrease the ability of the target firm to compete?

Answer: It depends. If the raider takes over a weak firm and installs better management, competition would increase. If the raider collects greenmail, the drain on the corporate treasury could weaken the firm's ability to compete, perhaps even driving it to bankruptcy.

Monopolistic Competition—All Around Us

The diary of a college student: "Walked to Blue and Green to purchase *Economics by Design* and my other textbooks. Picked up my designer jeans at Rubi's Dry Cleaners. Dropped in to House of Burgers for lunch. After class, had to drive to CompuWiz to buy more DataSave computer disks. Gassed up at Gas'n N Go'n, and got some Purrfection cat food for Kitty while I was there. Haircut at The Hair Team. Later, pizza at Piece-A-Da-Pie. Topped off the day with dancing and snacks at City Limits."

This college student has certainly had an active day. Much of it was spent dealing with firms operating in markets characterized by monopolistic competition, a market structure with many firms, product differentiation, and relatively easy entry of new firms. Many retailers operate in monopolistically competitive markets. In addition, many of the products they sell are also produced by firms in monopolistic competition.

Monopolistically competitive firms face downward-sloping demand curves because of product differentiation. They thus set their output and price in the same manner as a monopoly. However, monopolistically competitive firms also face a great deal of competition from other firms that offer close substitutes. Thus, each firm's demand is highly elastic, meaning that it slopes downward only slightly, such as the demand facing firm 2 in Figure 7A-3. This limits the market power of these firms.

Monopolistic competition is exciting, because easy entry and exit make it possible for entrepreneurs to test out their good ideas. If your version of an industry product is particularly appealing to the public, for example, you can open up shop and possibly grow rich. The downside is that your vision of the market could be clouded. For example, it seems that new restaurants are constantly opening. A few will catch on and grow, possibly even into national chains. Many more will allow their owners to scrape by. Others go out of business.

Advertising and Product Differentiation

The key to riches in monopolistic competition is successful **product differentiation** in such things as style, taste, shape, size, color, texture, quality, location, packaging, advertising, and service. For example, McDonald's differentiated its coffee by serving it very hot, at least until it faced negative publicity and a court verdict against it because of burns suffered by a drive-through customer. The trademarked golden arches are just one of many other features still differentiating McDonald's from its competitors, just as the 31 flavors helps differentiate Baskin-Robbins.

Monopolistically competitive markets are typically characterized by advertising and sales promotions. Some ads focus on facts, such as Yellow Pages ads with addresses, phone numbers, and hours of operation. On the other hand, much advertising is designed to work on consumers' imaginations and stick in their memories. Advertising slogans permeate our language. In the 1984 Democratic presidential primaries, for example, candidate Walter Mondale challenged front-runner Gary Hart with "Where's the beef?" That question struck a chord with Americans who had heard it in Wendy's television commercials, and Mondale won the nomination. More typically, successful advertising, slogans, and sales promotions increase the demand for a firm's version of the industry's output.

When advertising or otherwise differentiating its product, the profit-maximizing firm is still guided by the same principle that guides its choice of quantity of output: marginal cost equals marginal revenue. If the marginal revenue generated by advertising exceeds the marginal cost, advertising raises profits. Otherwise it does not. Similarly, the profit-maximizing firm will adjust its hours of operation, selection of merchandise, and every other aspect of product differentiation with this same principle in mind. For example, if a store's marginal revenue from staying open an extra hour in the evening exceeds the marginal cost of staying open the extra hour, the store will choose to stay open that extra hour.

OBSERVATION POINT: T-Shirt Talk—Free Speech in Monopolistic Competition

"Someday a woman will be President." That thought, printed on T-shirts for sale by a nationally prominent retailer, led to those shirts being pulled from the shelf after a customer protested. Subsequently, other customers protested the store's censorship. The T-shirts went back on the shelves, but did not stay there long. This time it was paying customers who seized the shirts—to make a statement!

Do you have a thought or a cause you would like to promote? Then perhaps the T-shirt business is for you. Since anyone can buy plain T-shirts and customize them with slogans, entry is easy. Your success in the market for T-shirt talk will depend upon how well you differentiate your product. Take caution, though. Your successful slogans and designs will quickly be imitated by competitors offering close substitutes. Stay alert for new ideas. That's the route to success in monopolistically competitive T-shirt talk.

When Does Detail Matter?

Monopolistic competition accurately describes many more markets than does perfect competition. On that basis, it appears that monopolistic competition ought to be the model of choice for analyzing markets. Appearances are deceiving.

The model of perfect competition is to be preferred over monopolistic competition when the details of product differentiation do not matter. Remember, the best model is the simplest model, so long as, in simplifying, we do not exclude details relevant to answering the questions we ask. The model of monopolistic competition is usually more useful than perfect competition only when analyzing questions specifically relating to the effects of product differentiation and advertising.

*P*rice Discrimination

Price discrimination is the selling of a good or service at different prices to various buyers, when such differences are not justified by cost differences. Examples include senior citizen and student discounts, differential rates for business customers for telephone and power, airline super saver fares, and prices that require the use of coupons. These examples of price discrimination are legal in the U.S. However, if price discrimination is used to create a monopoly or otherwise lessen competition, it is prohibited by the Clayton Act.

Price discrimination is feasible when different prices can be charged to different market segments. For example, it costs no less to screen a movie in a theater filled with children than to show it to adults. Yet adult ticket prices are usually twice those of children's, because adults are less deterred by higher prices—demand for adult tickets is less elastic than demand for children's tickets. That's one way that theaters practice price discrimination. Another is to offer cut-rate tickets for afternoon showings of a film. Price discrimination is not an act of charity; it maximizes profits. If theaters can fill otherwise empty seats, the revenue earned is all profit, because the cost of showing a movie to a packed theater and to an empty theater is the same.

Price discrimination cannot be practiced if there can be *arbitrage*, in which buyers who are offered goods at a low price can resell those goods to other buyers. Everyone would then wind up buying at or near the same low price. For example, pricing adult movie tickets higher than children's would accomplish nothing if adults could see a movie with a child's ticket. The only tickets that a theater could sell would be child's tickets, purchased by children and then profitably resold to adults at a price less than the regular adult price.

A

✔ **QUICKCHECK**

Differences between in-state and out-of-state tuition at public colleges and universities are usually substantial. Is this price discrimination? How can it be justified?

_____

Answer: It is no more costly to serve a student from one location than from another. Therefore, the custom fits the definition of price discrimination. It is justified by the logic that those whose tax dollars have built the schools deserve a lower price. Thus, this price discrimination is intended to satisfy the goal of equity.

EXPRESS STUDY TRUE OR FALSE

1. Perfectly competitive markets are characterized by ~~high~~ *no* barriers to entry.
2. An exclusive franchise is one example of a barrier to entry.
3. A four-firm concentration ratio equal to 100 always indicates a monopoly market. *or oligopoly*
4. Cartels are illegal in the United States.
5. Advertising provides a way to differentiate products.
6. Price discrimination occurs when a firm charges different customers different prices because there is a difference in the cost of serving those customers.
   when there is no

Module B

EXPLORING ISSUES

The United States Postal Service holds a special place in our hearts and in our history. It has politics on its side. What of economics? This Exploration considers whether the delivery of first-class mail is a natural monopoly, and whether privatization and competition would better serve the public interest.

Neither snow, nor rain, nor heat, nor gloom of night stays these couriers from the swift completion of their appointed rounds.
Inscription on Manhattan Post Office, adapted from "The Histories of Herodotus"

No Madison Avenue advertising agency could think up a better slogan for the post office than the motto adapted from the centuries-old writings of Herodotus. The mails must go through. That has been true since the post office was established on September 22, 1789.

What is probably the oldest monopoly in America is rich in tradition. The first postmaster general was Benjamin Franklin. In 1995 the post office earned $54.4 billion in revenue and had about 700,000 employees. That is big business, the 33rd largest company in the world according to *Fortune* magazine. Approximately 181 billion pieces of mail were sorted, routed, and delivered in 1995, 40 percent of the world's mail. Nonetheless, more and more, the following questions are being asked: Do we still need the post office? What could replace it?

The Postal Monopoly

All over the world delivery of mail is entrusted to governments. The U.S. Postal Service is a monopoly, guaranteed by the postal monopoly statutes and perhaps even the Constitution.

Critics of the post office have expressed disgust at how long it sometimes takes the mail to arrive, if it arrives at all. A few postal employees have even been known to dump mail into the garbage or take mail to their homes. Among the post office's other problems are occasionally rude employees and public worry over the rising costs of mailing a letter.

Will the delicate vase that we have mailed to Aunt Emma at Christmas arrive safely? What if she is at the doctor's office when delivery is attempted? Since the post office will not redeliver items and Aunt Emma no longer drives, how will she take delivery of the vase? The quality of service that consumers want is apparently not being delivered along with the mail. Could all these problems be related to the monopoly status of the Postal Service?

There is no private-sector firm exactly comparable to the U.S. Postal Service. Thus, legally and in practical terms, the Postal Service is a monopoly. Its colorful red, white, and blue vehicles rumble up and down the highways and byways of the country delivering mail to virtually every household and business in America. Full service to all communities is part of its tradition. No privately owned firm would deliver mail to communities if losses were the result. The post office must do so because of Congressional mandate.

Under penalty of law, deliveries to mailboxes are restricted to the Postal Service. Woe unto the youngster who unknowingly puts a hand-printed circular into a mailbox. That action, intended to help earn a little money from babysitting or mowing lawns, is a violation of federal law.

"Don't Fix What Ain't Broke"

Even if the postal monopoly laws did not provide barriers to entry, it is questionable whether a full-service competitor to the post office would enter the market. The reason is that, historically, the post office has required government appropriations to meet expenses. These appropriations have shrunk from 8.4 percent of total postal revenue in 1980 to 1.3 percent in 1991. The absolute dollar amounts are quite large, however, equaling $562 million in 1991, for example. Furthermore, the investment required to duplicate the fleet of vehicles, post offices, and equipment, and the recruiting and training of a work force, would mitigate against new competition.

Why does government deliver the mail, and not the private sector? Perhaps the best answer is that the public, while not entirely satisfied with the quality of service and its cost, has so far not pushed Congress to experiment with alternatives. Health care did not become a crisis until the cost of a one-day hospital stay reached the level of a month or two of the average worker's earnings. If the cost of mailing a letter reached an hour's pay, then perhaps more of us would want to see changes in the postal system. Even so, recent problems of deteriorating quality and increasing cost have caused renewed interest in privatization.

B

The Promise of Privatization

The benefits of privatization are realized when operating efficiencies are captured and passed on to consumers along with improvements in service. Numerous studies have documented the benefits of providing services through the private sector. Take weather forecasting, for example. The government's National Weather Service provides weather forecasts to farmers, seafarers, pilots, and others for whom accurate weather forecasts are a matter of life, death, and livelihood. But many businesses find it is worth the cost to subscribe to one of the many private forecasting services, such as Accuweather. At a minimum, private forecasts provide a useful second opinion. Worse for the government is the hypothesis that private forecasts are more complete and more accurate than government forecasts.

Localities that have replaced government-provided garbage collection with private-sector contracts have realized significant savings. Dozens of government-provided goods and services that have been turned over to the private sector show similar results. Towing of illegally parked cars, tree trimming along city streets, housekeeping and custodial services, forest management, private police protection, education, social services, family planning, and many more provide ample evidence. Furthermore, greater efficiency following privatization is a worldwide phenomena.

If the Postal Service were privatized—auctioned off to an owner who would run it on a for-profit basis—could consumers expect to benefit? Through cost savings and quality improvements, it would be possible to keep prices reasonable, make consumers happy with the service, and put profits into the pockets of the owner. However, it is also possible that a profit-maximizing monopolist would raise prices while allowing quality to deteriorate.

A privately owned post office monopoly would unquestionably raise public cries for regulation to provide incentives to operate with maximum efficiency while limiting profit to the level of normal profit. However, regulation is imperfect and is not likely to result in the capture of all efficiencies. Another possibility would be to repeal the postal monopoly statutes. There is plenty of competition in the market for package delivery. Without legal barriers preventing firms from delivering first-class mail, it seems likely that competition would emerge there, too.

Universal Access and Cross-Subsidies

If the postal service were privatized, would the public demand **universal access**? If universal access is preserved, the postal service would remain committed to the present practice of providing mail service to everyone. That adds to the cost. People who live in areas of sparse population are expensive to serve. An hour of a letter carrier's time and a gallon of gas can serve many more customers in a densely populated urban area than in a rural area. Would a privately owned postal service be tempted to cut off service to high-cost customers? Not if it were allowed to set a price that covered the cost of providing that service.

Certain services probably lose money for the Postal Service. In order to contribute to a higher level of national literacy, it reportedly delivers magazines and newspapers below cost. To reduce those losses, publishers agreed some years ago to standardize the size of their publications in accord with the desires of the Postal Service. That is why the *Ladies Home Journal* shrank in size, even as *Popular Mechanics* grew larger. A fully privatized post office would not continue to provide services at a loss. It would either raise prices, stop providing the service if profit proved impossible, or sell the facilities and equipment necessary to provide the service to another firm, which believed it could make a profit.

Postal authorities set prices on first class mail and on other services high enough to offset the losses on services that are underpriced. This practice is referred to as **cross-subsidization**. A problem is that these higher rates send customers searching for alternatives. As alternatives are found, the Postal Service loses customers. That means the remaining customers have to pay even higher rates. A vicious cycle is set in motion.

Stamping Out Innovation—At What Cost?

True monopoly involves the lack of close substitutes for a firm's product or service. Are there such substitutes for the services of the post office? Remember that the monopoly is a legal monopoly on first-class service, along with monopolization of the use of mailboxes. Private firms are allowed to compete against the post office on other kinds of service. United Parcel Service and Federal Express are examples of firms that have successfully taken on the competitive challenge.

Even with the rudimentary state of the information superhighway, snail mail, as the post office is derogatorily called by computer users, faces greater challenges in the future. Businesses are increasingly turning to their fax machines and e-mail because of lower cost and greater convenience. In this way, the market is circumventing the postal monopoly laws.

The choices facing the postal service are simple: (1) use its legal monopoly to eliminate innovative competitors, (2) innovate itself, or (3) do nothing and see its share of mail delivery continue to shrink. The first alternative is the simplest and possibly the most tempting. The result would be a twenty-first-century post office bearing a striking resemblance to its predecessor of the nineteenth century. The second alternative has been tried, but with mixed results. Competition is the spur to innovation, but with legal barriers to entry in first-class service, it remains to be seen how successful the Postal Service will be at remaking itself. One positive sign is that the Postal Service reduced its debt by $1.7 billion in 1995. The third alternative has little to recommend it, except for the power of the status quo. A national debate on the merits of privatization could help clarify alternatives and their costs as the information superhighway is expanded in the future.

The Power of Politics

Complicating privatization is the powerful postal workers' union. Postal workers are some of the nation's highest-paid unskilled workers. Privatization that increases the efficiency of delivery might involve layoffs, which would reduce the power of the union. Congress might find itself embroiled in controversy if privatization led to the loss of jobs.

One worry is that opening the Postal Service to competition would result in great rivalry in the most profitable segments of mail service, thus leaving the Postal Service with all the unprofitable segments. With unrestricted privatization, prices of each type of service would tend toward the marginal cost of that service. Prices would be efficient, but not necessarily fair. Politicians often worry about fairness rather than efficiency.

Perhaps the future will bring even newer technologies, which do away with postal services as we presently know them. Until that day, the economics of privatization paints a tantalizing picture of efficiency. Will that picture lose its allure? If privatization becomes a reality, time will tell.

PROSPECTING FOR NEW INSIGHTS

1. Do you believe that universal access is a legitimate philosophy to underpin the Postal Service? Should the rural population pay the full cost of providing service to the hinterlands?

2. If the post office is privatized, how should the government go about picking a new owner? What conditions, if any, do you think should be placed upon ownership? Would you prefer to see a privately owned, regulated postal service? If so, why? If not, why not?

Firms' costs are increased if they practice racial discrimination, gender discrimination, or other types of discrimination that is not motivated by the desire to minimize production costs. In competitive markets, these higher costs can force the exit of discriminating firms. Alternatively, government could punish discrimination directly. Which route is better? The experiences on two not-so-far-away planets may offer some guidance.[2]

Bartholomew Crockett sank into the velvet plush comfort of his favorite reading chair. He spilled a drop of steaming coffee on his left hand. No matter. He was holding a dog-eared copy of his favorite science fiction stories in that hand. His position as Chief Economist at the Washington think tank, more formally known as The Institute for Market Research, left him little time for pleasure reading. He was not going to let the slight burning sensation detract from the moment.

Because his work involved studying the effects of antidiscrimination policies, he felt a keen sense of excitement as he turned pages to find Stanton van Witt's classic *Directive 2082-50*. The story of two planets with different approaches to discrimination was thought-provoking as well as entertaining. Bartholomew took a sip of coffee and began to read.

B

Directive 2082-50

by Stanton van Witt

Rachel Abregon stared at the official document in her hand. Directive 2082-50 was short and to the point: Citizens of the planet Freemar have been granted the right to discriminate against any and all others, effective immediately.

So it has finally happened, Rachel thought. Resentment against the mass of beings from the dying planet of Bursa, who arrived on Freemar during the Great Migrations of the years 2051 to 2075, had raised the hackles of native Freemarians to this extreme. Rachel employed a number of Bursans in the firm she had founded not long after the migrations ended. Her decision to become an entrepreneur was made easier by the resulting increase in available labor. Besides, the newcomers, unlike Freemarians, were willing to tackle the dirty, dangerous job of halite mining. Abregon Mining exported halite to other worlds within the Realm of the Orb, the loose confederation of planets that

---

[2]In this story, Gary Becker and Milton Friedman are real people. All other names are those of fictional characters.

comprised a free trade area. She liked the migrants' work, although culturally, as the old saying goes, they might as well have been from another planet.

The smooth functioning of Abregon Mining forced Rachel to monitor in person its far-flung sales offices. The farthest reach of her travels was to Regula. Bursans had also arrived on that planet, creating resentment among the Regulans against the newcomers that equaled if not exceeded such resentment in Freemar.

In Regula, however, the ruling Council of Elders had a different policy toward discrimination. There, all forms of discrimination were outlawed. Antidiscrimination regulations were so numerous and complex on Regula that Rachel dreaded her periodic trips there, except for the opportunity to see her husband, Hagar. Much of the time that she spent on Regula had to be devoted to helping Hagar, sales manager on Regula, see to the tedious details of compliance with orders given to the firm by the Equality Police. They would have preferred to spend their precious time together rekindling intimacy. But sales on Regula were so great that she felt Hagar was the only person she could trust to handle the job.

Being a two-career family with the distance between them was not easy. Recently even greater care had to be taken since the police had been empowered by the Elders to burn on the spot any business that the police judged to be guilty of discrimination. Lately Regula's age-old nickname, "The Smoky Planet," was well justified. Giving too much power to bureaucrats was dangerous, Rachel concluded.

Rachel worried over how Freemarians would react to the Directive. Many were prejudiced against the newcomers. Until now, uncertainty about the law kept most from acting on that prejudice. But now discrimination was legal. She feared the effects of unfettered discrimination on the stability of her planet; she was also fearful for Hagar and for the future of her business on Regula, even though she knew in her heart that she was in total compliance with both the spirit and letter of the law.

B

Bartholomew placed the book on the mahogany side table and took another sip of coffee. From his previous readings of the story he knew quite well the fate that was to befall Rachel, and reacting to that knowledge, the hairs on the back of his neck bristled. Bartholomew continued to read.

As the years passed and cumulated to two generations, Rachel's worry had matured to alarm and finally to outright panic. Her travels to Regula and frequent conversations with Hagar over Interplanetary Bell had convinced her that Regulan society was disintegrating. The rate of disintegration had recently accelerated and had now reached the point that, as far as Rachel was concerned, would soon lead to the destruction of Regula. At first the drive to legislated equality on Regula had seemed to work. Fear of the burn-on-the-spot orders given the police had quickly eliminated the most visible forms of discrimination. But there was a price to be paid.

The perception arose among the Regulans that the newcomers ill deserved the job promotions and raises they received. Even worse was the per-

ception among the Regulans that their own wages and careers were on hold, as their employers attempted to satisfy the demands of the increasingly hard-to-satisfy Equality Police. Many Regulans thought the antidiscrimination policy was too harsh and economically harmful. Eventually grumbling gave way to intimidation of the newcomers by those Regulans who were willing to risk the penalties. Intimidation gradually turned into sporadic violence. Sporadic violence in turn gave birth to the well-organized terrorist organizations and then to the death squads. Defiance against authority and violent protest was the new credo by which Regulans lived.

Paradoxically, discrimination on Freemar had ceased to exist in the intervening years, and the planet was a model of peace and prosperity. At first, some business owners succumbed to temptation and indulged their baser inclinations by perpetrating various discriminatory acts against the newcomers. But those firms found themselves with higher costs and less ability to compete than their nondiscriminating counterparts. The competitive markets on Freemar ensured that firms with higher costs would either change their behavior or go out of business, to be replaced by nondiscriminating new firms, which would also experience lower costs. The competitive response, along with the inefficiencies introduced on Regula by its antidiscrimination laws, made Freemar the most productive, most efficient producer of goods and services within the Realm of the Orb.

Rachel knew what had to be done. She would go at once to Regula to bring Hagar home again. Abregon Mining could use his skills in a hundred different ways on Freemar. With Regula on the edge of collapse, the sales office had no reason to stay open anyway. There were still a few shuttle flights to Regula—enough to get Rachel there and the two of them back home.

Three moons after her arrival in Regula, Rachel and Hagar boarded the shuttle for the flight to Freemar. It was packed with Bursans fleeing Regula to join their relatives on Freemar. About ten seconds after the great craft lifted from the ground, the smoky atmosphere exploded with fire. The bomb had done its work well, instantly killing all aboard. The history books of Freemar were to record the event as the beginning of The Third and Final Equality War of the Dead Planet Regula.

Rachel and Hagar came to be honored on Freemar as martyrs sacrificed at the altar of unlimited government.

Bartholomew pondered the moral of the story with the help of a last swallow of coffee. He recognized that the thesis of the story was in accordance with the writings of the Nobel Prize–winning economist Gary Becker. Becker pioneered the economic study of discrimination. In his work, *The Economics of Discrimination* (1957), Becker used economic theory to demonstrate that competitive markets would lead to the elimination of discrimination in the long run. In the tradition of another "Chicago school" Nobel Prize winner, Milton Friedman, Becker's writings often acknowledged the unintended side effects of government policies. Perhaps Becker would have envisioned the destruction of the Regulan economy from its government's antidiscrimination policy, thought Bartholomew.

Bartholomew's brow wrinkled, revealing the depth of his thoughts. It was obvious to him that van Witt had written the story to make clear that there are economic advantages to not discriminating. The critical question is whether firms would give up profits to discriminate. Is profit king in the business world?

Bartholomew found himself pacing back and forth, dissatisfied with the outcome of van Witt's story. Then, in a flash, he knew what he must do. He must compose his own ending to replace the one offered by van Witt. Bartholomew eagerly sat at his desk and began to compose. This is what he wrote:

As the years passed and cumulated to two generations, Rachel became more and more withdrawn. The conflict on Freemar, which had intensified with the passage of time, had left her distraught and ultimately in shock. The directive issued long ago had unleashed wave after wave of destruction upon the economy, the culture, and the people of Freemar. In a self-indulgent orgy of discrimination, many of the largest firms in Freemar had been willing to put themselves at a competitive disadvantage relative to nondiscriminating firms on Regula. The price of discrimination proved high as massive numbers of business failures on Freemar gave birth to the Perpetual Depression. The Depression bred more conflict and destruction.

Meanwhile, Regula prospered. The Equality Police had succeeded in stamping out every last bit of discrimination on the planet. The plethora of antidiscrimination measures the Council of Elders imposed had met with resistance at first. But with the passage of time prejudice had faded. "Beings are just beings." was the slogan Rachel had seen everywhere on Regula. The slogans, the affirmative action plans, the quotas, and the equality acts had all been effective. Regula had entered the history books as a prime example of the good that government action can achieve. And with the elimination of discrimination came great prosperity. Firms that hire qualified employees without regard to color, shape, or planet of origin experience the lowest costs; firms that discriminate incur additional costs arising because of their refusal to deal with qualified minority beings. The competitive advantage held by firms on Regula allowed them to grow into the industrial giants of the Realm of the Orb.

Abregon Mining, following Rachel's better instincts, was a rare exception on Freemar. Her firm did not discriminate. It therefore maintained some modest prosperity while every aspect of life on Freemar was collapsing around it. Success in a sea of failure breeds resentment. And many resented Rachel's ability to keep her business going. When the violent finality that would later be referred to on Regula as the Ultimate Tribulations of Freemar exploded around her, Rachel was powerless. She was one of the first victims. Her death occurred at the hands of a mob—a mob that grew and turned upon itself until no one was left alive.

The people of Regula mourned the passing of Freemar, but saw it as the fiery hand of just retribution. Hagar never remarried, but sold what was left of Abregon Mining and devoted the rest of his life to the service of the Equality Police as a personal memorial to Rachel.

B

1. Explain why the model of perfect competition is central to this story. How might the story change if markets were to be monopolistically competitive?

2. When the newcomers are discriminated against, van Witt's story does not provide details. What are some specific actions that are discriminatory? The story suggests discrimination creates costs for the discriminator. Can you describe how a firm that discriminates puts itself at a disadvantage and increases its costs?

B

Module C

MASTERING ROADSIDE CHALLENGES

CHALLENGE 1
Long-Run Supply in Perfect Competition

In the short run, a perfectly competitive supply curve slopes upward because each firm's marginal cost curve slopes upward. In the long run, when there is time for entry and exit of firms, supply may slope upward, slope downward, or be totally flat. **Long-run supply** is the long-run equilibrium quantity that will be sold at each possible price.

The shape of long-run supply depends upon the behavior of input prices as industry output changes. There are three possible cases, as follows:

1. **Constant-cost industry:** An increase in the industry's output does not affect input prices.
2. **Increasing-cost industry:** An increase in the industry's output causes input prices to rise.
3. **Decreasing-cost industry:** An increase in the industry's output causes input prices to fall.

Figure 7C1-1 shows the effect of an increase in demand for the product of a competitive industry. The increased demand generates profits, which attract new entrants into the industry. Newly entering firms shift supply to the right. How far it shifts depends upon which of the three types of industries it is, as shown in the figure. The long-run supply curve connects the initial market equilibrium and the new market equilibrium. Long-run supply is seen to slope upward for an increasing-cost industry, to be flat for a constant-cost industry, and to slope downward for a decreasing-cost industry.

The typical scenario that identifies a constant-cost industry starts with an increase in demand for its output. Existing firms, which are assumed to be earning normal profits at this time, meet an increase in demand by increasing output. But the greater output carries a higher price, because the short-run supply curve slopes upward. The economic profits for existing firms created by the price increase causes entry of new firms. They contribute their output to industry production, thus shifting the short-run supply curve to the right. The movement in the short-run supply curve drives the price back down. In the case of a constant-cost industry, the price moves back down to its original level. Entry will stop at this point because firms are back to normal profits. This story unfolds in this way because new firms were able to enter the industry without affecting the average or marginal cost of production. The lack of impact of entry on cost is the substance of a constant-cost industry.

The story of an increasing-cost industry starts similarly to that of the constant-cost industry. An increase in demand drives up price and increases profits for existing firms, thus causing the entry of new firms. But something different happens at this point. The new firms, in their scramble for resources, cause input prices to rise for the whole industry. The cost curves shift up for all firms as a consequence. Higher costs mean that the price must end up higher than where it started in order for firms to reach normal profit.

Chapter Seven Market Models **267**

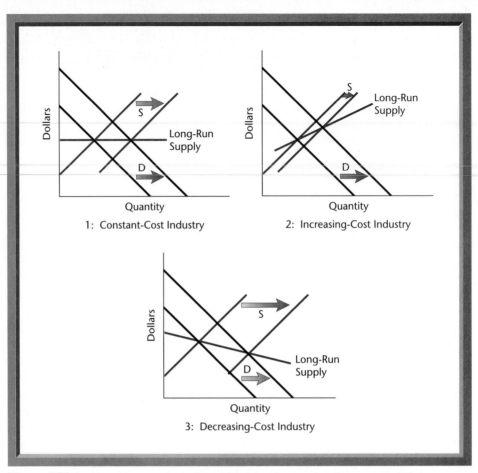

Figure 7C1-1 **Long-run supply is determined by changes in short-run equilibriums over time.** How far short-run supply (S) shifts over time in response to a change in demand (D) will depend upon whether an industry is constant cost, increasing cost, or decreasing cost.

For example, an increase in the demand for fresh shrimp would in the long run put more shrimp boats into the water. If more shrimpers seeking a catch caused the price of nets to increase, the industry would fit the increasing-cost model.

In a decreasing-cost industry, entry shifts the cost curves down. For example, as the electronics industry expanded in Silicon Valley in California, the movement of skilled labor to the area, the development of specialty suppliers, and increased transportation facilities contributed to lower production costs.

C

A monopolist or other firm that faces a downward-sloping demand curve chooses quantity and price according to the profit maximizing rule: **Produce the quantity where marginal revenue equals marginal cost.** Table 7C2-1 below shows the demand, revenue, and cost data required to master the logic of profit maximization for an imperfectly competitive firm.

Revenue data make up the first four columns. The price (P) and quantity (Q) columns show the firm's demand. Total revenue (TR) is price multiplied by quantity. Marginal revenue (MR) equals the change in total revenue divided by the change in quantity. The fifth column shows total cost (TC); the sixth shows marginal cost (MC); the seventh shows average cost (AC). The final column shows profit. Sighting down the final column reveals that maximum profit equals $24.50, which occurs at five units of output and a price of $7.00.

The firm's decision to produce five units can also be reached by comparing marginal revenue to marginal cost. The firm will produce the next unit of output so long as marginal revenue equals or exceeds marginal cost, which again leads to the output of five units. The firm would not produce the sixth unit since marginal cost exceeds marginal revenue.

Figure 7C2-1 shows graphically a profit-maximizing monopoly. Quantity (Q*) is set at the point where marginal revenue equals marginal cost. Price (P*) is set according to the demand curve. The average cost at quantity Q* is labeled AC*. Total profit is represented graphically as the area of the rectangle labeled Profit. This is a simple application of the length times width formula for the area of a rectangle. In the graph, length equals profit per unit, the difference between price and average cost, and width equals the quantity produced.

TABLE 7C2-1			*Revenue and Costs for a Firm with Market Power (Average cost rounded to the nearest penny)*					
P	**Q**	**TR**	**MR**	**TC**	**MC**	**AC**	**Profit**
$12.00	0	$0.00	Undefined	$3.00	Undefined	Undefined	$−3.00
11.00	1	11.00	$11.00	4.00	$1.00	$4.00	+7.00
10.00	2	20.00	9.00	4.50	0.50	2.25	+15.50
9.00	3	27.00	7.00	5.50	1.00	1.83	+21.50
8.00	4	32.00	5.00	7.50	2.00	1.88	+24.50
7.00	5	35.00	3.00	10.50	3.00	2.10	+24.50
6.00	6	36.00	1.00	15.50	5.00	2.58	+20.50
5.00	7	35.00	−1.00	24.00	8.50	3.43	+11.00
4.00	8	32.00	−3.00	36.00	12.00	4.50	−4.00
3.00	9	27.00	−5.00	52.00	16.00	5.78	−25.00
2.00	10	20.00	−7.00	70.00	18.00	7.00	−50.00
1.00	11	11.00	−9.00	92.00	22.00	8.36	−81.00
0.00	12	0.00	−11.00	120.00	28.00	10.00	−120.00

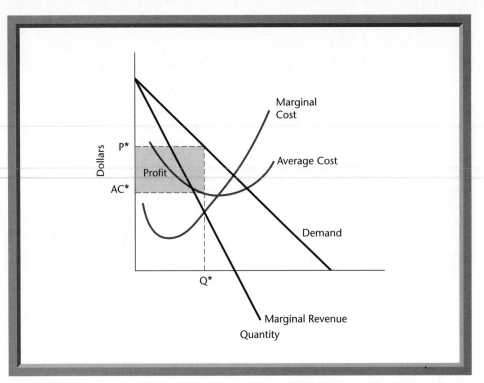

Figure 7C2-1   Total profit equals profit per unit multiplied by quantity. Total profit is illustrated graphically as the shaded area of the rectangle labeled Profit.

C

Study by Design

SpeedStudy

SpeedReview

Markets can be arranged by the degree to which firms have market power. The models of perfect competition and monopoly are extreme in their assumptions, but can be used to analyze many market situations for which other details do not matter. When those details become important, models of monopolistic competition or oligopoly may be more pertinent. Oligopoly is the only market structure containing numerous models, including cartel, game theory, and others. In any of the imperfectly competitive market structures, firms have some control over price. Sometimes they can segment the market and find it profitable to price discriminate.

SpeedStudy True or False Self-Test

A1. Long-run equilibrium in perfect competition is characterized by economic ~~profit~~. *breakeven*

A2. Economic efficiency is achieved in perfectly competitive markets.

A3. The best example of natural monopoly is a ~~taxi-cab company~~. *loc. publ. util.*

A4. Advertising may create a barrier to entry.

A5. A firm facing a demand curve that slopes downward to the right has market power.

A6. To maximize profit, a monopolist will set ~~price~~ *MR* equal to marginal cost. *another price associated with the correspondi... quantity*

A7. Fair-rate-of-return regulation of monopoly is designed to provide a monopolist with a normal profit.

A8. Cartels are found in ~~monopolistically competitive~~ markets. *oligopolistic*

A9. If one computer manufacturer merges with another computer manufacturer, the merger is termed ~~vertical~~ merger. *horizontal*

A10. Entry is ~~difficult in~~ monopolistically competitive markets. *easy*

B11. The postal monopoly laws are a barrier to entry.

B12. The U.S. Postal Service faces vigorous competition in the market for first-class mail.

B13. Economic analysis shows that discrimination cannot occur.

B14. Becker used the competitive model to show that market forces would eventually eliminate discrimination.

C15. The ~~demand~~ curve of a constant-cost industry is perfectly elastic. *supply*

C16. The supply curve of a decreasing-cost industry slopes downward in the long run.

C17. If a firm has market power, the firm's marginal revenue curve lies ~~above~~ its demand curve. *below*

C18. A monopolist's profit equals the difference between price and average cost, multiplied by the quantity produced.

The MasterMind

Selected Terms along the Way

perfect competition, 240
market power, 240
barriers to entry, 240
monopoly, 240
oligopoly, 240
monopolistic competition, 240
homogeneous products, 241
natural monopoly, 246
limit pricing, 249

deregulation, 250
mutually interdependent, 250
cartel, 250
game theory, 251
contestable markets, 252
price leadership, 252
horizontal integration, 253
vertical integration, 253
conglomerate merger, 253

product differentiation, 255
price discrimination, 256

universal access, 260
cross-subsidization, 260

long-run supply, 267
constant-cost industry, 267
increasing-cost industry, 267
decreasing-cost industry, 267

MasterMind Multiple Choice Self-Test

A1. Economic efficiency requires that quantity produced in a market be such that
   a. firms earn economic profits.
   b. firms at least break even.
   c. the last unit produced has a value to consumers equal to its marginal cost of production.
   d. average cost is maximized.

A2. Which is *not* a barrier to entry?
   a. High profits.
   b. An exclusive franchise.
   c. Natural monopoly.
   d. Import quotas.

A3. Price leadership describes a model of
   a. natural monopoly.
   b. monopoly.
   c. oligopoly.
   d. monopolistic competition.

A4. Which of the following is the best example of vertical merger?
   a. A computer manufacturer merges with a computer store.
   b. Two book publishers merge.
   c. A jewelry store merges with a furniture store.
   d. A cosmetics manufacturer merges with a pizza restaurant.

A5. Price discrimination
   a. results when an increase in costs forces a firm to raise its price.
   b. results when an increase in demand causes a price increase.
   c. is illegal in the U.S.
   d. occurs when one consumer pays a higher price than another, and there is no difference in cost to justify the price difference.

B6. Interest in privatization of postal services is prompted by concerns over
   a. privacy in the handling of mail.
   b. inequities in the delivery of mail.
   c. whether the free market could make a profit delivering mail.
   d. deteriorating quality and increasing cost.

B7. Gary Becker's view of discrimination is that
   a. it is not a problem.
   b. competition in markets will ultimately lead to its elimination.
   c. government action is the only way to stop discrimination.
   d. all firms will discriminate if given the chance.

C8. Which of the following would best explain an increasing-cost industry?
   a. Input shortages as output expands.

b. High barriers to entry.

c. Rapidly expanding demand.

d. Price discrimination.

C9. A monopoly can sell four units of output at $3 each and five units of output at $2 each. The marginal revenue of the fifth unit of output equals

a. $2.

b. $-2.

c. $12.

d. $10.

MasterMind Questions and Problems

A1. List the four forms of market structure and their characteristics. If you owned a firm, in which market structure would you prefer to operate? Why?

A2. You've decided you're going to live the simple life, which requires selling off your belongings. In which of the following instances, if any, would you be a price taker?

a. For sale: 1984 Escort.

b. For sale: 100 shares of General Motors common stock.

c. For sale: Panasonic 19″ color television.

d. For sale: apartment full of furniture.

Does it appear from this exercise that the classified for sale ads are populated with price takers?

A3. The mere fact of monopoly guarantees that a firm will earn economic profits. True or false? Explain.

A4. Product differentiation is found in oligopoly and monopolistic competition. What purpose does product differentiation serve from a firm's perspective? From society's perspective?

A5. Why is the model of perfect competition usu-

ally preferable to the model of monopolistic competition?

B6. What substitutes exist for the services of the U.S. Postal Service? Do you expect the Internet to be an even better substitute in the future? Why or why not?

B7. Milton Friedman, in *Capitalism and Freedom* and in other writings, argues that competitive markets are an effective force mitigating racial and other discrimination. For example, he claims that buyers of bread care only about getting their bread at the lowest price and not about the race of the baker. That allows anyone of any race to become a baker. Does Friedman's argument make sense to you? Why or why not?

C8. Identify some industries that would be approximated by the model of perfect competition. For each, indicate reasons to think the industry might be increasing cost, decreasing cost, or constant cost.

C9. Illustrate graphically a monopoly firm that is maximizing profit, but earns only a normal profit.

Future Explorations: Mapping out Term Papers

1. The Antitrust Laws—What's Legal and What's Not?

You will put the antitrust laws into practical perspective by identifying specific actions that legislation and the courts have ruled to be illegal. Your paper should be written in the form of a business report addressed to your boss, an executive who would like to become more informed on these matters. Your boss asks that you document your report with references to court cases.

2. **Barriers to Entry and Oligopoly**

   The goal of this research is to identify the barriers to entry in several oligopoly industries of interest to you. In addition to your own observations and conjectures, you will be required to consult the writings of industrial organization economists to identify industries commonly considered to be oligopolistic. What conclusions have these economists reached regarding the relationship between profitability and barriers to entry?

3. **Deregulation: Past, Present, and Future**

   This paper traces the history of deregulation since the 1970s and evaluates its success. The paper examines (a) whether more or less competition has been the outcome and (b) whether it appears that more industries will be deregulated or reregulated in the future. The paper provides evidence to support its analysis.

Answer Key

ExpressStudy True or False		SpeedStudy True or False Self-Test		MasterMind Multiple Choice Self-Test
1. F		1. F	10. F	1. c
2. T		2. T	11. T	2. a
3. F		3. F	12. F	3. c
4. T		4. T	13. F	4. a
5. T		5. T	14. T	5. d
6. F		6. F	15. F	6. d
		7. T	16. T	7. b
		8. F	17. F	8. a
		9. F	18. T	9. b

Income From Labor and Human Capital

A LOOK AHEAD

Labor matters affect people personally in their daily lives. Numerous stories spring to mind: Ralph, an unskilled worker, seizes the opportunity to enroll in skills training classes; Ethel, a factory worker, ponders joining a labor union in hopes of higher wages; Juanita, a middle manager, frets over the possibility of being laid off; Sam, who has been unemployed for two years, is so discouraged that he is ready to stop looking for work; Jane feels outrage at the wage gap between herself and male co-workers; and college students on the verge of graduation worry about finding their first real jobs in an overcrowded job market. These examples show that labor issues surely enter the everyday thoughts of millions of people. This chapter examines the labor market, with wages, employment, and wage differentials between individuals and among groups as the primary focus.

DESTINATIONS

Module A

As you zip along the Expressway you will arrive at an ability to

- state why the demand for labor is a derived demand;
- explain the link between the reservation wage and labor force participation;
- describe the roles of competitive and noncompetitive influences in labor markets;
- explain why wages differ among workers and relate this explanation to the earnings gap experienced by women and minorities;
- identify the extent and significance of poverty in the U.S. economy.

Module B

Upon leaving the Expressway to explore issues you will be able to

- discuss recent trends in the U.S. distribution of income and their significance;
- distinguish when it is appropriate to place a dollar value on human life.

Module C

Mastering Roadside Challenges will allow you to hone analytical skills by

- deriving a firm's demand and profit-maximizing employment of labor;
- using the human capital model to examine the decision to attend college.

Psychologists tell us that an adult's sense of self-worth is often closely tied to work. A job is akin to a membership card in society. People without jobs often feel incomplete. People with jobs often strive for better ones. For many students, the chief motive for attending college is greater future economic security.

Anyone who has ever had a job or tried to get one has been a part of the labor market. In 1995, of a U.S. civilian, noninstitutional population of 198.5 million people above the age of 16, approximately 125 million received income from employment, with the median (half above and half below) full-time worker earning $24,856. About five million business firms provided most of those jobs. Another eight million or so labor-market participants are unemployed.

The labor market comprises firms and individuals. Unlike the product market, in which firms are sellers and individuals are buyers, individuals sell their labor services to firms in the labor market.

The Price of Labor's Services: The Wage Rate

Individuals offer their services to employers to earn incomes. The size of their incomes depends upon two variables: the quantity of labor they supply and the amount they are paid. The quantity of labor supplied is usually measured in hours. The *wage rate* is the amount an individual is paid per hour. When the wage rate is multiplied by hours worked, the result is *wages*, the income from labor.

Most hourly wage workers who work more than forty hours a week receive time and a half for all hours over forty. Hours in excess of forty are called *overtime* hours. Overtime wage rates are 50 percent greater than the *straight-time* rate which a worker receives for the first 40 hours worked. The Department of Labor enforces these rules, which arise from the *Fair Labor Standards Act*, enacted by Congress in 1938.

Workers who are paid a *salary* receive a fixed amount of income, no matter how many hours they work. Employers expect salaried employees to work a minimum number of hours per week, typically corresponding to the regular operating hours of the business. If such employees work additional hours, they are not paid for those hours. For instance, certified public accountants (CPAs) are often expected to work sixty hours a week or more during the weeks before April 15 in order to prepare tax returns prior to the annual Internal Revenue Service filing deadline. Their salaries do not rise despite the longer hours worked during tax season.

Salaried workers may voluntarily seek extra duties from their employers, pushing their hours of work over the required minimum. Why would a worker who is not a workaholic toil additional hours for no additional pay? The answer is that future promotions and raises often depend upon a worker's willingness to work longer hours. Future financial gain accordingly provides the incentive to work longer hours in the present.

An employer's **total labor costs** are the sum of wages (and salaries) plus fringe benefits. Some benefits are voluntarily offered by employers; others are required by government. Typical benefits received by workers include paid vacations, sick leave, employer contributions to Social Security, *workers' compensation* coverage, which provides workers who are injured on the job with a stipend while they recuperate from their injuries, paid time off for lunch, and health benefits. Benefits account for about 28 percent of labor costs for the typical U.S. employer.

An individual's wage or salary ought to relate directly to his or her contribution to the firm's output. For many jobs it is difficult to calculate individual **labor productivity**, the amount of output produced by a worker during some time period. To see the difficulty, consider a hospital administrator who evaluates the work of staff physicians. In an average day one doctor sees 50 patients who have minor complaints. Another treats 10 patients with life-threatening illnesses. Which doctor is more productive? Simply looking at the number of patients is not very revealing. This example illustrates how difficult it is for personnel managers to set individual pay.

A worker's productivity can be easily measured only in a few instances. These occur when employees work individually rather than as part of a team, with each working under identical conditions with identical work to do. For example, a clothing factory that provides each employee with the same model sewing machine and the same pattern to sew, could compare the outputs of various workers. Even in this instance, however, true productivity differences might depend in part on other factors, such as workplace lighting, balky machines, and interruptions. Nonetheless, some workers are paid on a *piecerate* basis, meaning that their pay depends directly on their productivity as measured by how many units of something they produce.

*L*abor Demand

Business firms employ most workers. But over 10 million people were self-employed in 1995. A market demand curve for labor shows the quantity of labor that all employers in a labor market will employ at various wage rates. The quantity of labor is usually measured in hours rather than number of workers, because employers may increase or decrease the number of hours their employees work rather than hire or fire workers.

Market labor demand curves are downward sloping, as illustrated in Figure 8A-1. Higher wage rates decrease the quantity of labor demanded, whereas lower wage rates increase the quantity of labor demanded. The demand for labor varies by the following:

- **occupation:** The demand for accountants is distinct from the demand for attorneys, which is distinct from the demand for welders, which is distinct. . . . Well, you get the idea. Occupational demands are distinct for dissimilar occupations because labor is associated with human capital that is specific to the occupation—*specific human capital*. That makes it difficult to transfer skills from one occupation to another.
- **geography:** For instance, the demand curve for labor in your hometown would most likely differ from the demand curves in neighboring towns.
- **industry:** An industry demand curve for labor shows the quantity of labor employed by all firms in an industry at various wage rates. Various industries may compete for the same pool of workers. The concept of industry demand for labor is especially useful when the mix of occupations in an industry is taken into account. Growing indus-

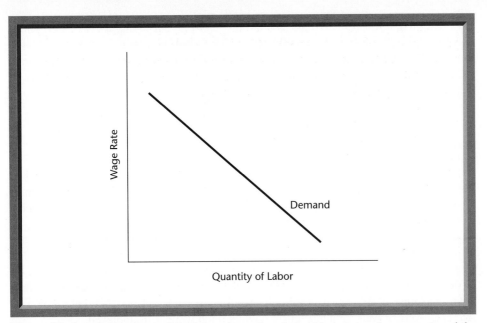

Figure 8A-1   Market demand for labor shows the relationship between the wage rate and the quantity of labor employed. For simplicity, the wage rate is assumed to include fringe benefits.

tries create new employment opportunities for workers who are trained in the occupations useful to those industries.

Labor demand curves shift to the left when business activity slows down. When the economy improves, labor demand curves shift to the right, as the demand for labor increases in the labor market as a whole and at individual firms and industries.

Labor demand is a **derived demand**, which means the demand for labor exists only because there is a demand for the firm's output. If a firm producing windows suddenly receives more orders because of an increase in new home construction, the firm increases its demand for hours of labor. It will either hire new workers or offer current employees the opportunity to work additional hours.

OBSERVATION POINT: Job Entrepreneurship—Finding What's Hot

The "hot" jobs of the future—jobs with openings and high pay—what are they and how do you get one? The U.S. Department of Labor publishes the *Occupational Outlook Handbook*, which projects future labor demand for numerous occupations. Recent projections show that most hot jobs, such as in medicine or computers, require advanced education or training. Unfortunately, projections of demand in specific fields can easily become as dated as yesterday's newspaper.

When "everybody" agrees on what will be hot, it's best to bet on something else. By the time you acquire the needed skills, so have a host of other people. Labor supply shifts out, and lucrative job opportunities become scarce. Instead, the secret to success may lie in being one of the first to identify hot job prospects of the future. There is risk in taking initiative. You might be wrong. If you follow that lonesome road, you may rightfully dub yourself a "job entrepreneur."

Labor Supply

Labor force participation concerns the decisions of individuals to offer their services in the labor market. To be counted as a member of the **civilian labor force**, a person must be sixteen years of age or older and either have paid employment or be actively looking for it. Examples of nonparticipants include full-time students and retirees. The **labor force participation rate** is the number of labor force participants divided by the population age 16 and over. In 1995 the overall labor force participation rate was 67 percent in the U.S. The rate for men was 75 percent, for women 57 percent, for whites 67 percent, and for African-Americans 64 percent. Of the approximately 125 million people earning income from employment, more than 7 million were multiple jobholders—they held jobs with two employers or were simultaneously holding a job while self-employed.

Individual preferences play a central role in explaining labor force participation. These preferences are evidenced in the individual's labor supply curve. Figure 8A-2 illustrates a typical labor supply curve. Below the **reservation wage**, individuals "reserve"

Figure 8A-2 **The backward bending supply curve** of an individual's labor services is explained by the tug of war between the income and substitution effects of a wage change.

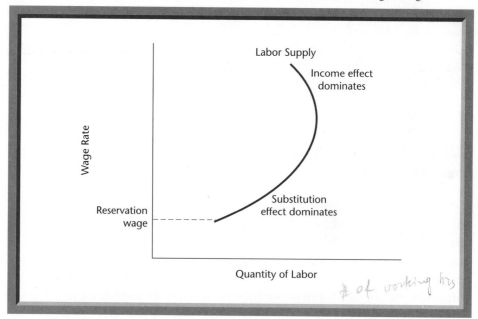

their labor—they choose not to work at all. Note that, unlike supply curves for other things, the individual's supply curve of labor services has a *backward-bending* portion. This shape can be understood by considering the substitution effect and the income effect of increasing wages.

As wages rise, the **substitution effect** of the change in wages causes individuals to work more—they substitute away from leisure, because the opportunity cost of leisure becomes higher as wage rates rise. The result is that people offer more hours in response to higher wages, causing the supply curve to slope upward. In place of leisure, workers consume goods and services with their increased earnings.

As wages rise, the **income effect** of the wage change tugs the worker in the opposite direction relative to the substitution effect. Higher wages bring higher incomes, which prompt workers to demand more of all normal goods. *Leisure*, time away from work, is a normal good. To buy more leisure, workers pay the opportunity cost of giving up the income from some work hours. The result is that, as wages rise, the income effect prompts workers to offer fewer hours of work. The supply curve bends backward when the income effect outweighs the substitution effect. This accounts for the huge decline in yearly hours of work for the average American worker during the twentieth century. The standard eight-hour work day and annual paid vacations have permitted workers to partake of more leisure as real incomes have risen this century. Self-employed workers, such as physicians and accountants with private practices, can increase their vacation time to enjoy their substantial income.

As seen in Figure 8A-2, the substitution effect tends to be stronger at lower wages, and the income effect stronger at higher wages. The result is a supply curve that first slopes upward and then bends backward.

Individuals' labor supply curves will vary depending on whether they are **primary workers**, the main source of income in households, or *secondary workers*, whose incomes are not as critical to their households' well-being. Primary workers are often called *breadwinners*. The labor supply curves of primary workers are nearly vertical, meaning that they will choose to work about the same number of hours, no matter the wages they are able to receive. The quantity of labor supplied by a primary worker is typically in the range of thirty-five to forty-five hours per week. In contrast, secondary workers have a much more pronounced upward slope and backward bend to their supply curves. Secondary workers are more likely to hold part-time jobs than primary workers.

As an example of an individual's labor supply decisions, consider Elena, a full-time college student. Graduating and earning good grades are her highest priorities. The $5.50 an hour paid by the local Burger Barn leaves her unimpressed. She could earn seven dollars an hour by occasionally modeling hair styles for Hair Trends, but she is still unwilling to take time away from her studies for that wage rate. The result is that she does not participate in the labor force.

If an employer was willing to pay Elena ten dollars an hour, she would go to work, but not for a penny less—ten dollars is her reservation wage. She figures that a few hours on the job each week would cause little harm to her grade point average. Elena would work even more hours if she was offered an even higher wage rate. If the wage she was offered soared to fifty dollars an hour, the opportunity cost of her leisure time would be too great to ignore; every hour of leisure time would cost her fifty dollars in lost earnings. She would then be willing to work twenty hours a week, which would still allow her to maintain passing grades.

Because of her commitment to her studies, Elena would not work more than twenty hours. That is the point where her personal labor supply curve bends back. For example, if she could earn a wage of seventy-five dollars per hour, she would reduce her hours of work because at that wage the income effect outweighs the substitution effect for her.

Elena's reservation wage could change. If she found herself short of tuition funds, she might even be willing to work at the Burger Barn for $5.50 an hour, if that was the only choice she had. When she graduates with a Bachelor's degree, her reservation wage is likely to go up because of her perception that the value of her labor services has been increased by her degree. If she doesn't receive a job offer in a reasonable period of time that meets that higher reservation wage, she might eventually lower her reservation wage. Reservation wages can change as individuals are unable to find work and as they learn more about the job market.

Labor supply curves may shift. Many persons receive *nonlabor income* from investments, pension funds, government transfer payments, interest on bank deposits, gifts from relatives, and so forth. The amount of nonlabor income received can affect labor market choices. Generally, a greater amount of nonlabor income will reduce the labor a worker supplies. When people have sufficient income from other sources, such as from Social Security, they often take early retirement, for example. If Elena did not receive income from home, it is likely that her labor supply curve would shift to the right and her reservation wage would decline.

The *market labor supply* sums the quantity of labor supplied at various wage rates for all the individuals in a labor market. Market supply curves of labor are upward sloping in the range of income that is usually relevant to employers. Because the market supply curve aggregates the labor offerings of all workers, its elasticity is between that typical of either primary or secondary workers.

An *industry labor supply* sums the quantity of labor supplied to a particular industry at various wage rates. Because higher wages in one industry attract workers from other industries, any particular industry supply curve of labor is nearly always upward sloping and usually quite elastic. For example, as wages rise in the trucking industry, some truckers might work less because of the income effect. However, it is likely that the reduction in worktime by individual truckers will be more than offset by an inflow of would-be truckers from other occupations.

Labor Markets

The exchange of labor services for wages occurs in *labor markets*. To some extent, each occupation, industry, and geographic area has its own labor market. Some labor markets are national in scope; others are local. For instance, the matching of professors to college and university employers typically occurs at national professional meetings. Professors and college administrators come from around the country to participate in job interviews at a central meeting place. Contacts made at these meetings lead to job placements. In contrast, colleges looking for clerical workers tap into their local labor markets for help. In the local area, colleges are likely to find clerks available for employment but few professors with specialized skills.

Labor market analysis may also highlight a geographic area. A particular town's labor market may be robust, providing its residents with good wages and job opportunities. At the same time, the labor market in a nearby town could be experiencing low wages and high unemployment. This scenario was played out in the western U.S. during the early 1990s. California's economy was in recession because of layoffs in defense industries, while neighboring Nevada's unemployment rate was significantly lower because of rapid growth in tourism there.

Differences in labor demand and supply across geographic areas create differences in wages and unemployment rates. Such differences arise because many jobs are filled using labor from a limited geographic area. Common sense says that the unemployed who live in areas where jobs are scarce ought to move to areas where labor shortages exist. Although some workers migrate, labor *immobility* also exists. Workers find that family ties, home ownership, and a preference for their present location inhibits their movement to places where job openings exist. In the 1970s work was plentiful and wages were high along the Alaska pipeline, but relatively few workers were willing to endure the harsh Alaskan winters.

OBSERVATION POINT: Build It and They Shall Come

In the late 1980s, America began to hear of the small town of Branson, Missouri. For seemingly inexplicable reasons, Branson was developing into a mini-Las Vegas, Ozark-style. Stars of country and middle-of-the-road music had found their home away from home. Theaters, gas stations, convenience stores, and fast-food restaurants sprang up rapidly to service the hordes of tourists who came to see and hear their favorite stars. Even Elvis was rumored to be hiding out there.

Where was the supply of workers who would fill the new, mostly unskilled jobs? Branson was growing so fast that job growth far outstripped the local labor supply. No problem! National publicity about Branson prompted a migration of the unemployed to the Ozark community. The lure of a job and the chance to rub shoulders with the stars provided a powerful incentive to move to Branson, thus demonstrating that labor immobility can be overcome.

Competitive—No Market Power

Like markets for output, labor markets can take several forms. The type of market in which a firm sells its output does not determine the type of market in which it buys its labor inputs. For example, oligopoly firms may purchase labor services in a competitive market.

A **perfectly competitive labor market** exists when the demand for labor and the supply of labor establish an equilibrium wage rate and quantity of labor. Characteristics similar to those that apply to perfect competition in the output market also apply to perfect competition in the labor market, including the following:

- There are many buyers and sellers of labor services in the market.
- The services of labor are homogeneous.
- The market is free of barriers to entry and exit.

The third characteristic means that workers are free to change jobs or move to labor markets that pay higher wages, if they wish to do so. Employers are also free to enter or exit labor markets. In practical terms, employers can freely relocate.

In a perfectly competitive labor market, employers are *wage takers*, which means that each will be able to hire as much or as little labor as it wishes at the going market wage rate. Figure 8A-3 shows the elements of a competitive labor market. The left panel shows the market demand and supply curves in a labor market. The intersection establishes the equilibrium wage rate and the equilibrium market quantity of labor hired. Since the labor market clears, there is neither a shortage nor surplus of labor. In common parlance, a surplus of labor is called *unemployment*.

The right panel in Figure 8A-3 shows a single, wage-taking employer. In perfect competition, the market wage rate equals the **marginal cost of labor**, the additional cost of employing one more unit of labor, which is also the supply of labor to the firm. Whatever the market structure in the labor market, one rule always holds: **Profit-maximizing firms hire to the point at which the marginal cost of labor equals the marginal value of labor to the firm.** In other words, a firm continues adding labor so long as the revenue it receives from the output produced by one more unit of labor is at least sufficient to cover the added cost resulting from employing that unit of labor.

Market Power in the Labor Market—Wages Could Be Driven Up or Down

The model of perfect competition assumes that both employers or employees are price takers, meaning that they have no market power. However, market power is often present in the labor market and can drive wages either up or down from the competitive level.

Figure 8A-3   **The competitive labor market** sets the wage, which implies a horizontal supply of labor to the firm. The firm's demand for labor will determine the quantity of labor it hires at that wage.

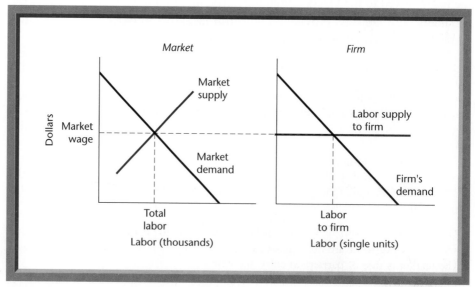

To the extent that workers gain control of the labor market, the wage rate will increase to more than the competitive level. The wage rate will decrease to less than the competitive level to the extent that employers dominate. These effects are captured in the following labor market models:

- **monopsony**—only one employer of labor;
- **monopoly**—only one seller of labor, a labor union;
- **bilateral monopoly**—only one employer and only one seller of labor.

Fewness of employers of labor creates *monopsony power* for firms. Such firms are able to pay workers less than the competitive wage. The extreme case of monopsony is *pure monopsony*—one buyer of labor's services. The best example of monopsony occurs in geographically isolated mill towns. The mill provides a reason for the town to exist because most of its citizens work there. As the major employer, the mill can offer less than the competitive wage rate to prospective workers. Highly specialized types of labor, such as astronauts or fighter pilots, may also face monopsony in their country's labor market.

Monopolies are said to possess market power because of their ability to raise prices above the level indicated by the intersection of supply and demand. *Labor unions*, discussed in the next section, are analogous to monopolies, in that unions eliminate competition for jobs among workers in order to raise the price of their members' labor. If they are successful in monopolizing the supply of labor's services, unions drive wages higher than would occur in competition.

Under a bilateral monopoly, the wage depends on whether the employer or employee bargains more effectively. Professional sports organizations often approximate bilateral monopoly. In the summer of 1994, for example, major league baseball players went on strike to protect their lucrative wages and benefits. The players union commenced to negotiate with the owners association—one seller and one buyer for players' services. After much acrimony, the two sides resumed playing baseball the following spring. It was not clear which side came out ahead. Because the strike generated ill will among fans, which reduced interest in the sport, it may be that both sides lost.

*W*hy Do Wages Differ?

Wage differentials among workers sometimes seem intuitive. We expect a heart surgeon to earn more than a janitor. Many wage differentials are not so easy to understand, however. Why should physicians earn more than teachers? Why should star athletes earn more than physicians? Individual wages differ because of a combination of market and other factors.

Occupational Choice and Change

Modern economies provide numerous occupational choices for workers. The U.S. government catalogs 801 occupations in the publication, *Occupational Employment Statistics*, and over 12,000 highly detailed occupations in the *Dictionary of Occupational Titles*. Occupational choice plays a significant role in earnings power. Generally, the highest-paying occupations are those that require the greatest skills, and the lowest paying are the unskilled occupations.

As economies grow more complex because of technological change, new job opportunities are created as old ones fade away. Just ask the thousands of (mostly) women who earned their living as keypunchers in the 1960s and 1970s how rapidly change can occur. In those days, data were entered into mainframe computers on paper cards that had been pierced with tiny holes by keypunchers. Punchcards and keypunch machines are hard to find outside museums today.

The skills required to keypunch were simple typing skills. No knowledge of computers was required. With retraining, many keypunchers were able to master the higher-level skills required by the new personal computers, which became common in the early 1980s. The keypunchers are a paradigm for today's labor market. Today, workers in most occupations are expected to possess more specialized skills and to keep their skills current.

✔ **QUICKCHECK**

Can you think of additional occupations that have disappeared or seen their numbers decline because of technological change?

_____

Answer: Elevator operators were supplanted by automatic elevators, switchboard operators by automated systems, longshoremen by mechanized containers, telegraphers by telephones, railway porters by airplanes, blacksmiths by automobiles, . . . the list is endless.

Compensating Wage Differentials

Different jobs have their own advantages and disadvantages. Most people would rather work at safe jobs in air-conditioned comfort rather than at dangerous jobs outside in the extremes of weather. Higher pay in the latter jobs will be necessary in order to equalize their attractiveness relative to the former jobs. Such increases in pay are termed **compensating wage differentials**.

Sanitation workers, coal miners, and others have unpleasant or dangerous jobs. To induce workers to take those jobs, employers must pay a compensating differential. Note that even with compensating differentials included, the pay in such jobs may still be relatively low, because skill requirements in many of these jobs are low.

People choose jobs on the basis of a spectrum of characteristics. Pay, the *pecuniary* attribute, is the most important characteristic for some. For others, job security, status, the likelihood of advancement, safe working conditions, the inherent interest of the work, or the flexibility of employers in matters of dress or hours is most important. Job features unrelated to pay are called the *nonpecuniary* attributes. Positive nonpecuniary features can offset low pay and vice versa.

Unions

Workers join unions to improve their pay and work environment. At the peak of union membership in 1953, 36 percent of U.S. workers belonged to a union. In 1994 that figure stood at 16.7 million members out of the civilian labor force of 131 million, or about 13 percent of the labor force. The percentage of workers who are represented by a union is slightly greater than this figure because workers in some unionized workplaces have the option to refrain from joining the union, and they exercise this option.

The decline in overall union membership masks the concentration of membership in several key industries that are heavily unionized. Indeed, government employee unionism reached record levels in the mid-1990s, with seven million government workers, equal to about 38 percent of such workers, belonging to unions. Table 8A-1 shows the percentage of workers belonging to a union in major industries.

Possibly the most important factor behind the deterioration in organized labor's strength in the private sector is increases in global competition in a number of industries where unions have historically been strong. Fewer U.S. workers in these industries mean fewer union members. Examples include steel and autos. Also contributing to the decline in unionism has been the increasing relative importance of white-collar jobs, in which the appeal of unions is relatively weak. Nonetheless, a recent nationwide survey of workers showed one-third of those surveyed who were not union members would like to be.

In order to survive, unions are facing up to today's economic environment and reaching out for new members. Efforts to organize workers, especially low-wage workers, have been stepped up during the 1990s. As a consequence, between 1992 and 1994 union membership increased 3 percent.

Union organizing efforts culminate in a secret ballot representation election, under the supervision of the National Labor Relations Board (NLRB). When more than half of a firm's employees vote in favor of a union, the NLRB certifies the union as the bargaining agent for the workers. Unions engage in **collective bargaining**, negotiations with employers aimed at improving the lot of workers. Legally, employers must bargain with a union but are not obligated to reach an agreement. Consequently, it sometimes happens that employers resist unionization by refusing to come to an agreement with the union.

When firms balk at union demands, which side will prevail? *Bargaining power* refers to the ability of a union to win an agreement with greater wages and benefits for its members. The primary weapon providing bargaining power to unions is the *strike*, or work stoppage. The ability to shut down an employer is a powerful weapon indeed, although strikers have the incentive to settle a strike because their employer will not pay them while they are on strike. Generally, a strike will be preceded by negotiations between the union and the employer. Thus a strike typically indicates the failure of negotiations. However, there are sometimes *wildcat strikes*, work stoppages that occur spontaneously because of workers' grievances against their employers.

TABLE 8A-1	*Percentage of Workers Belonging to a Union, by Major Industry, 1994*	
Agriculture		2.3
Private sector workers, excluding agriculture		10.9
Mining		15.6
Construction		18.8
Manufacturing		18.2
Transportation and public utilities		28.4
Wholesale and retail trade		6.2
Finance, insurance, and real estate		2.3
Services		6.2
Government		38.7

Source: 1995 Statistical Abstract of the U.S., Table No. 698.

Union bargaining power is reduced in the twenty-one states with *right-to-work laws*, which permit a unionized firm's workers the option of not joining the union. In these states, union and nonunion workers may work side by side on the job. Hence, workers in right-to-work states are less likely to present a united front when labor disputes arise, which decreases union bargaining power.

Another union weapon is the *boycott*, a campaign to persuade union members and the public to refrain from purchasing the output of a firm with which the union has a disagreement. Boycotts often go hand in hand with strikes.

When an employer faces a strike, its most powerful weapon is the freedom to hire permanent replacements for striking workers. Although firms have the right to replace strikers, that right is often not exercised because of fears of violence directed toward the firm or toward the scabs, as replacement workers are disparagingly called by organized labor. Perhaps the most widely known example of striking union workers permanently losing their jobs to replacements occurred in the 1980s when President Reagan replaced striking air traffic controllers.

How successful are unions at winning higher wages for their members? Median usual weekly earnings for union members in 1993 were $575, compared to $426 for those not represented by unions. On the face of it, it seems that unions increase earnings by approximately 35 percent. However, the issue is more complex than a simple comparison of wages. Higher pay means fewer jobs in the union sector, which increases the supply of labor to the nonunion sector and drives down wages there. Furthermore, the kinds of jobs held by union members differ from the kinds held by other workers. Some of the higher pay in union jobs is likely to be compensating differentials, which would be paid even in the absence of unions. The consensus of research into this complicated issue, after taking account of all other factors affecting wages, is that unions do raise wages for their members. However, estimates of the increase vary too widely to know its magnitude.

Human Capital and Signaling

The amount of human capital that individuals possess is another important determinant of earnings differentials. Human capital is the knowledge, skills, and other productivity-enhancing attributes embodied within individual workers. Attending college is a prime example of how to increase one's human capital. Sources of human capital include formal schooling, on-the-job training, and skills training in the classroom.

It is costly to build a stock of human capital. There are out-of-pocket, explicit costs, as well as the opportunity costs of forgone earnings. For many college students, opportunity costs far exceed the explicit costs. Is a college degree worth the investment? College graduates are less likely to be unemployed than high school graduates, and earn higher incomes over their adult lives. The $37,300 median 1995 salary for college graduates exceeds the median of $21,200 for those who have not graduated from college by about 75 percent. The statistics must be interpreted with caution, however, since those going to college may differ in other respects from those who do not.

Several studies indicate that the returns to the investment in a college diploma probably increased during the 1980s, which helps explain why an increasing fraction of high school graduates attend college. The increase in relative wages is due to many factors. One is the decline in the power of unions to raise wages above competitive levels for their mostly high school-educated membership. Other contributing factors include (1) the flow of relatively unskilled immigrants into the U.S., many of whom compete for jobs against high school graduates; (2) the increased desire of employers to hire college graduates for jobs that have not historically required advanced education; and (3) the high-tech economy, which places a premium on education.

The **signaling** hypothesis provides an alternative to the human capital explanation for the greater earnings of college graduates. Education is seen as providing information to employers about attributes of job applicants. Employers believe that someone with good credentials will quickly be able to learn what is needed to perform a job and will possess the reliability and other qualities necessary to succeed.

This view holds that most college courses do little to increase a person's productivity. In effect, college does not train people for the job market, but instead screens out the winners from the losers. Many economists believe that there is truth in both the human capital and signaling views.

Discrimination, Luck, and Other Market Imperfections

Discrimination is the unequal treatment of persons because of their race, gender, religion, or any other characteristic unrelated to the ability to perform the job. Labor market discrimination can take several forms: discrimination in hiring, discrimination in promotions, and wage discrimination. Regardless of the form, discrimination on the basis of race or gender is illegal in the United States. The Civil Rights Act of 1964 is the cornerstone of government efforts to fight discrimination. Additional legislation and several presidential executive orders attack specific forms of discrimination.

Discrimination in hiring can lead to segregated workplaces. A discriminating employer would hire only the members of one group to do a particular job. Racial and gender stereotyping plays a role in motivating this type of discrimination. The owner of a factory producing clothing would be discriminating if the owner refused to employ males, based upon the belief that women are better sewing machine operators than men. If there is discrimination in hiring in the high-paying occupations, then group differences in earnings will arise.

Promotions into jobs with greater skill requirements and more responsibilities provide workers with the means to improve their earnings. Discrimination in awarding promotions will have a negative effect on the earnings of those discriminated against. Discrimination in promotions is one possible explanation for why some groups earn less than others.

Where the work force is unionized, promotions are often granted on the basis of *seniority*, which refers to a worker's term of employment. To the extent that minorities and women have been discriminated against in employment in the past, their chances for advancement in a seniority-based system of promotions will be impaired. Nonetheless, unless the employer's intent is to discriminate, the practice is generally not illegal. However, many employers are under *affirmative action* plans, which involve a commitment to increase minority and female hiring and promotions. Affirmative action is controversial, with its critics charging that it promotes reverse discrimination. Its advocates respond that the intent of affirmative action is to make up for past discrimination, and that affirmative action plans only level the playing field with white males.

Wage discrimination occurs when a worker who is as productive as other workers is paid less because of race, sex, color, religion, or national origin. This discrimination is illegal in the U.S. It is difficult to ascertain what part of wage differences between workers occurs as a result of wage discrimination and what part occurs because of productivity differences.

Evidence accumulated by economists indicates that wage discrimination typically accounts for only a small part of wage differentials among racial and gender groups. An individual's age, intelligence, health, education, marital status, occupation, and number of years of experience affect his or her productivity and hence wages. The major part of the lower wages of minorities and women can be attributed to differences in these attributes, rather than to wage discrimination.

Wage differentials exist even among individuals who are identical in all measurable attributes that may affect earnings, including race and gender. For instance, race and gender discrimination cannot explain the substantial wage differences that exist among 40-year-old, college-educated, married white males who work as managers. Instead, we must acknowledge the effect of difficult-to-measure factors on earnings. Being in the right place at the right time and other forms of luck play a role in wage differences. Other possible factors include differences in looks, social skills, ambition, selection of marriage partner, and other intangible attributes.

For example, studies have found that good-looking people have an advantage in the labor market. For instance, when two people with identical credentials are sent to the same job interview, the good-looking applicant is usually offered the job while the average-looking one is not.

Market imperfections—deviations from the perfectly competitive labor market model—may also cause wage differentials. Unions and monopsony employers are examples previously mentioned. Additional imperfections include imperfect information, labor market immobility, cronyism, and occupational licensing laws that have the effect of limiting the number of people who pursue a line of work.

*P*overty

Low wages or lack of a job can create poverty. Poverty is associated with deprivation, which motivates government transfer programs to aid the poor. Some of these transfers are "cash," such as the well-known welfare check. About two-thirds of government transfers to the poor are **in kind**, meaning that valuable services are provided instead of money. In-kind benefits include health care, food stamps, subsidized housing, and subsidized school lunches. These programs seek to preserve a minimum standard of living for the poor and are commonly referred to as the *social safety net*.

Most households in poverty are very close to the **poverty line**, defined by the Social Security Administration as an income that is three times the amount of a nutritionally adequate diet. This income varies by household size and composition. Interpreting "nutritionally adequate" is controversial. A vegetarian diet that emphasizes grains and beans can be nutritionally adequate, for example, and cost far less than one third of the stated poverty line. Small changes in the definition of this line would result in large changes in the percentage of people classified as poor.

From 1960 to 1973 the number of persons falling below the poverty line decreased from 22 percent to 11 percent of the population, then stayed within the range of 11 to 15 percent over the following two decades. Poverty rates for children have been even higher—23 percent in 1993. Almost half of female-headed families with children fall below the poverty line. Conversely, with the safety net provided by Social Security, poverty among the elderly has fallen to less than 8 percent of the elderly population. Overall poverty rates have stayed in a stable range over the last two decades, even as spending on poverty programs has increased.

It would be unreasonable to expect extra spending on in-kind aid for the poor to reduce poverty statistics. The reason is that the official measure of poverty excludes the value of in-kind benefits. As the poor receive more subsidized health care, housing, and other in-kind benefits, it is not surprising that their earnings fail to rise. Higher earnings would cause a loss of eligibility for these valuable programs. If the value of in-kind transfers is included in poverty measures, the percentage of poor Americans drops to approximately 9 percent of the population.

OBSERVATION POINT: "Cut my Salary. Please!"

Incentives are changed by the existence of government transfer programs. It is not always easy to predict how people will respond to such incentives. Case in point: A few years ago, a professor asked his university's administrators to lower his annual salary by a few hundred dollars. His request was not frivolous. Its purpose was to make his children eligible for subsidized school lunches. The savings from subsidized lunches would have more than made up for his salary reduction. Moral: Those whose earnings are low may have an incentive to reduce their work effort in order to further lower their incomes and qualify for government assistance.

Earnings of Women and Minorities—The Wage Gap Remains

Concern over discrimination in the labor market highlights the significance of earnings differentials between males and females and between whites and minorities. Even though a substantial fraction of earnings differences are explained by factors other than labor market discrimination, these differences have important social implications. The primary focus in this section is on women, although many of the same issues arise concerning the earnings of minorities.

The average full-time female worker in the U.S. earns about seventy-two cents for every dollar earned by the average male. This figure is up from fifty-nine cents in 1978. The closing of the earnings gap in the 1980s is explained by women workers developing specialized job skills, thereby allowing women to move into professional and managerial jobs.

In the 1980s women workers also broke their historical pattern of *discontinuous labor force participation*, which occurs when someone leaves and later reenters the labor force. Many women would leave their jobs after childbirth and not return to work for several years in order to care for their children. This in-and-out pattern of labor force participation caused women's human capital to depreciate and reduced their years of labor-market experience relative to men. The result was lower earnings. As more and more women stay in the labor force throughout their lives, their earnings have risen relative to those of men and are expected to rise even more.

Explanations for the remaining earnings gap focus on women's occupational choices. Many occupations are dominated by females. Table 8A-2 compares the percentage of males in a select group of traditionally male occupations with the percentage of females in another group containing several traditionally female occupations. Many of these female-dominated occupations pay less than the male-dominated ones.

Occupational segregation, the concentration of women workers in certain jobs, such as nursing and teaching, is commonly cited as evidence that women are discriminated against in hiring. The reasoning is that women are forced into these jobs because other jobs are not open to them. However, many economists deem this view simplistic. Interruptions in women's careers because of childbearing, child rearing, and the need to change jobs because of a husband's job transfer may motivate women to select occupations where interruptions in labor force participation will be least harmful to their careers. The skills required in these traditionally female occupations are easily transferred from one employer to another and become obsolete only very slowly.

There are other possible explanations for occupational segregation. Gender-based differences in interests may be one factor. In addition, there might be discrimination against women by the educational system, such as school guidance that channels women away from subjects that lead to employment in traditionally male jobs. Employer discrimination in hiring women for some jobs is another explanation. It must be remembered that pay varies from one occupation to another. Unless women work in the various occupations in equal proportions as men and for as long as men, a wage differential will continue to be observed.

One controversial suggestion, which its advocates claim would raise women's earnings to the same level as men's, is called comparable worth. **Comparable worth** would replace market-determined wages with government-set wages designed to ensure pay equity across different jobs. Several states have passed comparable worth laws, but limit their applicability, such as to government jobs. Its champions propose a federal comparable worth law that would apply to all employers in the U.S.

If wages were determined by comparable worth, government would have to decide which occupations involve equal responsibilities and are therefore deserving of equal pay. Government would set higher wages in those female-dominated occupations determined to be equivalent to male-dominated occupations and make it illegal for employers to pay

TABLE 8A-2   *Selected Male-Dominated and Female-Dominated Occupations, 1994*

Male-Dominated Occupations (percentage of workers who are males)	Female-Dominated Occupations (percentage of workers who are females)
Engineers (91.7)	Librarians (84.1)
Dentists (86.7)	Registered nurses (93.8)
Clergy (88.9)	Elementary school teachers (85.6)
Firefighters (97.9)	Dental hygienists (100.0)
Mechanics (95.5)	Secretaries (98.9)
Construction workers (97.8)	Telephone operators (88.8)
Truck drivers (95.5)	Child care workers (97.3)

Source: 1995 Statistical Abstract of the U.S., Table No. 649.

less. Economists' analyses show that the effect would be similar to minimum wage laws—comparable worth would reduce the number of jobs in female-dominated occupations. Critics of comparable worth also worry that wages would be set in an unfair manner. After all, for comparable wages, would you prefer to introduce yourself as a janitor or secretary? These two occupations are often deemed comparable because subtle points of job status cannot easily be measured.

Table 8A-3 compares the earnings of men and women. The earnings data are provided by race; the figures include only full-time, year-round workers. Time series data are provided in order to show the progress that women and blacks have made in closing the wage gap with white males.

The data show a significant earnings gap between black and white males, with the average black male earning just over 75 percent of the amount earned by the average white male in 1994. While narrowing over time, this gap continues to be a source of concern. In contrast, black women earned 86 percent of the earnings of white women in 1994. African-American women show a greater attachment to the labor force than do white women, which increases the earnings of black women relative to white women. On average, black women stay in the job market longer than white women because the proportion of households headed by women is greater among black households than among white.

OBSERVATION POINT: Homespun—Promoting Family Values?

Is working at home right for you? You can earn an income, be your own boss, eliminate commuting and daycare expenses, and spend time with your children. There is one problem, however: legal barriers. The Fair Labor Standards Act of 1938 outlaws commercial *piecework* sale of women's garments sewn at home. Who would know if child labor laws were violated? What if your hourly earnings fell below the minimum wage? Society has an interest in preventing the abuse of labor, but it also has an interest in promoting family cohesiveness. Sometimes laws promote some values over others.

TABLE 8A-3 *Earnings of Year-Round, Full-Time Workers by Race and Gender, Selected Years 1976–1994* (percentages are of white male earnings for the same year)*

Year	White Males	Black Males	White Females	Black Females
1976	$35,608	$25,503 (71.6%)	$20,898 (58.7%)	$19,538 (54.9%)
1979	36,017	25,957 (72.1%)	21,275 (59.1%)	19,494 (54.1%)
1982	34,464	24,478 (71.0%)	21,466 (62.3%)	19,185 (55.7%)
1985	35,388	24,752 (69.9%)	22,701 (64.1%)	20,095 (56.8%)
1988	35,405	25,952 (73.3%)	23,580 (66.6%)	21,130 (59.7%)
1991	33,680	24,622 (73.1%)	23,454 (69.6%)	20,820 (61.8%)
1994	32,440	24,405 (75.2%)	23,894 (73.7%)	20,628 (63.6%)

*Adjusted for inflation; dollar figures expressed in 1994 dollars.

Source: 1996 Economic Report of the President, Table B-29.

1. The sum of all wages an employer pays reveals the employer's total labor costs.
2. The demand for labor is a derived demand.
3. People will participate in the labor market when their reservation wages exceed the market wage.
4. A monopsony labor market occurs when there are many employers in the market.
5. On-the-job training is an example of human capital acquisition.
6. On average, black women show a greater attachment to the labor force than do white women.

A

> **EXPLORATION 1**
> *Income Distribution—$20-Million-Dollar Paychecks and the Big Squeeze in the Middle*

This exploration examines the distribution of income between the rich, the poor, and the middle class. Explanations and possible solutions for income distribution problems are proposed.

What ever happened to economic security? It seems that most workers have to run faster and faster just to stay in place. Husbands were joined by their wives in the workplace in the 1970s and 1980s, but even with two incomes combined, median family income (half above and half below) has barely kept up with inflation. Even the booming economy of recent years did not always help. Inflation-adjusted median family incomes fell from $39,105 in 1991 to $38,632 in 1992 and to $37,905 in 1993 before rising to $38,782 in 1994. The behavior of family income over time is documented in Figure 8B1-1.

Two aspects of the problem of diminishing economic security must be disentangled. One is the slowdown in real income growth over the past two decades. The other is the increase in inequality in the distribution of income. The output of the economy is analogous to a pie. We first want to ensure that the pie keeps getting bigger, especially relative to population growth, and then we worry about the size of our slice of the pie relative to our neighbor's slice. While the pie has been growing, the pieces going to those at the top have gotten larger, leaving less for everyone else. These developments have financially squeezed the middle class.

*S*o *You're Gonna Be a Star*

One way to solve your personal economic security problem is to become a star actor, athlete, or singer. Comic actor Jim Carrey of "Ace Ventura" fame solved his economic worries when the high demand for his unique services caused him to be paid $20 million per picture. Other celebrities whose multimillion-dollar incomes have made headlines in recent years include the Superbowl-winning quarterback Troy Aikman, basketball stars Michael Jordan and Shaquille O'Neil, and singers Michael Jackson and Madonna.

Economists have coined a term, **economic rent**, to describe earnings in excess of opportunity costs. Economic rent is responsible for the incredible earnings reaped by many celebrities. People whose talents and abilities are exceptionally scarce are sometimes able to earn much more than their next best alternative. For example, Michael Jackson's talent is uncommon and in fixed supply. The combination of fixed supply and great demand

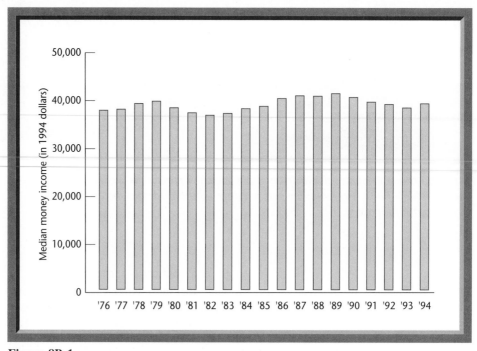

Figure 8B-1 **Inflation-adjusted median money income of families, 1976–1994.**

Source: 1996 Economic Report of the President, Table B-29.

for his music and concerts results in sky-high earnings. Yet his opportunity cost, his best earnings opportunity outside the entertainment industry, is not nearly so spectacular.

Wage determination and economic rent for a superstar or other person with unique talents are illustrated in Figure 8B1-2. The fixed supply of superstar-quality talents results in a vertical supply curve of labor with that talent. For example, the quantity of Madonna's talent does not increase even if her earnings rise. The position of the demand curve for the star's talents determines earnings. When demand is large relative to supply, high earnings are the outcome. The portion of earnings representing economic rent is indicated by the blue shaded area in the figure.

This model applies to a spectrum of workers. Success in many fields requires exceptional skills. The most successful heart surgeons, stockbrokers, economists, attorneys, and business executives, among others, earn economic rents. Some of these people become superstars in their fields. Examples include former mutual fund manager Peter Lynch, economists Paul Samuelson and Milton Friedman, attorney Johnny Cochran, and Michael Eisner, head of Disney.

Not everyone, even those with unique talents, is able to earn significant economic rents. Your favorite club band may possess enormous talent, which is in fixed supply just like Madonna's. Nonetheless, without sufficiently large public demand for that talent, the band members are doomed to work for cover charges until the band's inevitable breakup. Similarly, many minor league athletes are close to major league quality in their talents, but the public is willing to pay high ticket prices only for major leaguers. Hence, a mi-

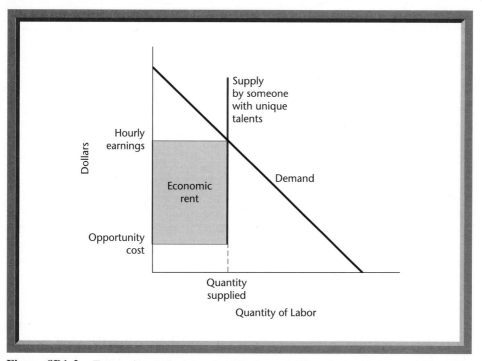

Figure 8B1-2   **Economic rent** is determined by demand. When demand is large relative to the fixed supply, earnings can be far above opportunity costs.

nor leaguer with 95 percent of the talent of a major leaguer may earn only 1 percent or less of the earnings of the major leaguer.

Clearly, the option of becoming a star is not open to most people seeking to boost their incomes. The theory of economic rent does, however, explain why some people end up in the group of highest paid workers, at the top of the income distribution. As predicted in 1981 by economist Sherwin Rosen, we increasingly live in a superstar economy, with a reward system of winner take all ever more common.

No More Middle Class?

The headlines bellow "More Layoffs Coming"; "Plant to Close"; "Inflation Up—Wages Fail to Keep Pace." Is the middle class dying a slow death? Some concepts related to the distribution of income can help clarify the answer to that question.

An *income distribution* reports the proportion of income each segment of the population receives. Since our biggest concern with the distribution of income is inequality, income distribution usually focuses on the fraction of total income received by different *quintiles*, where a quintile contains 20 percent of the population. If everyone's income were equal, each quintile of the population would receive 20 percent of total income. Where inequality exists, the quintiles show variation in the fraction of income received. A simple example will help. Consider a population of five persons, for which the total in-

| | | Lowest | Second | Middle | Fourth | Highest | Top 1 |
Year	Total	Quintile	Quintile	Quintile	Quintile	Quintile	Percent
1977	100.0	5.7	11.6	16.3	22.8	44.0	7.3
1989	100.0	4.3	10.1	15.1	21.5	49.9	12.4
1992	100.0	4.1	9.9	15.2	21.7	49.8	12.1

TABLE 8B1-1 *Shares of Total After-Tax Incomes (in percent)*

Source: Center on Budget Policy and Priorities, based upon Congressional Budget Office data.

come received by the whole population is $100. In this example, each person represents a quintile, one-fifth of the population. If each person earned $20, each quintile would show a 20 percent share of income received. There would be perfect equality.

Suppose instead that there is inequality in the incomes received among our population of five. Beginning at the bottom of the distribution and moving up, the first person earns $5, the second $10, the third $15, the fourth $20, and the top earner $50. The total is still $100, but now there is inequality. The lowest quintile receives 5 percent of income, the next quintile 10 percent, and so forth up to the highest quintile, which receives 50 percent of income.

In Table 8B1-1, data on the income distribution for the U.S. in 1977 is contrasted with similar data for 1989 and 1992. The lowest quintile of the population has seen its share of income fall from 5.7 percent of the total to 4.1 percent. At the same time, those Americans in the top 1 percent of the income distribution have seen their share increase from 7.3 percent to 12.1 percent. Middle America, those in the three middle quintiles, garnered 46.8 percent of the income, down from 50.7 percent in 1977. Between 1989 and 1992, there appears to have occurred a slight reversal of the trend to growing inequality, but nonetheless the average American remains uneasy over whether the rich are getting richer and the poor poorer.

*H*ow Equal Should Equal Be?

Is the income distribution in Table 8B1-1 good or bad? That is unclear. Two important points are not apparent from the data. The first is that in spite of growing inequality, the distribution nonetheless exhibits significant stability. The changes are slight in absolute terms. The second is that there is substantial movement within the distribution. Some people move up and others move down with the passage of time. For example, many younger workers who were at the bottom of the distribution in 1979 had moved up by 1993 after acquiring education and job experience. Meanwhile, many older workers who were at the top in 1979 had moved down because they retired. This dynamic movement in the distribution means that most people are not permanently stuck at the bottom. A final point can also help put inequality in perspective. The average estimated 1996 after-tax income of families in the top 1 percent is $438,000; that of families in the bottom quintile is $8,230. Without upward mobility, such a stark contrast would be hard to justify.

Income distribution is the outcome of a complex process involving numerous forces and depends heavily on what is counted as income. For example, there would be much less inequality apparent if in-kind government assistance to the poor were included in income. Nevertheless, it is reasonable to be concerned about the income distribution. If those who live in poverty come to believe that aspiring to the middle class is an impossible dream, then the frustration created could alienate potentially productive workers, thereby reducing their motivation to obtain schooling and work hard.

The income distribution can be made more equal. Indeed, changes in federal tax policy are capable of reducing the share of the well-to-do. Such policy changes must be tempered, however, by recognition that incentives to acquire human capital and be productive may be reduced by higher taxes. The problem is how to keep the pie growing while ensuring that everyone receives a fair slice.

Stumbling through the Culture of Success

Not everyone measures success in terms of money. For those many who do, perhaps the most encouraging fact is that the monetary returns to education have apparently been increasing in recent years. That is part of the reason the rich have been getting richer and the poor poorer. Those with more education have prospered; those without have suffered.

To what do economists attribute the premium placed on skilled labor? The most compelling argument seems to be the impact of technological change on the workplace, best exemplified by computerization during the 1970s and 1980s. Today's workers are forced to work smarter, not harder. Brain power has replaced muscle power as the most important determinant of success in the labor market, which suggests that education and job training could provide the answers to stagnating wages and income inequality.

PROSPECTING FOR NEW INSIGHTS

1. Is it fair for some people to earn huge economic rents? Should those rents be taxed away? Would taxing rents cause superstars to withhold their talents from the marketplace?
2. If education and job training are the answers to the problems discussed in this Exploration, what could prevent workers from obtaining more education and training? Could government devise policies to overcome those obstacles?

B

EXPLORATION 2
Preventing Workplace Negligence—The Price of Life and Limb

For the sake of cost-benefit analysis and lawsuits over negligence, economists are often called upon to place a value on human life. Different techniques are appropriate, depending upon the use to which the estimate is put.

A worker in an aluminum refinery falls into a vat of molten metal. Later, the company offers the grieving family $100,000 in compensation. Is that a fair settlement? An oil refinery explodes and burns, killing three employees. The employer accepts responsibility, but is not sure what fair compensation to offer the families of the deceased. An airliner crashes killing all aboard. Are all the lives lost of equal value?

These are examples of the issues facing economists who are called upon to place a dollar value on life and good health. Often these economists serve as expert witnesses in court proceedings that grow out of wrongful death lawsuits. Well-established and accepted methodologies exist for valuing life. It is these methodologies, explained below, that economists bring to bear.

Health and safety are regulated by government in an effort to save lives and reduce injuries. How much of such regulation is enough? This question also requires the application of economic principles to answer.

Ex post *versus* Ex ante—*Can Placing a Monetary Value on Human Life Be Justified?*

Some feel it is immoral to place a monetary value on human life. Indeed, few of us would fail to object if someone tried to tell us what our lives are worth or that some lives are worth more than others. We intuitively feel that the value of our life is beyond economic calculation and that it is just as valuable as that of the next person. For these reasons, economists do not place a monetary value on the life of any living human being.

When individuals suffer wrongful death, however, their survivors are deprived of the income that the deceased could have earned. At that point economics comes into the picture. Economists also recognize that the loss of loved ones goes beyond dollars and that economic analysis is not well suited to delve into the emotional costs attached to losses of loved ones. However, most would agree that restoring the incomes lost to those who have suffered the wrongful death of a loved one is equitable. Analyzing how much that reimbursement should be is aided by economic analysis.

The concept of human capital is used to place a value on lost earnings. Individuals invest in education and job training in the expectation that they will live long enough to reap the return from those investments. Investments in education often involve financial sacrifice for the individuals making them. The wrongful death of an individual prevents those returns from being realized. It thus seems fair that this loss should be compensated.

It may not seem as fair that the human capital approach discriminates among persons. Those with the most human capital are worth more than those with less human capital. That means children are worth less, because they have no labor market experience. The elderly are worth less, because their prime earning years are behind them. The physically and mentally challenged are also worth less because of their relative lack of earning power. The reason for these differences is that economic analysis of specific lives lost does not truly value that life; it only values productivity received by others. Valuing a human life in this way has a long history. For example, English common law has traditionally permitted the practice in court proceedings.

Measuring and Interpreting the Value of Lost Earnings

When a life ends, all that can be said about the future unfolding of that life must be based upon past evidence. When valuing that loss of life, the starting point is an examination of the record of the individual's past earnings.

The trend in earnings can be projected into the future. Such projections must be carefully crafted, however, because past earnings growth depended partially upon past inflation rates. If future expected inflation is lower or higher than past inflation, the projections must be adjusted accordingly.

When going to court, the economist brings a set of yearly net income projections, based upon expectations about future inflation and upon estimates of future promotions and other factors relating to the best guess about future earnings. These are sums of money that would have been received in the future. As such they must be placed in *present value* terms, which adjusts for the time value of money. The calculation of present value allows the economist to state the value of future net earnings as a single lump sum, payable today. Unfortunately, many court cases have been known to omit the concept of present value, thus overstating the value of lost earnings.

Earnings projections take account of the *life cycle*, which refers to the typical pattern of earnings over the course of a person's life. An individual who is young and inexperienced is at a point in the life cycle where current earnings are low. As the years go by, earnings typically increase, peak out in middle age, and decline slightly as health and other problems associated with advanced age become apparent. By making assumptions about the age a person would have retired, economists can estimate the number of remaining years of earning power.

Another component of loss is also estimated. This is the value of services provided to the household by the deceased. Examples include housework and child-rearing services. Courts accept the notion that survivors should be compensated for this loss as well.

Offsetting the loss of wages and household services is the value of the consumption the deceased would have undertaken. Examples include food, clothing, and medical services the deceased would have consumed. These sums of money are subtracted by the economist from the estimated value of wages plus household services.

There are problems with arriving at an indisputable value for a human life. Much of the economist's work is speculative, even when the economist attempts to be objective. Attorneys would not normally attack the methodology, which is well established, but could disagree with the earnings projections. It is left to the judge or jury to decide who is more persuasive.

B

Valuing the Chances We Are Willing to Take

Just how dangerous the workplace is can be gauged by referring to Figure 8B2-1. The data show the on-the-job death rate has been falling for some thirty or more years. Even so, in 1993, the death rate reveals an average of eight of every 1000 workers were killed

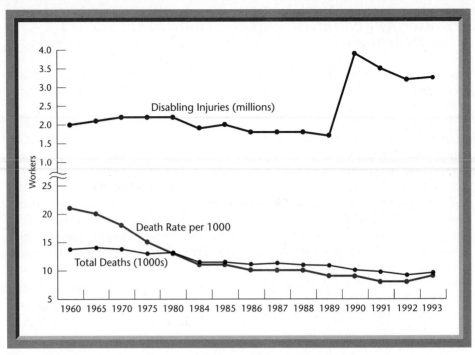

Figure 8B2-1 Workers killed or disabled on the job, 1960–1993.

Source: 1995 Statistical Abstract of the U.S., Table No. 688.

on the job. On top of those 9,100 deaths, 3.2 million workers suffered disabling injuries. Some jobs are clearly more dangerous than others. Obviously, the workplace can never be made perfectly safe. If employers are willing to spend enough money, though, the risk of injury and death can be reduced.

Alternatively, the employer can offer higher wages to compensate workers for workplace dangers. The theory of compensating wage differentials posits that employers will be forced to pay higher wages when jobs are dangerous. Higher wages are necessary to attract a sufficient supply of workers and to compensate them for the risk to life and limb. We can impute a value of life by observing the behavior of workers who willingly take the hazardous jobs in exchange for higher pay.

Suppose, hypothetically, that the risk of death among police officers is increased by one in one hundred over the risk of death among security guards. Also suppose that police officers are paid $10,000 in additional income to accept that risk. What value do police officers place on their lives in this example? An approximate answer can be had by dividing the additional income by the additional risk. $1,000,000 (10,000/.01) is the value that officers themselves place on their lives. Another way of looking at this calculation is to note that each group of 100 police officers employed costs $1,000,000 in extra wages ($10,000 multiplied by 100 police). That $1,000,000 in wage costs "pays" for the death of one police officer. Since no individual officer knows for sure who will die, the $1,000,000 reflects the value of a *statistical life*.

How much would you be willing to pay to reduce your risk of death on the job?

Suppose that you hold a job on an offshore oil rig that is dangerous, but that the risk of death can be reduced by 1 percent if you are willing to spend $100 for the purchase of a hard hat and steel-toe boots. Good deal? You bet. If you and your co-workers refused to make the purchases, then your statistical life is valued at less than $10,000 ($100/.01).

In reality, the Occupational Safety and Health Administration (OSHA), the Federal agency charged with enforcing health and safety rules, will probably force the oil rig operators to pay for your hard hat and boots and force you to wear them. How is safety regulation justified? Cost-benefit analysis is the key. An important benefit of safety regulation is the value of lives saved. Suppose a new regulation imposes safety measures that cost employers $100 million and is expected to save ten lives. Economic analysis suggests that the safety measures are worthwhile only if lives are worth at least $10 million each. If statistical lives were worth that much, the average worker would be willing to pay $100,000 for the hard hat and boots in the previous paragraph.

Safety in the Marketplace—What Role Government?

The search for profit motivates firms to implement numerous safety measures, even when no regulation forces them to do so. The rationale is that unsafe working conditions lead to various costs, such as costs associated with interruptions in production and higher costs of labor compensation. For example, a dangerous firm must offer higher wages and better benefits to attract workers. It would also be forced to pay higher insurance premiums to cover health care expenses and liability. If these costs exceed the cost of the safety measures, a profit-maximizing firm will undertake the safety measures.

There is also a role for government. The most clear-cut role for government occurs when there are external costs, costs borne by others. For example, highway speed limits and drunk driving laws can be justified on the basis of saving the lives of careful drivers who have the misfortune of being hit by a vehicle driven recklessly. To achieve economic efficiency, government must weigh costs and benefits of alternative regulations. Lowering the speed limit on interstate highways to twenty miles per hour, for example, would undoubtedly save lives. However, people are willing to accept some extra risk of injury or death voluntarily in order to receive the benefits from saving time in traveling.

Figure 8B2-2 shows in principle how to choose an efficient amount of safety. The idea is to keep adding safety measures so long as the marginal benefit exceeds the marginal cost. For example, the value of the statistical lives saved by lowering a speed limit from eighty to seventy miles per hour would usually exceed the cost of the extra time spent traveling. However, the marginal cost of lowering the speed limit from thirty to twenty would usually exceed the marginal benefit.

Figure 8B2-2 also applies to the firm. This section started by noting that profit motivates the firm to implement safety measures. However, there are questions about whether all of the benefits from safety improvements are captured in the firm's profits. If they are not, then firms will not choose to be safe enough. This situation might occur if workers have insufficient information about the value of safety improvements. For example, the workers might not realize how risky a job actually is and thus be unwilling to sacrifice much pay or other benefits in order to receive extra safety. In this case, the firm perceives less than the true marginal benefits from safety and implements too few safety measures. Figure 8B2-2 illustrates this possibility.

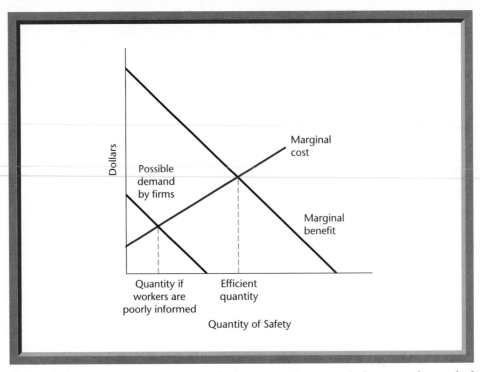

Figure 8B2-2   The efficient quantity of safety occurs where marginal cost equals marginal benefit. The quantity chosen in the marketplace would be less than that if workers underestimate the value of safety.

If firms do not undertake an efficient number of safety measures, there is a role for government regulators. Specifically, government regulators might estimate the efficient amount of safety and force firms to achieve that amount. However, it is difficult to estimate these marginal costs and benefits of extra safety, especially since different workers have different preferences when it comes to how much risk they are willing to accept in exchange for extra income.

It is impractical for government safety regulations to be tailored to the wants of different groups of workers. The result is that both firms and workers often complain about rigid work rules and safety measures. However, throwing the rules out risks that the marketplace might surprise workers with how unsafe their jobs can be.

There is an ongoing controversy over whether government should cut back its regulation of workplace safety. In that case, government could still make information on workplace safety available to workers so that they could choose more efficiently. On the other hand, backers of government safety regulation point out that there are economies of scale in evaluating information about safety. From that perspective, it seems sensible to let experts in government evaluate the information and make choices more efficiently than most workers could do themselves.

1. How much safety are you willing to pay for in the automobile you drive? Should people be forced to pay for safety or should it be voluntary?

2. If you were an attorney arguing a value-of-life case, what questions would you ask of the economist(s) testifying?

B

Module C

MASTERING ROADSIDE CHALLENGES

CHALLENGE 1
Derived Demand—How Much Labor Will the Firm Employ?

Consider a firm operating in a perfectly competitive output market, as shown in Table 8C1-1. The first two columns of the table show the relationship between labor and the firm's output. The third column, marginal product, is calculated as the change in output that results from a one-unit change in labor. This price-taking firm sells its output for $2 per unit, as seen in the fourth column. Note that price equals marginal revenue for a perfectly competitive firm. Total revenue is obtained by multiplying price by the quantity of output.

The **marginal revenue product of labor** is the increase in the firm's revenue arising from the employment of an additional unit of labor, as seen in the last column of the table.

$$\text{Marginal revenue product} = \frac{\Delta \text{total revenue}}{\Delta \text{labor}}$$

Marginal revenue product can also be calculated by multiplying marginal revenue by marginal product. **Marginal revenue product measures the value of an additional unit of labor to the firm.**

If we suppose that the firm operates in a perfectly competitive labor market, then the firm is a wage taker, purchasing labor's services at the going market wage rate. **The wage rate equals the marginal cost of labor for a wage taker.** For example, if the market wage rate is $16, adding one more unit of labor always increases the firm's total cost by $16. **For a wage-taking firm, the marginal cost of labor is constant and equivalent to the supply curve of labor to the firm.** The reason is that the firm can purchase as many units of labor as it wishes at the market wage rate.

TABLE 8C1-1 *Marginal Revenue Product for a Price Taker in the Labor Market*

Labor (L)	Output (Q)	Marginal Product	Price (P) (=marginal revenue)	Total Revenue (TR = P × Q)	Marginal Revenue Product (ΔTR/ΔL)
0	0	Not defined	$2.00	$0	Not defined
1	12	12	2.00	24.00	$24.00
2	22	10	2.00	44.00	20.00
3	30	8	2.00	60.00	16.00
4	36	6	2.00	72.00	12.00
5	40	4	2.00	80.00	8.00
6	42	2	2.00	84.00	4.00

A firm will employ the quantity of labor that maximizes profit. This quantity of labor can be determined by comparing the marginal revenue product of each unit of labor to its marginal cost: **Profit maximization requires a firm to hire labor so long as labor's marginal revenue product exceeds its marginal cost.** If the marginal revenue product is less than the marginal cost of labor, a firm will not hire that worker. For example, the firm in Table 8C1-1 would hire three units of labor at the $16 market wage rate. Since the fourth worker's marginal revenue product is less than $16, that worker will not be hired.

The firm in Table 8C1-1 is illustrated in Figure 8C1-1. The marginal revenue product curve is also the firm's demand curve for labor because it shows how much labor the firm will employ at various wage rates. Observe that the firm's labor demand curve shows an inverse relationship between the wage rate and the quantity demanded of labor.

The firm's labor demand curve may shift. An increase in labor demand would accompany

- an increase in the market price of the firm's output;
- an increase in the marginal product of labor. Labor's marginal product can increase (1) with technological improvements in production or (2) because labor's skills increase through education or training.

Labor demand would decrease if the price of output fell or if the marginal product of labor decreased.

The market demand for labor is the total amount of labor demanded by all firms at each wage rate. This demand can be influenced either by market power in the output market or by market power in the labor market. Consider first the output market.

Imperfectly competitive firms and monopoly firms possess market power over the

Figure 8C1-1   The marginal revenue product curve is a firm's labor demand curve. The firm will employ labor at the point where the marginal revenue product equals the marginal cost of labor.

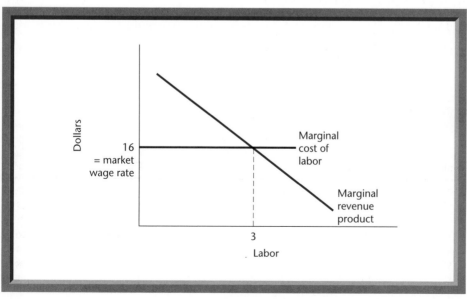

price of output, which results in higher output prices in these markets compared to the prices that would exist if the markets were perfectly competitive. Higher prices mean a smaller quantity demanded, which translates into less production and less demand for labor. **Thus, *ceteris paribus*, less labor is employed in markets where firms possess market power than in markets where market power is absent.**

In the labor market, a firm can have market power over the wage rate. In this case, the firm is a wage setter rather than a wage taker. This condition occurs when employers possess monopsony power. Consider a pure monopsony firm—the only employer of labor in a labor market. Data for such a firm is presented in Table 8C1-2. As the only employer of labor in this particular labor market, the monopsonist faces the market supply curve of labor, which is shown in the first two columns in the table. The firm's total cost of labor for each quantity of labor is obtained by multiplying the wage by the quantity of labor, and is seen in the third column.

In the next-to-last column of the table, the marginal cost of labor is shown. Marginal cost is calculated as the change in the total cost of labor resulting from a one-unit increase in the quantity of labor. Note that, unlike in the perfectly competitive labor market, the marginal cost of labor exceeds the wage rate in monopsony. The reason is that hiring extra workers increases the wage rate paid to all workers, not just to themselves. The final column of the table shows marginal revenue product data for this firm. The monopsonist will follow the profit-maximizing rule, which says to employ labor to the point where the marginal revenue product equals the marginal cost of labor.

How many units of labor will the monopsonist employ? The answer is three units of labor. Up to that point the marginal revenue product of labor is greater than the marginal cost of labor. Beyond that point, the marginal revenue product is less than the marginal cost. At three units of labor, the marginal revenue product and marginal cost are equal at $10. However, the monopsonist need not pay a wage rate of $10. Instead, the supply of labor figures in columns one and two show that the firm can attract three units of labor by paying a wage rate of only $8. Thus $8 is the wage the monopsonist will pay.

Figure 8C1-2 shows the market supply curve of labor, the marginal cost of labor, the demand for labor (marginal revenue product), and the profit-maximizing employment and wage rate. The monopsonist makes its hiring decision in the following two steps:

• Step 1: It employs the amount of labor for which the marginal cost of labor equals marginal revenue product.

TABLE 8C1-2 *A Monopsony Firm*

Labor	Wage Rate	Total Cost of Labor	Marginal Cost of Labor	Marginal Revenue Product
0	$5	$0	Undefined	Undefined
1	6	6	$6	$12
2	7	14	8	11
3	8	24	10	10
4	9	36	12	9
5	10	50	14	8
6	11	66	16	7

C

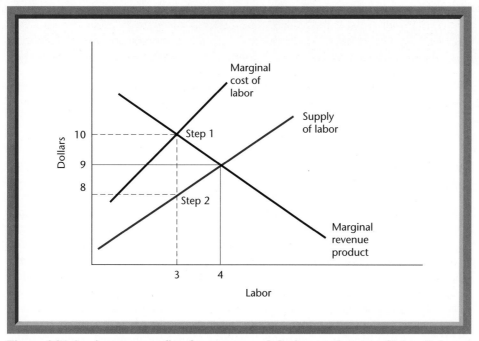

Figure 8C1-2   A monopsony firm faces an upward-sloping supply curve of labor. It chooses to employ 3 units of labor, based on the intersection of the marginal cost of labor and marginal revenue product (step 1). It pays a wage of $8, the minimum needed to attract 3 workers (step 2). This contrasts with the 4 workers paid $9 that would arise if the monopsony market could be magically transformed to perfect competition.

• Step 2: It pays as little as possible for that labor, where this wage rate is given by the supply curve of labor at the quantity chosen in step 1.

These choices are shown in Figure 8C1-2.

Figure 8C1-2 also illustrates a compelling point about monopsony that was raised earlier. If this monopsonized labor market could be transformed into a perfectly competitive one, the employment of labor would increase to the point where the supply and demand curves for labor intersect. Supply and demand show the competitive wage rate to be $9 and the competitive level of employment to be four units of labor. This demonstrates that **monopsony labor markets are characterized by less employment and a lower wage rate than are perfectly competitive labor markets.**

C

Human capital acquisition is an investment. Costs are incurred now that will pay future returns. Is it wise to invest in more education? If the answer is yes, then how much more? Let's sort out the costs, benefits, and principles explaining decisions about human capital.

The *private costs* associated with obtaining additional human capital are those costs borne by the individual. The *social costs* include taxpayer-provided subsidies that help individuals acquire more education and training. The *private returns* are benefits received by the individual who makes the human capital investment. *Social returns* include benefits received by society that result when human capital investment is undertaken. Examples include a lower unemployment rate and a more productive economy.

Consider the decision to go to college. The private costs of college are of two types: explicit costs paid out of pocket, and implicit opportunity costs, which are forgone earnings. If we assume that college takes four years to complete, that a student begins college at age eighteen, and that the student does not hold a part-time job, then the twenty-two-year-old college graduate will have spent four years incurring costs. During those same four years, a high school graduate will have been earning income.

The private benefits to obtaining a college degree are increased lifetime earning power and the value of education in terms of personal satisfaction. Two considerations help to drive up earnings. One is that college graduates are less likely to experience interruptions in earnings caused by unemployment. The second is that the wage rate or salary paid to a college graduate will usually exceed that paid to a high school graduate. As a result, college graduates can expect much higher earnings over their lifetimes than can high school graduates. For example, the lifetime earnings differential between the two groups was estimated in 1992 to equal $574,000. However, as shown below, merely looking at such raw data is not enough. Not only is there likely to be an *ability bias* as many of the most able and motivated high school students pursue higher education, but there is also a big difference in value between earnings received now and received in the future.

Suppose that when all the costs are summed, and all the benefits are also summed, that the total benefits are greater than the total costs. The individual should go to college, right? While this simple approach may seem correct, it has a fatal shortcoming. The problem is in the timing of the costs and benefits.

Investment theory teaches us that a sum of money received in the future, a *future value*, is worth less than the identical sum received today. To see that this statement is true, consider the choice between receiving a dollar today or a dollar sometime in the future. We would prefer to receive a dollar now, because we could invest that dollar at the current interest rate and receive more than a dollar in the future, composed of the sum we invested plus the return on the investment. In one year we would have $1.00 multiplied by (1 + interest rate). For example, if the interest rate equals 5 percent, we would have $1.05, which equals $1 multiplied by 1.05.

Another way of looking at the issue of timing is to consider how much we would be willing to accept now to give up some future sum. For example, if interest rates equal 5 percent, we could deposit about 95 cents in a bank account and in one year claim the original deposit plus about 5 cents in interest. The value of 95 cents is calculated by di-

C

viding $1.00 by 1.05. The example shows that an investor, facing a 5 percent interest rate, would be indifferent between an investment that paid 95 cents today and another investment that paid a dollar in one year. However, the investor would prefer to receive any amount greater than 95 cents today to a dollar in one year.

Another way of expressing this relationship is to say that the **present value** of $1.00 to be received in one year equals 95 cents, when the interest rate equals 5 percent. The present value of $1.00 to be received in two years equals about 90 cents when the interest rate is 5 percent, since 90 cents placed into a bank account now would grow to about a dollar over a two-year period. This example shows that the farther into the future a dollar is to be received, the smaller is its present value. In other words, the future value is *discounted* to achieve the present value. The rate at which discounting occurs—the **discount rate**—is just the interest rate used to calculate present value.

Since the costs and benefits of human capital investment are spread over the ages between eighteen and sixty-five (assumed to be the age an individual retires), those costs and benefits should be expressed in present-value terms. Dollars of cost, incurred early in a student's life, have a greater present value than dollars of income, which are received later. The *discount factor* used to calculate present values equals $(1 + i)^t$, where i equals the interest rate and t equals the number of years in the future the sum of money is spent or received.

For example, suppose the discount rate is 5 percent. Using this figure, it is possible to calculate the *net present value* of the investment in a college education. The procedure is to calculate the present value of the benefits and the present value of the costs, and then subtract the former from the latter. The calculation of net present value is illustrated below for four years of college expenses (beginning at age eighteen), followed by earnings which begin in the fifth year (age twenty-two) and continue for forty-three years, until retirement. Recognizing that major expenses are usually planned ahead of time, it is assumed that all expenditures and receipts are incurred in a lump sum at the end of the year indicated.

$$\text{Present value of benefits} = \frac{\text{fifth year benefits}}{1.05^5} + \frac{\text{sixth year benefits}}{1.05^6}$$

$$+ \frac{\text{seventh year benefits}}{1.05^7} + \ldots + \frac{\text{forty-third year benefits}}{1.05^{43}}$$

$$\text{Present value of costs} = \frac{\text{first year cost}}{1.05} + \frac{\text{second year cost}}{1.05^2}$$

$$+ \frac{\text{third year cost}}{1.05^3} + \frac{\text{fourth year cost}}{1.05^4}$$

Net present value = present value of benefits − present value of costs

If the net present-value calculation is a positive number, the investment in college should be undertaken, because a positive number indicates the present value of the benefits exceeds the present value of the costs. If the calculation reveals a negative number, the present value of the costs outweighs the present value of the benefits; the pursuit of a college degree would not be worth the expense.

Can you apply this analysis? The calculation of present values is tedious without a financial calculator. With such a calculator, the calculation is quickly accomplished by

C

entering estimates of costs and the incremental income earned from a college degree and assigning a value to the interest rate. Often the question is raised as to which of numerous market interest rates should be selected. The correct interest rate will reflect the individual's opportunity cost of moving funds from other investments to the human capital investment. For example, if the only other choice open to the investor is to leave the funds in a bank account paying 5 percent interest, and if the investor is certain of his or her estimates, then an interest rate of 5 percent would be reasonable.

A higher interest rate is appropriate to account for uncertainty about the future. The higher is the interest rate, the lower will be the present value of benefits in the future. For example, $100,000 of extra earnings forty years in the future is worth only $14,205 today at an interest rate of 5 percent. However, the present value of that $100,000 in the future falls to a mere $2,210 if a 10 percent interest rate is used.

C

Study by Design

SpeedStudy

SpeedReview

The labor market offers people the chance to earn incomes. Wages and salaries are augmented by fringe benefits to arrive at total labor costs. The fundamental determinant of the wage rate is demand and supply in the labor market. Labor demand varies by occupation, geography, and industry, and is derived from the demand for firms' outputs. Individual labor supply curves reflect personal preferences, which are shaped by economic need, knowledge of the labor market, and other factors. Market labor supply curves are upward sloping.

Labor services are exchanged for wages in labor markets. Individual labor markets have different characteristics. For example, wages will be lower in a monopsony labor market than in a perfectly competitive one, but higher in a labor market monopolized by a single union seller of labor services. Compensating wage differentials, differences in human capital, discrimination, and other factors cause wages to vary from one worker to the next.

SpeedStudy True or False Self-Test

A1. Paid vacations are an example of a fringe benefit.

A2. The reservation wage is the smallest sum of money that a person will work for.

A3. *Ceteris paribus*, the income effect of a wage increase will cause a person to work fewer hours.

A4. Right-to-work laws outlaw unions in the twenty-one states with such laws.

A5. Monopsony firms pay competitive wages.

A6. Under a bilateral monopoly, the wage rate will be higher than under monopoly.

A7. The theory of compensating wage differentials says that garbage collectors will be paid more in order to compensate them for the unpleasant aspects of the job.

A8. Occupational segregation is about the concentration of workers in certain occupations.

A9. Women earn about 50 percent of men's earnings.

A10. One of the widest pay gaps is between the earnings of black women and white women.

B11. Economic rent is income in excess of opportunity costs.

B12. The income share going to the highest quintile increased to over 50 percent between 1977 and 1992.

B13. The use of economic principles to place a value on life is a recent development.

B14. If you are willing to pay $10 to reduce your risk of death by 50 percent, then the value you place on your life is at least $10,000.

C15. A firm maximizes profit by hiring up to the point where the wage rate equals marginal revenue.

C16. If a firm sells its output at a constant price of $2 per unit, and if one more worker would add seven more units, then the worker's marginal revenue product equals $14.

C17. College students often find that the implicit opportunity cost of attending college exceeds the explicit cost.

C18. The present value of a stream of future income equals the sum of that income divided by the number of years involved.

The MasterMind

Selected Terms along the Way

total labor costs, 278
labor productivity, 278
derived demand, 279
civilian labor force, 280
labor force participation rate, 280
reservation wage, 280
substitution effect, 281
income effect, 281
primary workers, 281
perfectly competitive labor market, 283

marginal cost of labor, 284
monopsony, 285
monopoly, 285
bilateral monopoly, 285
compensating wage
   differentials, 286
collective bargaining, 287
signaling, 289
in kind, 290
poverty line, 290

occupational segregation, 292
comparable worth, 292
economic rent, 295
marginal revenue product
   of labor, 306
present value, 311
discount rate, 311

MasterMind Multiple Choice Self-Test

A1. The difference between salaried workers and workers who are paid a wage is

  a. the former receive fringe benefits and the latter do not.

  b. the former receive a fixed income, while the income of the latter depends on how many hours are worked.

  c. the former receive overtime pay, while the latter do not.

  d. the former are nonunion workers, while the latter are union members.

A2. Monthly labor costs at XYZ Manufacturing Company, which employs 1,000 workers, equal $10,000 in wages and $2,700 in fringe benefits. Total labor costs at XYZ are

  a. $12,700.

  b. $12.70.

  c. $10.00.

  d. not able to be determined from the information given.

A3. To say that labor demand is derived means that

  a. labor demand is fixed.

  b. labor demand is not related to the wage rate.

  c. labor demand arises from the demand for output.

  d. labor demand varies from city to city.

A4. Who is *not* a labor force participant?

  a. A seventeen-year-old working at Benny's Big Burger.

  b. A nurse employed at City Hospital.

  c. A retired telephone company employee.

  d. An unemployed welder looking for a job.

A5. Night shifts pay more than day shifts

  a. by law.

  b. due to occupational segregation.

  c. because a higher percentage of night shift workers are white.

  d. because of compensating wage differentials.

B6. A quintile equals

  a. 10 percent.

  b. 20 percent.

  c. 25 percent.

  d. 40 percent.

B7. In order to evaluate whether or not a regulation should be imposed or a project undertaken, it is often necessary to weigh the value of lives lost or saved. For this purpose, economists who estimate the value of a life look at

  a. the amount of insurance an average person buys.

  b. the emotional and financial losses suffered by family and friends.

c. how much money or other things of value people require in order to voluntarily accept extra risk.

d. the damages that juries have typically imposed on firms in wrongful death lawsuits.

C8. The marginal revenue product curve would definitely shift to the right if

a. average product increased.

b. marginal product decreased.

c. product price increased.

d. product price decreased.

C9. Which of the following is *not* a part of computing the net present value of a college education?

a. Estimating how much future earnings are increased by the college education.

b. Estimating the number of years of additional earnings and personal satisfaction.

c. Using a higher interest rate to the extent that the future looks more uncertain.

d. Multiplying earnings in the future by the interest rate to arrive at their value in the present.

MasterMind Questions and Problems

A1. Why do some employers offer fringe benefits that exceed those required by government mandates? Why do other employers choose not to offer such fringe benefits? Evaluate each of the following fringe benefits and state the advantage to an employer who offers:

a. free day care.

b. flextime—within limits, employees pick their own starting and quitting times.

c. employee lunchroom with lunches provided to employees at cost.

d. two weeks paid vacation.

A2. What is your reservation wage today? What will it be when you graduate from college? What could cause your reservation wage to change?

A3. How much monopsony power do you think each of the following employers has? Explain any qualifiers to your answers.

a. A fast food restaurant in a major city.

b. The only newspaper in a major city.

c. One of three television stations in a medium-sized city.

A4. Many community colleges pay professors solely on the basis of their educational attainments and their years of experience, which means every professor with the same amount of schooling and experience is paid the same salary. Four-year colleges and universities, on the other hand, usually have merit pay plans, so that professors with identical qualifications may be paid widely disparate amounts.

a. Why would community colleges reject the merit pay concept, but not four-year colleges?

b. "Basing pay raises on seniority rewards mediocrity." Evaluate.

c. "Merit pay plans allow bosses to reward their favorites and punish those they dislike." Evaluate.

A5. Since 1950, the overall labor force participation rate for men has declined slightly while that for women has risen dramatically. What could account for these facts?

B6. Are consumers responsible for the inequality in the income distribution? After all, if people refused to pay high prices for tickets to sports events, concerts, and the like, the amount of economic rents accruing to superstars would diminish. Are there other factors at work in creating inequality?

B7. Should cost-benefit analysis be used to craft workplace safety regulations, or should the economics be ignored and maximum safety in the workplace be our goal?

C8. Explain in your own words the meaning of marginal revenue product. How does this concept relate to derived demand?

C9. Is the model of investment in human capital applicable to decisions other than the decision to attend college? Provide some examples of instances for which the model would apply.

Future Explorations: Mapping out Term Papers

1. **Real Wages and the American Worker**

   Your research will focus on the average earnings of workers over time, after adjusting for inflation. Your purpose is to document the slow growth in real earnings during the last twenty years and possible causes. The government documents section in the library contains numerous useful U.S. Department of Labor and Census Bureau publications, which will provide you with data. The news media and professional journals such as the *American Economic Review* have also published articles on this topic, which you may wish to consult.

2. **Occupational Wages: The Best- and Worst-Paying Jobs**

   In this paper your goal is to identify the best- and worst-paying jobs, document average or median earnings in those jobs, and discuss the duties and educational qualifications needed to perform these jobs. Are your findings consistent with the theory of compensating differentials? Discuss.

3. **Women in the Labor Market**

   This paper is concerned with the increasing importance of women in the labor market. It will document the increasing labor force participation of women over time and women's progress at closing the wage gap with men. Alternative explanations of why a wage gap remains will be examined. The paper concludes by looking at the effect women have had on the labor market and how their roles within the family have changed.

Answer Key

ExpressStudy True or False	SpeedStudy True or False Self-Test		MasterMind Multiple Choice Self-Test
1. F	1. T	10. F	1. b
2. T	2. T	11. T	2. a
3. F	3. T	12. F	3. c
4. F	4. F	13. F	4. c
5. T	5. F	14. F	5. d
6. T	6. F	15. F	6. b
	7. T	16. T	7. c
	8. T	17. T	8. c
	9. F	18. F	9. d

CHAPTER

Nine

Government's Role in Production

317

A Look Ahead

Technology tells us what can be done. Economics tells us what should be done. Politics tells us what will be done.

This old saying sums up the dilemma facing economists. They are caught in the middle. Economists neither produce goods for consumers nor control public policy. Rather, economists attempt to identify how the intertwining actions of government and markets can offer citizens the best value.

The search for efficiency and equity can sometimes justify government intervention in the market economy. Economists seek to identify when public policy is needed to meet economic goals and the types of government actions that are appropriate. With these goals in mind, this chapter examines both **market failures**—instances in which free markets fail to achieve economic efficiency—and the policy designs that hold the most promise of remedying those failures.

Pointing out when government actions can promote efficiency is an ongoing task. Because subtleties of efficient policy design often get lost in the political process, examining the details of specific policies is equally important. Poorly designed policies can cause unintended problems elsewhere in the economy or even contradict the policies' intended objectives.

DESTINATIONS

*M*odule A

As you zip along the Expressway you will arrive at an ability to

- ascertain why the private marketplace fails to offer valuable public goods;
- provide an economic justification for some pollution, but not as much as is produced in the unregulated marketplace;
- discuss how policy instruments that can control pollution can also be used to protect water, fish, wild animals, and other common property resources;
- identify how private property rights promote conservation of resources;
- interpret why regulations are enacted and why they are resented.

*M*odule B

Upon leaving the Expressway to explore issues you will be able to

- discuss the issue of transborder pollution and the difficulties in finding solutions;
- distinguish several different ways in which economics affects criminal justice.

*M*odule C

Mastering Roadside Challenges will allow you to hone analytical skills by

- analyzing how taxes or marketable permits can control pollution efficiently;
- demonstrating how inappropriate assumptions can distort cost-benefit analysis.

Market Failure—What Role Government?

The United States contains over 80,000 separate governments. These range from education, sewer, and water districts through municipal, county, and state governments, on up to the federal government. Each government has its own administrative costs. What can justify so many governments? Should all these governments be abolished so the free market can reign supreme?

The invisible hand of the marketplace leads profit-seeking producers to offer an efficient variety of goods and services. Competition ensures that these goods and services are produced at least cost. The result is that waste is minimized and social surplus maximized. However, there are exceptions—instances of market failure in which markets do not lead to efficient levels of production. **Market failures occur frequently when goods are not purely private.**

The Spectrum of Goods

A **private good** is consumed by one person and one person only. Private goods are *excludable* and *rival*, meaning that people can be excluded from consuming the good and that one person's consumption diminishes the amount that is available for everyone else. For example, a swig of Kumquat Delight Fruit Drink would be a private good, because each swig that one person takes leaves that much less for someone else. The goods that we buy are almost always private in nature. However, we consume other goods that are public.

Public goods are just the opposite of private goods. A *pure public good* is both nonexcludable and nonrival. Different people place different values on public goods. However, we have no choice but to each consume the same amount. National defense provides an example of a nearly pure public good. Whether U.S. citizens are pacifists, hawks, rich, or poor, and no matter our race, gender, or ethnicity, we all consume the same amount of national defense.

Public goods are usually *impure*. For example, highways represent an impure public good, especially during rush hour when cars slow each other down. Some highways can also be designed for limited access, a means of exclusion. Still, for the most part, highways do offer the characteristics of a public good. Namely, one person's consumption of the services of a highway would not interfere with another person's consumption of those same services, and exclusion would be difficult.

Public goods can extend over a wide or limited area. A city's air quality is an example of a *local public good*. Local public goods provide an economic justification for local and regional governments. For instance, it is better to have local streets and highways under the control of municipal and state governments, respectively, than have decision makers in the nation's capital decide which potholes get repaired and where street lights are installed. The same would hold true for the many other public goods that are primarily local or regional in nature.

In between public and pure private goods are common property resources and private goods with externalities. Sometimes the ownership of something is *common property*, meaning that it is shared. Shared ownership occurs most frequently in connection with natural resources, thus leading to the term **common property resources**. For example, an oilfield could straddle two separate properties, with each property owner having the right to pump as much oil as the owner desires. A common property resource generates contention over who gets to use it.

Other times, the production or consumption of private goods lead to costs or benefits to third parties—people or businesses who were not party to the transaction. Such spillover effects onto third parties are termed **externalities**. Externalities can be either negative or positive. Pollution is an example of a negative externality. Negative externalities impose *external costs* on others. For example, to the extent that air pollution causes health problems or decreases people's enjoyment of outdoor activities, the pollution has imposed external costs on its victims. Conversely, positive externalities confer *external benefits*, such as when a neighbor kills all the mosquitos on her property, which also results in fewer in your own backyard. The external benefits are the greater enjoyment you derive from your backyard and the money you save on pest control.

Figure 9A-1 summarizes the range of goods and resources from the extreme of pure private goods to the other extreme of pure public goods. To reiterate, market failure occurs when goods are not purely private.

Public Goods and the Free-Rider Problem

Public goods are unique in that we all consume them jointly. We share national defense, fresh air, and even access to radio signals. Adding more consumers does not diminish the enjoyment we each get from these goods. This arrangement has repercussions on demand that prevent the marketplace from offering an efficient quantity. Unlike a private good, each unit of a public good is simultaneously consumed by everyone. The value of a public good is thus the sum of its values to all consumers.

Figure 9A-2 illustrates this idea, where the public good is worth $9 to Ana, and $12 to Bob, and so forth. It would be efficient to provide this good only if total social benefits exceed total social costs, where **social costs or benefits** are defined to equal all costs or benefits within the economy.

In most applications, the quantity of a public good can vary, which means we must

Figure 9A-1 **The spectrum of goods and resources** is based on the degree of rivalry and excludability, where the left extreme is completely rival and excludable and the right extreme is completely nonrival and nonexcludable.

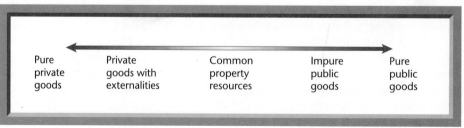

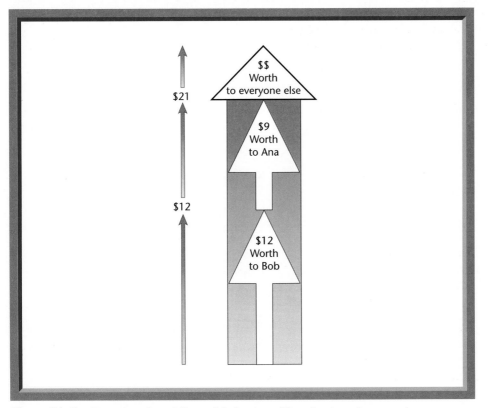

Figure 9A-2   **The value of a public good is the sum of its value to each person,** because everyone consumes the same amount.

compare the increment to social costs to the increment to social benefits from producing more of the public good. In other words, we must consider not only total benefits and costs, but also marginal social benefit and marginal social cost.

The efficient quantity of a public good is that for which marginal social cost equals marginal social benefit, because that quantity maximizes social surplus. *Social surplus* refers to benefits to consumers net of all production costs, seen as the shaded area in Figure 9A-3. Q* represents the efficient quantity of output.

The schedule of marginal social benefits is sometimes referred to as demand for the public good. The law of demand applies as much to public goods as to private goods. The greater is the quantity, the lower is the marginal social benefit from increasing quantity further. This means the marginal social benefit curve is downward sloping. However, this marginal social benefit schedule is demand only in the abstract. In practice, it would be extremely difficult to get people to pay anything voluntarily for a public good.

For private goods, you walk away with something in exchange for your money. With public goods, the amount you consume seems unaffected by how much you spend. Whether you offer a year's wages or nothing at all makes no discernible difference. You can still consume just as much of the public good as everyone else. The result is a **free-rider problem,** in which everyone has the incentive to let others pay the costs of providing the public good.

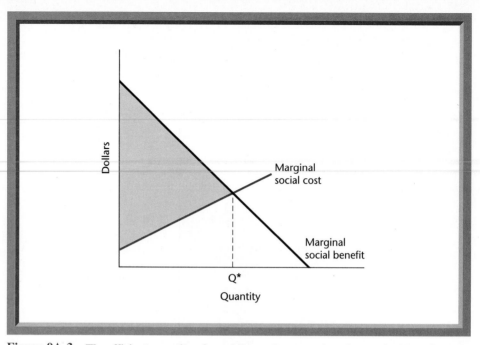

Figure 9A-3 **The efficient quantity of a public good** occurs when the marginal benefit of another unit just equals its marginal cost.

The solution to the free-rider problem ordinarily involves taxation. Government compels everyone to contribute, since everyone shares in consuming public goods. How much money people are forced to contribute is then at the discretion of government rather than the consumer directly. Thus nearly everyone would prefer either more or less government spending on any particular public good.

Sometimes, too, private entrepreneurs find ways to tie public goods to private goods that individuals or firms are willing to buy. For example, broadcast radio and television stations bundle their broadcasts with commercials. Because broadcasts are accessible to all, they are public goods and thus cannot be sold directly. However, commercials are private goods from the standpoint of advertisers. The more valuable is the public good aspect of programming, the more stations can charge advertisers for air time. In this and many other cases, there is at least some private provision of public goods. Unfortunately, there is nothing that compels private markets to produce the most efficient quantity or variety of these goods.

OBSERVATION POINT: "What's a Little Snow?"

The great blizzard of 1996 paralyzed much of the Northeast. Not Buffalo, New York, though. As one of the snowiest spots in the U.S., the people of Buffalo are used to the white stuff. "So what's another foot or two?" they ask as they slog to work, listening to the news reports of prolonged federal government shutdowns and other snow emergencies elsewhere.

True, Buffalonians are battle-hardened veterans of many a winter campaign. But there is more to the story. What's missing is the part about the efficient choice of a local public good—snow removal. Officials in Buffalo know it's going to snow hard, nearly every year. It is thus efficient for them to spend heavily on snow plows and other capital equipment. With snowfalls much less frequent in other parts of the country, officials there find it more efficient to devote that money to other needs. The result is that when the infrequent snowstorm does strike, the Buffalonians drive to work while the Washingtonians wait for a warm, sunny day.

Externalities—When Should There Be Action?

Externalities in the form of external benefits or external costs are all around us, although frequently of minor significance. Externalities occur when the **private costs or benefits** of an action—those borne by the ones taking the action—differ from social costs or benefits, which include both private and external costs and benefits.

$$\text{Social cost} = \text{private cost} + \text{external cost}$$
$$\text{Social benefit} = \text{private benefit} + \text{external benefit}$$

Significant external benefits are not as widespread as significant external costs. For example, constructing a beautiful new house in a shabby neighborhood will increase the value of other homes in that neighborhood. Likewise, people who successfully pull themselves out of poverty or other difficult situations serve as valuable role models for others seeking to escape similar situations. While there are many other examples of external benefits, external costs are more pervasive and worrisome.

The most obvious external cost is from environmental pollution. For example, fumes from the tailpipe of a diesel bus do not bother either the passengers or the bus company. Rather, the cost is external—the fumes bother the drivers behind. Would you wish to follow a gravel truck that drops sand and pebbles that threaten your vehicle? The cost of chipped paint on your Ford Bronco is of no concern to The Pits Gravel Company unless, perhaps, it fears a lawsuit or government reprisal.

Because external costs or benefits are not felt by the person or firm causing the externality, the free market price signal fails to generate efficient outputs. For example, Figure 9A-4 shows the supply and demand for a product that is associated with an external cost. The supply curve represents marginal private costs, but fails to reflect full marginal social costs. The difference between marginal social cost and marginal private cost is marginal external cost.

$$\text{Marginal social cost} = \text{marginal private cost} + \text{marginal external cost}$$

or

$$\text{Marginal external cost} = \text{marginal social cost} - \text{marginal private cost}$$

Thus, **when external costs are present, the free market produces too much**—output exceeds that which would be efficient. Conversely, **when there are external benefits, the free market produces too little.**

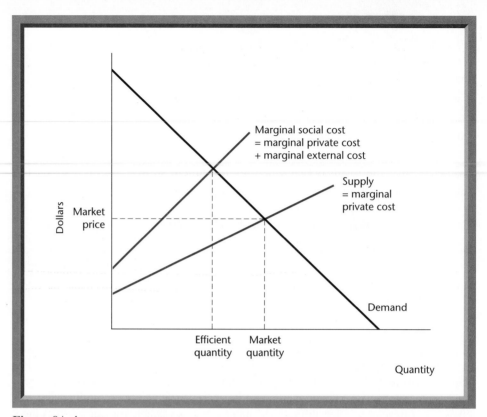

Figure 9A-4 **When external costs are present,** supply lies below marginal social cost, and the free market produces more than would be efficient.

The presence of external costs does not imply that the externality-generating activity should cease. It is efficient to have some pollution, for example. In the course of a day's living, we are each responsible for pollution, such as from the tailpipe of the vehicles that take us where we want to go. Additional pollution is generated in producing the products we buy.

Are manufacturers evil people, who pollute so that we will be miserable? Actually, pollution results from firms using common-property air or water to remove wastes. The principle of mass balance, a physical law, implies that some waste will always occur when inputs are transformed into outputs. This waste must go somewhere, and water and air provide excellent waste removal services.

Still, lacking government action, polluters pollute too much. The reason is that there is no market for many environmental services. However, there is a market for some. For instance, firms economize on the solid wastes they generate when they must pay the trash collector to have these wastes disposed of. In contrast, in the case of liquid and gaseous waste, firms have no incentive to cut back if they can use the publicly owned environment to remove these wastes for free.[1]

---

[1]An analysis of an external benefit can be found in chapter 14, Challenge 2.

When Markets Are Missing

If environmental services provided by common-property water and air were priced, as they would be if sold in a market, firms would economize and pollute less. They would compute how valuable pollution is to them in terms of the extra output it allows. They would also look for alternate ways to produce their output with less pollution. The upshot is that firms would pollute only when the value of that pollution exceeds its environmental costs. That would be efficient.

Occasionally, firms compete on the basis of how environmentally friendly—how "green"—their products are. For example, consumers may pay extra for recycled paper or nontoxic anti-freeze. However, consumers rarely seek information on how much pollution is generated in the production of a product, and are rarely willing to pay much of a premium for green products.

Typically, then, competition forces firms to be environmentally neglectful unless there are public policy incentives to be otherwise. Were a firm to go to the expense of cutting back its pollution, that firm would be at a disadvantage in competing against other firms in its industry. Only the heaviest polluters would survive. This is why pollution externalities represent a market failure, one calling for government action to change the rules of the game.

While reliance on public policy is commonplace, it is not the only means to resolve externalities. An alternative would rely upon legal safeguards against damage to the property of others. If pollution damages your property, sue for damages! Polluters will seek to avoid damages if they have to pay.

This school of thought is supported by the **Coase theorem**, named after Nobel Laureate Sir Ronald Coase. The Coase theorem holds that parties to an externality would voluntarily negotiate an efficient outcome, without government involvement. Government need merely define and clearly enforce property rights. For example, if the value of changing the amount of an externality exceeds its cost, a mutually beneficial agreement would be struck to accomplish this change. That would be efficient. If the value of change is less than the cost, an agreement would not be reached. That would also be efficient.

Few people believe the Coase theorem offers a general solution to externality problems. For example, imagine your neighbor playing her classic Bruce Springsteen album at top volume at 2 A.M. Are you likely to ask how much money that experience is worth to her, and compare the amount with your own willingness to pay to avoid hearing it? Would you offer to pay her enough to get her to turn the volume down? You're a reasonable person, aren't you? "NOT AT 2 A.M.!" you say?

Anyway, if you pay once, you'll wind up paying again, even if your neighbor decides that she no longer likes listening. She likes the money. That exemplifies the problem of *strategic behavior*, which interferes with the practical application of the Coase theorem. That problem becomes significantly worse when the effects of the externality are widespread. In addition, identifying specific culprits and bringing together victims becomes quite difficult when many parties are involved. **Transaction costs**, the expense of coordinating market exchanges, would be high. Thus, the Coase theorem applies only in the absence of transaction costs and strategic behavior. In practice, this means we either resort to public policy to remedy the externality or ignore the problem and let the market fail.

A

OBSERVATION POINT: Back in Time to Baker Street

A

Wouldn't you sometimes like to do away with those stinking internal combustion engines and return to the pristine past of horses and carriages? You could rub Ol' Paint's nose and wouldn't have to deal with smog and ozone alerts.

Dream on, for the reality of life prior to the horseless carriage was anything but pollution free. Witness Old London. Well before the invention of motor cars and lorries, the streets of London were beset with acid rain and choking air pollution. The source of many toxic particulates churned into the air by hooves and carriage wheels was, shall we say, just opposite from Ol' Paint's nose.

The skies over London were also black with sooty smoke from the many coal- and wood-burning fireplaces throughout the city. Now, more than a century later and several million people larger, London offers more breathable air and clearer skies.

Yes, London still sees pollution, because heat, transportation, and nearly every other product cannot be produced without it. The difference is better pollution-control technology spurred on by public policy. Compared with the good old days, then, production is up and pollution is down.

Common Property Resources—No Incentives for Conservation

Common property resources are owned jointly. Examples include groundwater, public lands, wild animals, and fish in the oceans, lakes, and rivers. The problem is that, when many people own the same resource, no one has any personal incentive to conserve it for the future. Owners have rights to take or use the resource, but have no way of ensuring its preservation.

For example, imagine sharing a very large joint checking account with all other students at your college. How much money would be left in the account by the end of the day? Most likely, each student would figure that others would quickly raid the account. The bank would see a stampede of students, each seeking to be the first to transfer the entire balance to a private account. Common property resources face much the same problem.

In a classic article entitled "Tragedy of the Commons" (*Science*, 1968), Garrett Hardin illustrates this problem with reference to the old English commons. The common land accessible to all quickly turned into a desolate expanse of dirt and mud, while private land nearby was lush and green. Grasses on the commons disappeared because shepherds allowed their sheep to overgraze. Shepherds had no reason to graze their flocks lightly, because the grass they saved would in all likelihood get eaten by someone else's flock. In contrast, on private land nearby, owners sought to conserve some grass to provide for future growth. The sheep were herded to fresh pastures before the grass was munched so short as to become endangered.

The common property resource problem is not a thing of the past. For example, overfishing along the coast of Maine and in many other ocean fisheries has caused catches to decline dramatically. Another concern is depletion of the ozone layer in the earth's upper atmosphere, as manufacturers in countries around the globe have little incentive to design ozone-friendly products. Likewise, irrigators and municipalities tapping into groundwater and river water resources have little incentive to practice conservation that would help each other out.

Government can solve common property resource problems by allotting the property to private users, such as through **privatization**. Most often, however, complete transfers would be impractical or politically unacceptable. For example, few would advocate selling rivers, lakes, and oceans to any single owner. The alternative is for government to act as the owners' agent and apportion use of the common property so that overuse is avoided. This is the rationale behind fishing and hunting permits, regulation of mesh size on fishing nets, mandated water-saving toilets, and various other restrictions and **user fees**—fees for use of a publicly owned good, service, or resource. As we shall see, some policy approaches are more promising than others.

*P*olicy *Tools*

This section highlights some prominent policy options for the control of externalities and allocation of common property resources. Although several applications will be mentioned, the focus will be upon pollution and water policy. This focus is warranted because pollution is the most prominent externality, and allocation of common-property water promises to become increasingly significant as population grows.

Moral Suasion

> *"Turn down that thermostat—Don't waste energy!" "Be water tight!" "Don't be a Litter Bug!" "Only* YOU *can prevent forest fires!"*

From U.S. Presidents to Smokey-the-Bear, we are exhorted to do the right thing. These appeals to our social conscience are the easiest form of public policy available to fight externality and common property resource problems. Unfortunately, **moral suasion** is rarely adequate to the task, and often has undesirable side effects.

There are some fundamental problems with moral suasion. First, it has no way of achieving any particular target, efficient or otherwise. Second, it imposes all costs of cutbacks on the "moral." This leads to a third and perhaps most troubling problem. Moral suasion can lead to a self-righteous intrusion on personal privacy.

OBSERVATION POINT: Water Waster?—Awarding David Robinson the Scarlet Letter

Remember all those "great books" you were forced to read in school? Perhaps one was *The Scarlet Letter*, by Nathaniel Hawthorne, which depicts life among the Puritans of early New England. The title is taken from a particularly effective technique of moral suasion. Those found guilty of adultery were forced to wear the scarlet letter *A*. Perhaps such a public humiliation would prevent others from engaging in this sinfulness.

Modern mass communication offers alternatives to the ignominious letter, as witnessed by Spurs' basketball star David Robinson. "Robinson near top of water-users' list," blared a front-page headline of San Antonio's daily newspaper (*Express-News*, June 18, 1994). Also splashed across the front page was a detailed listing of the names and neighborhoods of the ten residential customers paying the highest water bills. Their monthly bills were itemized in the range from $328 to $731, each completely legal.

Fear of public humiliation can provide a powerful incentive to conserve. No one wants the neighbors to point and whisper. No one wants to wear the shameful tag of water waster.

Technology Mandates

Have you noticed that newly installed toilets don't flush well? The reason is the U.S. Environmental Protection Agency's 1995 nationwide law prohibiting the sale of toilets with tank capacities over 1.6 gallons. This is an example of the administratively popular policy of **technology mandates**.

Technology mandates occur when government instructs producers as to the exact technology to install to remedy some public problem. Low-flow showerheads and low-flush toilets are examples of technology mandates designed to avoid wasting water. Catalytic converters on automobiles are mandated to reduce air pollution. Technology mandates are usually chosen because they are easy to observe and enforce, and seem like a very straightforward solution to the problem.

Sometimes the mandates are indirect, as with scrubbers on powerplant smokestacks, and other specific pollution control strategies. Here, the Environmental Protection Agency (EPA) specifies emission standards that must be met and suggests technologies that will meet these standards. Producers are free to use other technologies, but would be subject to serious penalties if the other approaches fail. If the EPA's suggested technologies fail, the producers avoid liability. There is thus much risk and little incentive to experiment with potentially better ways of pollution control.

Technology mandates are often much more expensive and annoying than other policy options. For instance, it is a waste of money and an annoyance to require high-tech, low-flush toilets in regions where water is plentiful. If external costs can be added directly to the price of products, the higher prices would induce conservation in ways that regulators might be unable to mandate. A higher price of municipal water might prompt consumers to wash larger loads of laundry and dishes, for example.

Using prices avoids the inefficiencies caused by the broad brush of technology mandates.

In the realm of pollution control, economic studies estimate that market-based alternatives to technology mandates can achieve the same amounts of emission cutbacks at roughly one-third the cost. For example, the EPA's bubble plan allows a firm to increase its emissions from some sources if it offsets those increases by decreasing its emissions from other sources. One Ohio utility plant responded by periodically hosing down its piles of coal to prevent wind-blown coal dust, rather than install expensive smokestack technology. The firm's particulate emissions dropped, while the cost of pollution control dropped even more. The EPA's offsets plan extends this flexible concept across firms to capture even more cost savings.

Government planners cannot be expected to foresee all of the options for pollution control. For example, what planner could have mandated that workers reduce pollution and congestion by abandoning their daily auto commute? Could planners in the 1970's have imagined the option of replacing commuters' automobiles with fiber optics? Yet, the recently available technologies of networked home computers have led many people to do just that by working at home. Allowing the market to choose this and other less costly strategies of pollution control means that we can have a cleaner environment at a lower cost.

Pollution Taxes—Environmental User Fees

Economists often advocate internalizing the costs of externalities directly into prices. If an activity generates damages, the value of those damages would be estimated, and a tax imposed equal to the amount of the marginal external cost at the efficient level of output. In this way, the tax causes perpetrators of the external cost to pay the full marginal social cost of their activities. This means that externalities become part of the decisions of those who cause them, and efficient choices will be made in the marketplace.

For example, if smoking a pack of cigarettes causes an average of $1 in health damages to others, then a tax of $1 per pack would represent those damages. Such a tax is sometimes referred to as an environmental user fee, since polluters are charged for using the common property environment.

Figure 9A-5 illustrates that a corrective tax on cigarettes shifts the supply curve up by the amount of that tax. The reason is that sellers now have to collect that extra payment and pass it along to government. The price would rise from the initial market price of $P_{no\ tax}$ to P_{tax}, but the price increase would not cover the full amount of the tax. The reason is that consumers respond to higher prices by purchasing fewer cigarettes, Q_{tax}, than the initial quantity of $Q_{no\ tax}$. If producers attempt to raise their price by the full amount of the tax, the law of demand would cause quantity demanded to fall, thus resulting in a surplus that would force prices to retreat somewhat. **Although price does not rise by the full amount of the tax, it does rise, which reduces consumption and its external costs.**

Using fees to remedy externalities often encounters difficulties. For example, external damages may depend upon time and place. Smoking at home does not impose the same externality as smoking in a restroom that many people must use. It is not possible to allow for this difference in imposing cigarette taxes. In other applications, such as taxes on water pollution from industrial effluent, fees could vary depending on such factors as season and time of day.

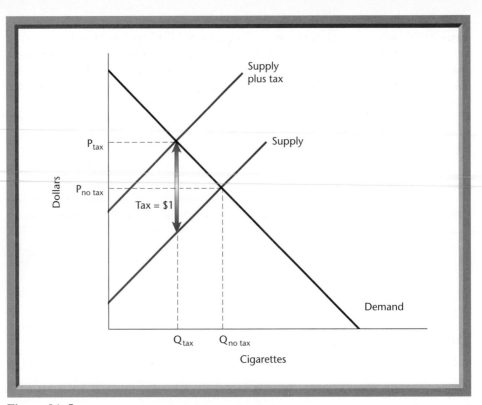

Figure 9A-5 **Using a tax to internalize an externality** requires that the tax rate be set equal to marginal external cost at the efficient quantity of output.

Measurement of pollution is another hurdle in the way of applying pollution taxes. For example, it may be difficult to constantly monitor the emission of pollutants, especially for autos and other mobile sources. For stationary sources like factories, one can imagine a system of periodic checks and penalties that would punish cheating. Of greater concern, however, is political acceptance of taxing pollution and providing effective penalties to ensure compliance.

Politicians often seek new revenue sources. In contrast to most taxes, those designed to remedy externalities actually promote economic efficiency. Yet, pollution taxes have proven to have little political support. On the one hand, some well-meaning environmentalists will not accept that the environment is an economic resource. They claim that pollution taxes are merely passed along to consumers, and that pollution is not reduced. This line of reasoning ignores the law of demand. It also ignores the role of competition. Competition forces firms to substitute cheaper inputs for the newly priced use of environmental services.

On the other hand, producers usually oppose pollution taxes. The reason is that those taxes result in significant transfers of revenues from polluters to the government, revenues that pay for the firms' ongoing emissions of pollutants. This revenue transfer is in addition to money spent directly on pollution control. Thus, pollution taxes lack powerful constituencies.

To overcome political barriers to pollution taxes, policy makers sometimes resort to paying for pollution abatement instead. For example, municipal waste-water treatment plants receive significant federal **subsidies**. Subsidies are appropriate to encourage actions causing external benefits. Unfortunately, subsidies for abating the external cost of pollution have undesirable side effects. Subsidies drain government revenues. They also reward polluters and can thereby lead to too many polluting firms.

OBSERVATION POINT: Second-Hand Smoke—To Ban or Not to Ban?

With worries about second-hand cigarette smoke abounding, antismoking laws have cropped up all around the country. Do these laws violate economic principles? After all, if all external costs are represented by cigarette taxes, people make efficient choices. In principle, a tax based upon the external costs of second-hand smoke seems hard to surpass.

Economic theory sometimes justifies **second-best policies**, such as a ban on smoking in certain public areas. This justification occurs when the preferred policy has undesirable effects in other areas due to entrenched inefficiencies elsewhere. For example, a high tax on cigarettes would raise the cost of smoking. Some addicted smokers might raid their children's food money or turn to theft to support their habits. If these secondary problems are serious and cannot be resolved directly, they might justify abandoning the tax in favor of smoking bans or other second-best alternatives.

However, it is easy to imagine all sorts of purported secondary effects. Applying these speculations to policy design could lead policy makers down the slippery slope of ever more command-and-control regulations. In the case of restaurant smoking bans, for example, will not diners vote with their feet? If so, they will go to restaurants that best satisfy their wants, including their preferences on smoking. Government intervention in this case would probably reduce efficiency, although some nonsmokers would not mind.

Marketable Permits—Whose Property?

Marketable permits offer the same economic advantages as taxes, but do so in a way that has much more political appeal. In application to pollution, marketable permits represent property rights to a certain amount of pollutant emissions. Government sets the overall quantity, and then divides up that quantity into a limited number of permits for the various polluters. While these permits could be auctioned, politics causes them more typically to be given away without charge.

Because the overall quantity of pollution is controlled directly, environmentalists are usually willing to acknowledge that marketable permits limit total pollution. Polluters prefer this approach to taxes because permits usually require no payment to government. However, polluters do sometimes worry that government might take away those rights or impose supplemental charges in the future.

Marketable permits are valuable property rights. The term *marketable* means that those rights can be bought and sold. This feature has appeal not only to producers, but also to economists. If pollution rights are traded, buyers would be firms with high costs of pollution abatement. Likewise, sellers would be firms with low costs of cutting back emissions. This means that emission reductions are undertaken by firms able to do so at least cost.

Trading in emission rights has mushroomed in recent years, so much so that it has formed an industry of its own. Markets for some pollutants are formal and well developed. For example, power plants and other emitters can buy and sell rights for sulfur dioxide emissions on the Chicago Board of Trade. Other pollutants have *thin markets*, where trades are few. When markets are thin, environmental consultants facilitate trading by keeping track of firms willing to sell their permits.

Marketable permits also provide a promising alternative in the allocation of common property resources. Here, a central authority determines how much of the resource can be used now, and still leave enough for the future. For example, the authority might estimate how much water can be pumped from a river without irreparable harm to the river's ecosystem. Pumping rights are then distributed among river users, perhaps in proportion to the users' historical levels of pumping. These rights are then good for each period into the indefinite future. Fluctuations in the river's ability to support pumping might cause the same percentage variations in the quantity allowed per permit.

By allowing permits to be marketable, those valuing water most highly would be the ones that would buy or retain the permits. This is just what economic efficiency prescribes. The main issues are distributional. For example, how are the permits to be initially distributed? Should we compensate feed store owners who lose their livelihoods when local farmers and ranchers sell their water rights to big cities? Political questions of this sort have been the largest obstacles to more widespread use of permitting.

OBSERVATION POINT: Airwaves at Auction

July 25, 1994, was a historic day in the history of American regulation. On that day, for the very first time, the Federal Communications Commission abandoned the use of bureaucratic criteria to assign airwave frequencies to potential broadcasters. Instead, on that July 25, the FCC commenced to sell these rights at auction. The rights were specified as ten-year, nationwide licenses to broadcast over each of ten separate band widths.

The judgment as to which broadcasters offer the most value is now left to the marketplace. That same market will dictate whether the bandwidths are used for two-way paging, messaging, personal communication devices, or any other service. Moreover, the government collects extra revenue. How much revenue had the Treasury been forgoing? When all was said and done, after forty-seven rounds of bidding, those ten licenses brought the U.S. Treasury over $600 million. Subsequent auctions of other frequencies have raised that total to over $8 billion.

*T*he Reach of Regulation

Regulation occurs whenever government acts to influence the specifications of goods and services or the manner in which they are produced. For example, the technology mandates discussed earlier are a type of regulation. Since competitive markets minimize production costs, the effect of regulations is to increase those costs. As such, regulations may be viewed as a form of taxation. Regulations increase economic efficiency only if the benefits they provide exceed their social costs.

The choice of what is to be regulated, and how that regulation is imposed, is at the discretion of the political process. Regulations are sometimes based on economic principles, such as the internalization of externalities. Other times, regulations lack a solid economic basis. Still, economics allows us to analyze the implications of alternative regulatory strategies, and thereby provides a benchmark by which to judge them.

A

Why the Controversy?

Speed limits, smoking bans, seat belt requirements, product standards, and workplace safety laws are but some of the many regulations that affect our daily lives. Should businesses be required to allow family leave time that gives workers time to nurture their young and care for sick parents? Should universities be granted public funds if the composition of their faculties, staff, and students fails to reflect that of the surrounding community? Perhaps you will agree—the extent to which various facets of our economy should or should not be regulated is one of the most controversial topics around.

When regulations apply uniformly across the country, they often lead to projects of little value that nonetheless impose heavy costs upon communities. For example, Great Bend, Kansas, has a population of about 15,000 residents. In 1980, in order to meet federal water quality standards, it upgraded its waste-water treatment plant. Fourteen years later, federal standards changed again. The town finds itself required to spend an additional $5.2 million in order to keep ammonia levels in its waste water from being toxic to fish in the Arkansas River. The fish? The Arkansas River at that point is little more than a trickle for most of the year. Its fish population consists mainly of minnows, minnows that seem exorbitantly expensive to local residents. Regulators do not bear the costs.

Regulation is sometimes hidden. For example, universities are required to satisfy social criteria pertaining to internal curriculum and policies or lose eligibility for federally funded student aid and other programs. In effect, this requirement places a hefty implicit tax upon deviating from federally sanctioned standards. Because there is punishment for violating these standards, regulation exists, whether it is called that or not.

Many people are concerned about overregulation, especially by the federal government. The more federal programs that are in place, the more weighty would be the consequences to states, municipalities, or private businesses of losing access to federal funding. Regional diversity decreases to the extent that federal funding depends upon conformity with national standards. Since markets operate by allowing consumers a diversity of choice, overregulation represents a threat to market efficiency.

Applying Regulations Judiciously

There are market-based alternatives to many forms of regulation. For example, this chapter has already discussed situations in which marketable permits can provide an efficient alternative to command-and-control regulation. In the design of public policy, the general rule is to target the problem in as precise and narrow a manner as possible, to hit the nail on the head. This is sometimes termed the **specificity principle**. By following the specificity principle, undesirable side effects are minimized.

Besides causing changes in the production and selection of goods and services, regulations have real economic costs associated with administrative and compliance. *Administrative and compliance costs* represent the regulations' transaction costs. For example, the Americans with Disabilities Act has been dubbed by detractors as the Full Employment for Lawyers Act. The paperwork and consulting fees spent on compliance with this and the myriad of other government regulations is enormous and a daunting hurdle for new and growing businesses. For example, a 1996 survey reported that one- and two-person businesses spent an average of 24 hours per month to comply with local, state, and federal laws.

Place yourself in the position of a business seeking to expand without breaking the law. One of your first tasks is to identify the many aspects of hiring, retention, and production that are subject to regulations. It is difficult to find them all. The task may even be so daunting that you choose to avoid expanding altogether.

If you plunge forward and succeed in identifying all areas in which regulation occurs, you still run the risk of unintentionally breaking the law. Table 9A-1 provides an example, taken from Equal Employment Opportunity Commission regulations on job interview questions, applicable to employers of fifteen or more persons. As you will note, legal and illegal forms of comparable job interview questions are difficult to tell apart.

The Americans with Disabilities Act (ADA) is a regulation defended on the basis that it provides a good that everyone merits. Such **merit goods** are those that consumers deserve to have, whether or not they would be willing to pay the costs of providing them.

In the case of the ADA, the merit good is access. Rather than provide public funding for this good, the ADA assigns responsibility to restaurant owners, store proprietors, and employers. Thus, establishments must offer wheelchair access, even the Lone Mountain Ranch cross-country ski lodge in Montana. It does not matter if the wheelchair-bound prefer extra cash in their pockets over special parking places, ramps, doors, and fixtures at a ski lodge restaurant. The option of trading away a merit good is not allowed.

Health care, safety, and information are also often viewed as merit goods. For ex-

---

TABLE 9A-1 *Regulations Regarding Interview Questions*

Legal Interview Questions	Illegal Interview Questions
Do you have 20/20 corrected vision?	What is your corrected vision?
How well can you handle stress?	Does stress ever affect your ability to be productive?
Can you perform this function with or without reasonable accommodation?	Would you need reasonable accommodation in this job?
Do you drink alcohol?	How much alcohol do you drink per week?

Source: EEOC, "Enforcement Guidance on Pre-Employment Disability-Related Inquiries," May 1994.

ample, workers might judge that higher wages would be worth more than costly safety equipment. Similarly, the sick might be willing to take a chance on an unapproved medical treatment. However, because safety is seen as a merit good, these trades are forbidden.

Unfortunately, there is no market check on which, if any, goods deserve the merit good designation. In other words, the concept of merit goods leaves the door wide open for regulations of almost any sort. Government places itself in the position of deciding which goods command this special status. Furthermore, if government chooses to provide these goods by way of regulation, there is no budgetary cost to the agency and thus little incentive for restraint.

✓ QuickCheck

Do you think it is legal for an employer to ask either of the following questions at a job interview? "What medications are you currently taking?" or "Are you currently using illegal drugs?" Also, what is the purpose of this exercise?

_____

Answer: It is legal to ask about illegal drug use, but not about medications in general. The exercise illustrates the difficulty of following government regulations.

EXPRESS STUDY TRUE OR FALSE

1. The free-rider problem causes common property resources to be overused. *is THAT consumers are unwilling to voluntarily pay for public goods*
2. The efficient quantity of a public good is that which maximizes social surplus.
3. The Coase theorem provides a theoretical justification for extensive use of taxes and permits to control pollution. *gov. to establish property rights, but otherwise leave pollution control to voluntary negotiations among effected parties*
4. Marketable pollution permits represent property rights that can be bought and sold.
5. Technology mandates usually achieve objectives of economic efficiency at the least possible social cost.
6. Regulations may be considered a form of taxation.

Module B

EXPLORING ISSUES

Trade between the U.S. and Mexico intensifies preexisting problems of transborder pollution. This Exploration looks at the very imperfect options available to resolve this issue.

The American Southwest

Wide open spaces, broad vistas, a freshening breeze—our vision of America's Southwest is one of expansiveness and freedom. It is a place to do and be as we please. The Southwest is part of our psyche; it's a state of mind. It's also a real place with real problems. As ever more people live in the vicinity of the Southwest, unlimited personal freedom comes into conflict with preservation of the environment that attracts them there. The environment of the Southwest is ill-suited to accommodate unrestricted pollution.

As in other parts of the country, citizens of the Southwest must abide by U.S. environmental laws, which means driving cars or operating factories with emission controls in place. The special problem of the Southwest, though, is that those controls apply to only a fraction of the sources of pollution. Much of the air and water pollution has its source in Mexico, an industrializing country with a rapidly growing population and less-stringent control over pollutants.

An American Medical Association group depicted parts of the U.S.–Mexico border as "a virtual cesspool and breeding ground for infectious diseases." (Council on Scientific Affairs). Exemplifying the problem of border air pollution, the city of El Paso, Texas, is in noncompliance with guidelines set by the U.S. Environmental Protection Agency (EPA). However, the EPA allows this noncompliance to continue without penalty. There is a reason.

If you have ever flown into El Paso and looked out the airplane window as you approached the city, you may have a good idea as to why the EPA makes exceptions for El Paso. On the south side of the Rio Grande is a polluted haze that greatly restricts visibility. The haze on the north side is much lighter. El Paso is on the north side and its twin, Ciudad Juarez, is on the south side. Ciudad Juarez has nearly triple the population and generates proportionally much more pollution than does El Paso. Unfortunately for El Paso, pollution knows no borders.

Transborder Pollution

Transborder pollution is a problem of growing magnitude around the world. The problems are worsening for two reasons. On the one hand, economic growth in the less-developed countries does not emphasize pollution control. Of greater concern to those countries are such tangibles as food, clothing, and shelter. On the other hand, the increased wealth of the developed countries has allowed them the luxury to focus beyond immediate necessities toward the quality and long-term sustainability of lifestyles. Environmental quality is important to both of those lifestyle goals.

Transborder pollution problems come in many forms. Some are global in nature, such as concerns that emissions of chlorofluorocarbons are depleting the earth's ozone layer. The pollution problem of most concern in America's Southwest is more local in nature. Here we have two countries, each of which feels the effects of the other's pollution. What trouble does this cause?

The problem of localized transborder pollution centers on incentives. There is much more incentive to control pollution that affects your own residents than there is incentive to control pollution absorbed elsewhere. For instance, cities along rivers routinely locate sewage treatment plants downstream and city dumps downwind from the city itself. When cities are all governed by one state or country, there are limits to how much pollution exporting is allowed. For example, while sewage from U.S. cities may be discharged downriver, at least U.S. law requires that it be treated. Given an absence of a world government, is there some other incentive for neighboring countries to be sensitive to each other's concerns?

Pollution Control Policies

It would be very difficult for the U.S. to apply any particular pollution control strategy to firms in Mexico. Options that work well within a jurisdiction don't work as well across jurisdictions. For example, one option long advocated by economists is for government to impose a tax on emissions of pollutants, such that the *external costs* of pollution are *internalized* into the production process. The idea is to make firms pay for environmental services. In other words, firms would be forced to pay for the waste-removal services of the air above or the river next door in the same way they pay for other types of services. In that case, you can rest assured firms would find ways to economize on smoke emissions and discharges into waterways.

A *second-best*, less desirable, alternative would be to tax the output of the firm. This approach would not give firms any incentive to reduce the amount of pollution per unit of output, but it would at least drive up the price of that output. Higher prices would mean fewer sales and thus less pollution. Could we apply either of these tax ideas to transborder pollution?

The answer is the U.S. probably could not effectively use pollution taxes on Mexican polluters. The U.S. could not tax pollution emissions effectively, because it lacks the authority to monitor pollution in Mexico and lacks the authority to impose taxes even if it could monitor that pollution. In principle, the U.S. could levy a pollution tax on output crossing the border. However, that tax could not effectively differentiate where in Mexico that output was produced. Furthermore, that tax would be politically unpalatable and violate international treaties.

Other policy instruments, such as pollution permits or mandated pollution control technologies, would also be infeasible for the same reasons taxes would not work. Where does that leave us?

Cooperation, Not Contention

The best solution may be voluntary cooperation between the U.S. and Mexico based on mutual self-interest. While both the U.S. and Mexico gain from trade between the two countries, the gains to Mexico are proportionally larger because it is the smaller country. This cooperative spirit is attested to by the 1994 implementation of the North American Free Trade Agreement (NAFTA), which incorporated Mexico into a revised and expanded free trade agreement between the U.S. and Canada.

NAFTA broke new ground in international trade by writing environmental safeguards directly into the treaty and side accords. For example, NAFTA signatories are obligated to maintain effective enforcement of their own environmental laws, even when the affected pollutants spill over the border. While NAFTA does not itself solve the problems of border pollution, it does provide a framework for cooperation on that issue.

What kind of cooperation can the United States legitimately expect from Mexico? Should we expect Mexico to maintain environmental standards equal to our own? Beware of environmental imperialism. The U.S. cannot expect the world to follow its standards, at least not without granting the rest of the world's citizens voting rights in U.S. elections. Moreover, uniform environmental standards would not make sense across all countries. After all, maintaining those standards is expensive, and incomes in some countries are much lower than in the U.S.

Mexico's per capita income is under $5,000 per year. Relative to the average U.S. citizen, the average citizen in Mexico thus consumes less in the way of high-quality food, clothing, shelter, medical care, and so forth. For Mexico to upgrade its control of pollution to match that in the U.S. would require further reductions in the quality of those goods.

One of the best ways for the U.S. to see greater control of pollution in Mexico is to see greater per capita income in Mexico. The reason is that environmental quality is a normal good, meaning that people want more as their incomes rise. The growth in income has been occurring in recent years and will be spurred along as NAFTA continues to be phased in. We are already seeing an increased interest in environmental improvement in Mexico. Over time, we can expect this interest to translate into concrete policy action.

In the meantime, there remain pollution problems along the U.S.-Mexico border. For example, sources of air pollution in the El Paso–Juarez airshed include the burning of tires to fuel brick kilns, dusty unpaved streets, and open-air spray painting of automobiles. The citizens of El Paso want action to clean this up sooner rather than later. So too do citizens of Juarez. Is effective action possible?

To answer that question, it must be noted that the environment is a *common property resource*, meaning that we can all use it, but that no one really owns it. This gives us no incentive as individuals to maintain it in the present or invest in its future. The way that government solves pollution problems is, in effect, to lay its own claim to the common property environment. Government then seeks to represent the interests of present and future users of the environment. Policy is implemented via such tools as carefully designed pollution charges, allocation of pollution permits, or mandated pollution controls.

Along the border, local governments have an incentive to cooperate in order to address the common pollution problem jointly. That is exactly what El Paso and Juarez have done. Specifically, those governments have formed a single international air quality management district for their region. This district is empowered with the authority to set air quality goals and employ market mechanisms to meet those goals.

For example, the market mechanism might grant limited emission rights to local polluters, but allow them to buy and sell these rights in the marketplace. In this way, overall pollution would be reduced and the firms that actually undertake pollution reduction would be those who can do so least expensively. The idea is for government to allocate property rights to the quantity of pollution that is permitted, and then let the free market determine which firms actually use those rights. For this approach to work, though, firms must not fear losing future allocations of pollution rights if they do not use those rights in the present. That has been a problem that has bedeviled such programs in the past. Markets function efficiently only when property rights are clear and reliable.

Conclusion

This Exploration has not dealt with all aspects of the transborder pollution problem. For example, much pollution is left over from the past, especially when it comes to toxins on the land and in the water. Therefore, controlling the flow of new pollutants is not enough; there is the stock of old pollutants to clean up. Who will pay for that cleanup? Part of the answer may be found in the recently established *North American Development Bank*, financed by the governments of Mexico and the United States to fund border cleanup projects. Yes, the hands of government and the pockets of taxpayers are likely to be major parts of any final resolution to the transborder pollution problems of the American Southwest.

PROSPECTING FOR NEW INSIGHTS

1. The production of many of the goods the U.S. imports from Mexico causes pollution within Mexico. Is this pollution fair to the Mexican people? Alternatively, would it be more equitable for the U.S. to import only those goods that are not associated with significant pollution or that abide by the pollution standards that U.S. industry is forced to face?

2. When firms in Mexico cause pollution that crosses the border, U.S. residents along the border are damaged. That pollution is an external cost, since the U.S. residents have no way to extract payment from the Mexican polluters. Explain how this sort of pollution raises a different set of issues than that discussed in question (1). What policies should the U.S. pursue?

Jurors, witnesses, defendants and attorneys all face economic incentives in the judicial process. Within the context of courtroom proceedings, there are issues concerning externalities, public goods, and cost-benefit analysis.

*T*he Arrest

SCREEEECH! Police cars pull up to your house. Next thing you know, officers in blue are reading you your rights and taking you in!

"What have I done?" you ask in bewilderment.

"Jury tampering!," barks the reply.

How did you get yourself into this mess, you wonder? In a way, the reason is clear—you did indeed offer money to a juror. But you only wanted to ensure an interview once the case was over. You'd drawn up the contract with the legal assistance program on your personal computer and specified explicitly that the contract did not depend on how the case turned out.

You just wanted a scoop. In a case as prominent as the trial of P. K. Timpken, the titans of the media would swarm all over those jurors the moment they delivered their verdict. All you had to offer was precious little money and a fledgling talk show on a public-access channel. You wouldn't have a chance of getting an interview unless you beat them to the punch. In hindsight, maybe you should have checked with an attorney. But that costs money!

It hardly seems fair. The most effective attorneys command the highest prices. Why should a wealthy person be allowed to buy better advice and a greater chance at a successful defense than can be obtained by a poor person? Then again, if there were no option to shop around, the alternative would be to provide everyone with tax-financed legal advice from salaried bureaucrats. Without the competitive motive for profit, what incentive would these bureaucrats have to do the best job? This is beginning to remind you of questions about physician incentives under health care reform . . .

"So, what's it gonna be? Public defender?"

You snap alert from your reverie and realize you have to make a choice. You don't have much money and don't know any good lawyers anyway. Oh well, here goes. "Public defender, please."

Attorney for the Defense

Hazel Chalmers was just out of law school and trying to work her way up the career ladder. This public defender job of hers wasn't what she had in mind for the long haul, but it was a start. Sure was a lot of work, though. Now that she'd gotten her Juris Doctor, her husband thought he might even see her sometimes. At least, that's how he put it. It's a good thing he wasn't expecting her to cook, clean, or any of that stuff. That's what her salary's for. That and paying off debts from law school. Kids? Maybe some day. "Can't wait to get that private practice, or at least onto the D.A.'s staff," she told herself.

"Hazel! We need to talk!" It was Fred Klein of the D.A.'s office.

"Hey Fred, what's up?"

"It's about that jury tampering case you've been assigned. I'll be prosecuting. I think we can settle. Got a minute?"

"Sure, let me close the door. What's the deal?"

"There is no question but that this client of yours offered money to a juror while the case was in progress. Whether that changed the verdict, I don't know. What I do know is that your client doesn't seem like a bad sort and probably just made an error in judgment. If you can provide a plea of guilty or no contest, I will recommend a suspended sentence. What do you say?"

"Thanks, Fred. That's really reasonable of you. Sounds like we can both lighten our load a bit. Of course, I'll have to talk this over with my client and get back to you."

You weren't happy about having to find so much money to cover bail. You wanted to put this whole thing behind you, you thought. Then again, you really weren't trying to bribe anybody, and it would offend your principles to say so. Or was it this other idea that was holding you back? Yes, a trial sure could offer some great publicity for your show!

"Hazel, I've thought it over, and I want to plead not guilty. That's my final decision."

You didn't see why the public defender was putting up so much argument. After all, she represents you, and you'd made up your mind. It was of no concern to you whether or not the D.A.'s office would question her competence if she brought you to trial. To trial it will be!

B

The Trial

Judge Lapetra Berry looked at her docket. Why was this jury-tampering case coming to trial? Was there something she didn't know about? Her schedule indicated that she was about to find out.

"Counsel, please meet me in my chambers."

"Mr. Klein, this court is busy. Couldn't you and Ms. Chalmers work something out?"

"Your Honor, the defendant has refused a plea bargain and has insisted on the right to a trial by jury. Off the record, it is my opinion that the defendant desires to use the procedures in this courtroom in order to generate publicity. I believe that, had the defendant been charged with bribing a juror in a less-publicized trial, the defendant would have been eager to accept a plea bargain."

Fred Klein wasn't happy about arguing routine cases that do little more than waste taxpayer dollars and the time of everyone involved. Fred had not always felt that way. He at first worried that plea bargains were too much like offering candy to little children—even innocent defendants might grasp for the chance to avoid the uncertainty of a trial verdict. Rightly or wrongly, most people want to get charges resolved as quickly as possible. Should prosecutors really push the accused into these plea bargains by threatening to throw the book at them if they don't cooperate?

Fred had changed his mind about plea bargains. Fred's boss, the district attorney, had driven home to him just how expensive actual trials could be—for defendants, jurors, and taxpayers alike. Looking at the formal assessment of costs and benefits provided by a *cost-benefit analysis*, Fred had come to understand why nearly 95 percent of criminal cases in the United States today are resolved by plea bargains. The adversarial system of justice involves such high transaction costs that, without plea bargains, the costs would be prohibitive. Why wouldn't Hazel cooperate?

"Your Honor, my client does indeed insist on a trial by jury. I respect that wish. There should be no prejudice against my client on that account." Hazel had not been happy with your decision at first, but found herself intrigued by your line of reasoning. It had been many years since she had taken economics courses. Could economic analysis really win this case for you?

*W*itness for the Prosecution

The jurors had been seated, and the case was progressing to Fred Klein's satisfaction. To Fred, the facts were clear—you had broken the law.

Curiously, Hazel also thought the case progressed well. As Hazel saw it, the case was like those economics problems she remembered from college. This case would revolve around interpreting the facts, rather than be a dispute over the facts themselves. She listened closely as Fred Klein put on his primary witness, jury foreman Joshua Ramirez.

"Mr. Ramirez, you say that the defendant passed you an envelope?"

"Yes, Sir."

"What did the envelope contain?"

"The envelope contained a contract offering me five hundred dollars if I agreed to be interviewed on a certain public-access television program."

"Did the subject of your offer arise during deliberations on the P. K. Timpken case?" continued Fred Klein.

"Yes, some of the other jurors used it as an example. There were some people holding out . . . looked like there might be a hung jury. But then we all got to talking about how lucrative it might be to be the ones to put this case to bed. You know, book contracts, talk shows, all kinds of things. But hey, we didn't take this public-access stuff very seriously. Five hundred dollars is peanuts. We figured we'd all get a bunch of really good offers after we gave our verdict."

"How did that affect your deliberations?"

"Well, it didn't influence me, personally, because I agreed with the way the verdict went."

"And you arrived at a pretty sensational verdict?"

Up jumped Hazel, "Objection! The witness cannot judge whether the verdict was sensational!"

"Sustained," intoned Judge Berry.

"Let me rephrase the question. The holdouts were persuaded by this line of reasoning?"

"Objection! The witness cannot read the minds of other jurors."

"Sustained. Watch yourself, Mr. Klein."

"Sorry, Your Honor." "Was there a verdict delivered after that discussion took place?"

"Yes, we arrived at a consensus within about ten minutes of the time of that discussion."

"Thank you. Prosecution rests."

"Ms. Chalmers, do you have any cross-examination of this witness?"

"Yes, Your Honor. Mr. Ramirez, were you aware when you accepted this jury assignment that you might have many opportunities to profit from telling your story?"

"Yes."

"Your Honor, I have no further questions of this witness."

"Redirect? No? Very well, the witness is excused. Ms. Chalmers, please proceed with the defense."

The next thing you know, you are being sworn in, and being made to recount the events once more. You wonder why you didn't plea bargain so as to avoid this unpleasant process. Too late now.

"Did you intend to influence the verdict?"

"No, I did not."

"Was there anything that led you to believe that offering payment to a sitting juror was acceptable behavior?"

"Yes, there were several things. For one, checkbook journalism has become commonplace among the major news agencies. You see, witnesses are often paid to give interviews, both on television and in print. This occurs while the trial is in progress. The public values knowing about what's going on, and people don't talk for free these days."

"What about jurors?" Hazel prodded.

"Oh yes, I have heard many reports that jurors are also paid for interviews after the trial is over. Some are even offered book contracts. My offer was like those—it would take effect once the trial was over."

Hazel took a moment to mull this over. "So in the market for interviews, you can't afford not to pay when your competitors are paying."

"That's right."

Closing Arguments

It wasn't long before Fred Klein had the opportunity to sum up his case.

"Members of the jury. There is no dispute about the facts in this case. The defendant offered money to a member of a jury actively considering the guilt or innocence of the accused in a criminal case. We have heard from witnesses that this offer may have materially influenced the outcome of that case.

"Service on juries is a civic responsibility, no less sacred than a person's vote. Just as we do not allow votes to be bought and sold for private profit, neither can we allow the profit motive to be waved in the face of jurors deliberating the fate of the accused. That is what the defendant is charged with. That, by all accounts, is what the defendant did. For that the defendant must be convicted!"

Hazel was ready. "Providing justice is for the most part a public good, and the public relies upon the ethics of the members of the jury to provide that good. If earning money from telling stories of the trial tempts participants to distort the judicial process, perhaps we need a law or constitutional amendment that restricts media payments. Until then, we cannot blame competitive news hounds for buying access to the news. It is worth something to the media because it is worth something to us."

*T*he Verdict

With a mischievous twinkle in her eyes, Judge Berry addressed the jury. "Members of the jury, I see you have a conflict of interest. You probably wish to find the defendant innocent so that you can sell your stories from this trial. I must declare a mistrial. You are free to go. Unless the prosecution has an angle to retry this case, so is the defendant."

PROSPECTING FOR NEW INSIGHTS

1. This case suggests that an externality arises in the competitive market for information. Specifically, competition for interviews may adversely affect the provision of justice.
   a. The case focused upon the effects on jurors. How could the prospect of money and publicity be even more troublesome as it pertains to witnesses?
   b. Policies that seem to resolve one problem can often cause additional problems in other areas. It becomes necessary to identify and weigh the benefits and costs of alternative policies. For example, should government ban media payments to witnesses and jurors? Should government ban television coverage of trials to remove incentives associated with publicity? What of free speech and the public's right to know?
2. A number of jurors have been dismissed from lengthy, high-profile cases on account of concerns that they might be writing books about those cases. Are such dismissals appropriate? Explain, with reference to the economic incentives involved.

CHALLENGE 1
Controlling Pollution With Taxes or Marketable Permits

According to the specificity principle, it is usually best to apply a tax or permit approach directly to pollution rather than to outputs. Sometimes this is difficult or impossible to do. For example, it would take an army of government agents to follow around potential smokers to collect a smoke emissions tax when they light up. In that case, it is far easier to monitor and tax cigarette sales.

When pollution control policy is applied to output, however, pollution is reduced only to the extent that output falls. In contrast, when pollution is taxed directly, polluters also have the incentive to reduce the amount of pollution per unit of that output. It is often feasible to tax pollution directly in cases of stationary-source polluters, such as factories. Such taxes require that the quantity of pollution emissions be monitored.

To correct pollution externalities, the simplest tax or permit systems require that regulators first estimate an efficient amount of each type of pollution that is to be controlled. That amount is likely to vary across pollutants, regions, and seasons. It is efficient for firms to pollute if the marginal social benefit of doing so exceeds the marginal social cost. The efficient quantity occurs when marginal social benefit equals marginal social cost. Figure 9C1-1 illustrates this point, where the efficient quantity of pollution emissions is labeled Q^*.

Social cost represents the value lost to victims of pollution externalities. Because all costs of pollution are external, the marginal social cost curve is labeled as marginal external cost in Figure 9C1-1. Marginal social benefits are given by the derived demand for emissions. Derived demand represents firms' willingness to pay for incremental rights to pollute. Firms are willing to pay because using the environment to remove wastes is a valuable service to them, just like the services of labor. Firms value this service because consumers value the output that the firms produce. Thus, the benefit of pollution is really the extra value that consumers receive because producers pollute.

Even though firms have a demand for environmental services, there is no one in the free market to charge them for those services, because no one can claim exclusive property rights to the environment. Thus, firms are free to pollute as much as they want. In Figure 9C1-1, the amount that firms pollute in the absence of government action is given by the intersection of derived demand with the horizontal axis, which is the quantity demanded at a price of zero. The difference between the free-market quantity of pollution and the efficient quantity is the amount of pollution abatement that government policy should aim for.

If the market functioned efficiently, the marginal external cost curve would become the market supply curve, and firms would face a price of P^* and emit a quantity of pollution equal to Q^* in Figure 9C1-1. However, because individuals do not personally own the environment, they cannot charge for its use. Thus the market is missing, because of a missing supply curve. Nevertheless, government can attempt to replicate this missing

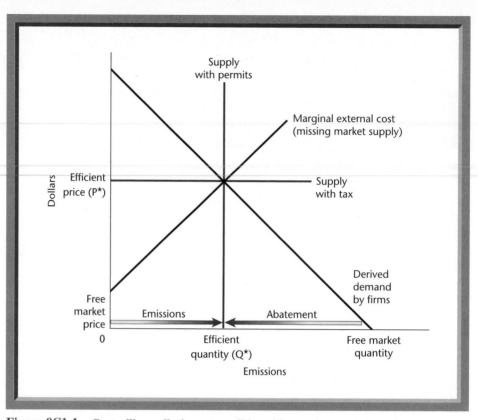

Figure 9C1-1   Controlling pollution externalities with permits or taxes requires an estimate of either the efficient quantity of emissions or of the external cost of those emissions at that quantity, respectively.

market by charging firms a fee per unit of emissions, where that fee is set to equal P*. This fee is commonly referred to as a pollution tax. **To remedy an externality with a tax, the tax rate must be set equal to marginal external cost at the efficient level of pollution.** Polluters would be forced to buy emission rights at that price. The effect of this tax is to offer a horizontal supply curve for emission rights, as shown in Figure 9C1-1. The market then chooses the efficient quantity, Q*.

Alternatively, regulators could issue marketable permits in the quantity Q*, which would have the effect of creating a vertical supply curve, as shown in Figure 9C1-1. So long as the derived demand curve remains unchanged, total emissions would be the same as under the tax approach. Revenues to government may differ from the tax approach, however, depending upon whether government distributes the permits at a competitive auction, at below market prices, or free of charge. Whatever the means of distribution, the market price of a permit would settle at P*. Producers able to obtain the most value from environmental services would be the ones to buy the emission permits. Thus, either the tax or permit approach allows regulators to create a market that allocates emission rights efficiently.

C

Everyone has heard of cost-benefit analysis. The term often conjures up a massive and very complicated report. However, at a basic level, cost-benefit analysis is something everyone does frequently but informally. Should you attend college? You weigh the costs and benefits. Given that you do attend college, should you attend class today? Again, you weigh costs and benefits. If you attend class, should you fight to keep awake and alert? It's cost-benefit analysis again.

Businesses use cost-benefit analysis for such applications as deciding whether to adjust output in the short run or long run. To perform cost-benefit analysis in business, marginal revenues and costs must be estimated along the dimensions of the quantity and product differentiation. For example, should a sugar company offer four-pound bags, five-pound bags, or both? Should the sugar be from sugar beets, sugar cane, or both? How should the bags be designed?

The guiding principle in this cost-benefit analysis is always to maximize profit, specifically the present value of the expected stream of profits over time. In finance, this is referred to as maximizing the value of the firm. In contrast, when government uses cost-benefit analysis, its goal is to maximize the present value of **net social benefits**, which are social benefits minus social costs.

Present value involves *discounting* future costs and benefits to the present-day equivalent. The rate at which discounting occurs is termed the **discount rate**, which is just an interest rate. For example, if the discount rate is 10 percent, then one dollar next year is worth only about ninety cents today. This is appropriate if that ninety cents could be invested in other projects to yield a dollar's worth of benefits next year. In a sense, then, ninety cents today would then be equivalent to a dollar next year.

In the private sector, firms discount future costs and benefits of a project according to the riskiness of the project and their cost of borrowing. Government undertakes such a large portfolio of diverse projects that, in the aggregate, there is little risk of projects failing. Since government is unlikely to default, borrowing costs are also lower, as can be seen by comparing corporate debt to government debt. The interest rates on corporate bonds are always higher and, depending upon the stability of the company, sometimes much higher than rates on government bonds.

For this reason, some people argue that government should use a lower discount rate than the private sector. Moreover, many people think that the private sector discounts the future too heavily. According to this line of reasoning, government should be more farsighted and thus employ a lower discount rate. The lower the discount rate, the more valuable benefits far into the future look from the vantage point of today.

This line of reasoning leads to a curious result. Any project with benefits extending into the future is computed to be more valuable if government undertakes it than if it is done in the private sector. This result is nonsensical, since the social value of a project should not depend upon who constructs it. For example, a grocery chain might reject building a new supermarket because population growth in the area is too slow. However, a cost-benefit analysis on that same store built by government might say to go ahead if government uses a lower discount rate.

C

Government borrows from the same pool of consumer savings as do private companies. If government uses low interest rates to justify undertaking projects that would not pass a cost-benefit test in the private sector, it drives up borrowing costs and competes away projects. Carried to an extreme, all new projects would be undertaken by the public sector, and the private marketplace would wither away. For these reasons, economists usually argue that government should use the same interest (discount) rate that prevails in the private sector.

For an example of cost-benefit analysis in the private sector and for the formula that applies, see Challenge 2 in chapter 8. In either the public or private sector, the computation of net present value is done with a financial calculator or computer spreadsheet software.

Cost-benefit analysis in government is more complex than in the private sector. Like private firms, government has various dimensions to its spectrum of choices. Along each dimension, economic efficiency requires that government seek to equate marginal social benefits and marginal social costs. For example, before determining the optimal size of the military budget, it is necessary to decide how incremental dollars would be spent, which in turn requires the assessment of alternative military strategies. Measuring the social benefits and costs along these dimensions is controversial and imprecise.

Unlike private firms, the government cannot observe the prices that its products sell for in the marketplace. What is the value of saving a wetland? No one offers to purchase public goods of this sort. What is the social cost of hiring workers who would otherwise be receiving unemployment compensation? There is a market price, but it ignores many social costs of unemployment. These are *intangibles*, yet they must be evaluated. To do so, government analysts impute social valuations through sometimes complicated techniques.

Some of the best techniques to reveal social benefits of intangibles involve observing other market prices that relate to the good in question. For example, the cost of noise pollution from airplanes can be estimated by observing how much less homes under take-off and landing flight paths sell for relative to comparable homes elsewhere.

Unfortunately, because of its complexity, cost-benefit analysis in government is often subject to distortion for political purposes. Because assumptions as to the values and significance of its many details are not etched in stone, analysts can often tweak cost-benefit analysis to influence its results.

In addition, errors may creep into the analysis, either inadvertently or intentionally. For example, the cost-benefit analysis of a water project might show as a benefit the increased values of nearby farmland. It might also show as a benefit the increased value of crop production. However, this would be the error of double counting. The increase in land values is itself caused by the increase in the value of crop production.

C

Study by Design

SpeedStudy

SpeedReview

Market failures can justify government action. This action can be to regulate or produce products directly. Direct production by government is often appropriate for public goods, because the free-rider problem causes these goods to be underproduced in the marketplace. Regulation is most appropriate for externalities and common property resources. Government can choose among various regulatory policy approaches, each of which has different characteristics and implications. Economists usually recommend taxes or marketable permits to control pollution or allocate common property. To enhance economic efficiency, policies must equate marginal social costs and marginal social benefits. However, government actions may cause undesirable side effects if not targeted precisely.

SpeedStudy True or False Self-Test

A1. A local public good is something that all localities across the country consume jointly.

A2. The value of a public good is computed by adding the quantity that each person desires at each price.

A3. If external costs are present, marginal social costs exceed marginal private costs.

A4. In daily life, most people will not encounter externalities.

A5. It is efficient to allow some pollution.

A6. The tragedy of the commons is a common property resource problem that could be resolved through regulation.

A7. If a pollution tax is imposed, polluters pass along all the expense of the tax to consumers and have no reason to cut back pollution.

A8. Polluters usually prefer taxes over marketable permits as a means of pollution control.

A9. If moral suasion persuades a paper mill to cut back its pollution, that paper mill will be at a cost disadvantage to its competitors.

A10. According to the specificity principle, policy should be directed as precisely as possible toward the problem at hand.

B11. An unrestricted free market will lead to the efficient amount of transborder pollution.

B12. In theory, a tax can internalize the external costs of pollution, although putting theory into practice is often quite difficult.

B13. The widespread use of plea bargaining has a basis in cost-benefit analysis.

B14. Interviews by the news media possess many characteristics of a competitive market, in which interviews go to those media buyers willing to pay the market price.

C15. A pollution tax in effect offers a vertical supply curve of pollution rights.

C16. Overall emissions, and the allocation of those emissions among polluting firms, can be the same under either an emissions tax or a system of marketable permits.

C17. Cost-benefit analysis is a technically precise means to eliminate controversy over whether or not government should undertake a project.

C18. Benefits of an irrigation project would include both the increased value of agricultural productivity and the increased value of the farmland.

The MasterMind

Selected Terms along the Way

market failure, 318
private good, 319
public good, 319
common property resources, 320
externalities, 320
social costs or benefits, 320
free-rider problem, 321
private costs or benefits, 323

Coase theorem, 325
transaction costs, 325
privatization, 327
user fees, 327
moral suasion, 327
technology mandates, 328
subsidies, 331
second-best policies, 331

marketable permits, 331
specificity principle, 334
merit goods, 334

net social benefits, 347
present value, 347
discount rate, 347

MasterMind Multiple Choice Self-Test

A1. Which of the following is the best example of a common property resource?

a. Groundwater.

b. National defense.

c. A highway.

d. Pollution.

A2. Private companies might be expected to provide public goods for any of the following reasons *except* the following:

a. The public goods can in some manner be tied to a private good.

b. Government mandates that the good be provided.

c. Government pays to have private producers provide the good.

d. The good is very valuable to consumers.

A3. Relative to users of a privately owned resource, users of a common property resource have _____ economic incentive to conserve that resource for the future.

a. more

b. the same

c. slightly less

d. no

A4. If consumption of a good causes an external cost,

a. the free market will produce too much of the good.

b. the free-market price of the good will be too high.

c. the best solution would be to impose a tax equal to total external cost.

d. the best solution would be to mandate changes in production technology.

A5. Marginal social cost equals

a. marginal private cost minus marginal external cost.

b. marginal external cost minus marginal private cost.

c. marginal private cost plus marginal external cost.

d. marginal external cost, except in cases of pollution.

B6. As countries develop, they pollute

a. more and more over time.

b. less and less over time.

c. more at first, and then less later.

d. less at first, and then more later.

B7. Media competition for interviewing jurors and witnesses in criminal cases is most likely to

a. encourage false claims of being witness to criminal events.

b. drive down the price of interviews.

c. make it easier for newspapers with small circulations to obtain interviews.

d. generate less information for the public at large.

C8. The optimal pollution tax would equal

    a. the difference between marginal social cost and the supply curve at the efficient quantity of output.

    b. the marginal external cost of pollution emissions at the efficient quantity of emissions.

    c. the difference between marginal social cost and the supply curve at the initial quantity of output.

    d. the marginal external cost of pollution emissions at the original quantity of emissions.

C9. In cost-benefit analysis, intangibles are usually

    a. listed separately, since they must be weighed separately from dollar benefits and costs.

    b. assigned dollar values based on their intrinsic worth, as determined by biological and physical science.

    c. assigned dollar values that are based upon related values in the private marketplace.

    d. omitted altogether, thus providing the basis for the most frequent criticism of the cost-benefit technique.

MasterMind Questions and Problems

A1. a. Assuming no market failures, briefly explain why the private marketplace is efficient. What does *efficient* mean in this context?

    b. Define and give an example of a public good. How does the condition for an economically efficient output of a public good differ from that for a private good? Explain how the free-rider problem causes private markets to provide too little of the public good.

A2. Suppose three communities would be served by a new sea water desalinization plant that costs $1 billion. Communities A and B each value this plant at $400 million. Community C values the plant at $100 million. Explain whether it is efficient for the plant to be built. Would the plant be constructed if each community shares the cost equally and the decision is made by majority rule? Explain.

A3. Affirmative action programs have led to higher salaries for professionals from minority groups. Using the concept of external benefits, explain how this effect might be justified. Explain how the concept of external cost might also apply.

A4. Stinkigunco, Inc., has a factory located upstream from a small community, which uses the river water for drinking. The plant's emissions of pollutants into the water forces the downstream community to treat the water in order for it to be drinkable. Describe the Coasian solution to this problem of externality and comment on its practicality.

A5. It is difficult to get a handle on the costs to firms of identifying and complying with regulations. For this reason, such costs are often ignored. Explain why the costs are difficult to compute and what problems arise when they are ignored.

B6. As per capita income rises in very poor countries, pollution also rises. However, as incomes continue to grow, pollution decreases. Explain.

B7. Rather than use the court system, more and more disputes are being resolved through mediators. Evaluate the motivation for this change and whether mediation makes economic sense.

C8. Consider again the Stinkigunko plant described in question 4. Using a graph you draw for reference, indicate precisely how an economist might advocate the use of an emission tax to deal efficiently with this issue. Note the value of the efficient tax. Also describe an alternative marketable permit approach to achieve the same ends as the tax.

C9. The presence of intangibles makes it much more difficult to estimate costs and benefits for public-sector projects than for private-sector projects. Give an example of an intangible that might need to be measured in a public-sector cost-benefit analysis, and suggest the lines along which the estimation might be performed.

Future Explorations: Mapping out Term Papers

1. **Unmasking the Faceless Regulators**
   This paper identifies the regulatory agencies of the federal government and summarizes their regulatory missions. Some regulatory strategies are identified. The growth of these agencies is highlighted by presenting an account of their budgets over time.

2. **Save the Whales!—An Economic Perspective**
   The focus here is on the worldwide destruction of rare, exotic, and lovable animals. What are people and governments doing to prevent species from becoming extinct? Alternative public policy approaches are considered, along with a discussion of their possible costs.

3. **Regulation and the Takings Clause of the Constitution**
   Regulations affect property values. For example, by restricting the use of land in certain areas, the Endangered Species Act has greatly reduced the market price of that land. This paper identifies other government actions that have affected land values, and interprets why even the discussion of regulation causes land prices to react. The paper notes that the *takings clause* of the U.S. Constitution prohibits expropriation of private property without compensation. This paper explains the public debate over how this clause should apply to government regulation.

Answer Key

ExpressStudy True or False	SpeedStudy True or False Self-Test		MasterMind Multiple Choice Self-Test
1. F	1. F	10. T	1. a
2. T	2. F	11. F	2. d
3. F	3. T	12. T	3. d
4. T	4. F	13. T	4. a
5. F	5. T	14. T	5. c
6. T	6. T	15. F	6. c
	7. F	16. T	7. a
	8. F	17. F	8. b
	9. T	18. F	9. c

$\mathcal{T}$axation and Public Choice

A Look Ahead

"Of the people, by the people, for the people,"—that is what we want from our government. That is why government is called the public sector—it is intended to represent the wishes of the public. To finance the many functions of government requires taxation, the types of which can vary widely. This chapter examines some of the array of taxes that exists in the United States and the rest of the world. The chapter also interprets the properties of those taxes and their alternatives.

While markets have their failings, so too does government. There is no invisible hand to guide government toward efficiency as there would be in a competitive market economy. Therefore, along with the many worthwhile programs of government, there come other programs of dubious merit. Even worthwhile projects tend to have inflated costs relative to the competitive ideal. This chapter examines how economic incentives within the public sector can lead to these and other government inefficiencies.

DESTINATIONS

$\mathcal{M}$odule A

As you zip along the Expressway you will arrive at an ability to

- list the major revenue sources in the United States;
- show why workers pay more Social Security tax than they think;
- distinguish two principles of tax equity, and explain why they conflict;
- justify why voters may be rationally ignorant of what goes on in government;
- infer why legislators engage in vote trading that leads to excessive government spending.

$\mathcal{M}$odule B

Upon leaving the Expressway to explore issues you will be able to

- interpret why the U.S. income tax is structured as it is, and why critics suggest changing it;
- identify why some commonplace policies toward water conservation are inefficient, and why the public sector chooses them anyway.

$\mathcal{M}$odule C

Mastering Roadside Challenges will allow you to hone analytical skills by

- analyzing the trade-off between efficiency and equity in the public budget;
- modeling why candidates shift their positions between the primary and general elections.

Taxation: *The Price of Government*

In this world nothing can be said to be certain, except death and taxes.
—*Benjamin Franklin*

Few things are less popular than taxes, since *taxes* represent money that is taken from us involuntarily by the government. Taxes go toward financing government activities, including the provision of public goods and the correction of market failures. Taxes are also used for **transfer payments** that redistribute income to the needy. Transfer payments include unemployment compensation, welfare, and other **safety net** programs that provide economic security. Transfer payments account for approximately 44 percent of total federal spending. Figure 10A-1 shows the growth in transfer payments and other components of federal spending over time.

Because taxes take roughly one-third of gross domestic product (GDP), taxpayers are acutely concerned that they not be taken advantage of—that all pay their fair share. This is the goal of *tax equity*. Because taxes can discourage work effort and investment, a second goal is *tax efficiency*. Tax efficiency implies that, unless taxes are targeted to correct an externality, they should be designed to raise revenues in a manner that affects our behavior the least. This approach would offer citizens the greatest possible incentive to be productive. With reference to these goals, this section looks at several types of taxes, with special attention to those used in the U.S.

Taxation in the United States

Figure 10A-2 illustrates the relative importance of revenue sources for the U.S. federal government. The personal income tax is the single largest source, providing 43 percent of all revenues. As U.S. citizens accumulate income over the course of the year, the federal personal income tax claims those earnings at incremental rates starting at 0 percent and increasing to 15 percent, 28 percent, 31 percent, 36 percent, and 39.6 percent as income rises higher and higher. This incremental rate is known as the **marginal tax rate**, which equals 28 percent for most Americans.

$$\text{Marginal tax rate} = \frac{\Delta \text{tax payment}}{\Delta \text{income}}$$

In other words, the average citizen pays twenty-eight cents to the IRS on each additional dollar he or she earns. Those taxes are withheld from income on the basis of the taxpayer's estimated *average tax rate*. The average tax rate equals a person's total tax liability divided by total income at the end of the year.

$$\text{Average tax rate} = \frac{\text{total tax payments}}{\text{total income}}$$

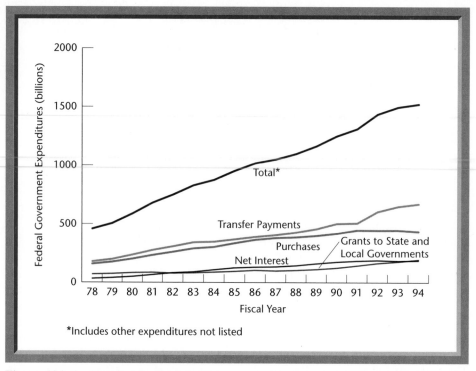

Figure 10A-1   Spending by the federal government has grown rapidly in recent years, especially spending on transfer payments, interest on the national debt, and grants-in-aid from the federal to state and local governments. Slightly over half of federal purchases are for national defense.

Source: 1995 Economic Report of the President, Table B-82.

As seen in Figure 10A-2, Social Security taxes account for 37 percent of federal revenues, quite close to the share of the personal income tax. The Social Security tax is a *payroll tax,* in which the government deducts a flat 7.625 percent from the amount of money the employer pays, plus another 7.625 percent from the amount of money the employee receives. Taken together, the Social Security tax collects 15.25 percent of payroll income, up to a maximum individual income of $61,200 in 1995.

Figure 10A-3 illustrates the supply and demand for labor in the aggregate. The seller is the worker who offers labor; the buyer is the employer. Labor demand represents the marginal value of additional units of work to the firm. Firms are unwilling to pay more than this value. Labor supply is shown as a vertical line, because the elasticity of labor supply by primary workers is nearly zero.

The portion of the Social Security tax paid by employers reduces their after-tax demand for labor by the same percentage as the tax, since the value of labor to the firm is reduced by the amount of tax that must be paid for that labor. This reduction is shown in the figure by a downward shift in labor demand, a shift that is just sufficient to cover Social Security taxes. This downward shift is not a constant dollar amount, which would result in a shift that would leave the after-tax demand parallel to the original demand. Rather, it is a constant 7.625 percent of each wage rate, which shifts after-tax demand down more

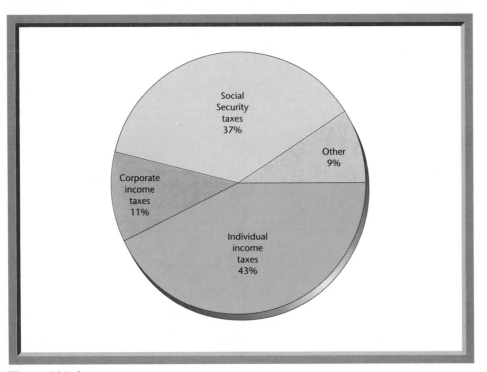

Figure 10A-2   Federal Revenue Sources, 1994

Source: *1996 Economic Report of the President*, Table B-76.

at higher wage rates, and thus causes the after tax demand to have a lesser slope than the original demand. The effect of requiring firms to pay Social Security taxes for the labor they employ is to reduce the amount they are willing to pay in wages. The portion of the Social Security tax paid by workers effectively reduces workers take-home pay still more.

As seen in Figure 10A-3, requiring the firm to pay Social Security taxes causes the equilibrium wage to be lower by exactly the amount of the tax. In effect, the tax burden has been *shifted* from employers to employees. The result is that workers effectively pay the full 15.25 percent Social Security tax. Many people are unaware of the true magnitude of the Social Security tax, because only half of the combined 15.25 percent rate appears on their pay stubs.

The Social Security budget is reported separately from that of the rest of government. Social Security tax receipts go into the Social Security trust fund, which provides a buffer between revenue inflows and revenue outflows to Social Security recipients, most of whom are currently retired. The Social Security trust fund contains approximately $400 billion as of this writing. However, this amount would only be enough to last just a little over one year if not supplemented by the Social Security tax. The Social Security trust fund is intended to grow over time to prepare for the increased Social Security outlays expected early in the twenty-first century when the large baby boom generation of the 1950s reaches retirement age.

The corporation income tax takes approximately 28 percent of corporate profits, and brought in revenues of $140.4 billion in 1994, equaling just over 11 percent of total fed-

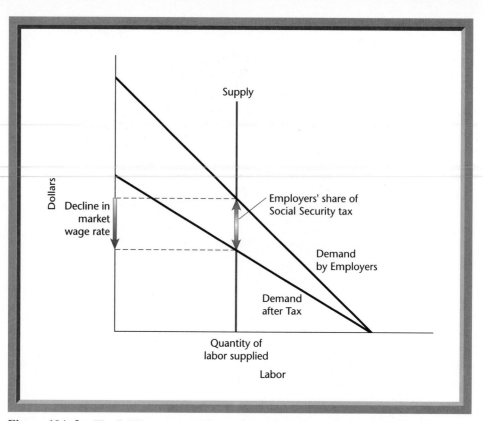

Figure 10A-3   The 7.625 percent employer share of the Social Security tax is passed on to workers in the form of lower wages. The employer share of the tax reduces employer after-tax demand for labor by that same 7.625 percent. To the extent that labor supply is completely inelastic, the market equilibrium wage also falls by 7.625 percent. Workers must then pay another 7.625 percent, which is the part that appears on their pay stubs.

eral revenues. The corporation income tax has proven to be quite controversial over time because, while it may seem fair to tax corporations as though they are people, the ultimate *incidence*—impact—of the corporation income tax is on the personal incomes of the owners or shareholders of the corporations. Since personal income is taxed by the personal income tax, many economists view the corporate income tax as double taxation of income and wonder what justification it has. However, few politicians would dare propose to tax individuals and not tax seemingly wealthy corporations. Thus the corporation income tax lives on.

Figure 10A-4 shows state and local revenue sources. Most states rely heavily upon a combination of individual income taxes, sales taxes, revenue from the federal government, and other charges. Major sources of revenue at the local level include property taxes and sales taxes.

Sales taxes collect a percentage of the value of the sale for government. Sales taxes are one form of **consumption tax**, which takes money as you spend it rather than as you earn it. This tax gives people a greater incentive to save, and may be partly responsible for the higher savings rates in other countries relative to the U.S. Most countries of the

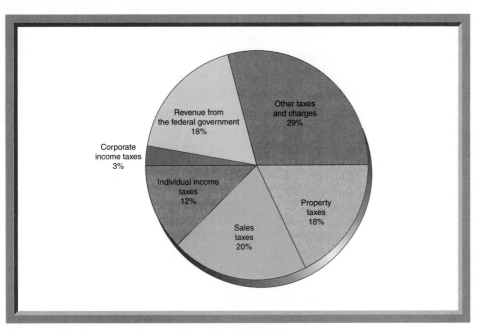

Figure 10A-4   Revenue sources for states and localities, 1991–1992.

Source: 1996 Economic Report of the President, Table B-82.

world, including Canada and countries of Europe and the Far East, rely much more heavily on consumption taxes as a source of public revenues than does the U.S.

States have to be careful not to tax any one source of revenue much more heavily than do other states, or that revenue source will migrate to the less-taxing state. This problem plagued New York State in the 1960s and 1970s, as the poor moved in to receive generous welfare benefits, while many of the wealthy moved away to avoid paying the high income taxes that financed those benefits.

When all the revenues we pay to all units of government are added together, the result is that government collects over one-third of the value of production in the U.S. Another way of looking at this is that the average American must work until tax freedom day in early May each year in order to have enough money to pay the government. Beyond that date, the money you earn is yours.

OBSERVATION POINT: "Don't Tax You, Don't Tax Me—Tax the Fellow Behind that Tree!"

In the abstract, taxes sound great. Higher taxes can eliminate the need for government borrowing and can pay for more of the public services we value. There is only one problem. We want to keep our own money and hence want those taxes to be paid by other people, not by ourselves.

Some localities have found a way to do just that through *tax exporting,* which is getting nonresidents to finance government. For example, speed zones on roads through small towns allow those towns to collect revenue from unsuspecting motorists. The payments on their speeding tickets keep property taxes down. The out-of-towner is never heard from again.

Bigger cities resort to surcharges on hotel and motel bills, since few people will change their travel plans because of a 15 percent tax on their lodging. The tourists and business travelers have probably left town before they know what's hit them. While the travelers grind their teeth and mutter about extortion, the locals can grow their government at a bargain price!

Possibilities for Tax Reform

The most common form of consumption tax in other countries is the **value-added tax (VAT)**. A VAT collects the difference between what companies earn in revenues and what they pay out in previously taxed costs. For example, the wheat farmer would pay a tax on the difference between revenues from the sale of the crop and the costs of fertilizer and other materials used to grow it. Taxing value-added yields the same tax revenues as a retail sales tax, since the price of a final product is nothing more than the sum of the values added.

Government can generally raise revenues more efficiently by broadening the **tax base** and lowering tax rates. In other words, **it is less disruptive to the workings of the economy to tax as wide a spectrum of income or consumption as possible at a low rate, rather than single out a few things for especially high rates of taxation.** By spreading taxes broadly, people have few ways to escape them and not as much incentive to try; inefficient changes in behavior are kept to a minimum. The Reagan-era income tax cuts put that principle into practice by closing various tax "loopholes" and cutting marginal tax rates to a maximum of 28 percent.

There are many alternatives to the particular set of taxes chosen in the U.S. For example, some have suggested that the U.S. should adopt a *flat tax*, the topic of Exploration 1 in this chapter, in which all income is taxed at the same rate. Others advocate a *consumed-income tax*, in which the value of savings is deducted from income before the tax is applied. The consumed-income tax would remove the bias against saving present in a more general income tax, which taxes money when it is earned and also taxes interest on that money when it is saved. The flip side is that, although a consumed-income tax would promote savings, some people view it as a tax deduction for the rich and not for the poor, because the ability to save rises sharply with income. That concern leads to the big question: How do we identify taxes that are both efficient and fair?

✔ QUICKCHECK

Would it be feasible to eliminate all of the many taxes we pay to different units of government, substituting instead a single, flat-rate tax equal to 16 percent of all consumption or income, without exception?

Answer: No, since governments at all levels currently collect just over one-third of the value of our output, replacing all taxes with a flat-rate tax would call for a rate closer to 34 percent. However, some estimates suggest that a flat-rate income tax of 16 percent would generate about as much revenue as our current multirate personal income tax and could finance most of the federal government.

Income Redistribution—How Much Is Too Much?

> *In general, the art of government consists in taking as much money as possible from one party of the citizens to give to the other.*
>
> *—Voltaire*

Taxes are intended to do more than collect government revenues efficiently. Taxes also redistribute income from the haves to the have-nots, and are used as a tool of public policy to remedy inequities that arise in a free market economy. Since people's views on equity vary widely, issues of tax equity become a matter of hot debate. Just because equity is difficult to pin down, however, does not mean that equity is not a valid economic objective of taxation and income redistribution.

Monitoring Tax Equity

There are two primary principles of tax equity, as follows:

- The **benefit principle** states that a fair tax is one that taxes people in proportion to the benefits they receive when government spends those tax revenues.
- The **ability-to-pay principle** states that those who can afford to pay more taxes than others should be required to do so.

The gasoline tax would appear to satisfy the benefit principle of tax equity, because gasoline tax revenues are *earmarked* for highway construction and repair. The more someone drives, the more government-funded highways the person drives on, and the more gasoline tax the person pays. In general, *user fees* are designed to meet the benefit principle of tax equity.

The benefit principle cannot be applied to programs whose purpose is to redistribute income. To see why not, consider food stamps. According to the benefit principle, food stamp recipients should pay for the cost of those food stamps. However, this would have the effect of defeating the fundamental purpose of the food stamp program, which is to help those in need. Food stamps are of no help if you have to pay for them! Thus, to justify redistributional programs, a different principle of tax equity is invoked—the ability-to-pay principle. This principle states that the more a person is able to pay, the more that person should pay.

Many people interpret the ability-to-pay principle to mean that taxes designed for redistributing income should be progressive. A **progressive tax** collects a higher percentage of high incomes than of low incomes. In contrast, a **regressive tax** collects a higher percentage of low incomes than of high incomes. A **proportional tax** collects the same percentage of income, no matter what the income is. The key is percentage. A tax that collects $1,000 from a poor person earning $10,000 and $10,000 dollars from a rich person earning $1 million is regressive, because the poor person pays 10 percent of his or her income, whereas the rich person pays only 1 percent.

Sometimes it is hard to determine whether or not a tax is progressive. For instance, the Social Security tax may be considered either proportional, regressive, or progressive, depending upon which aspects of the system are under scrutiny. Up to about $61,200 of payroll income in 1995, the tax is proportional at 15.25 percent. Because the marginal Social Security tax rate beyond that point drops to only 2.9 percent, for hospitalization insurance, the average tax rate declines with income and the overall tax is regressive. However, if Social Security benefits are included along with the taxes, the Social Security System as a whole is highly progressive. The reason is that Social Security recipients receive a much higher ratio of benefits to the taxes they paid if their earnings were low during their working years. Social Security thus redistributes income from the wealthy to the poor.

OBSERVATION POINT: *Progressive*—What's in a Word?

The economist who came up with the terms *progressive* and *regressive* knew which kind of tax he wanted. After all, who could argue against progress? Would you prefer to regress? That would be moving backward, not forward. Bear in mind, though, that there is no magic in the terms.

The ability-to-pay principle of equity says the rich should pay more than the poor to finance government. It does not specify whether the higher taxes should be less than, more than, or exactly in proportion to the higher income. For instance, it would make life simpler if we had one flat-rate income tax, with no exemptions, deductions, exclusions, etc. Such a tax would be proportional. Would it be fair? That judgment is entirely up to you.

Equity and Efficiency—The Big Trade-off

Economic efficiency involves getting the most valuable output from the inputs available. In effect, efficiency bakes the biggest economic pie. Taxes are efficient to the extent they do not change our behavior. The most efficient tax is one we cannot escape.

For example, as income taxes rise, we don't try as hard to get ahead in the workplace. Even if we work the same number of hours after a tax increase, we are less likely to invest our time and money to acquire more human capital. Likewise, the presence of estate and gift taxes means that we don't try to accumulate as much for our children. Higher corporate income taxes mean that businesses don't invest as much, either, because the corporation income tax cuts down on the return to business investment. None of these taxes is efficient.

For an efficient tax, we can turn to the *head tax*. In short, if you have a head, you pay the tax! Since head taxes are efficient and require virtually no paperwork, should all of our other taxes be replaced by head taxes? You probably see the problem. While the economic pie would be large, it would be sliced very unfairly. In other words, head taxes would not be equitable.

Not only are tax laws written with an eye toward equity, but government spending is often meant to promote equity directly through provision of a social safety net. This safety net targets the needy with both cash transfers and **in-kind benefits**, which are any benefits other than money. Social Security is far and away the largest cash transfer program, redirecting a significant amount of current earnings to current retirees. The next largest cash transfer program, and source of the oft-criticized welfare checks, is Aid to Families with Dependent Children (AFDC). The largest in-kind program is Medicaid, which provides health insurance for the impoverished.

A trade-off between efficiency and equity pervades our system of tax and spending programs. Ideally, to provide a broad and generous safety net, government might guarantee good housing, good food, and good health insurance for everyone. The better the guarantees, however, the more the programs will cost and the less will be the incentives to work and invest. There are three reasons for this inefficient reduction in work incentives, as follows:

- There is less need to better yourself to the extent that government guarantees you a comfortable lifestyle. As the saying goes, necessity is the mother of invention.
- If you choose to forge ahead anyway, your greater ability to take care of yourself causes you to lose eligibility for many welfare-type programs. Over some ranges of income, the loss of benefits from Medicaid, AFDC, subsidized housing, food stamps, and other welfare programs more than offsets the value of extra income earned.
- Obtaining the money for safety net programs requires either raising taxes or borrowing, which would require higher taxes in the future. With higher taxes comes less incentive to work and invest.

We could eliminate the second problem if we offer eligibility to everyone, regardless of income. However, that policy would accentuate the third problem.

There is no ready answer to the dilemma of choosing between a generous safety net and incentives for economic productivity. This is an area of seemingly endless political debate and compromise. The fate of the Communist economies in Eastern Europe and the former Soviet Union warn of the dangers of going too far in the direction of the social safety net. We don't want our economy to stagnate. On the other hand, we can afford to provide some economic security for the disadvantaged. Choices of this sort are why policymakers face "the big trade-off" between efficiency and equity in the design of government tax and spending programs. The processes by which they choose are the subject of the next section.

*T*he Public Choice Process

Democracy is the worst form of government . . . except for all the others.

Government policies can correct market failures. For this reason, economists have designed and analyzed numerous techniques to promote the goals of efficiency and equity. However, suggesting policy techniques is not enough. Because government accounts for nearly one-fifth of national output and employment, an understanding of the economy is not complete without an examination of the manner in which government makes its choices. For example, what are the incentives for government to design and implement its policies efficiently? The field of **public choice** examines economic incentives within government, including those that face voters, politicians, and the administrators of government programs.

Incentives within government are often inefficient, because the public sector lacks the guidance of market competition. Correcting market failures through government policy action thus brings up the problem of **government failure**—the inefficiency of government processes. Sometimes government policy action is desirable to remedy market failures. Other times, the cure is worse than the disease. While there is room for improvement, however, there is no known form of government that can completely do away with inefficiency. Improving incentives within government remains a worthy challenge for us all.

Why the Discontent?

In the elections of 1994, Republicans gained control of both the U.S. Senate and House of Representatives for the first time in forty years. This watershed event has been widely interpreted as a sign of growing disenchantment with government itself. Surveys bear this out, indicating a significant and rising level of hostility toward government.

For example, according to a very large sample survey conducted by the Times Mirror Center prior to the 1994 elections, 66 percent of Americans thought that government is almost always wasteful and inefficient. A different 1994 poll found that 68 percent of voters wanted a smaller government, and only 21 percent wanted a bigger one. Still another poll, conducted in mid-1995, found that 76 percent of the respondents rarely or never trust government to do what is right. Are there economic reasons for these negative attitudes?

Although more pronounced than in the past, suspicion of government is far from new. Part of the problem is in the nature of government decisions themselves. Because we delegate decisions collectively, none of us gets exactly what we want. Moreover, each candidate represents a *bundled good*, meaning that the voter cannot pick and choose which items on a candidate's agenda to support, and which to oppose—one vote buys all.

The result is a compromise that is not fully satisfying to anyone. In the case of public goods, for example, the quantity that is chosen by public officials must then be consumed by everyone, no matter their personal preferences. However, the culprit is not the public officials, but the nature of the public good itself—public goods are consumed jointly. Where possible, people prefer to make choices for themselves.

A second source of concern over government action has to do with the *principal-agent problem*. Over 19 million workers in this country are employed by government as public servants. Public servants range from teachers to Marines to, until recently, an official tea taster. No matter the job, they are all *agents* of the public (the *principal*). However, because the public is so large, no individual has direct control. For example, we do not advise informing the traffic officer preparing to give you a ticket that he or she is your servant and should follow your orders. This generalized accountability provides a great deal of leeway on the part of the agents to do as they please.

Although neither of these problems explains directly why antipathy toward government has grown, it might be reasonable to conclude that these concerns increase as government gets progressively larger, as has been the case in most of twentieth-century America. As government grows, choices made at the individual level decline in proportion to choices made collectively. Moreover, as we will see in the next few pages, there is a tendency for government spending to grow more rapidly than is efficient. Historical evidence suggests that the longer a government rules, the more entangling it becomes to a market economy.

Incentives in the Political Process

The size of the populace leads to a dilemma. People want to be involved in their government, but lack the time to do so effectively. Because there are so many voters and so many government policy actions, few voters have much incentive to become fully informed about issues or candidates. Voters delegate decisions to politicians, who in turn delegate to the administrative bureaucracy. The amount of detail involved in governing the country is too overwhelming to do otherwise. Thus citizens maintain what is known as **rational ignorance**, meaning that voters make the rational choice to remain uninformed on many public choices.

Unfortunately, this **rational ignorance means that politicians and bureaucrats can often safely follow their own personal agendas, even when those agendas conflict with what the public would want them to do.** For example, one item that is high on the personal agendas of most elected officials is to remain in office. Incumbent politicians routinely get reelected, even though *term limitations*—laws that restrict the number of sequential times a politician can hold one public office—are quite popular. How do these politicians do it?

One secret is to engage in **logrolling**—vote trading—in order to obtain projects of direct benefit to constituents in their districts. Logrolling results in massive spending packages that contain numerous clauses pertaining to local spending projects. These projects (often called *pork*) and other accomplishments are then reported back to constituents through a newsletter. Left out is any focus on cost, however, even though the pork does not come cheaply.

Remember, to obtain projects for their districts, legislators must vote for all of the other costly items in the legislation, including those of no benefit to their constituents. When voters focus on visible benefits from projects and ignore the less-obvious costs, they are said to suffer from **fiscal illusion**. Fiscal illusion leads to the Santa/Scrooge syndrome, emphasizing that legislators have incentives to spend more (Santa) and tax less to satisfy miserly voters (Scrooge).

Even when the costs of logrolling are considered, the costs are still likely to be of little concern to the electorate. After all, the costs are in terms of other districts' wasteful projects that are included in an appropriations bill. However, if a majority of other legislators are signing onto the bill, you don't want your district left out. In other words, if you are going to be paying for other districts' pork, you want pork of your own. Thus, constituents rarely hold pork-barrel politics against their own legislators, even though they may disapprove of the practice in general.

There is good reason to disapprove. *Pork-barrel politics* leads to excessive government spending, as the cost of the myriad of relatively small projects gets lost in the general budget. For example, the constituents in most districts would be delighted to accept federally funded projects, such as for highways or drainage. It does not matter whether the project would pass a cost-benefit analysis, because the costs are spread across the country, while the benefits are concentrated in that district. They are grateful to their elected representatives. For voters in other districts, the project is too small to focus on and has no bearing on the reelection of their own representatives. The result is too much government spending.

One check on logrolling can be found in the line-item veto. The *line-item veto* allows a president or governor to veto parts of appropriations bills, rather than having to accept or reject the bills in their entireties. If the president were to be a Democrat, for instance, he or she could veto all of the Republicans' pet projects, except projects of Republicans who support the presidential agenda. In turn, because Republicans would know their projects would not survive, they would not go along with voting for the Democrats' pet projects. The result would be much less pork. In the United States, the president and governors of forty-three states have some form of line-item veto authority.

Not all vote trading is inefficient. For example, a worthy project might serve only a portion of the country. Consider levees along a river that benefit the residents of only a few states. Without vote trading, the project would not pass through Congress, since a majority of states would perceive no benefits. Such projects could still be undertaken, however, if the affected states join forces and proceed on their own. Payment for the project would then come from the residents of those states instead of from general tax revenues.

✔ QuickCheck

Does the line-item veto authority of the president stop logrolling in the federal government?

Answer: Logrolling is reduced but not eliminated. For example, friends of the president would not have their pet projects vetoed. However, the presidents' friends would have a more difficult time lining up support for those projects in Congress, especially if the president routinely vetoes the pet projects of other legislators.

Interest Groups—Minority Rule?

The United States prides itself on its majority rule. Yet legislation is often influenced by small, well-organized minorities, aligned according to special interests. *Special-interest groups* are characterized by a tightly focused agenda and *lobbyists*—agents who promote that agenda within the political system.

The agendas of the special interests often conflict with the interests of most voters. Special interests are frequently able to get their way, however, by paying close attention to the details of legislators' votes. Legislators who vote against special interests know they lose their votes and campaign contributions. However, legislators who favor the special interests and vote against the wishes of the majority often face no adverse consequences. The reason is that general interest is often more diffuse, with few voters keying their votes around specific issues. In short, **when the benefits of an action are spread broadly and the costs are concentrated, special interests are frequently successful at preventing the action from occurring.**

For example, few people would vote against a legislator because he or she supports sugar import quotas, despite the consequent higher prices for sweeteners, which raises a broad array of food and beverage prices facing the average consumer. However, a legislator who votes to repeal sugar import quotas definitely loses the support of sugar growers, corn sweetener manufacturers, and other allied agricultural interests. While the number of voters who gain from sugar import quotas is minuscule relative to those who lose, the power of the gainers is magnified because they key their votes around this one special interest issue.

Lobbying by special interest groups is sometimes efficient in that it provides information that prevents legislative errors. When legislation targets the actions of a particular industry, for example, that industry's lobbyists are in the best position to provide relevant information on the industry's business practices. For example, Congressional staffers attempting to fashion sensible pipeline regulations might obtain information on oil and gas pipeline operations from the American Petroleum Institute, which lobbies for the oil industry. Other interested lobbyists would also submit information. Congressional staffers use this information to design policies that are cost-effective, an advantage to both the oil industry and the economy.

Unfortunately, special interest lobbying is frequently inefficient, because it involves wasteful rent seeking. **Rent-seeking behavior** occurs when lobbyists or others expend resources in an effort to come out a winner in the political process. Since economic efficiency looks at the size of the economic pie, not how it is sliced, the time and money lobbyists spend trying to get the pie sliced to their liking is inefficient.

Some observers contend that an emerging trend in Congress reduces the problems of special-interest lobbying and the rent seeking that comes with it. This trend is toward replacing federal programs with **block grants** to states, where the block grants represent sums of money designated to go toward a range of state-administered programs. For example, Congress designates a single block grant to finance many of the welfare programs administered in a state. By leaving the details up to the states, block grants mean that Congress need merely decide on the number of dollars to include in the grant, something that voters will monitor relatively closely. Lobbyists must then compete with each other, state by state, over the allocation of that money.

A

OBSERVATION POINT: Rent Seeking— A National Pastime

There is a big difference between competition in the marketplace and competition for favors from government. In the marketplace, the winner is the one that builds the better mousetrap and thereby increases the well-being of others. Lobbying for political favors is not productive in this way. It is more akin to fighting over a prize. The time and money wasted in fighting over who gets the prize is a form of rent seeking and serves little constructive purpose from the point of view of society at large. The value of government policies is often counteracted by the money that interest groups spend in trying to come out among the winners.

Most of us engage in rent seeking, too. You have done so yourself if you have ever returned a sweepstakes entry, such as in the Publishers Clearing House or American Family Publishers multimillion dollar sweepstakes. At the time, you probably wondered if it was worth the time and postage to apply, because you knew that millions of other people would be sending in their entries. That illustrates the problem of rent seeking—the value of the prize is offset by the cost of seeking it—the millions of dollars worth of time and postage all the entrants spend to be included in the drawing.

Incentives in Agencies

Administrative agencies face the task of translating general and often vague legislation into detailed programs that are actually implemented. Employees of the many agencies of government are commonly referred to as government *bureaucrats*. The term is not to their liking, however, since it calls up images of stodginess, red tape, and delays associated with bureaucracy. Are the employees of the government agencies unresponsive to the citizens they are supposed to serve?

The employees of government agencies have personal agendas that sometimes conflict with the intent of voters and their elected representatives. Most significantly, for both public-spirited and self-serving reasons, bureaucrats almost always desire budgets for their agencies that exceed what the average citizen and elected official would prefer.

To understand this phenomenon, consider who enters any particular government agency. For example, who joins the armed forces? Most likely, it's people of a military persuasion, who are convinced that the armed forces are more important than most people realize. Likewise, those who join the Environmental Protection Agency have keener interests and greater expertise in environmental matters than do most of the rest of us. They naturally tend to think that environmental protection deserves a higher priority than it gets.

More broadly, who enters government at all? For the most part, it's people who think government is relatively more important than most citizens realize. Thus, employees of government in general and agencies in particular truly believe that their missions are more deserving than the political process acknowledges. For these public-spirited motives, they seek to expand the size of their agencies beyond what is efficient.

There are also self-serving reasons why government employees want larger budgets for their agencies. From the top of the agency to the bottom, a larger budget is seen as good job protection. It opens up promotion opportunities and reduces the threat of layoffs. As a manager, the more budget under you, the more power and prestige you enjoy, and the better your qualifications look should you wish to switch jobs later. Indeed, it is usually considered disloyal for any agency personnel to advocate cutting the agency's budget.

Figure 10A-5 shows the marginal net benefit of increasing an agency's budget, where *marginal net benefit* equals marginal social benefit minus marginal social cost. At first, if the agency directs its spending toward its most essential missions, the value of agency spending far exceeds its budgetary cost. As the budget size is increased, however, the agency must fund programs of increasingly less merit. When the value of extra spending is less than the cost of that spending, the agency has spent too much.

To achieve economic efficiency, the agency budget should equal B^* in Figure 10A-5, the amount for which marginal net benefit is zero. The social surplus generated by this spending is given by the triangular area labeled Gain. If the agency spends beyond B^*, social surplus would decrease. For example, if spending were to equal $B_{too\ much}$, the area labeled Loss would need to be subtracted from this gain.

Turf-Building—Strategies for a Bigger Budget

It is one thing for bureaucrats to want an inefficiently large budget—to expand their turf. Getting that budget is another matter. Unfortunately, the struggle over the size of agency budgets is rather one-sided, because the agency is best positioned to know what its spending options are. If an agency is aware of ways to save money, for example, it has little incentive to reveal them. Such *informational asymmetries*, in which one party to a transaction knows more than the other, put legislators at a disadvantage in overseeing agencies.

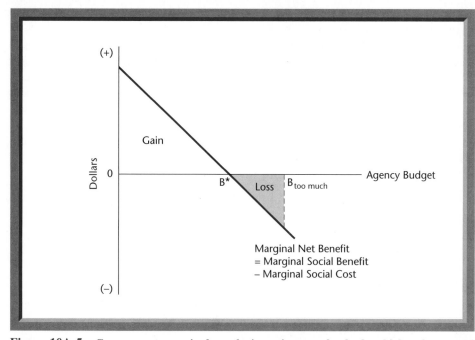

Figure 10A-5 **Government agencies have the incentive to seek a budget higher than would be efficient.** B* denotes an efficient budget. If the actual budget is $B_{\text{too much}}$, some of the gain from the agency's existence is offset by a loss from overspending. Gains and losses are shown.

There are various strategies by which government agencies have been known to obtain the budgets they want. For example, agency spending is commonly guided by "use it or lose it." Agencies want to avoid getting caught with extra cash at the end of the fiscal year when the budget expires. Extra cash might indicate to the legislators or public that the agency could accomplish its mission with a smaller budget next time. The response to use-it-or-lose-it incentives is a spending spree near the end of each fiscal year. If you are an agency employee with a pet project, it's a great time to get it funded.

When agencies submit their budgets for review, they are often told to provide a bare-bones alternative budget, perhaps representing a 20 percent reduction from the budget they claim to need. The idea is to give the legislative oversight committee an idea of what services would be sacrificed if the budget were to be reduced. If you are in charge of a government agency and are told to do this, could you manipulate the process to obtain a large budget? Remember, you know more about possibilities for reducing costs in your agency than do the legislators. Would you economize on travel, or on the number of times the trash is collected?

To preserve your budget, you would be better served by suggesting that something more visible and less acceptable be cut. The strategy of selecting widely supported projects for potential cuts has been used so often, it's acquired its own name—the **Washington Monument strategy**. Using this strategy, the agency offers a bare-bones budget that cuts its most popular functions. For instance, the Park Service might propose to save money by restricting access to the Washington Monument to between 9 A.M. and 5 P.M.

on weekdays, with no access at all on weekends. Evenings and weekends are cut because they are the times of peak tourist demand.

The Washington Monument strategy is used at all levels of government, but not always successfully. In 1992, for example, a school district in a major city claimed that it would be forced to eliminate all school crossing guards unless voters approved a tax increase. Surely the school board did not believe that children's lives deserved the lowest priority. This example of the Washington Monument strategy backfired, though, as voters rejected the tax increase. To safeguard the children's lives, a private individual donated the money needed to pay for crossing guards. In following years, the school district quietly appropriated the money needed to fund this essential service.

OBSERVATION POINT: Why Are They Tearing up a Perfectly Good Road?

What's wrong with the street? See, I don't think anything's wrong with the street. I think you're just trying to justify your inflated budgets. (Michael Douglas' character to highway construction worker in the movie, Falling Down)

Why do highway reconstruction crews always seem to tear up the best part of a road first? Could it be that the contractors want the public to see how the road continues to need work, so that future funding is not jeopardized? In the movie *Falling Down*, Michael Douglas' character responded by sending a bazooka blast at the highway equipment. In contrast, economics holds the promise of more constructive and long-lasting solutions. Finding them is the hard part.

Addressing Government Failures

Is there anything citizens can do to counter all the incentives within government to spend too much? The options are limited. For example, limiting the number of years legislators can serve might keep representatives more in touch with the voters. However, such term limits deprive government of experienced legislators, and also run the danger of focusing legislators' attentions on personal profit opportunities once they leave office.

A balanced budget amendment to the U.S. constitution has been proposed as a means to restrict excessive spending. The problem is that government itself defines what is counted in the budget. For example, when government sought to accomplish the social goal of providing access for the handicapped, it passed the Americans with Disabilities Act. This act represents billions of dollars in government-mandated spending, paid for by business. It is a large tax and spending program, but never shows up as such in the budget. Were there to be a balanced budget amendment, we could expect an upsurge in such unfunded mandates and other types of off-budget spending.

There is no easy way to provide the proper incentives for efficiency within government. That should come as little surprise. After all, if command and control worked well, there would be little reason to adopt competitive free markets. We resort to government when markets fail. Unfortunately, market failure does not imply government success.

OBSERVATION POINT: Primer for Big Government—How to Hide a Tax

Favorite Recipe: Unfunded Mandates

What is a mandate? No, it is not the counterpart to a woman date. **Unfunded mandates** occur when government requires the implementation of public policy actions, without providing the funding necessary to carry out those actions. For example, local telephone customers normally wind up paying a surcharge to fund federally mandated telephone services for the hearing impaired. That cost stays off the federal budget.

Private businesses are favorite targets of unfunded mandates, including family leave and health insurance requirements for employees, handicapped-accessibility requirements for customers, and many more. While mandated public services have value, it is hard to know whether the benefits are worth the costs. The costs are effectively hidden in the resulting inefficiencies and higher prices borne by firms and their customers.

A

EXPRESS STUDY TRUE OR FALSE

1. The combination of the personal income tax and Social Security tax accounts for approximately two thirds of federal tax revenues.

2. Government programs that are designed to redistribute income from the rich to the poor are usually justified on the basis of the ability-to-pay principle of taxation.

3. If a rich person pays more taxes than a poor person, the tax system must be progressive.

4. It is irrational for voters to select candidates without first examining in detail all of the information available about those candidates.

5. When lobbyists fight over who will benefit from government programs, they are engaging in wasteful rent seeking.

6. The professionals who staff government agencies provide an important safeguard against politicians' tendency to spend too much.

Module B

EXPLORING ISSUES

The income tax is complicated by many exemptions, deductions, and other so-called loopholes that lower tax revenues, but often have economic justifications. Replacing the complex tax code with a simple flat-rate tax also has a basis in economics, but would limit government's ability to accomplish social aims.

The Simple Tax

How much money did you make? $____.__

Send it in.

"Too complicated!" We hear that complaint every spring, as Americans once more delve into their financial records to prepare their tax returns. Why is it necessary to compute all the exemptions, deductions, exclusions, alternative minimum taxes, and so forth? Is it just a jobs program for tax accountants, tax lawyers, and Internal Revenue Service agents, or just breaks for special interests wanting to escape paying their fair share? Yes, many people long for a flat and simple tax. Such a tax would have a single rate, applicable to all income. Tax returns could be filled out on a postcard, although not quite the one represented above.

The flat tax has appeal for its simplicity, but there are other considerations that are argued to justify a more complicated system of taxation. These can be seen by asking the most basic question of all: What is the goal of an income tax? The goal is for government to raise revenues for its many programs and to do so in the most equitable and efficient manner possible.

A tax is efficient only if it does not *distort* relative prices within the economy, since price signals are what allocate resources to their highest-valued uses. By taxing all income equally, distortions are minimized. Efficiency thus calls for a *broadly based* tax, meaning one that it is difficult to escape. Much of the complexity of the current income tax code stems from innumerable provisions that remove income from taxation, thus narrowing the tax base.

The ability-to-pay principle of equity suggests that some income should be taxed more than other income, depending on how needy the person is. Exempting low incomes concentrates the tax base and leads to inefficiencies. Thus, the personal income tax is a compromise between efficiency and equity. Unfortunately, the compromise accomplishes neither goal fully and is also complicated.

*T*axing Personal Income, with Lots of Exceptions

The concept of income is not altogether easy to pin down, since income is more than money. For example, if you drill a water well in your back yard and inadvertently strike oil, your wealth spikes upward. That change in wealth is income, even if you do not sell any of that newly discovered oil until next year or beyond. A **comprehensive measure of income** would subtract a person's wealth at the beginning of the year from wealth at the end of the year, and then add back in the person's consumption during the course of that year. Consumption is added because it represents income that is spent.

Government does not use this comprehensive measure of income in computing the amount of personal income taxes to collect. It would be too complicated and intrusive for government to attempt assessing how valuable each person's assets are at the end of each year. After all, assets include homes, cars, stocks, stamp collections, and much more. Moreover, even if the government could assess these values, there is the problem of *liquidity*—of converting assets into cash. Liquidity is necessary to pay taxes. The federal government does not want to be responsible for kicking Grandma out of her house, just because property values around her have increased and she does not have the liquidity to pay the taxes on her rising comprehensive income.

The result is that the tax code looks at only a subset of comprehensive income, that which is liquid. If people sell their illiquid assets, they obtain liquidity and are subject to taxation on their **realized capital gains**, the increase in the value of assets between when they were bought and when they were sold. Even here, however, there are exceptions. For example, Grandma would fall under an exemption for the elderly, were she to sell her house. Throughout the tax code, there is special treatment for special interest groups. Yes, Grandma has a special interest loophole.

So-called *loopholes* include the various exemptions, deductions, exclusions, and credits that complicate the tax code. Despite their notoriety, there are often economic principles behind these **tax expenditures**, so termed because they sacrifice tax dollars. The basis of tax expenditures often revolves around equity.

For example, the concepts of vertical equity and horizontal equity are two ways to judge whether a tax meets the ability-to-pay principle. **Vertical equity** is hard to pin down, because it concerns the proper tax burden for people of differing abilities to pay. **Horizontal equity**, which suggests that people with equal means should pay equal taxes, is more straightforward. Yet, even ignoring differences in wealth, equal monetary incomes do not necessarily imply an equal ability to pay. Differences in the ability to pay explain why there are tax exemptions for children, major medical expenses, and other facets of life that hit some people harder than others.

The search for equity complicates the tax code and makes it less efficient. This inefficiency hurts us all by reducing our standard of living. Thus, in trying to allocate the tax burden fairly, government winds up increasing it for the average citizen. These efforts to be fair cause price distortions within the economy and waste our labor resources because of the paperwork, accountants, and tax lawyers associated with a tax code that often seems like an imponderable murky morass to the average citizen. Is it worth it? Has government even accomplished its fairness goals?

B

*T*he Flat Tax Sounds Appealing

Some people argue that a truly flat tax is not only efficient, but also quite fair. A tax that is truly flat would apply the same tax rate to everyone. As your income rises, you would still pay more taxes. However, as a percentage of income, each person would pay equally. Thus, if the tax rate is 15 percent and your income is $16,000, you would owe $2,400 in taxes. If your income is $160,000, you would owe $24,000 in taxes. A flat tax designed in this way is entirely proportional.

There is still the question of what constitutes income. Proponents of the flat tax often favor exempting income from savings and investment, since such income is generated by other income that has already been taxed. Such an exemption would be efficient, since it avoids penalizing income that is directed to savings and investment relative to that which is directed to consumption.

The biggest appeal of the flat tax is that it is transparent and easy to comply with. *Transparency* means that its operation is easily monitored. We know the rules, and those same rules apply to everyone. Thus we need not worry about clever tax dodges that we suspect others use to avoid paying their fair share of taxes. Moreover, we need not concern ourselves with keeping records and adjusting our behavior in ways that will minimize our own tax burdens. With the flat tax, we pay it when it comes due and ignore it for the rest of the year. That is appealing!

*H*ow Flat Is Flat?

In practice, flat tax proposals are not as simple as "Report your earned income, and send in 15 percent." Flat tax proposals usually include some exemptions and deductions. Most prominently, these proposals are made to be progressive by exempting the first many thousands of dollars from taxes altogether. For example, under some proposals, the first $16,000 of income would be exempted. By exempting some income from taxation, the tax rate must be higher because the tax base is smaller. While proposals for flat taxes differ in the amount of income they exclude, some would require rates over 20 percent to bring in as much revenue as the current personal income tax.

There are two reasons that some income is exempted from taxation. One reason concerns equity. For example, since low-income citizens are more needy, many people view it as unfair to take any of their money through taxation. The other reason is politics. Because changing the tax code results in both gainers and losers, care must be taken that more people gain than lose, or the change is not likely to happen. For these reasons, flat tax proposals typically exempt some income and certain popular deductions, such as the deduction for home mortgage interest payments. While there is no obvious economic reason for the tax code to favor homeowners over renters, the idea is to gain the support of special interests that pay attention—in this case, the homeowners.

Low-income citizens comprise another large group of potential voters. Since these people do not provide much tax revenue anyway, why not just promise them a zero tax burden? Exempting income at the low end of the scale has the potential to buy a great deal of public support at a relatively low cost. Of course, the higher up the income ladder those exemptions go, the higher the cost will be.

Not everyone supports the idea of exempting income. Even without exemptions, taking the same percentage of income from the rich and poor alike means that wealthier citizens pay a much higher price for government than is paid by the poor. Moreover, the poor receive benefits from redistributional programs, which are not offered to the more well-to-do. If the poor receive a totally free ride, will they still be responsible citizens? It would be rational for them to support inefficient and excessive government spending, since the costs are borne by others.

There is also a concern over what might be termed psychological issues. If low-income households pay no taxes whatsoever and are on the receiving end of government programs paid for by others, how will they view themselves and their country? Paying taxes denotes participation, being a part of the process.

In contrast, those who receive benefits without paying a dime in taxes may rationalize this situation by viewing themselves as disadvantaged victims of an unfair economy. That way, they can feel good about receiving back from society some part of what was rightfully theirs all along. After all, the powerful people who craft the tax code seem to be saying that those with more money owe amends to the poor, who owe nothing. The message is that the poor are victims and are not responsible for their plight. This message is probably true for some of the poor, but certainly not for all. We might prefer to avoid ensconcing that message in the tax code.

Should the Tax System Be the Tool of Government Policy?

Taxes are the price we pay for living in our country. Government needs the money, so it seems fair to pay. However, because government has a monopoly on the power to tax, it can practice price discrimination. In other words, it can charge some people more than others, irrespective of how much government service they consume. Government can price discriminate on the basis of its citizens' characteristics, such as income or family size, although supposedly not by race, color, or creed. Government makes use of this power to vary the prices it charges, just as the theater owner charges higher prices for adults than for children.

A truly flat tax without exclusions takes away from government much of its power to price discriminate. Its hands are tied. Would this loss of a government policy instrument be the country's loss as well? Perhaps the answer comes down to this: When the government adjusts the tax code to right social injustices, does it do a good job? Do the benefits outweigh the costs? If so, the current tax system is justified. If not, perhaps we should order up a flat tax and direct our attention to other matters.

PROSPECTING FOR NEW INSIGHTS

1. On balance, do you think it is a good idea to adopt a flat tax? If such a tax is adopted, how much income should be exempted? Explain your reasoning.
2. Income taxes provide government with information about your earnings. Information from tax returns has been used to convict bootleggers, narcotics smugglers, and others with large unreported incomes of tax law violations, even when government

could not prove that their income was obtained illegally. Some supporters of tax reform would prefer to abandon the income tax altogether and replace it with a value-added tax or other tax that leaves no paperwork trail and keeps individuals' affairs out of the eyes of government. Do you think the information contained in income tax returns should be used by government in prosecuting crime? Should we fear that government will go overboard and misuse tax information to infringe upon civil liberties? Explain.

EXPLORATION 2
Drinking Water—Stirring Together Markets and Government

Inclining block rates characterize the provision of municipal water supplies, even though this price structure is inefficient. Unfortunately, public officials are often motivated to prefer inefficient pricing over efficient alternatives, even when those alternatives appear to satisfy goals of equity.

The issue of drinking water is coming ever more to the forefront as populations grow while rainfall does not. Likewise, as we become more aware of the value of free-flowing streams and natural ecosystems, we are less willing to build new dams and reservoirs. For these reasons, municipal water supplies are likely to become increasingly scarce. In an efficiently functioning market, prices would rise to keep supply and demand in balance. Prices would also adjust to provide water of optimal quality, another issue in many areas.

*M*onopoly Brings in Government

Municipal water markets lack effective competition. Rather, they are characterized by monopoly, which means that customers buy from the one supplier or do without. The market for municipal drinking water is a natural monopoly, in that it occurs without any action of government. The reason arises from the very high cost of installing water lines relative to the cost of the water passing through those lines. The result is usually only one set of water lines into each house or apartment complex.

Suppose that water utilities are to be owned or regulated by government. What price or prices should water sell for? If government follows the lead of the competitive marketplace, it would set a single price that is just high enough to avoid either a surplus or shortage of water. In times or places when water is particularly scarce, however, the market-clearing price could be quite high. Would that be fair? After all, water is one of our most basic necessities of life.

When regulating or setting water rates, politicians respond to voters. Few voters are likely to look favorably on water rates that take in revenue beyond what is needed to cover water's production costs. That suggests some form of *average cost pricing*. In contrast, the economically efficient market-clearing price of water is based on **marginal cost pricing**, given by the intersection of marginal cost with demand. That marginal cost could exceed average cost by quite a bit if the most cost-effective water projects are already in place. The newest sources of municipal water are likely to be much more expensive than long-established sources, leading to a low average cost and a high marginal cost.

*P*olitical Action: Inclining Block Rates Look Fair

Pricing municipal water creates a political dilemma that policy makers often fail to address in an economic manner. For instance, the most common political solution is to offer **inclining block rates**, which present water customers with ever-higher water rates as their usage goes up. Inclining block rates give the appearance of fairness according to the ability-to-pay principle, since this rate structure punishes high-volume users by increasing their marginal rates, which causes their water bills to go up more than in proportion to their increases in water usage. The problem with inclining block rates is that such rates neither clear the market nor ensure that water goes where it is valued the most.

An inclining block rate structure often proves divisive and ineffective when water scarcity becomes severe. For instance, when Santa Barbara faced a drought a few years ago, the city-owned utility kept adjusting its inclining rate structure until there was a nearly thirtyfold difference between the marginal rates facing high- and low-volume water users—marginal water rates ranged from just about $1 to over $29 per 100 cubic feet. The result was that high-volume users did indeed cut back dramatically to avoid those rates. The problem is that the large majority of customers, those consuming under 500 cubic feet per month, saw no change in their rates and thus did not conserve.

By abandoning the price signal for most residents, Santa Barbara was forced to resort to the command-and-control alternative of telling their residents when and how they would be allowed to use water. Many conservation possibilities could not be brought about in this manner. For instance, it would not be feasible to monitor whether washing machines and dishwashers are full when they are run. Nor would it be feasible to monitor whether toilets are flushed too often or showers taken for too long. Indeed, even though Santa Barbara distributed low-flow showerheads free of charge, they could not monitor the shower to make sure that people truly sacrificed their higher-quality showerheads for the low-flow models. Nor could they monitor how long people stayed in the shower, even with low-flow showerheads.

While many conservation practices could not be mandated, those that were proved quite irritating. The result is that Santa Barbara wound up pouring massive amounts of money into a desalinization plant and other supplemental water sources. Santa Barbara could have saved at least some of that money and much of the irritation if it had chosen a more economical course of action.

Cities facing heightened water scarcity need not choose between onerous expenses for new water supplies or the wrath of the water police. There is a third alternative, one that employs economic incentives to achieve efficient usage of the water that is available. Only when cities are not wasting the water they already have should they shop for new water sources.

B

*M*arket-Based Alternatives: Big Brother Go Home!

The economic solution is to forgo political prices in favor of market prices, and accomplish equity goals separately. The invisible hand of the free market relies upon a single price to ensure that neither surpluses nor shortages occur and that goods go where they are worth the most. A single market price is unlike inclining block rate water prices, which differ from person to person for purely political reasons. Rather, a genuine market price would present each person with the same marginal cost of using water, equal to that price. We all pay the same price per gallon at gasoline stations—why not per gallon of tap water?

Water utilities can avoid collecting revenues in excess of costs and still maintain an efficient water market. To do so, however, there must be supplemental action. That action could take any of several forms. For example, water utilities could charge an efficient market-clearing price, and then rebate extra revenues to water customers. The rebate must not be tied directly to water usage, since to do so would lower the effective price of water and lead to excessive consumption. Instead, rebates could be based upon which category a customer falls under, such as small-lot residential, two-bedroom apartment, apartment complex, etc.

Another path is to adopt a trick of the retail trade—coupons. Price discount coupons provide an option to cut down on revenues without affecting market efficiency. Those coupons would offer customers low rates when the coupons are proffered along with payment of their water bills. To ensure efficiency, the coupons must be marketable. This marketability would allow customers to sell the coupons for the market price of the coupon. In this way, coupons would go to those who value the coupons most highly, who would be the same people as those who value water most highly. Corner stores would probably serve as *market makers* for a small margin between the price at which they would buy and sell coupons (the *bid/ask* price), much like currency traders along the U.S. borders.

A third option would employ "feebates" to avoid the transaction costs associated with keeping track of coupons. *Feebates* represent a combination of penalty fees on heavy users, which pay for rebates to light users. Under this option, each user is given a baseline usage amount, above which is assessed a per unit penalty fee or below which is rebated a per unit conservation reward. Baselines would add up to the municipality's water supply. The penalty and rebate rates would be set equal to each other and adjusted up or down as necessary until the market clears. In this way, water rates could be set to cover average cost only and still achieve an efficient market allocation because each user would face the same opportunity cost of water use.

Implementing any of these options would generate political dickering over the assignment of property rights to entitlements of rebates, feebates or coupons. The debate would be over defining appropriate usage categories, since defining categories affects the distribution of rebates, feebates, or coupons. However, categories need be established only once. The rebates, feebates, or coupons would continue month after month for as long as desired.

Using any of the market pricing plans would have significant advantages relative to adjusting the prices themselves to achieve equity. For instance, we would not need any heavy-handed government restrictions on how we use our water—no water police. New industry would find no restrictions on its water usage, just the price incentive to conserve. The value of supplementing water supplies would also be revealed.

The Political Barrier to Good Economic Policy

Why then do not more municipalities adopt market-based pricing plans? The answer involves the principal-agent problem, in which public servants (agents) have objectives that differ from those of the public they serve (principals). The public in this case consists of municipal water customers. Few of these customers wish to become experts on water rate possibilities. Instead, they would prefer to leave those things to people they perceive as experts. Unfortunately, they often assume the experts are those with hands-on experience.

Those with hands-on experience at publicly owned or regulated water utilities have little incentive to adopt new, more efficient ways. What's in it for them? Government employees are notorious for being risk averse. After all, if things go wrong, their jobs can be at stake. If things go well, in contrast, they might generate the resentment of other agency employees afraid of upsetting the apple cart. Moreover, public agencies rarely reward public employees for saving the public money, particularly if the savings lead to budget cuts.

The result is little incentive to avoid rate structures that lead to inefficiencies and wasteful new water projects. After all, the less effective is the rate structure at promoting conservation, the more will be spent on other approaches. Is it any wonder, then, that entrenched "experts" commonly reject innovative ideas. This close-mindedness is usually excused on the basis of a myriad of purportedly practical details left unaddressed in alternative proposals. Of course, the other choice would be for the experts to use their practical knowledge to resolve the details themselves.

Rather than adopt a cost-saving rate structure, the water utility is motivated to prefer expensive supplemental water projects or conservation programs. Conservation programs tend to be police and hardware oriented, such as programs to provide low-flow showerheads and toilets to public housing projects and other politically chosen recipients.

Separate conservation programs would be unnecessary with an efficient rate structure. Conversely, without efficient incentives to conserve water itself, recipients of low-flow showerheads will most likely remove or drill out the flow restricter to obtain a better feeling shower. After all, why not? Likewise, water-miser toilets will hardly save water if recipients flush them repeatedly for more effective cleaning. Again, where's the incentive not to?

The problem is ultimately one of incentives. We want to provide incentives for water customers to use water efficiently. Unfortunately, the incentives of publicly owned or regulated water utilities are at odds with this principle. The more crisis there is in water allocation, the higher is the profile of the water utility. With a higher profile comes more in the way of size, stature, budget, and job security—all in the self-interest of employees and management, but not of the public.

Still Hurdles to Leap

In the private, unregulated marketplace, competition for profit provides a powerful incentive for firms to provide what their customers want. No corresponding incentive exists in government. Thus, while there are valid reasons to mix government and markets, that mix rarely performs as well as it could. Providing the right incentives within government remains a formidable hurdle in the design of economic policy.

1. Would you object to charging all water customers a single water price? Would you object if this water price brought in extra revenue for the local utility? What if that utility were owned by government? Explain.

2. Studies show that less water is consumed as its price rises. Still, many people do not believe so. Ask yourself—Would you change your behavior in any way if you were to see a significant increase in water costs? If so, how? If not, why not?

B

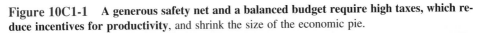

CHALLENGE 1
Trade-offs in Income Redistribution

There is a fundamental conflict between efficiency and equity when equity involves the redistribution of income from the haves to the have-nots. The conflict revolves around incentives for productivity, necessary to generate wealth. The economy sacrifices incentives for efficiency to the extent that government taxes productivity and rewards being unproductive. However, equity is also a valid economic goal, worth sacrificing some efficiency for. The question is how much. This Challenge illustrates the basic choices that must be made.

In the absence of government taxes and transfer payments, each person's pretax and after-tax earnings would be identical. The 45-degree line labeled "Without taxes or transfers" in Figure 10C1-1 shows this equality. With government there are taxes and, if income is low enough, transfer payments. Some of these transfers are cash, such as the welfare check associated with Aid to Families with Dependent Children, the earned income

Figure 10C1-1   A generous safety net and a balanced budget require high taxes, which reduce incentives for productivity, and shrink the size of the economic pie.

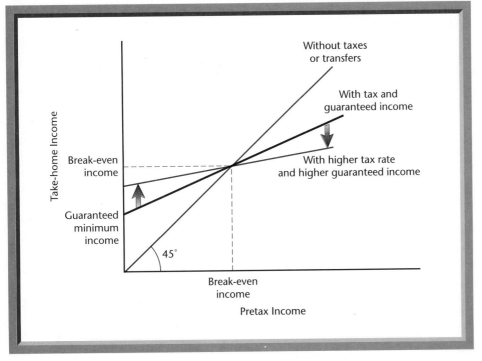

tax credit, unemployment compensation, and various other programs. However, roughly twice as much aid is provided in kind, including the value of such goods and services as Medicaid, subsidized housing, and food stamps.

Figure 10C1-1 illustrates the conflict between three goals of income redistribution. The goals are as follows:

- A generous social safety net;
- Work incentives;
- Budgetary balance.

The conflict is shown most directly by assuming a simplification of our mishmash of social spending programs and taxes. This simplification provides a social safety net on the basis of cash alone and is termed a **negative income tax**. Under the negative income tax, everyone is guaranteed a minimum income. All income above the guaranteed minimum income is then subject to an income tax. For low income levels, tax payments are less than the value of subsidies, so that the net effect is a negative tax.

Figure 10C1-1 shows the guaranteed minimum income and the possibilities for take-home pay after payment of income taxes—the line labeled "With tax and guaranteed income." This line must have a slope of less than one. Otherwise, everyone would receive transfer payments in excess of the taxes they pay, which would quickly bankrupt the system. Break-even income occurs at the level of pretax income for which the amount of taxes paid just equals the value of the transfers received. Above break-even income, workers are net tax payers. Below break-even income, they are net transfer payment receivers—beneficiaries of the negative income tax.

Now for the conflict. Note that if the safety net becomes more generous, *ceteris paribus*, both the guaranteed minimum income and break-even income rise. This effect could be shown by an upward shift of the "With tax and guaranteed income" line. Transfer payment recipients would receive more, and there are more of them. Thus, costs rise.

To combat rising costs, it is tempting to raise the tax rate. However, the effect of a tax increase would be to pivot clockwise the "With tax . . ." line, perhaps to where it intersects the "Without taxes . . ." line at the same break-even income. This change is shown by the arrows in Figure 10C1-1, pointing to the line labeled "With higher tax rate and higher guaranteed income."

There is a problem, though—a higher tax rate reduces the incentive to work, since extra work effort would have less of an effect on take-home income. Even though break-even income may not change, fewer people would opt to earn it, meaning the capacity of the economy to support the program would be questionable. Unfortunately, to the extent that the tax rate is kept low to retain work incentives, break-even income rises, which makes the program more expensive.

In practice, the take-home income line is not smooth; it even contains segments where additional income is more than offset by losses of cash payments and in-kind benefits. This occurs at different points for different people. For example, the income cutoff for Medicaid and the income matching percentage for the earned income tax credit both depend on the number of dependents in the household. There are numerous other *means-tested* (income-dependent) benefits that do likewise. While a simplification of the actual system of taxes and spending, the negative income tax serves to illustrate the inherent nature of the trade-offs among budgetary balance, work incentives, and spending on the social safety net.

C

The negative income tax is more than just a reference model, as evidenced by recent experience in Mexico. Unfortunately, the potential for fraud is a major deterrent to more widespread adoption. When benefits are in kind, those who don't actually need them are less likely to accept them. For example, the wealthy drug dealer with little income reported to the government would be unlikely to accept public housing, even if offered. Accepting cash would be another matter altogether.

CHALLENGE 2
Choice of Candidates—The Median Voter Model

A funny thing happens on the road to public office. In U.S. presidential campaigns, for example, Democratic and Republican candidates for president often sound much farther apart on the issues in the primaries than they do when it comes time for the general election. For an explanation of this and other aspects of election outcomes, we can turn to the *median voter model.*

The median voter model is applicable when voters—those who actually vote— can be lined up along a spectrum from left to right. Maybe the spectrum is political, ranging from the left wing to the right wing. Perhaps the spectrum is budgetary, ranging from a lower budget to a higher budget. In any case, the **median voter** is the one for whom 50 percent of the other voters prefer further to the right on the spectrum and 50 percent prefer further to the left. In an election in which all voters pick between two candidates, the candidate chosen by the median voter will win by garnering just over 50 percent of the vote. Note that voters are considered to be those people who do indeed vote.

Figure 10C2-1 illustrates the importance of the median voter in two-candidate elections. In this figure, nine voters and four candidates are lined up along the political or budgetary spectrum. Each voter is labeled with a *V* and also numbered. Candidates are labeled with the capital letters A, B, C, and D, standing for Ann, Bart, Chuck, and Darlene. Which candidate would defeat any opponent in a two-person race? The median voter holds the answer.

Voter 5 is the median voter and would vote for Bart against any opponent. If the opponent was to the left of Bart, Bart would also be preferred by voters 6 through 9 and thereby win with a majority of the vote. Likewise, if the opponent was to the right of Bart, voters 1 through 4 would side with the median voter to grant Bart the majority.

Suppose we divide voters into Democrats and Republicans and then hold primary elections to determine each party's candidate. For simplicity, we'll assign voters 1 through 5 and Candidates Ann and Bart to the Democrats. Voters 6 through 9 and candidates Chuck and Darlene go to the Republicans. In the Democratic primary, voter 3 now becomes the median voter and would vote for Ann. In the Republican primary, voters 7 and 8 tie for median voter honors. Their votes would go to Darlene. That means the general election would come down to a race between Ann and Darlene.

Voter 5 has not been forgotten. Between the primaries and the general election, the candidates turn their attentions toward the overall median voter, 5. They start sounding

C

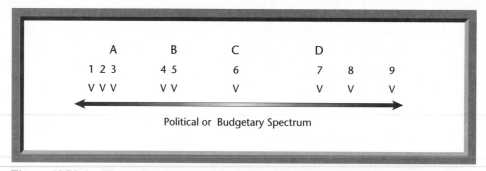

Figure 10C2-1 **The median voter model** helps explain the outcome of the political process.

more and more alike. The candidate best able to shift to the positions of voter 5 is thus most likely to win the election.

For example, President Clinton was known for his skill at shifting his public image. His ability to adapt to voter sentiment allowed him to remain at the median of the political spectrum and win the presidency in 1992. In contrast, in 1972 George McGovern lost to President Nixon by one of the largest margins of all time, winning the electoral votes of only Massachusetts. Holding to his principles, McGovern's message in the presidential election was nearly identical to the message that won him the Democratic primary. However, the median Democratic voter at that time was significantly to the left of the median voter in the general population.

C

Study By Design

SpeedStudy

SpeedReview

We pay for government through a variety of taxes, including the personal income tax, Social Security tax, corporation income tax, and various sales taxes. Some of the tax payments represent transfers that redistribute income from one group to another. The combination of taxes and transfer payments discourages work effort. In general, promoting equity will come at a cost in terms of efficiency. Competition leads free markets to achieve efficiency, except in the case of market failure. While market failure can be corrected by government action, government is subject to failures of its own. Incentives that lead to excessive spending is probably the most pervasive government failure. These incentives exist at each stage of the public choice process. For example, even though voters may disapprove of logrolling as a general concept, they rationally vote for candidates who are good at it.

SpeedStudy True or False Self-Test

A1. Corporation income taxes account for about 30 percent of the revenues collected by the federal government.

A2. Workers in effect pay the employer portion of the Social Security tax and often do not know it.

A3. Efficiency requires that companies be taxed at the same rate as individuals.

A4. The U.S. personal income tax is equitable according to the benefit principle of taxation.

A5. If your income increases from $10,000 to $30,000, and your tax payments increase from $2,000 to $4,000, the tax is regressive.

A6. A Representative's chances of winning reelection to a Congressional district would likely be enhanced if that Representative avoids vote trading altogether.

A7. The personal self-interest of employees of any government agency is normally furthered by a larger budget for that agency.

A8. If a government agency adopts the Washington Monument strategy, the agency will be totally honest in revealing all potential cost-saving measures.

A9. When you enter a contest, you are engaging in rent-seeking behavior.

A10. Unfunded mandates offer a means for government to accomplish its goals, without the spending showing up on the public budget.

B11. A flat tax would be regressive.

B12. A comprehensive measure of income would add the value of a person's consumption to the change in that person's net worth.

B13. An inclining block rate pricing structure for water usage represents a close approximation to efficient market pricing.

B14. Government employees responsible for setting water rates have little incentive to adopt efficient rate structures.

C15. The tax system trades off objectives of efficient work incentives, a social safety net, and budgetary balance.

C16. Under a negative income tax, even the lowest income households will pay at least some tax.

C17. The median voter model explains why candidates shift their positions between primary elections and the general election.

C18. According to the median voter model, a candidate will have the best chance of winning an election if he or she takes positions exactly in the middle, irrespective of where potential voters line up on the issues.

The MasterMind

Selected Terms Along the Way

transfer payments, 355
safety net, 355
marginal tax rate, 355
consumption tax, 358
value-added tax (VAT), 360
tax base, 360
benefit principle, 361
ability-to-pay principle, 361
progressive tax, 361
regressive tax, 361
proportional tax, 361

in-kind benefits, 362
public choice, 363
government failure, 363
rational ignorance, 365
logrolling, 365
fiscal illusion, 365
rent-seeking behavior, 367
block grant, 367
Washington Monument
  strategy, 369

unfunded mandates, 371

comprehensive measure
  of income, 373
realized capital gains, 373
tax expenditures, 373
vertical equity, 373
horizontal equity, 373
marginal cost pricing, 377
inclining block rates, 377

negative income tax, 382
median voter, 383

MasterMind Multiple Choice Self-Test

A1. The goal of tax equity is to see that
  a. everyone pays their fair share of taxes.
  b. taxes do not harm the incentive to produce.
  c. taxes are collected efficiently.
  d. government benefits are distributed efficiently.

A2. Of the following, the most efficient tax would be the
  a. corporate income tax.
  b. personal income tax.
  c. sales tax.
  d. head tax.

A3. Which of the following represents a government-mandated benefit provided by private employers?
  a. Access for the handicapped.
  b. Aid to Families with Dependent Children.
  c. Medicaid.
  d. The personal income tax.

A4. As applied to government, the essence of the principle-agent problem is that ——— are principals, ——— are agents, and ——— follow their own agendas.
  a. citizens; public servants; citizens
  b. citizens; public servants; public servants
  c. public servants; citizens; citizens
  d. public servants; citizens; public servants

A5. Logrolling is a term referring to how
  a. the public will sell their votes on election day for money.
  b. vote trading occurs among legislators who want to bring home the pork.
  c. lobbyists waste time and resources trying to influence government legislation.
  d. the lumber industry exerts an unreasonable amount of control over government legislation.

B6. Which of the following is a characteristic of "feebates"?
  a. Feebates are intended to duplicate the effects of an inclining block rate pricing structure.
  b. Feebates provide rebates to purchasers of low-flow showerheads, up to but not in excess of the purchase price.
  c. Feebates would normally generate more revenue for the municipality than the alternative of average-cost pricing.
  d. Feebates combine rebates and penalty fees in a manner that can achieve an efficient allocation of municipal water.

B7. Which of the following is the best example of a tax expenditure?
  a. Building a new interstate highway.

b. Deducting charitable contributions from income before taxes are assessed.

c. The Medicaid program, in which medical services are offered only to the poor.

d. Social Security payments to the elderly.

C8. Other things equal, an increase in the negative income tax rate will cause

a. an increase in work effort.

b. an increase in the guaranteed minimum income.

c. an increase in break-even income.

d. an increase in tax revenues, if work effort does not drop too much.

C9. In the median voter model, voters are required to pick between ———— alternatives, where the positions of the voters can be arranged along a ———— spectrum.

a. two; linear

b. any number of; linear

c. two; circular

d. any number; circular

MasterMind Questions and Problems

A1. Using a graph and labeling the axes, curves, and all relevant information, demonstrate how employees wind up paying the employer portion of Social Security taxes.

A2. Why it is difficult to design aid to the poor that provides work incentives? Explain with reference to cost and the level of the safety net.

A3. We allow people to buy and sell most of what they own, so should we also allow voters to buy and sell their votes? Alternatively, since most potential voters do not vote, should we eliminate voting and replace it with surveys that measure public opinions? Explain.

A4. Many governments have term limits to prevent so-called empire building by holders of public office. For example, the president of the United States can serve only two four-year terms. Is this a good idea? Should the idea be extended to other levels of government? What problems are likely to arise?

A5. Explain how logrolling can lead to excessive government spending. Would eliminating logrolling cause too little spending?

B6. Choosing your own numerical example, demonstrate why a flat tax with some income exempted would be progressive.

B7. Describe the characteristics of a market-clearing price for municipal water. Explain whether an increasing block rate price structure allocates water to the same uses.

C8. Consider a negative income tax with a guaranteed minimum income of $10,000 per year and a tax rate of 20 percent. What would be the break-even income? Why would it be impractical to implement this tax? How could the tax be revised to make it more practical?

C9. Using the median voter model, explain why candidates take positions in primary elections that are more extreme than the positions those same candidates take in the following general election. Also describe two reasons why, even in theory, the median voter may not obtain his or her most desired outcome.

Future Explorations: Mapping out Term Papers

1. **That Mind-Boggling Maze of Taxes**
   This paper identifies some of the many taxes Americans face. The paper looks most closely at the personal income tax. It is seen that tax lawyers, accountants, and other constituencies would have much to lose if the personal income tax were simplified. The paper examines arguments for and against tax simplification. In conclusion, the paper points out reasons why advocates of tax simplification always seem to lose in the political process.

2. **Media Sound Bites and the Political Process: Can We Think for Ourselves?**
   This paper uses economic analysis to examine whether the media shape our opinions or merely respond to our desires. The paper starts by viewing the media as responding to market demand. It appears that most consumers prefer short colorful news pieces to in-depth analysis. The news is then viewed as a form of entertainment and not taken seriously when people are actually called upon to make decisions. The paper proceeds to examine whether candidates design their commercials to exploit rational ignorance on the part of voters. The paper concludes by exploring whether public prohibitions on certain types of advertising are warranted, or whether such government involvement would cause more harm than good.

3. **Sleeping with the Government: Have Special Interests Captured Our Bureaucracies?**
   This paper looks at the economic role of lobbyists. On the one hand, lobbyists provide a voice for those who feel so strongly about an issue, they are willing to part with their own money. On the other hand, lobbyists seek to capture value from the various laws that are passed and rules and regulations designed to put those laws into action. If lobbyists behave rationally, they expect to benefit from influencing legislation and its interpretations more than the lobbying costs. The paper concludes by asking whether lobbying is socially desirable or if there is a better alternative.

Answer Key

ExpressStudy True or False		SpeedStudy True or False Self-Test		MasterMind Multiple Choice Self-Test
1. T		1. F	10. T	1. a
2. T		2. T	11. F	2. d
3. F		3. F	12. T	3. a
4. F		4. F	13. F	4. b
5. T		5. T	14. T	5. b
6. F		6. F	15. T	6. d
		7. T	16. F	7. b
		8. F	17. T	8. d
		9. T	18. F	9. a

CHAPTER

Eleven

Measuring the Macroeconomy

389

A LOOK AHEAD

How do we live now? How did we live in the past? How will we live in the future? By looking around we can gain impressions of how we're living now. Historians can shed light on the past. Futurists can peer into their crystal balls and tell us their visions of the future. But the keepers of the government's statistics may very well be the ultimate font of knowledge.

This chapter is about economic measurement. Obviously, numbers can never tell the entire story, and so statisticians will never replace social observers, historians, and the like. Nonetheless, economic statistics are quite useful. We have goals as a society: economic growth without inflation, for example. Various macro measures are used to monitor whether we are achieving our goals. Other measures indicate what we can expect in the future, thus allowing us to plan more effectively.

DESTINATIONS

Module A

As you zip through the Expressway you will arrive at an ability to

- present some widely-accepted goals for the macro economy;
- distinguish how GDP and GNP measure output;
- understand how price indices are used;
- explain how the unemployment rate is calculated;
- divide unemployment into different types and explain the implications of each.

Module B

Upon leaving the Expressway to explore issues you will be able to

- identify the advantages and disadvantages of static and dynamic scoring;
- relate some shortcomings of government statistics.

Module C

Mastering Roadside Challenges will allow you to hone analytical skills by

- considering two alternate means of calculating GDP;
- working through examples of how to calculate price indices.

*M*acroeconomic Goals

Macroeconomics deals with the economy as a whole. The performance of the macro-economy thus affects everyone. Government tax policies, spending policies, and monetary policies are aimed at achieving several desirable ends. **Economic growth, full employment, and low inflation are three widely accepted goals of macro policy.** Since these goals may at times conflict with each other, there is sometimes disagreement over which goal should receive first priority in the design of government policies. For example, policies that promote full employment may be inconsistent with low inflation, so one or the other goal must take priority.

Economic growth occurs when the economy's total output of goods and services increases. Higher living standards are a by-product of economic growth. In effect, growth enlarges the economic pie, allowing many people bigger slices. Table 11A-1 illustrates some of the ways in which economic growth has increased the U.S. standard of living.

It is generally believed that the economy can sustain a long-term growth rate of 2.5 percent per year. However, some optimists argue that twice that rate is possible. Over the long run, small differences in the growth rate can make a large difference in living standards. It would take twenty-nine years for aggregate output to double at a 2.5 percent growth rate, but only half that time in the more optimistic case.

Doubling times, such as that for aggregate output, can be estimated using the **rule**

TABLE 11A-1 *Some Illustrative Changes in the U.S. Standard of Living, 1970–1990*

Feature	1970	1990
Average size of new home	1,500 square feet	2,080 square feet
New homes with central air conditioning	34 percent	76 percent
Homes with color TV	34 percent	96 percent
Homes with cable	4 million	55 million
Homes with VCRs	0	67 million
Homes with 2 or more cars	29 percent	54 percent
Households with microwave ovens	Less than 1 percent	79 percent
Homes without telephones	13 percent	5 percent
Median household net worth	$24,217	$48,887
Average work week	37.1 hours	34.5 hours
Annual paid vacation, holidays	15.5 days	22.5 days
Number retired from work	13.3 million	25.3 million
Life expectancy	70.8 years	75.4 years

Source: Federal Reserve Bank of Dallas Annual Report, 1993.

of seventy-two Whatever the continuously compounding percentage growth rate of a variable is, dividing that number into seventy-two will reveal the approximate doubling time. For example, a 5 percent growth rate means that output doubles about every 14.4 years, because 72/5 equals 14.4.

In practice, economic growth does not occur in a smooth fashion. The economy surges and stumbles at periodic intervals. These ups and downs in the growth of output sometimes put the economy above, and other times below, its long-run sustainable growth rate.

When economic growth falls short, unemployment is usually the result. High employment is a major goal of public policy. Concerns over unemployment motivate the development of macro models designed to better understand its causes and identify policies to achieve full employment.

Policymakers also seek to preserve the value of money by keeping the inflation rate low. In practice, the economy has experienced some inflation every year since 1955. Annual inflation reached a peak of 12 percent in the 1970s before declining sharply in the 1980s and stabilizing at about 3 to 4 percent so far during the 1990s. At these inflation rates, public concern over inflation has subsided. However, a 3 percent inflation rate will cause prices to double in about 24 years. If inflation were to reach 10 percent, a level reached during the 1970s, it would take little more than 7 years for prices to double. This explains why increases in the inflation rate merit concern, especially among those living on fixed incomes.

*M*easuring National Output

From the earliest days of American history, government has kept statistical records. As the economy has grown larger and more complex, the importance of keeping track of the economy has increased. Policymakers rely upon government data to design policies that will improve economic performance.

The value of goods and services produced is the single most important measure of the nation's output. According to the circular flow of income, the value of national output must be identical to the value of national income. This equality occurs because every dollar that buyers spend on output represents income to the sellers of that output.

The economy's output is diverse, running the gamut from A to Z, including the proverbial kitchen sink. One way to measure output is to classify it according to who's doing the purchasing. To this end, purchases are classified by sector: households, businesses, government, and foreigners. Each unit of output finds its way to one of these sectors. The output is valued at *market value*, which is measured by market prices. Apples, oranges, the kitchen sink, and all other goods and services are valued by the common dollar-denominated yardstick of market prices.

Output is measured by tallying the value of *final goods and services*—those which are sold to their final owners. The most widely reported measure of the economy's output is **gross domestic product (GDP)**, the market value of the final goods and services produced in the economy within some time period, usually one quarter or one year. Spending on *intermediate goods*—goods used to make other goods—is not included so as to avoid double counting, the counting of the same output twice. For instance, a new car purchased by a consumer includes a new battery and tires. Since the total value of the car includes the value of its components, the output and the inputs should not be counted separately. On the other hand, since replacement batteries and tires are purchased by their final user, it is appropriate to count these expenditures in consumer spending.

Consumption

Consumption spending is purchasing by households. Household spending makes up the majority of spending in the U.S. economy, about 68 percent of total spending in 1994. This spending may be on services or on consumer durable or nondurable goods. Nondurables are goods that are consumed quickly, by definition in one year or less. Food is an example. Durables are goods that have an expected lifespan of more than one year, such as automobiles.

Investment

Investment—spending now in order to increase output or productivity later—is the most variable component of GDP. While there are many forms of investment, such as a college student's investment in the human capital provided by an education, GDP statistics record only three measurable types:

- purchases by firms of **capital,** such as new factories and machines;
- consumers' purchases of **new housing**, a form of consumer capital;
- the market value of the **change in business inventories** of unsold goods.

Purchases of capital allow firms the opportunity to increase their future outputs of goods and services. As such, a pickup truck purchased by a firm is counted as investment. If that same truck had been purchased by you for your personal use, it would have been included in consumption. New homes are included under investment because they provide an ongoing stream of housing services over many years.

To see why the change in business inventories is included as investment, consider an increase in business inventories. Inventories increase when firms deliberately produce more than can be immediately sold. Inventories also increase when demand falls short of firms' estimates, as in a recession. Clearly, inventory investment is qualitatively different from investment in capital, in that an increase in inventories may be unintended. Nonetheless, accumulations of inventory represent investment because they allow for increased sales in the future. When goods in inventory are sold, inventory investment shows a decrease and consumer spending an equivalent increase.

Investment may be either gross or net. *Gross investment* is the total amount of investment. Gross investment in the private sector of the economy amounted to about 14 percent of GDP in 1994. **Net investment** is gross investment minus depreciation. Because plants and machines wear out or become technologically obsolete, net investment will be less than gross investment. A positive value for net investment measures the increase in the economy's productive capacity. A negative value for net investment means that depreciation exceeded the total amount of investment, which implies that the productive capacity of the economy declines. When the focus is on net investment, **net domestic product (NDP)** is a more appropriate measure than GDP. NDP equals GDP minus depreciation.

Government

A

Governments at the federal, state, and local levels account for about 19 percent of total purchasing in the U.S. economy. Governments purchase a wide range of goods and services from businesses. While estimates differ, perhaps one-tenth of that government spending could be classified as investment, such as in new highways and other infrastructure. Examples include government-owned buildings, such as schools, offices, and airports. Government also pays for social services provided by teachers, social workers, parole officers, and others. These are civilian goods and services. Defense goods, such as tanks and missiles, are also purchased. Defense spending has comprised about two-thirds of federal government purchases in recent years.

Government purchases of goods and services should be distinguished from government transfer payments. *Transfer payments*, such as Social Security and unemployment benefits, are received by individuals who do not provide goods and services in return. Including all levels of government, government transfer payments to persons totaled $950 billion in 1994, or 43 percent of total government expenditures. To the extent that transfer payments are used by households to buy goods and services, they are counted as consumption spending.

Foreign Commerce

Some of the output produced by the economy is purchased by foreigners in the form of exports. Because a portion of spending by consumers, businesses, and government is on imports, it is useful to subtract imports from exports.

Exports minus imports defines *net exports*. A negative figure for net exports means that spending on imports is greater than spending on exports; a positive figure means that spending on imports is less than spending on exports. Net exports varies from year to year, with the deficit exceeding 3 percent of GDP in 1987. More recently, the deficit has been closer to 1 percent. For example, in 1993, exports equaled 10.4 percent of GDP and imports equaled 11.4 percent of GDP, leaving exports minus imports equal to -1 percent of GDP.

OBSERVATION POINT: Are Disasters Good for the Economy?

Hurricanes, floods, and earthquakes are good for the economy, right? After all, they force people to spend more, which increases output. Isn't an increase in output a reason to rejoice?

Clearly, something is amiss with this reasoning. The key to understanding this faulty logic? Spending on additions to our stock of goods and services increases living standards. However, spending that follows natural disasters merely replaces goods in order to bring living standards back to some semblance of their former levels.

Gross Domestic Product—A Closer Look

GDP is the sum of purchases by the four sectors of the economy. Therefore we can write the following equation for GDP:

$$\text{GDP} = \text{consumption} + \text{gross investment} + \text{government purchases} + \text{net exports}$$

$$\quad\;\; (68\%) \qquad\qquad (14\%) \qquad\qquad\quad (19\%) \qquad\qquad\quad (-1\%)$$

In this equation, government purchases include government investment, so that only private sector investment is counted under gross investment. Gross investment includes U.S. investment undertaken by foreign citizens as well as U.S. citizens. Thus, if a citizen of France purchases a new condominium in New York City, the transaction is entered as investment. However, if this same person purchases U.S.-made business machines and ships them to France, the transaction is entered in net exports.

GDP may also be viewed as the sum of value added in the economy. Each firm takes inputs of materials and intermediate goods and increases their value through the firm's production process. **Value added** equals the revenue from the sale of output minus the cost of purchased inputs. For example, a farmer who purchases $3,000 worth of seed and fertilizer to grow a crop that is subsequently sold for $10,000 has added value equal to $7,000.

Potential GDP is the value of GDP that would exist if all resources in the economy were fully and efficiently employed. When actual GDP is subtracted from potential GDP, the value of lost output due to unemployment and inefficiencies in the economy is revealed. Actual GDP equals potential GDP only if there is no unemployment or underemployment of resources.

Per capita GDP is GDP per person. The total U.S. GDP of $6.93 trillion ($6,930,000,000,000—a trillion is a million millions or a one followed by twelve zeros) in 1994 is more easily placed into perspective when divided by the population of 260,660,000 persons. Per capita GDP for that year was $26,580. This is the amount of output produced and divided equally among every man, woman, and child living in the U.S.

Until 1992, the main measure of the economy's output was **gross national product (GNP)**. GNP differs from GDP in that the value added to production by resources located outside the U.S., but owned by U.S. citizens, is counted in GNP. Unlike GDP, GNP excludes value added within the U.S. by foreign-owned resources. Typically, U.S. GDP and GNP differ by less than one percent, so that either can be used to evaluate the performance of the economy.

The nation's statisticians ignore some output, sometimes deliberately. For example, goods and services that we produce for ourselves at home are not counted. So, if you cook your own dinner tonight, the value of that service does not appear in GDP. But if you eat out, those services are counted. That's because there is a market price for a restaurant meal but not for a home-cooked meal.

There are other outputs statisticians would like to measure, but are unable to. These involve economic activity in the **underground economy**—market transactions that go unreported. Some of these goods and services are illegal and thus not recorded in GDP. Others are not reported so that their producers avoid paying taxes on the output.

✓ QUICKCHECK

Are each of the following included in computing U.S. GDP?

1. New Corvettes built in Bowling Green, Kentucky;
2. New Honda Accords produced in Marysville, Ohio;
3. New Accords produced in Japan, but purchased by U.S. residents;
4. New Ford cars produced in Ford plants in Great Britain and purchased by residents of Britain.

Answers: (1) Yes, although the value of any imported components would be subtracted. (2) Yes, since the nameplate or ownership of the company does not matter. As in (1), the value of imported engines, transmissions, or other components are not part of U.S. GDP. (3) No. Japanese-built Accords purchased by American consumers are an import. Recall that imports are subtracted from exports in the calculation of GDP. (4) No. U.S. GDP measures U.S. production.

OBSERVATION POINT: Shhh! Want a Rolex?
How about a "Honey Do"?

While it is obviously difficult to measure illegal activity, estimates place the underground economy at from 3 percent to 15 percent of total economic activity in the United States. Other countries see even higher percentages. As a general rule, the more burdensome are a country's taxes and regulations, the larger will be its underground economy.

Most people think that the underground economy consists of prohibited goods and services, such as drugs and prostitution, along with stolen or counterfeit items. Yes, that Rolex watch being hawked on the street corner is probably fake or stolen. But there is much more. A significant portion of the underground economy consists of legal goods that are sold off the record in order to avoid taxes or regulatory requirements.

Examples of this type of underground activity include toxic wastes illegally dumped, workers illegally employed, goods sold without the collection of sales taxes, and services sold without required paperwork. Yes, the underground economy may include that friendly fellow willing to take on the "honey-do-this, honey-do-that" odd jobs. No license inspected, no credit cards accepted, and no tax collected.

*M*easuring *Inflation*

GDP can change because the quantities of various outputs in the economy change, or because prices change. Usually, GDP changes in response to a combination of both reasons. Since only increases in output make us better off, we would like to know how much of any change in GDP is due to price changes and how much is due to output changes. A price index can tell us.

Price Indices

A *price index* measures the average level of prices in the economy. There are several price indices, each created for a specific purpose, with a different set of prices measured.

- The **consumer price index (CPI)**, the best known index, measures prices of typical purchases made by consumers living in urban areas.
- The **producer price index (PPI)** measures wholesale prices, which are prices paid by firms.
- The **GDP deflator** is the most broadly based price index because it includes representative prices across the spectrum of GDP.

To understand a price index, the concept of the base period is critical. The *base period* is an arbitrarily selected initial time period against which other time periods are compared. The price index is arbitrarily assigned a value of 100 during the base period. For instance, the base period for the CPI is presently 1982 to 1984, and the CPI has been assigned an average value of 100 over that period of time.

Table 11A-2 reproduces selected values for the CPI. The table shows, for example, that the CPI for 1951 equals 26. That value means that a dollar's worth of consumer purchases in the base period would have cost twenty-six cents in 1951. The table also shows that the CPI for 1989 equals 124. On average, a consumer would have needed $1.24 to pay for the purchases that cost a dollar during the base period.

If it were possible to count all the prices in the economy, the number of different prices would likely be in the millions. It is unrealistic to expect so many prices to be used

TABLE 11A-2	*Selected Values of the Consumer Price Index*
Year	**Consumer Price Index**
1951	26
1961	29.9
1971	40.6
1981	90.9
1989	124.0
1990	130.7
1991	136.2
1992	140.3
1993	144.5
1994	148.2
1995	152.4

Source: *1996 Economic Report of the President,* Table B-56.

in the construction of price indexes. Indeed, the calculation of the CPI is based upon only about two hundred and fifty items that consumers purchase. This collection of goods and services used in the calculation of the CPI is called the *market basket*. The market basket represents a sampling of the most important items that consumers buy.

The items included in the market basket are periodically examined, with some items discarded and new items included, as the pattern of consumer spending changes. When this action is taken, a new base period and CPI series is declared, since measuring the prices of different market baskets would literally involve comparing apples to oranges.

Because the CPI has updated the market basket only about once a decade, it has not captured the efforts of consumers to substitute cheaper goods for more expensive ones. Nor does it catch the introduction of new goods. Because of these distortions, it has been estimated that for at least the last decade, the CPI has overstated inflation by one percent per year or more. Since Social Security and other payments are adjusted upward with increases in the CPI, the federal budget deficit has been magnified.

When there is a continuing increase in a wide variety of prices, the economy is said to experience ongoing inflation. An **inflation rate** for any year is calculated by taking the percentage change in a price index as follows:

$$\text{Inflation rate} = \frac{\text{change in price index}}{\text{initial price index}} \times 100$$

For example, from Table 11A-2, the CPI equaled 140.3 in 1992 and equaled 144.5 in 1993. The change in the CPI was 4.2 units, equal to 144.5 minus 140.3. When 4.2 is divided by 140.3, the annual rate is inflation is seen to be 2.99 percent. If the inflation rate is negative, *deflation* is said to occur. That would happen if the CPI declined in value from one year to the next.

Disinflation differs from either inflation or deflation. *Disinflation* means that the rate of inflation declines. For instance, if we observed a time series of inflation rates of 7 percent and 2 percent in two consecutive years, disinflation would have occurred. Disinflation occurred during some years of the 1980s.

Real versus Nominal Values

Increases in economic variables may occur as a consequence of inflation, which "pumps up" the value of macro variables. An increase in GDP due solely to price increases does not increase economic welfare, just as an increase in wages that is completely offset by higher prices leaves workers no better off. We can use a price index to adjust economic measures for the effects of inflation.

The **nominal value** of a variable is expressed in current dollar terms. Nominal values may be considered as "what you see is what you get," because nominal values are not adjusted for inflation. The **real value** of a variable adjusts for inflation. The real value is expressed in terms of the value of the dollar during a selected base period. The time period chosen as the base period is not very important. What is important is that each year's measuring units be the same—dollars with the same purchasing power. A time series of real GDP would reveal how much output actually grows over time.

The distinction between real and nominal values is important to individuals. Consider a worker whose weekly pay increases from $100 to $110. That worker has experienced a 10 percent increase in nominal income. If prices have remained constant, the worker's real income is also 10 percent greater. However, if prices have increased by 10 percent, the $110 of current income will purchase only as much as $100 purchased in the past. That means that the real income has not changed.

The following formula shows how to use a price index:

$$\text{Real value} = \frac{\text{nominal value}}{\text{price index}} \times 100$$

This formula applies to our personal economy. For example, suppose Jack earned $39,000 in the base year and $40,500 in the current year, a 3.8 percent increase. If the price index in the current year equals 105, Jack's real income in the current year is ($40,500/105) × 100 which equals $38,571.43. Jack's real income, which measures his purchasing power, has fallen since the base year.

The same formula applies to aggregate economic measures. To calculate the real value of GDP, we would use the price index designed for that purpose, the GDP deflator, as follows:

$$\text{Real GDP} = \frac{\text{nominal GDP}}{\text{GDP deflator}} \times 100$$

For example, as seen in Table 11A-3, nominal GDP equaled $6.931 trillion in 1994. The GDP deflator, with 1987 as the base year, equaled 126.3 (rounded to one decimal place) in 1994. Real GDP thus equaled $5.488 trillion, about 20.9 percent higher than the $4.540 trillion figure for GDP in the base year. Note that nominal GDP grew more rapidly than real GDP. Nominal GDP will always grow more rapidly than real GDP when inflation pumps up the nominal figure. Thus, the difference of $1.443 trillion between real and nominal GDP in 1994 is due solely to inflation. Table 11A-3 shows rounded values for nominal and real GDP for selected years. The real GDP figures have been "deflated" using the GDP deflator.

TABLE 11A-3   *Nominal and Real Gross Domestic Product*

Selected Years	Nominal GDP (in trillions)	GDP Deflator	Real GDP (in trillions of 1987 dollars)
1961	$0.532	26.3	$2.023
1971	1.097	37.1	2.957
1981	3.031	78.9	3.842
1987	4.540	100.0	4.540
1988	4.900	103.9	4.716
1989	5.251	108.5	4.840
1990	5.546	113.3	4.895
1991	5.725	117.6	4.868
1992	6.020	120.9	4.979
1993	6.343	123.5	5.136
1994*	6.931	126.3	5.488

Source: Adapted from *1995 Economic Report of the President,* Tables B-1 and B-3, and *1996 Economic Report of the President,* Tables B-1, B-3, and B-4.

*1994 data computed with different methodology than in previous years.

Measuring Unemployment

An economy with unemployment is wasting resources and producing at a point inside the production possibility frontier. The concept of unemployment applies to any resource that lies idle. In common usage, however, unemployment refers to idle labor rather than idle capital.

The Labor Force

The U.S. **civilian labor force** is composed of persons age sixteen and over, excluding those in the military, who are either employed or actively looking for paid work. The labor force typically expands as the population of persons over age sixteen increases and as job opportunities improve.

Table 11A-4 shows population, civilian labor force, and unemployment data for 1979 to 1995. When the ratio of the civilian labor force to the population age sixteen and over is calculated, the result is the *labor force participation rate*. The most notable aspect of the data in the table is the consistent increase in the participation rate. This trend is primarily due to the increase in the participation of women in the U.S. labor force.

TABLE 11A-4 *Population, Labor Force, and Unemployment 1979–1995*

Year	Population Age 16 and Over (millions of persons)	Civilian Labor Force (millions of persons)	Labor Force Participation Rate (in percent)	Number of Unemployed (in millions)	Unemployment Rate (unemployed/ civilian labor force)
1979	164.9	105.0	63.7	6.1	5.8
1980	167.7	106.9	63.8	7.6	7.1
1981	170.1	108.7	63.9	8.3	7.6
1982	172.3	110.2	64.0	10.7	9.7
1983	174.2	111.6	64.0	10.7	9.6
1984	176.4	113.5	64.4	8.5	7.5
1985	178.2	115.5	64.8	8.3	7.2
1986	180.6	117.8	65.3	8.2	7.0
1987	182.8	119.9	65.6	7.4	6.2
1988	184.6	121.7	65.9	6.7	5.5
1989	186.4	123.9	66.5	6.5	5.3
1990	188.0	124.8	66.4	6.9	5.5
1991	189.8	125.3	66.0	8.4	6.7
1992	191.6	127.0	66.3	9.4	7.4
1993	193.6	128.0	66.2	8.7	6.8
1994	196.8	131.1	66.6	8.0	6.1
1995	198.6	132.3	66.6	7.4	5.6

Source: 1996 Economic Report of the President; Table B-33.

Unemployment Rates

To be counted as unemployed a person must be at least sixteen years of age and without work, but actively looking for a job. Separating the employed from the unemployed would seem easy, but there are many details to consider. For example,

- Does an individual who works only an hour per week for pay have a job? Yes, because people are counted as employed regardless of how few hours they work, just so long as it's one hour a week or more for pay.
- Can someone who works without pay be counted as employed? Again, yes, just so long as that person is working in a family business for at least fifteen hours a week.
- Does going to school count as having a job? No. For students, school may seem to be a full-time job, but it's not considered in that light by government statisticians. Neither are students counted among the unemployed, unless they are looking for jobs.

The Bureau of Labor Statistics (BLS) estimates the number of employed and unemployed, and hence the unemployment rate, through the results of a monthly survey of 60,000 households. As a check on the accuracy of that survey, the government also surveys business establishments to count the number of jobs. The number of jobs and the number of people employed ought to match, if these two surveys are accurate. Unfortunately, in 1994 the BLS was forced to tinker with its household survey methodology because of discrepancies in the results of the two surveys. As of this writing, labor economists remain disturbed over the possible lack of accuracy of the unemployment data.

The unemployment rate is the ratio of the number of unemployed persons to the number of persons in the labor force. The last column in Table 11A-4 shows yearly average unemployment rates. The unemployment rate, while useful, does not tell us all we would like to know about the labor market. Some workers who have part-time jobs would like to have full-time jobs. Those workers are *underemployed*. Other workers would like to have a job, but have tried unsuccessfully to find one in the past and have given up looking. Because they have stopped looking, they are not counted in the unemployment statistics. Such would-be workers are called **discouraged workers**. **If discouraged workers were counted as unemployed, the reported unemployment rate would rise**. Discouraged workers were estimated by the Labor Department to number 550,000 persons in 1994.

Concerns over the accuracy and meaning of the unemployment rate have led economists to have a saying about it: "The unemployment rate is like a hot dog. It's hard to tell what's in it." People are unemployed for a variety of reasons, with some reasons of more concern than others. For example, some people are unemployed because they have voluntarily left their jobs. These unemployed persons are of less concern than the unemployed who have been involuntarily laid off. Some other people who are unemployed are actually earning incomes in the underground economy. **The underground economy causes the reported unemployment rate to overstate true unemployment.**

The unemployment rate does not tell us the duration of unemployment—how long people have been unemployed. Short spells of unemployment among workers are of less concern than long-term unemployment. An examination of the unemployed reveals that most unemployment is of short duration; a 1990 survey revealed only 1.3 percent of the unemployed were without work for more than fifteen weeks. In 1994 one-third of all cases of unemployment lasted less than five weeks.

OBSERVATION POINT: Demography and the Twenty-First Century Labor Force

Demography is the study of population statistics. Demographers offer us small glimpses of the future in which we can have a great deal of confidence. Birth rates and death rates change slowly. Therefore, demographers can predict how many people of various ages will comprise the labor force in ten, twenty, even thirty years into the future.

Demographers tell us to expect an aging work force. The large numbers of baby boomers born from 1946 to the mid-1960s were followed by the much smaller number of babies born in the 1970s and 1980s. As the baby boomers grow older, with fewer young workers entering the labor force, the average age of the labor force must rise. That fact has important consequences for labor productivity, Social Security, the health care system, and other aspects of life in the twenty-first century. Demographers warn us that we should begin to plan for those consequences now.

Identifying Various Types of Unemployment

Unemployment can be divided into the following four types:

- *Frictional*—associated with entering the labor market or switching jobs;
- *Seasonal*—unemployment that can be predicted to recur periodically, according to the time of year;
- *Structural*—caused by a mismatch between a person's human capital and that needed in the workplace. This mismatch can be caused by an evolving structure of the economy as some industries rise and others fall. It can also be caused by minimum wage laws or other structural *rigidities* that inhibit job creation or the movement of workers into new jobs;
- *Cyclical*—resulting from a downturn in the business cycle and affecting workers simultaneously in many different industries.

Structural and cyclical unemployment are usually of most concern, because they represent *involuntary unemployment*, meaning that employees have little choice in the matter. In contrast, frictional and seasonal unemployment frequently represent *voluntary unemployment*, which can be planned for and more easily overcome.

SEASONAL AND FRICTIONAL—WAITING FOR THE OLD OR SWITCHING TO THE NEW   Seasonal unemployment affects workers in agriculture, many tourism-related occupations, education, tax accounting, professional sports, and some other industries. There is usually little concern over this unemployment, because it can be planned for—it is part of the job. Workers are not even counted as unemployed if they have labor contracts that restart after the off-season, such as often occurs in teaching and professional sports.

Frictional unemployment occurs when people are between jobs, either because they were fired and have yet to line up new jobs or have quit voluntarily, such as in preparation for moving somewhere else or trying something new. Either way, their stay on the unemployment roles is likely to be brief. Frictional unemployment also includes many young people entering the labor market for the first time and older workers reentering the workforce after an absence, such as for rearing children.

Changing jobs does not imply frictional unemployment. Most voluntary job switching is done without it; people line up new jobs before leaving their old ones. However, involuntary job changes, such as in response to layoffs and firings, commonly do result in frictional unemployment. In the case of involuntary frictional unemployment, publicly provided unemployment compensation acts as a safety net. It allows the job seeker to hold out longer in search of the best job opportunity.

STRUCTURAL—HUMAN CAPITAL MISMATCHES AND LABOR MARKET RIGIDITIES Changes in the structure of the economy can give rise to **structural unemployment**, as demands for some types of goods and services give way to demands for others. This change in structure arises from such factors as technological change, international trade, and changing ways of doing business. For example, computers and telecommunications have opened doors to many types of jobs, but have cost many types of jobs, too.

Former telegraph operators exemplify structural unemployment. Once a valuable skill, the ability to speedily send coded messages over telegraph lines now has no market. Telegraph operators who were displaced by the technology of telephones could not easily find other employment at comparable wages. Their skills were not in demand. Until they retrained or found new jobs (usually at much lower wages), the ex–telegraph operators were structurally unemployed.

Rigidities that inhibit labor movement and the creation of new jobs can also cause structural unemployment. For example, the federal minimum wage law introduces a rigidity by making it difficult for workers with little human capital to find a job. Further rigidities arise from the regional nature of many jobs. For example, there may be pockets of unemployment in inner cities and some regions of the country, while there are plenty of job openings in suburbia or other states. If regional migration were without cost, such locational rigidities would vanish.

Human capital is often specific to a particular firm or kind of job—**specific human capital**—and does not apply readily to other firms or in other jobs. As telegraph operators learned the hard way, workers with specific human capital are most prone to structural unemployment. It is a risk that people take voluntarily, since the best-paying jobs usually involve specific human capital. In contrast, *general human capital* involves such skills as communication, reasoning, and math. General human capital is easily transferred from job to job. Those who possess it are less likely to be structurally unemployed. For most students, an economics education represents general human capital. However, graduate training in economics is more specialized, and thus represents specialized human capital.

Structural unemployment is a necessary part of economic evolution. Without structural unemployment, there would be no progress—no industrial revolution, no railroad, no automobile, no computer. Those skilled workers who lose their jobs often find the transition to new jobs difficult, since economic change has depreciated the human capital that supported their incomes. They are usually forced to evaluate their alternatives, and either take a job with lower pay or drop out of the labor force to retire or learn new skills.

A

Examples of structural unemployment are frequently poignant, involving older workers who have advanced high up career ladders that collapse out from under them. Sometimes the reason involves imports. For example, the U.S. imports much of its steel from countries of Europe and the Far East. Blast furnaces in America's "rust belt" that were built before World War II could not compete with the newer, more technologically advanced facilities in other countries. In response, America's primary steel producers laid off many highly skilled workers. Those skills and a powerful union had combined to increase steelworkers' earnings to levels far above what they could earn in other occupations. Does a fifty-year-old exsteelworker go back to school and start over, compete with teenagers for a minimum-wage job, or retire early and hope the money holds out? The choices are painful.

Structural unemployment is not only in blue-collar jobs. Corporations have eliminated many white-collar managerial jobs in corporate downsizings in recent years. Like their blue-collar counterparts, former managers find that job openings are few and competition is fierce. Their choices are often little better than those of the fifty-year-old steelworker just mentioned.

Government sometimes offers job-training programs to cushion the blows of structural unemployment. The question arises, though, as to the form of that training. For example, should government train hair stylists? That would take the jobs of other hair stylists or force them to work at lower wages. Such human capital is also so specific that it would not be pertinent for many of the structurally unemployed. The fifty-year-old steelworker would probably not enroll.

CYCLICAL—A SYSTEMIC DISORDER   A troublesome form of unemployment is caused by downturns in the business cycle, *panics* as they were called in the nineteenth century. In these periodic downturns, people in numerous sectors of the economy lose their jobs simultaneously. As incomes drop, spending drops, and the panics feed on themselves in a vicious cycle. There just does not seem to be enough spending to go around, at least for awhile. Cyclical unemployment is thus a systemic disorder felt throughout the economy. The question of how to ameliorate the business cycle and the cyclical unemployment it brings has motivated a seemingly endless debate among macroeconomists. Alternative perspectives on this issue will be discussed in chapter 12.

*M*easuring the Business Cycle

Stages of the Business Cycle

The term **business cycle** refers to the expansions and contractions in economic activity that take place over time. Figure 11A-1 shows the stages of a business cycle as a smooth curve. The low point in economic activity is called the *trough*. Following the trough is the *expansion* stage. When the expansion is ready to end, the economy reaches its *peak*, and then falls into *recession*. Officially, recessions are defined as three consecutive quarters of declining GDP. An especially severe recession is termed a *depression*. Subsequently, another trough will mark the point where the process begins repeating itself.

In the real world, the ups and downs in the economy do not occur in such a smooth fashion. Expansions typically last much longer and are much stronger than recessions.

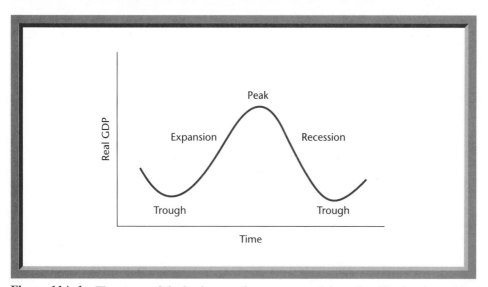

Figure 11A-1 **The stages of the business cycle** are not smooth in reality. The duration and intensity of stages can differ dramatically over time.

Thus the business cycle occurs within the context of a rising trend. Figure 11A-2 reveals the upward course of GDP over time.

Seasonal Adjustments—Helping to Isolate Cyclical Effects

Many economic variables move either up or down at the same time each year. For example, construction activity slows down during the winter because of bad weather and picks up during the warmer months. Retail sales increase during the Christmas season. Agriculture follows seasonal patterns. Thus, downswings in economic activity do not always indicate recession, just as upswings do not always signal expansion.

These seasonal effects make it difficult to disentangle actual growth in economic variables from changes due to seasonal volatility. That is why most published data are seasonally adjusted, using statistical models to make the adjustments. Seasonal adjustments to data help reveal the underlying trends. For example, when construction activity drops off in January, the seasonally adjusted data can tell us whether the decline is merely the usual winter slowdown or whether construction is stronger or weaker than usual for that time of year.

Seasonal adjustments can reveal unusual strength or weakness in the economy. For example, if the seasonal adjustment shows that the January decline in construction is not as sharp as usual, and many other economic measures are also above their seasonal norms, we have compelling evidence that the economy is expanding.

Reading the Indicators—Leads and Lags

Who decides when the economy leaves one stage of the business cycle and enters the next stage? Surprisingly, that job is not left to government economists, whose judgment might be swayed by political considerations. Instead, an independent organization, the National

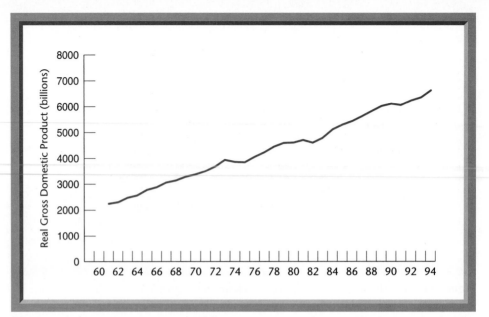

Figure 11A-2   **The rising trend of GDP** becomes apparent when real GDP is viewed over many years.

Bureau of Economic Research (NBER), is entrusted with the dating of business cycle turning points.

Because important indicators of the economy such as GDP, employment, and industrial production sometimes move opposite to each other, the job of the NBER is a difficult one. In many instances, the NBER will not announce the onset of a recession until it has observed the indicators for months. There are also often delays in dating the beginning of expansions. The NBER clearly does not wish to suffer the embarrassment and loss of confidence that would occur if it called the economy wrong.

There are hundreds of economic indicators capable of illuminating various aspects of the economy. Experience has shown that some of these indicators, called **leading indicators**, will usually change direction before the economy does. Examples include the index of building permits, housing starts, and manufacturers' new orders for durable goods. These data series and several others are combined to form a composite index of leading indicators, which receives much attention from the media. Other indicators, the *lagging indicators*, usually change direction only after the economy has already done so. The unemployment rate and expenditures on new plants and equipment are examples. Many indicators change direction about the same time the economy changes direction. These are called *coincident indicators*. Examples include the index of industrial production and the prime interest rate charged by banks.

Investors and businesspersons find the concept of the leading indicators to be especially interesting. If the leading indicators always worked with perfection, people could profit from the knowledge that the economy was going to change direction. Unfortunately, the leading indicators do not always give an accurate prediction of the future direction of the economy, and thus must be used with care.

OBSERVATION POINT: What Ever Happened to the Great Depression of 1990?

Prophets of gloom and doom have always prospered, at least until enough time passes for everyone to see that their predictions were wrong. Perhaps there is a part of human nature that likes a good scare. Modern-day Chicken Littles tend to be more concerned with the economy than with a falling sky. There always seem to be new volumes on the shelves of bookstores that predict impending disaster for the economy.

In the late 1980s, economist Ravi Batra's *The Great Depression of 1990* reached best-seller status by scaring readers with predictions of another Great Depression. Many such doomsday books refer to the theories of Nicholai Kondratiev (1892–1938), a Russian business cycle theorist who was banished to Siberia during the reign of Stalin. Kondratiev believed that capitalist economies moved in long, predictable cycles. Some of his modern-day disciples interpret his work as predicting a catastrophic, worldwide downturn in economic activity in the 1990s. Although a minor recession did occur in 1991, we are still waiting for the big one!

EXPRESS STUDY TRUE OR FALSE

1. GDP does not count intermediate goods.
2. Net investment equals gross investment minus ~~taxation.~~ *depreciation*
3. The consumer price index is calculated for a market basket of about 250 goods.
4. The labor force includes the unemployed who are seeking work.
5. A person with general human capital is ~~more~~ *less* likely to be structurally unemployed than a person with specific human capital.
6. The unemployment rate is a ~~leading~~ *lagging* indicator of economic activity.

EXPLORATION 1
*Assessing Economic Performance—It's Hard to Know the Present,
So Dare We Predict the Future?*

*Measures of economic performance are highly imperfect. Government must use
these measures, though, so that it can evaluate its own performance. This raises
a concern. If too much weight is attached to economic measures, will the
measures themselves become corrupted?*

*A*re You Better Off?

"Are you better off now than you were four years ago?" Every presidential election, one
candidate or another suggests that we ask ourselves that question. After all, there is no
one better positioned to know how we are doing than we are. Nevertheless, as you have
seen in this chapter, government does attempt to compute objective measures of economic
performance.

Measures of GDP, inflation, unemployment, and other standards of economic performance often seem straightforward. Interpreting them is the tricky part. Consider the
CPI, representing the price of a bundle of many different items purchased by consumers.
According to the CPI calculation, computers have been subject to deflation, because the
price per unit of computing power has declined dramatically over the last quarter century.
Thus, computers are responsible for lowering the inflation rate in the overall CPI index
below what it otherwise would have been.

Along with the reduction in computer prices, however, has also come a behavioral
change. Specifically, more powerful equipment has become a necessity to stay computer
literate. In other words, computer users who wish to communicate in the modern world
must be proficient on modern equipment running modern software. The money and time
needed to keep up with these ever-multiplying changes has risen, not fallen. Thus, while
computer prices have fallen in a microeconomic sense, they may have risen in the macro
sense of staying connected in the information economy.

This situation brings up the question of lifestyle. Microeconomics tells us that both
buyers and sellers gain when purchases are made. Thus, our quality of life would seem
to have risen dramatically, judging by the huge sales of cars, phones, calculators, computers, and other items embodying modern technology. Yet, the myriad of choices we
make as individuals have an effect on the world we must cope with every day. Inventions
have changed this world dramatically from what it used to be. Along with greater efficiency have come many more things to know and do. Tasks have gotten simpler, but life
has gotten more complex.

Just looking at aggregate economic statistics, it might be hard to fathom how anyone could be nostalgic for the past. After all, GDP is up, and so is the variety of goods and services we can buy. Yet, price indices and GDP measure only goods and services sold in the marketplace, valued at their market prices. There is more to life.

Unmeasured *intangibles* of value include simplicity, love, freedom, harmony, neighborliness, and many other qualities. By the same token economic statistics also ignore intangible "bads," such as pollution, feeling trapped, loneliness, and traffic congestion.

Then there are the things that are measured, but that do not actually indicate that the economy is better off. For example, increases in military spending increase GDP, but do nothing to directly increase a country's welfare if the spending merely offsets that of its enemies. Increased spending on cigarettes could ultimately do harm, yet such spending increases GDP in the same way as increased spending on education and health care. Some spending increases pollution, traffic congestion, and public health problems, or otherwise makes us worse off.

A single *measure of economic welfare (MEW)* that could take into account the effects of spending on the overall standard of living would be an informative adjunct to the GDP statistics. Although economists and social scientists have tried to develop such a measure, their efforts have failed to lead to a widely accepted MEW. The upshot is that, while macro measures are useful handles on the economy, they cannot answer that ultimate question: Are you better off?

*H*olding the Line on Federal Spending—The Tyranny of the Budget

The federal government must have answers, even if they are not the ultimate answers. It must know whether there are macroeconomic problems. If there are problems, it must know how serious those problems are. Otherwise, government cannot know which actions to take, or even whether to take action at all. Thus, it turns to economic statistics.

Some economists would say that government should ignore the aggregate economy, and just focus on prudent budgetary practices. If the government follows sensible rules, they say, the economy will take care of itself. However, whether or not the government's best macro policy strategy is active or passive, it is still necessary to track economic performance. The reason is that government policies affect the rest of the economy, which in turn affects government revenues and expenses. Without knowing revenues and expenses, government cannot budget effectively.

Of course, just knowing economic data does not mean that government will choose to budget sensibly. The ongoing federal budget deficit—a shortfall of federal revenues below expenses—is evidence. The federal government has incurred a budget deficit every year since 1969. In response to citizen outrage over this, Congress has revised its budgetary practices. As we will see, the result has been to give economic statistics a more central role than ever before.

In 1985, in an attempt to lead the federal budget into balance, Congress passed the Gramm-Rudman-Hollings Act. This legislation set specific deficit-reduction targets. Each time targets were not met, the act called for across-the-board budget cuts that would bring spending into line with those targets. According to the Gramm-Rudman targets, the federal deficit was to be eliminated by 1991.

When 1991 rolled around, the federal budget deficit was $267 billion dollars, higher than it had ever been before. What happened? Well before 1991, Congress had modified and then abandoned the Gramm-Rudman-Hollings approach. The across-the-board budget axe was not used. It fell victim to special interests, especially the interests of Social Security recipients. Too much spending was exempted from cuts.

Congress has instead instituted a different set of budgetary procedures to add some integrity to the budget process. Specifically, in the Budget Enforcement Act of 1990, Congress legislated that policy changes should not increase the budget deficit. Thus, policy changes that would add to the budget deficit must be balanced by other changes that would offset that effect. Doing so sounds reasonable, but brings back that basic statistical problem—measuring the effects on government revenues and expenses of alternative public policies. As we will see, these statistics are not immune from politics.

*S*tatic Assumptions about a Dynamic Economy

Is government able to forecast the effects of policy changes? In 1990 Congress imposed a surcharge on luxuries, including among other things, new yachts and other luxury boats. Immediately after the so-called luxury tax took effect, orders for new yachts all but disappeared. Although the tax rate was higher, government revenue from boat sales was much lower. Overall the luxury tax did bring in more money, but the amount was about $13 million by 1993, rather than the $76 million over that period that was designated in the Congressional budget.

Although the revenue effect of the luxury tax could have been predicted with much greater accuracy, the Budget Enforcement Act did not allow Congress to do so in its budgetary calculations. Thus, the luxury tax surcharge was assumed to bring in $76 million dollars of extra revenue, which then allowed Congress to pass an additional $76 million of new spending programs.

This traditional manner of computing the effects of federal actions is known as **static scoring**, also termed *static revenue estimation*. Static scoring assumes no general change in behavior as a result of government policy changes. Hence, the effect of the luxury tax on demand was ignored. The alternative is called **dynamic scoring**, or *dynamic revenue estimation*, which does allow for consideration of all behavioral changes caused by changes in government policy.

Static scoring has led to other serious problems. Prior to its final passage in December 1994, for example, Congress was nearly forced to abandon the internationally negotiated revisions to the General Agreement on Tariffs and Trade (GATT). Negotiations over the GATT had dragged on for over seven years, as countries around the world sought to retain their special trade protections. The final agreement dramatically lowered trade barriers, thereby promoting free trade, which had been America's objective all along. The problem was those static scoring rules.

Although the entire purpose of reducing trade barriers was to promote trade, static scoring rules assumed that the volume of trade would remain constant. Thus, any tariff cut was automatically scored as a revenue-loser by the same percentage that the tariffs were cut. Budget rules meant that tariffs could not be cut without other policy changes that would add revenues or cut expenditures in other areas to offset the purported revenue loss. It was only through an extraordinary act of juggling user fees and

B

other elements of the budget that the Congressional budgetary rules were finally satisfied.

Static scoring is stupid, you might say. Everyone knows that taxes can change our behavior. For example, anticipating higher taxes after taking office in 1993, President and Hilary Clinton chose to receive Mrs. Clinton's sizable income from her law partnership on December 31, 1992. Conventionally, law firm partners would have received such income the next day, on January 1, 1993. Other Americans also anticipated a tax increase and acted accordingly.

Static scoring has been a budgetary mainstay because it provides an obvious baseline estimate, the baseline being the status quo. Analysts may know that behavior will change, but are unlikely to agree on exactly what forms the changes will take or how significant will be their effects. Because of such disagreement, dynamic scoring must inevitably lead to controversy.

*R*ecognizing *Reality, But Whose?*

Everyone in the budget process knows that static scoring gives wrong answers. Still, as the saying goes, the devil you know is better than the devil you don't know. If the government were to follow a dynamic scoring standard, who could tell what questionable assumptions would lie buried beneath the surface?

Consider the possibilities. In the early 1980s, *supply siders* sought to cut taxes in order to spur economic growth. Some members of this group, including ex-Congressman and then-current Budget Director David Stockman, based their arguments on the idea that cutting taxes would spur so much investment and extra work effort that tax revenues would go up. Although most economists at the time doubted that tax rates were so high that tax revenues would rise if rates were lowered, the idea that we could have our cake and eat it too was very appealing. Thus, taxes were cut in the hope that economic growth would so increase the size of the **tax base**—that which is taxed—that tax revenues would actually increase. After all, since

$$\text{Tax revenues} = \text{tax rate} \times \text{tax base}$$

a sufficiently large increase in the tax base could more than offset a decline in the tax rate.

After adjusting for inflation, tax revenues from the highest income group did indeed increase following the cut in tax rates. However, from other income groups, real tax revenues fell. In this case, Stockman's speculation was incorrect. More generally, do we wish to incorporate speculation into the budget process? If so, what would be the meaning of budgetary discipline?

The problem of budgetary discipline also arises on the spending side. As debate over static versus dynamic scoring heated up in 1995, advocates of social programs often found themselves attracted to the dynamic standard. For example, the director of an arts project in Saint Louis argued vehemently that balancing the federal budget by cutting back social programs could easily have the opposite effect. The idea is that money spent on art programs for inner-city youth fosters self-respect and self-confidence, which leads these youths into lives as productive, taxpaying citizens who give back many times more than they received. Thus, cutting social spending would threaten to increase rather than decrease budget deficits.

The issue of static versus dynamic scoring underscores the old adage that politics makes strange bedfellows. Conservatives seeking to cut taxes find themselves allied with liberals seeking to expand government spending on social programs. Both support dynamic scoring. On the other side are conservatives and liberals who fear political manipulation of the budget process. Whatever the immediate outcome of this tug-of-war, the issue will remain with us.

To Think or Not to Think, That is Government's Question

Is it better to continue with static scoring that we know gives wrong answers or to allow our elected officials the leeway to use their best judgments as to which forecasts to accept? Do we trust them to think well? Is it better to analyze and maybe get it wrong than not to analyze at all? That is the question.

PROSPECTING FOR NEW INSIGHTS

1. List some of the events in your personal life that have made you particularly happy or unhappy. To what extent were these goods and bads recorded in government statistics on the health of the economy? To the extent that government statistics failed to catch these occurrences, what was the reason?

2. As a taxpayer, do you support static or dynamic scoring? Which do you think is more likely to lead to lower taxes? To higher taxes? Explain your answers.

B

EXPLORATION 2
EDUCATIONAL SHORT STORY
Hitchhiking Across the Economy

An old expression says there are lies, damned lies, and statistics. In this story the defects of statistical data are pointed out. The characters and plot are fictional, but the issues relating to the calculation and reporting of statistics are accurately detailed here. The National Bureau of Economic Research, referred to in the final section of the story, really exists and performs the functions described.

"It's not supposed to happen like this. Not to me. I've done everything I was supposed to," I slowly murmur to no one in particular, one thought disconnected from the other. Then, dazed, I lean forward, accept the proffered pen, and sign the papers that are stripping me of my final connection to the mainstream economy.

Now that the bank has taken back the house, I'm a statistic—again! First, I lost my job as a financial analyst on Wall Street. Then Ellen left and took little Jill and Jason. Now, I'm homeless, a far cry from my starry-eyed youth an eternity ago. I wonder—is the government accurately recording my troubles in its statistics?

Aggregate Income and the Hitchhiker

Twenty-four hours and three rides after taking pen in hand I am in Dayton. First stop: a five-dollar-a-night bunkhouse for a night's sleep on a thin, lumpy mattress, and a chance at a job the next morning.

After a fitful rest, I am woken abruptly at 6:00 A.M., the brightness of the florescent ceiling lights in my eyes, the clanging of the wake-up bell in my ears. My last two dollars are paying for the "bunkhouse breakfast special"—lots of steaming hot coffee, toast, grits, and greasy eggs and sausage. Now bring on that job!

I have never seen such a mountain of clothing, eight feet high, shirt sleeves jumbled with pants legs—thrift shop donations all. I will spend the next nine hours sorting the good from the bad, the dirty from the clean, the torn from the mended. My mind wanders. I recall the economics that was ever present on Wall Street. I remember the time I stood in the boss's office explaining the intricacies of national income accounting. How could I explain it to Jim Say, the manager here at the thrift store?

I play the scene out in my mind as I sort. "Jim, the sale of castoff goods that keep the thrift store economy going is not recorded in gross domestic product. These goods do not result from current production. However, the value of my sorting services are included in GDP since that does contribute to current production." Hmm. I still know my stuff.

I already have extra work lined up. Mrs. Ogden, the heavily made-up seventy-year-old widow marches up to me while I am putting out T-shirts and declares, "Young man, Jimmy Say likes your work, and I need someone to paint my house. I'll give you five dollars an hour if you want to earn some money on your days off."

We soon strike a deal. It turns out that her late husband had prepared the walls for painting before he died. I wonder if she is aware that if she had hired me to do that job, the GDP would grow by whatever she would have paid me. Should I explain to Mrs. Ogden that do-it-yourself activities are similar to volunteer work for charitable organizations, and similar to housework, because none are included in GDP? No, but I do have an urge to talk economics with someone. Old habits die hard, I suppose.

The small, bent woman certainly knows at least a little economics. Before striding out of the store, she warns me, "You are going to be paid by check! I will not be a party to making the underground economy any bigger than it already is. The TV news people said that cash is unlikely to be reported as income on peoples' tax returns. I think everyone ought to pay their fair share of taxes!" Perhaps I will tell her later that unreported cash payments are omitted from official national income accounting statistics such as GDP. Economists are acutely aware that the income from illegal activities, and other income that is not reported to the Internal Revenue Service, is substantial enough to significantly bias the official GDP statistics.

A *Strange Encounter with Price Indices*

A few weeks in Dayton is enough. The cold winds of winter have begun to blow, and I need the succor of the Southern sun. So I'm hitching a ride south. Folks heading for Birmingham seem to be the most willing to give a poor hitchhiker a ride, so Birmingham it is.

On the last leg of the trip, my eyelids get heavier and heavier as the miles tick by in a blur. Soon I am asleep. With sleep comes a dream of being home with Ellen. My slumbering brain relives a scene from my marriage, a real-life incident that began when Ellen opened the envelope. "Hon, this is a bounced check notice from the bank. What happened to the checking account?"

"Let me see . . . uh-oh. My fault. I didn't make allowance for the big jump in property taxes this year, so I didn't pay close enough attention to the account balance when I wrote the check."

Ellen responded, "I thought inflation was running at less than 3 percent this year. Where could the money be going? We've never bounced a check before."

"That's true, but our personal price index is up over 10 percent, 10.4 percent to be exact. You see, the consumer price index is calculated on certain assumptions about how people spend their incomes. Our spending patterns do not match those in the CPI. Furthermore, the CPI does not include taxes in its calculation. Remember the controversy over the big increase in school taxes voted by the school board. Remember too that our car and homeowner's insurance took bigger jumps than the national average because of all the crime that's been happening locally. That's why I calculated our personal CPI."

"Wait a minute," Ellen objected. "I was watching a story on CNN last night that said the CPI overstates the inflation rate. People change their behavior to try to offset the effects of rising prices. For example, they buy more from discount stores and less from department stores. The CPI doesn't measure these kinds of changes in behavior, and that has serious effects on the budget deficit. Several members of Congress were interviewed for the story, and they noted that a number of government expenditures are tied to changes in the CPI. For example, Social Security payments rise in line with the CPI. Because the CPI overstates inflation, Social Security recipients receive bigger government checks than they are rightfully entitled to. The story concluded with a defense of the CPI by an economist at the Bureau of Labor Statistics, who basically said that it is impossible to design a price index that is completely accurate."

"Right, Ellen. Sounds like CNN did a good job on that story. And that Bureau economist is correct. It is quite expensive to survey consumers to see what they actually buy. Such surveys are normally taken at intervals many years apart. So the CPI doesn't really measure what people actually buy, and that creates problems. Even though the CPI overstates inflation for most consumers, for our family it understates inflation. Some families experience more inflation than others."

The blare of a horn wakes me. For a moment, in that nether world of half-sleep and half-consciousness, I thought I was home. What I wouldn't give to really be there.

Of Victims, Deadbeat Dads, and Statistics

Birmingham is warmer than Dayton, but the haze that screens out the sun is not what I need. So I drop the $20 I have earned into an envelope addressed to Ellen and the kids. Later, I stand at the edge of I-59 with thumb extended. I know where I want to go: New Orleans, Houston, San Antonio, Phoenix, and ultimately the big L.A.—the quicker the better!

I have skipped too many meals in order to send money to Ellen. I need to eat. After several days and 900 miles on the road, hunger prompts me to stop and scout around San Antonio for work. I spend the next few days working as a handyman. To save money I sleep in what has to be the cleanest, quietest dumpster in town.

With enough cash in my pocket to feel confident of avoiding starvation, I am ready to go. The sun directly above me, heading for I-10, I am tramping along a little-used railroad track that is surrounded by brush country. Then it happens. In a flash, he jumps from behind a small tree and swings the empty whisky bottle, catching me square in the forehead. I don't have time to duck, and I am unconscious before I hit the ground.

The sun is low in the sky when I come to. Blood is still oozing from the throbbing cut on my forehead, but I know I will live.

My precious meal money! Of course it is gone. I am afraid he might come back, so I stagger a hundred yards or so in the direction of the highway, and move away from the tracks as darkness sets in. I sit with my torso propped against a scrubby live oak and fall asleep. Next morning, my head is clear and I think of reporting the assault and robbery to the police, but I am afraid. I thus join the ranks of millions of Americans who fail to report crimes. Some people don't bother because they understand that some crimes are unlikely to be solved. Others simply don't trust the police. Either way, it biases the crime statistics downward. In my case I am afraid I might be arrested. Yes, I confess. I may be a criminal.

When Ellen left with the kids she sued me for child support. In my heart, I know she did it for my own good. She thought that a court order might motivate me to try even harder to get a good job. The judge ordered me to pay up. The size of the monthly payment was based upon the income I had earned as a financial analyst. My protests that I couldn't find a job and that Ellen still had her job fell on deaf ears. The judge blamed me rather than the economy for my unemployed status, and warned me that I could be jailed for nonpayment. But the court's order is for an amount that seems infinitely more than I can make now.

Will I be arrested if I report the crime? I don't know for sure, but I don't want to find out. So I keep walking until I see a gas station. As I clean up in the restroom I pray that the cut will heal without becoming infected. I don't know how I could pay for medical treatment.

Vignettes of an Economy in Transition

Now my journey is over. Life for me can begin again in Los Angeles, as it has for the hundreds of thousands who have made it their destination. The sounds of dozens of foreign tongues excite my senses. This model of the city of the future teems with those who began their new life here more disadvantaged than me. If they can make it, so can I!

As night falls, I spy a vacant lot that a group of the homeless have turned into a refuge. They welcome me. A small fire to ward off the chill, a dilapidated sofa and chair, and flattened cardboard box beds with crumpled newspaper pillows provide evidence of the effort to supply the comforts of a real home. An article catches my eye on one of the pages of my pillow. It says the National Bureau of Economic Research, the private, not-for-profit association of economists that the government relies upon to interpret the business cycle, has just concluded that the recession ended thirteen months ago. The economy has entered the recovery phase that always follows a recession. That's good news, but it reminds me of how difficult it is to make sense of an economy.

If the economy is really recovering, why did I meet so many discouraged workers during my journey. There was Martha, for example. When the clothing factory she worked at in San Antonio moved to Haiti, she tried to find another job. She was a part of the unemployment statistics then. Now, since she quit looking for work, she is not counted as unemployed. Is that the right way to measure unemployment? And with so many Marthas, is the economy really in recovery? In spite of the official declaration that the recession has ended, one never really knows.

I turn my attention to more optimistic thoughts—maybe tomorrow I'll get a job. When I do, I'll take my first dollar and put it in the slot in that "three-minutes-for-a-dollar" long-distance phone I saw up the street. It will be good to hear the voices of Ellen and the kids. In GDP the value of my call will be recorded as one dollar. To me, it will be worth so much more than that.

PROSPECTING FOR NEW INSIGHTS

1. Some people will believe that what happened to the main character in this story could never happen to them. Do you think that the economy is an important determinant of poverty and homelessness, or do you think that poverty and homelessness are more the fault of the individual? Discuss.

2. Converting cardboard boxes into beds is a part of the underground economy that escapes government statistics. You have probably also observed or participated in the underground economy. List some examples.

B

CHALLENGE 1
The National Income and Product Accounts

The purpose of national income accounting is to summarize the millions of daily economic transactions in a form that economists, government planners, politicians, and others can easily use and understand. The development of the national income and product accounts began in the 1930s in response to the need to evaluate depressed economic conditions, and the growing realization that the government's existing collection of data meant that it already possessed the primary data that could be used to construct the accounts.

The Bureau of Economic Analysis (BEA), an arm of the U.S. Department of Commerce, is responsible for the preparation of the final reports detailing the national income and product statistics. These reports are prepared using data obtained from other government agencies. Individual tax returns, obtained from the Internal Revenue Service, are an important source of data. Survey data are also extensively employed.

Users of BEA data are familiar with the notion of preliminary and revised data. Preliminary data are estimates that are subject to change. Revised data incorporate changes in data made necessary as more complete information becomes available with the passage of time. Data may be revised several times before the BEA is satisfied with its accuracy. The process of revision can occasionally drag on for years.

Most data is available at quarterly or annual intervals, although some data is available monthly. The monthly Commerce Department publication, the *Survey of Current Business*, is the primary source of national income and product data. BEA-developed data can also be found in other government publications, including the annual *Economic Report of the President*.

In calculating GDP it is useful to recognize that every dollar of production creates an equivalent dollar of spending. **Since every dollar of spending generates a dollar of income for someone, the value of production and income are also equal.** Goods and services are produced and sold, with the dollars spent by purchasers being collected by businesses. These dollars go toward the payment of incomes—wages to workers, for example.

The equality of production and income means that GDP can be calculated in two ways, as seen in Table 11C1-1. On the left side of the table, GDP is obtained by measuring the total value of production. The **expenditures approach** sums spending on consumption, investment, government purchases, and the value of net exports. On the right side of the table, the **incomes approach** sums various income items plus other charges against GDP. Proprietor's income is received by persons who own unincorporated businesses, such as farmers and physicians. Net interest is interest received by individuals minus individuals' interest payments.

Because of imperfections in data collection, product and income are not exactly equal. This necessitates the inclusion of the statistical discrepancy as part of the "other charges" on the income side. Other complications associated with the income approach force the inclusion of several additional other charges. Capital consumption measures de-

TABLE 11C1-1 *Two Approaches to Measuring GDP*

Expenditures Approach	Incomes Approach
Personal Consumption Expenditures	**Compensation of Employees**
Durables	Wages and salaries
Nondurables	Supplements
Services	+
+	**Proprietor's Income**
Gross Private Domestic Investment	+
Business capital investment	**Rental Income of Persons**
New housing	+
Inventory change	**Corporate Profits**
+	+
Government Purchases	**Net Interest**
Federal	+
State and local	**Other Charges against GDP**
+	Capital consumption
Net Exports	Indirect business taxes
	Other items, net
	Statistical discrepancy
=	=
Gross Domestic Product	**Gross Domestic Product**

Source: Adapted from Federal Reserve Bank of Richmond, "The National Income and Product Accounts," *Macroeconomic Data: A User's Guide*, 3rd ed, 1994.

preciation in the nation's capital stock. Indirect business taxes are federal excise taxes and state and local sales taxes included in the value of purchases. These complications make the income approach less useful than the more straightforward expenditures approach for most macro analyses.

By making adjustments to GDP, other measures of aggregate economic activity can be calculated, as follows:

- *Gross national product (GNP)*

$$\text{GNP} = \text{GDP} + \text{income received by U.S. firms and workers outside the U.S.}$$
$$- \text{ income received by foreign firms and workers within the U.S.}$$

- *Net national product (NNP)*

$$\text{NNP} = \text{GNP} - \text{capital consumption}$$

- *National income (NI)*

$$\text{NI} = \text{NNP} - \text{indirect business taxes} - \text{business transfer payments} - \text{statistical}$$
$$\text{discrepancy} + \text{subsidies less surplus of government firms}$$

- *Personal income (PI)*

$$\text{PI} = \text{NI} - \text{corporate profits} - \text{net interest} - \text{social security taxes} - \text{wage accruals less}$$
$$\text{disbursements} + \text{government transfer payments to persons} + \text{personal interest}$$
$$\text{income} + \text{personal dividend income} + \text{business transfer payments to persons}$$

• *Disposable personal income (DPI)*

$$DPI = PI - \text{personal tax and nontax payments}$$

As the adjustments show, national income accounting can be quite complex. Each of the measures defined above is used for a specific purpose, thus justifying the effort. For example, disposable personal income shows how much income people actually have available to spend. Economists who forecast consumer spending find DPI to be useful in making predictions.

A detailed, nontechnical explanation of the national income accounts and subaccounts is contained in the article, "The National Income and Product Accounts" in *Macroeconomic Data: A User's Guide* (1994), published by the Federal Reserve Bank of Richmond. This article contains suggestions for further reading, including sources for detailed definitions of the items comprising the accounts and discussions of the justification and methodology for national income accounting.

CHALLENGE 2
Computing Price Indices—Chain Weights Link the Future to the Past

The consumer price index (CPI) and producer price index (PPI) are examples of **fixed-weight price indices**. This means that the indices begin by defining a base period during which the consumption of selected goods and services, called the market basket, is measured. The indices are then constructed assuming that the market basket remains unchanged, or fixed.

A simple example in which the CPI is calculated for a market basket of three goods can help clarify the procedure. Suppose we wish to calculate the CPI for a market basket of apples, oranges, and bananas. In the base period 5 apples, 4 oranges, and 2 bananas are purchased. The prices in the base period were 30 cents each for apples, 20 cents each for oranges, and 10 cents each for bananas. Now, apples are still 30 cents each, but oranges have also risen to 30 cents each, while bananas have risen to 20 cents each. The CPI calculation is as follows:

$$CPI = \frac{(30 \times 5) + (30 \times 4) + (20 \times 2)}{(30 \times 5) + (20 \times 4) + (10 \times 2)} = \frac{310}{250} = 1.24$$

In the base year the market basket cost $2.50. Now that same market basket costs $3.10. The index number of 1.24 indicates that the market basket costs 24 percent more than in the base year.

The CPI follows the practice of assigning a base-year value equal to 100, which merely involves multiplying all computed values by 100. The index we calculated would become 124. A comparison of the index number of 124 to the base year value of 100 still shows that the market basket costs 24 percent more now than in the base year.

C

To compute the inflation rate between two years, when neither is the base year, the formula is as follows:

$$\text{Inflation rate} = \frac{\Delta \text{CPI}}{\text{starting CPI}}$$

multiplied by 100 to put the value in percentage terms. To adjust Social Security payments or other payments for inflation, government increases them by this percentage.

Note that if people change their consumption patterns between the base year and the current year, this change has no effect on the CPI. For example, if people bought more apples and fewer oranges and bananas because the price of apples did not increase, while the prices of bananas and oranges did, the CPI would still be 124. In this instance, the CPI is misleading and biased. In fact, as prices change, people typically substitute relatively cheaper goods for goods that have become relatively more expensive. The inaccuracy introduced into the CPI by this behavior is termed the **substitution bias**. The CPI is also biased because it fails to account for quality changes and the introduction of new products. Both biases cause the CPI to overstate inflation in the actual cost of living. These biases are in the nature of price indices that use quantities as fixed weights.

Another type of price index, called an **implicit price deflator**, is a fixed-weight index that uses current quantities rather than base-period quantities. The GDP implicit price deflator is an example of this type of index. This method takes current quantities and calculates what they would have cost at prices prevailing during the base period.

An implicit price deflator embodies changes in quantities from year to year. This method is superior to that used to calculate the CPI in one respect; it more accurately portrays actual behavior. However, this type of index has its own disadvantage. When two periods other than the base period are compared, the index is difficult to interpret because the index mixes both price and quantity changes. If the CPI were calculated in this manner, it would understate the effects of inflation, because it would ignore expensive goods that people stopped buying. For example, our example earlier would use current-year quantities. If consumers in the current year bought 8 apples, 2 oranges, and 1 banana, our example would be changed to read:

$$\text{CPI} = \frac{(30 \times 8) + (30 \times 2) + (20 \times 1)}{(30 \times 8) + (20 \times 2) + (10 \times 1)} = \frac{320}{290} = 1.10$$

This manner of computation says that prices have risen by 10 percent rather than 24 percent under the other formula.

Beginning in 1996, the calculation of real GDP switched to using a **chain-weight index**. The chain-weight index eliminates the need to select a base year. In any given year, the chain-weight index averages two component indexes, the first using the current-year market basket, and the other using the prior-year market basket. The idea is to reach a middle ground between sole reliance on current-year quantities and sole reliance on base-year quantities. If the CPI were computed in this way, it would better approximate true inflation.

The term *chain weight* comes about because this index links quantities (weights) in two successive years, then moves forward a year and does that link again, and so forth. This continuous linking, two years at a time, forms a chain, and hence the name. For example, the calculation of 1995 GDP involves quantities for 1994 and 1995. Similarly, the calculation of 1996 GDP involves quantities for 1995 and 1996.

C

The introduction of the chain-weight index will reduce the bias inherent in the old fixed-weight method. For example, since the 1987 base year used in the fixed-weight calculation, the price of electronics has declined substantially. The drop in price has caused more electronic devices to be sold. Using the base-year price of electronics overstates the value of electronics, and thus causes real GDP to be overstated. Calculations by the Federal Reserve Bank of St. Louis show that between 1991 and 1994, the fixed-weight method overstated average annual real GDP growth by 0.44 percentage points. That is, the fixed-weight method showed that real growth averaged 3.16 percent per year, while the chain-weight method showed a 2.72 percent growth rate.

We can use our CPI example to illustrate how to compute a chain-weight index. To do so, we must assume that the base year in the example is one year prior to the current year. We also note that the chain-weight index uses a geometric average, which means we must multiply the two component indexes together and then take the square root of the product. Specifically,

$$\sqrt{(1.24 \times 1.10)} = \sqrt{1.364} = 1.17$$

In other words, rather than reporting inflation to be either 24 percent or 10 percent, the chain-weighted computation reports inflation to be 17 percent, which is likely to be a better approximation to the actual change in the cost of living.

A nontechnical reference to price indices is the subject of the article "Macroeconomic Price Indexes" in *Macroeconomic Data: A User's Guide* (1994), published by the Federal Reserve Bank of Richmond.

C

Study by Design

SpeedStudy

SpeedReview

In order to know whether the nation is meeting its macro goals, government collects data that measure the aggregate economy. Spending is categorized as consumption, investment, government purchases, and net exports. GDP is the most widely reported measure of the aggregate economy, although for many purposes, per capita GDP is useful. GDP is an imperfect measure of a nation's well-being, because it misses such things as the underground economy and many household services. Several price indices, including the CPI, the GDP deflator, and the PPI, measure inflation.

The unemployment rate must also be interpreted carefully, because of the existence of an underground economy and discouraged workers. Unemployment of labor comes in four basic types: seasonal, frictional, structural, and cyclical. Cyclical unemployment follows the business cycle, which is the sequence of recession, trough, expansion, and peak. Adjusting data seasonally can help interpret this cycle, and leading indicators can help predict it.

SpeedStudy True or False Self-Test

A1. Investment is the ~~most~~ *least* stable component of GDP.

A2. Generally, gross investment would be ~~less~~ *more* than net investment.

A3. Net exports equal imports minus exports. *imports*

p. 206 A4. The difference between GDP and GNP is that GDP includes net exports while GNP does not.

A5. *Per capita* GDP is GDP per person.

A6. The GDP deflator is the most broadly based price index because it includes prices of a wider assortment of outputs than the other indices.

A7. Inflation rates of 5 percent, 4 percent, and 3 percent in succeeding years indicate deflation. *disinflation*

A8. Demography is the study of population statistics. *p. 206*

A9. Whenever a person switches from one job to another, frictional unemployment must occur.

A10. The measured rate of unemployment might ~~overstate~~ *understate* actual unemployment due to the presence of discouraged workers.

B11. Intangibles are measured in the GDP statistics.

B12. The Gramm-Rudman-Hollings approach to balancing the budget has been especially successful.

B13. The sale of used goods is not included in GDP.

B14. The cash income earned from illegal activities is not included in GDP.

C15. To revise data means to adjust it for the effects of inflation.

C16. The only valid method to calculate GDP is to add up consumption, investment, government purchases, and net exports.

C17. The CPI and the GDP deflator are calculated in the same manner.

C18. Were the CPI to become a chain-weighted index, it would be less likely to overstate inflation.

The MasterMind

Selected Terms Along the Way

rule of seventy-two, 391
gross domestic product
  (GDP), 392
investment, 393
net investment, 393
net domestic product
  (NDP), 393
value added, 395
potential GDP, 395
gross national product
  (GNP), 395
underground economy, 396
consumer price index (CPI), 397

producer price index
  (PPI), 397
GDP deflator, 397
inflation rate, 398
nominal value, 398
real value, 398
civilian labor force, 400
discouraged workers, 401
frictional unemployment, 402
structural unemployment, 403
specific human capital, 403
business cycle, 404

leading indicators, 406
static scoring, 410
dynamic scoring, 410
tax base, 411

expenditures approach, 417
incomes approach, 417
fixed-weight price indices, 419
substitution bias, 420
implicit price deflator, 420
chain-weight index, 420

MasterMind Multiple Choice Self-Test

A1. Consumption spending is approximately
_____ percent of GDP.

  a. 30
  b. 40
  c. 50
  d. 70

A2. If all married couples were to divorce and pay
for household services performed,

  a. it would make no difference to the GDP accounts, since the government is not interested in private affairs of households.

  b. welfare of the average person would increase, because there would be more
  incomes.

  c. personal income would be unaffected, but
  the income distribution would change.

  d. GDP would increase.

A3. The underground economy in the U.S.

  a. is insignificant.

  b. measures the potential output forgone due to
  the existence of discouraged workers.

  c. causes measured unemployment rates to
  overstate actual unemployment.

  d. was in existence primarily in the years prior

to the Civil War, and was associated with
the movement of slaves by abolitionists.

A4. A year ago the price index equaled 125. Today
it equals 130. The inflation rate over the last
year is

  a. 130 percent.
  b. 125 percent.
  c. 5 percent.
  d. 4 percent.

$$\left(\frac{130-125}{125}\right) \times 100$$

A5. The stage of the business cycle that follows a
recession and precedes an expansion is called a

  a. peak.
  b. trough.
  c. recession.
  d. U-turn.

B6. The traditional technique the federal government uses to compute the effects of its actions
is termed

  a. dynamic scoring.
  b. static scoring.
  c. equilibrium scoring.
  d. hogwash.

B7. The consumer price index (CPI) generally
   a. states the inflation rate accurately.
   b. overstates the true inflation rate.
   c. understates the true inflation rate.
   d. measures the reactions of consumers and retailers to a variety of possible rates of inflation or deflation.

C8. The national income and product accounts statistics are published by the

   a. Office of Management and Budget.
   b. Council of Economic Advisors.
   c. Bureau of Economic Analysis.
   d. Internal Revenue Service.

C9. The CPI is computed as a _____ index.
   a. variable-weight
   b. fixed-weight
   c. heavy-weight
   d. chain-weight

MasterMind Questions and Problems Self-Test

A1. After obtaining the most recent copy of the *Economic Report of the President* from your library, compare the discussion of macroeconomic goals in this chapter with those discussed in the *Report*. Are all the goals mentioned in the chapter also in the *Report*? What statistics are quoted in the *Report* to buttress the views of its authors?

A2. The misery index is defined as the sum of the inflation rate plus the unemployment rate. Some people who are not economists claim that the misery index is a good measure of economic welfare. Evaluate the misery index against per capita GDP as a measure of economic well-being.

A3. Explain how, as actual consumption varies from the market basket, the CPI becomes distorted.

A4. Can you think of a logical reason for excluding persons under the age of sixteen from the labor force statistics, but not excluding persons over age sixty-five or even age seventy from the statistics?

A5. List three instances in your own life when you or someone you know have been unemployed. For each, explain the type of unemployment, such as frictional, seasonal, structural, or cyclical.

B6. What are the problems with static and dynamic scoring? What are the advantages of each? After evaluating the advantages and problems, which method of scoring do you believe the government should use?

B7. Improving the accuracy of economic statistics and the speed with which they become available is costly. But policy decisions that go awry because of statistics that are inaccurate or misinterpreted are also costly.
   a. When should the government spend more to improve economic statistics?
   b. Select a particular economic statistic and assess its usefulness. What mistakes could users of the statistic make?
   c. How much of the detail of how government statistics are calculated should users know?

C8. If you manage a major chain of retail stores, and are developing your plans on how much inventory to stock for the Christmas season, in which of the national income and output measures would you be most interested in? Why?

C9. Some businesses grant employees yearly cost of living raises equal to the percentage increase in the CPI. Why is it important for the managers of such businesses to know how the CPI is constructed? Explain.

Future Explorations: Mapping out Term Papers

1. **The Unemployment Rate: Should It Carry So Much Weight?**
   Why does a single economic indicator, the unemployment rate, have so much influence over public policy? Does the unemployment rate deserve this much attention? What alternate definitions of unemployment does the government calculate? Some of the answers to these questions will become apparent when you produce a table of the average annual unemployment rate in the U.S. since 1929. You may also wish to examine unemployment rates for various groups—whites, blacks, and so forth.

2. **Firm Start-ups: Does the Business Cycle Matter?**
   When the economy expands, do more businesses get started? The purpose of this paper is to (a) gather data on the number of new firms started each year for the last twenty years and (b) relate the data to the business cycle.

3. **The Great Budget Battle of 1996: Rely on Projections or on Psychics?**
   The federal government started 1996 in an inauspicious way. Because Congress would not allow an increase in the federal debt ceiling until an agreement was reached to balance the budget in seven years, federal agencies were forced to partially shut down, a history-making event. Part of the reason for the shutdown had to do with disagreements over projected economic growth. The purpose of this paper is to research the role that projections played in the effort to reach an agreement to balance the budget. Among the questions you will answer are the following: Which government agencies produce projections? What methods are used to arrive at projections? How does the government use projections in its planning? Do most projections prove to be accurate?

Answer Key

ExpressStudy True or False	SpeedStudy True or False Self-Test		MasterMind Multiple Choice Self-Test
1. T	1. F	10. F	1. d
2. F	2. F	11. F	2. d
3. T	3. F	12. F	3. c
4. T	4. F	13. T	4. d
5. F	5. T	14. T	5. b
6. F	6. T	15. F	6. b
	7. F	16. F	7. b
	8. T	17. F	8. c
	9. F	18. T	9. b

*E*mployment, Output, and Fiscal Policy

A Look Ahead

You've probably heard the joke. "If you line up all the economists in the world, end to end, you still won't reach a conclusion!" It sometimes seems that there are as many perspectives on the macroeconomy as there are economists. Perhaps this lack of agreement is not surprising. After all, since all kinds of things happen at once in the economy as a whole, what causes what is often not obvious. Value judgements will also differ about how much weight to attach to alternative policy goals. This said, macroeconomists actually share a great deal of common ground, especially within two broadly defined schools of thought—Keynesian and classical.

This chapter looks at the interplay between expenditures, output, employment, and the price level. To do this, a distinction is drawn between the long run and short run. Using the long run as a reference point, this chapter focuses primarily on the short-run macro equilibrium. The analysis is done within the framework provided by the model of aggregate supply and aggregate demand.

DESTINATIONS

*M*odule A

As you zip along the Expressway you will arrive at an ability to

- justify why there is a natural rate of unemployment of 5 or 6 percent;
- present the contrasting perspectives of Keynesian and classical economists;
- explain how inflationary expectations can lead to inflation;
- describe how new spending can have a ripple effect throughout the economy;
- identify ways in which fiscal policy might stabilize the economy automatically.

*M*odule B

When you leave the Expressway to explore issues you will be able to

- interpret how government regulations and lawsuits can cause cost-push inflation, and how this effect may be masked by technological change;
- analyze rationales for a federal budget deficit, explaining why the twin trade deficit raises doubts about the rationale for expansionary fiscal policy.

*M*odule C

Mastering Roadside Challenges will allow you to hone analytical skills by

- detailing alternative interpretations of why wages and prices might be "sticky";
- demonstrating how Keynesian analysis of the expenditure equilibrium underlies aggregate demand.

Module A

TRAVELING THE ECONOMICS EXPRESSWAY

If you find a job you love, it won't be work at all.

People derive sustenance, both material and spiritual, from the work they do. It is of great concern, then, when jobs are hard to come by. Economists are quite aware of the suffering associated with unemployment and the loss of productivity that goes with it. Yet, when it comes to choosing the proper public policy toward aggregate employment and output, well-meaning economists disagree sharply. The differences commonly revolve around economists' different perspectives on the trade-off between short-run and long-run goals. It is because the issues are so important that the controversy becomes so intense.

*T*he Route to Full-Employment Output

Employment can be viewed from a long-run or short-run perspective. The long-run view is associated with **classical** economics, so called because that had been the standard approach until the 1930s. According to the classical view, unemployment is nothing more than a transitory *disequilibrium* in the marketplace—a time markets take to adjust to their market-clearing equilibriums. Specifically, there is a surplus of workers in the labor market. The market response is for wage rates to fall until the surplus is absorbed. In response to lower labor costs, competition forces output prices also to fall. These wage and price adjustments are supply and demand in action.

One of the earliest expressions of the classical viewpoint was by the French economist, Jean Baptiste Say (1767–1832). According to Say, the aggregate value of what is produced will provide the income with which to buy it. Periods of unemployment are thus disequilibriums that will be corrected when the marketplace figures out the profit-maximizing mix of goods and services to produce. Put another way, *Say's law* states that supply creates its own demand.

The 1936 publication of *The General Theory of Employment, Interest, and Money* by British economist John Maynard Keynes revolutionized the study of the macroeconomy. Keynes sparked the emergence of macroeconomics as a separate field of study. In response to the pressing problems of the Great Depression, Keynes offered a new, short-run perspective, which came to be termed **Keynesian** economics. Both classical and Keynesian perspectives are used today. However, the two viewpoints suggest very different roles for a government that wishes its workforce to be fully employed. Consider first the long run.

The Natural Rate of Unemployment

In countries around the globe, unemployment rates average significantly closer to zero than to one hundred percent. This is no coincidence. People look for ways to work because work puts food on the table. Even in the Great Depression of the 1930s, unemployment in the United States reached as high as 25 percent of the workforce for only one year, 1930, and as high as 20 percent for only three years, 1930 to 1932. Given that income is critical to living, however, it does not take many percentage points of unemployment to cause severe human trauma.

Periods of relatively high unemployment, such as occurred in the Great Depression, are the exception rather than the rule. In the last eighty years, U.S. unemployment has averaged just over 6 percent of the work force. Most episodes of relatively high unemployment in the U.S. and around the world have been associated with a breakdown of the monetary system. In the U.S., the Great Depression was precipitated by a banking system collapse that shattered people's confidence in the security of their bank deposits. *Hyperinflation*, in which governments print so much money that its value seems to diminish daily, has been the culprit in other countries. For example, hyperinflation was a problem in Germany between World War I and World War II.

Other reasons for upward spikes in unemployment also revolve around systemic collapses. For example, recent threats to the security of property rights in Russia have led to relatively high unemployment in that country. However, these are exceptions. More generally, **the desire of people to receive income keeps unemployment down.** This is a long-run tendency that is subject to a variety of short-run disruptions, such as those just mentioned.

Even in the long run, the unemployment rate does not tend toward zero, exactly. Rather, the long-run tendency is for unemployment to settle at a few percentage points above zero, due to the inevitable presence of seasonal, frictional, and structural unemployment. The minimum long-run sustainable level of unemployment is termed the **natural rate of unemployment**, and is thought to be in the vicinity of 5 or 6 percent of the U.S. work force today.

The economy would tend toward a lower natural rate in the absence of social *safety net* programs, which include unemployment compensation, Medicaid, food stamps, and additional programs designed to cushion the impact of unemployment, poverty, or other mishaps. Without the safety net, the unemployed would be subject to greater misery, and a correspondingly greater incentive to grasp at any job offer, without regard to its long-term consequences. From the employer's perspective, minimum wage laws, liability laws, and many other policies discourage job formation because of the cost of complying with them. Thus, government policies can and do affect the long-run equilibrium level of employment. Because of government actions, it is likely that the natural rate of unemployment has risen from a little over 2 percent a century ago to 5 or 6 percent today.[1]

The flip side of the natural rate of unemployment is **full employment,** which equals 100 percent minus the natural rate of unemployment. Because the natural rate of unemployment exceeds zero, **full employment occurs when the employment rate is less than 100 percent.**

---

[1] We have defined the natural rate of unemployment to include the long-run impact of government policies. We note that some economists prefer a more precise term, such as the nonaccelerating inflation rate of unemployment (NAIRU), since they do not wish to suggest that government influences are natural.

OBSERVATION POINT: Forecasting Jobs Lost to Imports—No Market for the Natural Rate?

We must have an income, and so we work. If we're out of work, we offer to work for less pay, which drives the wage level down. As the wage level falls, the price level falls. Our incomes then buy more goods, and more people can work to produce them. The process continues until all but 5 or 6 percent of us have jobs. That is the logic of the natural rate of unemployment.

When it comes to international trade, though, the public has no patience for logic—it wants numbers! How many jobs do we gain from trade? How many do we lose? The public's media servants eagerly seek out professionals who are willing to provide numerical forecasts that international trade cuts down on aggregate employment. Exporters and others with interests in free trade respond with professionals willing to provide numerical forecasts that trade increases aggregate employment.

Imports cost jobs in import-competing industries. However, the logic of a natural rate of unemployment leaves no room for international trade to have any long-run effect on unemployment in the aggregate. If imports were to cause unemployment, unemployed workers needing an income would pressure wages and prices lower until full employment was reached. Actually, because the dollars spent on imports bounce right back into the U.S. to buy U.S. exports and investments, full employment can even continue without a drop in wages. Unfortunately, logic lacks the eye-popping magic of numbers, and therein lies the market!

Long-Run Aggregate Supply

Full-employment output, also termed *full-employment GDP*, is the real GDP the economy produces when it fully employs its resources. The economy can temporarily exceed full-employment output if workers accept overtime or find new jobs exceptionally quickly. Whether actual GDP is above or below its full-employment amount, however, the existence of a natural rate of unemployment implies that the long-run tendency is for output to move in the direction of full-employment GDP. Full-employment output does not depend on the price level or upon changes in the price level associated with inflation or de-flation.

The economy supplies full-employment output in the long run, no matter the price level, as shown by the vertical **long-run aggregate supply** in Figure 12A-1. Long-run aggregate supply would shift to the right if the economy's productive capacity increased, such as through more resources or better technology. Long-run aggregate supply would shift to the left if productive capacity were to decrease.

As evidence that the price level does not matter in the long run, consider that the price level today is more than triple that of the late 1960s. However, market wages have also adjusted upward. Other than requiring that we earn and spend about three times as much to obtain the same goods and services, the rise in wages and prices has little long-run significance for the aggregate economy.

Aggregate Supply Meets Aggregate Demand

Aggregate supply reveals how much real GDP the economy will offer at various price levels. But what determines what that price level will be? To answer this question, we must add aggregate demand. **Aggregate demand** relates how much real GDP consumers, businesses, and government will purchase at each price level.

A conventional demand curve tells the quantity of a good or service that will be purchased at each of various possible prices. For example, as the price of Pepsi rises, the

Figure 12A-1 **Long-run aggregate supply** shows that full-employment output, measured by real GDP, does not depend on the price level.

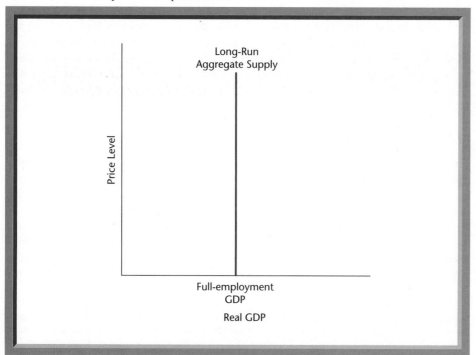

quantity demanded falls because consumers substitute Coca-Cola and other beverages. In the event of a general inflation in the prices of all goods and services, though, consumers can no longer merely substitute away from products whose prices have risen. Yet, consumers can no longer buy as much as before, either, because the inflation has eroded their wealth and the purchasing power of their income. Thus, other things equal, an increase in the price level will cut back the aggregate quantities that consumers purchase, and a decrease in the price level will increase aggregate purchases. To summarize, two central reasons that aggregate demand slopes downward are as follows:

- The **purchasing power effect**—at lower price levels, money goes further. In other words, even if all of us continue to spend the same amount of money, a lower price level causes the real GDP we purchase to be greater. Note that if additional purchasing power is added to the economy in any other way, such as by extra government spending, the entire aggregate demand curve will shift to the right.
- The **real balances effect**—a lower price level increases the real, inflation-adjusted value of money that has been saved, and thus increases people's willingness to make purchases.[2]

Figure 12A-2 shows a downward-sloping aggregate demand curve, along with long-run aggregate supply. The long-run equilibrium price level occurs where the two curves intersect. At any higher price level, aggregate spending will be insufficient to support full employment. Unemployed workers will compete for jobs, which will drive down wages. Competition in the output market will force firms to lower prices in response to these lower wages. The lower price level this brings means that spending will buy more output and thus lead to greater employment. The process continues until the economy reaches full employment and the corresponding full-employment GDP, as shown in Figure 12A-2.

If the actual price level were below the equilibrium shown in Figure 12A-2, the economy would "overheat," with aggregate purchasing power exceeding the economy's ability to produce. Firms would compete for workers, thus driving their wages up. Competitive firms would pass on these higher wages to consumers by raising their prices. The resulting increase in the price level would soak up the excess purchasing power, thus leading the economy back to its long-run equilibrium.

"In the Long Run, We Are All Dead"

This is perhaps the most famous saying of John Maynard Keynes. What is the significance of his oft-quoted observation? If you have ever been involuntarily out of a job, perhaps you know. Long-run trends toward full employment are little consolation to someone struggling to find enough work to keep body and soul together.

The macroeconomic views of John Maynard Keynes came to prominence during the Great Depression of the 1930s. This decade was characterized by both stubbornly high unemployment rates and the lack of a secure safety net of social programs to assist those who found themselves without any means of support. This combination lends itself to a

---

[2]A number of authors also include an international substitution effect, which says that a lower price level reduces imports and increases exports. However, since foreign exchange markets ensure that currencies quickly bounce back to their respective countries, the international substitution effect has little effect on aggregate purchasing power.

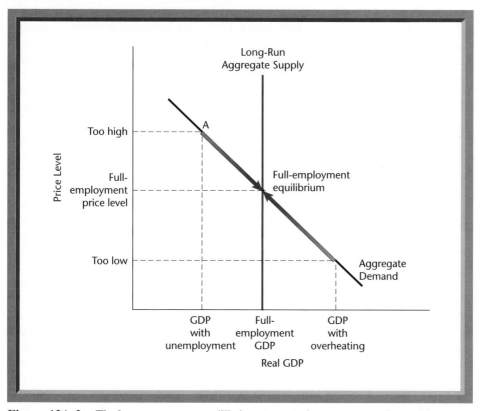

Figure 12A-2   The long-run macro equilibrium occurs where aggregate demand intersects long-run aggregate supply. Competition prevents the price level from remaining either too high or too low.

short-term view of the world. Economic policies that are merely long-term tendencies cannot match the allure of public policy action to correct problems in the here and now. If short-term fixes are expected to have long-term costs, so what? "In the long run, we are all dead." Keynes thus chose to ignore long-run tendencies toward full employment.

In contrast to classical economists, Keynesians dismiss the significance of wage and price adjustments to a market equilibrium. Their rationale is the existence of **sticky wages** and **sticky prices**, where *sticky* refers to an inflexibility in a downward direction. If wages are very sticky, the downward movement in wages required to reach a long-run equilibrium could take so many years that it becomes irrelevant. This downward stickiness could be due to labor contracts between unions and employees. It could also be due to human psychology—when firms cut wages, their workers resent it. The result is lower quality and lower productivity. Firms thus hesitate to cut wages.

If aggregate demand is insufficient to bring about full employment at the current price level, Keynes assumes that neither wages nor prices can fall. In Figure 12A-2, for example, sticky wages and prices would block any downward movement along aggregate demand from a price level that is too high, such as at point A. Rather, point A would remain an **unemployment equilibrium**, at which the economy continues to produce less than full-employment GDP. In contrast, if the price level is too low, inflation would soon cool off an overheating GDP.

Since the price level cannot fall to correct an unemployment equilibrium, the only solution is to shift aggregate demand rightward by increasing spending power. To accomplish this shift, Keynesians look to **fiscal policy**, which is government policy toward taxation and spending. Keynesians commonly advocate using *expansionary fiscal policy*—increased government spending or reduced taxation—to *stimulate* aggregate demand. The Works Progress Administration and other New Deal programs of President Franklin Roosevelt are examples of stimulative fiscal policies. Indeed, World War II seemed to prove the validity of Keynesian economics, since the massive amount of government spending it involved paved the way from the Depression of the '30s to the prosperity of the '50s.

Keynes' assumption that wages and prices cannot fall at all in the short run is too extreme. These days, wage cuts are reported in a variety of industries. Labor unions are not as powerful as they were in the 1930s. Indeed, it is often unionized employees who see the most dramatic wage cuts. In the late 1980s, for example, President Frank Lorenzo of Continental Airlines succeeded in slashing the pay of Continental's pilots, mechanics, and other workers drastically, sometimes to less than half of their previous salaries. Continental found that pilots paid in the $50,000 range could fly planes just as competently as those paid over $100,000.

However, wage cuts do not come easily. Continental's actions precipitated several years of confrontations with organized labor. When Frank Lorenzo attempted to start another airline after leaving Continental, the unions effectively lobbied the federal government to block him on the grounds of his past practices toward labor. Thus, while wage cuts do happen, downward stickiness also occurs. It should be noted that classical economists disagree with the contention that wages and prices are sticky, particularly if there are also competitive sectors of the economy that offer other job opportunities to those who would otherwise be unemployed.

Macro Adjustment—The Short and the Long of It

The presence of wage and price stickiness leads to a floor below which the price level will not fall in the short run. This is seen in **short-run aggregate supply**, which tells how much output the economy will offer in the short run, at each possible price level. Short-run aggregate supply holds all labor supply curves of individual workers constant, meaning that worker expectations about wage opportunities are also constant.

Short-run aggregate supply slopes upward, as shown in Figure 12A-3. Two reasons for its upward slope are as follows:

- *Structural rigidities*—as new spending power is added to the economy, it tends to raise wages and prices where it first hits, before eventually diffusing throughout the economy. Thus, an increase in spending cannot move the economy in the direction of full-employment output without bidding up wages and prices in some sectors, which in turn leads to a higher overall price level along with higher output.
- *The production effect*—when the price level rises and labor supply curves remain fixed, firms can profit by increasing output and employment. If the economy is already at full employment, they will employ workers overtime, thus allowing the economy to exceed full-employment output temporarily.

Suppose the economy starts at the unemployment equilibrium given by the intersection of aggregate demand and short-run aggregate supply in Figure 12A-3. To combat unemployment, government spends an extra $1 billion to buy a new Poseidon-class de-

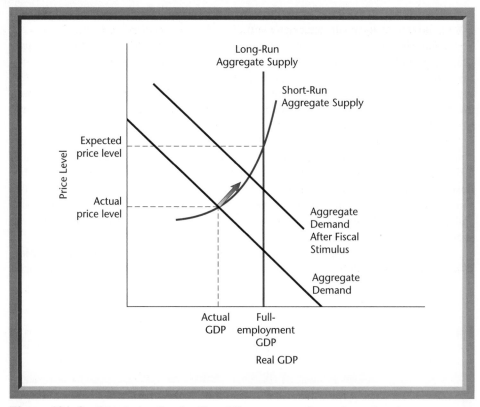

Figure 12A-3 Stimulative fiscal policy shifts aggregate demand, moving the economy up the short-run aggregate supply curve. The result is an increase in output along with demand-pull inflation.

stroyer. The additional spending shifts aggregate demand to the right and increases employment, as shown by the arrow in Figure 12A-3.

The fiscal stimulus is inflationary because the short-run aggregate supply curve slopes upward, due at least in part to structural rigidities—the spending does not diffuse rapidly throughout the economy. Rather, the added demand for jobs is concentrated in the defense industry. Industries that compete for workers with the human capital used in defense contracting find that their costs rise and that they must in turn raise the prices of their outputs. Job seekers without the required skills remain unemployed.

The sequence of events described in the above paragraph is an example of demand-pull inflation. **Demand-pull inflation** occurs when a rightward shift in aggregate demand moves the economy up short-run aggregate supply. **Demand-pull inflation causes higher output and a higher price level.**

The production effect relies upon workers being fooled by inflation or deflation. After all, if the price level changes, workers should adjust their own labor supply curves accordingly. In the event of inflation, for example, individual wage requirements should rise, thus shifting each worker's labor supply curve upward. However, while it is easy for workers to know past rates of inflation, it is much more difficult to recognize contemporaneous price-level changes. For the economy to be in long-run equilibrium, workers must have accurate wage and price expectations. For this reason, **short-run aggregate supply always intersects long-run aggregate supply at the expected price level.**

Because the short-run aggregate supply curve intersects long-run aggregate supply at the expected price level, a change in that price level will shift short-run aggregate supply vertically. For example, if the expected price level increases, short-run aggregate supply shifts vertically upward until its intersection with long-run aggregate supply occurs at the new expected price level. Likewise, if the expected price level decreases, short-run aggregate supply shifts downward.

Such shifts are likely because workers revise their expectations over time. For example, as inflation rose significantly from 2 percent in 1960 to 6 percent in the early 1970s, most people commenced to factor inflation into their labor supply decisions—they developed **inflationary expectations**, and could be fooled only by actual inflation that turned out differently from what they came to expect. Thus, stimulative fiscal policies that shifted aggregate demand to the right were offset by upward shifts in the short-run aggregate supply curve.

When aggregate supply shifts up and to the left, the result is **cost-push inflation,** as shown in Figure 12A-4. **Cost-push inflation reduces output and increases the price**

Figure 12A-4   An increase in inflationary expectations causes an upward shift in short-run aggregate supply. The result is cost-push inflation, in which output falls and the price level rises, as illustrated by the movement from point B to point C.

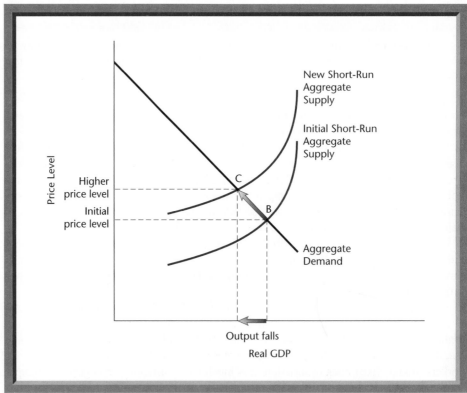

level, which leads to staflation—the simultaneous occurance of inflation and economic stagnation. The shifting short-run aggregate supply becomes a moving target for government policymakers. If government chases an upwardly shifting aggregate supply with ever more stimulative policies that shift out aggregate demand, the result would be the reinforcement of inflationary expectations. As inflationary expectations rise, short-run aggregate supply shifts up and output falls, which prompts more fiscal stimuli in an ever-repeating cycle. The result is an ongoing inflationary spiral of rising and falling output along with continually accelerating inflation.

Figure 12A-5 depicts a sustainable long-run macro equilibrium, in which the expected and actual price level are equal. The expected price level is given by the intersection of short- and long-run aggregate supply. The actual price level is given by the intersection of short-run aggregate supply and aggregate demand. Because these intersections both occur at the same point, a point on long-run aggregate supply, the economy is at full employment.

In the absence of inflationary expectations or anything else that would shift short-run aggregate supply upwards, the economy will remain at full employment without in-

Figure 12A-5 **Macro policy aims to achieve the full-employment output and a stable price level**, which occurs when the actual price level equals that which is expected. The actual price level is given by the intersection of short-run aggregate supply and aggregate demand. The expected price level is given by the intersection of short-run supply and long-run aggregate supply.

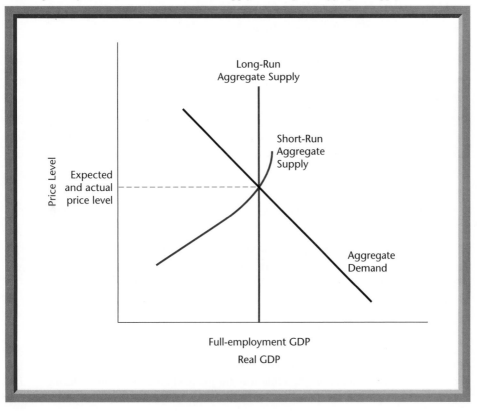

Classical	Keynesian
The focus is on the long run.	The focus is on the short run.
Prices and wages will adjust upward or downward as needed to reach a full employment equilibrium.	Prices and wages adjust upward without difficulty, but are downwardly sticky and thus unable to lead the economy from an unemployment equilibrium to full employment.
Government should not attempt to manage aggregate demand.	Government should actively adjust taxes and spending in order to manage aggregate demand.
Shortcoming: Remedying unemployment requires patience.	Shortcoming: Remedying unemployment can lead to demand-pull inflation and possibly an inflationary spiral.

flation. Whether achieved through government policy intended to manage aggregate demand, or through a hands-off policy of giving short-run aggregate supply time to adjust on its own, this long-run macro equilibrium is usually considered to be the ideal outcome of macro policy. Table 12A-1 summarizes the differences between classical and Keynesian perspectives on reaching this outcome.

OBSERVATION POINT: Breaking Inflationary Psychology—Call in the Wage-Price Marshal!

"Freeze!" shouts the wage and price marshal, .44 Magnum at the ready. Figuratively speaking, anyway, that is the idea behind wage and price controls. These controls are designed to assure an inflation-weary public that the government means business. They can put their inflationary expectations to rest. Would you?

Resorting to wage and price controls is serious medicine, and the public knows it. They figure that there must really be a serious malady to warrant such treatment. Furthermore, the public expects that the controls are only temporary, because of the cheating, shortages, and other economic distortions they lead to. Rather than eliminate inflationary expectations, then, wage and price controls may be more likely to prepare the public for a jump in inflation when the controls are lifted. That is just what happened upon elimination of the 1971 wage and price controls declared by President Nixon. That was the last time such controls were imposed in the U.S.

Keynes' Call to Action

Although classical analysis is respectable today, it fell into disrepute during the Great Depression of the 1930s and remained that way for the next quarter-century. During the Depression era, people did not understand why high unemployment persisted year after year despite falling prices. The public wanted government action to correct the problem. Keynesian macroeconomic theory provided the intellectual basis for such action. Keynesian economics focuses on the demand side of the economy, and is thus sometimes referred to as *demand-side economics*. Economists today are likely to say that aggregate demand is only part of the picture. However, nearly all will agree that it is an essential part.

Behind Aggregate Demand: The Expenditure Equilibrium

Behind the aggregate demand curve lies spending by consumers, government, and investors. We will focus initially on consumer spending, since consumption accounts for nearly 70 percent of GDP. To determine how much this spending will be at any given price level, Keynes examined what motivates people to spend and the amount of spending these motivations lead to. Keynesian analysis focuses on spending, because one person's spending is another person's income—the two go hand in hand. Likewise, the circular flow model tells us that aggregate income and output must be equal.

Aggregate national income = aggregate national output

Money spent on a hamburger, for example, is split into income to the employees and owners of the hamburger store, as well as to the various suppliers of the other inputs that go into that burger. Thus, gross domestic product can be viewed as a measure of both output and income.

Spending can be divided into the following two types:

1. **Autonomous spending:** spending that does not depend on income;
2. **Induced spending:** spending that depends on income.

Autonomous spending includes investments people make and things that people buy, even if they have no income. For example, if it became necessary, people would draw upon their wealth to buy such necessities of life as food and shelter. Even college students without any earnings have been known to draw down their parents' bank accounts in order to pay for room and board at school!

Autonomous spending causes induced spending, because money that one person spends autonomously adds to someone else's income, thus inducing them to spend more. As others receive more income, they buy more output, leading to an ongoing cycle of greater income and output. The only thing that slows down these ongoing rounds of induced spending is savings.

For example, Dawn spends her wages for boots at Bubba's Boot Boutique, which provides Bubba with income that he spends at J-Mart, which provides Jerome with income that he spends at. . . . This process is termed the *multiplier effect* of spending. Through this multiplier effect, autonomous and induced spending add up to **an expenditure equilibrium,** which **is the level of GDP that the economy tends toward in the short run, at a given price level.**

At the expenditure equilibrium, actual spending equals *intended spending*—how much consumers, businesses, and government desire to spend. For businesses, actual and intended spending often differ. The reason is that businesses intend to spend enough to maintain their inventories at desired levels, but cannot predict exactly how much of their products consumers will buy. For example, toy sellers cannot predict exactly how many Mighty Warriors, Nintendo games, and other toys consumers will buy at Christmas.

An expenditure equilibrium implies that there are no unintended inventory buildups or drawdowns that would prompt a change in business plans. Thus, all businesses must correctly forecast demands for their products. The world is not that precise. Because there will always be some forecasting errors, the economy will achieve an equilibrium only approximately.

The strength of the multiplier effect depends on how much of their incomes people spend. To the extent that people save their incomes, those savings represent a *leakage* out of the multiplier process. Taxation is another leakage from the spending stream. The fraction of additional income that people save is termed the **marginal propensity to save (mps)**. Likewise, the fraction of additional income that people spend is called the **marginal propensity to consume (mpc)**. Together,

$$mpc + mps = 1$$

The mpc and mps must sum to one because consumption and saving are the only possible uses for an extra dollar of income.

If autonomous spending rises, the expenditure equilibrium will rise by the amount of autonomous spending multiplied by the **expenditure multiplier**. The expenditure multiplier is the amount by which equilibrium GDP grows as a result of an increase—an *injection*—of new autonomous spending. If autonomous spending were to decrease, the expenditure multiplier would reveal how much GDP would fall.

If people always spend every penny of income they receive, the expenditure multiplier would be infinity. For example, if Ann were to receive $1,000 in income, she would spend $1,000. That would provide others with $1,000 in income, which they would spend, thus providing others with $1,000 in income, and so forth. In practice, however, there are leakages, such as savings and taxes. Most centrally, considering only the leakage of savings, the expenditure multiplier is the reciprocal of the marginal propensity to save, as follows:

$$\text{Expenditure multiplier} = \frac{1}{mps}$$

The expenditure process is summarized as follows:

$$\Delta \text{ Autonomous spending} \times \frac{1}{mps} = \Delta \text{ expenditure equilibrium}$$

where Δ denotes "change in."

The change in autonomous spending could be by government, businesses, or consumers. If autonomous spending changes, **the change in autonomous spending multiplied by the expenditure multiplier gives the change in equilibrium expenditures.** For example, if government spending rises by one billion dollars, and the marginal propensity to save is 0.2, the expenditure equilibrium will rise by (1/0.2) multiplied by $1 billion, which equals 5 multiplied by $1 billion, or $5 billion.

Note that there is nothing here to indicate whether the expenditure equilibrium occurs at full employment. However, **there must be some idle resources for the multiplier effect to occur.** If an injection of new spending occurs when the economy is already at full employment, consumers and others bid up prices by seeking to buy more output than the economy is capable of sustaining. The result is inflation, implying a rising price level that offsets the multiplier effect. Thus, without unemployed resources and a constant price level, the multiplier effect is thwarted.

If the expenditure equilibrium occurs below full-employment GDP, there will be unemployment, and thus downward pressure on prices until full-employment GDP is achieved. However, this is where Keynes draws the line from his classical predecessors. As discussed earlier, Keynesians view prices as downwardly sticky. Keynes went so far as to dismiss any possibility for prices to fall, because that process would only occur in the long run. As you have heard before, "in the long run, we are all dead." Thus, **the expenditure multiplier assumes a constant price level.**

✔ **QUICKCHECK**

Suppose the marginal propensity to consume is .75. Using the expenditure multiplier, what is the effect on equilibrium GDP of an extra $10 billion federal spending program?

Answer: If the economy is below full employment, and the price level remains constant, the effect equals $40 billion. This result is obtained by multiplying $10 billion by the expenditure multiplier. Since the mpc equals .75, and since the sum of mpc and mps must equal 1, the mps must equal .25. The multiplier thus equals $1/.25 = 4$.

The Role of Multipliers in Fiscal Policy Design

To prevent an unemployment equilibrium, in which the economy is stuck in recession, Keynesians argue that either autonomous spending or the multiplier itself must be increased. The multiplier will increase to the extent that people decrease their marginal propensity to save. Since savings represent a leakage out of the multiplier process, Keynesians emphasize the value of consumption. If people consume a greater fraction of their income, the multiplier increases and equilibrium occurs at a higher GDP.

For example, if the marginal propensity to save were to equal 1, that would mean that people save every dollar they receive. In that case, the expenditure multiplier would equal $1/1 = 1$, meaning that the effect of an extra dollar of spending is that dollar and no more. If the mps equals 0.2, in contrast, people save only twenty cents per dollar of additional income. In that case, an extra dollar of spending would generate $1 multiplied by (1/0.2), giving a result of $1 multiplied by 5, which equals a $5 increase in equilibrium spending and output. Thus, a decrease in the marginal propensity to save means that equilibrium income will be a greater multiple of autonomous spending.

Keynesians argue that the most powerful tool at government's command is its fiscal policy. Keynes was thus a strong advocate of increasing government spending during recessions. Keynesian analysis also suggests that the economy could be stimulated through tax cuts. However, Keynesians note that people might save some of their tax refunds rather than spend them to stimulate the economy. In other words, the *tax multiplier*—the expansionary effect of a tax cut or contractionary effect of a tax increase—would be less than the expenditure multiplier. Thus, Keynes viewed extra government spending as the most effective policy to cure a recession.

According to Keynesian analysis, financing extra government spending with an equivalent increase in taxation would have an expansionary effect, because the expenditure multiplier exceeds the tax multiplier. The **balanced budget multiplier** combines the expenditure multiplier for an increase in government spending and the tax multiplier for the increase in taxes to finance that spending. It can be shown that this multiplier equals 1, meaning that, when financed by a tax increase, an increase in government spending increases equilibrium GDP by the amount of that extra spending and no more.[3]

Critics of Keynesian analysis contend that Keynesian multiplier analysis is flawed because it ignores the impact of financing government spending. Specifically, the tax multiplier and balanced budget multiplier assume that higher taxes have no effect on incentives to work or invest. The critics disagree. For example, since higher taxes reduce the expected return on investments, tax increases are likely to reduce investment, and thus impede the growth of worker productivity and output over time. If government spending is financed by borrowing, critics contend that the borrowing is likely to drive up interest rates, thus causing *crowding out*—reduced borrowing in the private sector—which reduces investment and consumption spending, but is not factored into multiplier analysis. Chapter 14 more fully investigates the determinants of investment.

OBSERVATION POINT: The Paradox of Thrift—Does Saving More Save Less?

The baby boomers are getting old. Retirement looms, and their lifestyles are threatened. Guess what? Now they all want to start saving their money! At last, the U.S. may see the national savings rate grow! More savings means more investment, you know, . . . or does it?

According to Keynes, investors are unimpressed with the increased availability of investment monies and the consequent lower interest rates. Rather, investors are dismayed to see the demand for goods and services shrinking. They will invest no more than before, and maybe even less. That heightened urge to save merely reduces the multiplier and lowers equilibrium GDP. The country winds up saving a higher fraction of a smaller national income. Thus, the fraction of income that people save may be higher, but national income will drop so much that total savings will be the same or lower—that's the *paradox of thrift*. The baby boomers should keep on spending!

If you believe in unemployment equilibriums, you are a Keynesian, and frugality is something to worry about. Otherwise, go classical, save your money, and sleep tight.

Implementing Fiscal Policy

When the economy overheats, Keynesians call for *contractionary fiscal policy* to slow it down. When unemployment is the problem, Keynesians suggest expansionary policy to reach the full employment equilibrium. Unfortunately, even the best intentioned *discretionary* public policy—policy adjusted at the discretion of lawmakers—is unlikely to fol-

---

[3]The tax multiplier formula equals $-mpc/mps$. When combined with the autonomous expenditure multiplier formula of $1/mps$, the result is $(1 - mpc)/mps = mps/mps = 1$.

low the Keynesian policy prescription. The reason has to do with the three **fiscal policy lags**:

- The *recognition lag*—It takes time to know that a recession is at hand. Officially, it takes three consecutive quarters of declining GDP before a recession is declared.
- The *action lag*—Tax and spending bills are not passed overnight.
- The *implementation lag*—It's great to build a highway, but most people expect to have it planned out before crews are sent to lay asphalt! Planning government spending takes time. It also takes time before tax changes can take effect.

Because of fiscal policy lags, the business cycle may have turned by the time the money starts flowing. The spending may be more likely to cause inflation than to reduce unemployment. Policy lags make it very difficult, if not impossible, to *fine tune* the economy to even out the ups and downs of the business cycle.

Instead of discretionary policy, lawmakers can rely upon **automatic stabilizers**, which are features embedded within existing fiscal policies that act as a stimulant when the economy is sluggish and act as a drag when it overheats (grows so fast that inflation threatens). The U.S. economy has automatic stabilizers imbedded within its system of taxation and spending. On the tax side, government tax revenues decline when output slows, because tax revenues are a percentage of that output's value. When tax revenues decline, the effect is expansionary. Likewise, if the economy overheats, the same percentage tax collects more revenues, which is contractionary. No policy action is necessary.

On the spending side, payments for welfare, unemployment compensation, and other public programs rise as the economy slows and more people seek these safety net services. Conversely, this spending falls when the economy heats up, just as Keynesian policy prescribes. Again, the action to stabilize the economy is automatic; no policy adjustments are needed.

Taken as a whole, the automatic stabilizers should be expansionary when the expenditure equilibrium is less than full employment and contractionary when the reverse is true. In practice, however, there is a significant tilt toward the expansionary side. For example, the economy has been in the vicinity of full employment in recent years. Even so, there have been substantial annual budget deficits, $203 billion in 1994 for example. If the automatic stabilizers were designed to match the Keynesian policy prescription, government would run neither a surplus nor a deficit when the economy is at full employment.

✓ **QUICKCHECK**

(A) Once federal spending is approved, why is there an implementation lag? Use a new highway as an example. (B) Must all fiscal policies have a long implementation lag? Explain.

Answer: (A) Projects must first be planned. A new highway requires a considerable amount of surveying before the specifics of its route and features are established. Land must then be acquired. There continues to be a sequence of employing different types of labor and other inputs for different phases of the construction. The final product may not be completed for several years. (B) Projects that require little planning will have a shorter implementation lag.

OBSERVATION POINT: Spend, Spend, Spend

Keynesian policy is often seen as providing politicians with an excuse to justify doing what is closest to their hearts—spend! Unfortunately, putting the brakes on an overheating economy is another matter altogether—politicians do not like to raise taxes and cut the "pork." So, while politicians talk of balancing the budget over the business cycle, it somehow never seems to happen. The federal budget has not recorded a surplus since 1969!

EXPRESS STUDY TRUE OR FALSE

1. The natural rate of unemployment has risen due to an increase in social safety net programs.
2. Short-run aggregate supply intersects long-run aggregate supply at the expected price level.
3. When the economy starts from less than full employment, demand-pull inflation is usually associated with a higher GDP.
4. The expenditure equilibrium occurs when GDP equals ~~GNP~~. *actual* ~~that~~ which was intended
5. The formula for the expenditure multiplier assumes that the price level is constant.
6. The three policy lags are termed the recognition lag, action lag, and implementation lag.

EXPLORATION 1
Stagflation and Malaise: Ghost from the Past or Specter of the Future?

Firms face expenses associated with government mandates regarding employment and production. These expenses increase the real opportunity costs of production, thus providing an impetus for cost-push inflation. However, other forces are also at work in the macroeconomy. Specifically, innovations in production techniques reduce real production costs.

In 1980 inflation in the U.S. exceeded 12 percent, and unemployment hovered over 7 percent. OPEC had succeeded in shocking the U.S. economy with another round of oil price increases. Something was wrong with the country. As President Jimmy Carter put it, there was a malaise across the land.

Since those days, technological progress has put downward pressure on **real production costs**, meaning the opportunity cost of producing outputs has gone down. This, along with monetary restraint, led to an expanding economy with low inflation throughout the 1980s and into the 1990s.

All is not rosy, however. Leaving aside productivity-enhancing technological improvements, recent years have witnessed a number of worrisome increases in real production costs. Most notably, firms have seen their real production costs increase in response to higher indirect employee costs, higher costs of complying with government regulations, and higher legal costs. The result could easily be cost-push inflation in which real GDP and per capita living standards drop, even as inflation takes root. To see this, consider the macro forces at work in the labor market.

*C*ostly Changes in the Labor Market

Firms across America have been hit with increases in the payroll costs that lead to neither greater output nor to higher real incomes for their employees. Rather, the costs are associated with hiring new employees, matching these employees to the right job, accommodating existing employees, and, when necessary, terminating employment.

Hiring new employees is no longer as simple as advertising a job, interviewing the applicants, checking the references, and making the best choice. Great care must now be taken to avoid lawsuits in this process. The lawsuits could come from the federal government, perhaps guarding against discrimination. Lawsuits could also come from some of the many people involved, such as someone who was not hired. Such a lawsuit might allege an unfair hiring process.

Jobs nowadays must be advertised exactly. Whereas in the past, if a particularly appealing applicant came along, the job could be tailored to suit that applicant's unique abilities, such actions today would wave the red flag of lawsuit over discriminatory treatment of those who were not hired. Hiring exactly according to the written advertisement avoids this problem, but also lowers the expected payoff to the firm from advertising a new opening. This caution increases the cost of producing the firm's output. These costs are not measured in official statistics.

Information about prospective employees is increasingly hard to come by. The Equal Employment Opportunity Commission issues detailed guidelines about questions that are or are not appropriate to ask of job candidates. The same questions must be asked of each candidate. The employer cannot revise the list once interviewing has started, even if it becomes obvious that some pertinent questions have been overlooked. This very formal process makes it difficult for an employer to get a feel for whether an employee will fit into the organization.

Little help is obtained from letters of recommendation. These letters are often nearly devoid of meaningful information. The threat of lawsuits bears much of the blame. After all, previous employers or others who know of reasons why someone should not be hired have no incentive to reveal it. Even if their information is true, they might still be sued for slander, defamation of character, or some other charge. There could even be dangers of lawsuits from future employers if letters of recommendation are misleadingly glowing.

Since the certain expense and uncertain outcome of a lawsuit is something few letter writers wish to face, letters of recommendation are often little more than reports on such dry, objective facts as a job applicant's previous position and duration of employment. The upshot is that, when hiring, firms face an increasingly risky process, and are less likely to find the best-qualified person for the job. This process increases per unit production costs. It also affects the marginal decision about whether to hire. The result is fewer employees per unit of output.

Government regulations and mandates have also increased employment costs. For example, the Americans with Disabilities Act mandates that firms accommodate a variety of employee disabilities. Thus, a firm cannot simply fire a worker for showing up to work inebriated, since that might be a symptom of alcoholism. Alcoholism is a covered disability. Health and safety regulations, antidiscrimination laws, family leave requirements, and other government actions are intended to make the workplace better. They are also inflationary because they increase per unit real production costs.

Such cost increases even arise from government-mandated protections for employees about to lose their jobs. For example, consider the requirement that firms notify their employees at least sixty days prior to closing a production facility and laying off employees that work there. In those sixty days, firms can expect to see both productivity and quality drop, perhaps precipitously. After all, employees are not usually motivated to do their best if they know that they will be out of work shortly. If they choose to produce at all, firms must be prepared for high absenteeism, low productivity, and even sabotage. In these ways, legislation designed to cushion the blow of unemployment has the unintended side effect of increasing firms' real production costs.

The Cost-Push Specter—Not a Short-Term Visitor?

The previous section focused on the increasingly costly process of creating and maintaining jobs. The many items mentioned tell only a small fraction of the story of how government legislation and private litigation have combined to raise the real cost of doing business. The result is a reduction in real GDP, as we measure it. However, to the extent that the legislation and litigation is worth doing, then it has countered that loss of measured GDP with unmeasured intangible benefits. The idea is to make the workplace safer, fairer, and less disruptive to private lives. In the process, however, purchasing power falls and prices rise.

Figure 12B1-1 illustrates the effect of higher real production costs on the macro-economy. Since the changes are structural, they shift the long-run aggregate supply curve to the left. Long-run aggregate supply shifts to the left because the combination of legislation and litigation has increased structural rigidities in the employment process, thereby increasing the natural rate of unemployment. Mostly, however, it is that resources are taken away from the production of goods and services measured in GDP.

Figure 12B1-1   **Long-run cost-push inflation** can arise from changes in employment practices that lead to higher real production costs.

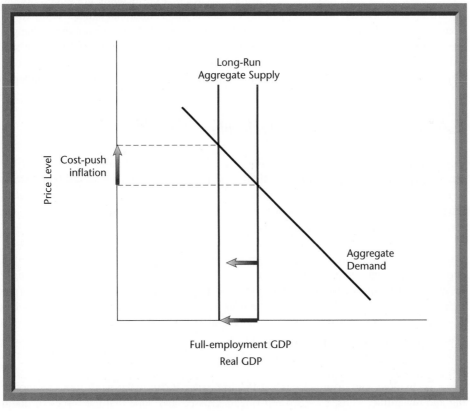

The leftward shift in long-run aggregate supply causes *long-run cost-push inflation*, as shown by the increase in the price level in Figure 12B1-1. The result of the long-run cost-push inflation is that the same amount of money buys fewer goods at higher prices.

Job Stress and the Elusive Forty-Hour Workweek

Despite all the "helpful" government presence in the employment process, it often does not seem that life on the job is any easier. This is not surprising. The same incentives that reduce the number of employees firms wish to hire also motivate firms to obtain more productivity from the employees they already have. From the employees' perspective, finding new jobs is more difficult. Since all employers face similar incentives to increase productivity, employees have little recourse but to bear down and be more productive. Thus, we see the rise of workweeks that are much longer than the traditional forty hours.

Incongruously, we also see more temporary and part-time positions. The reasons for both trends are similar. Part-time and temporary workers are easier to hire and fire and require fewer federally mandated benefits. For example, firms will go to extraordinary lengths to stay below fifty full-time employees. Firms that exceed that threshold find themselves subject to an array of costly mandates and regulations. Part-time and temporary workers often provide the flexibility to avoid that threshold.

Taken as a whole, then, the increasing presence of well-meaning laws pertaining to the workplace is threatening that mainstay of middle-class American existence, the forty-hour workweek. Part-time and overtime work is on the rise. Whether or not these changes are for the long-term good, is it any wonder that jobs seem stressful? Employment statistics measure the quantity of employment. We have no federal measure of its quality. The increasingly common reports of violence in the workplace give reason to wonder.

B

Doom and Gloom or a Technology Boom?

Inflation arising from the cost-push inflationary forces described so far would lower the purchasing power of our incomes. Real GDP would fall. Government would be reluctant to fight this inflation too vigorously, since that would require it to shift aggregate demand leftward, which would compound that falling GDP. We are thus left with stagflation and the malaise of more stressful jobs. This is a gloomy prognosis, indeed.

We can take comfort, however, in observing that many of the cost-push forces described in this Exploration have been growing stronger for many years, while inflation and unemployment remained modest for most of those years. One prominent reason might be that, even as firms are faced with higher costs per employee, they are also incorporating more efficient technologies and modes of operation. Technological progress has been an ongoing process that tends to reduce real production costs and thereby lower the price level and increase output. The result is just the opposite of stagflation. Ongoing technological improvements offer the prospect of offsetting the costly structural changes in the workplace.

Technology can even help defeat malaise, since it can make work more invigorating and rewarding. Thus, we keep our fingers crossed and hope that the forces of doom and gloom will be kept in check by a technology boom.

1. The macroeconomic orientation of this Exploration is best characterized as supply side, since it highlights the effects of legislation and litigation on productivity and notes that technological change might counter these effects. Keynesian economists might choose to highlight other features of the macroeconomy. Identify some additional forces at work in the macroeconomy. Would they support or counter concerns over stagflation and malaise?

2. This Exploration notes that laws and regulations are enacted in order to accomplish some worthy end. However, because these benefits are not elaborated upon, the reader might get the impression that legislation and litigation have imposed costs in excess of their benefits. Have they? Justify your answer with some specific examples.

EXPLORATION 2
Budget Deficits and Trade Deficits—Do We Spend Too Much?

Both the federal budget deficit and the federal debt can be justified to a limited extent, since the U.S. offers future taxpayers valuable assets in addition to the debt. There is also a Keynesian justification, although the effect of the twin trade deficit and other factors call this justification into question.

> *I place economy among the first and most important virtues, and public debt as the greatest of dangers.*
>
> —*Thomas Jefferson*

B

Why do babies cry? You would cry, too, if you were born nearly $18,000 in debt. That is how much debt Uncle Sam had already rung up by 1995 for each new baby born as a United States citizen. The federal Government continues to add to that **national debt** each year in which it runs a **budget deficit**, that is, a shortfall of revenues below expenditures. The national debt can be thought of as the *stock* of accumulated past budgetary imbalances, and the deficit as a *flow* that adds to that debt. By 1995 the budget deficit was $203 billion, and the national debt stood at over $4.6 trillion. That debt represents 70 percent of the annual value of U.S. output. Interest payments alone account for about 14 percent of total federal government spending.

Is this fair? Is our government doing the right thing by spending our next generation's money, without them having any voice in the matter? After all, the colonists of Massachusetts rebelled against unjust English taxes in the 1773 Boston Tea Party. Their rallying cry, "Taxation without representation is tyranny!" provided one more spark to the fire that formed the United States of America. Is our government engaging in tyranny against future American citizens?

Why Borrow?

To answer these questions, ask yourself when debt is justified. You may run up debt to pay for a college education. If you expect a payback in the form of a better income down the road, some debt while in college seems justifiable. What if you "own" a home? Few people own their homes outright. Yet most homeowners, even those with hefty mortgages to pay off, do not consider themselves debtors. Government statisticians count them as debtors, though.

Most people are willing to take on debt when that debt allows the purchase of assets of greater value. The homeowner who takes on a mortgage and the lender who offers that mortgage figure that the value of the house is more than enough to cover the balance due on the mortgage. Indeed, most homeowners with mortgages view the difference between the value of their homes and what they still owe as a primary source of their savings.

Government statisticians take a different view. When the government measures how much Americans save, it subtracts from that savings figure the amount that is owed on mortgages. The value of the homes is left out because it is difficult to measure. Since there are so many homeowners with mortgages in the U.S., America's savings rate then appears artificially low when compared with that of other countries.

Likewise, when the government reports its own debt, it does not offset this debt with the value of the assets it owns. After all, how do you value assets of the government? Those assets include such things as parks, highways, military bases, military equipment, a judicial system, and much more. Taken as a whole, we know the value is quite high. We also know that new babies born as U.S. citizens will obtain benefits from these assets for years to come. From this perspective, expecting future citizens to bear some of the costs does not seem so bad.

Would the next generation accept this deal—to be born with both the privileges and obligations of being a U.S. citizen? While we cannot ask them, we can observe their parents answering that question with their actions. It would be most unusual to find an expectant mother seeking to leave the U.S. so that her baby would be born elsewhere. In contrast, many expectant parents from other countries attempt to enter the U.S. so their babies can become U.S. citizens.

Just because most people believe that, on balance, there is a positive value to living in the U.S. does not tell us that the U.S. has the right amount of debt. If the accumulation of debt exceeds the accumulation of assets, the value of our country diminishes over time. If the U.S. holds down debt by cutting back on public investments, the country runs the risk of missing out on investment opportunities that would look good in hindsight. U.S. opportunities for economic growth would diminish, meaning that long-run aggregate supply would not shift rightward as rapidly as it could.

Macroeconomics also emphasizes the importance of reaching long-run aggregate supply. If the economy starts from an unemployment equilibrium, then Keynesian economists argue that government should engage in deficit spending. The idea would be to shift aggregate demand to the right until a full-employment output is reached.

*T*he Twin Deficits

As a country, we often accuse ourselves of being on a spending binge, one we will have to pay for later. As evidence, we point to both the federal budget deficit and the U.S. **trade deficit**. The trade deficit is the amount by which the value of goods we import exceeds the value of goods we export. Because we spend more of our dollars on foreign goods than foreigners return in exchange for American goods, foreigners have extra dollars left over to invest in the U.S. Those investments represent future obligations of this country to other countries. Yet, while it is the collection of our individual actions that leads us to a trade deficit, we don't usually consider ourselves to engage personally in irresponsible spending.

While the 1994 budget deficit of $259 billion is much larger than the trade deficit of $166 billion, the two are closely related, so much so that they are often called the **twin deficits**. By running a budget deficit, the U.S. government leaves more money in the pockets of consumers, some of which they spend on imports. Those U.S. dollars that consumers spend on imports come back to the U.S., such as when foreigners buy U.S. exports or invest in the U.S.

When the government borrows money to finance the budget deficit, that borrowing tends to draw more investment dollars into the U.S. in response to the expanded investment opportunities. To obtain dollars to invest in the U.S., foreign investors must bid them away from other uses, such as foreign purchases of U.S. products. Thus, other things equal, the higher is the federal budget deficit, the higher is the trade deficit.

The existence of the twin deficits throws cold water on the Keynesian idea that government can spend the economy out of an unemployment equilibrium. The problem is illustrated in Figure 12B2-1. If the government attempts to shift aggregate demand to the right through deficit spending, it generates offsetting effects that shift aggregate demand back to the left. Specifically, the higher U.S. trade deficit reflects a reduction in spending on U.S. goods.

By the same token, the same higher interest rates that caused foreigners to invest in the U.S. rather than buy our goods will also prompt U.S. citizens to save more and spend less. Higher interest rates also cut down on private investment, another component of aggregate spending. Together, these effects offset government's expansionary fiscal policy and leave the economy back where it started, as seen in Figure 12B2-1.

Over 80 percent of government debt is owed to U.S. citizens. Nevertheless, as the federal government adds to its debt, so too do U.S. citizens. Attracting additional foreign investment accumulates obligations to repay that debt in the future, even if the debt is in the form of foreign ownership of land, buildings, and factories. After all, it becomes their assets that we hold in this country. Is that dangerous? The problems many third-world countries had in repaying their debts are legendary. Is that problem in store for the U.S.?

B

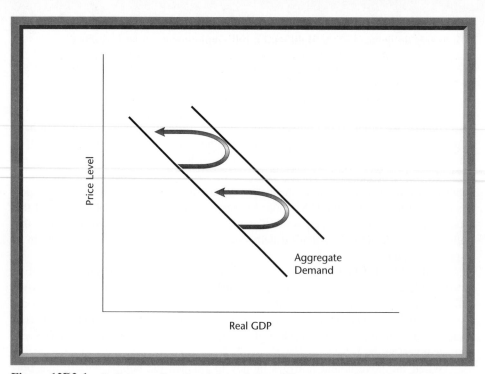

Figure 12B2-1 **Deficit spending that is intended to shift aggregate demand to the right may in practice be offset by an enlarged trade deficit,** together with less consumption and investment spending by U.S. citizens.

*T*he Overstated Dangers of Foreign Debt

Third-world countries ran into problems repaying their debt because that debt was denominated in U.S. dollars. They had to acquire those dollars. To the extent that the U.S. owes financial debt to citizens of other countries, that debt is also denominated in dollars. The critical difference is that those are our dollars; we control the presses that print the money.

Some people worry over a sudden exodus of foreign investment, possibly as a means to exert political pressure. Such worries are unfounded. If foreigners for some reason wish to stampede out of the U.S., they would have to leave behind all but a small fraction of their assets. Likewise, foreign holdings of our currency pose no threat to us, since that currency will either be spent in the U.S. or could be replaced by newly minted bills. The U.S. is thus largely immune to the problems that plagued third-world debtor countries.

The other worry is whether, by borrowing and spending so much, we are selling out our heritage. Indeed, some wonder if we are somehow in another world war, this time one we are losing to the Japanese and other countries of the Far East. Are we about to lose our country to their money instead of their guns? Should we protect ourselves by not allowing foreigners to buy so many investments here?

To answer those questions, we must recognize that when foreigners invest in the U.S., they are allowing us political and economic control over things of great value to them. In that way, foreigners acquire a strong interest in having our economy perform well and in maintaining good political relations.

Also, unlike in a military defeat, all investment transactions are voluntary. For instance, when Japanese investors purchase golf courses in the U.S., the U.S. sellers of those golf courses think that they benefit, or they would not sell. In fact, so far, Japanese investors have not proven very astute at making real estate investments in the U.S.

We have seen that a budget deficit and consequent increase in the federal debt can be justifiable. We have also seen that this expansionary fiscal policy tends to increase the trade deficit and international debt, but that the consequences of those increases are not as worrisome as many people think. Just how much debt is the right amount, however, remains an open question.

No Clear Route to Balancing the Budget

Suppose the public decides that government should trim or eliminate the federal deficit. How is it done? Should taxes be raised? Taxes take away our personal control over the money we earn. Raising taxes also tends to cut into productivity, since it reduces the rewards for work effort and taking business risks. Then there is that other problem: Those in favor of higher taxes rarely think that the extra tax burden should be borne by themselves.

The other alternative is to cut spending. Which spending? After all, everyone has their pet projects, especially when it comes to Congress. The problem is that, in the abstract, everyone wants to cut the budget because no one likes to pay. When it comes to particulars, though, the public can't agree.

There is no easy way out. Meat cleaver approaches, such as legislation or a constitutional amendment to balance the budget, are unlikely to live up to the hopes of their supporters. The problem is that Congress can hide its taxes and spending, because it has no accounting firm overseeing its budget. The budget of the United States is a long way from meeting generally accepted accounting standards. There are reasons.

The U.S. budget contains a current accounting of revenue inflows and outflows, along with an accounting for debt. Missing, however, is any capital account, listing the value of assets and liabilities. For example, taxpayers faced huge liabilities from federal insurance of bank and savings and loan deposits in the 1980's, but the potential for those liabilities was never recorded in the federal budget when the insurance was granted. How many more such liabilities lie in wait for us?

Conversely, the vast wealth of land and capital owned by the federal government is also not accounted for. Thus, should it wish to do so, Congress could reduce the budget deficit by selling federal land and capital to whoever would pay the most. There is no ledger of the value lost when these sales occur. Thus, it would be tough to force Congress to adhere to a budget, when it has so much leeway over what that budget contains.

Hush-a-Bye Little Baby

In summary, the newborn baby need not cry over the bill from Uncle Sam. After all, Uncle Sam is handing over a lot of valuable assets along with that bill. Nor need the baby lose a great deal of sleep over international debt, as the dangers are overstated. Giving government the incentive to economize, however, will continue to be a challenge in the years ahead.

PROSPECTING FOR NEW INSIGHTS

1. Keynesian economics suggests that deficit spending can be justified to pull the economy out of an unemployment equilibrium. Yet deficit spending has occurred every year in recent memory, despite the economy being at or near full employment in the large majority of those years. What are some likely explanations for this expansionary fiscal policy? Should Keynesian economics take any blame?

2. JUAN: It makes me mad sometimes to realize that so many U.S. workers are working for foreign-owned companies. We are becoming a country of servants who won't ever have much chance of making it to the top of those foreign firms.

   TERRI: What's the alternative? Should we refuse to buy foreign products unless they are made abroad?

   What do you think? Are we becoming a nation of servants because of increased foreign investment? Is this a consequence of our choice to borrow and spend so much?

B

CHALLENGE 1
Wage and Price Stickiness—Do Markets Clear or Don't They?

Microeconomics focuses on market equilibrium prices and quantities, almost ignoring the possibility for a disequilibrium. If a market is not at equilibrium, microeconomics teaches that the forces of supply and demand will cause price to change rapidly until the equilibrium comes about. Yet when markets are aggregated into the macroeconomy, there is concern about wage and price stickiness that can lead to protracted periods of unemployment below the long-run equilibrium natural rate. How can this be?

Economists offer up two sorts of answers. One view is that some critical markets do not move to equilibrium easily. Changes in demand for outputs make it appropriate for some wages and prices to rise or fall relative to other wages and prices. However, there are rigidities within both labor and output markets. Stores have leases and contracts that are not easily adjusted. In some cases, the contracts are with unions that refuse to negotiate wage cuts.

The problem is often exacerbated by a lack of information and trust. When employers attempt to downsize or close operations, employees often balk. Conversely, when things are looking good, management may be reluctant to believe that it will last. Thus, necessary adjustments in employment and output occur in a slow, "sticky" manner.

The other view is that markets move to equilibrium rapidly, but that there are misperceptions on the part of market participants, which cause them to adjust their behaviors over time as they learn the truth. The result of this second view is that short-run equilibriums will give way to a long-run macro equilibrium over time as supply and demand curves shift.

This view highlights the confusion that both workers and firms can experience when confronted by changes in inflation. For example, if there is a general inflation in wages and prices that workers and firms are not conscious of, both will be pleasantly surprised. In the case of workers, it will incorrectly appear to them that the competitive wage rate has risen, and they will offer a greater quantity of labor at what they mistakenly think to be a higher wage rate. By the same token, firms will be anxious to increase output because demand for their products appears to have shifted out. In reality, the increased quantity demanded does not result from a shift in demand, but rather from the firm failing to increase its price to keep pace with inflation. At a lower real price, consumers buy more.

As workers and firms learn the errors of their expectations, they adjust their supply and demand curves until, ultimately, a long-run equilibrium is reached. This process, too, can explain how wages and prices can appear to be sticky.

Underlying this second view of wage and price stickiness is the notion of how workers and firms form their expectations of future inflation. If they have **adaptive expectations**, they are basing their prediction of the future upon what has happened in the past. In this case, they are more likely to be fooled than if they have **rational expectations**, in which they base their expectations upon the best available information, such as news analyses and reports of macro data.

The more that workers and firms find themselves fooled, the more likely they are to pay attention to such news analyses, and the more rational their expectations are likely to be. This view suggests that the more experience people have with inflation, the less serious the problem of wage and price stickiness is likely to be.

CHALLENGE 2
The Keynesian Cross Behind Aggregate Demand

Keynesian analysis of the demand side of the macroeconomy can be understood with the help of the *Keynesian cross* model, also called the **income-expenditure model**, which relates intended spending to actual GDP. This model, illustrated in Figure 12C2-1, has two components: the forty-five degree line and the aggregate expenditure function, to be discussed in the following paragraphs.

Figure 12C2-1 The Keynesian cross. When the value of autonomous and induced spending just equals the value of actual production, the economy is at an expenditure equilibrium.

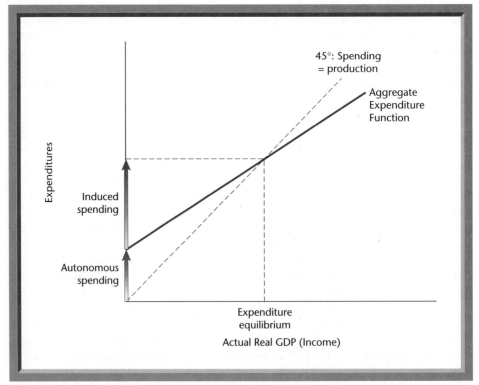

The forty-five degree line shows how much spending can be sustained by any given amount of production. If intended spending and production are equal, then the economy must be at some point on that forty-five degree line.

The **aggregate expenditure function** shows how much is intended to be spent at each possible level of real GDP. Actual GDP will always be the same as aggregate expenditures, except for unintended changes in business inventories. Unintended inventory changes show up as the difference between intended and actual investment, as follows:

$$\text{Aggregate expenditure} = \text{consumption} + \text{intended investment}$$
$$+ \text{government} + \text{net exports}$$

$$\text{Actual GDP} = \text{consumption} + \text{actual investment} + \text{government} + \text{net exports}$$

Because of autonomous spending, the aggregate expenditure function has a positive vertical intercept, as shown in Figure 12C2-1. The autonomous spending leads to production, which leads to induced spending through the expenditure multiplier effect described in the Expressway. The result is an expenditure equilibrium, in which the value of spending and production are equal. This equilibrium occurs at the intersection of the aggregate expenditure function and the forty-five degree line.

To see why this intersection represents an equilibrium, consider what would happen if real GDP were either above or below it. If the economy produced less than the equilibrium, intended spending would exceed output and inventories would be drawn down. Firms would then increase output in order to replace those inventories. Likewise, if production exceeded the equilibrium, intended spending would not keep pace with production and inventories would build up. Firms would cut back output until the equilibrium was reached. When intended spending and actual output are identical, inventories are neither drawn down nor built up, and thus the economy is in an expenditure equilibrium.

The Keynesian model is now thought to tell only part of the story, however, since it omits any mention of supply-side features. The modern tool of aggregate supply and aggregate demand analysis incorporates the Keynesian cross implicitly. The Keynesian cross lies hidden behind the aggregate demand curve. To see how, consider Figure 12C2-2.

The top portion of Figure 12C2-2 shows that an increase in the price level shifts the aggregate expenditure function downward. This shift occurs because the higher price level represents inflation that erodes the purchasing power of both autonomous and induced spending. For example, consumers without income will spend less if inflation has diminished the value of their savings. There is then less of a multiplier effect, and the expenditure equilibrium drops to a lower GDP, such as from GDP_1 to GDP_2 in Figure 12C2-2.

The bottom part of that figure merely notes that the higher price level, P_2, is associated with the lower expenditure equilibrium, GDP_2. By the same token, the lower price level, P_1, is associated with the higher expenditure equilibrium, GDP_1. This relationship between the price level and the expenditure equilibrium is nothing more or less than aggregate demand.

C

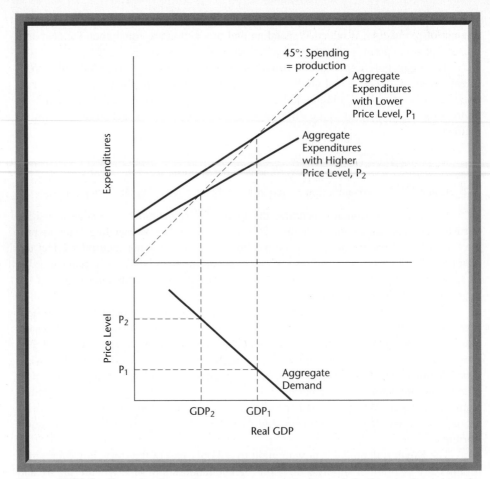

Figure 12C2-2 From the Keynesian cross to aggregate demand. As the price level rises, the real purchasing power of both autonomous and induced spending falls, thus lowering the expenditure equilibrium from GDP₁ to GDP₂. Aggregate demand shows the expenditure equilibrium for each price level.

C

Study by Design

SpeedStudy

SpeedReview

Government cannot eliminate all unemployment, especially that which is voluntary. The long-run tendency in the marketplace is toward the natural rate of unemployment and its associated output. That is the classical focus, but the process takes time.

In the short run, unemployment could be higher or lower than the natural rate. Sticky wages and prices might hinder the economy's adjustment to full-employment output, if the economy starts at a short-run unemployment equilibrium. To remedy this situation, Keynesians focus on stimulating aggregate demand. Aggregate demand is underlaid by intended spending, which can be autonomous or induced. Induced spending multiplies autonomous spending to reach an expenditure equilibrium, which is a point on aggregate demand associated with the current price level. If the expenditure equilibrium is at less than full employment, Keynesians advocate additional government spending until the economy reaches a full employment equilibrium. The resulting stimulus to aggregate demand could lead to inflation and develop inflationary expectations that are hard to break.

SpeedStudy True or False Self-Test

A1. Full employment requires an unemployment rate of zero.

A2. Classical economists argue that the desire of people to work will eventually lead to full employment, even if the unemployment rate is temporarily quite high.

A3. Keynesian economists argue that sticky wages will prevent the economy from reaching full employment in the long run. *short run*

A4. Short-run aggregate supply will shift upward if people have inflationary expectations.

p. 223

A5. The production effect on short-run aggregate supply requires that workers be fooled with either more or less inflation than they expect.

A6. Demand-pull inflation is associated with an increase *less* in unemployment.

A7. Keynesian analysis focuses primarily on the supply side of the economy.

A8. Induced expenditures depend on actual GDP.

A9. Keynesian analysis encourages less saving and more consumption if the economy is at an unemployment equilibrium.

A10. Automatic stabilizers are contractionary when the economy is at less that a full employment equilibrium.

B11. Cost-push inflation is caused by firms claiming higher costs than they actually have.

B12. The threat of lawsuits can cause an increase in real production costs.

B13. The value of a country's capital can be used to justify a national debt.

B14. Unless the U.S. trade deficit declines, there is a real danger that the U.S. government will be forced to default on its debt.

C15. Adaptive expectations are more likely to result in wage and price stickiness than are rational expectations.

C16. If markets move to equilibrium rapidly, there cannot be wage and price stickiness.

C17. The axes of the Keynesian cross model show GDP and the price level.

C18. The Keynesian cross model underlies the idea that aggregate supply slopes upwards in the short run.

The MasterMind

Selected Terms Along the Way

MasterMind Multiple-Choice Self-Test

A1. Aggregate demand slopes downward because
   a. as prices rise, people substitute less expensive goods and services.
   b. as the price level rises, people begin to expect inflation.
   c. as the price level rises, people are fooled because they did not expect it.
   d. an increase in the price level reduces real intended spending, which causes the expenditure equilibrium to occur at a lower real GDP.

A2. In the long run, starting from full employment, an increase in aggregate demand will
   a. cause aggregate supply to decrease as people become pessimistic.
   b. cause inflation, but have no impact on unemployment.
   c. cause severe unemployment, but leave prices unchanged.
   d. lead to an increase in real output as spending rises.

A3. Keynesian analysis emphasizes that
   a. government can best achieve its objectives of high employment and low inflation by staying out of the marketplace and by keeping its budget balanced.
   b. equilibrium in the economy can occur at less than full employment.
   c. it is better for government to cut taxes than to increase spending.
   d. the government should always balance its budget.

A4. The formula for the expenditure multiplier
   a. applies only when there are some idle, unemployed resources.
   b. implies that the price level rises as spending rises.
   c. indicates that the multiplier will be 5 if the marginal propensity to consume is 1/5.
   d. assumes full employment.

A5. Automatic stabilizers have an advantage over discretionary fiscal policies in that they largely avoid the problem of
   a. inflation.
   b. government interference in the private marketplace.
   c. multiplier effects.
   d. policy lags.

B6. Cost-push inflation is associated with
   a. lower real GDP.

b. lower prices.

c. tax cuts.

d. automatic stabilizers.

B7. The difference between the federal budget deficit and the national debt is that the budget deficit represents

a. the accumulation of past debts, while the national debt is the amount by which spending exceeds revenues each year.

b. the amount by which spending exceeds revenues each year, while the national debt represents the accumulation of past deficits.

c. the amount of money the country owes that it cannot pay back.

d. the amount of money the U.S. owes foreign countries, while the national debt represents the amount of money the U.S. owes in total.

C8. Wages may be sticky for each of the following reasons *except*

a. the natural rate of unemployment is higher now than it was a century ago.

b. labor supply and demand curves adjust over time as market participants adjust their expectations about inflation to reflect their recent experience.

c. union contracts prevent firms from lowering wages.

d. workers and firms may be slow to accept evidence that conditions in the labor market have changed.

C9. Unintended depletion of inventories

a. indicates that real output is likely to fall, as price increases drive away consumers.

b. indicates that real output is likely to increase as firms seek to replenish those inventories.

c. is unrelated to output, as inventories are pre-existing, and thus not a part of current or future production.

d. would be impossible in the Keynesian model, as intended and actual investment must always be equal.

MasterMind Questions and Problems

A1. Identify four reasons why the natural rate of unemployment is higher now than it was a century ago.

A2. Identify the essential difference between classical and Keynesian schools of thought. If you were a public policymaker and received conflicting advice from a classical and a Keynesian economist, how would you choose?

A3. On separate graphs, show demand-pull and cost-push inflation, labeling the axes, curves, and changes in output and the price level. Explain how cost-push inflation might prompt policymakers to cause demand-pull inflation. Then explain how this demand-pull inflation could lead to another round of cost-push inflation.

A4. a. Suppose the marginal propensity to save is 0.4 and autonomous spending is $1 trillion. Identify the expenditure equilibrium.

b. To increase the expenditure equilibrium by $1 trillion, what change in autonomous spending would be needed? Why is this amount less than $1 trillion?

A5. Identify some federal programs that act as automatic stabilizers. In each case, explain why.

B6. a. From your own experience, identify some inefficiencies in the workplace that raise the costs of production. Do any of them involve government? Do they show signs of getting better or worse over time?

b. Using a graph of aggregate demand and long-run aggregate supply, show the effect of increasing inefficiencies on the macro equilibrium. Also show the countervailing effect of technological progress. Label the axes, all curves, and the equilibrium points.

B7. "Our federal government exploits babies. It does so by slapping them with a huge debt upon birth—a debt they did not ask for, but will be forced to repay. Let's care for our children and grandchildren. It's time for government to stop running budget deficits and to start repaying our massive public debt!" Evaluate, including in your discussion an assessment of the proper role of debt in the public sector.

C8. List some instances in which you have observed what might be wage or price stickiness. Explain why each instance might have occurred, or alternatively, why the seeming stickiness did not really happen.

C9. Using two possible price levels, show how aggregate demand can be derived from the Keynesian cross diagram. Label the axes and all curves and equilibrium points on both the Keynesian cross graph and the aggregate demand graph.

Future Explorations: Mapping out Term Papers

1. **Stuck by Sticky Wages**
   This paper looks at labor practices in different industries and highlights unionization or other features of these industries which might lead to sticky wages. The paper discusses which types of industries are more prone to wage and price stickiness. The paper concludes by looking at unemployment from the perspective of someone without work because wage rates in his or her industry are too high. The paper attempts a realistic discussion of what this person might do.

2. **Jobs Ontario—Your Highway Dollars at Work**
   Ontario advertises its highway spending as a jobs program. Many other units of government in the U.S. and Canada do the same. This paper examines whether there is a macroeconomic basis for that claim, or whether spending on highways merely reduces spending elsewhere. It is shown that the answer depends upon whether the macroeconomic assessment is based on Keynesian or classical economic theory. The issue of policy lags is also included in the analysis.

3. **Cost-Push Inflation or Its Reverse—Conflicting Trends in the Workplace**
   This paper identifies various changes that have occurred in the modern workplace. Some changes, such as compliance with expensive government regulations, are shown to decrease productivity, and thus generate cost-push inflation. Others of these changes enhance productivity, and thus lead to cost-push deflation—the opposite of cost-push inflation. The paper uses a graph of aggregate supply and aggregate demand to illustrate these conflicting tendencies.

Answer Key

**ExpressStudy
True or False**

1. T
2. T
3. T
4. F
5. T
6. T

**SpeedStudy True
or False Self-Test**

1. F
2. T
3. F
4. T
5. T
6. F
7. F
8. T
9. T

10. F
11. F
12. T
13. T
14. F
15. T
16. F
17. F
18. F

**MasterMind Multiple
Choice Self-Test**

1. d
2. b
3. b
4. a
5. d
6. a
7. b
8. a
9. b

A LOOK AHEAD

The large number of colorful slang words for money suggests that it is never far from peoples' minds. How else can such synonyms as "moolah," "simoleons," "dough," "lettuce," "bucks," and "boodle" be explained? Further evidence is found in the numerous sayings that concern money. You probably recognize these samples: Time is money. Money doesn't grow on trees. Money to burn. Money is the root of all evil.

Money is also at the heart of the macroeconomy. Monetary policy affects interest rates, inflation, unemployment, and economic growth. Because of its broad effects, there is often contention over what monetary policy should be. Monetary policy is established by the Fed, short for the **Federal Reserve System**. The Fed is the U.S. central bank—the most powerful institution in U.S. money and banking. Commercial banks—those on Main Street—also play a prominent role.

DESTINATIONS

*M*odule A

As you zip along the Expressway you will arrive at an ability to

- identify the types, functions, and liquidity of various money measures;
- use the model of aggregate supply and aggregate demand to explain the effects of a change in the quantity of money;
- describe the structure, functions, and policy tools of the Federal Reserve System;
- recite the equation of exchange and explain its role in the conduct of monetary policy;
- relate the behavior of real and nominal interest rates to the level of inflation.

*M*odule B

Upon leaving the Expressway to explore issues you will be able to

- explain how price stability and the independence of the central bank are related;
- discuss problems created by inflation, and possible solutions.

*M*odule C

Mastering Roadside Challenges will allow you to hone analytical skills by

- working through an example of multiple deposit expansion;
- interpreting why interest rates can vary widely among countries, despite international competition for financial investments.

*M*oney

Money facilitates the exchange of inputs and outputs and is integral to the circular flow of income between households and firms. To put money into perspective, imagine a world in which it did not exist. To fulfill our wants, we would have to either barter or produce on our own all the goods and services we consume. Both alternatives are inefficient. Money provides us with higher living standards. That's why money is no fad and never goes out of style. In one form or another, money has been in continuous use from the earliest days of civilization.

Money is a type of wealth. *Wealth* consists of all the things of value that we possess. Previous generations often preferred to hold wealth in the form of land and gold. For centuries gold was synonymous with money, but land was not. Land could not perform the functions of money because of important qualities that it lacks—*portability* and *divisibility*. Money should be easily transportable and divisible to make it convenient to spend and receive change.

What Is Money?

Everyone knows what money is. It's the rectangular pieces of paper with pictures of presidents and the shiny metallic coins that we carry with us when we go shopping, right? Not quite. If it has value, is portable, and doesn't turn to mush, it has probably served as money. In prisoner of war camps during World War II, cigarettes served as money. Among Native Americans, wampum (seashells) was used as money. Tobacco and furs were money at various times in frontier America.

Gold has served as money for thousands of years. Paradoxically, gold is not money in the U.S. today. What then performs the role of money? Government-issued currency and coins are money, but they are most assuredly *not* the largest component of the U.S. money supply. The electronic notations of bankers representing checking account money hold that distinction, as will be discussed shortly.

Money is used as the following:

- *Medium of exchange.* That is, money is used to make purchases. Money must be acceptable to sellers, who will find it so only if they believe that others will too.
- *Store of value.* Money is a means of holding wealth, but by no means the only one. Real estate, jewelry crafted of precious stones and metals, and stocks and bonds also serve as stores of value, because they are not perishable and are expected to retain their value. Conversely, food and clothing are not used as money.
- *Unit of account.* The market values of goods and services are expressed as prices, which are stated in terms of money. The monetary unit varies from one nation to another. These monetary values are used for a variety of purposes, such as to measure GDP or to make comparisons among goods.

Fiat money is money by government decree. Paper currency and current U.S. coins are examples. Because government accepts fiat money, others do too. Gold and silver coins, once a staple of the U.S. money supply, are examples of *commodity money*. Commodity money was made from precious metals.

Unfortunately, commodity money is subject to *Gresham's law*—bad money drives out good. In other words, people have the incentive to nick, shave, or otherwise reduce the metallic content of coins. Anyone possessing such an altered coin tries to spend it first and hoard the better, unaltered ones. This practice forces recipients of commodity money to examine it carefully, such as by weighing it and even biting it. People do not wish to examine their money this closely, and thus turn to fiat money instead.

The governments of virtually all nations today hold a monopoly on the production of fiat money. The profit from the difference between the value of money and the cost of producing it is called **seignorage**. For example, if a $100 bill costs five cents to print and place into circulation, the government's profit from the issuance of that bill is $99.95.

A

✓ QuickCheck

Many people refer to their credit cards as plastic money. Do credit cards perform any of the functions of money?

Answer: No. Credit cards are not a medium of exchange. Credit card balances must be paid off with the medium of exchange, usually checking account money. Credit cards are also neither a store of wealth nor a unit of account. Credit cards make it more convenient to spend money, but are not themselves money.

OBSERVATION POINT: Cash in Your Cash

You can bring your "greenbacks" to the U.S. Treasury or the Federal Reserve and redeem them for something of value. Until the 1930s that something was gold. For a while, Silver Certificates circulated as paper money. Silver coins remained a possibility until 1965, when the U.S. Treasury started replacing them with less valuable "sandwiches" of copper covered by nickel. The Treasury still mints a gold coin, the American Eagle, but it is not used as money because its value as gold is too high.

You can still cash in your cash, and receive something valuable in exchange. You can exchange your Federal Reserve Notes for . . . more of the same! A twenty dollar bill will net you two tens, four fives, or twenty ones, at your request.

Liquidity: M1, M2, and M3

When paper money and coins are deposited in banks, money changes form. Deposits into checking accounts create **demand deposits**, also termed *checkable deposits*. More money is held in the form of checkable deposits than in any other form. These deposits are money because checks—orders to a bank to make payment—are generally accepted by sellers. Traveler's checks are also generally accepted by sellers. In addition, currency may be transformed into any of several "near monies," such as balances in savings accounts.

The Federal Reserve has three definitions of money, termed the *monetary aggregates,* which categorize money according to how liquid it is. **Liquidity** refers to the ease, speed, and cost of converting an asset into spendable form. An asset is completely liquid if it is spendable without delay. The monetary aggregates include M1, M2, and M3. **M1** is the most liquid and totaled $1.1 trillion in 1995. **M2** is slightly less liquid and totaled $3.8 trillion in 1995. **M3** is much less liquid and totaled $4.6 trillion in 1995. The specific components of each category are as follows:

M1: the sum of currency and coin in the hands of the public, demand deposits, and traveler's checks. These forms of money are the most easily and immediately spendable. **Currency owned by banks is not counted as money because it is not available to make purchases.**

M2: M1 plus savings deposits and "small" time deposits and money market mutual funds. **Time deposits** are certificates of deposit (CDs), which can be withdrawn without penalty only after some period of time, such as one or five years. The Fed considers CDs small if they are less than $100,000!

M3: M2 plus large time deposits (at least $100,000), and several other near monies. These additional components of M3 are even less spendable than the items in M2.

Because currency and coin are immediately spendable, they are completely liquid. Demand deposits are only slightly less liquid, since businesses often require check writers to present some form of identification before the check is accepted. Savings account deposits are slightly less liquid than demand deposits, but can be converted into demand deposits or currency with relative ease.

Financial assets, such as stocks and bonds, are not counted in the money supply figures. They are nonetheless relatively liquid because they can be readily sold in the financial marketplace at fair market value, although brokerage fees reduce their liquidity. In contrast, most nonfinancial assets are not very liquid. For example, automobiles, furniture, and personal belongings are difficult to sell quickly at their market value. Similarly, the sale of real estate usually involves large broker's fees.

OBSERVATION POINT: Money Watch—Keeping an Eye on the Aggregates

Who keeps an eye on the growth of money? Money supply data are closely watched by the president, Congress, Wall Street, and even Main Street. Tracking the money supply statistics is easy, as the Fed's latest figures are published weekly in the press. Interpreting the statistics, however, is an art as well as a science. Ideally, there should be just enough grease for the wheel to keep the economy growing without inflation. Because investors in bonds have the most to gain or lose from inflation, the reaction of bond prices to the latest money supply data is especially useful at shedding light on how close to the ideal the actual numbers are.

Unemployment, Money, and Aggregate Demand

If you've been unemployed, you know the problem—not enough money to spend! If unemployment in the macroeconomy exceeds the natural rate, the problem is the same: Aggregate unemployment stems from too little money being spent to sustain the full-employment output, given the current price level. An unemployment equilibrium occurs when aggregate demand intersects short-run aggregate supply at less than full-employment GDP, as illustrated by point A in Figure 13A-1.

Classical economists suggest the remedy for unemployment is to let the price level fall, so that the money in circulation can buy more real output. In this view, the problem is not one of too little money, nor of insufficient aggregate demand, but of too high a price level. Once the price level falls sufficiently, employment will increase to the full-employment level, as illustrated by point C in Figure 13A-1.

In the Keynesian view, unemployment is caused by insufficient aggregate demand. **Aggregate demand shifts with changes in the quantity of money in circulation.** Thus, the remedy of Keynesians for unemployment is to increase aggregate demand by additions to government spending, which puts more money into circulation. With more government spending, aggregate demand shifts to the right, as shown in Figure 13A-1. The

Figure 13A-1 Increasing the amount of money in circulation shifts aggregate demand to the right, which can move the economy from unemployment equilibrium A to full-employment equilibrium B. Alternatively, full-employment equilibrium C can be reached by waiting for prices to drop.

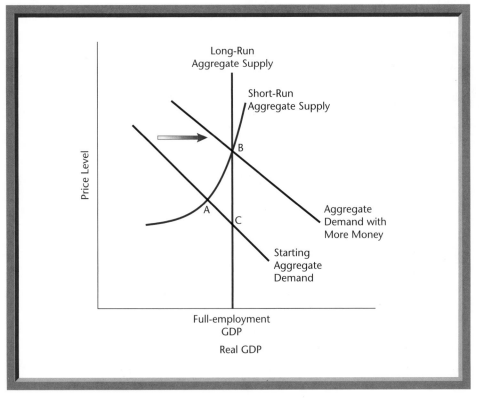

price level rises as the economy moves to full-employment at point B in the figure. **Note that the position of both short-run and long-run aggregate supply is independent of the quantity of money. Only aggregate demand is directly affected by money.**

According to Keynesians, the key to bringing the economy out of a depression is not merely to increase the quantity of money in the hands of consumers, because consumers cannot be relied upon to spend it. Instead, Keynesians advocate government spending on goods and services as the way to directly increase the amount of money in circulation. But what is the proper monetary policy when the economy is not in a depression? To answer this and other monetary questions, we first turn our attention to banking.

*M*oney and Banking in the U.S.

The Banking System

In 1995, 10,000 U.S. commercial banks accepted deposits and made loans. Recent years have seen a rise in bank mergers and interstate banking as legal barriers against banking across state lines have fallen. Electronic banking from home, such as via the Internet, looms on the horizon. The fact is that banks are becoming ever more national and even international institutions.

Banks are regulated by both state and federal governments. Bank regulation is designed to protect against unsound banking practices that could bankrupt both depositors and government insurance funds. For example, unsound lending practices contributed to the multitude of bank failures in the 1980s.

Banking regulation is quite controversial. Since regulations inhibit banks from responding to the demands of their customers, regulations can lead to inefficiencies. For example, under the Glass-Steagall Act of 1933, banks are barred from offering insurance and brokerage services. Yet consumers value one-stop shopping, and diversification might actually reduce the risk of bank failure. This explains why there are regular calls for repeal of the act.

Table 13A-1 lists the major assets and liabilities of banks. The assets are things that banks own and show how banks use funds. The liabilities show how banks raise funds.

The most liquid asset is cash. A portion of cash assets are currency and coin held by banks as vault cash. Additional cash assets are held as deposits with the Federal Reserve. The sum of vault cash plus deposits with the Fed is called *bank reserves*. Bank reserves are available immediately to meet depositor withdrawals.

Bank loans go to both the household and business sectors. Banks lend in order to

TABLE 13A-1 *Major Assets and Liabilities of Banks*	
ASSETS (Uses of Funds)	**LIABILITIES** (Sources of Funds)
Vault cash	Deposits
Deposits held by the Federal Reserve	Federal funds
Loans	Discount loans
Securities	
Other	

earn income in the form of interest. *Securities*, in the form of *bonds*, are government interest-bearing assets that the government issues when it borrows. Interest payments on securities also provide banks with income.

Bank deposits are liabilities because they are funds owed to depositors. Banks also raise funds by borrowing. Funds borrowed from other banks are called *federal funds*. The interest rate they charge is called the **federal funds rate**. Borrowings from the Federal Reserve are called *discount loans*. This is because the Federal Reserve discounts its loans by charging interest on loans when they are made. The rate of interest charged is termed the **discount rate**.

Banks hold some fraction of their deposits on reserve to meet the cash needs of their customers. The remainder is available for investment, such as to make loans. Individual banks are required by law to meet **reserve requirements** imposed by the Fed. The current reserve requirement of approximately 10 percent for demand deposits means that banks must hold at least $10 in reserves for every $100 of deposits. Hence, banks are free to invest most of their deposits, but must hold a relatively small fraction of total deposits in the form of reserves. Reserves in excess of the required amount are called **excess reserves**. Hence, total reserves equal required reserves plus excess reserves.

The possibility that banks might not be able to pay off depositors motivates the *Federal Deposit Insurance Corporation (FDIC)* to insure deposit accounts up to $100,000. This insurance reduces the possibility of bank runs, in which numerous depositors simultaneously seek to withdraw funds because of fears about the financial soundness of a bank. However, critics of FDIC insurance point out that the existence of this insurance permits banks to make riskier loans because depositors know that they will not lose those deposits no matter how many unsound loans a bank may make.

In this section, we have discussed banks. There are also other *financial intermediaries* that raise funds in order to make loans or investments. With minor exceptions, the discussion of banks also applies to credit unions and savings and loans. Insurance companies, mutual funds, pension funds, and finance companies are examples of nonbank financial intermediaries, because, although they are not banks, they invest the funds they raise.

✓ **QUICK**CHECK

A bank has $1,000 in deposits and holds $250 in reserves. If the reserve requirement is 20 percent, how much are excess reserves?

Answer: Required reserves equal 0.2 multiplied by $1000, or $200. Since total reserves equal $250, excess reserves must be $50.

OBSERVATION POINT: Do Banks Discriminate in Making Loans?

"Redlining!" Some banks have been accused of refusing to extend home loans in minority neighborhoods. Minorities have been turned down for home loans as much as twice as often as whites, evidence in the eyes of bank critics of discrimination. Banks defend themselves by noting that the profit motive prompts banks to make sound loans and reject risky ones. Which argument is most convincing? Some banks—those unable to demonstrate that they applied risk criteria in a colorblind fashion—have been convicted in courts of law of illegal redlining. Other banks, however, have been found innocent.

How Banks Create Money

When a bank makes a loan, the quantity of money increases. To see how, suppose you hope to borrow the cost of a new Dodge Neon, $10,000, from your bank, Homestate University National Bank. After discussing your loan request with loan officer Softheart, the loan is approved. Soon you'll be behind the wheel of your first new car.

If you receive the loan as currency, the amount of currency in the hands of the public, which includes you, is greater than before the loan. Recall that this currency, while inside the bank's vault, was not included in the money supply. Once you receive the $10,000, the M1, M2, and M3 money supplies increase by that amount.

You might not feel safe with $10,000 cash on your person. For this reason, you probably received the loan in the form of a $10,000 check deposited in your checking account. Again, the M1, M2, and M3 money supplies increase by $10,000.

When borrowers repay bank loans, the quantity of money falls. If a loan is repaid with currency, the money supply decreases because there is less currency in the hands of the public. If a loan is repaid by writing a check, the money supply falls due to fewer demand deposits.

Meet the Fed

Structure and Functions of the Federal Reserve

The Federal Reserve was created by the *Federal Reserve Act of 1913* in response to recurring problems of bank failure and the belief that a central bank could contribute to U.S. economic stability. With its creation, Congress sought to provide the banking system with the stabilizing influence of a central bank. To this end, the Fed does the following:

- Functions as a **banker's bank**. The Fed holds reserves for commercial banks.
- Functions as a **lender of last resort**. The Fed lends reserves to sound banks that are temporarily short of reserves. Withdrawals by depositors deplete reserves. If depositors become concerned about a bank's ability to pay, the rush to withdraw funds can create a bank run.
- **Supervises banks.**
- **Conducts monetary policy**. The Fed was established for the purpose of providing an elastic money supply—a quantity of money that responds to the demands of the economy. A tighter monetary policy constrains the quantity of money, perhaps to fight inflation. A looser monetary policy expands the money supply in order to stimulate economic growth. Fed influence over the money supply is a critical element in the conduct of monetary policy.
- **Issues currency.**
- **Clears checks.**

The Fed has the following three primary components:

- The **Board of Governors**, which is responsible for the overall direction of the Federal Reserve and its policies.
- The **Federal Open Market Committee (FOMC)**, which is charged with the conduct of monetary policy.
- The **Federal Reserve Banks**, which regulate and provide a variety of services for banks.

There are seven members of the Board of Governors. They are appointed to fourteen-year nonrenewable terms by the president, with the advice and consent of the Senate. Terms are staggered so that one term expires every two years, which minimizes political influence over the Fed. One of the seven is named by the president to chair the Board. The chairperson serves a four-year renewable term. The chairperson is the most powerful individual in the Fed and one of the most powerful people in the country. As of 1996, economist Alan Greenspan held the position.

The FOMC consists of twelve members, the seven members of the Board plus four rotating district bank presidents, and the president of the New York District Bank. The president of the New York Fed is always a member of the Committee because New York City is the hub of the nation's financial markets. The FOMC usually meets at intervals of approximately four to six weeks, making adjustments in the conduct of monetary policy in accordance with its assessment of economic conditions.

There are twelve regional Federal Reserve Banks, as shown in Figure 13A-2. Together with their branches, these Banks perform the routine functions of the Fed. Chances are that you have benefitted from their services today. Federal Reserve Banks issue currency, which bears the location of the issuing bank. Commercial banks within a district make deposits of reserves into their district's Federal Reserve Bank. Federal Reserve Banks also operate the Fed's check-clearing operations, which allows funds to be expeditiously transferred from check writers' accounts to the accounts of the banks that cash the checks. These banks also participate in the supervision of commercial banks in their districts.

National banks—those chartered by the federal government—are automatically members of the Federal Reserve. Banks with state charters may join at their option. Whether or not they are members of the Federal Reserve System, however, all banks have nearly equal access to the Fed's services and are subject to its regulations. Thus, although only about 4,000 banks are formal members, in practical terms all banks fall under the purview of the Federal Reserve.

Open Market Operations

The principal method used by the Fed to influence the money supply is open market operations. **Open market operations** occur when the Fed enters the financial marketplace to buy or sell government securities, such as treasury bonds. The Fed does not itself issue government securities; the U.S. Department of the Treasury issues Treasury bonds, for example. The Fed can only obtain them in the open market, hence the name. Open market operations allow currency, in the form of Federal Reserve Notes, to make its way into circulation.

For example, suppose your Aunt Elvira sells a bond to the Fed for $10,000. The Fed issues a check written on itself, payable to Aunt Elvira. When she deposits the check in her checking account at Investors' National Bank, demand deposits in the banking

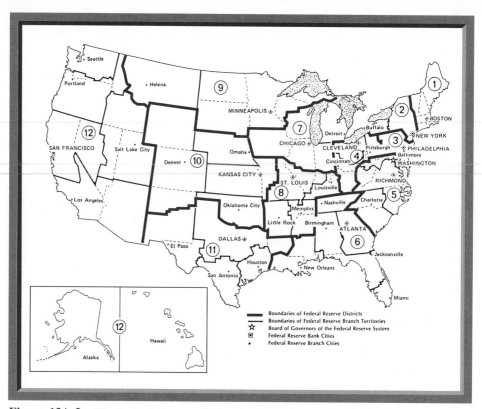

Figure 13A-2 **The Federal Reserve System** is divided into twelve districts.

system increase by the amount of the check. Thus, the money supply increases. If she had cashed the check instead, currency in the hands of the public would have increased. Either way, the money supply rises.

When an individual buys a bond sold by the Fed, the money supply decreases. Suppose the buyer pays for the bond by writing a check. When the buyer's bank pays the Fed, the buyer's checking account is reduced by the amount of the check. Thus, demand deposits decrease, as does the money supply.

The bulk of the Fed's open market operations involve banks directly. An open market sale to a bank by the Fed decreases bank reserves. Fewer reserves mean that the bank is able to do less lending. Thus, open market sales tend to reduce the money supply. A greater volume of open market sales is consistent with a tighter policy.

An open market purchase by the Fed from a bank increases bank reserves, which in turn tends to increase the money supply, as banks have more money to loan. A greater volume of open market purchases is consistent with a looser monetary policy. However, whether loans are actually made and the money supply actually increased depends upon the willingness of banks to make loans and upon the desire of the public to borrow. **Thus, the Fed influences but does not control the money supply.**

However, by conducting open market operations, **the Fed controls the monetary base.** The **monetary base** is the sum of currency held by the public plus bank reserves.

An open market purchase by the Fed increases the monetary base by the amount of the purchase; an open market sale decreases the monetary base by the amount of the sale.

✔ **QUICKCHECK**

If Aunt Elvira deposited the Fed's check into her savings account, would the money supply increase?

Answer: The M1 money supply would remain unchanged. However, M2 and M3 would rise, because these measures include savings accounts.

A

The Money Multiplier and the Monetary Base

The effects of open market operations do not stop with the initial purchase or sale. Secondary effects magnify changes in the money supply. For example, an open market purchase from an individual increases the money supply once when the seller receives the proceeds of the sale. If those funds are deposited in a bank, and then loaned to someone, the money supply increases again. This process can continue over and over.

The money multiplier shows the total effect on the money supply of each dollar of open market operations. To see how the money multiplier works, return to Aunt Elvira's sale of a bond to the Fed. When her checking account increased with the deposit of the Fed's check, we saw that demand deposits in the banking system increased.

If we assume for simplicity that Investors' National Bank was just meeting a 10 percent reserve requirement prior to the $10,000 deposit, then the bank will find itself holding excess reserves of $9,000. Actual reserves have increased by $10,000, but the bank is only required to hold 10 percent of that amount, equal to $1,000, as required reserves. The bank is thus able to make loans up to the amount of excess reserves and still meet the reserve requirement.

As it happens, your best friend wishes to borrow $9,000 to finance the purchase of a used Saturn automobile. After speaking with loan officer Pushover at Investors' National Bank, your friend's loan is approved. That loan increases the money supply by $9,000. When the dealer is paid, your friend's check will be deposited into the dealer's bank. That bank will then have excess reserves to lend. The amount of required reserves equals $900, so excess reserves equal $8,100, the amount that can be loaned.

This lending-depositing-lending sequence could continue. Someone can borrow $8,100. When the loan is spent, and someone else deposits the $8100 in their bank, that bank will have excess reserves, which it is able to lend. At each succeeding step in the process, the sum of money loaned, which is new money, grows smaller because each succeeding bank in the sequence must hold a portion as required reserves. Thus the process is eventually exhausted when the last bank in the sequence has essentially nothing left to lend.

What is the total of new money created when the expansion of the money supply is complete? The answer depends on the money multiplier.

$$\text{Money supply} = \text{money multiplier} \times \text{monetary base}$$

The money multiplier can vary according to loan prospects and people's behavior, and is thus hard to calculate with precision. However, an upper bound can be found by calculating the **deposit multiplier—the maximum possible value of the money multiplier.** The deposit multiplier is calculated by assuming that all money is held as demand deposits and that banks do not hold excess reserves. In practice, the true value of the money multiplier will be less than the deposit multiplier.

The deposit multiplier is the reciprocal of the percentage reserve requirement, meaning

$$\text{Deposit multiplier} = \frac{1}{\text{reserve requirement}}$$

For example, if the reserve requirement equals 10 percent, then 1 divided by 10 percent equals 1/0.1, which gives a deposit multiplier of 10. To use this multiplier, multiply the Fed's original open market purchase of $10,000 by the multiplier, 10. The total of new money in that case is $100,000.

The following three factors affect the money multiplier, and thus the actual expansion of the money supply:

- **The reserve requirement:** Changes in the reserve requirement would change the deposit multiplier, and thus the maximum value of the money multiplier. A lower reserve requirement means that banks are able to lend a greater fraction of deposits; a higher reserve requirement has the opposite effect.
- **The public's desire to hold currency instead of deposits:** If people hold more of their money as currency and less as deposits, banks will have fewer dollars to lend. If Aunt Elvira had taken the original $10,000 from the sale of her bond as currency and buried it in her back yard, the multiple expansion of the money supply would not have taken place.
- **The desire of banks to hold excess reserves:** Excess reserves may be held in order to meet unexpected depositor withdrawals, or because lending opportunities seem poor. Reserves that are not loaned out do not add to the money supply.

Other Tools of the Fed

In response to unexpected customer withdrawals or other reasons, banks may wish to borrow from the Fed in order to maintain their required reserves. Recall that loans from the Fed to banks are called discount loans, and the rate of interest charged is called the discount rate. An increase in the discount rate makes it more costly for banks to borrow; a decrease makes it less costly.

Increases in the discount rate tend to decrease the quantity of money by prompting banks to borrow less from the Fed. Conversely, a decrease in the discount rate leads banks to borrow more from the Fed, which tends to increase the amount of money in circulation. Thus, **a change in the discount rate tends to cause the money supply to change in the opposite direction.**

Changes in the discount rate are typically front-page news because they are an easily understood signal of the Fed's policy intentions. A decrease in the discount rate signals a looser monetary policy. The Fed may wish to see the money supply grow faster to stimulate growth and employment. An increase in the discount rate signals a tighter policy. Perhaps the Fed would like to slow down monetary growth to fight inflation.

TABLE 13A-2 *The Fed's Monetary Policy Options*

Tighter Monetary Policy	Looser Monetary Policy
Open market sale of securities	Open market purchase of securities
Increase in discount rate	Decrease in discount rate
Increase in reserve requirement	Decrease in reserve requirement

The Fed could change the money supply dramatically by altering the reserve requirement. A decrease in required reserves would increase the money multiplier and spur monetary growth. An increase in the reserve requirement would reduce the money multiplier and thus decrease the money supply. Excess reserves, which banks are able to loan out, would become required reserves, which cannot be loaned out.

The Fed is reluctant to increase reserve requirements because banks without sufficient excess reserves would be forced to sell securities or call in loans—actions that could prove disruptive to the bank and its customers. Thus, while potent, changes in reserve requirements are rarely used as an instrument of monetary policy. Table 13A-2 summarizes the Fed's options in setting monetary policy.

✔ QUICKCHECK

When the Fed lowers the discount rate, why does it become more likely that the money supply will increase?

Answer: A lower discount rate lowers the cost to banks of borrowing reserves from the Fed. Banks that are short of reserves are more likely to borrow reserves from the Fed and less likely to borrow from other banks. Thus, more funds are available in the banking system to lend to the public.

Guiding Monetary Policy

The goals of Federal Reserve monetary policy are high employment, low inflation (price stability), and economic growth. Successful monetary policy must steer a course that keeps inflation in check without creating an unacceptably high level of unemployment. The Fed maintains some secrecy over exactly how it strives to reach these goals. In recent years, observers of the Fed speculate that the Fed has followed a **price rule**, by which it adjusts the money supply up or down in order to keep the prices of certain basic commodities within a target range.

The Fed also designates *monetary targets*, which are acceptable ranges for the growth rates for the M1, M2, and M3 money supplies. In practice, the Fed often misses its targets because it has no direct control over the money supply; it controls only the monetary base. Moreover, monetary targets may sometimes conflict with the Fed's price rule or other objectives.

In 1995 the range of target growth for M2 was 1 percent to 5 percent, and for M3, 0 percent to 4 percent. Target ranges such as these represent the Fed's best guess about the amount of monetary growth that is best for the economy. When economic conditions change, the Fed can change the targets. For example, in mid-1995 the Fed raised the M2 targets to 2 to 6 percent. Such adjustments are made bearing in mind that too much growth in the money supply has the potential to set off higher inflation; too little, a recession.

The Equation of Exchange—Money and Prices

The **equation of exchange** was originally proposed in the nineteenth century as a means of explaining the link between money, prices, and output. The equation of exchange reveals that the amount of money people spend must equal the market value of what they purchase, as follows:

$$M \times V = P \times Q$$

The left side of the equation represents total spending in the economy. What is spent? Money (M in the equation). But the dollar you spend today was spent by someone else earlier, and will be spent again later. The typical dollar will change hands more than once as the economy's output is purchased. The average number of times money changes hands in a year is called the **velocity of money** (V), which was 1.9 in 1994 for the M2 definition of money. Total spending is calculated by multiplying the money supply by velocity.

On the right side of the equation, P is a price index showing the average level of prices. The aggregate output of goods and services is represented by Q. When P and Q are multiplied, the result is the dollar value of purchases, which is equivalent to nominal GDP. Because the value of what is bought must equal the value of what is sold, the equation of exchange is always true.

The equation of exchange forms the basis for the **quantity theory of money**. The quantity theory contends that velocity and aggregate output are unaffected in the long run by a change in the money supply. Thus, the effect of a change in the quantity of money must be a proportional change in the price level. An increase in the money supply brings inflation. Conversely, a decrease in the money supply brings deflation. Except for determining the price level, the quantity theory suggests that money does not matter, because the economy will always operate at the full-employment level of real GDP.

The quantity theory can be illustrated with the model of aggregate supply and aggregate demand, as shown in Figure 13A-3. An increase in the money supply shifts aggregate demand to the right, because additional money provides greater purchasing power at any given price level. The long-run effect is to increase the price level but leave real output unaffected. The movement from point A to point B in Figure 13A-3 illustrates this effect.

> ✓ **QUICKCHECK**
>
> If the money supply doubles, what does the quantity theory predict?
>
> _____
>
> *Answer:* The quantity theory predicts the price level would double. If the money supply tripled, prices would triple, and so forth.

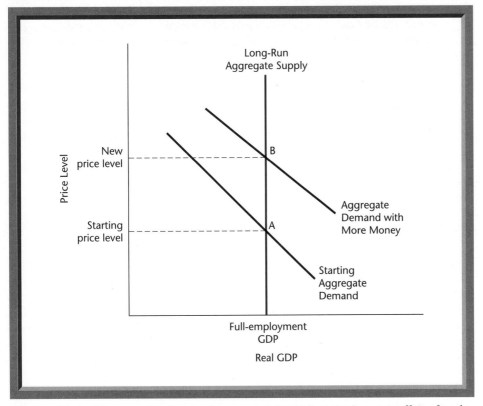

Figure 13A-3 **The quantity theory of money points out that the long-run effect of an increase in the money supply is merely to increase the price level.** An increase in aggregate demand increases the price level by moving the economy from equilibrium A to equilibrium B.

OBSERVATION POINT: Taxation through Inflation— What a Money Maker!

The Fed's ability to affect the money supply provides the federal government with opportunities to collect an "inflation tax," which occurs when the Fed escalates its purchases of government bonds. Because fewer bonds are in circulation, government debt to the public decreases, just as it would if government collected more taxes.

This way to reduce federal debt is appealing, except for one thing. The Fed's purchases of government bonds increase the money supply and may lead to inflation. This inflation further reduces the real burden of federal debt, because it allows government to repay its remaining debt with cheaper dollars—dollars that have less purchasing power than those originally borrowed. In effect the government would have tricked the buyers of bonds, and those buyers will not forget.

Future government borrowings would become much more expensive, meaning that future government bonds would be forced to pay much higher interest rates.

The Monetarist Prescription

Monetarism is a school of economic thought, founded by Nobel-winner Milton Friedman, that offers a modern version of the quantity theory. Monetarists readily agree with one contention of the original quantity theory: Velocity and aggregate output are independent of the quantity of money in the long run. However, unlike the quantity theory, monetarism acknowledges the existence of a short run.

According to the monetarist view, the quantity of money may indeed affect velocity and aggregate output in the short run. For example, a reduction in the growth rate of the money supply may cause a reduction in aggregate output. This effect could occur if people cut their purchases of goods and services because bank loans become more costly or difficult to obtain. If that happens, the economy slows down.

To avoid the recession that could result from too little money, or the inflation that could result from too much money, the monetarist policy recommendation is for the Fed to increase the money supply at a steady rate, equal to or slightly greater than the long-run growth in aggregate output. Since long-run growth of output tends to be about 2.5 to 3 percent, a steady annual monetary increase of about 3 percent or slightly higher is called for. The idea is to provide sufficient money so that the economy's additional output could be purchased without setting off significant inflation. This long-run focus places monetarism within the classical school of macro thought.

Implementing Monetarism—Some Practical Impediments

The Fed announces a range of monetary targets that are adjusted infrequently, which is consistent with monetarism. However, the Fed also makes ongoing adjustments in monetary policy that cause the actual growth in the money supply to deviate from its targets, at least in the short run. Thus, the Fed is accused by monetarists of being too quick to increase or decrease the growth rate of the money supply. Monetarists claim that this activist policy accentuates economic instability; they have compared the Fed to a driver who jerks a car's steering wheel first one way, and then the other, before accidentally steering the car off the road.

There are some practical problems in implementing monetarism. The most basic problem is that the Fed does not control the money supply. The Fed only controls the monetary base. Growing the monetary base at a slow and steady rate does not mean that the money supply will do likewise. Spirits of pessimism or optimism can greatly affect the money multiplier, which relates the monetary base to the money supply.

For example, the federal government partially shut down in November, 1995, laying off sixty percent of its employees. That shutdown lasted only one week. Had it continued, it would probably have generated widespread economic uncertainties, which would have prompted bankers to hold off on making many loans. The reduction in loans would have reduced the money multiplier, and thus the money supply. It is likely that the economy would have entered a recession, even if the monetary base remained the same. The Fed could counter such a drop in the money supply with an increase in the monetary base. However, that requires the Fed to predict national mood swings, which may be beyond its abilities.

Two other factors also complicate the Fed's search for stable prices. One is that changes in the money supply affect inflation with, as Milton Friedman put it, a "long and variable lag." Today's change in monetary policy may not take effect for months or even years, at which time economic conditions may be quite different from what they were at the moment the policy was implemented. Therefore, the effects of monetary policy are hard to predict.

The second problem is that there is disagreement over whether the M1 or M2 measure of the money supply should be the primary Fed target. M2 seems to have been the Fed's primary focus in recent years. Ideally, the Fed should emphasize the money supply variable that is most closely associated with economic performance. Which money supply measure this implies, however, is not obvious. Thus, while monetarism provides general guidance for monetary policy, it is difficult to implement with precision.

*I*nterest Rates

If people were picked at random and asked to recite the money supply figures, the response would be many blank stares. On the other hand, if asked about interest rates, people might mention the interest rate paid by their bank on savings deposits, the interest rate on their car loan, their mortgage interest rate, or even the interest rate on some government securities.

Interest rates represent the cost of borrowing and the reward for saving or lending. Conventionally, interest rates are expressed as annual percentages. For example, a bank depositor who receives a 10 percent interest rate on deposits will receive $10 per year in interest payments for each $100 deposited; a borrower who borrows at 10 percent would pay $10 per year in interest for each $100 borrowed.

Real versus Nominal Rates

Inflation affects the reward for saving and the true cost of borrowing. To see how, suppose that Lydia has agreed to lend Jon $100 at 10 percent interest, with a loan maturity of one year. Jon will thus repay Lydia $110 one year after the loan is made. If inflation increases prices by 10 percent during the year, the $110 that Lydia receives from Jon will buy only as much as the original $100. If effect, Lydia's true reward for giving up the use of her dollars is zero. If Lydia had expected a 10 percent rise in prices, she would not have accepted a 10 percent interest rate on the loan. Only a higher interest rate would have increased her purchasing power at maturity relative to its original value and given her a real reward for making the loan.

A *nominal interest rate* is an interest rate that is stated without reference to the inflation rate. The nominal rate on Lydia's loan to Jon is 10 percent. A *real interest rate* adjusts a nominal rate for inflation in order to show the true cost of borrowing and the true reward for lending. If inflation is 10 percent, the real rate on Lydia's loan is 0 percent. The following equation sums up this relationship:

$$\text{Nominal interest rate} = \text{real interest rate} + \text{inflation rate}$$

Before deciding upon the interest rate on her loan to Jon, Lydia should have used this equation. If she expected 10 percent inflation, and she was only willing to make the loan in exchange for a real return of 5 percent, then she should have set a 15 percent rate on the loan. Upon being charged 15 percent by Lydia, Jon should use the equation to calculate the real rate. The real rate would tell Jon the true cost of the loan. Jon would algebraically manipulate the equation to read as follows:

Real interest rate = nominal interest rate − inflation rate

Figure 13A-4 shows the nominal and real federal funds rate since 1979.

✓ QUICKCHECK

(A) What is the real interest rate if thirty-year government bonds pay 8 percent interest, and bond investors expect inflation to average 3 percent over the next thirty years? (B) What is the real rate on $100 kept in a bank account that pays 2 percent interest, and inflation is 3 percent?

Answers: (A) Use the real interest rate equation: 8 percent is substituted for the nominal rate and 3 percent for inflation. The real rate equals 5 percent. (B) Substituting in the real rate equation, the real interest rate is −1 percent. A negative real interest rate shows a loss of purchasing power.

Figure 13A-4   The nominal and real federal funds rate, 1979–1994.

Real federal funds rate calculated as the nominal rate (Table B-69) minus the change in the GDP implicit price deflator (Table B-4).

Source: 1996 Economic Report of the President.

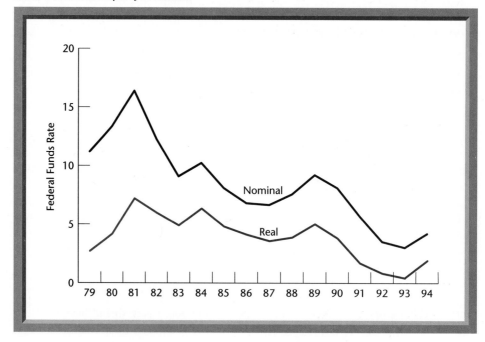

Monetary Policy toward Interest Rates

To a degree, monetary policy works through interest rates. A key interest rate is the federal funds rate, the interest rate on reserves banks lend to each other. The Fed does not directly set the federal funds rate, but can influence it by changing the quantity of bank reserves through the conduct of open market operations. Open market sales by the Fed dry up bank reserves, and thus result in a higher federal funds rate. The higher cost of reserves may be passed along to borrowers in the form of higher interest rates on bank loans. Conversely, open market purchases by the Fed tend to reduce the federal funds rate, and can thus lead to lower interest rates on consumer and business loans.

Monetary policy often targets short-term interest rates. A tight policy causes real interest rates in the economy to rise, with the goal of keeping inflation in check. If successful, then, a tight monetary policy would lead to nominal interest rates that are not much higher than the real rates. A loose policy causes real short-term rates to fall in order to stimulate the economy. A loose policy is usually advocated when inflation is not a problem.

Because interest rates are of direct concern to households and businesses, some people argue that the Fed should aim to keep them low. Although the Fed could aim to keep real rates low, the result would likely be inflation that causes nominal interest rates to soar as time passes. The reason is that in the long run, open market purchases used to drive down interest rates will increase the money supply and thus inflation. **Monetary policy cannot lower interest rates in the long run, except through lower inflation.** A Fed policy that ignored this principle is often held responsible for the upsurge of inflation in the 1970s. Monetarists argue that the Fed ought to target the money supply with the goal of keeping inflation under control and let interest rates adjust on their own.

EXPRESS STUDY TRUE OR FALSE

1. Changes in the quantity of money shift the aggregate ~~supply~~ *demand* curve.
2. Currency in bank vaults is *not* included as part of the M1 money supply.
3. Part of the Fed's job is to provide services to banks.
4. The primary tool of monetary policy is open market operations.
5. If the reserve requirement equals 20 percent, the deposit multiplier equals ~~20.~~ *5*
6. Monetarists prefer an ~~activist policy at~~ the Fed. *to maintain slow, steady growth in the money supply*

Module B

EXPLORING ISSUES

Independence—nations strive for it; young people can't wait for it; the Fed tries to keep it. The Fed vigorously defends its independence in spite of attacks from critics. Does Federal Reserve independence benefit the economy, or is the defense of its independence just a ploy unjustifiably to retain powers that should not ever have been granted to the Fed?

Discretionary power over monetary policy makes the Fed the 1500-pound gorilla of the economic jungle. When expansionary monetary policy is given credit for growing the economy and for lowering the unemployment and interest rates, Americans feel good about the Fed. People's jobs are secure, their incomes are growing, and low interest rates mean the monthly payments on that new car they've been wanting are now affordable. But when interest rates are high, and bankruptcies and unemployment are rising, the Fed gets the blame. What right does the Fed have to create economic pain? After all, the leaders of the Fed were not elected to office. Should not the Fed be held more closely accountable in the political process?

*T*he Independent Fed

The Federal Reserve is unique among government agencies in being subject to relatively few explicit government directives. The Fed has a great deal of independence to conduct monetary policy as it pleases, without interference from Congress or the president.

The fear that originally motivated Congress to insulate the Fed from politics is that political pressures could influence the Fed to pursue an expansionary monetary policy at the wrong moment, a policy that would ultimately lead to inflation. Evidence suggests that the inflationary effects of monetary policy do not set in immediately, but appear only after a time lag. Thus, if the Fed were subject to political pressure, decision making could favor short-term expediency over long-term economic goals.

One source of the Fed's independence from political pressure relates to the structure of the Board of Governors. Governors are appointed by the president of the United States to fourteen-year nonrenewable terms. Governors thus are given the freedom to make policy decisions without the worry of reappointment. Once on the Board, a governor is free to follow the dictates of conscience rather than the decrees of the president or Congress.

Typically, government agencies are funded by Congress. In contrast, the Fed funds itself. By retaining independent control of its own purse strings, the Fed retains independence of action. The Fed's secret of financial independence? The Fed is a banker's bank, and as such earns interest from the discount loans it makes to commercial banks. However, the major source of the Fed's earnings is interest from its holdings of treasury securities, securities it may have purchased with newly printed Federal Reserve Notes! In recent years the Fed's net income after expenses has totaled a whopping $15 billion each year, much of which it is required to turn over to the U.S. Treasury.

Another factor in Federal Reserve independence is found in the financial markets. The Fed's policy actions have the potential to roil the markets, providing substantial gains or inflicting massive losses on the owners of stocks, bonds, and other financial instruments. Financial market participants, called "bond market vigilantes" in the press, stand ready to bail out of investments when they perceive the Fed is acting irresponsibly, and hence threatening the value of those investments. That threat influences the Fed, helping free it from political pressure.

Even homeowners help keep the Fed independent. With the advent of adjustable-rate home mortgages, some homeowners' monthly payments are pushed up by the upward surge in interest rates that accompanies expected inflation. Hence, this segment of the public has a vested interest in seeing that the Fed acts responsibly.

These considerations mean that lots of people have an interest in a stable monetary policy. Thus, the President's appointments to the Board do not go unnoticed. In 1983, for instance, pressure from financial markets forced Republican President Reagan to reappoint then Board chairman Paul Volcker despite Volcker having first been appointed to the Board by President Carter, a Democrat. Volcker was perceived by the markets as an experienced policymaker, independent and above politics, and thus a stabilizing influence on the economy.

*R*eining *in the Fed Aristocracy—Accountability in Practice*

Critics argue the Fed has too much power and charge it with decision making that favors its own self-interests and those of special interests, such as bankers. In this view, the Fed is akin to an aristocracy exercising power at the expense of the greater economic welfare. Ostensibly, however, the Fed operates in the public interest. But what is the public interest? Possible goals include stable prices, stable interest rates, a stable foreign exchange value of the dollar, and stable overall economic activity, at a level sufficient to ensure high employment. Unfortunately, these economic variables fluctuate over time, sometimes severely.

One school of thought with definite views about the sources and implications of such economic instability is monetarism. Monetarists usually believe that market economies are inherently stable and that fluctuations in economic activity are the result of unstable monetary policies. If the monetarist view is valid, then the Fed must be reined in, since its exercise of power through the conduct of discretionary monetary policy not only is not in the public interest, but is certainly harmful. Thus, proponents of monetarism seek to harness the Fed aristocracy.

Monetarism provides a theoretical foundation for the paltry limits that do exist on the Fed's independence, and offer the justification for even stronger Congressional action for stripping the Fed of its powers to conduct monetary policy. The importance of the quantity of money in monetarist thought led Congress to pass House Concurrent Resolution 133 in 1975. This resolution calls for the Fed to announce target ranges for growth in the M1, M2, and M3 monetary aggregates. Furthermore, the 1978 Humphrey-Hawkins bill, which commits the U.S. to full employment, requires the Fed to act in a manner consistent with that goal.

In addition to being required to report to Congress on a periodic basis about its monetary policy actions, the Fed is regularly at risk of losing at least part of its current, reduced level of independence. Proposals advanced by critics of the Fed would, if enacted into law, strip the Fed of a portion of its discretion in the conduct of policy.

Two other aspects of accountability deserve mention. One is the Fed's penchant for secrecy. The Fed has lobbied unsuccessfully to be allowed to make monetary policy decisions behind closed doors and keep those decisions from the public for months or even years. Its justification seems to be that if the public knows what the Fed is doing, investors and others might be able to take actions that would mitigate the effects of monetary policy.

A final consideration is the accusation that the Fed churns its portfolio of securities. *Churning* means unnecessary buying and selling. In practice, the Fed disguises its intentions by buying and selling securities at the same time. Securities dealers make large profits from the Fed's dealings in government bonds. Critics of the Fed would like to increase the amount of money the Fed turns over to the Treasury by taking a chunk out of those profits.

*G*o for the Gold!

Some congressional critics of the Fed wish to vest Congress or the U.S. Treasury with the powers of oversight over monetary policy. Others wish to take monetary control out of government's hands altogether. This change could be accomplished by adoption of a monetary rule, as discussed in the Expressway, or a gold standard. In this way, the money supply would be truly free of politics.

"Gold bugs" would like to reestablish the convertibility of currency into gold, thus establishing a **gold standard** that would transform the dollar from fiat money to commodity money. Those who advocate a gold standard focus on the potential for the Fed to create inflation under the current system of fiat money. Tying the dollar to gold would limit the Fed's ability to create excess dollars. The current system of fiat money makes it possible for the Fed to finance government deficits by printing money. Too much fiat money means inflation—a hidden tax. Those advocating a gold standard prefer the monetary discipline inherent in tying the quantity of money to something beyond the reach of politics.

A gold standard would not necessarily make for a stable value of money, however. For example, the accumulation of gold from the New World by Spanish Conquistadors led to a centuries-long gradual decline in the price of gold in Europe. Supply shifted out and the price went down. Since gold was used as money, and it gradually lost value, the result was inflation.

These days, the value of gold also changes dramatically. After reaching a peak of nearly $800 in 1979, for example, the price of gold fell to less than half of that amount by 1994. Although the price of gold recovered to about $400 per ounce by 1996, the lesson is clear. Any currency that can be exchanged for gold at a fixed rate will find that its value in the world marketplace fluctuates just as much as the value of gold. Tying the U.S. dollar to gold in the period over which gold's value fell by half would have meant that the dollar's value would have also fallen by half. That would have caused an approximately one hundred percent inflation rate!

In the Fed We Trust

Perhaps the above motto should be printed on U.S. paper currency. Owners of dollars, both at home and abroad, surely place their trust in the Fed to maintain the value of the dollar. Is this trust well placed?

If the American people are the true owners of the Fed, and thus principals, then the seven members of the Board can be viewed as the people's agents. The *principal-agent problem* is that agents sometimes put self-interest ahead of the best interests of principals. Do the governors make decisions that enhance their own future employment prospects? Most appointees to the Board have chosen not to serve out their full fourteen-year terms, and have instead accepted attractive job offers outside government. Because the services of these highly qualified people would naturally command a high price in the marketplace, we cannot presume a problem. We might nonetheless temper our absolute trust in the Fed with a dose of caution.

Is the economy better off because of the Fed's independence? According to evidence summarized by Patricia Pollard in the July/August 1993 issue of the *Federal Reserve Bank of St. Louis Review*, nations whose central banks are more independent have had better inflation records than nations whose central banks are less independent. Furthermore, on the whole, independent central banks are able to control inflation more effectively, without hindering economic growth.

The lesson to be learned from experiences with central bank independence around the world is that price stability must be the number one policy goal of a central bank. Granting the central bank some measure of independence appears to promote this objective. After all, if the central bank does not pursue the goal of stable prices, who will?

B

PROSPECTING FOR NEW INSIGHTS

1. How does the existence of twelve regional Federal Reserve banks, rather than a single central bank, contribute to the Fed's independence? Explain.
2. The president nominates individuals to the Board of Governors, subject to the advice and consent of the Senate. Should the people elect members of the Board of Governors by direct vote, or is the present system preferable? Explain.

Money can lose value quickly or slowly. What causes money to lose value? Who is harmed the most by that loss of value? Does anyone benefit? In this Exploration the objective is to examine the issue of inflation.

Historically, gold has probably served as money more often than any other commodity, because of its beauty, permanence, and scarcity. It was the scarcity of gold that helped to establish its relative value and maintain the stability of that value.

Monetary systems today are based upon fiat money, which has no intrinsic value. Such money is vulnerable to losses in value due to inflation, because governments may be tempted to finance expenditures through the issuance of more printing-press money, rather than through borrowing or taxation. Thus, public concern over the value of money is legitimate.

*H*yperinflation

Hyperinflation is inflation out of control. With hyperinflation, money loses its value quickly. Take an annual inflation rate of 10,000 percent, for example. What would a dollar be worth after just one year of such hyperinflation? The answer: Less than a penny. To put it another way, it would take over $100 at the end of a year of such hyperinflation to purchase what $1 would have purchased at the beginning of the year.

The most widely documented episode of hyperinflation occurred in post-World War I Germany in the years 1922–1923. Germany had been held responsible by the victorious allies for the payment of war reparations. That responsibility overburdened the government's ability to tax and borrow. The only avenue of escape left for the German government was the printing press. Before the presses stopped and currency reform occurred, prices had increased by a factor of 1.5 trillion (a trillion equals one followed by twelve zeros). If the U.S. suffered an inflation of similar magnitude, a $50 textbook would rise in price to $75 trillion.

Imagine a hyperinflated world. Your purse or wallet would not be large enough to transport enough money to make a simple purchase. You might demand that your boss pay your wages at the end of every workday, or even more often than that. A dollar received now would have more purchasing power than a dollar received later. You would also want to budget enough time to spend that money. During hyperinflation, money is like a hot potato. Everyone wants to get rid of money as quickly as possible, thus increasing the velocity of money.

Hyperinflation is much more than pages out of a history book. Many modern countries have gone through the same problems. For example, imagine yourself peering from your apartment window in Buenos Aries, Argentina, in 1989. You spy an armored car pulling up to La Dora Restaurant down the street, and carting away sacks of money. It is midnight. You recall seeing the same event the previous midnight and the midnight before that. Come to think of it, you'd seen bags of money carted away from that same restaurant every day at noon. Are you alarmed? Should you call the police to report a money laundering operation? Actually, these events were real, but represented nothing more than the restaurant seeking to get its money into an interest-earning bank account as quickly as possible. At a 1989 inflation rate of 100 percent per month, it did not take long for the Argentine currency to lose its value.

With prices changing so rapidly, imagine the effort that would have to be devoted to keeping track of price changes in supermarkets, restaurants, and other retail establishments. Some people would wish to opt out of the monetary economy as completely as possible by arranging to participate in barter arrangements with others. Overall, hyperinflation would be a giant headache to deal with. The efforts of people to cope with hyperinflation would reduce labor productivity, thus resulting in real reductions in the standard of living.

*I*nflation and the Rule of 72

In recent decades, hyperinflation has occurred only in less-developed economies. Why, then, is a certain nervousness over inflation detectable in most advanced industrialized nations? One insight can be gained by applying the rule of 72 to various inflation rates. The rule of 72 allows an estimate of how many years it would take prices to double for any rate of inflation. The calculation involved in the rule of 72 is simple: Take an inflation rate and divide it into 72. Table 13B2-1 shows the outcome of applying the rule of 72 to selected annual inflation rates between 1 percent and 16 percent.

The calculations in Table 13B2-1 show that an increase in the inflation rate from levels that are initially low can have dramatic long-term effects. For instance, a sustained 2 percent inflation rate, such as was the approximate norm in the U.S. during the 1950s, would mean that it would take almost half of the average person's lifetime for prices to double. At a 4 percent inflation rate, a figure in line with recent U.S. experience, prices would double about four times over a lifetime. At a 10 percent inflation rate, prices would double over and over a total of ten times. At that inflation rate, newborns had better not become used to the idea of dollar-a-loaf bread. In their golden years, bread would be expected to cost $10 a loaf.

TABLE 13B2-1   *Applying the Rule of 72*

Annual Inflation Rate	Estimated Number of Years for Price Level to Double
1%	72
2%	36
4%	18
8%	9
10%	7.2
16%	4.5

Unanticipated Inflation and Indexing

As long as average incomes keep up with inflation, no one is hurt, right? So why not adopt *Mad Magazine*'s Alfred E. Neuman attitude of "What, me worry?" A partial answer to that question involves making the distinction between *anticipated inflation* and *unanticipated inflation*. Anticipated inflation is expected by the public. Unanticipated inflation is inflation that catches the public by surprise.

Anticipated inflation, when everyone's crystal balls are working properly, can be taken into account in wage negotiations, mortgage loans, and a variety of other contractual agreements. In theory at least, everyone is thus able to defend against losses imposed by anticipated inflation.

When inflation is unanticipated, the story changes. An increase in inflation, which makes inflation higher than expected, provides borrowers with a windfall resulting from a lower-than-expected real interest rate. Because borrowers win, lenders lose. To see this relationship, suppose I borrowed $1,000 from you to be repaid in one year. We both anticipate an inflation rate of 2 percent over the year, and agree that a 3 percent real return on your loan is fair. Thus, we strike a deal that I will repay you $1,050, the original sum I borrowed, plus $20 to make you whole for the loss of purchasing power you suffer because of inflation, plus another $30 for giving up the use of your money for the year.

Now suppose inflation proves greater than we anticipated. For example, suppose inflation rises to 5 percent. The real interest rate on the loan drops to zero. The $1,050 I repay you provides you with no reward for giving up the use of your money. You lose. I win, because I was able to use your money without having to pay you a real return. In other words, I used your purchasing power, and returned the same purchasing power to you. If inflation had risen to a rate greater than 5 percent, I would have returned less purchasing power to you than you had to begin with. You would be an even bigger loser.

A solution to the problem just discussed is called **indexing**—automatically adjusting the terms of the agreement to account for inflation. If we indexed our loan agreement, we would agree to adjust the amount I repaid you according to some price index, say the consumer price index (CPI). If the CPI showed an inflation rate of 5 percent over the year of our loan agreement, I would be required to repay you $1,080, equal to the $1,000 I borrowed, plus the 3 percent real return you wanted, or $30, plus the 5 percent, or $50, to make up for the reduction in purchasing power caused by inflation.

A number of high-inflation countries, such as Brazil and Israel, have resorted to indexation to deal with inflation. In the U.S., variable-rate home mortgages are a form of indexing. When market interest rates rise because of inflation, home buyers find their monthly payments also rising because the interest rate built into their mortgage agreement rises accordingly. Traditional fixed-rate home mortgages are not indexed. Lenders who make fixed-rate loans take the risk of inflation-induced losses in exchange for a higher interest rate than is initially attached to a variable-rate mortgage of the same duration and risk.

In the 1970s, when U.S. inflation was relatively high and rising, cost of living adjustment (COLA) clauses in labor agreements were a popular form of wage indexing. COLAs call for periodic upward adjustments in the wages of covered workers to match increases in the CPI. With unions losing power and inflation losing steam during the 1980s, COLAs lost popularity. Social Security payments, however, are still indexed to the CPI.

B

Indexing can lead to problems. One is that indexing attaches extraordinary importance to the index numbers used. As noted in chapter 11, indexes are approximations that can easily overstate the true inflation rate. The CPI's overstatement of inflation partly explains why Social Security benefits have become more generous in real terms over time. Indexing is also criticized for feeding the very inflation it is intended to fight. In 1995, for example, Brazil began a deindexation program that outlaws indexation in a variety of scenarios. Brazil recognized that indexation contributes to a vicious cycle of ever-rising inflation.

*W*hy Not Zero Inflation?

If hyperinflation is potentially destructive, and even a little inflation requires adjustments in the form of indexing, why do not governments pursue policies of zero inflation? If inflation is, in the widely-quoted words of Milton Friedman, "always and everywhere a monetary phenomenon," then why can't inflation be eliminated?

One answer is political—it takes willpower to endure the disruptive effects of limiting monetary growth. The other is operational—central banks can influence, but not control, the rate of inflation. Figure 13B2-1 plots the inflation rate and money growth in the

Figure 13B2-1   Monetary growth and inflation are closely tied, but not identical, as is illustrated by the growth rate of the CPI and of M2.

Source: 1996 Economic Report of the President, Tables B-56 and B-65.

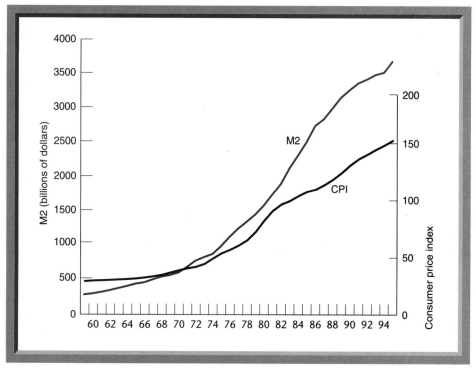

U.S. for 1979 to 1995. The figure shows that lower money growth is not always associated with lower inflation. A portion of the inflation rate is outside the control of monetary policy, at least in the short run.

1. Why do you think the U.S. has not experienced hyperinflation? If the U.S. did experience hyperinflation, what changes in money and banking do you think the voters would demand?

2. Would you prefer to see the Fed adopt the goal of zero inflation or have it accept a little inflation? If there is a trade-off between inflation and unemployment, should the goal of low inflation or low unemployment carry more weight? Explain.

B

CHALLENGE 1
From the Mathematical to the Behavioral—Deposit and Money Multipliers

The deposit multiplier shows the maximum amount by which deposits in the banking system will expand after reserves in the system are increased by Federal Reserve open market operations or discount loans to banks. An expansion of deposits occurs because banks make loans, and people who receive money deposit it in banks, and so forth. The mathematical formula for the simple deposit multiplier is the reciprocal of the reserve requirement. When multiplied by some initial change in reserves, the result is the maximum possible change in the money supply.

Table 13C1-1 illustrates how a deposit multiplier works. This table tracks the chain reaction that occurs after the Fed purchases $1,000 of securities from a bank, thus providing it with $1,000 of excess reserves. We will refer to this bank as the Initial Bank, and to subsequent banks as Bank One, Bank Two, and so forth. The Initial Bank loans the $1,000 of excess reserves to a customer, who spends the funds. The recipient of the $1,000 deposits that amount in Bank One. Each bank in the table loans the maximum amount consistent with a 10 percent reserve requirement, and all monies received are assumed to be deposited in the next bank in the sequence.

The deposit multiplier process shown here represents the maximum value of the money multiplier. The money multiplier is the actual proportion by which the money supply increases in response to Fed actions that change the monetary base. The public and bankers play a significant role in determining the value of this money multiplier. For ex-

TABLE 13C1-1	*Multiple Expansion of Deposits, Given a 10 Percent Reserve Requirement*		
Bank	**Deposits Received**	**Loans Made**	**Change in Reserves**
Bank One	$1,000.00	$900.00	$100.00
Bank Two	$900.00	$810.00	$90.00
Bank Three	$810.00	$729.00	$81.00
Bank Four	$729.00	$656.10	$72.90
Bank Five	$656.10	$590.49	$65.61
Bank Six	$590.49	$531.44	$59.05
Bank Seven	$531.44	$478.30	$53.14
Bank Eight	$478.30	$430.47	$47.83
.	.	.	.
.	.	.	.
.	.	.	.
Total for the banking system	$10,000.00	$9,000.00	$1,000.00

ample, if bankers are pessimistic about future economic prospects, they may be reluctant to make loans. In this case, they will maintain a sizable cushion of excess reserves. This cushion is termed the **excess reserves-to-deposits ratio (e/d)**. In contrast, in the simple deposit multiplier, new deposits are always loaned to the maximum extent possible, and thus do not generate excess reserves. The ratio (e/d) is hence assumed to equal zero in the simple deposit multiplier.

In addition, another ratio comes to bear. This ratio, termed the **currency-to-deposits ratio (c/d)**, reflects the behavior of the public. If the public is pessimistic about the security of the banking system, the public will hold more currency and smaller bank accounts. When people receive payments, they will deposit only some of those payments into their banks. In contrast, the simple deposit multiplier requires that they deposit all payments into their banks, and thus assumes (c/d) equals zero.

Both the excess reserves-to-deposits ratio and the currency-to-deposit ratios will be affected by changes in expectations about the future of the economy. The result is that actions by the Fed cannot have a fully predictable effect upon the money supply, because the Fed cannot control these expectations. Other factors can also affect e/d and c/d. For example, e/d will increase if bankers worry about unexpected withdrawals. Likewise, the existence of the underground economy, which operates on a largely cash basis, causes c/d to be higher than it otherwise would be. Anything that affects these ratios also affects the money multiplier.

CHALLENGE 2
Interest Rate Differentials over Time and across Countries

Economists often speak of "the interest rate" as if there were only one, when there are actually many interest rates. This custom is acceptable because the spectrum of interest rates within a country usually moves together. Still, interest rates can and do differ. Reasons include differences in the following:

- *Default risk*—the chance that the payer of interest will be unable to make those payments, or even return funds invested. There is little default risk in depositing funds into an insured bank account or investing in bonds issued by the federal government. In contrast, corporate bonds involve higher default risks, and hence pay higher interest rates than do bank accounts and government bonds.
- *Liquidity*—Since liquidity is of value, savers must be rewarded for giving it up. Savings account deposits are both safe and highly liquid. Interest rates on these accounts are thus relatively low.
- *Term to maturity*—the time before the investment will be repaid. Typical savings and checking accounts have terms to maturity of zero, meaning that repayment is immediate upon the request of the depositor. Bills, notes, bonds, and certificates of deposit each represent IOUs repayable only at a later date. Bills have shorter terms to maturity than notes and bonds. Terms to maturity among U.S. government bills, notes, and bonds range from three months to thirty years. Bonds, which have longer maturities, customarily pay higher interest rates.

- The currency in which the interest is paid—Competition for investment forces interest rates higher in countries with high inflation rates or high risks.

The relationship between the term to maturity and interest rates is illustrated by a *yield curve*, such as shown in Figure 13C2-1. Current yield curves can be found in most financial newspapers and on-line financial services. The yield curve ordinarily slopes upward, such as shown in Figure 13C2-1. Interest rates normally rise along with terms to maturity because investors must be compensated for being locked in for a long time.

Although not the norm, it is also not very unusual to find yield curves that are inverted over some ranges of maturities. This inversion occurs when investors expect lower interest rates on bonds bought in the future. Investors are then willing to lock in long-term rates that are below current short-term rates because they want to avoid having to reinvest their money in the future at what they believe will be lower rates. Figure 13C2-2 illustrates a yield curve that is inverted over a range of maturities. Specifically, the interest rates are inverted for maturities of up to one year in duration.

The numbers illustrated in Figure 13C2-2 represent actual data for January 1996. Events and expectations at that time exemplify why the yield curve is sometimes inverted. Specifically, the Fed maintained a relatively tight monetary policy, which kept short-term interest rates relatively high. Because investors thought that the Fed's policies had succeeded in preventing inflation from taking root, they expected the Fed to ease in the future. A *Fed easing* would loosen up credit and lead to lower real interest rates. Since in-

Figure 13C2-1   **A typically shaped yield curve** shows that bonds with longer maturities offer higher yields.

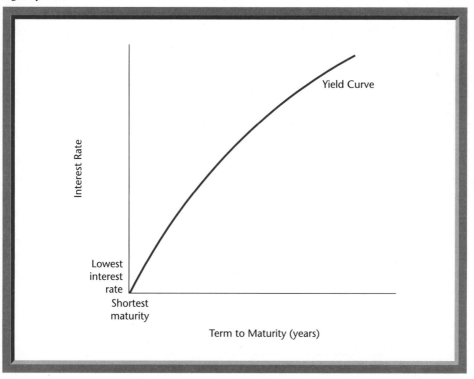

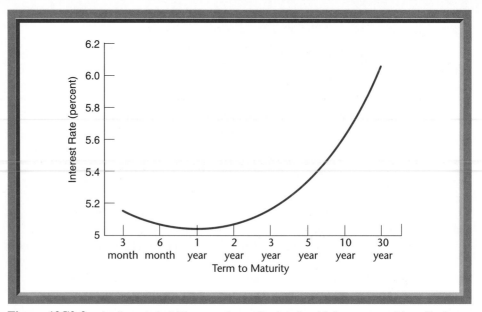

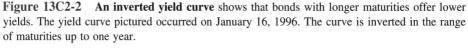

Figure 13C2-2   An inverted yield curve shows that bonds with longer maturities offer lower yields. The yield curve pictured occurred on January 16, 1996. The curve is inverted in the range of maturities up to one year.

Source: Prodigy.

vestors did not perceive inflation to be a problem, they expected nominal interest rates to fall also. The result was an inverted yield curve.

Interest rates among countries also vary, often quite dramatically. While some of this variation is associated with differences in investment risk, there are also dramatic differences in *risk-adjusted rates*—rates that have the risk premium factored out. Would not investors direct all of their money into countries with the highest risk-adjusted interest rates? After all, in competitive markets, sellers who set their prices above the competition have no sales.

As it turns out, **the risk-adjusted interest rates are equal among countries when those rates are expressed in any single currency.** Put another way, the interest rate differentials among countries are exactly offset by expected exchange rate differentials.

For example, suppose an American investor buys a Mexican bond that earns a risk-adjusted return of 25 percent, versus the 5 percent risk-adjusted return available in the U.S. The Mexican bond is denominated in pesos, since that is Mexico's currency. Thus the investor must buy pesos in order to buy the bond. The American investor will also receive pesos as future bond payments, and will thus be faced with converting them back into dollars.

To do this conversion, the investor can wait until the payment arrives and then exchange pesos into dollars at the **spot rate**, which is the exchange rate of the moment. Alternatively, since the investor would know how much payment would be coming, he or she could enter the *futures market* to lock in a future exchange rate. However, that investor might be in for an unwelcome surprise: The cost of a **futures contract** that guarantees today's exchange rate in the future would wipe out the gain from the higher Mexican interest rate.

In this example, the market's best guess is that the peso is going to depreciate against the dollar at a rate of exactly 20 percent. In other words, the expectation in the marketplace is that the interest rate differential that makes the Mexican bond look attractive is exactly offset by the expectation of a deteriorating Mexican currency. Otherwise, investors would seek to buy pesos with dollars and force the peso higher or Mexican interest rates lower today, until there was no more opportunity for profit.

In sum, the difference in risk-adjusted interest rates among countries is exactly offset by the expected rate at which the country's currency appreciates or depreciates. This equality is called **interest rate parity**. Competition in the worldwide market for investments is what makes it happen.

C

Study by Design

SpeedStudy

SpeedReview

Money affects the macroeconomy through its effects on aggregate demand. The M1, M2, and M3 money supplies are defined according to decreasing liquidity, respectively. The Federal Reserve controls the monetary base and thereby influences the quantity of money. The bulk of the money supply is created by banks when they make loans. An initial deposit of new money into a bank results in an expansion of money through the money multiplier effect.

The Federal Reserve is composed of three primary parts: the Board of Governors, the Federal Open Market Committee, and twelve regional Federal Reserve District Banks. Most monetary policy is conducted through open market operations. Monetarists argue that the Fed should target a slow and steady growth path for the money supply, so as to provide enough money for economic growth, but not so much as to cause an unacceptable level of inflation. The Fed also influences interest rates, which in turn affect other aspects of the economy. If the Fed is successful at controlling inflation, real and nominal interest rates will be close together.

SpeedStudy True or False Self-Test

A1. Fish could not serve as money.

A2. Seignorage is a source of government revenue.

A3. Gresham's law states that ~~good~~ money drives ~~bad~~ money out of circulation.

A4. The assets side of a balance sheet shows the uses of funds.

A5. When banks borrow from other banks, the borrowings are called federal funds.

A6. Currency plus bank reserves equals the monetary base.

A7. Increasing the discount rate will probably decrease the money supply.

A8. In practice, the effects of changes in monetary policy are nearly instantaneous.

A9. According to the quantity theory, the only effect of an increase in the money supply is to shift aggregate supply to the right.

A10. The real interest rate is ~~the sum of~~ the nominal interest rate ~~plus~~ the inflation rate.

B11. Federal Reserve independence is guaranteed by the U.S. constitution.

B12. Nations with independent central banks tend to have lower inflation and equally good economic performance otherwise.

B13. Anticipated inflation is expected by the public.

B14. Indexing is designed to be a solution to problems created by inflation.

C15. The deposit multiplier equals the minimum value for the money multiplier.

C16. When banks hold more excess reserves, the money multiplier is reduced in value.

C17. When stated with reference to each country's local currencies, the percentage interest rates in various countries are identical.

C18. Interest rate parity means that the U.S. dollar will buy the same amount of goods and services, no matter what country it is spent in.

The MasterMind

Selected Terms Along the Way

Federal Reserve System, 465
seignorage, 467
demand deposits, 467
liquidity, 468
M1, M2, M3, 468
time deposits, 468
federal funds rate, 471
discount rate, 471
reserve requirements, 471
excess reserves, 471

open market operations, 473
monetary base, 474
money multiplier, 475
deposit multiplier, 476
price rule, 477
equation of exchange, 478
velocity of money, 478
quantity theory of money, 478
monetarism, 480

interest rate, 481
gold standard, 486
indexing, 490

excess reserves-to-deposits
   ratio (e/d), 494
currency-to-deposits ratio
   (c/d), 494
spot rate, 496
futures contract, 496
interest rate parity, 497

MasterMind Multiple-Choice Self-Test

A1. Other things equal, which of the following would immediately decrease the money supply?
   a. A borrower repays a bank loan.
   b. A borrower receives a bank loan in the form of a check.
   c. The Fed conducts an open market purchase of securities.
   d. The Fed lowers the discount rate.

A2. If the Fed wishes to expand the money supply, it would
   a. increase the discount rate.
   b. conduct an open market purchase.
   c. increase the reserve requirement.
   d. authorize additional Federal Reserve Notes to be deposited into the U.S. Treasury.

A3. The Fed has direct control over
   a. M1 only.
   b. M1 and M2 only.
   c. M1, M2, and M3.
   d. the monetary base.

A4. The equation of exchange is
   a. $MP = VQ$.
   b. $MV = PQ$.
   c. $PV = MQ$.
   d. $\dfrac{1}{\text{percentage reserve requirement}}$.

A5. Monetarism is a form of _____ economics.
   a. Keynesian
   b. classical
   c. supply-side
   d. Marxist

B6. The Fed's major source of funding is
   a. Congress.
   b. the president.
   c. the United Nations.
   d. its investments.

B7. Those most likely to be harmed by unanticipated inflation are
   a. the Fed.
   b. the federal government.
   c. lenders.
   d. borrowers.

C8. Which does *not* affect the value of the money multiplier?
   a. The ratio of currency to deposits.
   b. The required reserve ratio.
   c. The ratio of excess reserves to deposits.
   d. The ratio of coins to paper money.

C9. If Alphaland offers higher interest rates than Betaland on comparable risk-adjusted investments, then the theory of interest rate parity suggests that

    a. Alphaland's currency is expected to depreciate over time relative to Betaland's currency.

    b. Betaland's currency is expected to depreciate over time relative to Alphaland's currency.

    c. investors will stop investing in Alphaland until interest rates fall there to equal those in Betaland.

    d. investors will stop investing in Betaland until interest rates rise there to equal those in Alphaland.

MasterMind Questions and Problems

A1. Suppose it became lawful for anyone to issue money without any government restrictions of any kind. What factors would influence an individual to either accept or reject privately issued money?

A2. On your personal balance sheet, what is the ratio of liquid assets to illiquid assets? Since illiquid assets often pay higher rates of return than liquid ones, why bother to hold liquid assets? Explain.

A3. What Fed actions are consistent with a looser monetary policy? Which are in accord with a tighter policy?

A4. Suppose M = the money supply = $200, V = velocity = 2, and Q = quantity of output = 100 units. What is the price level? According to the quantity theory of money, what happens to the price level if the money supply triples to $600?

A5. What is your bank's current nominal interest rate on savings deposits? What is the real interest rate on savings deposits? If the real rate is negative, would people continue to hold dollars in savings accounts? Why?

B6. Discuss how you or someone in your family has been affected by Federal Reserve monetary policy. Do Fed-induced changes in interest rates help or harm you or your family members? Why?

B7. Suppose that you anticipate a significant upward move in the inflation rate next year. List at least five actions you could take to protect yourself from inflation's negative effects.

C8. Suppose you attached radio transmitters the size of microdots to 100 one-dollar bills, deposited those dollar bills into your bank, and monitored their locations as they circulate. Write a one-page educational short story describing the route that those dollar bills would take, assuming that all banks have a 20 percent reserve requirement.

C9. Using a numerical example, explain how exchange rate changes can offset an interest rate differential between two countries.

Future Explorations: Mapping out Term Papers

1. Bank Regulation: How Much Is Enough?
In this paper you will trace the history of bank regulation back to the New Deal of the 1930s. What motivated the regulations imposed on banks? Are these regulations still needed? Did these regulations play a role in the increased number of bank failures in the 1980s? You will identify specific regulations, including the details of the

Glass-Steagall Act and the workings of federal deposit insurance. You will also present the views of the Federal Reserve on reforming bank regulation.

2. **Money and Monetary Policy: A Look at the Last Thirty Years**
The last thirty years have been turbulent ones for the Federal Reserve. Problems of inflation, slow economic growth, recession, and more have challenged the Fed's policy makers. In this paper you will identify the individuals who have served as chairpersons of the Fed and contrast their successes and failures.

3. **Central Banking around the World**
In this paper you will contrast the Federal Reserve with its counterparts in other major countries. You will also discuss the international component in the job that central bankers perform. For example, what does it mean for a central bank to defend its country's currency? Is there much cooperation between the central banks of the world? Illustrate the answers to these questions with historical instances of central bank behavior.

Answer Key

ExpressStudy True or False	SpeedStudy True or False Self-Test		MasterMind Multiple Choice Self-Test
1. F	1. T	10. F	1. a
2. F	2. T	11. F	2. b
3. T	3. F	12. T	3. d
4. T	4. T	13. T	4. b
5. F	5. T	14. T	5. b
6. F	6. T	15. F	6. d
	7. T	16. T	7. c
	8. F	17. F	8. d
	9. F	18. F	9. a

Fourteen

Policy for the Long Run

Module A

TRAVELING THE ECONOMICS EXPRESSWAY

Module B

EXPLORING ISSUES

Module C

MASTERING ROADSIDE CHALLENGES

$\mathcal{A}$ Look Ahead

Economic growth was once symbolized by more railroads and smokestacks. Now, growth is likely to result from new ways of transmitting and processing information. Either way, growth offers the only way to maintain or improve living standards in the face of an expanding population. Since labor is a resource, an increase in population can itself bring economic growth. However, along with the additional output come additional mouths to feed. Thus, economies turn to capital formation as a way to increase the value of output per capita.

While economists have long sought to maintain consistent noninflationary growth, that focus has intensified lately. In a sense, focusing on the long run is a luxury allowed by recent years of relative peace and prosperity. In contrast, Keynes developed his theories amid the pressures of the Great Depression of the 1930s. It is not surprising that Keynes dismissed the long run so as to focus more intensely upon short-term cures for the economy's ills.

This chapter starts by examining some micro foundations of macro theory that pertain to capital formation. These foundations provide insight into how the marketplace generates the investment needed for economic growth. With this as background, the chapter proceeds to explore the long-run implications of alternative macro policy prescriptions.

DESTINATIONS

$\mathcal{M}$odule A

As you zip along the Expressway you will arrive at an ability to

- identify the determinants of savings and investment;
- describe how government policies unintentionally discourage capital formation;
- recount classical theory and its modern development;
- use aggregate supply and aggregate demand analysis to integrate and distinguish the various schools of macroeconomic thought;
- discuss why liberals embrace Keynesian theory, and conservatives embrace classical theory.

$\mathcal{M}$odule B

Upon leaving the Expressway to explore issues you will be able to

- interpret how taxation and spending associated with Social Security reduce incentives for productivity and capital formation;
- draw out the implications of a country's fundamental choice between short-run comfort and long-run prosperity.

$\mathcal{M}$odule C

Mastering Roadside Challenges will allow you to hone analytical skills by

- explaining how the tax code's biases against saving can be offset by adjustments to other policies in theory, but probably not in practice;
- modeling appropriate values for research subsidies, and discerning practical difficulties in implementing those subsidies.

503

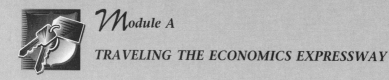

There is much less focus these days than there used to be upon policies to correct short-run unemployment. Some of the reasons include the following:

- Yearly unemployment rates in single digits since 1940;
- Social safety net programs that reduce the impact of the unemployment that does occur;
- Past public policies that offered short-term cures for unemployment, but which ultimately lost their effectiveness and proved inflationary;
- The high fraction of spending controlled by government, causing citizens who would rather be spending their money themselves to be suspicious of activist policies.

In response, macroeconomics has recently focused on long-run incentives for growth, as well as upon the microeconomic foundations of these incentives. These are the topics of this chapter.

Growth through Capital Formation—Savings and Investment

The U.S. has a history of increasing real GDP. However, recent years have seen that GDP growth diminish. For example, from 1947 to 1973, the GDP growth rate was near 4 percent. From 1973 to 1992, however, the growth rate was only 2.3 percent. The U.S. growth rate has fluctuated, as has that of other countries, as shown in Figure 14A-1.

Since 1972, U.S. economic growth has declined relative to what it was in the prior quarter-century. This decline is shown in Figure 14A-2. Figure 14A-2 also points out that most economic growth in the U.S. is attributable to increases in labor and capital, and to technological change. Both technological change and additional capital increase labor productivity.

Unfortunately, as seen in the table, the contribution of capital and technology has declined over time. For example, if technological change had continued at the pace seen in the earlier period, growth would have averaged over 3.5 percent in the later period rather than the actual figure of 2.3 percent.

Using index numbers, Figure 14A-3 illustrates relative labor productivity in the United States and selected other countries over time. Note that some other countries have seen more rapid rates of productivity growth than has occurred in the U.S. Some scholars attribute this disparity to technological catch-up, as other countries adopt technological changes pioneered in the U.S.

Labor productivity is primarily associated with how much capital—both physical capital and human capital—labor has to work with. The labor productivity statistics suggest correctly that the United States has been quite successful at accumulating capital. The creation of new capital is termed **capital formation**. What is it that brings about this capital formation? What can be done to encourage more? What sort of capital is needed?

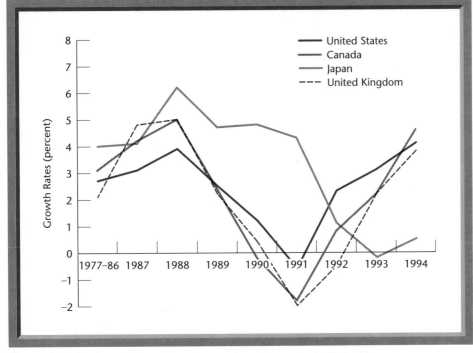

Figure 14A-1   Growth rates in real gross domestic product, 1977–1994.

Source: 1996 Economic Report of the President, Table B-108.

Capital formation requires investment. Investment can be coordinated centrally, through government. For example, government ordinarily finances the construction of highways, because it would be very difficult for private investors to acquire rights of way or to charge for highway usage. Indeed, rebuilding highways, especially bridges on the U.S. interstate highway system, is thought to be one of the major investment needs in the U.S. today.

Typically, investment is a decentralized process that responds to supply and demand in the marketplace. Investors finance the capital formation that is necessary to take advantage of market opportunities. For example, investors who expect to profit from the sale of gum balls, livestock feeders, big-screen televisions, or any other product must first finance the capital necessary to produce that product. Firms invest when they wish to do the following:

- Expand their scale of operations;
- Implement better production techniques; or
- Produce new goods that their old plants are ill suited to manufacture.

To acquire human capital, individuals invest in themselves. This investment includes the time and money it takes to attend college or otherwise acquire new skills.

Private investors have a strong personal incentive to invest wisely. Because their own resources are on the line, private investors can be relied upon to investigate closely

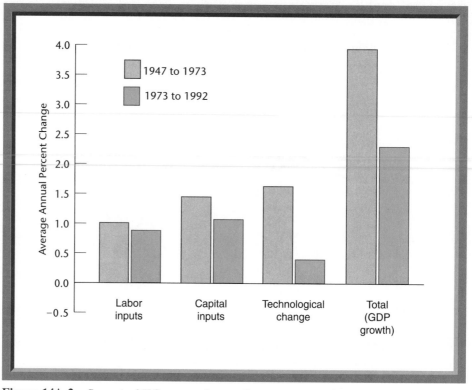

Figure 14A-2 **Sources of U.S. economic growth, average annual percent change.**

Source: 1994 Economic Report of the President, Table 1-7.

which products are likely to succeed and which are not. While no one can foresee the future with certainty, investors who judge the best are rewarded in the marketplace with additional funds for further investment.

Central to understanding the process of capital formation is the observation that **funds for investment come from savings.** In general, the more savings, the more investment. Sometimes people invest their savings themselves, such as when they buy houses or stocks. Other times, savers deposit their money into financial intermediaries, such as banks and mutual funds, which are then responsible for investing that money.

Savers look to invest for good returns without excessive risk. Without aiming to do so, government reduces private savings and investment. This reduction happens in two ways. First, government taxes away income that might be saved. Second, government taxes the returns on investments, thus making them less attractive. In contrast, **government also adds to investment to the extent that it directly invests the tax revenues it receives.**

Without government, aggregate savings and investment would be equal. With government, the total amount saved plus the total amount taken in taxes must equal the sum of private investment, government investment, and government spending on consumption

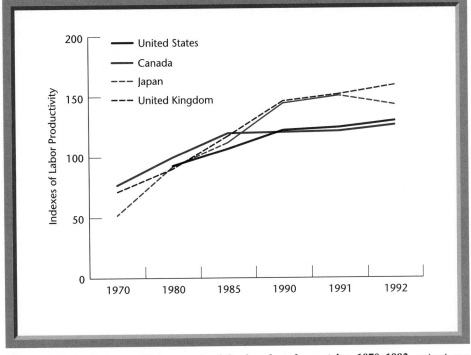

Figure 14A-3 **Indexes of labor productivity in selected countries, 1970–1992, output per hour.**

Source: 1994 Statistical Abstract of the U.S., Table No. 1390.

items. Lumping together private and government investment, we have the following equality:

$$\text{Investment} + \text{government consumption} = \text{savings} + \text{taxation}$$

or, equivalently,

$$\text{Investment} = \text{savings} + \text{taxation} - \text{government consumption}$$

To avoid too much complexity, the preceding analysis ignores international investment. In reality, some of an economy's investment money comes from foreign investors. The reverse also holds; a country's citizens often invest their savings in other countries, in the hope of obtaining a higher return than is available in their own country. In the U.S., investment inflows from other countries exceed investment outflows.

Not all private investment goes to capital formation. For example, accumulating business inventories for the purpose of selling them in the future is a form of investment. Because it is not possible to forecast sales accurately, businesses often find that they accumulate more or less inventory than they intend. Thus, while actual savings and actual investment are equal, it is not necessarily true that actual investment equals **intended investment**—the amount intended by the investors themselves. Unintended investment in the form of unplanned inventory changes are often pointed to as the cause of the business cycle, since firms adjust their production orders to make up for those inventory changes.

Extra production may occur when inventories unexpectedly decrease; production slow-downs are typical of unexpected increases in inventories.

In addition, some investment goes to replace existing capital that has depreciated. **Depreciation** occurs when capital wears out, becomes technologically outdated, or otherwise loses some or all of its usefulness. Thus

Investment = new capital + replacement of depreciated capital + inventory changes

Investment involves current expenses, in the expectation of receiving income in the future. When firms borrow to finance new investment, the expected future income must be sufficient to pay off the amount borrowed, plus interest. Higher interest rates raise the cost of investing. Some investments that would be undertaken at low interest rates will not be undertaken when interest rates are high. This result causes the investment demand curve to slope downward, as seen in Figure 14A-4.

Investment is also affected by other factors, such as business confidence, which encompasses expectations about the future. Further influences include current economic growth and opportunities presented by technological change. Changes in any of these variables would shift the investment demand curve.

Figure 14A-4   The interest rate equilibrium occurs at the intersection of investment demand and savings supply. This rate determines the quantity of actual savings and investment. The equilibrium will change if either demand or supply shifts, such as in response to changes in confidence about the future.

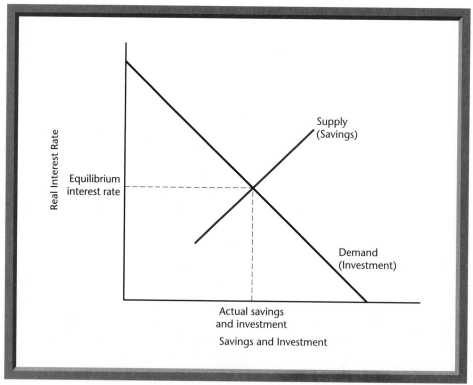

Government fiscal policy can shift investment demand. An expansionary fiscal policy can stymie the capital formation needed for economic growth. Specifically, when government increases spending or cuts taxes in order to stimulate the economy, it finances the difference with borrowing. It does this by selling government bonds to investors. Unless the Federal Reserve accommodates this increased borrowing by increasing the money supply, the government borrowing drives up market interest rates, thereby causing a **crowding-out effect**. The crowding-out effect represents money that would have gone to private-sector investment, but instead goes to finance government borrowing. Thus, if the money supply is held constant, expansionary fiscal policy is counteracted by a reduction in private investment spending.

Along with investment demand, Figure 14A-4 also shows supply and the market equilibrium. *Ceteris paribus*, the higher is the real interest rate, the more savings dollars will be offered to investors through financial markets. The higher the real interest rate, though, the fewer investment projects will actually be undertaken. The reason is that the interest rate represents both the price of borrowing and the reward for saving. For the saver, the higher is the reward, the more savings will be offered. For the borrower, the higher interest rate cuts down the quantity of borrowing demanded. The equilibrium interest rate clears the market by equating the quantity of savings supplied to the quantity of investment demanded.

Figure 14A-4 highlights how the actual amount of savings and investment depends on market interest rates. Additional real-world detail may be introduced into the model. For example, there are actually many interest rates, including a spread between the interest rate charged to borrowers and paid to savers. This spread is typically included to reward financial intermediaries for their services. There are also different rates reflecting different degrees of investment risk. This latter complication has some broad-reaching implications, as we shall see in the next section.

OBSERVATION POINT: Reining in Inventories—Big Blue's World Is Not What It Used to Be

The hot new trend in manufacturing is to produce products immediately after orders are received, as a way to combat unintended changes in inventories. Underestimating demand once meant forgoing sales of a popular product, while overestimating demand meant warehouses full of rapidly depreciating equipment. Consider IBM. "Big Blue" inventory overstocks totaled $700 million worth of extra computers at the end of 1994. IBM erred in the other direction on its Aptiva line of home computers, forgoing many millions more in revenue by not having enough product to ship.

That was then. Like other manufacturers, computer makers are turning to flexibility. This just-in-time production method often includes standardized parts and just-in-time inventories of those parts. One PC manufacturer, AST Research, even went so far as to merge with its supplier, Samsung.

Then there is Compaq Computer. By changing its assembly lines to cells of workers who can easily retrain from assembling one type of computer to another, Compaq aims to manufacture 95 percent of its computers just in time to ship within five days of a customer's order. IBM has also adopted Compaq's cell approach, hoping to match the nearly 25 percent jump in worker productivity that came with it.

Supply-Side Policy

The Investment Decision—Risk and Return

> *Success represents the 1 percent of your work that results from the 99 percent that is called failure.*
> — *Soichiro Honda, founder, Honda Motors*

Private investors do not know with certainty which products will sell and which will not. They accept some risk, in the hopes of getting a return that compensates for that risk. There is always risk ex ante, meaning before the outcome is known. Investors assess the **expected return**—the value of the investment if successful, multiplied by the probability of success. The *actual return* can be viewed ex post, meaning after the fact. Ex post, an investment might have turned out fabulously, or it might have failed miserably.

As an example of the difference between expected return and actual return consider the emergence of video cassette recorders in the 1980s. Sony Corporation invested vast sums of money into Beta-format video cassette recorders. A consortium of other electronics companies poured even more money into the competing VHS format. Consumers in the marketplace preferred the VHS format, rendering Sony's investment nearly worthless. By the same token, the investments of the VHS investors paid off handsomely.

Investment is discouraged by government regulation that ignores ex ante risk or otherwise decreases expected returns. For example, suppose government decides to regulate the price of pharmaceutical drugs to ensure that no company makes excessive profits. Government might compute the cost of producing a drug and the cost of researching and developing it, and then allow the price of the drug to cover this cost plus a "fair" return on investment. If that is the end of the calculation, however, few new drugs would be researched. Investors would be unwilling to risk losing all of their money on an unsuccessful drug in the hopes of making a so-called fair return that ignores the risk of failure. For example, the pharmaceutical industry is littered with failed companies that once had bright prospects. Their downfall? The promising new drugs that swallowed the companies' research money did not live up to expectations.

OBSERVATION POINT: Regulating Safety or Regulating Growth?

Do you want to gorge on rich foods, yet gain no weight? Perhaps Procter and Gamble's new fat substitute, Olestra, is for you. Then, too, there are troublesome side effects, including possible gastrointestinal and other problems. The studies to investigate these took so long that Procter and Gamble's 1987 request for government permission to sell Olestra was not acted upon until 1996. Even then, questions remained, which is one reason why Olestra is today only approved for snack foods.

Olestra provides just one example of the many products that must pass regulatory tests before going to market. Regulators at the Food and Drug Administration and other federal agencies pronounce products that affect health and safety to be unsafe until proven safe. In contrast, the free market offers products for sale with no proof that they are safe or accomplish anything useful. Let the buyer beware!

In response to imperfect information, people sometimes buy things they don't want, or that are even harmful or fatal. To avoid doing so, consumers may rely on a company's reputation, the desire of companies to avoid legal liabilities, or upon the approval of Underwriters Laboratories or other independent testers. When government regulators step in, though, watch out! Not only is the wait longer for new drugs and other products, but fewer new drugs and other products are even researched and developed. The certainty of many years of costly tests, together with uncertain revenues in the distant future, means that many investment dollars go to finance other things. Thus, there is a trade-off. Is it better safe than sorry? Consumers could end up safe and sorry too.

The Incentive Effects of Taxation

The U. S. federal government relies upon the personal income tax for the bulk of its revenues. This tax takes a fraction of an individual's income. If the taxpayer uses the remaining income to buy goods and services, no additional income tax is collected from that person. However, if the taxpayer saves some of the remaining income, the government comes back to tax the interest or other return on that savings. The result is that the personal income tax discourages savings. This tax has the effect of driving up interest rates to cover some of that tax cost, thus also discouraging investment.

Figure 14A-5 highlights the effect on private savings and investment when interest income is taxed. Figure 14A-5 ignores whether tax revenue might itself be used for investment. Note that savers respond to the interest they actually get to keep, which is the "no tax" supply curve shown in Figure 14A-5. This means that, for any given quantity of savings that is offered, the presence of the tax increases the required before-tax interest rate. The effect of the tax is to shift the supply curve upward by the amount of the tax. The result is a higher market equilibrium interest rate, which leads to less savings and investment, as shown in Figure 14A-5. In this way, taxation of the return on savings discourages both savings and investment.

Savings are taxed because government wants the revenue. While government does allow tax-deferred retirement accounts, it currently limits how much money can go into these accounts. Debate continues over whether the political focus on short-term revenues is too shortsighted. As of this writing, Congress is considering some proposals that would reduce taxes on savings.

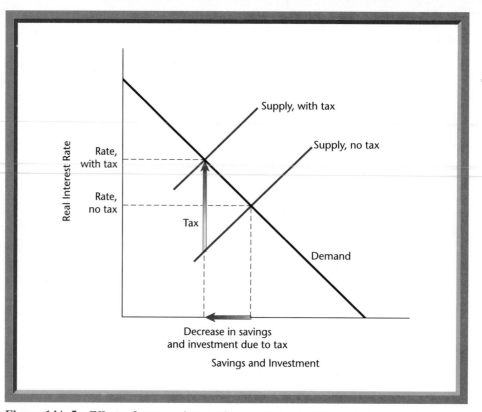

Figure 14A-5 Effects of a tax on interest income. This tax shifts the savings supply curve up to cover the amount of the tax, which leads to a higher equilibrium interest rate and less actual savings and investment.

Investment is also discouraged by other taxes, such as the tax on capital gains. **Capital gains** represent the difference between the current market value of an investment and its purchase price. The *capital gains tax* takes a percentage of this difference when the investment is sold. Since investors know about the capital gains tax when making investment decisions, it too has a chilling effect on capital formation. The reduction in investment demand means that banks pay lower interest rates on savings. Likewise, individuals who invest directly in stocks or anything else subject to capital gains taxation also see their expected returns reduced. The upshot is that the capital gains tax leads to less savings and investment.

The public usually supports provisions in the tax code that discourage investment, because they see investors as wealthy people who should pay more. The ability to save and invest is much greater among the wealthy than among the poor. Hence, reducing the capital gains tax or moving from an income tax to a consumption tax would initially benefit the rich more than the poor. However, investment bakes a larger economic pie that is shared between both the investor and consumer, because investors can be successful only by offering something of value in the marketplace. In the process, capital is formed and the economy grows.

Subsidizing Research and Development

Even without the inhibiting effects of taxes and regulations, the private sector may not devote an efficient amount of financial capital toward increasing future productivity. This shortfall occurs when there are external benefits from investment in research and development *(R & D)*. Recall that an external benefit occurs when some benefits are received by third parties who are not directly involved in a market transaction. In effect, these third parties siphon off benefits that would otherwise have gone to the firms undertaking the R & D. This reduces the expected benefit to investors, and is thus likely to reduce the amount of resources they devote to R & D.

While often lumped together, there is a significant distinction between research and development. **Research** is aimed at creating new products or otherwise expanding the frontiers of knowledge and technology. **Development** occurs when that technology is embodied into capital or output. For example, research may be aimed at uncovering a superconducting material that allows electricity to flow unimpeded at ordinary temperatures. If the research is successful, many companies could then incorporate the advance in knowledge to design their own products, such as transmission lines, electromagnets, or computers.

External benefits are most prominent at the research stage, especially when the research involves creation of knowledge that can be applied to the production of many different products, as in the example just given. It is difficult for any one investor or group of investors to assert property rights over the range of applications from basic advances in knowledge. For this reason, given that the odds of achieving a significant knowledge breakthrough are quite small, private investors usually avoid investments in basic research.

To correct this market failure, and perhaps as a counterweight to the general distortion against investment in the tax code, government subsidizes research. Sometimes government funds research directly, such as cancer research at the National Institutes of Health. Sometimes subsidies are indirect, such as public support of universities that require faculty to conduct research along with their teaching. There is controversy over how generous these subsidies should be, however, since the diffusion of knowledge throughout the economy makes measuring the value of basic research practically impossible.

Much more controversy exists when government subsidizes development. For example, the Federal Department of Energy funded a variety of alternative energy demonstration projects after the dramatic rise in world oil prices in 1973. However, most of the investments in windmills, solar energy, shale oil, and other forms of alternative energy were never commercially viable. Even gasoline blended with ethanol (alcohol made from corn) survives in the marketplace only because of ongoing government subsidies.

Such investments are development rather than basic research. Development by one firm does give other firms ideas about what will be successful and what will not, and thus involves external benefits. However, this situation holds true for airline services, fast-food locations, new toys, and a host of other goods and services offered in the marketplace—competitors learn from each others' successes and mistakes. Such minor external benefits pervade any market economy. For such minor externalities, it would be inefficient to single out some and not others.

The importance of research is a cornerstone of **new growth theory**, associated with the work of economist Paul Romer. New growth theory highlights the association between productivity growth over time and technological advances that are embodied in new capital. Since no one can know beforehand which lines of research will prove fruitful and which will fail, economies that handsomely reward productive ideas will grow the fastest. Productive ideas can include all sorts of things, including how to make lightweight concrete, how to genetically engineer a healthier potato, how to organize a firm, and any number of other thoughts.

According to new growth theory, the ideas behind new technologies are promoted most effectively by allowing individuals to claim property rights, and the associated monopoly power, over ideas they have. The excess profit associated with monopoly power provides the incentive to create ever better ways of doing things.

Supply Siders—Furthering the Classical Tradition

With inflation and unemployment becoming less of an economic threat as the 1980s progressed into the 1990s, the focus in macroeconomic policy turned toward furthering incentives for productivity and economic growth. Economists who emphasize these incentives have become known as **supply siders**. Supply-side analysis focusses on long-run growth, which places it squarely in the classical tradition.

The objective of supply-side policy is to ensure that the long-run aggregate supply curve is associated with the greatest possible amount of output. Supply-side policies are designed to generate capital and increase productivity, which has the effect of shifting the long-run aggregate supply curve to the right, as shown in Figure 14A-6. Any decrease in the natural rate of unemployment would also shift long-run aggregate supply to the right.

Long-run aggregate supply shifts in response to changes in structural features of the economy. Structural features include resources, technology, demography, and labor practices. Structural features also include government policies that change how workers and firms behave. Examples include unemployment compensation, minimum-wage laws, and other public policies that affect the natural rate of unemployment.

Supply siders are concerned with any government policies that might cut productivity and lead to structural unemployment. They look with suspicion at the work disincentives imbedded in many safety net programs, and at regulations that make it more costly for firms to hire and fire employees. However, they are most known for their focus on tax policies.

Supply siders recommend keeping marginal tax rates low, so as to leave a higher fraction of incremental earnings in the hands of individuals and investors. In this way, there is more incentive to invest and be productive. The result is that full-employment output is greater. The reason is partly that there will be more work effort provided at the full-employment equilibrium in response to greater marginal rewards for that effort.

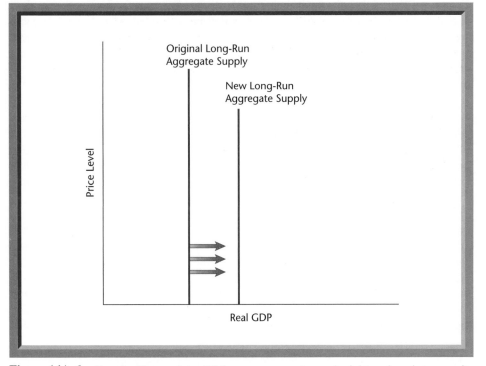

Figure 14A-6 **Supply siders** seek to shift long-run aggregate supply rightward, so that per capita GDP will grow.

Mostly, however, output will be greater because investors will have greater incentives to build up the economy's stock of physical and human capital, and thereby increase the productivity of its labor.

Supply-side theory is commonly associated with *Reaganomics*, the economic policies of President Ronald Reagan. Because the concern of the supply siders is with the long run, they have little use for activist fiscal policies designed for short-run goals. Supply siders often see an expansionary fiscal policy as an excuse for a greater government presence in the economy, and worry about the increased regulatory and tax burdens that presence may bring.

Tax policies in the 1980s largely followed the supply-side agenda of cutting marginal tax rates in order to promote growth. Such growth was intended to provide greater prosperity in the future, as well as a greater tax base over time. The evidence is favorable. Beginning in 1983 and lasting into the 1990s, the economy witnessed low inflation and real economic growth nearly every year. Relative to the prior decade, the 1980s saw a tripling in the rate of productivity growth and almost a doubling of real investment in new businesses.

Concurrently, however, the government ran a large budget deficit, because it did not cut spending proportionally. The budget deficit exceeded 6 percent of GDP in 1983, although it fell to just under 3 percent by 1989. The Reagan-era budget deficits look like

Keynesian fiscal policy run amok, with the fiscal stimulus of a tax cut applied to marginal tax rates at the high end of the income spectrum, rather than to rates paid by those struggling to make a good life for themselves. Critics of Reaganomics thus refer to supply-side policies as *trickle-down economics*. This term suggests that the policies are intended to make the rich richer, so that they might spend a bit more and help the rest of us.

The economy grew, and the rich got disproportionately richer, at least in terms of the income they reported to the IRS. However, while Reagan-era tax cuts reduced real federal tax revenues from most groups in the economy, the tax cuts greatly increased tax revenues from the highest income groups. The top 5 percent of income earners increased their share of total income tax payments from 36 percent in 1980 to 43 percent in 1990. Tax revenues from the wealthy increased because the tax cuts gave them the incentive to skip tax shelters and invest in economically productive ways.

In this manner, the economic pie grew and the U.S. Treasury gained more money. Upward mobility became commonplace. Looking at the lowest fifth of the income distribution in 1980, for example, 86 percent had advanced beyond that by 1988, with 16 percent even making it all the way to the top fifth of the income distribution. Supporters of Reaganomics thus say its critics are motivated by the politics of envy, because the critics ignore the intended purpose of the tax cuts, which is to target growth and opportunity. These supporters blame the lingering deficit on the political difficulty of cutting welfare, Social Security, and other entrenched spending programs.

OBSERVATION POINT: The Laffer Curve—Who Will Laugh Last?

At a tax rate of zero percent, government collects no revenue. It can increase revenues by increasing tax rates, but there are limits. After all, a tax rate of 100 percent would also generate no tax revenue—no one would bother to earn money if Uncle Sam takes it all. Arthur Laffer, a young UCLA economist, discussed this at lunch one day in the 1970s. He sketched the hump-shaped relationship between tax rates and tax revenues on the back of his napkin. Ever since, for better or worse, that sketch has been called the Laffer curve.

Promoted by supply siders, the Laffer curve proved to be a potent idea in the early 1980s. It surely would be nice if government could cut its tax rates and see both the economy and its tax revenues grow. Congress went on to cut tax rates in 1982, and—lo and behold—the economy grew and the rich wound up paying more taxes. They paid more taxes because economic growth meant there were more of them and they had more income.

Unfortunately, although overall federal tax revenues increased by $1.1 trillion in the 1980s, that was not enough to overtake government spending. The Laffer curve became a laughing stock among the I-told-you-so crowd. Yet, no one can dispute its logic. Will the Laffer curve rise to prominence again if the right tax is found to cut? The capital gains tax, perhaps? As the saying goes, he who laughs last, laughs best!

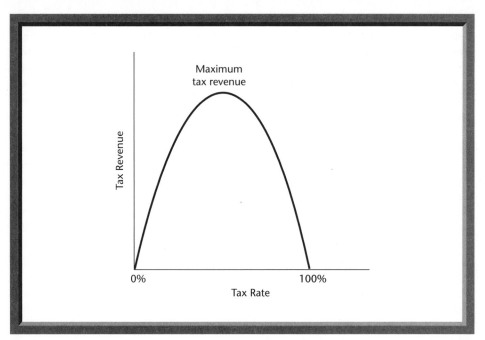

The Laffer Curve

Policy in Practice

Perhaps because macroeconomists offer conflicting advice, macroeconomic policy tends to follow the course of *pragmatism*; policies are used when they seem to work, and discarded when they do not. However, there is much more concern now than in the mid-twentieth century over long-run implications of macro policies.

New Age Macro

The Great Depression was ended by World War II, which involved a massive amount of government spending. Thus, in the prosperous decades following the War, Keynesian analysis was thought to have been proven correct. As President Richard Nixon phrased it, "We are all Keynesians, now." However, the 1960s proved to be the last decade in which Keynesian economics was widely held in such high esteem.

In the decades that followed the 1960s, macroeconomics has moved in the direction of emphasizing its microeconomic foundations, such as the incentives facing investors discussed earlier. In general, the focus has been on examining economic incentives facing individuals and firms that, when looked at collectively, can influence the performance of the overall economy. This orientation has led **new Keynesians** to offer evidence from the labor market that suggests Keynesian analysis is valid in the short run. However, new Keynesians are more willing than traditional Keynesians to acknowledge the importance of long-run tendencies toward full employment.

New classical economists, in contrast, acknowledge that free markets will lead to a full-employment equilibrium, but emphasize factors that may cause short-run disequilibriums. With lines between Keynesians and classical economists blurring, economists frequently term themselves as *eclectic* or *agnostic*, meaning that they accept insights from a variety of perspectives, and prefer not to pigeonhole themselves into any single category.

A recurring theme among these "new age" macroeconomists is their focus on information flows and market responses. New Keynesians emphasize practical issues in the workplace that inhibit adjustments to full employment. New classical economists emphasize that public policy cannot be expected to work if it assumes that government knows more than participants in the marketplace. Specifically, new classical economists point to the concept of rational expectations. **Rational expectations** occur when, on average, people correctly predict the implications of government policy action. The idea of rational expectations served as the basis for the award of the 1995 Nobel Prize in Economics to Professor Robert Lucas of the University of Chicago.

To understand the implications of rational expectations, suppose government pumps extra money into the economy in order to stimulate employment. In the 1950s and 1960s, the extra monetary growth caused a reduction in unemployment together with an increase in inflation. The reduction in unemployment is thought to have occurred because people were misled into thinking that their wage and profit opportunities were rising, when in fact the extra wages and profits were being eaten away by the concurrent inflation that people did not anticipate. Because of the prolonged period of time in which the public was tricked by inflation that was higher than expected, we can conclude that the public did *not* have rational expectations.

In contrast, once burned, twice shy. As people and businesses have learned to factor the effects of inflation into their personal and business plans, government can no longer inflate its way to lower unemployment. This limitation on government's ability to manage the economy was shown by the combination of inflation and unemployment—**stagflation**—experienced in the 1970s. People had learned to predict more accurately the impacts of public policy. Their expectations had become more rational.

If people have rational expectations, government policy that is intended to be expansionary or contractionary will have no predictable effect on the expenditure equilibrium. In other words, the best guess is that fiscal policy actions will not change the economy much in either direction. Public policies that have been debated in Congress, commented on by the media, and passed into law are not likely to surprise us. Because new classical economists emphasize the significance of rational expectations, they usually suggest that government should step back and let the macroeconomy take care of itself.

In practice, there will occasionally be **supply shocks** that affect production possibilities. Shocks may take various forms, such as changes in technology, labor productivity, or input availability. The result is a change in full-employment output, and hence in long-run aggregate supply.

For example, long-run aggregate supply would shift to the left in response to a natural disaster or other supply shock that increases production costs. A leftward shift in long-run aggregate supply would cause it to intersect aggregate demand at a lower output and higher price level, thus causing *long-run cost-push inflation*, as shown in Figure 14A-7. While not shown in the figure, recall that short-run cost-push inflation would occur when the short-run aggregate supply curve shifts leftward and upward, such as due to changes in inflationary expectations. Whether long-run or short-run, **cost-push inflation leads to less output and a higher price level.**

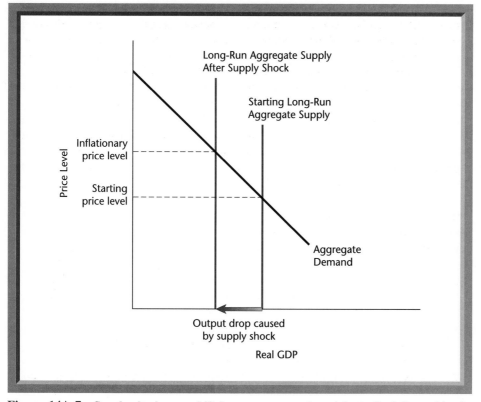

Figure 14A-7   **Supply shocks can shift long-run aggregate supply to the left,** resulting in long-run cost-push inflation.

New classical economists emphasize the existence of a **real business cycle,** where variations in macro output and the price level over time tend to be caused by unexpected shocks to aggregate supply or aggregate demand. For example, when OPEC dramatically raised the price of oil in 1972, and again in 1979, the economy was shocked into inflation and recession each time. Since trying to counter the unpredictable is bound to fail, this line of reasoning leaves no place for government to attempt either expansionary or contractionary policies.

OBSERVATION POINT: The Real Business Cycle—Some Shocking Surprises

Cars, wars, oil cartels, and computers may not seem to have much in common, but they do. They have all shocked the economy one way or another. How could ordinary citizens foresee the potential of the auto or the carnage of World War II? We did not know of the oil crisis of the 1970s before it happened, and we did not forecast its disappearance in the 1980s. Even now, who knows what new technologies will lead to, or when catastrophe will strike? All of these things and more jolt the economy, either to make it more productive, or to knock it back a notch. Policymakers can predict these events no better than the rest of us.

Maneuvering into a Soft Landing—Monetary Policy in the '90s

Applying macro models to the more complex real world takes finesse. In February 1994, for example, the Federal Reserve surprised the markets by commencing a series of increases in the cost of borrowing money as part of a drive to ward off inflation by reducing aggregate demand. The low market interest rates of the time indicated that the public had not previously seen any danger of inflation. However, the Fed tightening signaled the public that the experts at the Fed were worried about future inflation, and this signal translated into increased inflationary expectations in the marketplace.

The Fed seems to have predicted correctly. 1994 saw robust economic growth, especially in the last quarter. This growth put upward pressure on prices, resulting in an uptick in inflation. The Federal Reserve maintained an increasingly contractionary policy, which resulted in higher interest rates throughout 1994. By the end of 1994, however, long-term interest rates started falling. These are rates on such investments as thirty-year Treasury bonds. The decline in those rates indicated that the market believed that Fed policy to keep inflation down would be successful. The reduction in inflationary expectations meant that people were willing to accept a lower interest rate on long-term investments.

The Fed had to walk a fine line because, while it wanted to prevent inflation, it was also concerned about output and employment. In other words, it was attempting to maneuver the economy into a *soft landing*, characterized by just enough contractionary policy to prevent inflation, but not so much as to cause unemployment.

Political Ideology and Policy Perspectives

Economic analysis influences people's politics and vice versa. For example, Keynesian policy prescriptions are often adopted by people whose politics are liberal. The reason is presumably not because most liberals have studied the economy in detail and are convinced of the validity of the Keynesian economic model. More likely, political liberals tend to believe that an activist government can be a powerful force for good in the world. Keynesian economics calls for government to be just such a force. It provides justification for a large government, but leaves open specific categories of spending.

A similar analysis applies to political conservatives, who tend to adhere to a classical perspective on the role of government. Conservatives usually distrust big government, preferring instead a more laissez-faire approach. Classical analysis suggests that much government action does more harm than good to the macroeconomy, which is in keeping with the conservative perspective.

While some controversy in macroeconomics is positive, concerning factual issues of cause and effect, most disagreement among macroeconomists is normative. For example, modern Keynesian models incorporate classical analysis of the long run. What makes these economists and their models Keynesian is that they discount the significance of the long run, preferring instead to emphasize wage and price stickiness and other short-run phenomena. Thus, the disagreement between modern Keynesians and classical economists often boils down to the degrees to which they are willing to trade off short- and long-run objectives.

1. Savings plus investment equals taxation plus government spending.

2. The capital gains tax discourages investment by reducing the expected after-tax return on that investment.

3. It is usually more efficient for government to subsidize development rather than subsidize basic research.

4. A country's labor productivity is primarily related to its culture.

5. The term *trickle-down economics* suggests a Keynesian interpretation of supply-side tax policies.

6. New classical economists suggest that government policies cannot counter supply shocks.

A

EXPLORATION 1
Social Security—Questions of Savings and Investment

Social Security is subject to stresses that bring its future into question. There are likely to be changes that affect national savings and economic growth, as well as individuals' incentives to be productive.

According to a recent survey, college students today are more likely to believe in alien visitors from outer space than in the future of Social Security. What is wrong with Social Security that its very existence is called into question? What does the future really hold? While time will tell, we can nonetheless make some intelligent predictions. We can see the stresses, as well as suggestions on how to relieve those stresses. The consequences are significant, both for individuals and the country. Choices about Social Security will affect productivity for years to come.

*T*he Pay-As-You-Go Puzzle

The fundamental problem with Social Security is that it is **pay-as-you-go**, meaning that current workers pay for people who are currently retired. This arrangement was fine when the program was first established in the 1930s. At that time, the ratio of workers to eligible retirees was quite high. Now that ratio is down to about three workers per retiree. By the year 2030, the ratio is predicted to drop to only about two workers per retiree. Advances in medicine and the aging of the baby boom generation take the blame for these demographic trends.

If the present structure of Social Security were to be offered by any private business, the owners of that business would be prosecuted for fraud for running an illegal **pyramid scheme**, in which the money from current investors is used to finance paybacks to longer-term investors. Pyramid schemes are very risky; if new investors ever stop coming, the most recent investors lose their money.

Social Security has a significant advantage over the typical pyramid scheme. New investors are forced into the system by government and its power to tax. However, if government changes its mind down the road, investors who have yet to receive a payback could lose out. Even if Social Security were fully financed, though, the low returns it offers would dissuade potential investors. Figure 14B1-1 illustrates these returns. Note that the return to those born before 1945 greatly exceeds the return to those born in later years. For this reason, Social Security is said to be redistributional across generations, in addition to being redistributional within each generation.

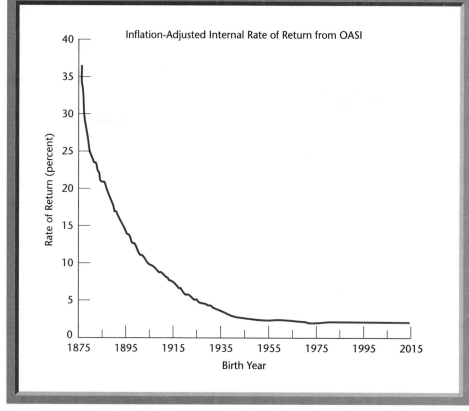

Inflation-Adjusted Internal Rate of Return from OASI

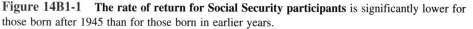

Figure 14B1-1   The rate of return for Social Security participants is significantly lower for those born after 1945 than for those born in earlier years.

Source: Economic Trends, Federal Reserve Bank of Cleveland, April 10, 1996, p 13.

Social Security collects taxes on all payroll income, and allots the proceeds for *OASDHI*, which stands for old age, survivors, disability, and hospitalization insurance. As of this writing, the combined employer and employee Social Security tax rate is 15.25 percent of the first $61,200 of that income, where the threshold is adjusted upward over time for inflation. For income over that threshold, the Social Security tax is eliminated except for the 2.9 percent hospitalization insurance.

If population projections are correct, and if no changes are made in the structure of Social Security itself, the combined payroll tax rate of 15.25 percent would have to rise to over 22 percent in the next twenty years. However, workers might balk at redistributing nearly a quarter of their incomes to the elderly, especially when there is no guarantee that they will see equivalent benefits when they retire. That's why people mistrust the staying power of Social Security.

There is a **Social Security trust fund**, which collects excess revenue and *earmarks* it for the payment of benefits in the future. However, the approximately $400 billion size of that trust fund is quite small relative to the demands against it. The trust fund would run out in a little over one year if not continuously supplemented by the Social Security tax payments of current workers and the firms who employ them. Moreover, if the trust fund is to become a meaningful resource for the future, Social Security tax rates would need to be increased in the present. This action would leave current workers paying not only for current retirees, but also for themselves as well. Few workers would support this double taxation. They would rather save their money themselves, instead of entrusting those savings to government.

No Real Savings—No Real Alternative?

The issue of savings is quite troublesome in a macroeconomic sense. As it stands, all savings held in the Social Security trust fund take the form of special government bonds. Since a bond is merely a promise to pay in the future, savings within the Social Security trust fund are nothing more than government IOUs.

To pay those IOUs, government must either create extra money via the Federal Reserve or collect extra tax dollars in the future. Either way, future taxpayers pay. If the government increases the monetary base, taxpayers pay the tax of inflation that eats away the value of their earnings. Otherwise, the trust fund bonds would be redeemed out of general tax revenues, which would require higher personal income taxes or other general taxes. Even if the Social Security trust fund were to stack a warehouse full of its special government bonds, it would still be up to future taxpayers to pay them off. Thus, for the macroeconomy, balances in the Social Security trust fund are not real savings.

Not only does the Social Security system fail to augment the country's savings, it actually lowers national savings to the extent that people expect to receive Social Security checks in the future. Workers substitute government's promises for their own savings. Moreover, because the Social Security tax reduces take-home pay, current workers have less money that could be saved. The reduction in the national savings rate because of Social Security implies less money for investment, and thus less capital formation. With less capital, the country's production possibilities grow more slowly. The result is that, when current workers retire, the economic capacity of the country to support them will be smaller than if Social Security never existed in the first place.

For the Social Security trust fund to represent real savings, it must generate real capital that will increase the country's production possibilities in years to come. The amount of savings needed for the Social Security trust fund to be **fully funded**—able to pay off all its future obligations without recourse to future taxation—would be well over a year's worth of GDP. In other words, the buildup of savings in the Social Security trust fund must represent more than a doubling of the country's current productive capacity.

If government were to invest the Social Security trust fund into the production of real capital, it could take one of two routes. It could produce the necessary capital itself. Government production may be justified to the extent that the needed investment applies to the provision of public goods, such as highway infrastructure needed for smoothly flowing traffic. Beyond this, however, direct government investment would lead the economy in the direction of command and control. Alternatively, government could invest the money in the marketplace, perhaps buying stock offerings of private companies. Imagine the consequences of that!

If the government were to enter the private marketplace, politics would undoubtedly affect the direction of its investment. Thus, we could expect to see politically correct industries and those with powerful constituencies thrive, while other industries would be denied access to government coffers. The result would be an **industrial policy**, in which government picks the industries in which to stake the country's future. Workers interested in real savings for their retirements might prefer that such investment choices be left to private investors guided by profit rather than by politics.

*P*ersonal Security Accounts—Who Holds the Reins of Investment and Growth?

Individuals do save for their own retirement. *Individual retirement accounts (IRAs)* promote that savings by allowing tax-free contributions of up to $2,000 per year, depending upon income. Government has been reluctant to increase that limit, since any increase in tax-free savings would deplete current tax revenues. Government has also been content to accumulate bonds in the Social Security trust fund, because selling those bonds to the trust fund transfers any extra money collected by Social Security taxes into general revenues that can be spent elsewhere.

If government so chooses, it can promote private savings for the future. It can do this in varying degrees. It could start by increasing or eliminating the contribution cap on IRAs. It could go further by eliminating the taxation of all savings. It could even go so far as to require that individuals save some fraction of their earnings for their own retirement. This savings would be placed into *Personal Security Accounts (PSAs)*, which would be financed by a payroll tax but be under the individual's own control and ownership. Because Social Security depends upon current workers to support current retirees, PSAs could only supplement, not replace, Social Security as it now stands.

Workers who get to keep control of their own savings might be more inclined to accept the double tax of paying for current retirees and also building up savings for their own retirement. Such an approach has the economic advantage of maintaining a free-market allocation of investment. Companies that offer mutual funds and other forms of investment would compete for savings, and the winners would be those companies that offer the best services and investments.

B

*C*oming Welfare for the Aged

The strategy of promoting savings and investment by inducing individuals to save for their own retirements does not provide for income redistribution from wealthier workers to poorer ones. As Social Security now stands, it is highly redistributional in this respect. The ratio of payments to retirees relative to the amount they contributed in their working years is much higher for the low income than for the high income. Payments are also adjusted on the basis of need, such as indicated by the number of dependents. Thus, even though the Social Security tax took out the same portion of each person's income when they were working, the percentage that Social Security gives back is much higher for the poor.

On an after-tax basis, Social Security may even pay the retired low-income worker more than he or she earned when working. A worker at the maximum income subject to Social Security tax, in contrast, is likely to receive only about 30 percent as much as when employed. The upshot is that, when Social Security taxes and payments are combined, the Social Security system is highly progressive. Low-income workers have money redistributed their way from the tax dollars paid by higher-income workers.

The redistribution from higher-income workers to lower-income workers is one reason participation in Social Security is required by law. If it were optional, workers with above-average incomes would all quit, leaving no money to redistribute. Workers would also be deterred from joining voluntarily by intergenerational redistribution, which gives current retirees a much better deal than can be expected by current workers.

If individuals are poor, suffer financial misfortune, or for any other reason have little savings when they retire, what are they to do? It seems clear that society will demand some safety net to prevent indigent retirees from a life of abject poverty. Thus, there will continue to be redistributional Social Security taxes. However, as people are forced to save for their own retirement, and as Social Security as we know it becomes merely a fallback for those in need, Social Security becomes ever more a welfare program.

In the past, Social Security has been viewed as something that people deserve to have, because they have been forced to pay Social Security taxes all their life. The more redistributional Social Security becomes, however, the less sense this view makes. If workers see their payroll taxes rise in order to pay for the rising proportion of the elderly, there is likely to be an outcry against paying for those who can afford to pay for themselves. The better-off Social Security recipients will be cut from the roles, and the taxes they paid will not save them. As Social Security advances down this road, it will become known as welfare for the aged. The question will be asked: "Why is there a separate tax earmarked for this welfare?" If this scenario is correct, the country will probably see the demise of the Social Security payroll tax, and its replacement by higher income taxes and other taxes.

*W*hether to Work or Not to Work—That is the Question

This prediction of the future suggests that workers have some serious thinking to do. Do they struggle to acquire human capital and increase their earnings? If they do, they will face paying for the Social Security welfare of others. The alternative is to live it up and avoid the hard work necessary to earn a high income. After all, living into retirement years is not ensured. Those who live for the moment, acquire little human capital, and save nothing for retirement would have the safety net of Social Security to cushion their fall. If that cushion is too appealing, the future of the U.S. economy will not be appealing at all.

PROSPECTING FOR NEW INSIGHTS

1. This exploration notes that current workers might not have the incentive to be as productive as they could be. The same has been said of current retirees, who see the value of their Social Security payments fall as the incomes they earn between ages sixty-five and sixty-nine increase. Why are Social Security payments reduced for those who earn money in their retirement years? Is this fair? How does your answer

depend upon whether Social Security is an entitlement that people have earned, or a welfare program?

2. The retirement age, at which a person will become eligible to receive Social Security benefits, is scheduled to rise from sixty-five to sixty-seven or more. This rise is to be phased in over the next fifteen years. What political reason prevents a more rapid phase-in? What will be the effect of this change on productivity?

EXPLORATION 2
EDUCATIONAL SHORT STORY
Winds of Change in Caribia

Poor countries can choose macroeconomic policies that provide a social safety net and equity. However, their need for growth may prompt more radical policies. The direction these macro policies should take is a matter of hot debate, in which the assessments of well-meaning people can reasonably differ. In this choice, economic policies become intertwined with political philosophies.

September 12

Dear Diary,

Not since Caribia declared its independence in the nineteenth century has this small country experienced such revolutionary fervor. At noon today, I venture up from the coast, following the Oxtaluca highway into the mountain strongholds of the Front for People's Liberation. If I am lucky, I will probe the thoughts of Jessica Botello, herself, and discover what drives her and the revolutionary army she leads. If I am unlucky, I could be held hostage or even die. My editor at the *Dispatch* thinks I do this for the pay. He must be crazier than I am!

I feel like I, Pamla Boles, am living history in the making. It is as though, after awakening from a long slumber, Caribia has tried to catch up in a few years with changes that the rest of the world made over the course of an entire century. First there was the coup. Long a single-party "democracy," Caribians were jolted by the toppling of President Morant. As a populist, President Morant was widely praised for his middle-of-the-road policies, in which the government maintained jobs by protecting local industries from foreign competition and provided help to the poor with revenues from hefty taxes on personal and businesses income. While touted for its egalitarianism and activist role for government in promoting prosperity, though, standards of living remained low. The economy seemed to be going nowhere.

Then came the coup that ousted Morant and installed President Frederico Campos and his "supply-side boys." This group of economic consultants emphasized growth above all else, with free markets providing the engine for that growth. Warmed-over, discredited Keynesianism was what they called Morant's policies.

In two short years, the safety net of the welfare state was torn away. Tax rates were slashed on business income, so as to encourage investment in new capital. All the exemptions, exclusions, and deductions that complicated the old personal income tax code were discarded, too. Instead of recognizing the special needs of the sick, those with children, and others in need, the income tax was abolished and replaced with a national sales tax. Less paperwork, fewer loopholes, and stronger incentives to work and invest, they said. The supply-side boys wanted to get the most out of Caribia's current resources and build more capital for the future. But they had no heart!

Life under Campos was full of disruption. Foreign investments poured in, and local industry was forced to sink or swim in the world marketplace. Many sank. New industries were springing up, but were often owned in part by foreign investors. Some people were getting rich. Many more suffered.

After two years of this, and the formation of an illegal leftist revolutionary army that promised to expropriate and divide up the country's wealth, the army staged another coup. This time, they returned the populist Morant to power and promised elections within the year. The elections are around the corner, and the revolutionaries have even agreed to participate. I look forward to visiting these revolutionaries turned democrats.

September 13

Between the mosquitos, the rain, and the excitement, I will not soon forget last night. The one bright spot was meeting my host for the night, Enriqué Garcia. Enriqué speaks a little English, which helps him in his job selling handicrafts to tourists. The living is pretty meager, but no worse than for others in his village of Traxalacah. The villagers are surprisingly well informed about life in the capital and elsewhere in the world. You can taste the discontent in their voices when they contrast the lifestyles they imagine in the United States with their own scant opportunities. They also resent the "financialeros" who get rich in the capital while they are stuck without opportunity.

Morant has nationalized industries and restricted competition from imports. He's taxed away business profits and prevented foreign investors from taking their money home with them. Of course the foreign investors don't like him, and neither does business, but those kinds of policies are meant to appeal to both the poor and the old-money rich. Yet, Enriqué doesn't trust him—too "elite." "Morant looks down his nose at us," he says. As for Campos, Enriqué suggests a lack of proper parenting in his boyhood.

Enriqué introduced me to Jessica Botello's top economic advisor, a heavily bearded, pipe-smoking character named Russell Jeffries. Russ was a transplanted Yankee like me, and we immediately hit it off. It turns out that he obtained his political science degree the same year I got my journalism degree, although the schools were two thousand miles apart. I asked him why, since his specialty is economics, he did not obtain an economics degree.

"You are so naive. The economics programs in the U.S. won't teach you about the real world. All they talk about is abstract models that deal with incentives for individuals and business. Or, if they jump to the bigger picture, they jump so far as to be meaningless. Why talk about multipliers and savings, when the real issue is control. The economics programs don't want to teach that. They don't want us to know about the inter-locking directorships and the buddy-buddy system called politics. If you've got control of business and media, you can get people to think anything you want them to."

I asked him what he thinks about Jessica Botello entering this election.

"Why not? If we win, that'll be great for the country. We will do away with com-petition, and instead cooperate for the common good. Do you know how much money is wasted in competition? It's mind boggling. In competition, one person's gain is someone else's loss. If we stop trying to outdo the other guy, if we stop trying to get ahead by grabbing somebody else's market or job, then we can have an economy that really grows, and is good to live in, too."

"That sounds great, Russ, but what if Jessica loses?"

"I guess it's back to revolution from the mountains."

"I don't get it. You're an idealist. Surely, you wouldn't wage war against a gov-ernment that most citizens voted for. Wouldn't that be immoral?"

"Pamla, Pamla," he said sympathetically, "you've been brainwashed by the very media you are a member of. I have studied the matter for years. We have got to stop fight-ing and start cooperating. But you can't teach that to people overnight, not when they've spent a lifetime being told the virtues of competition.

"We may have to beat them at their own corrupt game, before they will acknowl-edge that there is a better way. No, Pamla, revolution is a necessary evil. It is a stage to go through before we can reach our goal of a society based on celebrating human worth. We want to tear down the society that has us tear each other down. This is for the good of us all, even those who don't know it yet."

"What school of economic thought do you fall under, Russ? Are you a Keynesian?"

Russ laughed. "In your establishment textbooks, they'd call me a radical economist. They want to put people like me off to the fringe so they can ignore us. We make them uncomfortable. I guess we hit too close to home!"

*S*eptember 14

I'm still shaking. I was admiring the rocky, yet lush, terrain and remembering the pleas-ant conversation with Enriqué and Russ of the night before. We were deep in the moun-tains, supposedly very near to Jessica Botello's camp. Our Land Rover was struggling up what passed for a road, but looked more like a washed out gully. Next thing I know, a tree crashes across our path, and what appear to be uniformed Federal soldiers surround the Rover. They did not seem friendly. Was I being set up? Were government soldiers going to murder me and blame it on the revolutionaries? As it turned out, the incident was just a security precaution. The uniforms were being worn by some of Botello's men, who then took us to her encampment.

*S*eptember 15

It seems like weeks since I've been in a decent bed, but the people are great! There is a real sense of camaraderie here. A sense of purpose fills the air. Their mission is clear. The people must take charge and rip the riches of the land from the bourgeoisie elite.

Why should some live in luxury, while so many others must scrape to live at all? There is a little bickering over tactics, but all share a belief in the nobility of their goals. I do not believe I have ever encountered such brave spirits. These people accept that their lives are on the line. Their leader, Jessica Botello, is no small part of their inspiration.

When I met Jessica, I was taken aback. I had seen the pictures of her with her rifle held at the ready. Yes, her colorful outfit was still there. But in real life Jessica Botello was quite small. She hardly seemed the type to lead an army. Talking with her, though, caused me to forget about looks and get caught up in the power of her vision. I wish she would have talked longer.

"I was born into that tiny group they term the middle class," Jessica confided. "Mine was not a struggle to find food to eat, but nor was it an easy life. My mother worked hard to bring in the money to raise us. She had to do this alone, because my father was killed in an industrial accident, or so the company said. In truth, he had been too honest for his own good. In some jobs it is dangerous to turn down a bribe.

"I resolved when I was very young that I would devote my life to a cause. That cause is not political. The cause is people. We are born; we cry. It does not matter if our parents are poor or rich. We cry the same. We deserve the same. Our opportunities must be the same.

"They say that opportunity knocks. Maybe it is us who should do the knocking. If we all knock together, opportunity will have no choice but to answer! You hear us knocking. The rest, you will see."

September 19

Jessica Botello appeared at the door of my tent and offered me a Nehi. "Pamla, the time has come for us to break camp. The election is tomorrow. If we win, I shall make a grand appearance. If we lose, well, perhaps we should not be so easy to find. Oh, I see you like the Nehi. Do not drink too fast."

I started to reply that Nehi was my favorite soft drink, but could not seem to form the words.

"Do not try to talk, now. We have drugged your drink, but you will not mind. Perhaps you have had enough, though. Please, do not take this personally. You are part of the media, and. . . ." I do not remember the rest.

That was two days ago. Now, I awake to find myself back here in Enriqué Garcia's house, with a morning *Dispatch* by my bed. On the front page, I see the lead story:

It's Revolution at the Ballot Box in Caribia

In a resounding defeat for the status quo and a repudiation of the leftist candidate Jessica Botello, voters in Caribia today ousted President Hector Morant. By a convincing margin, voters selected former dictator Frederico Campos to be their next President.

Frederico Campos, who returned from exile only last month, offers the voters an austere economic program that emphasizes the importance of private property and free markets. Campos promises that, while hardships can be expected in the short term, the future will see expanding opportunities and higher standards of living. His chances of victory had been widely dismissed, with opponents emphasizing that the supply-side policies advocated by Campos would increase income inequality within the country.

Some analysts now suggest that, in electing Campos, voters may be hoping that a rising tide will lift all ships. Others suggest that, by accepting greater economic risk in exchange for increased economic opportunities, voters are expressing a willingness to shoulder more responsibility for their own lives. Central to both notions is that, through sacrifice in the present, Caribia's economy will grow more vibrant over time.

I wonder about Jessica, and the future of this country. Most of all, though, I wonder what became of the last two days, and if this pounding head of mine will ever be the same again.

PROSPECTING FOR NEW INSIGHTS

1. Why do different ideas about a country's economic path lead to such antagonism in the political process that people are willing to risk their lives for their opinions? Do you think there were economic motives behind the U.S. Civil War? Explain.

2. Russ Jeffries describes himself as a radical economist. He claims that the economics profession will not allow the teaching of the radical perspective because it is a threat. Is there another plausible explanation besides a conspiracy to suppress threatening thoughts? Do the economic arguments of Russ Jeffries make sense? Explain.

B

Module C

MASTERING ROADSIDE CHALLENGES

CHALLENGE 1
Second-Best Efficiency When Taxes Discourage Investment

Why settle for second best? **Second-best efficiency** is the most efficient outcome possible, given that there is some inefficient policy or situation that will not be changed. For example, we might want to provide incentives for the efficient amount of capital formation, despite the tax system discouraging the investment that finances new capital.

Before proceeding, it is worth noting why taxes discourage investment. The personal income tax double-taxes the return on savings—income that is spent on consumption goods and services is taxed only once, when it is earned, but income that is saved is taxed both when it is earned and again on the earnings it generates when it is saved. Along the same lines, the return to those who save is reduced by taxes on the earnings of corporations and by taxes on capital gains to owners of stock or other assets.

The prospect of changing all these taxes might seem implausible. If so, second-best efficiency calls for the adjustment of other things. Those other things include nearly every price and public policy in the economy! The reason is that, by overtaxing capital, the tax system penalizes goods and services that employ a lot of capital; this causes higher prices and substitutions toward other goods and services that use capital less intensively or not at all.

Since very few goods and services are produced with an exactly average amount of capital relative to other inputs, second-best efficiency suggests that the invisible hand of the market will get nearly all prices wrong when taxes are biased against capital. Specifically, second-best efficiency would call for decreasing the prices of capital-intensive goods and services relative to those that use less capital. The effect would be an increased return to capital, thereby countering somewhat the effects of the tax system.

The notion of second-best efficiency is often criticized as providing a dangerous excuse to avoid addressing the root causes of problems, and instead to embark upon a wide-ranging course of action that could potentially cause more problems than it solves. Seeking second-best efficiency is like trying to balance a table with one leg that is a little too short. Instead of propping up or replacing the short leg, second-best efficiency would have government attempt to saw off a little bit from each of the other legs. The odds of success would not be good.

The development of new information can confer significant external benefits, particularly if the advance in knowledge can be applied to producing new or better goods and services. Such advances shift long-run aggregate supply to the right, by allowing more or better output from the economy's resources. The existence of external benefits implies a market failure that keeps the quantity of research inefficiently low, thus short-circuiting this economic growth. The market failure occurs because the demand for research fails to capture external benefits, thus causing a suboptimal payoff in the marketplace.

Figure 14C2-1 illustrates the existence of external benefits from research and the suboptimal quantity this brings about. The efficient quantity, for which marginal social benefit equals marginal social cost, is also noted. To correct this market failure, government can offer to subsidize each unit of research in an amount equal to the marginal external benefit at the efficient quantity, where marginal external benefit equals the difference between marginal social benefit and demand. This action has the effect of shifting

Figure 14C2-1   External benefits from basic research create a market failure that can be corrected with a subsidy. The subsidy must be set equal to marginal external benefits (the difference between marginal social benefit and demand) at the efficient quantity.

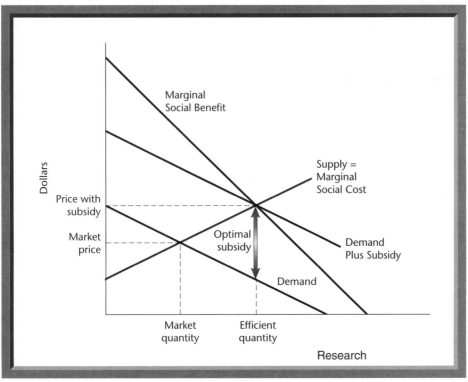

demand upward by the amount of the per-unit subsidy, so that the new demand intersects supply at the efficient quantity. In principle, this approach corrects the market failure.

In practice, life is not so simple. It is impossible to know the value of basic research until long after it has been completed and, researchers hope, applied. Thus, government resorts to a broad-brush approach, in which it subsidizes the research process rather than the research product. These subsidies are pervasive within higher education, in which faculty must "publish or perish." Publication in peer-reviewed journals is used as the measuring rod as to whether or not research is of value.

Government also subsidizes research by private companies through provisions in the tax code, such as the research and experimentation tax credit. To minimize the magnitude of subsidies going toward research that would have been done anyway, the tax credit applies only to research expenditures over a threshold amount. Since government cannot know how much research and experimentation would have been done in the absence of the credit, it is difficult to know whether this tax credit has been effective.

C

Study by Design

SpeedStudy

SpeedReview

Economies grow though accumulating resources. They have the most control over capital, which in turn improves labor productivity. Current tax policies discourage savings, which finances the investment necessary for capital formation. Some current regulations also discourage investment. Conversely, government promotes technological advance through subsidies for basic research, such as is conducted at colleges and universities. Otherwise, the existence of external benefits would lead to too little of such research.

Supply siders are modern classical economists who seek to minimize structural features of the economy that discourage work effort and capital formation. Reducing regulations and marginal tax rates have been two of their emphases. New classical economists point out the failings of activist government policy, while new Keynesians emphasize that short-run Keynesian insights can be seen within a long-run context. Each of these modern schools of thought acknowledges the importance of microeconomic foundations to the study of macroeconomics. Political liberals tend to adopt Keynesian economics, and conservatives tend to adopt classical economics. In practice, policymakers often put aside their ideological hats and follow a pragmatic approach when designing macro policies.

SpeedStudy True or False Self-Test

A1. Actual investment equals the replacement of depreciated capital, plus capital formation, plus inventory changes.

A2. Most investment comes from government.

A3. Government taxes the return on savings in order to bring in extra revenue.

A4. An increase in capital increases labor productivity.

A5. If prices on pharmaceutical drugs are controlled to allow the producer to cover manufacturing expenses plus a slight profit, the marketplace

p. 261

will ensure an efficient amount of investment into new products.

A6. The capital gains tax discourages investment because it takes away some of the expected return on that investment.

A7. The objective of supply-side policy is to ensure that long-run aggregate supply is associated with the greatest possible amount of output.

A8. Reaganomics is associated with a supply-side agenda.

A9. Keynesians emphasize the importance of lower tax rates, so that long-run aggregate supply will shift to the right over time.

A10. If people have rational expectations, government fiscal policy is an effective means to combat unemployment and inflation.

B11. The Social Security trust fund has enough savings built up to last for approximately fifteen years.

B12. Social Security redistributes income both within and between generations.

B13. In *Winds of Change in Caribia*, the supply-side boys emphasize economic growth above all else.

B14. All macroeconomic views can be categorized as either Keynesian or classical.

C15. The government actions necessary to achieve second-best efficiency are often so complicated that they would probably not be performed correctly in the real world.

C16. Second-best efficiency represents the most efficient outcome possible, subject to some inefficient constraints.

C17. The value of research is often evaluated by whether it is published in a refereed journal.

C18. The competitive marketplace produces the efficient quantity of new knowledge.

The MasterMind

Selected Terms Along the Way

MasterMind Multiple Choice Self-Test

A1. Without government or foreign commerce, the amount saved is about the same as the amount

  a. invested.

  b. consumed.

  c. taxed.

  d. earned.

A2. The investment demand curve illustrates how the amount of investment depends on

  a. the price of capital, such as plants and equipment.

  b. the nominal interest rate.

  c. the real interest rate.

  d. the inflation rate.

A3. Government subsidies for basic research can be economically justified on the grounds that basic research

  a. redistributes income to the poor.

  b. provides external benefits, but less than would development.

  c. provides external benefits, more than would development.

  d. would otherwise be monopolized by the private sector.

A4. Which school of macroeconomic thought is most likely to emphasize policies that increase full-employment output?

  a. Keynesians.

  b. New Keynesians.

  c. Supply siders.

  d. New classical economists.

A5. Political liberals are most likely to be

  a. Keynesians.

  b. supply siders.

  c. new classical economists.

  d. communists.

B6. Which of the following is *not* a problem in converting Social Security financing from pay-as-you-go to fully funded?

  a. Current workers would face double taxation.

  b. There would be less ability to redistribute income within a generation.

  c. Social Security investments are in government bonds.

  d. Future taxpayers would be forced to pay higher payroll taxes.

B7. The winning candidate in Caribia promised to

  a. provide a wide safety net.

  b. remove the safety net and lower taxes.

  c. divide up the country's wealth among its citizens.

  d. keep out foreign investors.

C8. The principle of second-best efficiency suggests that

  a. government should not settle for second best.

b. if the tax system is inefficient and cannot be changed, then most free market prices will need to be changed in order to be efficient.

c. the goal of equity should come first, followed by the goal of efficiency.

d. government policies designed to promote efficiency should be backed up with other government policies designed to accomplish the exact same goals.

C9. To achieve an efficient amount of research, a subsidy per unit of research should equal

a. total external benefits.

b. total external costs.

c. total social benefits.

d. marginal external benefits.

MasterMind Questions and Problems

A1. Identify three different opportunities for investment in physical capital. Discuss how a higher real interest rate could make these opportunities less attractive.

A2. List three examples of government spending that might be considered investment. Would the private sector have undertaken these projects if government did not? Explain.

A3. a. Graph aggregate demand and long-run aggregate supply. Label (1) the axes of the graph, (2) each curve, and (3) the long-run equilibrium.

b. On the same graph, show aggregate demand shifting to the left in response to some shock, such as a crisis in banking. Indicate the new long-run equilibrium. Assuming sticky wages and prices prevent a rapid movement to this equilibrium, show the amount by which equilibrium GDP might drop below its full-employment level.

A4. Economists are reluctant to call themselves Keynesians or supply siders because of negative connotations associated with those terms. What are some of these connotations? Are they deserved?

A5. Explain what distinguishes supply siders, new classical economists, and new Keynesians.

B6. How is the Social Security trust fund invested? Explain why the trust fund must be invested differently if it is to represent real savings. How could the buildup of real savings be accomplished in a way that would avoid political influence on where those savings go?

B7. In *Winds of Change in Caribia*, little was said about the current government, except that the economy seemed to be stagnating. Some people claim that Keynesian policies cause stagnation by focusing on government spending and automatic stabilizers while ignoring aggregate supply. Does this claim have any basis? Explain.

C8. Suppose the tax code is reformed to eliminate any bias against capital formation. Identify another possible source of inefficiency, and explain how second-best analysis might apply if that inefficiency is to remain. Also discuss why putting the principle of second-best efficiency into practice could easily cause more problems than it solves.

C9. Identify two advances in knowledge that have led to economic growth. Was government funding involved?

Future Explorations: Mapping out Term Papers

1. No More Surprises!

This paper starts by reporting examples of how firms have predicted future demand for their products and instances in which these predictions have proven wrong. The paper then examines new ways of inventory control that are intended to better match predicted and actual demand. Of particular interest is just-in-time-production that minimizes the buildup of undesired inventories. The paper concludes by noting how participants in the macroeconomy can be surprised by supply- or demand-side shocks and ways in which these shocks can affect individual firms.

2. Taxes Are Always Changing

This paper reviews tax changes that Congress has contemplated in the last few years. For each, the paper discusses the motivation behind the tax change, the implications upon savings and investment if the changes were to occur, and postulates why the changes were enacted or rejected.

3. Planning for Retirement—The Impact of Social Security

This paper looks at the general manner in which Social Security is financed and how benefits are determined. It also uses some specific examples to illustrate the Social Security benefits you might receive upon your own retirement, assuming the Social Security system remains unchanged. The paper goes on to discuss what changes in Social Security are probable and what impact they are likely to have on your personal plans.

Answer Key

ExpressStudy True or False	SpeedStudy True or False Self-Test		MasterMind Multiple Choice Self-Test
1. F	1. T	10. F	1. a
2. T	2. F	11. F	2. c
3. F	3. T	12. T	3. c
4. F	4. T	13. T	4. c
5. T	5. F	14. F	5. a
6. T	6. T	15. T	6. d
	7. T	16. T	7. b
	8. T	17. T	8. b
	9. F	18. F	9. d

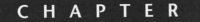

C H A P T E R

F i f t e e n

*G*lobal Economic Themes

539

A LOOK AHEAD

The watershed events of history are often linked to economic forces. In 1989 the free world witnessed a wall come down in Berlin, shattering the symbol of a globe divided into two armed, hostile camps. Subsequently, we observed the collapse of the empire that erected that wall, a collapse directly tied to the failure of its economic system. The cold war ended, and new challenges took center stage.

As Soviet communism was collapsing, millions of personal computers were deployed on desktops in homes and workplaces around the world. Information and an ability to communicate cheaply with others now has the potential to create a new global neighborhood of peace and prosperity. Yet other forces, including crime and terrorism at home, and genocidal warfare abroad, threaten these bright visions.

As the world continues its never-ending struggle between chaos and peace, between destruction and prosperity, can a greater understanding of economics be a stabilizing force? The possibilities are exciting. This chapter illuminates significant economic opportunities and problems that spill beyond the borders of any one country. Common to each of the five themes is the contribution that an analysis of costs and benefits can make in explaining these global issues.

DESTINATIONS

$\mathcal{M}$odule A

As you zip along the Expressway you will arrive at an ability to

- assess the effects of technological change on the optimal amount of information;
- apply the model of supply and demand to see how immigration affects wage rates;
- interpret how expected costs and benefits influence the decision to engage in criminal activity;
- relate the role economics can play in motivating war and peace;
- discuss how the choice of economic systems can affect resources and the environment.

$\mathcal{M}$odule B

Upon leaving the Expressway to explore issues you will be able to

- identify economic incentives for virtue or vice;
- describe how government threats to property rights hinder economic development and how the private sector offers imperfect alternatives.

$\mathcal{M}$odule C

Mastering Roadside Challenges will allow you to hone analytical skills by

- explaining how immigration affects a country's pattern of international trade;
- analyzing the role economics plays in your life today and in the future.

The 1969 Apollo moon mission sent home dramatic pictures. For the first time we were witness to the brilliant beauty of a fragile, life-filled earth hanging alone in the darkness of space. The planet appeared as a lifeboat, sustaining precious existence in a vast, empty universe. Those pictures instilled a realization that we are all citizens of one planet.

The forces of economic change leave no one unaffected. From economically primitive third-world villages to country clubs dotting suburbs across the United States, people's lives are shaped by the global economy. As information technology turns distant peoples into our global neighbors and economic competitors, all must adapt to change. Immigration makes our global neighbors our literal next-door neighbors, and that too alters economies. We want our global neighborhood to be peaceful and safe from crime. We also want other lands to prosper. This chapter identifies five themes relating to the new world economy.

Theme 1: The Earth Keeps Shrinking

Ever since the first human beings gazed upon the earth, there has been curiosity about what lies over the horizon. For thousands of years, people were forced to rely upon their own legs in order to glimpse beyond. Subsequently, the legs of horses and camels served as more efficient substitutes for human legs. Harnessing the power of the wind with sails meant that great bodies of water were no longer barriers to questioning minds.

Today, in the historical blink of an eye, humanity stands ready to adopt ever newer electronic technologies, which move minds rather than bodies. Fax machines, e-mail, and the Internet give us a preview of the future. This global meeting of minds in the marketplace for ideas offers both promise and peril. Will the information we share with each other create information overload, or will we use our access to information to increase economic efficiency and for other good purposes?

The Birth of the Information Age: The Road Ahead

Whether for consumers or businesses, information is required to make good decisions. The model of perfect competition assumes that market participants possess perfect information, which means that perfectly competitive markets work smoothly. However, in the real world, information is not perfect and is in fact costly. The consequence of costly, imperfect information is greater uncertainty in making decisions.

In our lifetime we have witnessed an explosion of information technologies that have already altered the decision-making process. Purveyors of technology promise even more advanced, easier-to-use information goods and services. To understand the significance of these changes, consider a model of information acquisition shown in Figure 15A-1. The marginal benefit curve is equivalent to the demand curve for information. Actually measuring a market demand curve would be difficult, however, since it would be

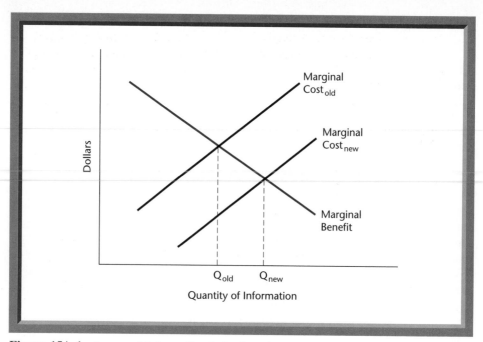

Figure 15A-1 **Improved information technology** increases the equilibrium quantity of information. The marginal cost curve shifts to the right, increasing the quantity from Q_{old} to Q_{new}.

difficult to measure units of information. Correspondingly, marginal cost is equivalent to the supply of information.

The marginal benefit of each additional unit of information declines, reflecting the decreasing usefulness of succeeding bits of information. People do not continue to acquire information to the point where the next bit of information is worthless, because information is costly. **The optimal amount of information occurs where the marginal benefit from using information equals the marginal cost of acquiring it.**

For example, the purchaser of a computer would greatly value information about its price, warranty, and capabilities. On the other hand, information about the country of origin of each component inside the computer would be of only passing interest. The value of the time it would take to ascertain the country where each computer component was manufactured means that few of us seek that information before making the purchase.

Computer networks, personalized electronic newspapers, interactive information services, and other new and proposed technologies offer us the prospect of improved decision making. How—by lowering the marginal cost of acquiring additional information. In Figure 15A-1 technological change has shifted the marginal cost curve to the right, indicating that information has become cheaper and more available. The point where the marginal benefits curve intersects the new marginal cost curve thus results in a new equilibrium quantity of information that is greater than the old equilibrium quantity.

As technology continues to improve, consumers, firms, and government can expect the marginal cost curve to continue to shift to the right, and the optimal amount of information to continue to edge closer to its outer limits. Distance learning provides an example. Persons living in areas not served by educational institutions now have the opportunity to attend nearby classes taught by faculty who may be lecturing hundreds of miles away, with the educational experience delivered to learners via high speed digital links. Don't care to leave home to attend class? Rudimentary distance learning on your home computer via the Internet is an option even today. Such possibilities are especially promising for less-developed countries where education is still something of a luxury.

Technological Change, Markets, and Antitrust

The ultimate impact of technological change upon the marketplace is difficult to evaluate. Joseph Schumpeter, legendary twentieth-century economic thinker and Harvard professor, hypothesized in *Capitalism, Socialism, and Democracy* (1942) that new technology provides the impetus for economic growth and higher living standards. While this concept may seem obvious, other issues are not so clear.

The "perennial gale of creative destruction," as Schumpeter termed it, has supplanted the state-of-the-art personal calculating power of the slide rule with first the pocket calculator and then the laptop computer. This progression took a mere twenty years or so. Numerous firms ceased to exist because of an inability to adapt to this technological change. Slide rule makers had no expertise in the electronics required to manufacture calculators. The destruction of existing firms and industries occurred concurrently with the emergence of new industries and firms that possessed or acquired electronics expertise.

Schumpeter hypothesized that a prerequisite to innovation is the market power conferred upon firms by oligopolistic market structures. Pure monopoly and perfectly competitive market structures are not well suited to initiate innovation, in his view. He saw large firms as possessing the wherewithal to conduct research. But monopoly firms lack the competitive pressures felt by firms in oligopoly markets, while perfectly competitive firms lack the pool of economic profits required to finance research and development.

The implications of Schumpeter's insights of more than fifty years ago are still of significance in the antitrust area. **Antitrust policy** is about ensuring effective competition. The question then arises as to how antitrust policy should be applied to markets in which innovation reduces competition. On the one hand, innovation brings higher living standards. On the other, innovation may reduce competition, at least in the short run. Do the benefits of innovation outweigh the costs to society associated with the reduction of competition? The antitrust problem is to answer this question by weighing benefits and costs.

Difficulties in striking the proper balance are illustrated by antitrust concerns over the Microsoft Corporation, whose operating software runs at least 80 percent of the world's personal computers. Microsoft's strategy for success is to add innovative features to each new-generation operating system. This practice potentially squeezes out makers of competing systems. For example, prompted by worries expressed by on-line services such as Compuserve, the Justice Department pondered the potential anticompetitive effects prior to the August 1995 introduction of Windows 95, with its easy access to the Internet via Microsoft Network. They feared that Microsoft would eventually monopolize access to the Internet. Should Microsoft have been barred from offering these services? Technological innovation raises these kinds of questions, the answers to which are often unclear.

The birth of new technologies and the effects of technological change may no longer be as predictable as they once were. The eroding importance of national boundaries brought about by the globalization of the economy is forcing governments to rethink beliefs about the significance of bigness of firms in the marketplace. Is it likely that the Schumpeter model still applies? New technologies quickly become available worldwide, aided by modern information technology. Oligopoly industries within a country are often no longer protected against foreign competition, as was once true. Increasingly, economists believe that U.S. antitrust policy should take a global, rather than national, perspective. That perspective means that foreign competition as well as domestic competition should be acknowledged when antitrust issues arise.

There are additional difficulties with the Schumpeter model. For example, the early development of the personal computer was inconsistent with the predictions of the model. Much of the original innovation in PCs came from small start-up firms, of which the most notable survivor is Apple. The personal computer also appears to have partially leveled the playing field between large firms and small ones. Small businesses today have access to information and other computer-related inputs that allow them better to compete with larger rivals. This change means that innovation may occur in more competitive markets, in addition to the oligopolies that Schumpeter had in mind.

At the other extreme, from cable TV to local telephone service, once stalwart monopolies find themselves challenged by newly arisen competition. In contrast to the thoughts of Schumpeter, the threat of **potential competition** may motivate monopolies to innovate. The bottom line is that firms today must concern themselves with innovation, regardless of which type of market they operate in.

More Choice, Less Diversity?

Will one of the changes wrought by technology be a more homogenized, less diverse world? Will individual cultures blend into one global culture, part American, part European, part Asian, spiced with elements of other cultures? Within the U.S., regional diversity diminished as the American experience involved us all eating the same fast food, watching the same television programs and movies, reading the same books, and so forth. Will the same happen throughout the new global village?

The loss of distinct cultural traits, beliefs, accents, foods, and customs is often viewed as a high price to pay for progress. In France the desire to maintain a distinctively French culture has caused the government to involve itself in restricting the influence of foreign books, movies, television, music, and language within the country.

Wherever in the world we live, our individuality is important to us. Economic changes and the globalization of the economy and culture have chipped away at that. On the one hand, we celebrate diversity by pointing with pride at our unique heritages. On the other hand, we worry that overemphasizing our differences will unravel the social fabric that binds us together. Striking the proper balance remains a challenge.

✓ **QUICKCHECK**

What are some examples of costs and benefits that accompany a government policy to maintain cultural purity, such as the policy in France?

Answer: Costs include the costs of the "culture police"—government bureaucrats who are paid to enforce such policies, and the loss of utility to consumers who would enjoy foreign books and movies. Benefits might include a more cohesive citizenry. However, repressive policies also run the risk of costly divisiveness. For example, many listeners objected when, in 1996, their government forced radio stations to devote forty percent of air time to playing French music.

*T*heme 2: *Immigration and The Melting-Pot World*

We came over on different ships, but we're all in the same boat now.

Traditionally, the U.S. has been referred to as the melting pot of the world. U.S. citizens are proud of their diverse ancestries and the symbolism of the welcoming arms of the Statue of Liberty. Today immigrants account for about 8 percent of the U.S. population.

The U.S. is not alone in its role as melting pot. People of different races, religions, languages, and customs have come to live together in more and more nations. Jamaicans, Hindus, and others from countries within the old British Empire fill the sidewalks of London, Algerians those of Paris, and Turks those of Berlin. Increasingly, however, many countries, including the U.S., are ambivalent about the ideal of the national melting pot.

Why Immigration Is a Concern

John F. Kennedy, the great-grandson of an Irish immigrant, published *A Nation of Immigrants* in 1958. The future President of the U.S. struck a reverent stance toward immigration in his book, respectfully praising the economic and cultural contributions to the nation from immigrants. Subsequently, the Immigration Act of 1965 opened the door to a new wave of mass immigration into the U.S., totaling about 800,000 persons per year. Today, in many other countries as well as the U.S., governments are witnessing challenges by the public to open-door immigration policies. There are numerous reasons for this opposition to further immigration, arising from the following two root causes:

- Ethnic tensions emanating from issues relating to the assimilation of the newcomers into the existing culture;
- A backlash stemming from concerns that immigration has high economic costs.

The U.S. Census Bureau estimates that by the year 2050, the immigration rates established by the 1965 act will result in a U.S. population of up to 500 million people, which is about twice the population counted in the 1990 census. The nation wonders how the economy can absorb that much population growth without social and environmental stress and reduced standards of living.

If the melting pot is not to boil over into ethnic warfare on our streets, as has happened in other countries, can a role model for immigrants of the future be identified? It could be Albert Einstein, whose skills were deployed during World War II in the development of the atomic bomb; or Werner von Braun, whose knowledge of rocketry played a key role in enabling the U.S. space program to reach the moon.

But superstar immigrants are few and far between. Perhaps the country seeks immigrants of the sort profiled in a series of *Saturday Evening Post* and *Country Gentlemen* articles in the 1940s: the Chinese-American Wongs of San Francisco, the Mexican-American Gonzalezes of San Antonio, the Norwegian-American Offerdahls of Wisconsin, and the half-dozen otherwise anonymous families able to succeed with their individual visions of the American Dream.

If it is success that we ask of immigrants, then the economy of today leaves little room for the unskilled. Economist George Borjas' research shows that it takes 100 years, or four generations, for immigrant families to achieve an economic status equal to that of native-born Americans. This research is based upon evidence accumulated over a period earlier in this century when education was significantly less important to labor market success than it is today. The implication of Borjas' research is striking: immigration of low-skilled and relatively uneducated workers is likely to create a nearly permanent underclass.

Immigration and Wage Differentials

The choice of immigration policy affects wage differentials between skilled and unskilled labor, as seen in Figure 15A-2. The left-hand side shows the labor market for unskilled workers, while the right-hand side shows the skilled labor market. Unskilled workers earn a lower wage than skilled workers, but the difference in wages is subject to change. A country that bars immigration will show a wage differential equal to $W^*_s - W^*_u$. However, the admission of only unskilled immigrants will lower the wage rate paid to unskilled workers to W^{**}_u as seen on the left, thus widening the wage differential with skilled workers. Conversely, the admission of only skilled immigrants will lower their wage rate to W^{**}_s as seen on the right, thus reducing the skill differential in wages.

Such skill differentials in wages are of concern because a widening skill differential implies that society could split into an upper income class and a lower income class, with the middle class disappearing. Such a development would bring the stability of society into question. However, wage differentials are not the whole story. **The optimal immigration policy, from an economic perspective, allows immigration up to the point where the expected marginal benefit to the economy from the last immigrant just equals the expected marginal cost.** The creation of the wage differential just discussed is only one of many possible costs and benefits from immigration.

Figure 15A-2 **Immigration policy affects skill differentials in wages.** Immigration of the unskilled increases wage differentials, whereas immigration of the skilled decreases such differentials.

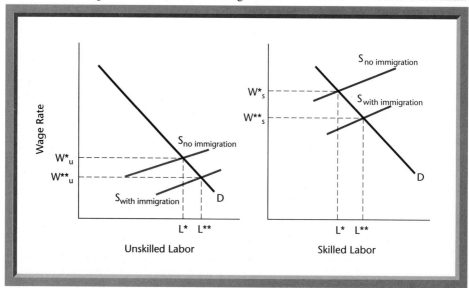

OBSERVATION POINT: Import the Young to Care for the Old?

The aging of the U.S. population will result in a crisis by the year 2030, unless action is taken soon. The number of retirees will explode, while the number of younger workers supporting the elderly with their Social Security contributions will shrink. Thus, while three workers support each retiree today, only two will do so by 2030. To keep Social Security solvent, the U.S. could greatly increase payroll taxes on younger workers, cut benefits drastically, or raise the retirement age.

There is another option that involves the return to a grand old American tradition—increased immigration. We would be offering foreigners a stake in America in exchange for their tax contributions. If there are not enough younger workers, import them!

A

Theme 3: The Economics of Crime and Punishment

Do unto others as you would have others do unto you. (The golden rule)

If we truly practiced the golden rule that we teach our children, there would be neither crime nor war. The brotherhood of humanity would prevail. Try as we might, we have not yet reached that level of perfection. Crime threatens our global neighborhood. In the U.S., about 94,000 crimes per day were committed in 1992. The exact number is unknown because many crimes go unreported. The economic model of crime highlights the role that economic incentives—specifically, expected costs and expected benefits—play in motivating, as well as reducing, crime.

A Worldwide Crime Wave?

On November 21, 1994, 120 nations met in Naples, Italy, to participate in a United Nations conference on international organized crime. That conference was prompted by a growing recognition that crime in one nation is increasingly transferred across international borders. U.S. Senator John Kerry has described today's global network of organized crime as "the new communism, the new monolithic threat."

From the Columbian drug cartel to the emerging "mafias" of Asia and Eastern Europe, the tentacles of organized crime reach across national frontiers—manipulating banking systems, laundering money, and corrupting economies and government officials. While crime takes many forms, the largest single activity is the production and sale of illegal drugs, with annual global revenues estimated by Interpol at $400 billion.

Sometimes innovation by criminal enterprises goes "back to the future." In Asia today, piracy on the high seas is a threat to ships and a problem for the insurance companies that insure their cargos. Modern-day pirates have access to sophisticated information technologies and weaponry, which allow profit-maximizing pirates to target the most lucrative container ships. Meanwhile, shippers who rely upon government police agencies to control piracy have been shocked by revelations that some governments may have actually sponsored the pirates.

Computer technology makes new forms of global crime possible. Criminals might not even need to leave home. In 1995 six Russian computer hackers were arrested for allegedly stealing $10 million from the then-largest U.S. bank, Citibank. They had purportedly accessed Citibank's electronic money transfer system, which enabled them to wire funds to their own accounts around the world. Citibank's technological safeguards fell behind the technology available to hackers. Such innovation in crime forces law enforcement to reallocate resources away from traditional crimes and toward the development of appropriate responses to high-tech lawbreakers. Tomorrow's cop on the beat may need to know as much about computers as guns!

The costs of crime and crime prevention take many forms. People pay higher taxes to support the police and criminal justice system. They also pay for deadbolts, alarm systems, guard dogs, and the like. Some flee to the suburbs or small towns or behind the walls of security-gated subdivisions in hopes of escaping crime. Hidden costs include psychic costs associated with the fear of becoming a victim and the loss of freedom when that fear limits one's activities.

Economic Incentives in Action

Recall that economics is about choice. Those who commit crimes make that choice. Thus, the scope of economic analysis includes the economic aspects of crime and its prevention. That analysis focuses on incentives.

What makes an individual turn to a life of crime? From an economic perspective, a prospective career criminal would consider the relative monetary returns. In other words, **the expected opportunity costs associated with taking up a life of crime guide the decision.** For example, if a person expects that an income of $30,000 a year can be earned from illegal actions, but $40,000 by legal means, common sense says to steer clear of criminal activity. The expected opportunity cost of becoming a criminal would be $40,000, but the income only $30,000.

Even if the calculation were reversed, with $40,000 of expected earnings from illegal activities compared to $30,000 from legal ones, it is still not certain that one would choose to become involved in crime. Criminals incur direct costs associated with their activities. For instance, there is the probability of being apprehended, convicted, and fined or imprisoned. Then, of course, there is the cost imposed by a guilty conscience. These considerations are illustrated in Figure 15A-3. **Because there is uncertainty attached to the outcome of criminal activity, the economic model of crime posits that criminals make decisions based upon the** *expected marginal benefits* **and** *expected marginal costs* **of criminal activity.** Expected values are especially important in the economics of crime because of the great uncertainty attached to rewards and punishments arising from a life of crime.

The challenge we face is to find new deterrents to crime that raise the cost to criminals of committing crimes, without a commensurate rise in cost to taxpayers. Some economists have recently begun to explore the effectiveness of community activism in raising costs for potential criminals. This approach considers the role that the residents of a neighborhood organized to fight crime can play in reducing crime. Preliminary results indicate that this approach has high benefits and low costs to the residents.

Apprehension and punishment of criminals also provides a deterrent—a costly one. "Doing time" is one form of punishment. Some critics of the criminal justice system have

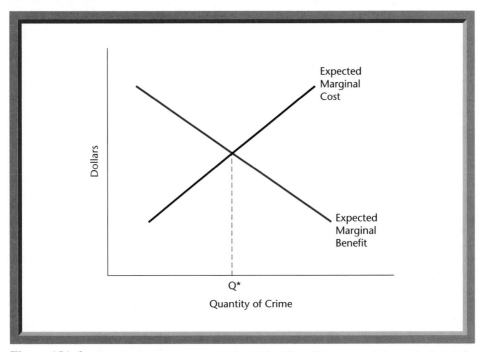

Figure 15A-3 Criminals compare expected marginal benefits to expected marginal costs in deciding how much crime to commit. Increasing the costs and/or lowering the benefits would reduce the amount of crime.

argued that the approximately $25,000 per prisoner per year cost of incarceration in the U.S. is not cost effective. They suggest that most of those in prison should be released and offered job training and other social services. However, economists' estimates of the benefits to society of incarcerating criminals suggests that the value of lives saved, assaults prevented, and homes left untouched by burglary are up to three times the cost of incarceration. That does not prove that imprisonment is the best alternative. The ratio of benefits to costs from attacking such root causes of crime as poverty, discrimination, and lack of opportunity could be greater than the three-to-one ratio from imprisonment. Unfortunately, such benefit to cost ratios are themselves fraught with uncertainties.

Although crime occurs everywhere, crime rates in some other countries fall substantially below those in the U.S., including in countries where poverty is more pronounced than in the U.S. There is still much to learn from the cultures and experiences of other nations. Such insights, while useful, are not in and of themselves a panacea. Difficult policy choices involving the allocation of resources among prevention and punishment must be made.

*T*heme 4: *A Just and Lasting Peace*

In the late 1960s President Richard Nixon referred to his efforts to end the Vietnam conflict as a search for "a just and lasting peace." That phrase became part of the common vernacular of the time. Today, more than twenty-five years later, another similar phrase, this time repeated by civil rights leaders, is "no justice, no peace." Clearly, justice and peace are linked. Because economic justice is an important part of justice as a whole, the achievement of world peace cannot ignore economics.

For thousands of years, neighbor has attacked neighbor in order to gain control of raw materials, goods, and property. Can a nation be secure, even when it suffers no conflict, if its neighbors covet its prosperity? While it is in the interest of every nation to see that prosperity spreads to all nations of earth, there will inevitably be disagreements about how best to achieve that result.

Prosperous industrialized nations support efforts to raise global living standards as part of a strategy to keep the peace. The Organization for Economic Cooperation and Development (OECD), World Bank, International Monetary Fund (IMF), and other organizations transfer resources from prosperous countries to poor countries to spur economic development. Nonetheless, nations also expend substantial resources on protection. The U.S., for example, spends about 4 percent of its gross domestic product on defense. In fact, most nations spend between 1 and 5 percent of their GDPs on military expenditures.

A few countries spend an extraordinarily large fraction of their GDPs on the military, either because they feel threatened, or because they wish to threaten other countries. For example, in 1991, the year of the Gulf War, Kuwait spent 102 percent of its GDP on the military, Iraq 75 percent, Saudi Arabia 30 percent, North Korea 20 percent, and Syria 18 percent. Military expenditures this large impose significant burdens on a nation's consumers and are thus difficult to sustain for very long.

New and different threats to peace and security loom on the horizon. A worldwide **trade war**, an event not witnessed since the Great Depression era of the 1930s, would have the potential to destroy prosperity as surely as conventional war, because import and export flows are vital to world affluence. Although economists recognize that trade wars are futile, such a trade war between the U.S. and Japan was narrowly averted in the summer of 1995. The U.S. threatened to place high tariffs on Japanese luxury cars in retaliation for what the U.S. believed were unfair trade policies in Japan.

A second threat is innovative, cheap, cost-effective terrorism. A thousand dollars of fertilizer and fuel oil transported in a rented truck makes a bomb capable of giving a small group of terrorists power to influence public policy far beyond what their numbers would indicate. Kidnapping is also cheap and cost effective and has been widely practiced in Europe for that reason. Even terrorists consider the economics of their actions!

Fighting over Global Property

Common property resources, such as the air, the ocean, and groundwater, are scarce and valuable resources that are jointly owned. Sometimes nations disagree over who has the right to those resources. For example, when the ships belonging to the fishing fleets of two friendly nations converged upon a school of whales swimming in midocean some years ago, violent conflict nearly resulted. "We have the right to harvest these whales," cried both sides. In such disagreements, who speaks for the world, or for that matter, the whales?

Closer to home, suppose you are a rancher and your land is traversed by a river that supplies your family and your cattle with drinking water. Would you fight if your upstream neighbor dammed the river, thus depriving you of the opportunity to enjoy the use of the water and your land? Such battles over water occurred among settlers in the parched lands of the western U.S. until water rights became firmly established. Even today the issue of water rights is a source of contention among countries in Europe and the Middle East.

In disputes over common property or any other issue, there is an incentive for economically powerful nations to become militarily powerful. While military power can be used for self-defense, it can also be employed for aggression. Consider Figure 15A-4 which shows production possibilities frontiers for two neighboring countries, Myland and Urland. These curves show the trade-off between military goods and civilian consumption goods. Thus, the axes are labeled Guns and Butter. The economy of Myland is more productive than the economy of Urland, since Myland's frontier is farther from the origin than Urland's.

Myland can produce more guns than Urland. If Urland devotes all its resources to the production of guns, it can produce the amount indicated at point A on the vertical axis of Urland's frontier. Urland produces no butter at point A. By contrast, Myland's productive capacity is sufficiently great that it can match Urland's production of guns by producing at point A′ on its frontier, a point that simultaneously allows the production of some butter, too. Myland could alternatively produce more guns than Urland by producing above point A′ on its frontier, and still have some butter.

Myland could use its economic superiority to commence a short-run military buildup designed to force Urland to the point of economic collapse. Discontent among the citizens of Urland with their government would occur because of the low living standards arising from the *arms race* between the two countries. This was the U.S. strategy that led to the disintegration of the Soviet Union.

Alternatively, Myland could use its military muscle to bully Urland into providing resources or goods and services to Myland at prices less than those of the free market. In another option, Myland could attack Urland and gain direct control over the resources.

What can Urland do to protect itself from its threatening neighbor? The formation of a mutual security pact with a third country would allow Urland some measure of security. Urland and a third country could agree to come to each other's defense if attacked by Myland. In effect, **a mutual-security pact increases the expected cost of aggression to the aggressor while reducing the expected benefits.**

Figure 15A-4   Economic power may translate into military power. Myland can produce more guns than Urland by locating above point A′ on its production possibilities frontier. Myland can use its power for good or for ill.

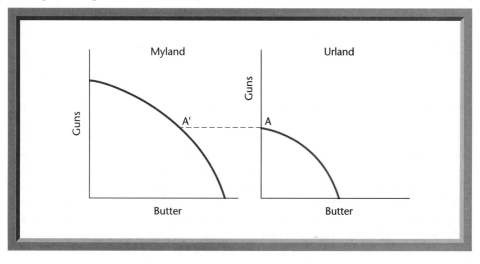

In the real world, mutual security pacts do protect nations. The U.S. is allied with many European countries in the North Atlantic Treaty Organization (NATO), and with other countries through other mutual-security pacts. However, such alliances are subject to the free-rider problem in which some members can avoid paying their fair share. For example, smaller countries that are members of NATO do not pay their fair share of costs, giving rise to the so-called exploitation of the big by the small. Japan bears only a small fraction of its defense costs, which are mostly paid by the U.S. Many taxpayers in the U.S. resent these circumstances.

Cooperation on military matters by the European members of NATO also spurred cooperation on economic matters, which led to the creation of the European Union (EU). The EU free-trade area competes fiercely in world markets with the U.S., the prime force behind the creation of NATO. Ironically, in its efforts to create a safer world, the U.S. helped give birth to a major economic competitor.

Ideally, nations realize that economics provides the incentive to seek peace. Moving down the production possibilities frontiers toward more butter makes both countries better off in the long run. In the short run, there are problems with transferring resources from defense to the civilian sector of the economy. In recent years, the downsizing of the U.S. military has left communities across the country keeping their fingers crossed in hopes that their military bases would not be among those marked for closure. When bases are closed, the civilian workers suffer unemployment. Generally, that unemployment will be temporary, but the transition to new work can be painful.

OBSERVATION POINT: A War to Control the Oil Fields

The long Iran-Iraq War of the 1980s proved that the leader of Iraq, Saddam Hussein, could maintain power while conducting a bloody, destructive war. After the war with Iran ended in a stalemate, Hussein turned his attention to another target for his aggression—one that could help pay the enormous costs of the just-ended war. This time, he reasoned, the victim will be small enough and weak enough to not be able to fight back.

The prize was Kuwait, a nation sharing a common border and a common property resource with Iraq. Pools of oil, lying deep underground, recognize no international boundaries. Iraq could argue that the oil pumped by Kuwait's wells really belonged to it. In August 1990, Iraq attacked. While a great coalition of the world's nations united to drive Iraq from Kuwait in the Gulf War, Hussein continued to rule Iraq with an iron hand after the war and continued to threaten neighboring lands.

Territorial Disputes and Tribal Warfare

Borders between nations are often ill defined. Centuries of warfare have shifted borders back and forth. Thus disputes over which nation owns a particular piece of land are common. Adolf Hitler promised the world in the 1930s that all he wanted was the Sudetenland, which was tied to Germany by language and culture. Sadly, that territorial dispute provided the springboard for Hitler's aggression and World War II.

Another form of territorial dispute is exemplified by the 1995 conflict in Chechnya.

The people of the region wished to be an independent country, but Russia, which has historically dominated the region, did not agree. The sympathies of most Americans were with the Chechynians. Would we feel the same if it were the people of Montana who demanded their independence? The difficulty with settling territorial disputes is that both sides usually believe that their side is right.

Tribal conflicts are not conducted to obtain raw materials, living space, or for any other seemingly rational reason. Fighting between Protestants and Catholics in Ireland, between Serbs and Bosnians in the former Yugoslavia, between tribes within Rwanda, and within other less-developed countries are examples. The economic devastation arising from these conflicts was seen on the evening news and measured with economic statistics. The price in terms of human sorrow is not so easily ascertained.

OBSERVATION POINT: The United Nations: What's All That Talk about Peace?

World War II was nearly over by June of 1945, as representatives from fifty nations hammered out a charter for the United Nations. The UN was established with high hopes that a forum for working out problems between nations could eliminate future wars. Since then, at least 1,000 wars, conflicts, and police actions have occurred. In the period from 1985 to 1995, the UN report "State of the World's Children, 1996" says 2 million children were killed, 4 to 5 million disabled, and 12 million made homeless by war.

Perhaps the UN's difficulties at peacekeeping stem from restrictions on its powers to change incentives among potential combatants. International condemnation of aggressor nations by the UN relies upon moral suasion to change behavior. Economic sanctions, such as bans on exports and imports, should carry more weight, but often prove ineffective. The problem is that sanctioned nations find ways, such as through smuggling, to escape sanctions. Thus, the UN is relatively powerless to stop war.

*T*heme 5: Free Markets or Central Planning?

In much of the world, communism has died of its own weight, with a whimper rather than a bang. Now the world waits to see whether the poor will embrace promises of government-provided economic security in exchange for government control of the economy—*central planning*.

The Price System—Finding New Resources

The earth's expanding population will need resources to prosper. Three billion citizens of earth, with additional billions on the way, seek warmth in the winter, cool breezes in the summer, and transportation year-round. All these services take resources. If resources are not to be exhausted, either new resource supplies must continually be found or produced, or better ways to utilize existing resources must be developed.

The lessons taught by the price system are germane to the question of where those resources will come from. The price system responds to scarcity. The scarcer are resources, the higher their prices, other things equal. Higher prices caused by a decrease in supply reduce the quantity demanded now. Higher prices caused by an increase in demand draw forth a greater quantity supplied. Furthermore, in the long run, higher prices make it profitable to find or develop substitutes, which would not be economical at lower prices. Higher prices also promote recycling. In this way the energy crisis of the 1970s was overcome by the free market, as consumers conserved and as producers found new supplies.

Does the price system always respond? The energy crisis of the 1800s was tied to a shortage of whale oil, which supplied the fuel for reading lamps. The shortage arose from the overharvesting of whales and from increasing energy demands. Because the need for power to turn the wheels of industry was more than whale oil could ever supply, the price system dangled the lure of profit to successful innovators who could find new energy sources. This incentive eventually brought about the age of petroleum. We can only speculate whether the next energy age will be of solar power or some resource we currently are not even able to imagine.

✓ **QUICKCHECK**

What are the differences in the way the price system works between nonrenewable resource markets, such as for petroleum, and renewable resource markets, such as for timber?

_____

Answer: Over the very long run, as nonrenewable resources are used up, the supply curve must shift to the left. Shifts to the right in the supply curve can only be temporary, as when a new oil field is developed. For nonrenewable resources, rising prices stimulate the search for substitutes. For renewable resources, the supply curve can be shifted to the right in the short run as well as the long run, as when new fish or timber farms are established.

Central Planning: Legacies of Environmental Destruction, Lessons for a Mixed Economy

When government has unchecked power, the ability to damage the environment is magnified. Government can become the polluter rather than the pollution fighter. The environmental legacy of communism provides a tragic illustration. Environmental devastation in Communist Europe and the Soviet Union ranged from the ecological death of rivers and lakes to the radioactive contamination spread over hundreds of square miles by the explosion at the Chernobyl nuclear power plant.

Communist governments largely ignored the environment for at least two reasons. First, poor nations are often unable to bear the costs of getting a clean environment, and Communism was never capable of generating much wealth. Second, the secretive, bureaucratic governments were unresponsive to their citizens' environmental concerns.

With communism in retreat, environmental worries have come to the forefront of public consciousness among the citizens of the formerly Communist nations. **An efficient environmental policy weighs the new jobs, greater output, and other benefits of eco-**

nomic activity against the environmental costs of that activity. Implementing such a policy in these countries would lead to a cleaner world.

Central planning is in retreat for another reason too. The economic performance of countries that centralized decision making within government has came under increasing scrutiny, as economic growth in these countries falls short of that in more free market–oriented countries. There are lessons to be learned for all countries, however, since all countries combine government and market forces. In other words, all countries have mixed economies. Sometimes the mix emphasizes free markets and other times government.

For example, Europe has endured a condition termed **Eurosclerosis**, referring to high unemployment rates and sluggish economic growth in some countries of Western Europe. Economic growth in Europe in the 1950s through the 1970s outstripped growth in the U.S. But during the 1980s that scenario reversed itself. Many economists attribute the problems in Europe to economies rife with bloated bureaucracies and characterized by costly social welfare programs that reduce the incentives of workers to work and of firms to invest. Other analysts also point out the hardships imposed upon Germany, the leading European economy, by the integration of prosperous West Germany with stagnant East Germany.

Because of Eurosclerosis, the nations of Europe have discovered that the generosity of the welfare state does have limits. A number of countries have begun the long march down the road to more market-based economies with less generous benefits for workers, students, and pensioners. The primary focus of these changes is the restoration of incentives in the private sector. While the social safety net has allure, so too do the opportunities offered by a vibrant, growing economy.

OBSERVATION POINT: Killer Bees, Fire Ants, and Hungry Rabbits

Never underestimate the ability of humans to inflict environmental disaster. Take the case of Australia's rabbits, which do significant damage to crops on the island continent. Rabbits are not native to the country, but were introduced when an immigrant youngster's pregnant pet rabbit escaped into the wilds where no natural predators existed. Then there are the fire ants and "killer bees" spreading throughout the U.S., threatening people, pets, crops, and the relatively gentle native ants and bees. The ants arrived on boats from South America and found a hospitable climate free of predators. The immigrant bees are the result of a scientific experiment in breeding that went awry when thousands of the pesky critters escaped into the wilds of Brazil and then decided to move north.

Economic Development: Choosing the Best Model

The appeal of orderly government planning of the economy versus the perception of the chaos of the marketplace—is that the choice facing developing economies today? The choice of order over chaos seems obvious. Unfortunately, the alternatives as presented are bogus. Government planning is often disorderly and wasteful.

The 1950s through the 1970s were the heyday of government central planning in less-developed countries. For all that effort, there are far too many countries still mired in poverty. Figure 15A-5 shows annual life expectancies and per capita gross national product for selected countries, running the gamut from the lowest to the highest GNP.

Which role model should less-developed lands adopt in order to join the ranks of the developed countries? Certainly, it would be wise at least to consider the development strategies of high-growth nations and see what they have in common. Table 15A-1 presents data on the average annual growth rates of selected high-growth countries and, for contrast, a group of selected countries that experienced negative growth during the period. A careful study of the high-growth countries shows a common factor that accounts for their rapid growth—a significant role for the price system. There may also be cultural values that play a role, however, which economics is ill-equipped to identify and evaluate. Virtues such as integrity, industriousness, generosity, and respect for others may play a major role in development and yet go unmeasured.

OBSERVATION POINT: The Best-Laid Plans of Mice and Government

Consider the outcome of government planning in Nigeria in the 1970s. To bring the nation up to modern standards required roads, bridges, airports, and other in-

Figure 15A-5 **Annual per capita gross national product (GNP) and life expectancy, selected countries, 1993.**

Source: World Development Report, Table 1.

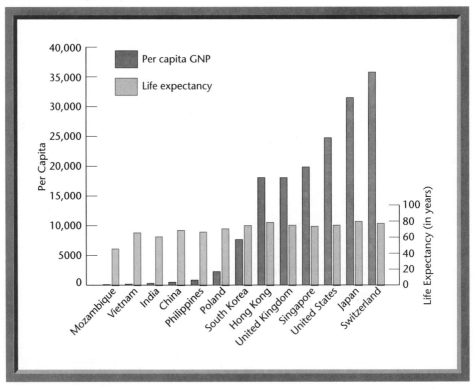

TABLE 15A-1	*Average Annual Growth Rates, 1980–1993, Selected Countries*		
High-Growth Countries	**Growth Rate (in percent)**	**Negative-Growth Countries**	**Growth Rate (in percent)**
China	9.6	Georgia	−6.1
South Korea	9.1	Trinidad-Tobago	−3.6
Thailand	8.2	Armenia	−2.8
Singapore	6.9	Estonia	−2.6
Hong Kong	6.5	Lithuania	−2.2
Malaysia	6.2	Azerbaijan	−2.2
Pakistan	6.0	Nicaragua	−1.8
India	5.2	Albania	−1.8
Japan	4.0	Niger	−0.6
United States	2.7	Peru	−0.5

Source: World Development Report, Table 2.

A

frastructure. This modernization called for massive quantities of cement, much more than the nation could produce domestically. Thus, Nigeria's government planners ordered the needed cement, which was shipped in the holds of freighters from cement-producing nations around the world.

Oops! One slight oversight threw these best-laid plans into disarray. The Nigerian docks were incapable of handling such quantities of cement. In fact, at one point it would have taken nearly thirty years to unload the cement that lay in the holds of ships anchored offshore. Ultimately much of the cement solidified within the ships, thereby providing a concrete example of the dangers inherent in centrally planned development.

EXPRESS STUDY TRUE OR FALSE

1. People consume information until its marginal benefit is zero. *equals its marginal cost*
2. According to Schumpeter, oligopoly promotes innovation.
3. The wage differential between skilled and unskilled workers would be expected to widen if more unskilled immigrants are admitted to the U.S.
4. Criminals are irrational and thus ignore incentives. *sometimes but often respond to incentives*
5. The only strategy open to a large country that covets the resources of a small neighboring country is to build up its stock of military goods and then attack.
6. When economic development has been guided by a large-scale master plan, it has usually proven more successful than when left to the free market. *282*

$\mathcal{M}$odule B
EXPLORING ISSUES

EXPLORATION 1
The Economics of Virtue

Economic incentives affect how easily people acquire the virtues that we value. The modern world is characterized by a number of features that make virtue less likely.

> *"Fiddle-de-dee." "Tomorrow is another day!"*
> —Scarlett O'Hara in Gone with the Wind

Scarlett had pluck and an upbeat attitude. Rhett Butler added a dash of suave sophistication. Together, this attractive couple captured the imagination of millions. Both Scarlett and Rhett had weak points, too, as any movie buff can report. Like Rhett and Scarlett, we each have our own set of virtues and vices. These virtues are developed through nature, nurture, and personal choice. They are also influenced by our opportunities and experiences, which are shaped by economic considerations.

Today we find ourselves bombarded with news reports of reprehensible deeds. We shake our heads and wonder what the world is coming to. At a personal level, we seek to overcome the many hurdles life puts before us. These are issues of morality and personal responsibility.

These are also issues of economics. After all, do we not acknowledge the role of advantages and disadvantages in explaining behavior? For example, some say that children's disadvantages must be offset by public assistance, or we cannot expect those children to grow to productive citizens who are able to shape their own destinies and to provide for themselves and their children. Others point to great men and women from history who built character by overcoming obstacles on their own.

$\mathcal{T}$he Market for Virtue

Virtue is a good. We value it in ourselves—virtue is its own reward. We value it in others, too. Unlike a physical good, though, virtue cannot be manufactured and is impossible to trade. We cannot go to the marketplace and offer to buy or sell two units of patience or three units of honesty. In large part, we must produce these things ourselves. However, we do acquire many inputs that assist us in this process. We also acquire inputs that make our job tougher, although we would do without these if we could.

On the positive side, we can purchase good books, tickets to uplifting movies, pleasant restaurant meals, and many other things to brighten our outlooks and dispose us to act virtuously. We can also select our friends, and visit places to get away. Although there is no direct market for friendship, the marketplace does offer places to meet and things to do. Government helps, too, by providing parks and other public goods that allow us to renew our spirits.

Then there is vice. The marketplace also assists us here, if we so desire. Of course, since we have all heard the saying that one man's virtue is another man's vice, who is to say what constitutes virtue and what constitutes vice. Sometimes, though, the vice is not of our own choosing—it is a negative externality. We do not want the vice of fear or of crime against our person or property. We do not want the vices of racism, discrimination, nepotism, or cronyism. We do not want the vice of children lured into pornography. We do not want the vice of mind-numbing noise. Then, too, while a loud rock concert in the park may be vice for some, it is virtue for others.

Just as government provides some inputs that promote virtue, it is also responsible for others that facilitate vice. Sometimes the two go hand in hand. Consider liability laws, for example. These laws are supposed to protect us from carelessness and other vices that do us harm. Yet, **lawsuit abuse** has become a vice in its own right. These days, people are often afraid of doing constructive things, for fear that there might be a slip-up for which they will be sued. Even if they have a valid defense, they know that a lawsuit could easily monopolize their time and other resources.

For example, a few years ago a Texas doctor delivered twins who were three months premature. One twin died, and the other lived, but in poor health. The doctor was concerned over the deteriorating condition of the mother, and promptly commenced exploratory surgery. Upon examining the mother, he discovered a rare complication of delivery that had been documented only three times previously. In each case, the mother had died. The doctor performed an emergency operation in time to save the mother's life. He was a hero! He was sued.

The lawsuit alleged that the doctor should have done more, and should have done it sooner. Although the doctor defended himself successfully against these charges, it cost him a great deal of time and stress. It drained his spirit. He had to resist the incentive to work less diligently. After all, if the savings from his many years' worth of work were at risk, and his reward for doing the best he could do was to face charges, why not back off? Those are not the kinds of rewards that promote virtue.

Companies also file lawsuits that are designed to thwart potential competitors. The fairness of these lawsuits is often open to question, especially when large companies with deep pockets direct their litigation against small, upstart companies that may be unable to weather the costs and uncertainties. When faced with potentially devastating lawsuits, such companies often find that their investors pull out, banks withdraw credit, and major customers go with competitors who have a more certain future. Thus, the lawsuit wreaks its damage, no matter the verdict in court.

A nonymity in the Information Age

To excel in the competitive marketplace, firms must provide what customers want. How then can we explain our many experiences with firms that do not? Why do we complain that our homes are shoddily built or our cars poorly serviced? In large part, the answer revolves around a lack of information. This lack is a failure of the free marketplace and promotes vice over virtue.

Take the case of going to a repair shop to have our car's brakes serviced. Since few of us specialize in the details of brakework, we pay attention only when problems arise. When our car's brakes start squeaking, we may ask acquaintances to recommend a repair shop. We may also look for coupons in the newspaper, recall commercials from TV, or merely check the Yellow Pages. None of these procedures provides reliable information.

View brake repair from the perspective of the repair shop. Many customers are only semiliterate when it comes to brakes, and they rely on the shop's expertise. You know that, since brake work is done only occasionally, the odds of any one customer returning are not good. Thus, your actions are not likely either to increase or decrease your future business very much. Is it surprising that "You need new brakes" is almost a cliché for trickery. Telling a customer that the squeak is nothing to worry about and to check again in another 10,000 miles is almost sure to cost you business.

Should you choose virtue or vice? In this case, the economic incentives are to be dishonest, to shade your assessments toward recommending actions that will bring in the most money. True, there is a market niche for firms with reputations for honesty and good quality. The customers of those firms will pay more for the work they have done, though, because that work is not subsidized by a lot of other needless work performed on the cars of the less careful shoppers. This situation leads to another moral dilemma, this one on the part of the shoppers.

In many lines of business, it is possible for the customer to acquire information from one supplier and then make use of that information to actually make the purchase from a different supplier. For example, many service providers offer free estimates as a marketing tool to bring in customers. This offer gives customers the opportunity to get free estimates from dealers with the best reputations for honesty and then get the actual work done at lower-cost, less-reputable establishments.

Along the same lines, customers can go to full-service stores to acquire information about products from furniture to electronics to computer software. Customers who have freely used the full-service store's resources often turn around and make their actual purchases from discount stores and mail-order catalogs. This market failure does not promote virtue. Has it always been this way?

As both population and mobility grow, it becomes ever easier for both people and businesses to escape their reputations. In a way, this ability of people to get away from what they have done is a virtue. America is supposed to be the land in which anyone can leave the past behind and get a fresh start.

In another way, though, being able to escape our reputations makes us less concerned with what we do. The result can be vice. We can honk our horns and make vulgar gestures and not have to live with any consequences. No one recognizes us. Since our reputations provide other people with information about whether and how to deal with us, the lack of that information reduces the incentives for virtue.

For example, would we enter a store carrying a sign that told sales clerks that we intended to buy from a deep-discount catalog-order company? Of course not, because we would get no service. By the same token, if we were known by reputation to be that kind of buyer, we would also get no service. Thus, despite the many information links available in the modern economy, there is also an increase in anonymity that provides incentives that tempt us away from virtue.

What's Different?

There have always been con artists and others who take advantage of imperfections in the flow of information. Still, it seems that society is facing ever more stresses on its virtues. Where are these stresses coming from?

One obvious culprit is population growth and its associated stresses. We have already mentioned the problem of ever more anonymity. Population growth causes other problems, too. For example, population stresses many of the environmental intangibles of life. The world is a noisier and more crowded place. As more people take up ever more space on this planet, we see our natural environment become congested and degraded. It becomes that much harder to find our Walden Pond to sit and contemplate. The result? More stress and less virtue.

Stress can come from freedom itself. Take the increased freedoms that broadcast television, music, and other forms of entertainment enjoy today. The major television networks no longer censor violence, sex, and foul language as they once did. Record companies today promote music that many consider vulgar and irresponsible. Parents who seek to instill other values in their children find themselves pitted against this pervasive music. Does society become coarsened in the process? Entertainment companies argue that they are merely responding to demand.

Stress also comes from restrictions on our freedoms. As both population and government grow, we find our actions increasingly limited by government regulation. This regulation may be necessary to protect us from each others' externalities. However, it also causes us to chafe and yearn for the freer world of the past. At least we can escape to the privacy of our own homes, can't we?

Modern technology makes our homes ever less private. This encroachment upon our privacy comes from a variety of sources. On the one hand, there is government. For example, a Missouri man was recently convicted of growing marijuana in his home. Government was alerted to his illegal acts by modern technology, which picked up the infrared signatures of the grow lamps he was using in his house. Law enforcement officers had become suspicious because he subscribed to *High Times* and was a member of NORML (National Association for the Reform of Marijuana Laws).

On the other hand, private firms have also become adept at using modern technology to invade our homes. Telephone directories that list numbers for people all across the country can be purchased on computer disk for very little money. As a selling point, these directories feature extensive listings of what are supposed to be unlisted numbers. In this world of today, a person cannot safely put a phone number on even the most innocuous of applications or information sheets without risking that the number will be sold for inclusion in such a database. Even greater invasions of our privacy are possible in the future. Proposed new telephone services do much more than simply "ID" a caller. These services are also able to provide name, address, income, marital status, and much more information about callers.

With random and sequential dialing, modern computers allow firms to blanket entire neighborhoods with phone calls. Is it any wonder, then, that we no longer expect a cordial, polite greeting when we call someone. The etiquette has changed. Today, rather than volunteering a friendly hello to whoever may call, people screen their calls with answering machines or Caller ID and only answer the ones they feel like answering. Al-

B

though the information provided by Caller ID reduces anonymity and thus reduces the vice of harassing phone calls, however, this impersonal monitoring can be viewed as a vice of its own.

Losing That Which Cannot Be Measured

Economics acknowledges the existence of intangibles. In the case of environmental pollution damages, the value of such intangibles is often measured in dollar terms for inclusion in the cost-benefit analysis of specific government programs. However, there is a wide array of intangibles that escapes measurement altogether. For example, is it a vice to gamble? Gambling can be addictive and difficult for some people to control. Moreover, if parents use their children's milk money to pay gambling bills, most would call that wrong for the sake of the children. However, when no third parties are hurt, is it not a vice to pass judgment on each other's behavior? Is it a vice for state governments to promote and profit from gambling? What if the funds raised will be spent on virtuous goods, such as public education? Evaluating such intangibles can seem mind-boggling.

As a society, we must be cautious. If we focus too much on promoting growth in the output that we measure, we will undoubtedly sacrifice output of intangible goods and services that we do not. We must seek the virtuous middle ground between the vice of being overly judgmental of others and the vice of using no judgment at all.

PROSPECTING FOR NEW INSIGHTS

1. Do you think virtue is rewarded in the modern world? Are the rewards to virtue now any different than they were in the past? Explain.
2. Some would say that technology promotes virtue. For example, Caller ID makes it less likely that people will make harassing phone calls. Identify some other examples in which technology affects the incentives for virtue or vice.

EXPLORATION 2
Prices and Property Rights—Do Russians Know the Secret to Prosperity?

To develop economically, Russia is transforming itself from the premier example of a centrally planned economy to a market economy. However, private property rights are an important part of this transformation, a part that remains uncertain.

*T*hat Was Then

Unlike capitalist countries, the former Communist countries of Eastern Europe and the Soviet Union had no competitive market prices to ensure an efficient allocation of resources. Prices were set for purposes of equity and political expediency, not for efficiency. Soviet planners tried to match resources to outputs and outputs to needs, but faced a difficult problem. To allocate efficiently, planners must know how much value consumers place on alternative outputs. They also must compute the opportunity costs of inputs. In contrast, free markets reveal this information automatically; it is implicit in market prices.

To acquire the information they need, the Soviet planners estimated **shadow prices**, which are what the market prices would have been if there had been free markets. This undertaking is something like trying to answer the old riddle, "How much wood would a woodchuck chuck, if a woodchuck could chuck wood?" Although the planners resorted to complex mathematical models, the estimated shadow prices were still only rough approximations to true market prices. When planners imposed incorrectly estimated prices, people and businesses were led to many wrong decisions about what and how to produce.

Even if the shadow prices were accurate, they would not have been the prices people actually pay. Thus, we saw such strange occurrences as children using loaves of bread as footballs, even though the bread did not last long in that usage, and even though the cost of the ingredients to make the loaves far exceeded their value as footballs.

The problem was that bread was priced very cheaply for political reasons, and customers bought it in much larger quantities than they would have if bread prices reflected the costs of the foodstuffs, labor, and other items used in producing that bread. Still, for political reasons, government attempted to turn out as much of this necessity as consumers would choose to buy.

Politically set prices had one interesting positive effect. They forced Russian authorities to exercise monetary restraint. Too many rubles would just add more purchasing power, which consumers would spend on underpriced goods. The Soviet Union did not have the wherewithal to produce enough of these goods as it was. With the exception of bread and a few other items, shelves were often bare. The only way to prevent even greater shortages was to keep additional money from circulating in the economy. Thus, in the former Soviet union, price inflation was kept low because government set the prices, and monetary growth was restrained in order to allow the policy of low prices to work. In contrast, when markets are free, the process is reversed. Monetary restraint must be exercised to keep inflation from taking hold in the marketplace.

The policy of holding prices to artificially low levels proved troublesome when it came to foreign trade. The Soviet Union was forced to maintain two sets of prices for each good. One set denominated prices in rubles, the local currency. The other set consisted of prices in dollars or another foreign currency. This second set was intended to correspond to the shadow prices estimated by the Soviet government.

By law, the ruble was **nonconvertible**, meaning that foreigners were not allowed to make purchases in rubles. To have done otherwise would have allowed foreigners to take advantage of the artificially low prices offered to Soviet citizens. The Soviet government would in this way have been subsidizing foreigners, which was not their intent.

The nonconvertibility of the ruble led to many interesting and convoluted barter trades, in which seemingly unrelated items were offered in exchange for each other. For

B

example, in order to do business in the Soviet Union, the Pepsi Company agreed to accept Russian vodka rather than cash. Once Pepsi imported the vodka into the U.S., it sold it to liquor wholesalers in exchange for cash. Barter deals were hard to arrange and often fell through. For example, Sikorsky Helicopter opted against accepting children's toys in exchange for helicopters. Children's toys were too far outside Sikorsky's area of expertise.

It was small wonder that the Russian economy spiraled downward over time. The arms buildup of the 1980s hastened that decline and prompted an overthrow of the central planners. First, there was Mikhail Gorbachev, would-be reformer of the communist system. Then came Boris Yeltsin, a free-market revolutionary who extricated Russia from the splinters of the Soviet Union. Many thought that, with markets freed from the central planners, living standards would quickly rise. The statistics said otherwise, and for good reason.

Protecting Russian Property

Russia embraced capitalist ideas, but failed to impose a key ingredient necessary for the success of free markets. That ingredient is certainty over **property rights**. If individuals and businesses have no confidence that they will be able to keep the fruits of their labors and investments, the profit motive is lost. Sure, we all want to profit, but only if we can keep or spend those profits for our own sakes. Few would seek profit in order to turn it over to the government. Unfortunately, in Russia today, that is a danger.

It is possible to make deals with the Russian government. The problem is, which government? Russia is presently characterized by too many governments, with uncertainty over which governments have jurisdiction over which places and activities. For example, it is possible to buy land in Russia. However, it is nearly impossible to obtain a clear title to it. One government may grant that title, while another government lies in wait to claim the land as its own somewhere down the line. At least one U.S. entrepreneur has seen this situation as a profit opportunity, and seeks to offer title insurance to remedy the problem.

Some Russian entrepreneurs have a different strategy. They specialize in having connections with both legitimate and illegitimate authorities. For example, Ben and Jerry's found these entrepreneurs extremely helpful in establishing a network of Russian "scoop shops" to sell its ice cream.

With all the governments come a host of taxes. To some extent, all taxes represent an expropriation of private property. Russian taxes sometimes carry this expropriation to an absurd extreme. Specifically, when taxes from the various jurisdictions are added together, they often sum to over one hundred percent. This means that, for every dollar of profit a business makes, it owes more than a dollar to the government.

It would seem that no business would voluntarily choose to operate under these conditions. Yet business does go on in Russia. The reason is twofold. First, many profits are hidden from the tax collector, either through bribery or techniques of accounting. Second, and related to the first, there is a thriving underground economy that is not reported to authorities.

Much of this underground economy is ruled by organized crime. There are thought to be hundreds of criminal organizations in modern Russia. Oftentimes, their leaders are former officials of the communist government, officials who know networks of "enforcers." In a way, these former officials are entrepreneurs. They provide a service for which there is a strong demand. That service is the protection of property rights. For a price, the local crime boss will protect your property from other criminals. Through his connections, he can also offer some protection from excessive government regulation and taxation.

It is thus not surprising to find that statistics from the Russian government show that the transition to free markets caused the Russian economy to shrink. Statistics measure the economy that is reported. Judging from the upbeat attitudes and spending seen on the streets of Russia's cities, the underground economy appears to be thriving.

When economic activity is not reported, government can collect no taxes on it directly. There is a way in which it can be taxed indirectly, however. That way is through inflation. Authorities in Russia's central bank no longer need to worry about sustaining artificially low prices. Rather, by printing money freely, they allow government to spend without collecting taxes. Instead, the tax is inflation that erodes purchasing power in the legitimate and underground economies alike.

There is a danger, though, that Russian central bankers seemed to overlook. Indeed, some say that the Russian central bankers saw the danger and were attempting to sabotage market reforms. The danger is that too much inflation of the ruble could drive the marketplace to forgo using the ruble as its currency. By requiring payment in dollars or barter, for instance, Russia's underground economy can sidestep the tax of inflation.

*N*ot *Just in Russia*

Around the world, countries have turned to free markets as a means of adding vitality to economies that must support ever more people. Still, free markets are often embraced half-heartedly, with reluctance. In this age of media sound bites, good economics often does not make for good politics. Indeed, for autocratic rulers, free-market economics may be downright threatening.

Free markets promote free thought. To get ahead in the marketplace requires savvy and foresight. It requires that people think about the choices they make. It is but a short step for people used to thinking about their own choices to start also thinking about the choices their country makes. It is only another short step for people to want involvement in decisions affecting their country and its economy. That step can be threatening to the status quo and invoke increasingly harsh crackdowns in order to intimidate people into submission. The Tienammin Square massacre and subsequent crackdowns in China provide examples.

Although free markets may promote democracy, it is not as obvious that democracy promotes free markets. Participation in making choices collectively is quite different from making choices individually in the marketplace. In the marketplace, individuals live with the consequences of their own personal choices rather than with the consequences of the majority's choice. The property rights that free markets rely upon to function efficiently can be both protected and undermined by a government responding to collective democratic choice.

For example, taxation and regulation both represent government **takings** of private property. These takings may be a necessary trade-off in obtaining goals of equity, or may promote market efficiency if they correct market failures. Unfortunately, a democratic political process is free to go further and cross the fine line between government actions that correct market failures and government actions that short-circuit market successes.

B

In the U.S., for example, controversy swirls around the Federal Endangered Species Act, which can at any time place severe restrictions on the free use of land. The motives are well intentioned—to protect the habitat of spotted owls, Texas wild rice, California kangaroo rats, or any other of numerous endangered species. However, the results can be extremely costly to the landowners, who see both the use and resale values of their properties plummet. Although government could in principle pay for such takings, taxpayers might be reluctant to foot the high bills that would result. The result is a less efficient market; the economic incentive for landowners who find an endangered species is to destroy it before the government can find out it's there.

*T*he Story Unfolds

Russia has undergone a dramatic upheaval, in which the old order of communism was thrown out to make way for the new order of capitalism. However, capitalistic free markets cannot function without the ownership of private property. There has been movement in this direction, such as the privatization of Russian car and truck maker ZIL and other companies. Still, because ownership of private property in Russia is tenuous, its free markets flounder.

The future can take different paths. One path is for an autocratic ruler to take charge, perhaps exploiting the passion of nationalism in the same way that Lenin exploited the passion of communism. Restoring order can add certainty to property rights. However, if the transition is tumultuous, who is to say that more revolution would not be around the corner? Tumultuous change adds uncertainty, which casts the staying power of property rights into doubt.

The other path is less exciting, but might offer more stability and certainty over property rights. That path is to fight the problems of the Russian economy battle by battle, without the upheaval of revolutionary warfare. The question would remain, however, as to which side would come out victorious. Would a democratic Russia battle for sound economic policy? Or would the public be swayed by feel-good sound bites that undermine the principles of private property that support free-market efficiency? We need only wait to see the answer, as the story unfolds before the Russian people and the world.

PROSPECTING FOR NEW INSIGHTS

1. Consumers like low prices. Yet the transition from government-set prices to free-market prices leads to higher prices of many items, such as bread, milk, and other heavily subsidized products. How can it be in the consumer interest to accept the transition from command-and-control pricing to free-market pricing? Do you think the typical consumer would recognize your reasoning?

2. Free markets rely on private property rights, but those rights are not absolute. In other words, it would not be in the social interest to allow private property to be put to any use whatsoever, without any restriction. What are some examples of legitimate government restrictions on the use of private property? Should the property owners be paid to accept these restrictions?

Guest workers are temporary immigrants, granted limited rights to work and live in a country. Switzerland depends upon its Italian guest workers. Saudi Arabia depends on guests from the Philippines and numerous other countries. Sometimes, guests become permanent, as with many of the Turkish workers invited into Germany. Then, too, rather than use guests, countries often resort to permanent immigration. Does this immigration serve a country well?

In the modern world, both capital and labor can move among countries, although there are often some barriers to this migration. Migration of either resource affects patterns of international trade. If this migration were carried to the extreme in which all countries have identical ratios of capital to labor, world trade would be greatly diminished, because differences in the relative abundance of resources provide the basis for specialization and trade.

As discussed in chapter 2, countries tend to export goods that employ inputs they have in abundance. If a country has abundant capital relative to labor, for example, it tends to export goods that are produced with a relatively high proportion of capital and import goods that employ more labor in their manufacture. Likewise, labor-abundant countries tend to export labor-intensive goods and import goods that are capital-intensive.

Countries have an alternative. For example, a capital intensive country could allow free immigration of labor and greatly reduce its need for the imports from labor-intensive countries. Is this alternative just as good?

The answer has to do with the ownership of resources and the distribution of income. If immigrants can claim property rights or subsidies from longer-term citizens, the well-being of those citizens could easily fall, even as the country's GDP goes up. Thus, the answer to the question in this challenge depends on the country's objective. If it seeks to maximize the well-being of its longer-term citizens, the answer is probably that immigration does not substitute well. If it seeks to expand its production possibilities and the power that they bring, the answer could easily be that it does.

You've heard it before—You cannot escape death and taxes. You also cannot escape economics. True, this book has come to an end, and we hope you enjoyed it. We also hope you enjoy recognizing the many ways that economics will influence your future and that of the world around you.

Recall some of the ways economics affects the personal lives of us all. We have individual decisions to make throughout our lives. Whether it be to buy a house or rent an apartment, get married or stay single, or watch TV or go to the movies tonight, the examples of decisions where economics can help are innumerable. A clear grasp of opportunity cost and a willingness to think in terms of costs and benefits can go a long way.

Then there are those decisions we make jointly with our friends, neighbors, and family. The choices we make affect not only our own welfare or satisfaction, but the satisfaction of those close to us. If the choices we make are arrogant or rude, we may increase our personal short-run welfare but risk decreasing our long-run welfare by alienating friends and family. Intuitively, most of us recognize the benefits of compromise and cooperation.

Finally, there is our participation in collective decision making as we go to the polls and vote. The economic policies implemented by our elected officials can have a real impact on us. It is therefore imperative that we be knowledgeable enough to gauge the likely outcomes of putting our favorite candidates in office.

Merely discussing economic issues with friends, or reading about economics in newspapers and magazines may not be enough. Perhaps you want to pursue an undergraduate economics degree. In that case, you will take intermediate-level classes in price theory (microeconomics) and macroeconomics. You will probably also be required to take at least one class in mathematical economics and another in econometrics. Many economics majors find classes in finance, accounting, and mathematics to be useful. Economics majors are sought after in the job market because of their analytical abilities—the ability to recognize how to tackle problems and formulate solutions—which means that you should be able to make a career for yourself in a diverse set of workplaces.

Should you choose to attend graduate school, you might wish to aim for a master's degree. Master's degrees require at least one and one-half to two years of study beyond the bachelor's degree. Going still further, you might seek a Doctor of Philosophy (Ph.D.), which would qualify you to become a university professor. That degree would mean two or three years of course work beyond the bachelor's, plus however long it takes you to write an original dissertation. If you take the courses, but do not write the dissertation, there are still many opportunities open to you; some are in academia, but more are in business and government.

Whether you choose additional formal study within the field of economics or are content to leave with a general understanding of how economic forces shape our destinies, we are confident of one thing. Relative to most people, you are now the expert.

C

Study by Design

SpeedStudy

SpeedReview

As the world's economic journey continues into the future, new problems, opportunities, and choices will present themselves, for which economics provides insights. The greater availability of information promises to make decision making more efficient, which seems likely to force government antitrust policies to adapt. Open-door immigration policies face opposition because of ethnic tensions and economic costs. The skill differential in wages will widen with greater immigration of the unskilled, but narrow with additional immigration of skilled workers.

Crime is a worldwide problem, with new forms of crime arising from changes in technology. Criminals compare the expected marginal benefit of criminal activity to its expected marginal cost. By refining policies that decrease expected benefits and increase expected costs, the prospect that crime can be reduced is enhanced. In spite of humanity's efforts to end all war, conflict remains possible. Common property resources, territorial disputes, and tribalism provide motives for war. With communism in disrepute, nations that have relied in the past on central planning to spur economic development must rethink their hostility toward the price system.

SpeedStudy True or False Self-Test

A1. The curve illustrating the marginal benefit of additional information is downward sloping.

A2. Schumpeter viewed the "gale of creative destruction" as a positive economic force.

A3. Schumpeter's model takes account of the globalization of the economy.

A4. In the U.S., the evidence suggests that unskilled immigrants typically catch up economically with native-born Americans within ten years.

A5. Crime rates would probably be the same in every country, if the probability of being caught, and the punishment, were the same.

A6. The greater availability of high-paying jobs would be expected to have no effect on the crime rate.

A7. Peace and economic justice go hand in hand.

A8. Whales swimming in the oceans are an example of common property.

A9. The price system offers the hope that resources will never be completely devoured regardless of how great earth's population becomes.

A10. Communist countries were highly effective at keeping the environment clean.

B11. Economic analysis acknowledges the existence of intangibles.

B12. Our virtues are shaped by our opportunities and experiences, which in turn are influenced by economics.

B13. Shadow prices are politically set and usually lie below what market prices would have been.

B14. Taxation and regulation can be viewed as a partial government expropriation of property rights.

C15. If a capital-intensive country allows the free immigration of labor, it can greatly reduce its need to import labor-intensive products.

C16. A country's citizens are as well off by allowing immigration of unskilled workers as by allowing the import of goods made with cheap foreign labor.

C17. The primary career path open to a student with a bachelor's degree in economics is to become an economist.

C18. Employers value the analytical skills of economics majors.

p. 282

The MasterMind

Selected Terms Along the Way

antitrust policy, 543
potential competition, 544
expected opportunity costs, 548
trade war, 550
common property resources, 550

Eurosclerosis, 555

lawsuit abuse, 559
shadow prices, 563
nonconvertible, 563

property rights, 564
takings, 565

guest workers, 567

MasterMind Multiple Choice Self-Test

A1. The equilibrium quantity of information occurs at the point where
   a. the marginal cost of information is at its minimum.
   b. the marginal benefit from more information equals zero.
   c. marginal benefit equals marginal cost.
   d. people have acquired all available information regardless of its cost.

A2. Schumpeter viewed innovation as most likely arising in
   a. monopoly markets.
   b. perfectly competitive markets.
   c. oligopoly markets.
   d. government laboratories.

A3. Borjas' view of U.S. immigration is that
   a. immigrants typically attain an economic status equal to that of the average American within a few years.
   b. it takes one generation for typical immigrant families to reach equal economic status with the average American family.
   c. it takes one hundred years for the typical immigrant family to reach an economic status equal to that of the average American family.
   d. immigrant families never catch up to the same economic level as average American families.

A4. Which of the following is least related to the amount and type of terrorism?
   a. The amount of market power held by oligopolists.
   b. The availability of information.

c. Technological change.
   d. The probability of being arrested and punished.

A5. Eurosclerosis refers to
   a. medical problems created by environmental pollution.
   b. slow economic growth in Europe that is related to generous welfare programs.
   c. a strategy for economic development in the Balkans.
   d. cultural factors that influence economic growth.

B6. From an economic perspective, virtue is a good that
   a. can be produced and sold in markets just like any other good.
   b. is unaffected by government actions.
   c. responds to the amount of information in the marketplace.
   d. is tangible.

B7. Which of the following government actions is most likely to help markets operate efficiently?
   a. Price controls.
   b. Tax collection.
   c. Enforcement of property rights.
   d. Income redistribution.

C8. Immigration will cause a country to
   a. import more labor-intensive goods.
   b. import fewer labor-intensive goods.
   c. invest more in other countries.
   d. increase its trade deficit.

C9. Which is *not* a valid reason for studying economics?

    a. Economics can provide a framework for individual decision making.

    b. Voters often need to be informed about economic matters.

    c. People who have not studied economics are incapable of making choices that improve the welfare of their families.

    d. Economics can provide a framework for joint decision making.

MasterMind Questions and Problems

A1. What three areas in your own life do you think would benefit the most from having access to more information? Why do you personally not seek more information about these areas? Does opportunity cost matter?

A2. Since immigrants supply the resource of labor, and since more resources cause the economy to grow, explain why there are objections to increasing immigration.

A3. Suppose a string of burglaries has occurred in a dormitory at your university. How could the economic model of crime be applied to reduce these burglaries?

A4. Explain the link between peace and economic justice.

A5. If you were to join the Peace Corps after graduating from college, and you were sent to a less-developed country, what single most important economic principle would you wish to share with the people of that country? Could you explain that principle in common-sense terms?

B6. Name and discuss at least three virtues. Explain how they might relate to economic behavior.

B7. What are shadow prices, and why are they used? Give an example of a problem that might arise were the government of a command-and-control economy to ignore shadow prices.

C8. If a nation such as Japan makes it difficult for U.S. firms to sells goods there, should the U.S. retaliate by barring immigrants from Japan? More generally, should trade policies and immigration policies be linked?

C9. How much do newspapers, magazines, and TV news contribute to your understanding of economics? Would you prefer to see more news reports on economic matters? Why or why not?

Future Explorations: Mapping out Term Papers

1. **Crime and Poverty: How Strong Is the Linkage?**
   Are crime rates positively related to poverty rates? In this paper you will take an interdisciplinary perspective by researching and contrasting the views of economists, criminologists, and sociologists on this important issue. You will also examine the FBI's publication, *Uniform Crime Statistics,* for any light that can be shed. Do poor cities have higher crime rates than wealthier ones? If they do, does that prove that crime is caused by poverty? Have crime rates dropped over time as poverty has lessened. In writing the paper, set aside any personal beliefs you have on the issue and focus on the most convincing evidence to provide an answer to the question in the title.

2. **Immigration: How Much Is Enough?**
   You will seek out quantitative dollar estimates of the costs and benefits of immigration in this paper. Why does the *Wall Street Journal* favor essentially unlimited im-

migration? Why do others, such as 1996 presidential candidate Pat Buchanan, favor cutting off further immigration? In addition to economic considerations, do cultural and other values play a role in the debate over immigration policy?

3. **Finding the Role Model for Economic Development**
   In this paper you will identify several countries that have succeeded in developing economically since 1960. You will present time-series data that show growth and the increase in living standards in the countries you select. You will familiarize yourself with the history and culture of these countries in an effort to see what they have in common. Finally, you will assess the likelihood that developing countries could use the countries you selected as role models.

Answer Key

ExpressStudy True or False	SpeedStudy True or False Self-Test		MasterMind Multiple Choice Self-Test
1. F	1. T	10. F	1. c
2. T	2. T	11. T	2. c
3. T	3. F	12. T	3. c
4. F	4. F	13. F	4. a
5. F	5. F	14. T	5. b
6. F	6. F	15. T	6. c
	7. T	16. F	7. c
	8. T	17. F	8. b
	9. T	18. T	9. c

Glossary

ability-to-pay principle   states that those who can afford to pay more taxes than others should be required to do so.

absolute advantage   the ability to produce a good with fewer resources than other producers.

adaptive expectations   when people predict future inflation or other economic variables based upon their recent experiences.

adverse selection   those who seek out insurance coverage are the most likely to need it; makes it difficult for individuals to get affordable health insurance and thus promotes employer group insurance.

aggregate demand   relates how much real GDP consumers, businesses, and government will purchase at each price level; graphically, aggregate demand slopes downward.

aggregate expenditure function   shows how much is intended to be spent at each possible level of real GDP.

allocative efficiency   involves choosing the most valuable mix of outputs to produce.

antitrust policy   laws and regulations designed to ensure effective competition.

appreciation   when a currency buys more of other currencies than previously; makes imports cheaper and exports more expensive.

arbitrage   the practice of buying low and selling high; directs goods to their highest-valued uses.

automatic stabilizers   features embedded within existing fiscal policies that act as a stimulant when the economy is sluggish and act as a drag when it is in danger of inflation.

autonomous spending   expenditures that do not depend on income.

average cost   per unit cost; total cost/output.

average product (of labor)   the average amount of output a firm receives per unit of labor; output/labor.

average revenue total revenue divided by output; equals price for firms that do not price discriminate.

balance of payments accounts measure a country's economic interactions with other countries; contains the current account and capital account.

balance of trade the monetary value of exported goods minus the monetary value of imported goods.

balanced-budget multiplier the effect on equilibrium GDP per dollar of additional government spending, when that spending is paid for by additional taxation; equals 1 in the simple Keynesian model.

barriers to entry when investors or entrepreneurs find obstacles to joining a profitable industry.

barter the exchange of goods and services directly for one another, without the use of money.

benefit principle states that a fair tax is one that taxes people in proportion to the benefits they receive when government spends those tax revenues.

bilateral monopoly a market with only one buyer and only one seller; usually refers to a labor market.

black market an illegal market, which could be for illegal goods or for legal goods when buyers and sellers seek to avoid government taxes or regulations.

block grant a sum of money transferred from the federal government to state or local governments, usually conditional upon it financing specific types of programs.

bonds promises to repay borrowed funds with interest at a specified future date.

budget deficit the annual shortfall of government revenues below government expenditures.

business cycle the uneven sequence of trough, expansion, peak, and recession that the economy follows over time.

capital anything that is produced in order to increase productivity in the future; includes human capital and physical capital.

capital account records the monetary value of capital inflows from other countries (foreign investment in the U.S.) and outflows to other countries (U.S. investment abroad).

capital formation the creation of new capital.

capital gains the difference between the current market value of an investment and its purchase price.

cartel a form of oligopoly characterized by collusion; intended to increase profits, but illegal in the U.S.

caveat emptor let the buyer beware; consumers are not protected by government-set product standards.

ceteris paribus holding all else equal.

chain-weight index when used to compute a price index, geometrically averages two component indexes, the first using the current-year market basket and the other using the prior-year market basket.

circular flow   a model of the economy that depicts how the flow of money facilitates a counter flow of resources, goods, and services in the input and output markets.

civilian labor force   the population age sixteen or over who are either employed or actively seeking employment.

classical   a macroeconomic school of thought that emphasizes the long run; relies upon market forces to achieve full employment.

Coase theorem   holds that parties to an externality would voluntarily negotiate an efficient outcome without government involvement when property rights are clearly defined.

collective bargaining   negotiations between labor unions and employers aimed at improving the lot of workers.

command and control   government decrees that direct economic activity.

common property resource   a jointly owned resource, such as groundwater; people have little incentive to conserve common property resources, but rather seek to capture them for their own private use.

comparable worth   the idea that government should set wages to ensure pay equity across different jobs, with comparable pay for jobs requiring comparable training effort and responsibility.

comparative advantage   the ability to produce a good at a lower opportunity cost (other goods forgone) than others could do.

compensating wage differentials   higher pay that compensates for undesirable aspects of a job.

complement   something that goes with something else, such as cream with coffee; the cross elasticity of demand is negative.

comprehensive measure of income   subtracts a person's wealth at the beginning of the year from wealth at the end of the year, and then adds back in the person's consumption during the course of that year.

conglomerate merger   brings together firms whose lines of business have no obvious relationship to each other.

constant returns to scale   when the long-run average cost remains constant as the firm proportionally expands its use of all its inputs.

constant-cost industry   when an increase in an industry's output does not affect input prices; in perfect competition, results in a horizontal long-run supply curve.

consumer price index (CPI)   measures prices of a market basket of purchases made by consumers living in urban areas.

consumer surplus   the difference between the maximum amount that a good or service is worth to consumers and what they actually pay for it; in brief, demand minus market price.

consumption possibility frontier   shows combinations of goods and services that could be consumed, given possibilities for production and trade.

consumption tax   a tax on spending rather than on income.

contestable markets   when new rivals can enter or exit the market quickly and cheaply; could characterize either oligopoly or monopoly.

corporation a type of firm that is a legal entity separate from the people who own, manage, and otherwise direct its affairs.

cost-push inflation occurs when a leftward shift in either short-run or long-run aggregate supply moves the economy up aggregate demand; associated with less output.

cross elasticity of demand measures the response of quantity demanded of one good to changes in the price of another good; computed by dividing the percentage change in the quantity demanded of one good by the percentage change in the price of the other good.

cross-sectional data the value of a variable at a given moment in time for a number of states, countries, or other separate entities; for example, unemployment rates in 1996 for each of the fifty states would be cross-sectional data.

cross-subsidization when prices on some goods or services are set high enough to offset losses on other goods or services; may be required by government, such as for postal services.

crowding-out effect represents money that would have gone to private sector investment, but instead goes to finance government borrowing.

currency-to-deposits ratio (c/d) the ratio of currency in circulation to deposits in financial institutions; the higher is c/d, the lower is the money multiplier.

current account records the monetary value of imports and exports of goods and services.

deadweight loss the value of the decline in efficiency to the economy as a whole, rather than merely a transfer of benefits from one component of society to another, such as from taxation or monopoly.

decreasing-cost industry when an increase in an industry's output causes input prices to fall; in perfect competition, results in a downward-sloping long-run supply curve.

demand relates the quantity of a good that consumers will purchase at each of various possible prices, over some period of time, *ceteris paribus*.

demand deposits checking account balances.

demand-pull inflation occurs when a rightward shift in aggregate demand moves the economy up short-run aggregate supply; associated with greater employment and output.

deposit multiplier the maximum possible value of the money multiplier; equals the reciprocal of the reserve requirement.

depreciation a decrease in the value of capital, such as from capital wearing out or becoming technologically obsolete; also, a decline in the purchasing power of a currency when it is exchanged for other currencies, which makes imports more expensive and exports cheaper.

deregulation the scaling back of government regulation of industry.

derived demand the demand for labor; exists only because there is a demand for the firm's output.

development when technology is embodied into capital.

direct (positive) relationship when a change in one variable leads to the same direction change in another variable.

discount rate the interest rate; the rate at which future values are reduced to their present value equivalents; also the rate of interest charged by the Federal Reserve on short-term loans to member banks.

discouraged workers people who would like to have a job, but have given up looking; not counted as unemployed because they are not included in the labor force.

diseconomies of scale when the long-run average cost rises as the firm proportionally expands its use of all its inputs.

dumping the selling of a good for less than its cost of production; prohibited by the General Agreement on Tariffs and Trade.

dynamic scoring allows for consideration of all behavioral changes caused by changes in government policy.

economic growth the ability of the economy to produce more output.

economic rent earnings in excess of opportunity costs.

economics studies the allocation of scarce resources in response to unlimited wants.

economies of scale when the long-run average cost declines as the firm proportionally expands its use of all its inputs.

efficiency means that resources are used in ways that provide the most value, that maximize the size of the economic pie; economic efficiency implies that no one can be made better off without someone else becoming worse off. Economic efficiency is divided into two types: allocative efficiency and technological efficiency.

egalitarianism the idea that an economy's output should be divided equally among all its citizens.

elastic refers to either demand or supply, where the value of the elasticity exceeds 1.

elasticity measures the responsiveness of one thing (Y) to another (X), specifically, the percentage change in Y divided by the percentage change in X.

elasticity of demand measures the responsiveness of quantity demanded to price, specifically, the percentage change in quantity demanded divided by the percentage change in price, expressed as an absolute value.

elasticity of supply measures the responsiveness of quantity supplied to price, specifically, the percentage change in quantity supplied divided by the percentage change in price.

employer mandates employee or customer benefits that government requires businesses to offer.

entrepreneurship personal initiative to combine resources in productive ways; involves risk.

equation of exchange an identity that shows that the amount of money people spend must equal the market value of what they purchase: Money supply multiplied by velocity of money equals the average price of output multiplied by aggregate output ($MV = PQ$).

equilibrium see market equilibrium.

equity fairness.

Eurosclerosis structural rigidities in Europe that have resulted in high unemployment rates and sluggish economic growth.

ex ante before the fact.

ex post after the fact.

excess reserves deposits banks hold as reserves in excess of reserve requirements established by the Federal Reserve.

excess reserves-to-deposits ratio (e/d) ratio of excess reserves to deposits in financial institutions; the higher is e/d, the lower is the money multiplier.

exchange rate price of one currency in terms of another.

exit when a firm goes out of business; the firm no longer has either fixed or variable costs.

expected opportunity costs opportunity costs that are predicted, but not known with certainty; used to guide decisions.

expected return the value of an investment if successful, multiplied by the probability of success.

expenditure equilibrium the level of GDP that the economy tends towards in the short run, at a given price level.

expenditure multiplier the reciprocal of the marginal propensity to save in the simple Keynesian model; when multiplied by a change in autonomous spending, gives the change in equilibrium GDP.

expenditures approach computes GDP by summing spending on consumption, investment, government purchases, and the value of net exports.

exports goods and services a country sells to other countries.

external costs value lost to third parties that is not included in market supply and demand, such as the costs of pollution.

externalities side effects of production or consumption that affect third parties who have no say in the matter; these can involve either external costs, such as from pollution, or external benefits, such as from a neighbor maintaining an attractive yard.

federal funds rate the interest rate on reserves banks lend to each other.

Federal Reserve System the U.S. central bank, established in 1913; contains three primary components: the Board of Governors, the Open Market Committee, and Regional Federal Reserve Banks; conducts monetary policy and participates in bank regulation.

firm's supply curve the amount of output offered by the firm at each price; equals the firm's marginal cost curve in excess of average variable cost; applies only to price-taking firms.

firms businesses that produce goods or services with the intention of earning a profit.

fiscal illusion when voters focus on visible benefits from projects and ignore the less-obvious costs.

fiscal policy government tax and spending policy; can be either expansionary, such as through lower taxes and higher spending, or contractionary, such as through higher taxes and reduced spending.

fiscal policy lags the time it takes between when a macroeconomic problem occurs and fiscal policy action takes effect to correct it; consists of a recognition lag, action lag, and implementation lag.

fixed cost   the cost of fixed inputs, which are those that cannot be changed in the short run.

fixed-weight price indices   indexes, such as the consumer price index, that track the price of a fixed market basket of selected goods and services.

float   when exchange rates are determined by market forces, without much intervention by governments.

free markets   the collective decisions of individual buyers and sellers that, taken together, determine what outputs are produced, how those outputs are produced, and who receives the outputs; free markets depend on private property and free choice.

free-rider problem   the incentive to avoid paying for a public good, because no one person's payment will have any appreciable effect on the quantity of the public good.

frictional unemployment   unemployment associated with entering the labor market or switching jobs.

full employment   occurs when the economy is at the natural rate of unemployment.

fully funded   used in the context of Social Security, describes an ability to pay off all future Social Security obligations without recourse to future taxation; in reality, Social Security is primarily pay-as-you-go.

futures contract   a contract to guarantee delivery of a currency or other commodity in the future at a specified price.

game theory   the notion that market participants use strategies to play economic "games," similar to strategies used in winning at bridge, poker, chess, and other games.

GDP deflator   index of representative prices across the spectrum of GDP; used to compute real GDP.

General Agreement on Tariffs and Trade (GATT)   an agreement signed by most of the major trading countries of the world, which limits the use of protectionist policies; enforced by the World Trade Organization.

gold standard   government promise to redeem its currency for gold at a specified rate; implies that the money supply would depend upon the amount of gold, rather than upon Federal Reserve policy.

government failure   the inefficiency of government processes.

gross domestic product (GDP)   the market value of the final goods and services produced in the economy within some time period, usually one quarter or one year.

gross national product (GNP)   the same as gross domestic product, except that the value added to production by U.S.-owned resources located outside the U.S. is counted in GNP, and the value added to production by foreign-owned resources within the U.S. is excluded.

guest workers   temporary immigrants, granted limited rights to work and live in a country.

homogeneous products   units of output that are identical across firms in a market.

horizontal equity   the idea that people with equal well-being before paying taxes should have equal well-being after paying them.

horizontal integration when a firm merges with another in the same line of business.

housing vouchers government grants that the recipient can spend only on housing.

human capital acquired skills and abilities that increase the productivity of labor.

implicit opportunity costs the monetary value that capital investments and the entrepreneur's time would have in their best alternative uses; also, the value of any best forgone alternative.

implicit price deflator a price index, such as the GDP deflator used to calculate real output and prices; calculated using current quantities rather than base-period quantities.

imports goods and services a country buys from other countries.

in-kind benefits government grants of goods or services, rather than of money.

incentive pay a pay structure in which workers profit if their actions add to the profit of their employer; intended to counter the principal-agent problem.

inclining block rates when water or other utility customers are faced with higher rates as their usage goes up.

income effect (of a wage increase) when wages rise, real income also rises, thus causing workers to choose more leisure and offer less labor, *ceteris paribus*; the actual change in the quantity of labor supplied will also depend on the substitution effect.

income elasticity of demand measures how the quantity demanded responds to income; computed by dividing the percentage change in quantity demanded by the percentage change in income.

income-expenditure model relates intended spending to actual real GDP; used to show how the economy arrives at an expenditure equilibrium, which is determined by the point at which actual GDP and intended expenditures are equal; also called the Keynesian cross, because it is emphasized by Keynesians.

incomes approach computes GDP by summing various income items, such as wages and profits.

increasing-cost industry when an increase in an industry's output causes input prices to rise; in perfect competition, results in an upward-sloping long-run supply curve.

indexing automatically adjusting the terms of an agreement to account for inflation.

induced spending expenditures that depend on income; rises if income rises, and falls if income falls.

industrial policy involves the government promoting certain industries; in principle, industries would be selected on the basis of their long-term promise.

industry the collection of firms producing a similar output.

inelastic refers to either demand or supply, where the value of the elasticity is less than 1.

infant industries start-up industries that might be unable to survive the rigors of competition in their formative years.

inferior goods demand for these goods varies inversely with income; their income elasticities of demand are negative.

inflation rate   the percentage change in a price index.

inflationary expectations   predictions about future inflation that people factor into their current behavior.

informational asymmetries   occur when one person has access to more information than another on a subject of mutual interest.

intended investment   the amount of investment planned by investors; often differs from actual investment due to unplanned inventory changes.

interest rate   represents the cost of borrowing and the reward for saving or lending.

interest rate parity   occurs when the difference in risk-adjusted interest rates among countries is exactly offset by the expected rate at which the country's currency appreciates or depreciates.

inverse (negative) relationship   when a change in one variable leads to the opposite direction change in another variable.

investment   spending now in order to increase output or productivity later; can be in either human or physical capital.

invisible hand   the idea that self-interest leads the economy to produce an efficient variety of goods and services, with efficient production methods as well. As described by Adam Smith in *The Wealth of Nations* (1776), the invisible hand of the marketplace motivates producers in search of profit to provide consumers with greater value than even the most well-intentioned of governments could do.

J-curve   shows a typical time path taken by the balance of trade in response to a currency depreciation; resembles the letter "J".

Keynesian   any economist subscribing to the macroeconomic perspective of John Maynard Keynes; emphasizes the short run and the importance of fiscal policy.

labor   people's capacity to work, exclusive of any human capital they possess.

labor force   normally refers to the civilian labor force.

labor force participation rate   the ratio of the civilian labor force to the population age sixteen and over.

labor productivity   the amount of output produced by a unit of labor during some time period.

land   all natural resources, in their natural states; gifts of nature.

law of diminishing marginal utility   the first unit of a good is the most satisfying, after which additional units provide progressively less and less additional utility.

law of diminishing returns   when additional units of labor or any other variable input are added to the production process in the short run, the marginal product of the variable input must eventually decrease.

law of increasing cost   says that as an economy adds to its production of any one good, the marginal opportunity cost of that good will rise.

lawsuit abuse   the inefficient misuse of lawsuits as a means of obtaining an unjustified verdict or extorting a settlement.

leading indicators   housing starts, manufacturers' orders, and other statistics that are expected to change direction before the economy at large does.

limit pricing charging the highest price customers will pay, subject to the limit that the price not be so high that potential competitors enter the industry.

liquidity how easy it is to convert an asset into a spendable form; highly liquid assets are often used as money.

logrolling when politicians trade votes in order to obtain projects of direct benefit to constituents in their districts.

long run period of time sufficiently long that all inputs are variable.

long-run aggregate supply the idea that, in the long run, the price level does not affect the amount of GDP the economy produces; graphically, long-run aggregate supply is vertical at full-employment GDP.

long-run supply the equilibrium quantity an industry offers for sale at each possible price in the long run.

M1, M2, M3 three measures of the money supply, defined in order of decreasing liquidity.

macroeconomics analyzes economic aggregates, such as aggregate employment, output, growth, and inflation.

marginal incremental; additional.

marginal benefit the value obtained by consuming one additional unit of a good.

marginal cost the cost of producing one more unit of output; Δtotal cost/Δoutput, or, equivalently, Δtotal variable cost/Δoutput.

marginal cost of labor the additional cost of employing one more unit of labor.

marginal cost pricing an efficient price, determined by the intersection of marginal cost and demand; achieved in a perfectly competitive market; an efficient regulatory objective under conditions of market failure.

marginal product (of labor) additional output produced by the addition of one more unit of labor; Δoutput/Δlabor.

marginal propensity to consume (mpc) the fraction of additional income that people spend.

marginal propensity to save (mps) the fraction of additional income that people save.

marginal revenue the increase in revenue to the firm from selling one more unit of output; Δtotal revenue/Δoutput.

marginal revenue product of labor the increase in the firm's revenue arising from the employment of an additional unit of labor; Δtotal revenue/Δlabor.

marginal social benefit marginal benefits to all members of society; includes marginal private and marginal external benefits.

marginal social cost marginal costs to all members of society; includes marginal private and marginal external costs.

marginal tax rate tax rate on additional income; Δtax payment/Δincome.

marginal utility the change in utility associated with consuming one more unit of a good; Δutility/Δquantity consumed.

market equilibrium a situation in which there is no tendency for either price or quantity to change.

market failures when markets fail to achieve efficiency, as in the case of public goods, externalities, and sometimes, market power.

market power when individual sellers have at least a bit of control over the prices of their outputs; arises from barriers to entry.

marketable permits property rights to a specified amount of an activity, such as groundwater pumping or air pollution, where those property rights can be bought and sold; can efficiently achieve quantity targets set by government.

market a coming together of buyers and sellers that expedites the voluntary exchange of resources, goods, or services.

median voter the voter at the median of the political or budgetary spectrum—50 percent of the other voters prefer farther to the right and 50 percent prefer farther to the left.

merchandise trade account records the value of imports and exports of goods.

merit goods outputs that consumers deserve to have, whether or not they would be willing to pay the costs of providing them; a normative economic concept based on equity—highly controversial, because different people have different views concerning what is equitable.

microeconomics concerns the individual components of the economy.

midpoint formula percentage change is computed from a point midway between the starting and ending observations; used in the computation of elasticity.

mixed economies the mixture of free-market and command-and-control methods of resource allocation that characterize modern economies.

models simplified versions of reality that emphasize features central to answering the questions we ask of them.

monetarism view that the Federal Reserve should maintain a slow and steady growth of the money supply, because monetary policy cannot effectively counter short-run economic fluctuations.

monetary base the sum of currency held by the public plus bank reserves; can be controlled by the Federal Reserve.

money a medium of exchange that removes the need for barter; also a measure of value and a way to store value over time; defined by the Federal Reserve as M1, M2, and M3.

money multiplier the amount by which a new deposit is multiplied to arrive at the actual increase in the money supply; maximum value is given by the deposit multiplier.

monopolistic competition a market with numerous firms selling slightly differentiated outputs.

monopoly a market with only one seller of a good without close substitutes.

monopsony a market with only one buyer; usually a labor market with a local or highly specialized employer.

moral hazard the temptation for consumers to increase their consumption of an insured good or service, such as healthcare, if insurance covers part of the cost; more generally, a distortion of price signals under insurance plans, resulting in inefficient behavior.

moral suasion exhortations to do the right thing, as defined by public policymakers; often associated with public humiliation of those who fail to comply.

mutually interdependent when the individual actions of firms in an industry have direct effects on market conditions facing other firms in that industry.

national debt how much money the government owes; in recent years, has been about two-thirds of U.S. GDP.

natural monopoly when one firm can supply the entire market at a lower per unit cost than could two or more separate firms; associated with economies of scale.

natural rate of unemployment the minimum long-run sustainable level of unemployment.

negative income tax the idea that all income above a guaranteed minimum income is subject to an income tax; if the guaranteed income is more than a person's actual income, the tax payment would be negative, which means that the taxpayer would collect money from the government.

net domestic product (NDP) gross domestic product minus depreciation.

net investment gross investment (total investment) minus depreciation.

net social benefits social benefits minus social costs.

new classical economists school of thought acknowledging that free markets will lead to a full-employment equilibrium, but emphasizing how the economy can be shocked into short-run disequilibriums.

new growth theory emphasizes the importance of new ideas in generating economic growth, and of intellectual property rights in providing the profit incentive to generate those ideas.

new Keynesians more willing than traditional Keynesians to acknowledge the importance of long-run tendencies toward full employment.

nominal values data that are not adjusted for inflation; for example, the interest rate posted in the bank is the nominal interest rate.

nonconvertible refers to the currency of a country that does not allow anyone but its own citizens to use that currency to buy the country's goods and services.

nontariff barriers to trade (NTBs) any of a variety of actions other than tariffs that make importing more expensive or difficult.

normal goods demand for these goods varies directly with income; the income elasticity of demand is positive.

normal profit the accounting profit just sufficient to cover implicit opportunity costs.

normative having to do with behavioral norms, which are judgments as to what is good or bad.

North American Free Trade Agreement (NAFTA) trading bloc that includes the United States, Canada, and Mexico.

occupational segregation the concentration of women workers in certain jobs, such as nursing and teaching.

Occam's razor the idea that all nonessential elements should be stripped away from a model.

oligopoly   a market with more than one seller, where at least one of those sellers can significantly influence price; usually characterized by a few significant sellers.

open market operations   when the Federal Reserve enters the financial marketplace to buy or sell government securities, such as Treasury bonds.

opportunity cost   the value of the best alternative opportunity forgone.

original position   occurs prior to when we have assumed identities as separate people—we do not know who we will become; attributable to philosopher John Rawls.

pay-as-you-go   the aspect of Social Security that finances payments to current retirees from the taxes of current workers.

per capita   per person.

perfect competition   a market with many identical sellers offering homogeneous products at the same market price.

perfectly elastic   refers to either demand or supply, where the value of the elasticity is infinity.

positive   having to do with fact, concerning what is, was, or will be. In principle, the accuracy of positive statements can be checked against facts.

potential competition   firms that could become competitors to a monopoly or oligopoly firm if the monopolist or oligopolist sets excessively high prices.

potential GDP   the value of GDP that would exist if all resources in the economy were employed efficiently.

poverty line   defined by the Social Security Administration as an income that is three times the cost of what it considers to be a nutritionally adequate diet.

present value   involves discounting future costs and benefits to the present-day equivalent.

price ceiling   a law that restricts price from rising above a certain level.

price discrimination   the selling of a good or service at different prices to various buyers when such differences are not justified by cost differences.

price floor   the lowest legal price; most commonly associated with farm price supports or minimum wage laws.

price freeze   a law that restricts a wide array of prices from rising above their current levels.

price gouging   the practice of raising prices to exploit temporary surges in demand; often illegal.

price leadership   a model of oligopoly in which, when one firm changes its selling price, the remaining firms in the industry copy that change.

price rule   a policy rule that has the Federal Reserve adjust the money supply up or down in order to keep the prices of certain basic commodities within a target range.

price taker   an individual, firm, or country with no influence over the market price.

primary workers   the main source of income in households.

principal-agent problem   the difficulty of making agents, such as managers or public servants, act in the interests of principals, such as shareholders or voters.

private costs or benefits costs or benefits that are borne by the decision maker, such as a buyer or seller.

private good consumed by one person only—excludable and rival; most goods and services are private.

privatization transferring property rights from government to individuals or firms; can also refer to government contracts for work done in the private sector.

producer price index (PPI) measures wholesale prices, which are prices paid by firms.

producer surplus the difference between revenue and short-run costs; in brief, market price minus supply.

product differentiation unique features of a firm's product that distinguish it from that of other firms.

production function the relationship between the amounts of inputs and the quantities of output a firm produces.

production possibility frontier model that shows the various combinations of two goods the economy is capable of producing.

profit total revenue minus total cost; unlike accounting profit, economic profit defines cost to include implicit opportunity costs.

progressive tax a tax that collects a higher percentage of high incomes than of low incomes.

property rights the ownership of private property.

proportional tax a tax that collects the same percentage of high incomes as of low incomes.

public choice examines economic incentives within government, including those that face voters, politicians, and the administrators of government programs.

public goods goods such as national defense or clean air that are nonexcludable and nonrival, meaning that a person's consumption of the good does not reduce its quantity for others; most public goods are impure, meaning that they are not completely nonexcludable and nonrival.

purchasing power effect at lower price levels, a particular income will buy more, thus providing a major reason that aggregate demand slopes downward.

purely competitive a market in which there are numerous firms, all of which are price takers, although not all of which are otherwise identical.

pyramid scheme an arrangement in which the money from current investors is used to finance paybacks to longer-term investors.

quantity demanded the quantity that consumers will purchase at a given price.

quantity supplied the quantity that will be offered for sale at a given price.

quantity theory of money contends that velocity and aggregate output are unaffected in the long run by a change in the money supply, implying that a change in the quantity of money causes a proportional change in the price level; based on the equation of exchange.

quota quantity limit on imports.

rational expectations occur when, on average, people correctly predict the implications of government policy actions; people base their expectations of future inflation or other economic variables upon the best available information.

rational ignorance when voters make the rational choice to remain uninformed on many public issues.

real balances effect the change in expenditures caused by the effect of a change in the price level upon the real value of some types of savings; for example, a higher price level lowers the purchasing power of money saved in banks, leading consumers to spend less.

real business cycle variations in aggregate output and the price level over time caused by unexpected shocks to aggregate demand or aggregate supply.

real production costs the opportunity costs of producing an output.

real values data that are adjusted for inflation; for example, the real interest rate equals the nominal interest rate minus the inflation rate.

realized capital gains the increase in the value of assets between when they were bought and sold.

regressive tax a tax that collects a lower percentage of high incomes than of low incomes.

regulations government laws that influence the specifications of goods and services or the manner in which they are produced or sold.

rent controls a price ceiling on apartment rents.

rent-seeking behavior occurs when lobbyists or others expend resources in an effort to come out a winner in the political process.

research aimed at creating new products or otherwise expanding the frontiers of knowledge and technology.

reservation wage the lowest wage at which an individual will offer labor services.

reserve requirements the percentage of deposits banks must retain as cash in their vaults or as deposits at the Federal Reserve; set by the Federal Reserve.

risk premium the portion of a price that compensates suppliers for the risks involved in production and distribution of a good.

rule of seventy-two states that doubling time equals seventy-two divided by the rate of growth.

safety net government programs to provide economic security.

satiation point the quantity of consumption at which marginal utility is zero.

scarcity a situation in which there are too few resources to meet all human needs.

search costs the value of the time and resources spent seeking, such as for a job or apartment.

second-best efficiency the most efficient outcome possible, given that there is some inefficient policy or situation that will not be changed.

second-best policies sometimes suggested when the most efficient policy would exacerbate entrenched inefficiencies elsewhere in the economy.

seignorage a government's profit from the difference between the value of money and the cost of producing it.

services account records the value of imports and exports of services.

shadow prices what market prices would be if there were free markets; used in command-and-control societies to improve the efficiency of resource allocation.

shift factors   anything that would move an entire curve on a graph.

short run   period of time in which at least one input is fixed.

short-run aggregate supply   tells how much output the economy will offer in the short run, at each possible price level.

shortage   the excess of quantity demanded over quantity supplied, which occurs when price is below equilibrium.

shutdown   when a firm ceases operations in the short run, but still incurs fixed costs; occurs when price is less than average variable cost.

signaling   sending a message, such as a college degree signaling that the recipient is an achiever.

social costs or benefits   the sum of all costs or all benefits to all members of society, usually associated with the production of a specific good.

Social Security trust fund   Social Security tax receipts in excess of those needed to fund Social Security payments to current retirees; by law, the Social Security trust fund must be held in the form of special government bonds.

social surplus   the sum of consumer and producer surplus.

specific human capital   human capital that is specific to a particular firm or kind of job.

specificity principle   the idea that policies should be targeted as narrowly and directly at a problem as possible.

spot rate   in foreign exchange markets, refers to the exchange rate of the moment.

stagflation   the combination of high inflation and high unemployment.

static scoring   assumes no general change in behavior as a result of government policy changes.

sticky wages and prices   wages and prices that are inflexible in a downward direction, possibly caused by labor contracts or inflationary expectations.

strategic dumping   selling a good for less than its cost of production, with the intention of driving competitors out of business.

strategic trade initiatives   government plans to attract, protect, and develop targeted industries.

structural rigidities   impediments within the economy that slow adjustment to a long-run equilibrium; examples include minimum wage laws, specific human capital, and unemployment compensation.

structural unemployment   unemployment caused by a mismatch between a person's human capital and that needed in the workplace.

subsidies   payments from government that are intended to promote certain activities.

substitutes   something that takes the place of something else, such as one brand of cola for another; the cross elasticity of demand is positive.

substitution bias   because people typically substitute relatively cheaper goods for goods that have become relatively more expensive, a fixed-weight price index overstates increases in the cost of living.

substitution effect (of a wage increase)   when wage rates rise, the opportunity cost of leisure rises, thus causing the quantity of labor supplied to rise, *ceteris* *paribus*; the actual change in the quantity of labor supplied will also depend on the substitution effect.

superior goods   normal goods that people increase their purchases of more than in proportion to increases in their incomes.

supply   relates the quantity of a good that will be offered for sale at each of various possible prices, over some period of time, *ceteris paribus*.

supply shocks   unexpected changes in technology, labor productivity, input availability, or other factors that affect production possibilities.

supply siders   economists who emphasize incentives for productivity and economic growth, such as lower marginal tax rates and less regulation.

surplus   the excess of quantity supplied over quantity demanded, which occurs when price is above equilibrium.

takings   government taxation or regulation that takes away from the value of private property.

tariff   tax on imports.

tax base   that which is taxed.

tax expenditures   exemptions, deductions, exclusions, and credits in the tax code that sacrifice tax dollars.

technological efficiency   implies getting the greatest quantity of output for the resources that are being used; for any given output, then, a least-cost production technique must be chosen.

technology   possible techniques of production.

technology mandates   occur when government instructs producers as to the exact technology to install to remedy some public problem.

terms of trade   the price of a country's exports relative to the price of its imports.

"the dismal science"   economics, viewed from the perspective of Thomas Robert Malthus, in which population growth must eventually reduce us all to no more than a subsistence existence.

the margin   the cutoff point; decision making at the margin refers to deciding on one more or one less of something.

time deposits   certificates of deposit (CDs), which can only be cashed in without penalty after a stated period of time, such as one year.

time-series data   the values of a variable over a period of time.

total labor costs   the sum of wages (and salaries) plus fringe benefits.

total product (of labor)   the total amount of output produced by a firm's labor.

total revenue   price multiplied by the quantity sold; when a variety of goods and services are sold, the price of each one is multiplied by its respective quantity, and the results are added together.

trade creation   efficient specialization and trade caused by lower trade barriers among members of a trading bloc; implies a greater amount of world trade.

trade deficit   a negative balance on the merchandise trade account, given when the dollar value of imported goods exceeds the dollar value of exported goods.

trade diversion trade among members of a trading bloc that would more efficiently be conducted between trading bloc countries and other countries outside of the bloc.

trade war a situation in which countries impose high trade barriers against each other, usually in retaliation for perceived unfair trading practices on the part of the other country or countries involved.

trading blocs agreement among a group of countries that provides for lower trade barriers among its members than to the rest of the world.

transaction costs the expense of coordinating market exchanges; reduces the number of those exchanges.

transfer payment the redistribution of income from one group to another.

transparent when a public policy's effect on market prices is readily apparent.

twin deficits refers to the federal budget deficit and the trade deficit, which tend to move together; the reason is that a higher budget deficit leads to higher interest rates, which drives up the value of the dollar in foreign exchange markets, and thus makes imports cheaper and exports more expensive.

underground economy market transactions that go unreported; associated with black market activity.

unemployment equilibrium a short-run equilibrium GDP that is less than full-employment GDP; the amount of real GDP that occurs when aggregate demand intersects short-run aggregate supply at a price level above the price level at which aggregate demand intersects long-run aggregate supply.

unfunded mandates occur when government requires the attainment of public policy goals by firms or lower units of government, without providing the funding necessary to carry out those actions needed to achieve those goals; access for the disabled is an example.

unit elastic refers to either demand or supply, where the value of the elasticity equals 1.

universal access the requirement that all citizens face the same prices and access to services, regardless of the cost of serving them; most commonly associated with the provision of postal services.

universal coverage a situation in which everyone has equal access to health insurance; eliminates the problem of adverse selection.

user fees charges for use of a publicly owned good, service, or resource.

utility a conceptual measure of consumer satisfaction; also refers to a firm that provides basic public services, such as water or electricity.

value added the difference between the price of output and the materials cost of inputs.

value-added tax (VAT) a form of consumption tax that collects the difference between what companies earn in revenues and what they pay out in previously taxed costs.

variable cost the cost of variable inputs; in the long run, all costs are variable.

velocity of money the average number of times money changes hands per year.

venture capitalists   private investors willing to fund start-up companies that look to become profitable in the future.

vertical equity   the proper tax burden for people of differing abilities to pay; difficult to agree upon.

vertical integration   when a firm acquires another firm that supplies it with an input, or acquires another firm which can sell the first firm's output.

voluntary export restraints (VERs)   an alternative to import quotas in which exporting countries agree voluntarily to limit their exports to the target country; has an effect similar to an export cartel, such as OPEC.

vouchers   provide spending power, but only on certain categories of goods of services, such as food or housing.

Washington Monument strategy   when a government agency offers a bare-bones budget that cuts its most popular functions; intended to increase the chances that a more generous budget will be approved.

World Trade Organization (WTO)   international organization formed to administer the General Agreement on Tariffs and Trade.

zero-sum game   a situation in which the winner wins only what the loser loses; in contrast to voluntary economic transactions, in which both parties gain.

$\mathcal{I}$ndex

DuPont, cellophane monopoly by,
246–247
Dynamic scoring (dynamic revenue estimation), 419

E

Earnings. *See also* Wages
  of college graduates, 310
  international trade and, 53
  retained, 201, 202
  Social Security and, 526
  value of lost, 301
Eclectic economists, 518
Econometrics, 15
Economic activity, measures of, 417–419
Economic analysis, 12–13
Economic class, middle class, 297–298
Economic development, models for,
    555–556
Economic efficiency, 57
Economic growth. *See* Growth
Economic indicators, 405–406
Economic measurement, 390
Economic mix, in United States and
    globally, 10–12
Economic modeling, 14–15
Economic objectives, 7–8
Economic policy, for long run, 502–538
Economic profits, as excess profits, 207
Economic rent, 295–296
Economic Report of the President, 31,
    417
Economics
  communist philosophy and, 18–22
  of crime and punishment, 547–549
  defined, 3
  as dismal science, 61
  experimental, 15
  global themes in, 539–568
  impact of, 567–568
  political philosophies and, 12–15
  politics and, 24–25
  role of, 23–27
  study of, 25–27
  of virtue, 558–562
Economic schools, political ideology
    and, 527-531. *See also* Classical
    economics; Keynesian economics;
    Monetarism and monetarists
Economics of Discrimination, The
    (Becker), 264
Economic systems, spectrum of. *See also*
    Economics
Economies of scale, 213
  in farming, 221–224
Economists, 16–17
  roles of, 23–24

Economy
  command and control, 6
  domestic, 162
  effect of disasters on, 394–395
  measures of, 408–412
  mixed, 6, 10
  poverty in, 47–48
  questions answered by, 6–8
  static and dynamic scoring of, 410–411
  supply siders and, 411
  in transition, 415–416
  underground, 396
Education. *See also* College education
  consumers of, 102–107
  for economists, 25–26
  returns on, 288
  supply and demand for, 102–107
Efficiency, 57
  as economic objective, 7–8
  income tax reform and, 372
  market failures and, 9–10
  and political prices, 120–160
  redistribution of income and, 381–383
  second-best, 532
  in taxation, 362–363
Efficient choice, of public good,
    322–323
Efficient quantity, of public good, 321
Egalitarianism, 19
Elasticity, 90–96. *See also* Elasticity of
    demand
  computing along demand curve,
    111–114
  of supply, 95
Elasticity of demand, 90–95
  dumping and, 184
  imports and, 191
Elastic supply, 95
El Paso, Texas, transborder pollution
    and, 336
Embargo. *See* Oil embargo
Employees, government bureaucrats as,
    367–368
Employment. *See also* Jobs; Labor
  full, 391
  international trade and, 173–174
  trade and, 53
  unemployment and, 428–429
Energy security, 182
Enforcement, of drug laws, 99
Engels, Friedrich, 18
Entrepreneurship, 41, 216–219
  determining field for, 279–280
  as resource, 40
Entry barriers. *See* Barriers to entry
Environment. *See also* Externalities;
    Government; Pollution

central planning and, 554–555
  green products and, 325
  policy tools for, 327–328
  in Southwest, 336–339
  technology mandates and, 328–329
  water availability and, 376–380
Environmental pollution. *See* Pollution
Environmental Protection Agency (EPA),
    328
  transborder pollution and, 336
Environmental standards, trade and,
    182–183
Equal Employment Opportunity Commission, 446
  regulations of, 334
Equality, of income distribution,
    295–299
Equation of exchange, money, prices,
    and, 478
Equilibrium, 86–90. *See also* Market
    equilibrium
  expenditure, 439–441
  unemployment, 433
Equity
  as economic objective, 7–8
  efficiency and, 121
  redistribution of income and, 381–383
  in taxation, 362–363
  vertical and horizontal, 373
Estate tax, 362
Eurodollars, 169
Europe, beef imports and, 177
Excess profit, 207
Excess reserves, 471
Excess reserves-to-deposits ratio (e/d),
    494
Exchange, equation of, 478. *See also*
    Foreign exchange
Exchange rates
  fixed, 170
  market equilibrium, 168–170
Exclusive franchise, 243
Expansionary fiscal policy, 434
Expansion stage, of business cycle, 404
Expected return, 510
Expenditure equilibrium, aggregate demand and, 439–441
Expenditure multiplier, constant price
    level of, 441
Expenditures approach, to income accounting, 417, 418
Experimental economics, 15
Explicit costs, 206
Exports, 52. *See also* Balance of payments accounting; Imports; Tariffs
    and GDP
  net, 394

in long run, 213–215
in short run, 208–209, 231
Profit-maximizing firms, labor and, 284
Progressive tax, 361, 362
Property
  fighting over, 550–552
  private, 6
Property resources, common, 326–327
Property rights
  in former Soviet Union, 564–565
  intellectual, 179
  marketable permits and, 332
Proportional tax, 361
Proprietorship, sole, 200
Protection, of jobs, 53–54
Protectionism, 174
PSAs. *See* Personal Security Accounts
  (PSAs)
Public choice
  median voter model and, 383–384
  process of, 363–371
  taxation and, 354–388
Public goods, 319, 320–322
  efficient choice of, 322–323
  and free-rider problem, 321–322
  market failures and, 9
Public policy, political ideology and, 520
Public utilities
  as monopolies, 246
  water availability and, 376–380
Public works project, 55
Punishment, economics of, 547–549
Purchasing, by government, 394
Purchasing power effect, 432
Purely competitive markets, farming and,
  221
Pure monopsony, 285
Pure public good, 319
Pyramid scheme, Social Security and, 522

Q

Quantity
  produced by monopoly, 247–248
  profit maximization and, 269
Quantity demanded, 77
Quantity supplied, 83
Quantity theory of money, 478
Quintiles, income distribution and, 297–298
Quotas, 175–177
  distributional implications of, 191–193
  on imports, 174

R

Race, wage discrimination and, 289–290
Rate-of-return regulation, of monopolies,
  249–250

Rates. *See* Measurement; Public utilities;
  Unemployment
Rates of interest. *See* Interest rates
Rational expectations, 518
Rational ignorance, 365
Rationing, 8
Ratios, excess reserves-to-deposits, 494
Rawls, John, 21–22
Reagan, Ronald
  antitrust law and, 246
  supply-side theory and, 515
  tax loopholes and, 360
Reagonomics, 515
Real balances effect, 432
Real business cycle, 519–520
Real estate, rent controls and, 126–128
Real interest rates, and nominal interest
  rates, 481–482
Realized capital gains, taxation on, 373
Real opportunity cost, 154
Real value, 398–399
Recession, 404
Recognition lag, 443
Redistribution of income. *See* Income
  distribution
Redlining, 471–472
Regional trading blocs, 178
Regressive tax, 361, 362
Regulation. *See also* Deregulation; Mo-
  nopoly; Price discrimination
  application of, 334–335
  of banks, 470
  controversy over, 333
  of employment interviews, 334
  and information economy, 57–58
  safety vs. growth and, 510–511
  in Southwest, 336–339
  of water, 376–380
Relationships, on graphs, 28
Rent, economic, 295–296
Rent controls, 126–128
  problems of, 129–132
  Trump Tower and, 128–129
Rent-seeking behavior, 367
Research. *See* Measurement; National
  Bureau of Economic Research
  (NBER); Research and development
Research and development
  subsidizing, 513–514, 533–534
Reserve requirements, 471, 476, 477
Reserves, foreign, 172
Resource allocation, 4
  nationalism and, 20
  after World War II, 4–5
Resources, 40–41. *See also* Labor

choice and, 3
common property, 320, 326–327
nonrenewable, 64
price system and, 553–554
Restraints of trade, 245
Retained earnings, 201, 202
Return(s)
  diminishing, 202–205
  of human capital, 310
  negative, 205
  risk and, 510
Revenue. *See also* Marginal revenue
  average, 229
  demand and, 111–112
  of late-night television, 212–213
  marginal, 209–210
  of U.S. government, 355–359
Right-to-work laws, 288
Risk, and return, 510
Risk-adjusted rates, 496
Risk averse, suppliers, 98
Risk premium, drug use and, 98, 100
Robinson, David, public humiliation of,
  328
Robinson-Patman Act (1936), 245
Rolling Stones, price gouging and, 132
Romer, Paul, 514
Roosevelt, Franklin Delano
  expansionary fiscal policy of, 434
  farm aid and, 220–221
Rule of 72, 61, 391–392, 489

S

Safety
  government role in, 303–304
  vs. growth, 510–511
  trade and standards of, 182–183
  in workplace, 299–305
Safety net programs, 355, 429. *See also*
  Income distribution
  government transfers as, 290
Salary, 277, 278
Sales taxes, 358–359
Savings
  capital formation and, 504–510
  and investment, 506
  Keynes on, 442
  personal accounts, 525
  Social Security and, 522–527
Say, Jean Baptiste, 428
Scalping, 132
Scarcity
  and choice, 39
  modeling, 42–45
  prices and, 8–9
Schools, inequalities in, 105–106